CORPORATE COMPUTER AND NETWORK SECURITY

Second Edition

CORPORATE COMPUTER AND NETWORK SECURITY

Raymond R. Panko
University of Hawaii

Prentice Hall

Boston   Columbus   Indianapolis   New York   San Francisco
Upper Saddle River   Amsterdam   Cape Town   Dubai
London   Madrid   Milan   Munich   Paris   Montreal   Toronto
Delhi   Mexico City   Sao Paulo   Sydney   Hong Kong
Seoul   Singapore   Taipei   Tokyo

Editorial Director: Sally Yagan
Editor in Chief: Eric Svendsen
Acquisitions Editor: Bob Horan
Editorial Project Manager: Kelly Loftus
Technical Content Editor: Julia Panko
Director of Marketing: Patrice Lumumba Jones
Marketing Manager: Anne Fahlgren
Project Manager: Renata Butera
Operations Supervisor: Renata Butera

Creative Art Director: Jayne Conte
Cover Designer: Axell Designs
Manager, Rights and Permissions: Charles Morris
Cover Art: Getty Images, Inc.
Full-Service Project Management: Shiny Rajesh
Composition: Integra Software Services Pvt. Ltd.
Printer/Binder: Courier Westford
Cover Printer: Demand Production Center
Text Font: Palatino

Library of Congress Cataloging-in-Publication Data

Panko, R. R.
    Corporate computer and network security/Raymond R. Panko.—2nd ed.
        p. cm.
    Includes index.
    ISBN-13: 978-0-13-185475-8 (alk. paper)
    ISBN-10: 0-13-185475-5
    1. Computer security.   2. Computer networks—Security measures.
3. Electronic data processing departments—Security measures.   I. Title.
QA76.9.A25P36 2010
005.8—dc22

                                    2009019292

10 9 8 7 6 5 4 3 2 1

Prentice Hall
is an imprint of

ISBN 13: 978-0-13-185475-8
ISBN 10:   0-13-185475-5

Dedication

To Julia Panko, my long-time networking and security editor and one of the best technology minds I've ever encountered.

BRIEF CONTENTS

CONTENTS

PREFACE

INTENDED COURSE

This book is written for a one-term course in IT security at the upper division undergraduate level or graduate level. Its design assumes that this is the only IT security course the student will have. It is designed to tell general information systems majors what they need to know about IT security, and it should give students going into IT security a solid foundation. If a school has more than one IT security course, this book can serve in the introductory course. It can also serve as a network security text.

PREREQUISITE?

The book can be used by students who have only taken an overview course in information systems. However, taking a networking course before using this book is strongly advisable. For students who have not taken a networking course, Module A is a review of networking with a special focus on security aspects of network concepts. In my school, networking is a prerequisite or co-requisite, but I still cover Module A. It helps students get the rust out.

BALANCING TECHNICAL AND MANAGERIAL CONTENT

Our students are going to need jobs. For the last few years, I have been asking working IT security professionals what they look for in a new hire. They always say that they want a strong business focus, meaning that they want proactive workers, not lumps waiting for directions.

But a business focus does not mean a purely managerial focus. Companies want a strong understanding of security management. But they also want a really solid understanding of defensive security technology. A common complaint is that students who have taken managerial courses don't even know how stateful packet inspection firewalls operate or what other types of firewalls are available. "We aren't hiring these kids as security managers," is a common comment. This is usually followed by, "They need to start as worker bees, and worker bees start with technology."

Overall, I've attempted to provide a strong managerial focus along with a solid technical understanding of security tools. Most of the course deals with countermeasures, but even countermeasure chapters reflect what students need to know to manage these technologies.

By the way, you can "throttle" the amount of technical content by using or not using the chapter material in boxes. These boxes have more advanced technical content that you can skip without causing problems for students understanding in the rest of the chapter.

STRONG TEACHER SUPPORT

This is a hard course to teach. I've tried to build in as much teacher support as possible.

- PowerPoint Lectures. There is a PowerPoint lecture for each chapter. They aren't "a few selected slides." They are full lectures with builds for complex figures. And they aren't made from figures that look pretty in the book but that are invisible on slides. I've also tried to create the PowerPoint slides to be pretty self-explanatory.
- Teachers Manual. The Teachers Manual has suggestions for the way to teach the chapters. For instance, the book begins with threats. In my first class, I have students list everybody who might attack you. Then I have them come up with ways each group is likely to attack you. Along the way, I sneak in things like the distinction between viruses and worms and other things that do not come up spontaneously.
- E-mail me. I'm Ray@Panko.com. If you have a question or you need support from Prentice-Hall, please contact me. I'd also love suggestions for the next edition of the book and suggestions for additional support for this edition.
- Website. Go to my personal website, http://panko.com. There you will find additional materials and other information for the book. Not a full blog, but "bloggy."
- Pearson Prentice-Hall website (http://www.pearsonhighered.com/panko). It has the PowerPoint lectures, along with answer keys, test item files, TestGen software, and the other usual suspects.

STRONG STUDENT SUPPORT

The text is designed for reading. Most notably, I break up the text with a lot of headings. Teachers often dislike that. Students love it because it helps see where they are in the flow of material.

After each section or subsection, there are Test Your Understanding questions. This lets students check if they really understood what they just read. If not, they can go back and master that small chunk of material before going on.

For homework, you can assign specific Test Your Understanding questions and end of chapter questions (which require students to integrate what they have learned). The test item file questions are linked to particular Test Your Understanding questions. If you cut some material out, it is easy to know what multiple choice questions not to use.

The PowerPoint lectures cover nearly everything, as do the figures in the book. Study figures even summarize main points from the text. This makes the PowerPoint presentations and the figures in the book great study aids.

My writing style has received some nice compliments from students. They often remark that I am good at making difficult concepts clear. I hope that is true.

NINE BIG CHAPTERS

Although there are only nine chapters plus the appendix), they are big chapters. When I teach the material, I take between one and one and a half semester week per chapter. For Chapter 2, I take two weeks. I know it is odd to have so few chapters in a textbook, but the material just broke out that way.

HEY! WHERE'S ALL THE ATTACK SOFTWARE?

This book does not teach students in detail how to attack. Nor does it teach them any hacker software. The main reason for this lack of focus on offense is that we are training students for the defense. Defense is really complicated and getting more so. It needs the entire book. I sometimes demonstrate a few offensive tools in my own class, but I try to keep my course worthy of its informal title, *Defense against the Dark Arts.*

　　With only nine chapters, you have time to introduce some offense. However, if you do teach offense, do it carefully. Attack tools are addictive, and students are rarely satisfied using them in small labs that are carefully air-gapped from the broader school network and the Internet. A few publicized attacks by your students can get IT security barred from the curriculum.

ORGANIZATION OF THE BOOK

I think that the book has a pretty nice flow. It starts with the many threats facing corporations today. This gets the students' attention levels up. The rest of the book follows the good old plan–protect–respond cycle. Chapter 2 deals with planning, and Chapter 9 deals with incident and disaster response. All of the chapters in the middle deal with countermeasures.

　　The countermeasures part starts with two chapters on cryptography because crypto is important in itself, and because cryptographic protections are parts of many other countermeasures. Subsequent chapters introduce access control, firewalls, host and data security, and application security. In general, the book moves from network stuff to computer stuff.

COMPARISON WITH THE FIRST EDITION

Actually, there isn't any comparison. This is a completely new book. Thank all of you who used my first edition for too many years. I sincerely apologize for taking so long to create the second edition.

Aloha, Ray

CORPORATE COMPUTER AND NETWORK SECURITY

Chapter 1

The Threat Environment:

Attackers and their Attacks

LEARNING OBJECTIVES:
By the end of this chapter, you should be able to:

- Define the term *threat environment*.
- Use basic security terminology.
- Describe threats from employees and ex-employees.
- Describe threats from malware writers.
- Describe traditional external hackers and their attacks, including break-in processes, social engineering, and denial-of-service attacks.
- Know that criminals have become the dominant attackers today, describe the types of attacks they make, and discuss their methods of cooperation.
- Distinguish between cyberwar and cyberterror.

INTRODUCTION

The world today is a dangerous place for corporations. The Internet has given firms access to billions of customers and other business partners, but it has also given criminals access to hundreds of millions of corporations and to far more individuals. Wireless transmission has brought new mobility but has also allowed attackers to enter corporations surreptitiously, bypassing firewalls designed to keep intruders from coming in through the Internet.

Basic Security Terminology

There are several pieces of terminology that we will use throughout the book.

THE THREAT ENVIRONMENT   If companies are to be able to defend themselves, they need an understanding of the **threat environment**—that is, the types of attackers and attacks companies face. "Understanding the threat environment" is a fancy way of saying "Know your enemy." If you do not know how you may be attacked, you

---

The Threat Environment
  The threat environment consists of the types of attackers and attacks that companies face

Security Goals
  Confidentiality
      Confidentiality means that people cannot read sensitive information, either while
      it is on a computer or while it is traveling across a network
  Integrity
      Integrity means that attackers cannot change or destroy information, either while it is on
      a computer or while it is traveling across a network. Or, at least, if information is changed
      or destroyed, then the receiver can detect the change or restore destroyed data
  Availability
      Availability means that people who are authorized to use information are not prevented
      from doing so

Compromises
  Successful attacks
  Also called incidents and breaches

Countermeasures
  Tools used to thwart attacks
  Also called safeguards, protections, and controls
  Types of countermeasures
      Preventative
      Detective
      Corrective

FIGURE 1-1 Basic Security Terminology (Study Figure)

cannot plan to defend yourself. This chapter will focus almost exclusively on the threat environment.

> *The threat environment consists of the types of attackers and attacks that companies face.*

SECURITY GOALS   Corporations and subgroups in corporations have **security goals**—conditions that the security staff wishes to achieve. Three common core goals are referred to collectively as **CIA**. This is not the Central Intelligence Agency. Rather, *CIA* stands for confidentiality, integrity, and availability.

- **Confidentiality**. Confidentiality means that people cannot read sensitive information, either while it is on a computer or while it is traveling across a network.
- **Integrity**. Integrity means that attackers cannot change or destroy information, either while it is on a computer or while it is traveling across a network. Or, at least, if information is changed or destroyed, then the receiver can detect the change or restore destroyed data.

- **Availability**. Availability means that people who are authorized to use information are not prevented from doing so. Neither a computer attack nor a network attack will keep them away from the information they are authorized to access.

Many security specialists are unhappy with the simplistic CIA goal taxonomy because they feel that companies have many other security goals. However, the CIA goals are a good place to begin thinking about security goals.

COMPROMISES   When a threat succeeds in causing harm to a business, this is called an **incident**, **breach**, or **compromise**. Companies try to deter incidents, of course, but they usually have to face several breaches each year, so response to incidents is a critical skill. In terms of our business process model, threats push the business process away from meeting one or more of its goals.

> *When a threat succeeds in causing harm to a business, this is called an incident, breach, or compromise.*

COUNTERMEASURES   Naturally, security professionals try to stop threats. The methods they use to thwart attacks are called **countermeasures**, **safeguards**, **protections**, or **controls**. The goal of countermeasures is to keep business processes on track for meeting their business goals despite the presence of threats and actual compromises.

> *Tools used to thwart attacks are called countermeasures, safeguards, or controls.*

Countermeasures can be technical, human, or (most commonly) a mixture of the two. Typically, countermeasures are classified into three types:

- **Preventative countermeasures** keep attacks from succeeding. Most controls are preventative controls.
- **Detective countermeasures** identify when a threat is attacking and especially when it is succeeding. Fast detection can minimize damage.
- **Corrective countermeasures** get the business process back on track after a compromise. The faster the business process can get back on track, the more likely the business process will be to meet its goals.

TEST YOUR UNDERSTANDING

1. **a.** Why is it important for firms to understand the threat environment?
   b. Name the three common security goals.
   c. Briefly explain each.
   d. What is an incident?
   e. What are the synonyms for *incidents*?
   f. What are countermeasures?
   g. What are the synonyms for *countermeasure*?
   h. What are the goals of countermeasures?
   i. What are the three types of countermeasures?

The TJX Data Breach

If this terminology seems abstract, it may help to look at a specific attack to put these terms into context and to show how complex security attacks can be. We will begin with the largest loss of private customer information (at least at the time of this writing). This is the TJX data breach.

THE TJX COMPANIES, INC. (TJX)   The TJX Companies, Inc. (TJX) is a group of over 2,500 retail stores operating in the United States, Canada, England, Ireland, and

---

The TJX Companies, Inc. (TJX)

A group of over 2,500 retail stores companies operating in the United States, Canada, England, Ireland, and several other countries

Does business under such names as TJ Maxx and Marshalls

Discovery

On December 18, 2006, TJX detected "suspicious software" on its computer systems

Called in security experts who confirmed an intrusion and probable data loss

Notified law enforcement immediately

Only notified consumers a month later to get time to fix system and to allow law enforcement to investigate

Two waves of attacks, in 2005 and 2006

Company estimated that 45.7 million records with limited personal information included

Much more information was stolen on 455,000 of these customers

The Break-Ins

Broke into poorly protected wireless networks in retail stores

Used this entry to break into central processing system in Massachusetts

Not detected despite long presence, 80 GB data exfiltration

Canadian privacy commission: poor encryption, keeping data that should not have been kept

The Payment Card Industry–Data Security Standard (PCI-DSS)

Rules for companies that accept credit card purchases

If noncompliant, can lose the ability to process credit cards

12 required control objectives

TJX knew it was not in compliance (later found to meet only 3 of 12 control objectives)

Visa gave an extension to TJX in 2005, subject to progress report in June 2006

The Fall-Out: Lawsuits and Investigations

Settled with most banks and banking associations for $40.9 million to cover card reissuing and other costs

Visa levied $880,000 fine, which may later have been increased or decreased

Proposed settlement with consumers

Under investigation by U.S. Federal Trade Commission and 37 state attorneys general

TJX has prepared for damages of $256 million as of August 2007

FIGURE 1-2   The TJX Data Breach (Study Figure)

several other countries. These companies do business under such names as TJ Maxx and Marshalls. In its literature, TJX describes itself as "the leading off-price retailer of apparel and home fashions in the U.S. and worldwide." With this type of mission statement, there is strong pressure to minimize costs.

DISCOVERY   On December 18, 2006, TJX detected "suspicious software" on its computer systems.[1] Three days later, TJX called in security consultants to examine the situation. On December 21, the consultants confirmed that an intrusion had actually occurred. The next day, the company informed law enforcement authorities in the United States and Canada. Five days later, the security consultants determined that customer data had been stolen.

The consultants initially determined that the intrusion software had been working for seven months when it was discovered. A few weeks later, the consultants discovered that the company had also been breached several times in 2005. All told, the consultants estimated that 45.7 million customer records had been stolen. This was by far the largest number of personal customer records stolen from any company.

The thieves did not steal these records for the thrill of breaking in or to enhance their reputations among other hackers. They did it so that they could use the information to make fraudulent credit card purchases in the names of the customers whose information had been stolen. These fraudulent purchases based on the stolen information did, in fact, take place.

In its defense, TJX noted that in most of the records stolen, most personal information had been masked (replaced by asterisks).[2] It also noted that most of the credit cards about which information had been stored had expired and that the company generally did not collect social security numbers (SSNs). However, for 455,000 customers who had been given refunds without a receipt, a much larger amount of personal information had been collected, and this information had been stolen as well.

TJX did not inform customers about the data breach until nearly a month later. The company said that it needed time to beef up its security. The company also said that law enforcement officials had told TJX not to release information about the breach immediately to avoid tipping off the data thieves about the investigation. Of course, the delay also left the customers ignorant of the danger they faced.

THE BREAK-INS   How did the breaches occur? It is believed that the data thieves broke into poorly protected wireless networks in some retail stores to get into the central TJX credit and debit card processing system in Massachusetts.[3] There, poor firewall protection[4] allowed the data thieves to enter several systems and to install a sniffer that listened to the company's poorly encrypted traffic passing into and out of the processing center. Another problem was that TJX retained some sensitive credit

---

[1] This paragraph is based on TJX, "Frequently Asked Questions," http://www.txj.com/tjx_faq.html.

[2] This paragraph is based on TJX, "Frequently Asked Questions," http://www.txj.com/tjx_faq.html.

[3] Mark Jewel, "Encryption faulted in TJX hacking," *MSNBC.com*, September 25, 2007. http://www.msnbc.msn.com/id/20979359/.

[4] Ross Kerber, "Details Emerge on TJX Breach," *The Boston Globe*, October 25, 2007.

card information that should not have been retained; it is this improperly retained information that the data thieves found valuable.[5]

How did the thieves remain undetected despite having a sniffer operate for over half a year and despite exfiltrating over 80 GB[6] of data? And how did the attackers place a sniffer on the TJX network that went undetected for seven months?[7] The answer to that question appears to be that TJX did not have an organized intrusion detection capability.

In its defense, the company said that it "believes our security was comparable to many other major retailers."[8] Its purpose in saying this may have been to prepare for a defense against lawsuits based on negligence. Proving negligence usually requires proof that a perpetrator was lax based on general practice in the field.

The Canadian Privacy Commission, which was the first governmental bureau to release findings about the break-in, gave the following assessment of TJX's security at the time of the breach:

> The company collected too much personal information, kept it too long and relied on weak encryption technology to protect it—putting the privacy of millions of its customers at risk. . . . The company did not manage the risk of a breach, it failed to encrypt data strongly enough, it did not monitor its systems well enough, it did not act in accordance with payment card industry standards and it collected too much information.[9]

THE PAYMENT CARD INDUSTRY–DATA SECURITY STANDARD (PCI-DSS)   A number of earlier (and smaller) data breaches had prompted the major credit card companies to create the **Payment Card Industry–Data Security Standard (PCI-DSS)**. This standard specified 12 required control objectives that must be implemented by companies that accept credit card purchases. Failure to implement PCI-DSS control objectives can result in fines and even the revocation of a company's ability to accept credit card payments.

At the time the data breach was discovered, TJX was far behind in its PCI-DSS compliance program. The company only complied with 3 of the 12 required control objectives. Internal memos[10] revealed that the company knew that it was in violation of the PCI-DSS requirements, particularly with respect to its weak encryption in retail store wireless networks. However, the company deliberately decided not to move rapidly to fix this problem. In November 2005, a staff member noted prophetically that "saving money and being PCI-compliant is important to us, but equally

---

[5] Mark Jewel, op. cit. http://www.msnbc.msn.com/id/20979359/.

[6] SANS Institute, "Unflattering Details Emerge in TJX Case," *SANS Newsbytes*, e-mail newsletter (9:86) October 20, 2007.

[7] Ibid.

[8] Ross Kerber, "Details Emerge on TJX Breach," *The Boston Globe*, October 25, 2007.

[9] OUT-LAW.com, "Canadian Privacy Commissioner Slams TJ X data policy" (OUT-LAW.COM is part of international law firm Pinsent Masons.), THEREGISTER.CO.UK, September 27, 2007. http://www.theregister.co.uk/2007/09/27/tjx_data_leak_report/.

[10] Evan Schuman, "VISA Fined TJX Processor for Security Breach," *Eweek.com*, October 28, 2007. http://www.eweek.com/article2/0,1895,2208615,00.asp.

important is protecting ourselves against intruders. Even though we have some breathing room with PCI, we are still vulnerable with WEP as our security key. It must be a risk we are willing to take for the sake of saving money and hoping we do not get compromised."

When the staff member noted that "we have some breathing room with PCI," he probably was referring to the fact that TJX had been given an extension allowing it to be compliant beyond the standard's specified compliance date.[11] This additional time, ironically, was given *after* the data breaches had already begun. This extension was dependent upon evaluation of a TJX report on its compliance project by June 2006. It is unknown whether TJX complied with this requirement. The letter that authorized the extension was sent by a fraud control vice president for Visa. It ended with "I appreciate your continued support and commitment to safeguarding the payment industry."

THE FALLOUT: LAWSUITS AND INVESTIGATIONS   The company quickly became embroiled in commercial lawsuits and government investigations. These lawsuits involved the filing of briefs that shed additional light on the break-ins. For instance, sealed evidence from Visa and MasterCard placed the number of account records stolen at 94 million—roughly double TJX's estimates.[12]

TJX was sued by seven individual banks and bank associations. In December 2007, TJX settled with all but one of these banks, agreeing to pay up to $40.9 million. This would reimburse the banks for the cost of reissuing credit cards and other expenses.

The company also received a large fine from Visa. Actually, Visa could not fine TJX directly but could only fine TJX's merchant bank, the Fifth Third Bank of Ohio. (Merchant banks are financial institutions that serve—and should control—retail organizations that accept credit card payments.) However, merchant banks typically pass on the fine to the retailer, in this case TJX. During the summer of 2007, Visa fined TJX's merchant bank $880,000 and announced that it would continue to impose fines at $100,000/month until TJX had fixed its security problem. However, in the TJX settlement with the seven banks and banking associations, this fine was to be reduced by an undisclosed amount.

In this battle of corporate giants, consumers were handled last. At the time of this writing, TJX has proposed a settlement that would only involve active measures such as help with ID theft through insurance and other measures for the roughly 455,000 victims who had given personally identifiable information when they returned goods without a receipt. Other victims would be given a modest voucher or the opportunity to buy TJX merchandise at sale prices.[13]

For the longer term, TJX is under investigation by government agencies.[14] This includes the U.S. Federal Trade Commission, which has the authority to punish

---

[11] Evan Schuman, "In 2005, Visa Agreed To Give TJX Until 2009 To Get PCI Compliant," *StorefrontBacktalk*, November 9, 2007. http://storefrontbacktalk.com/story/110907visaletter.

[12] Ross Kerber, "Court Filling in TJX Breach Doubles Toll," *The Boston Globe*, October 24, 2007.

[13] John Leyden, "TJX Consumer Settlement Sale Offer Draws Scorn," *TheRegister.com*, November 20, 2007. http://www.theregister.co.uk/2007/11/20/tjx_settlement_offer_kerfuffle/.

[14] Se Young Lee, "Credit Card Headaches from TJX Breach Remain," *The Boston Globe*, August 9, 2007.

companies that do not protect private customer information. In addition, attorneys general from 37 states are conducting investigations. Federal and state investigations could lead to large fines.

To deal with these legal problems, TJX set aside cash and recorded losses. As of August 2007, the bank had prepared for damages of $256 million (up from only $25 million three months earlier).[15]

PROSECUTION   On August 25, 2008, the Department of Justice charged 11 individuals with conducting the TJX break-in and the subsequent use of the stolen information.[16] Three were Americans, and they were jailed rapidly. Two more were in China. The rest were in Eastern Europe. The indictment underscores the international nature of cybercrime. Although the three Americans conducted the actual data theft, they fenced the stolen information overseas. Two of the American defendants rapidly entered plea deals to testify against the alleged ringleader Albert Gonzalez of Miami, Florida.

Although prosecution is continuing at the time of this writing, the evidence confirms that the break-ins were done through wireless access points secured by wired equivalent privacy (WEP).[17] Once in, the attackers installed password sniffers to capture credit card numbers and passwords for critical servers. At one point, they even opened a secure Virtual Private Network (VPN) connection from hacked TJX servers to their own servers. The three attackers created some fake credit cards and used them to buy merchandise, but they fenced most of the information overseas for sale on the black market.

One surprising thing about the indictment is that this criminal gang had plundered not only TJX of customer information. According to the indictment, other firms that had information stolen by the crime ring included BJ's Wholesale Club, OfficeMax, Boston Market, Barnes & Noble, Sports Authority, Forever 21, and DSW.[18]

TEST YOUR UNDERSTANDING

2. **a.** Who were the victims in the TJX breach? (The answer is not in the text, and this is not a trivial question.)
   b. Was the TJX break-in due to a single security weakness or multiple security weaknesses? Explain.
   c. Why would meeting the PCI-DSS control objectives probably have prevented the TJX data breach? This is not a trivial question.
   d. Would meeting the PCI-DSS control objectives have ensured that the data breach would not have occurred? Think about this carefully. The answer is not in the text.
   e. Which of the CIA goals did TJX fail to achieve in this attack?

[15] Ross Kerber, "Cost of Data Breach at TJX Soars to $256m," *The Boston Globe*, August 15, 2007.

[16] U.S. Department of Justice, "Retail Hacking Ring Charged for Stealing and Distributing Credit and Debit Card Numbers from Major U.S. Retailers," August 5, 2008. http://www.usdoj.gov/criminal/cybercrime/gonzalezIndict.pdf.

[17] Ibid.

[18] Ibid.

EMPLOYEE AND EX-EMPLOYEE THREATS

Having looked at threats in general, at key security terminology, and at a particular compromise, we will now look at specific elements of the corporate threat environment. We will begin by looking inside the firm, at the threats created by employees. When firms began getting their own computers in the 1960s, they soon found and have continued to find that disgruntled and greedy employees and ex-employees are serious security threats. As Walt Kelly's cartoon character Pogo said on Earth Day in 1970, "We has met the enemy, and they is us."

Why Employees Are Dangerous

Employees and ex-employees are very dangerous for four reasons:

- They usually have extensive knowledge of systems.
- They often have the credentials needed to access sensitive parts of systems.
- They know corporate control mechanisms and so often know how to avoid detection.
- Finally, companies tend to trust their employees. In fact, when security insists that an employee behave in a particular way or explain an apparent security violation, it is common for the employee's manager to protect the employee against "security interference."

Employees and ex-employees are very dangerous because they have extensive knowledge of systems, have the credentials needed to access sensitive parts of systems, often know how to avoid detection, and can benefit from the trust that usually is accorded to "our people."

These factors often eliminate the need for sophisticated computer knowledge. In fact, in 23 financial services cybercrimes committed between 1996 and 2002, 87 percent were accomplished without any sophisticated programming.[19]

IT employees are particularly dangerous because of their extraordinary knowledge and access. IT security employees are the most dangerous of all. The Department of Justice has a website, http://www.cybercrime.gov, which lists federal cybercrime prosecutions. Roughly half the cases have defendants who are IT and even security employees and ex-employees. The Romans asked, *"Quis custodiet custodes?"* This translates as "Who watches the watchers?" This is one of the most difficult issues in IT security management.

Employee Sabotage

One of the oldest concerns about employees is **sabotage**, which is the destruction of hardware, software, or data. *Sabotage* comes from the French word for *shoe* because disgruntled workers in the early years of the Industrial Revolution supposedly threw their wooden shoes into machines to stop production.

---

[19] Keeney, et al., *Insider Threat Study: Illicit Cyber Activity in the Banking and Finance Sector*, United States Secret Service and the CarnegieMellon Software Engineering Institute, August 2004.

Employees and Ex-Employees Are Dangerous
  Dangerous because
      They have knowledge of internal systems
      They often have the permissions to access systems
      They often know how to avoid detection
      Employees generally are trusted
  IT and especially IT security professionals are the greatest employee threats (*Qui custodiet custodes?*)

Employee Sabotage
  Destruction of hardware, software, or data
  Plant time bomb or logic bomb on computer

Employee Hacking
  Hacking is intentionally accessing a computer resource without authorization or in excess of authorization
  Authorization is the key

Employee Financial Theft
  Misappropriation of assets
  Theft of money

Employee Theft of Intellectual Property (IP)
  Copyrights and patents (formally protected)
  Trade secrets: plans, product formulations, business processes, and other info that a company wishes to keep secret from competitors

Employee Extortion
  Perpetrator tries to obtain money or other goods by threatening to take actions that would be against the victim's interest

Sexual or Racial Harassment of Other Employees
  Via e-mail
  Displaying pornographic material
  . . .

Employee Computer and Internet Abuse
  Downloading pornography, which can lead to sexual harassment lawsuits and viruses
  Downloading pirated software, music, and video, which can lead to copyright violation penalties
  Excessive personal use of the Internet at work

Non-Internet Computer Abuse
  Access to sensitive personal information motivated by curiosity
  In one survey at a security conference, one in three admitted to looking at confidential or personal information in ways unrelated to their jobs

Data Loss
  Loss of laptops and storage media

Other "Internal" Attackers
  Contract Workers
  Workers in Contracting Companies

FIGURE 1-3   Employee and Ex-Employee Threats (Study Figure)

Tim Lloyd, a computer systems administrator, was fired for being threatening and disruptive. In retaliation, Lloyd planted a logic bomb program on a critical server. When pre-set conditions occurred, the logic bomb destroyed the programs that ran the company's manufacturing machines. Lloyd also took home and erased the firm's backup tapes to prevent recovery. Lloyd's sabotage resulted in $10 million in immediate business losses, $2 million in reprogramming costs, and 80 layoffs. The attack led to a permanent loss of the company's competitive status in the high-tech instruments and measurements market because the company could not rebuild the proprietary design software it had been using.[20]

Sabotage can also have financial motives. When Roger Duronio sabotaged 2,000 servers at UBS PaineWebber, he was not just punishing his ex-employer. He also sold UBS PaineWebber shares short to take advantage of the subsequent drop in the company's share price. Although the attack did extensive damage, the stock price did not drop, and Duronio lost money. Found guilty of computer sabotage and securities fraud, 63-year-old Duronio was sentenced to eight years in federal prison.[21]

In another case, two traffic engineers working for the City of Los Angeles pleaded guilty to hacking the city's traffic center and disconnecting signals at four of LA's busiest intersections. They then locked out the controls for these intersections, so that it took four days to restore control. They did this a few hours before their union's scheduled job action against the city in support of contract negotiations. For this infraction, they received 240 days of community service and were required to have their computers at home and work monitored.[22]

Employee Hacking

Another concern is that employees will hack (break into) the company's computers using stolen credentials or some other ploy. They can then steal money, steal intellectual property, or just look up embarrassing information.

As we will see in Chapter 10, U.S. law provides the following definition of **hacking**—intentionally accessing a computer resource without authorization or in excess of authorization. Definitions of hacking in other jurisdictions tend to be very similar.[23]

---

[20] Sharon Gaudin, "Computer Saboteur Sentenced to Federal Prison," *Computerworld*, February 26, 2002. www.computerworld.com/itresources/rcstory/0,4167,STO68624_KEY73,00.html.

[21] Sharon Gaudin, "Ex-UBS Systems Admin Sentenced to 97 Months in Jail," *InformationWeek*, December 13, 2006. http://www.informationweek.com/news/showArticle.jhtml?articleID=196603888.

[22] Dan Goodin, "LA Engineers Cop to Traffic System Sabotage," November 6, 2008. http://www.theregister.co.uk/2008/1106/traffic_control_system_sabotage.

[23] The first documented use of the term *hacker* was in Steve Levy's book, *Hackers*, in 1984 (Penguin Books). Levy actually decried the use of the term *hacker* to mean someone who breaks into computers illicitly. Rather, he argued that hackers were people who managed to hack out creative solutions to difficult computer problems. Some people in security continue to argue for Levy's viewpoint, using the term *cracker* as someone who breaks into computers. However, this is not the dominant usage in security and is certainly not widespread in the popular literature. The term *cracking* is now used primarily to refer to the breaking of passwords or encryption keys.

> *Hacking is intentionally accessing a computer resource without authorization or in excess of authorization.*

Note that the key issue is **authorization**.[24] Were you explicitly (or implicitly) authorized to use the resource that you accessed? Were you authorized to use part of the resource but not the specific part that you accessed? Note that your motivation for hacking is irrelevant. Penalties are the same whether you were attempting to steal a million dollars or were merely "testing security."[25]

Employee Financial Theft and Theft of Intellectual Property (IP)

There are many reasons for employees to access resources without permission or in excess of permission. Sometimes employees do so out of mere curiosity or to find information that could embarrass the company. At other times, however, they have purely criminal goals, such as **financial theft**, which involves the misappropriation of assets (say by assigning them via computer to themselves) or the theft of money (such as the manipulation of an application in order to be paid a bonus).

In one case of financial theft, two accountants at Cisco Systems illegally accessed a corporate computer to issue themselves $8 million worth of Cisco stock. In fact, they successfully issued themselves stocks three times before being caught. They committed the crime by exploiting the company's poorly controlled procedures for issuing stock to employees.[26]

In another case, Quitugua Sabathia, 31, of Vallejo, California, used her computer to embezzle more than $875,000 from the North Bay Health Care Group. A former accounts payable clerk at North Bay, she accessed the firm's accounting software and issued approximately 127 checks payable to herself and others. To conceal the fraud, she altered the electronic check register to make it appear that the checks had been payable to North Bay's vendors. This particular theft obviously required a good knowledge of the computer system.

Another criminal motive is the theft of the company's **intellectual property (IP)**, which is information owned by the company and protected by law. IP includes formally protected information such as copyrights, patents, trade names,

---

[24] In their defense, hackers can claim that they did not realize that authorization was required because the computer system that they hacked was public, like a free news website. Consequently, firms that have login screens or even public home pages should have a prominent warning that specific authorization is needed to use a site.

[25] Most hacking laws require damage to pass a certain level before the hacking can be prosecuted. However, it is quite possible for a hacker to do the requisite amount of damage accidentally, even if he or she did not intend to do damage. While access has to be intentional, damage does not.

[26] U.S. Department of Justice, "Former Cisco Systems Accountants Sentenced for Unauthorized Access to Computer Systems to Illegally Issue $8 Million in Cisco Stock to Themselves," November 26, 2001. http://www.cybercrime.gov/Osowski_TangSent.htm.

and trademarks. Although many companies have no such formal intellectual assets, IP also includes **trade secrets**, which are pieces of sensitive information that a firm acts to keep secret. These include plans, product formulations, business processes, price lists, customer lists, and many other types of information that a company wishes to keep secret from competitors. If another company obtains trade secrets in an illicit way, that company will be subject to prosecution. Nevertheless, some employees steal trade secrets to sell to another company.

> *Intellectual property (IP) is information that is owned by the company and protected by law.*
>> *Trade secrets are pieces of sensitive information that a firm acts to keep secret.*

Another case illustrates the theft of intellectual property. A paralegal employee in one law firm copied the company's plans for a plaintiff in a large court case. These plans cost several million dollars to develop. The employee attempted to sell the plans to one of the firms representing the defendants.[27]

When scientists and engineers change jobs, there is always a danger that they will take trade secret information with them. One former DuPont research scientist admitted downloading trade secrets worth $400 million. Only when he announced his intention to leave was his downloading behavior analyzed. The analysis found that he had downloaded 16,700 documents and even more abstract—15 times the volume of the second-highest downloader. Most of these documents had nothing to do with his primary research area.[28]

Employee Extortion

In some cases, an employee or ex-employee will user his or her ability to damage systems or access confidential information to extort the firm. In **extortion**, the perpetrator tries to obtain money or other goods by threatening to take actions that would be against the victim's interest. For instance, an employee might plant a logic bomb on the company's computer. If the employee or ex-employee tells the company to pay money to avoid suffering damage, this is extortion. Stealing intellectual property and demanding money in exchange for not passing on the information is also extortion.

> *In extortion, the perpetrator tries to obtain money or other goods by threatening to take actions that would be against the victim's interest.*

---

[27] U.S. Department of Justice, "Manhattan Paralegal Sentenced for Theft of Litigation Trial Plan," January 30, 2002. www.cybercrime.gov/farrajSentence.htm.

[28] Jaikumar Vijayan, "Scientist Admits Stealing Valuable Trade Secrets," PC World, February 16, 2007. http://www.pcworld.com/article/129116-1/article.html?tk=nl_dnxnws.

Employee Sexual or Racial Harassment

Although hacking, theft, and extortion are critical issues, employee sexual or racial harassment is an even more common problem. Sexual harassment, for example, can include making physical threats, taking revenge after a romantic break-up, downloading and displaying pornography, and retaliating against an unwilling sexual partner by withholding promotions and raises.

> One such case began when a female employee spurned a male employee, Washington Leung. He left the firm and later logged into his ex-firm's servers using passwords given to him while employed there. He deleted over 900 files related to employee compensation. To frame the female employee, he gave her a $40,000 annual raise and a $100,000 bonus. In addition, he created a Hotmail account in her name and used the account to send senior managers at the company an e-mail containing some information from the deleted files. However, the frame failed. On his work computer at his new place of employment, authorities found evidence of the e-mail he sent to senior managers.[29]

Employee Computer and Internet Abuse

INTERNET ABUSE   The term **abuse** is used for activities that violate a company's IT use policies or ethics policies. In some cases, employees abuse their Internet access, most commonly by downloading pornography, downloading pirated media or software, or wasting many hours surfing the Internet for personal purposes. Abuse ranges from mildly damaging behavior to criminal acts.

Abuse *consists of activities that violate a company's IT use policies or ethics policies.*

Downloading pornography can lead to sexual harassment lawsuits against the firm as well as against the responsible individual. Downloading pirated music, videos, and software, in turn, can result in extensive copyright violation penalties.[30] Downloading any unapproved files can also lead to expensive malware infections.

While many employers do not mind a small amount of personal Internet use, some employees become addicted to Internet use and spend tens of hours a week on personal Web surfing at work.[31] In addition, when employees download numerous files from the Internet, they are likely to download a virus or some other malicious software.

IT security departments usually dislike searching for evidence of pornography and excessive personal websurfing, but this is part of the job in most firms.

---

[29] U.S. Department of Justice, "U.S [sic] Sentences Computer Operator for Breaking into Ex-Employer's Database," March 27, 2002. www.cybercrime.gov/leungSent.htm.

[30] In addition, pirated software often contains viruses that infect the downloader's computer and then infect other computers in the firm.

[31] Raymond R. Panko and Hazel Beh. "Monitoring for Performance and Sexual Harassment," *Communications of the ACM*, in a special section on Internet Abuse in the Workplace, January 2002.

NON-INTERNET COMPUTER ABUSE   Another aspect of employee abuse is unauthorized access to private personal data on internal systems by curious employees. This type of behavior was detected in the 2008 U.S. presidential election campaign and in several celebrity hospitalizations.[32]

> During the 2008 presidential campaign, contract employees at the State Department employees looked without permission at the passport histories of candidates Obama, Clinton, and McCain.[33] "According to Infoworld.com: a breach was flagged by the State Department's in-house computer system; but supervisors downplayed the alarm."[34] Two of the contract workers have been fired by their employers. Later, Verizon announced that Obama's phone records had been accessed illegally.[35]

The abuse of internal corporate systems for voyeuristic purposes is not limited to general office employees. For example, a survey of 300 senior IT administrators in a London security conference and trade show found that one in three admitted to looking at confidential or personal information in ways unrelated to their jobs.[36]

Data Loss

The damaging employee behaviors we have looked at so far involve deliberate improper actions. However, employees can endanger the security of their firms through simple carelessness, by losing laptops, optical disks, and USB RAM drives. The release of data on these computers and media can be devastating to the firm. Even if the data is not actually used, the fact that it may be used may require the firm to take expensive actions.

> A Ponemon survey in 2008 found that 630,000 laptops are lost in airports each year. Although only some of these are corporate computers, airports are not the only place that laptops are lost, and lost media can be just as damaging.[37]

Other "Internal" Attackers

Employees are not the only threats inside a firm's walls. Many businesses hire **contract workers**, who work for the firm for brief periods of time. Contract workers often get access credentials that are not deleted after their engagement ends. In fact,

---

[32] Charles Ornstein, "UCLA Workers Snooped in Spears' Medical Records," *Los Angeles Times*, March 15, 2008. http://www.latimes.com/news/local/la-me-britney15mar15,0,1421107.story.

[33] Anne Flaherty and Desmond Butler, "Obama, Clinton And McCain's Passports Breached: Two State Dept Officials Fired, Investigation Underway," *Associated Press*, March 21, 2008 07:53 p.m. EST; published in the *Huffington Post*, January 14, 2009.

[34] Prolog, "Obama's Phone Records, Passport Documents Breached by Verizon Employees, Dept of State Contractors," Press Release, December 14, 2008.

[35] Ibid.

[36] Gregg Keizer, "One in Three IT Admins Admit Snooping," *Computerworld*, June 22, 2008. http://www.computerworld.com/action/article.do?command=viewArticleBasic&articleId=9101498.

[37] Ponemon Institute, "Airport Insecurity: The Case of Missing & Lost Laptops," June 30, 2008. http://www.dell.com/downloads/global/services/dell_lost_laptop_study.pdf.

companies often hire other companies to do contracting work that takes place inside the original company's walls. These other companies and their employees also often receive temporary credentials. These contract workers and contracting firms create risks almost identical to those created by employees.

Claude Carpenter, a 19-year-old employee of a firm managing servers for the U.S. Internal Revenue Service (IRS), planted a logic bomb on the servers when he learned he was about to be fired. Although he was seeking vengeance on his own company, the IRS would have been the real victim had his logic bomb succeeded. He also planted the code on his supervisor's computer to frame the supervisor. The company successfully defused the logic bomb, but other firms in similar situations have not been so lucky.[38]

TEST YOUR UNDERSTANDING

3. **a.** Give four reasons why employees are especially dangerous.
   b. What type of employee is the most dangerous?
   c. What is sabotage?
   d. Give the book's definition of hacking.
   e. What is intellectual property?
   f. What two types of things are employees likely to steal?
   g. Distinguish between intellectual property in general and trade secrets.
   h. What is extortion?
   i. What is employee computer and Internet abuse?
   j. Who besides employees constitute potential "internal" threats

TRADITIONAL EXTERNAL ATTACKERS I: MALWARE WRITERS

Although employees and other "internal" threats can be extremely dangerous, firms must also be concerned with **traditional external attackers**, who use the Internet to send malware into corporations, hack into corporate computers, and do other damage.

Malware Writers

The first external malware attackers were malware writers. The term **malware** generically means "evil software." The most widely known type of malware is the virus, but there are many other types, including worms, Trojan horses, RATs, spam, and several other types that we will see in this section.

Malware is a generic term for "evil software."

---

[38] U.S. Department of Justice, "Lusby, Maryland Man Pleads Guilty to Sabotaging IRS Computers," July 24, 2001. http://www.cybercrime.gov/carpenterPlea.htm.

Malware is a very serious threat. In June 2006, Microsoft reported results from a survey of users who allowed their computers to be scanned for malware.The scan found 16 million pieces of malware on the 5.7 million machines examined.

Viruses

Viruses are programs that attach themselves to legitimate programs on the victim's machine. Later, when infected programs are transferred to other computers and run, the virus attaches itself to other programs on those machines.

Viruses are programs that attach themselves to legitimate programs.

Initially, most viruses spread through the transfer of programs via floppy disks. Today, in contrast, most viruses are spread via e-mail messages with infected attachments. However, instant messaging, file sharing programs, users innocently downloading infected programs from malicious websites, and users deliberately downloading "free software" or pornography are also common ways to spread viruses. Through networked applications, viruses can spread very rapidly today.

Malware
   A generic name for any "evil software"

Viruses
   Programs that attach themselves to legitimate programs on the victim's machine
   Spread today primarily by e-mail
   Also by instant messaging, file transfers, etc.

Worms
   Full programs that do not attach themselves to other programs
   Also spread by e-mail, instant messaging, and file transfers
   In addition, direct propagation worms can jump to from one computer to another without human intervention on the receiving computer
      Computer must have a vulnerability for direct propagation to work
   Direct propagation worms can spread extremely rapidly

Blended Threats
   Malware propagates in several ways—like worms, viruses, compromised webpages containing mobile code, etc.

Payloads
   Pieces of code that do damage
   Implemented by viruses and worms after propagation
   Malicious payloads are designed to do heavy damage

FIGURE 1-4   Classic Malware: Viruses and Worms (Study Figure)

When Macintosh users searched BitTorrent sites in early 2009, they found that they were able to download the newly released Adobe Photoshop CS4. They would also download a program installed on the download CS4 on the down-loader's computer. The copy of CS4 was clean, but when the downloader ran the cracking program, he or she got a dialog box saying that "Adobe CS4 Crack [intel] requires that you type your password." The dialog box had Name and Password data entry boxes, plus some cryptic details that made it look more authentic.[39]

Worms

Viruses are not the only type of malware. One particularly important type of malware is the **worm**. Unlike viruses, worms are full programs that do not attach themselves to other programs.

> *Worms are full programs that do not attach themselves to other programs.*

In general, worms act much like viruses and can spread via e-mail and in other ways that viruses spread. However, some worms have a far more aggressive spreading mode—jumping directly from one computer to another without user intervention on the receiving computer. Such **direct-propagation worms** take advantage of vulnerabilities (security weaknesses) in software. When a direct-propagation worm jumps to a computer that has the specific vulnerability for which the worm was designed, the worm can install itself on that computer and use that computer as a base to jump to other computers—all without any action on a user's part.

> *Direct-propagation worms jump directly to computers that have vulnerabilities; they then use these computers to jump to other computers.*

Direct propagation can be very rapid, enabling the worm to do tremendous damage before it is noticed by humans. Researchers at the University of California at Berkeley estimated that a worst-case direct-propagation worm could do $50 billion in damage in the United States alone.[40]

> *Direct propagation requires no user action, so direct-propagation worms can spread extremely rapidly.*

---

[39] Andrew Nusca, "Mac Trojan Horse Found in Pirated Adobe Photoshop CS4," January 26, 2009. http://blogs.zdnet.com/gadgetreviews/?p=856&tag=nl.e539.

[40] Gregg Keizer, "Worst-Case Worm Could Rack Up $50 Billion in U.S. Damages," *CMP Techweb*, June 4, 2004. http://www.techweb.com/wire/story/TWB20040604S0006.

On January 25, 2003, the Slammer worm exploded across the Internet. In ten minutes—before more than a handful of people knew it existed—Slammer had infected 90 percent of all vulnerable computers on the entire Internet.[41] Despite the fact that Slammer did not erase hard disks or do other deliberate damage to the computers it infected, Slammer still caused massive damage by spreading so rapidly that it overwhelmed parts of the Internet. Around the world, ATMs became unusable, police departments lost their ability to communicate, and most Internet users in Korea lost their service.[42] Had Slammer been deliberately malicious, it could have produced tens of billions of dollars in damage worldwide. Although Slammer's rapid flooding of the Internet was unprecedented, we now know that even faster "blitz worms" are possible.[43] Worms and related threats such as viruses are no longer weapons of mere mass annoyance. They can cause incredible losses.

Blended Threats

If viruses and worms were not bad enough, a growing number of **blended threats** propagate both as viruses and worms. They can also post themselves on websites for people to download unwittingly. By propagating in multiple ways, blended threats increase their likelihood of success.

MessageLabs (http://www.messagelabs.com) keeps data on viruses, worms, and blended threats. MessageLabs reported that in August 2006, 1.0 percent of all e-mail messages contained viruses, worms, or blended threats. During major outbreaks, one in ten e-mail messages may contain viruses, worms, or blended threats.

Payloads

After viruses and worms propagate, they often execute **payloads**, which are pieces of code that do damage. Benign payloads merely pop up a message on the user's screen or do some other annoying but nonlethal damage. Unfortunately, some viruses and worms that have apparently benign payloads or even no payloads at all can do substantial damage. For example, although Slammer did not contain a payload, it spread so rapidly that it clogged networks with so much traffic that it effectively shut down parts of the Internet.

In turn, **malicious payloads** can do extreme damage, for example, by randomly deleting files from the victim's hard disk drive or by installing some of the other types of malware described later in this section.

Virus and worm payloads also frequently "soften up" the computer by disabling its antivirus software and taking other actions that leave it highly vulnerable to subsequent virus and worm attacks.

---

[41] David Moore, Vern Paxson, Stephan Savage, Colleen Shannon, Stuart Stainford, and Nicolas Weaver. "The Spread of the Sapphire/Slammer Worm," 2003 (Slammer was also called Sapphire.) http://www.caida.org/outreach/papers/2003/saphire/saphire.html.

[42] Raymond R. Panko, "Slammer: The First Blitz Worm," *Communications of the AIS*, 11(12), February 2003.

[43] Vern Paxson, Stuart Stainford, and Nicholas Weaver, "How to Own the Internet in Your Spare Time," *Proceedings of the 11th USENIX Security Symposium (Security '02)*, 2002.

In 2004, the Aberdeen Group (http://www.aberdeen.com) surveyed 162 companies. They found that each firm lost an average of $2 million per virus or worm incident and spent an additional $100,000 to clean up computers after an attack. Both numbers increased with company size. Most companies reported enduring an average of one incident per year, although many firms reported multiple incidents. To give another data point, the security firm Mi2g (http://www.mi2g.com) estimated that damage from malware in 2004 alone averaged $290 per PC in the firms it studied.

TEST YOUR UNDERSTANDING

4. a. What is malware?
   b. Distinguish between viruses and worms.
   c. How do most viruses spread between computers today?
   d. Describe how directly propagating worms move between computers.
   e. Why are directly propagating worms especially dangerous?
   f. What is a virus or worm payload?

Trojan Horses and Rootkits

NONMOBILE MALWARE   Viruses, worms, and blended threats are not the only types of malware, but they are the only types of malware that can forward themselves to other victims. Other forms of malware can only spread to a machine if they are placed there. Examples of ways to get nonmobile malware include the following:

- Having a hacker place it there.
- Having a virus or worm place it there as part of its payload.
- Enticing the victim to download the malware from a website or FTP site by portraying the malware as a useful program or data file.
- Attaching hostile mobile code (described later) to a webpage and executing it on a victim's computer when the victim downloads the webpage.

TROJAN HORSES   Most nonmobile malware programs are Trojan horses. Early Trojan horses were programs that pretended to be one thing, such as a game or a pirated version of a commercial program, but really were malware. Many of these classic Trojan horses still exist. Today, however, when we talk about a **Trojan horse**, we mean a program that hides itself by deleting a system file and taking on the system file's name. Trojan horses are difficult to detect because they look like legitimate system files.

A Trojan horse is a program that hides itself by deleting a system file and taking on the system file's name. Trojan horses are difficult to detect because they look like legitimate system files.

REMOTE ACCESS TROJANS (RATS)   One common type of Trojan horse is the **remote access Trojan (RAT)**. A RAT gives the attacker remote control of your computer. The attacker can remotely do pranks, such as opening and closing your CD drive or typing things on your screen. However, they can also engage in more malicious activities.

Nonmobile Malware

Must be placed on the user's computer through one of a growing number of attack techniques

Placed on computer by hackers

Placed on computer by virus or worm as part of its payload

The victim can be enticed to download the program from a website or FTP site

Mobile code executed on a webpage can download the nonmobile malware

Trojan Horses

A program that replaces an existing system file, taking its name

Remote Access Trojans (RATs)

Allow the attacker to control your computer remotely

Downloaders

Small Trojan horses that download larger Trojan horses after the downloader is installed

Spyware

Programs that gather information about you and make it available to the adversary

Cookies that store too much sensitive personal information

Keystroke loggers

Password-stealing spyware

Data mining spyware

Rootkits

Take control of the super user account (root, administrator, etc.)

Can hide themselves from file system detection

Can hide malware from detection

Extremely difficult to detect (ordinary antivirus programs find few rootkits)

FIGURE 1-5   Trojan Horses and Rootkits (Study Figure)

There are many legitimate remote access programs that allow a remote user to work on a machine or do diagnostics. However, RATs typically are stealthy in order to avoid detection by the owner of the machine.

DOWNLOADERS   Some Trojan horses are downloaders. They usually are fairly small programs, which makes detection difficult. After they are installed, however, they download a much larger Trojan horse capable of doing much more damage.

SPYWARE   The term **spyware** refers to a broad spectrum of Trojan horse programs that gather information about you and make it available to an attacker.[44] There are several types of spyware.[45]

---

[44] Although the biggest problem with spyware is the theft of information, spyware also tends to make computers run sluggishly.

[45] One new form of spyware is *camera spyware*, which spies on the victim visually by turning on a computer's camera and perhaps also its microphone.

- Websites are allowed to store small text strings called **cookies** on your PC. The next time you go to the website, the website can retrieve the cookie. Cookies have many benefits, such as remembering your password each time you visit. Cookies can also remember what happened last in a series of screens leading to purchases. However, when cookies record too much sensitive information about you, they become spyware. (Cookies are not Trojan horses per se, but we include them with other types of spyware.)
- **Keystroke loggers**, as the name suggests, capture all of your keystrokes. They then look through the collected keystrokes for usernames, passwords, social security numbers, credit card numbers, and other sensitive information. They send this information to the adversary.
- More directly, **password-stealing spyware** tells you that you have been logged out of the server you are visiting and asks you to retype your username and password. If you do, the spyware sends your username and password to the attacker.
- **Data mining spyware** searches through your disk drives for the same types of information sought by keystroke loggers. It also sends this information to the adversary.

ROOTKITS   Trojan horses replace legitimate programs. A deeper threat is a set of programs called rootkits. In Unix computers, the root account is a super user account that has complete power over the computer. Although this super user account is called Administrator on Windows computer, super user accounts are referred to generically as root accounts. **Rootkits** take over the root account and use its privileges to hide themselves. They do this primarily by preventing their operating system's file-viewing methods from detecting their presence. Rootkits are seldom caught by ordinary antivirus programs, and rootkit detection programs often are specific to particular rootkits.

In 2005, Sony BMG downloaded a rootkit onto the PCs of people playing Sony BMG media disks. The discovery of this digital rights management rootkit generated extreme negative publicity. This negative publicity increased when it was learned that the rootkit left the PC open to attack by anyone.[46]

TEST YOUR UNDERSTANDING

5. **a.** How can nonmobile malware be delivered to computers?
   b. What is a Trojan horse?
   c. What is a RAT?
   d. What is a downloader?
   e. What is spyware?
   f. Why can cookies be dangerous?
   g. Distinguish between keystroke loggers, password-stealing spyware, and data mining spyware.
   h. Distinguish between Trojan horses and rootkits.
   i. Why are rootkits especially dangerous?

[46] Robert Lemos, "Hidden DRM Code's Legitimacy Questioned," *SecurityFocus*, November 2, 2005. http://www.securityfocus.com/news/11352.

Mobile Code

When you download a webpage, it may contain executable code as well as text, images, sounds, and video. This is called **mobile code** because it executes on whatever machine downloads the webpage. Javascript is a popular language for writing mobile code. Microsoft Active X controls are also popular. In most cases, mobile code is innocent and often is necessary if a user wishes to use a website's functionality. However, if (and only if) the computer has the vulnerability used by a particular piece of mobile code, hostile mobile code will be able to exploit this vulnerability.

Social Engineering in Malware

Social engineering attacks take advantage of flawed human judgment by convincing the victim to take actions that are counter to security policies. For instance, if an employee receives an e-mail message warning about a mass layoff being immanent, he or she may open an attachment and therefore download a virus, worm, or Trojan horse. Although technology can provide many protections, it is very difficult for companies to protect against human misjudgment.

> *Social engineering attacks take advantage of flawed human judgment by convincing the victim to take actions that are counter to security policies.*

SPAM   The bane of all e-mail users is **spam**, which is defined as unsolicited commercial e-mail. Although ISP, corporate, and personal spam filters have reduced the volume of spam greatly, people are still bombarded constantly by spam. In addition to being annoying, spam messages often are fraudulent or advertise dangerous products. In addition, spam has become a common vehicle for distributing viruses, worms, Trojan horses, and many other types of malware. According to MessageLabs (http://www.messagelabs.com), 73 percent of all e-mail messages were spam in March 2009.

Mobile Code

  Executable code on a webpage

  Code is executed automatically when the webpage is downloaded

  Javascript, Microsoft Active-X controls, etc.

  Can do damage if computer has vulnerability

Social Engineering in Malware

  Social engineering is attempting to trick users into doing something that goes against security policies

  Several types of malware use social engineering

    Spam (unsolicited commercial e-mail)

    Phishing (authentic-looking e-mail and websites)

    Spear phishing (aimed at individuals or specific groups)

    Hoaxes

FIGURE 1-6   Other Malware Attacks (Study Figure)

Even the load on networks caused by simply transmitting and storing spam can be significant. This is especially true because many spammers now send spam that has image bodies instead of text bodies as a way to avoid detection from spam scanning programs. Image spam messages are much larger than traditional text spam messages.

PHISHING   In **phishing attacks**, victims receive e-mail messages that appear to come from a bank or another firm with which the victim does business. The message may even direct the victim to an authentic-looking website. The official appearance of the message and website often fool the victim into giving out sensitive information. A small but significant fraction of all people who receive phishing messages respond to them because these messages seem so authentic. A Gartner survey in 2007 indicated that U.S. consumers were scammed out of $3.2 billion through phishing that year. Phishing also leads to many expensive help desk calls within firms.

In 2004, when phishing was fairly new but already well known to consumers, a study showed consumers a group of e-mail messages and asked whether each message was a phishing attack or not. The consumers judged 28 percent of the phishing messages to be legitimate messages.[47] They also believed that a fair number of legitimate messages were phishing messages.

SPEAR PHISHING   Normal phishing attacks tend to appeal broadly to many people so that they can dupe as many victims as possible. In contrast, spear phishing attacks are aimed at single individuals or small groups of individuals. For instance, if an attacker's goal is to get the CEO of a corporation to download a Trojan horse, the attacker may craft an e-mail message that deals with a pressing issue for the CEO, appears to come from a trusted person, and contains specific details that only the trusted person is likely to know.

In one case, a number of CEOs received a message disguising itself as a court order. The message directed the CEO to a website, uscourts.com. There, the CEO could find court documents could be downloaded, along with a plug-in to read the documents. The plug-in, of course, was spyware that searched the CEO's valuable computer.[48]

HOAXES   Some e-mail messages contain **hoaxes**. In some cases, these hoaxes simply make the victim feel stupid when they tell other people what they "learned,"

---

[47] Bob Sullivan, "Consumers Still Falling for Phish," *MSNBC News*, July 28, 2004. http://www.msnbc.com/id/5519990/.

[48] Scott Nichols, "Spear Phishing Targets CEOs," *PC World*, April 16, 2008. http://blogs.pcworld.com/staffblog/archives/006805.html?tk=nl_spxblg.

but in other cases, the hoaxes try to persuade the victim to damage their own system.

The Sulfnbk.exe hoax told computers that a virus called AOL.EXE was traveling around the Internet. The hoax said that they should delete the file sulfnbk.exe. Victims who did so were really deleting their AOL access. Other hoaxes have tried to persuade victims to delete their antivirus protection and even critical operating files needed for their computer's operation.

TEST YOUR UNDERSTANDING

6. a. What is mobile code?
   b. What is social engineering?
   c. What is spam?
   d. What is phishing?
   e. Distinguish between normal phishing and spear phishing.
   f. Why are hoaxes bad?

TRADITIONAL EXTERNAL ATTACKERS II: HACKERS AND DENIAL-OF-SERVICE ATTACKS

In the 1970s, malware writers were joined by external hackers, who began to break into corporate computers that were connected to modems. Today, nearly every firm is connected to the Internet, which harbors millions of external hackers.

Traditional Motives

Most traditional external hackers did not cause extensive damage or commit theft for money. They were motivated primarily by the thrill of break-ins, by the validation of their skills, and by a sense of power. In addition, external hackers often communicated with one another. By demonstrating their ability to break into well-defended hosts, hackers could increase their reputations among their peers.[49] This type of attacker still exists.

Often, traditional hackers focused on embarrassing the victim. In 2009, for example, vandals broke into a computerized road sign in Austin, Texas and changed its message to read, "The end is near! Caution! Zombies ahead!"[50] However, many traditional external hackers did and continue to engage in some direct theft, extortion, and other damage to support their "hobby."

---

[49] Others have weirder motivations. British hacker Gary McKinnon reportedly broke into 73,000 U.S. government computers looking for evidence of extraterrestrial contacts. Ian Grant, "Garry McKinnon broke into 73,000 U.S. government computers, Lords Told," *ComputerWeekly.com*, June 16, 2008. No longer available online.

[50] Dan X. McGraw, "Austin Road Sign Warns Motorists of Zombies," *The Dallas Morning News*, January 29, 2009. http://www.dallasnews.com/sharedcontent/dws/news/localnews/transportation/stories/013009dnmetzombies.1595f453.html.

Traditional Hackers
  Motivated by thrill, validation of skills, sense of power
  Motivated to increase reputation among other hackers
  Often do damage as a byproduct
  Often engage in petty crime

Anatomy of a Hack
  Reconnaissance probes (Figure 1-8)
      IP address scans to identify possible victims
      Port scans to learn which services are open on each potential victim host
  The exploit
      The specific attack method that the attacker uses to break into the computer is called the attacker's exploit
      The act of implementing the exploit is called exploiting the host

IP Address Spoofing
      Attackers often use IP address spoofing to conceal their identities (Figure 1-9)
      Putting false source IP addresses in reconnaissance and exploit packets
      Hiding the attacker's identity
      However, the attacker cannot receive replies sent by the victims to the false IP address

Chain of attack computers (Figure 1-10)
      The attacker attacks through a chain of victim computers
      Probe and exploit packets contain the source IP address of the last computer in the chain
      The final attack computer receives replies and passes them back to the attacker
      Often, the victim can trace the attack back to the final attack computer
      But the attack usually can only be traced back a few computers more

Social Engineering
  Social engineering is often used in hacking
      Call and ask for passwords and other confidential information
      E-mail attack messages with attractive subjects
      Piggybacking (walking through a door opened by another who has access credentials)
      Shoulder surfing (watching someone type his or her password)
      Pretexting (pretending to be someone and asking for information about that person)
      Etc.
  Often successful because it focuses on human weaknesses instead of technological weaknesses

Denial-of-Service (DoS) Attacks
  Make a server or entire network unavailable to legitimate users
  Typically send a flood of attack messages to the victim
  Distributed DoS (DDoS) Attacks (Figure 1-11)
      Bots flood the victim with attack packets
      Attacker controls the bot

Bots
  Updatable attack programs (Figure 1-12)
  Botmaster can update the software to change the type of attack the bot can do
      May sell or lease the botnet to other criminals
  Botmaster can update the bot to fix bugs

Skill Levels
  Expert attackers are characterized by strong technical skills and dogged persistence
  Expert attackers create hacker scripts to automate some of their work
  Scripts are also available for writing viruses and other malicious software
  Script kiddies use these scripts to make attacks
  Script kiddies have low technical skills
  Script kiddies are dangerous because of their large numbers

FIGURE 1-7   Traditional External Attackers: Hackers (Study Figure)

Raymond Torricelli, known as "Rolex," hacked into NASA computers and ran chat room discussions on the hacked computers, using up processor time, memory, and disk resources. Torricelli's goal was to get participants to go to a pornographic website. He admitted to being paid $0.18 for each participant who went to the website. This earned him $300 to $400 per week.[51]

TEST YOUR UNDERSTANDING

7. **a.** What were the motivations of traditional external hackers?
   b. Did traditional external hackers engage in theft?

Anatomy of a Hack

Although there are many different ways to hack a computer, there is a general broad process that attackers often follow when they are attempting to hack a company's computers.

RECONNAISSANCE PROBES   Before a thief breaks into a home, he or she often "cases" the neighborhood to look for vulnerable houses. The attacker then gathers information about potential victim houses to decide which ones to break into. Hackers also tend to do reconnaissance before breaking into a computer.[52] As Figure 1-8 shows, the attacker often sends probe packets into a network.[53] These probe packets are designed to elicit replies from internal hosts and routers. If internal hosts or routers respond to these probe packets, their responses can tell the attacker a great deal about the network.

    IP Address Scanning   The first round of probe packets is designed to find hosts that are active because active hosts can be attacked. Before scanning, the attacker must learn the firm's IP addresses range. (Firms are given contiguous blocks of IP addresses to assign to their computers.) The attacker can then send **IP address scanning** probes to all IP addresses in this range. These probes often use the Internet Control Message Protocol (ICMP) Echo and Echo reply messages discussed in Module A. When a host receives an ICMP Echo message, it should send back an ICMP Echo reply message. When the attacker receives an ICMP Echo reply message from an IP address, it knows that there is a live host at that IP address.

    Port Scanning   Once the attacker knows the IP addresses of live hosts, it needs to know what programs the identified hosts are running because most attacks rely on vulnerabilities in specific programs. On server hosts, applications correspond to port

---

[51] Department of Justice, "Hacker Sentenced in New York City for Hacking into Two NASA Jet Propulsion Lab Computers Located in Pasadena, California," September 5, 2001. www.cybercrime.gov/torricellisent.htm.

[52] In one study in 2005, only about half of all attacks were preceded by scans, but if scans were done, the probability of a follow-on attack was high. Jaikumar Vijayan, "Port Scans Don't Always Precede Hacks," *Techworld,* December 13, 2005. http://www.techworld.com/security/news/index.cfm?NewsID=4991. Last accessed December 15, 2005.

[53] In 2003, it was found that 45–55 percent of all suspicious activity found by intrusion detection systems was hackers scanning for targets. Christine Burns, "Danger Zone," *Network World*, August 25, 2003. http://www.nwfusion.com/techinsider/2003/0825techinsiderintro.html.

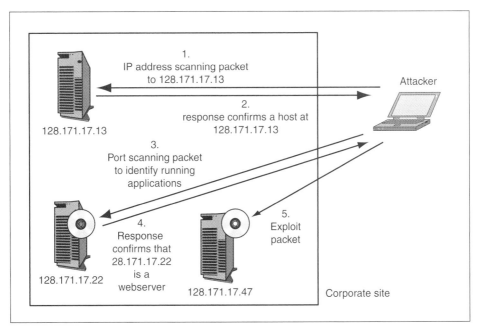

FIGURE 1-8   Probe and Exploit Attack Packets

numbers. For example, 80 is the well-known port number for HTTP webservers. If Port 80 is open, then the computer probably is a webserver. There are many well-known port numbers between 0 and 1023. Each indicates the presence of a particular type of application. The attacker sends **port scanning** probes to each identified host in order to determine which applications the host is running. Typically, a port scanning program requests a connection to a program on a particular port number.[54] If the target sends back an agreement to proceed, the attacker knows that the target host is running a program on that port number.

THE EXPLOIT   Once potential victim hosts are identified, the attack can begin. In this case, the attacker sends exploit packets to victim hosts, instead of probe packets. The specific attack method that the attacker uses to break into the computer is called the attacker's **exploit**, and the act of implementing the exploit is called **exploiting** the host. If the exploit succeeds, the attacker "owns" at least an account and may "own" the computer itself. **Owning** a computer allows the attacker to do anything that he or she wishes.

SPOOFING   Each packet carries a source IP address, which is like the return address on an envelope. The source IP address is dangerous for hackers because it allows corporations to locate the attackers. As Figure 1-9 shows, attackers can frustrate efforts to find them by **spoofing** the source IP address, that is, placing a different IP address in the source IP address field. This way, the victim cannot learn the attacker's true IP address.

---

[54] If the program uses TCP at the transport layer, TCP segments requesting connections have their SYN bits set. Replies indicating a willingness to proceed set both the SYN and ACK bits.

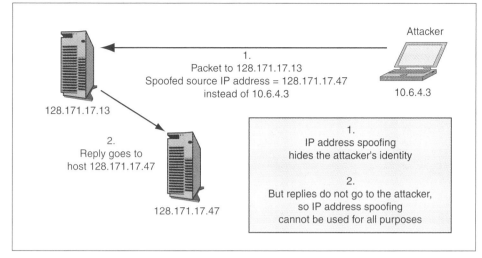

FIGURE 1-9   Source IP Address Spoofing

Not all packets can be spoofed. For instance, the attacker usually must be able to read replies to probe packets. Victim replies are always sent to the host whose IP address is in the probe's source IP address field. If the attacker spoofs the IP address in probe packets, it will not receive the replies. Many exploit packets also need to receive replies.

Figure 1-10 shows that attackers who need to receive replies often work through a **chain of attack computers** previously compromised by the attacker.[55] Commands are passed through the chain to the final computer, which sends the probe or attack

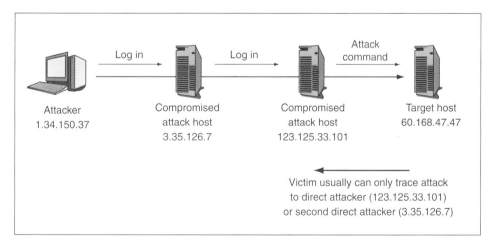

FIGURE 1-10   Chain of Attack Computers

---

[55] For example, the attacker may use Telnet to get from one computer to another. In the end, the attacker will be able to type commands that go directly to the final computer. To the attacker, it is not even apparent during operation that there are multiple computers between the attacker and the final computer.

packets. Replies are also passed through the chain back to the attacker. The victim usually will be able to trace the attack back to the last computer in the chain and perhaps to one or two more hosts in the chain, but the victim can rarely trace the attack all the way back to the attacker's host.

TEST YOUR UNDERSTANDING

8. **a.** Distinguish between IP address scanning and port scanning.
   b. What is an exploit?
   c. What does "owning" a computer mean?
   d. What is IP address spoofing?
   e. Why is IP address spoofing done?
   f. When can an attacker not use IP address spoofing?
   g. When attackers must use valid IP source addresses in probe or exploit packets, how do they conceal their identities?

Social Engineering

Many external (and internal) attacks use social engineering, which, as we saw earlier, is attempting to trick users into doing something that goes against the interests of security. Compared to technical protections, human gullibility often is far easier to exploit.

In one social engineering ploy, a hacker calls a secretary claiming to be working with the secretary's boss. The hacker then asks for sensitive information, such as a password or even a restricted file.

> In one study, U.S. Treasury Department inspectors posing as computer technicians called 100 Internal Revenue Service employees and managers. The treasury agents asked each target for his or her username and asked the user to change his or her password to a specific password chosen by the "technician." This was a clear violation of policy, yet 35 percent fell for the ruse in 2005. As bad as this was, it was an improvement over 2001, when 71 percent changed their passwords.[56]

Other examples of social engineering including following someone through a secure door without entering a pass code (this is called **piggybacking**) and looking over someone's shoulder when he or she types a password (this is called **shoulder surfing**). In **pretexting**, the attacker calls claiming to be a certain customer in order to get private information about that customer.

> In 2006, senior executives at Hewlett-Packard (HP) attempted to find the source of an information leak that must have come from someone on the board. A firm hired by HP allegedly used pretexting to get telephone call records about suspected leakers from the telephone company by pretending to be the suspected leakers.[57]

---

[56] Mary Dalrymple, "Auditors Find IRS Workers Prone to Hackers," *Washington Post*, March 16, 2005. http://www.washingtonpost.com/wp-dyn/articles/A42115-2005Mar16.html.

[57] Robert Lemos, "HP's Pretext to Spy," *Security Focus*, September 6, 2006. http://www.securityfocus.com/brief/296.

Although the leaker was found, the revelation of pretexting used against board members sparked a fury. The board's chairperson, Patricia Dunn, and several other executes were forced to resign, and HP had to pay a $14.6 million fine to the State of California.[58]

TEST YOUR UNDERSTANDING

9. **a.** How can social engineering be used to get access to a sensitive file?
   b. What is piggybacking?
   c. What is shoulder surfing?
   d. What is pretexting?

Denial-of-Service (DoS) Attacks

Another type of external attack is the **denial-of-service (DoS) attack**. A DoS attack attempts to make a server or network unavailable to legitimate users. In terms of the CIA security goal taxonomy discussed earlier, DoS attacks are attacks on availability.

A denial-of-service (DoS) attack attempts to make a server or network unavailable to serve legitimate users by flooding it with attack packets.

Figure 1-11 illustrates the most common type of DoS attack, a **distributed denial-of-service (DDoS)** attack. In this exploit, the attacker first places programs called **bots** on many Internet hosts (clients, servers, or both). Later, when it is

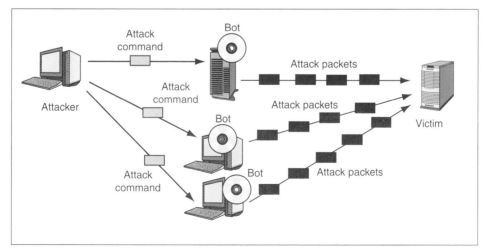

FIGURE 1-11   Distributed Denial-of-Service (DDoS) Flooding Attack

---

[58] Kelly Martin, "HP Pretexting Scandal Comes to Partial Close," *Security Focus*, December 8, 2006.

time to begin the DoS attack, the botmaster sends a message to all of the bots. The bots then begin to flood the server or network listed in the attack message with attack packets. Soon, overloaded servers and networks cannot serve their legitimate users.

In 2001, the Code Red virus attacked the U.S. White House website. Fortunately, the attacks were made against the website's IP address instead of its host name. The White House merely changed the IP address of whitehouse.gov.

To attack a server, for instance, the bots might flood the server with TCP connection-opening requests (TCP SYN segments). A server reserves a certain amount of capacity each time it receives a SYN segment. By flooding a computer with SYN segments, the attacker can cause the server to run out of resources and therefore crash or be unable to respond to further connection-opening attempts from legitimate users. If the attack stream is especially heavy, the victim corporation's entire network will be unable to communicate over the Internet.

As Figure 1-12 shows, the botmaster is not limited to sending attack commands to installed bots. The botmaster can also send software updates to the bots. The simplest updates are sent to fix bugs in the program code. In the past, malware releasers often discovered after the release that the program had unforeseen bugs that prevented it from working properly. These flaws made it possible for antimalware firms to destroy many of these programs. However, the ability to download updates allows malware vendors to fix errors.

The figure also shows that the botmaster can send updates that give new functionality to bots. For instance, many bot armies are originally programmed to send spam. Later, when antispam efforts lock out the IP addresses of these bots, the botmaster can send updates to make the bots capable of implementing DoS attacks. The botmaster can then use them to make attacks or lease the botnet to other criminals

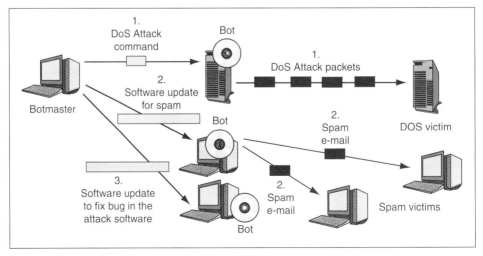

FIGURE 1-12 Fixing and Updating Bots

for DoS attacks. In 2003, botnets with 10,000 computers could be purchased outright for $500.[59]

Jeanson Ancheta was indicted for crimes involving a large botnet. Ancheta was charged with creating the botnet and installing adware programs, which constantly pop up advertisements, on these computers for a fee. He also was charged with renting parts of his botnet to others criminals for spam and denial-of-service attacks.[60]

TEST YOUR UNDERSTANDING

10. **a.** What is a DoS attack?
    b. Describe a DDoS attack.
    c. Describe a SYN flooding attack in some detail.
    d. What two types of updates can a botmaster send to bots?
    e. Why do many botnets have multiple owners over time?

Skill Levels

Hollywood movies often portray hackers as geniuses who can break into tightly protected servers in a few seconds. In reality, highly skilled **wizard hackers** usually need days or even months of hard work to break into a well-protected system—if they succeed at all. During this time, they will try many different attacks. In other words, skilled hackers are characterized both by high technical expertise and dogged persistence.

To automate some aspects of their attacks, hackers often write programs called **hacker scripts**. The term *script* traditionally has denoted a fairly crude program written in a simple language. Today's hacker scripts, however, often have easy-to-use graphical user interfaces and look like commercial products.

In addition, many scripts are available on the Internet. These easy-to-use hacker scripts have created a new type of hacker—the **script kiddie**. This is a derogatory term that skilled hackers give to relatively unskilled hackers who use these pre-made scripts. Although individual script kiddies are much less likely to succeed in breaking into a computer than skilled hackers, there are far more script kiddies than skilled hackers. This makes script kiddies as a community extremely dangerous.

Furthermore, the large number of script kiddie attacks makes it difficult for corporations to identify the small number of highly dangerous attacks that companies face from very skilled attackers and that need special attention. In July 2002, Riptech examined data from 400 of its customers in detail. It noted that only about 1 percent of attacks were sophisticated aggressive attacks. However, when sophisticated aggressive

---

[59] John Leyden, "Phatbot Arrest Throws Open Trade in Zombies," *The Register*, May 12, 2004. http://www.theregister.com/2004/05/12/phatbot_zombie_trade.

[60] Department of Justice, Central District of California, "Computer Virus Broker Arrested for Selling Armies of Infected Computers to Hackers and Spammers," November 3, 2005. http://www.cybercrime.gov/anchetaArrest.htm.

attacks did appear, they were 26 times more likely to do severe damage than even moderately sophisticated aggressive attacks.

> In February 2000, a number of major firms were subjected to devastatingly effective DDoS attacks that blocked each of their e-commerce systems for hours at a time. Victims of this series of attacks included CNN.com, eBay, Yahoo.com, Amazon.com, Dell.com, eTrade, ZDNet, and other major firms. At first, the attacks were thought to be the work of an elite hacker. However, the culprit was found to be a 15-year-old script kiddie hacker in Canada, who was caught only because he bragged online about the attack.

Virus and other malware writers also have long written programs for creating new malware. Viruses have become so easy to create with these tools that Sven Jaschan, an 18-year-old German student who had never written a virus before, was responsible for 70 percent of the virus activity in the first half of 2004 (http://www.sophos.com).

Today, tools are available for creating all types of exploits. One of the most important is the Metasploit Framework, which makes it easy to take a new exploitation method and rapidly turn it into a full attack program. Metasploit is used both by attackers to launch attacks and by security professionals to test the vulnerability of their systems to specific exploits.

TEST YOUR UNDERSTANDING

11. a. What are the two primary characteristics of skilled hackers?
  b. Why are script kiddies dangerous? (Give two reasons.)
  c. Why are malware and exploit toolkits expanding the danger of script kiddies?

THE CRIMINAL ERA

Dominance by Career Criminals

Prior to about 2003, most external attackers were employees, ex-employees, or traditional external attackers. Today, however, *most* external attackers are **career criminals**, who attack to make money illegally. Although hacking is always a crime, even when done by a traditional wizard hacker interested only in fame and a feeling of power, today's criminals have traditional career criminal motives, and many of their attack strategies are computer adaptations of traditional crimes.

Today, most external attackers are career criminals.

Contrary to some popular beliefs, criminals are not slow to take advantage of new technologies. In 1888, Inspector John Bonfield of the Chicago police said, "It is a well-known fact that no other section of the population avail themselves more readily and speedily of the latest triumphs of science than the criminal class."

The Criminal Era
   Today, *most* attackers are career criminals with traditional criminal motives
   Adapt traditional criminal attack strategies to IT attacks (fraud, etc.)
   Many cybercrime gangs are international
      Makes prosecution difficult
      Dupe citizens of a country into being transshippers of fraudulently purchased goods to the attacker in another country
   Cybercriminals use black market forums
      Credit card numbers and identity information
      Vulnerabilities
      Exploit software (often with update contracts)

Fraud, Theft, and Extortion

Fraud
      In fraud, the attacker deceives the victim into doing something against the victim's financial self-interest
      Criminals are learning to conduct traditional frauds and new frauds over networks
      Also, new types of fraud, such as click fraud

Financial and Intellectual Property Theft
      Steal money or intellectual property they can sell to other criminals or to competitors

Extortion
      Threaten a DoS attack or threaten to release stolen information unless the victim pays the attacker

Stealing Sensitive Data about Customers and Employees
   Carding (credit card number theft)
   Bank account theft
   Online stock account theft
   Identity theft
      Steal enough identity information to represent the victim in large transactions, such as buying a car or even a house

Corporate Identity Theft
   Theft of a corporation's identity

FIGURE 1-13   The Criminal Era (Study Figure)

During the 1930s, John Dillinger and many other criminals took advantage of newly affordable automobiles to rob banks and disappear before the police could apprehend them. License plates were introduced primarily to help police reduce the advantages of mobile criminals.

In addition, criminals do not make strong distinctions between various types of crimes. In 2003, for example, VeriSign examined IP addresses from which attacks came. It found a high correlation between the IP addresses used in hacking and those used in fraud.[61] To give another example, police who searched locations used in

---

[61] Carolyn Duffy Marsan, "VeriSign Correlates Hacker, Fraud Activity," *NetworkWorldFusion*, November 19, 2003. http://www.nwfusion.com/newsletters/isp/2003/1117isp2.html.

identity theft found meth pipes and other material indicating that the criminals were meth addicts using online identity theft to support their meth addictions. They were stealing information and selling it to other criminal groups.[62]

CYBERCRIME   Cybercrime—the execution of crimes on the Internet—has become an extremely large problem in a very short period of time. According to the U.S. Treasury Department, cybercrime proceedings surpassed those from illegal drug sales in 2005.[63] In 2004, Internet crimes accounted for only 1.3 percent of all recorded crimes in Germany but accounted for 57 percent of the material damage caused by crimes.[64] In 2006, the FBI estimated that cybercrime costs businesses $67 billion a year. Cybercrime is not *becoming* an important problem for Internet security. It *has already become* the dominant problem.

INTERNATIONAL GANGS   With the Internet, national borders are irrelevant. As a result, cybercrime is fully international, thwarting attempts by countries to prosecute crimes committed against victims within their borders. When prosecution does result, it typically is only because of creativity on the part of prosecutors.

> Russian hacker Vasiliy Gorshkov stole credit card numbers and other personal information from numerous computers in the United States. He received a job offer from a U.S. recruiting firm, Invita. He was required to demonstrate hacking skills against a test network before coming to the United States. At a job interview with Invita in Seattle, he discussed hacking freely. When asked about his concerns with the FBI, he said that the FBI was no problem because the FBI could not get him in Russia. Yes, you guessed it. Invita was an FBI front. Gorshkov was tried and convicted.[65]

One problem that international gangs have is that many online sellers will not ship to addresses outside of the United States. To get around this problem, criminal gangs engage **transshippers** in the United States. These people receive shipped goods at U.S. offices and then ship them to the criminal gang in another country. Transhippers are paid a fee for each package they transship. Often, the transshippers are solicited over the Internet and never realize that they are doing anything to help criminals. Similarly, international gangs use **money mules** to transfer money (in return for a small percentage fee paid to the money mule). Often, transshippers and money mules are recruited through online job sites.

---

[62] Byron Acohido and Jon Schwartz, "'Meth Addicts' Other Habit: Online Theft," *USA Today*, December 15, 2005. http://www.usatoday.com/tech/news/internetprivacy/2005-12-14-meth-online-theft_x.htm?loc= interstitialskip.

[63] *Money.cnn.com*, "Record Bad Year for Computer Security," December 29, 2005. http://money.cnn.com/2005/12/29/technology/computer_security/index.htm.

[64] *Associated Press*, "Europe Council Looks to Fight Cybercrime: Group Pushes Ratification of International Treaty," September 15, 2004.

[65] U.S. Department of Justice, "Russian Computer Hacker Convicted by Jury," October 10, 2001. www.cybercrime.gov/gorshkovconvict.htm.

Thomas Pae received a 33-month prison sentence for participating in an international fraud ring. Romanian hackers broke into Ingram Micro's online ordering system and placed illegitimate orders for hundreds of thousands of dollars' worth of goods. These goods were delivered to Pae and other American conspirators, who shipped the goods to Romania.[66]

BLACK MARKETS AND MARKET SPECIALIZATION   Traditional criminals have always worked cooperatively. For example, fences buy stolen goods from thieves at a discount and then resell the stolen goods as apparently legitimate outlets where the origin of the goods will not be obvious.

Internationally, there are many **black market websites** for stolen consumer information.[67] There are even going rates for credit card numbers, with price being determined by how well the credit cards numbers have been validated, for instance, by making a small purchase with each card number to ensure that the number is "live."[68]

Researcher Dan Clements of CardCops (http://www.cardcops.com) posted fake credit card information on a website.[69] He leaked information about the website to a few chat rooms frequented by hackers. Within 15 minutes, the website had been visited by 74 carders from 31 different countries. By the end of the weekend, 1,600 carders had visited the site.

In 2007, the Symantec Corporation (http://www.symantec.com) reported typical prices in late 2006 hacker forums. U.S. credit cards with the card verification value went for between $1 and $6. Full identity theft information (U.S. bank account with password, credit card information, date of birth, etc.) went for between $14 and $18. Verified PayPal account information with balance went for $50 to $500, depending on the balance. Access to a compromised computer cost $3. A list of 29,000 e-mail accounts went for $5.

Most black markets deal in credit card and identity information, but these are not the only black markets. When an analyst discovers a security vulnerability in a piece of software, he or she usually notifies the software company, which credits the analyst when a patch is released to fix the vulnerability. However, software companies rarely pay vulnerability discoverers. As a consequence, a growing number of analysts sell vulnerability discoveries on one of several vulnerability black market.

Other programmers write exploitation software and sell it on black markets. In most cases today, exploitation software is sold with a provision for online support

---

[66] Federal Bureau of Investigation, "Los Angeles Man Sentenced to Prison for Role in International Computer Hacking and Internet Fraud Scheme," http://www.cybercrime.gov/paeSent.htm.

[67] Byron Acohido and Jon Schwartz, "Cybercrime Flourishes in Online Hacker Forums," *USA Today*, October 11, 2006.

[68] Carders and identity thieves also prey on one another. One practice is ripping—selling credit card numbers that are known to be invalid.

[69] Bob Sullivan, "Net Thieves Caught in Action," *www.MSNBC.com*, March 15, 2002. http://www.cardcops.com/msnbc/msnbc5.htm.

and free updates. For purchases, payments may even be held in escrow until the buyer has tested the exploitation software.

In 2007, an employee of SecurityFocus.com talked via ICQ instant messaging with a principal member of the Russian group that produced the Mpack infection kit that was widely sold beginning in 2006. The kit sold for between $700 and $1,000 and was constantly improved by its developers. A Russian, who went by the handle DCT, said that Mpack was created and primarily maintained by a three-member group called the Dream Coders Team. DCT said that the group paid for exploits that it used to continually upgrade its product. He said that the average price for a zero-day exploit (a vulnerability with no patches) was $10,000. DCT objected to the name "cybergang," maintaining that "We are just a group of people working together, but doing something illegal." He said that nobody in the group had connections with "real-life criminals." DCT also said that he has a legitimate job as well as working on Mpack and other projects. The Russian also said that because of all of the notoriety that Mpack was getting, the group would probably have to shut down Mpack soon.[70]

In many ways, cybercrime is maturing like many traditional markets. At the beginning, all-in-one companies usually dominate in a new market. Later, vertical and horizontal specialization appeared. In cybercrime, some criminals search for exploits, others develop toolkits, others specialize in distribution and botnet management, others run markets for identity theft and credit card numbers, and others create shared codes and libraries. Over time, new market niches continue to appear rapidly.

Although criminals often cooperate, they also tend to engage in wars against each other. For instant, the Srizbi Trojan Horse spread by the Mpack infection kit removed Storm Bot infections from hosts that Srizbi infected. It did this because Srizbi and Storm Bot were rival spamming services. In retaliation, the Storm Bot botnet conducted a denial-of service attack against the Mpack servers so that Mpack users could not download updates.[71]

TEST YOUR UNDERSTANDING

12. **a.** What is the dominant type of attacker today?
   b. Is cybercrime negligible today compared to non-computer crime?
   c. Why are international gangs difficult to prosecute?
   d. Why do international gangs use transshippers?
   e. How do they use transshippers?
   f. How do they use money mules?

---

[70] Robert Lemos, "Newsmaker: DCT, Mpack developer," *SecurityFocus*, July 20, 2007. http://www.securityfocus.com/news/11476/.

[71] Dan Goodin, "Rival Malware Gangs Wage Turf War," *The Register*, July 1, 2007. http://www.theregister.co.uk/2007/07/01/malware_gang_war/.

Fraud, Theft, and Extortion

Fraud, theft, and extortion are traditional criminal attacks. Today, criminals have learned to execute these crimes over networks.

FRAUD   Criminals attempt to get money illicitly in a number of ways. We will list just a few in this chapter. One characteristic of many of these criminal attacks is that they involve fraud. In **fraud**, the attacker deceives the victim into doing something against the victim's financial self-interest. For example, in the T-Data example given later in this chapter, the attacker defrauded a company into giving him equipment by pretending to be a real company that would pay.

> *In fraud, the attacker deceives the victim into doing something against the victim's financial self-interest.*

There is nothing new about fraud. In the physical world, of course, fraud has been perpetrated since the beginning of humankind. Criminals are simply learning how to conduct fraud over networks. In many cases, in fact, they merely execute classic frauds long practiced face-to-face over networks. Most spam messages, for example, use classic fraud methods and have classic fraud goals.

In other cases, criminals are creating new network-specific frauds. For instance, many websites get paid by advertisers on a per-click basis. Every time a website visitor clicks on an advertising link at the website and is taken to the advertiser's website, the advertiser pays the original website a small fee. In **click fraud**, a criminal website owner creates a program to click on the link repeatedly. Each of these bogus clicks takes money from the advertiser without generating potential customers.

FINANCIAL AND INTELLECTUAL PROPERTY THEFT   Just as career criminals have long burgled homes and robbed banks, career criminals on the Internet engage in financial theft.

> In perhaps the most ambitious attempted theft to date, the Mafia in Sicily attempted to steal over $400 million by creating a fake branch of the Banco di Sicilia.[72] The police learned about the attempt from informants who heard that the Mafia was seeking the help of dishonest bank officials. A police officer posed as a dishonest bank official and cracked the case. If not for informants, a massive theft might have been executed.

In other cases, career criminals steal a firm's intellectual property for sale to other criminals or to corporate competitors. As noted earlier in the chapter, IP consists of formally protected information such as patents and other information and

---

[72] Phillip Willan, "Mafia Caught Attempting Online Bank Fraud," *IDG News Service*, October 3, 2000. No longer online.

trade secrets, which are sensitive pieces of information that the company acts to protect, such as corporate plans and even price lists. Even as far back as 1999, Fortune 1,000 companies lost more than $45 billion through the theft of trade secrets, according to a Price Waterhouse Coopers survey. This was long before the theft of intellectual property via the Internet became a serious threat.

> A paralegal employee in one law firm copied the company's plans for a plaintiff in a large court case. These plans cost several million dollars to develop. He attempted to sell the plans to one of the firms representing the defendants. That firm, however, notified the authorities.[73]

EXTORTION AGAINST CORPORATIONS   **Extortion** is the using threat of harm to get the victim to pay money to avoid the harm. Extortion has long been a staple of criminal attacks in the real world. One way to use IT to extort a firm is to threaten to attack it unless protection money is paid.

> One Russian gang threatened online betting sites with denial-of-service attacks unless the betting sites paid protection money.[74] The demanded tributes ranged between $18,000 and $55,000. Many online betting sites paid the extortion money.
>   In another case, a hacker brought down a critical server during a low-activity period and threatened to do it again during a peak-activity period unless paid extortion money. This company paid the extortionist.[75]

Sometimes, when a criminal steals information, he or she extorts the firm by threatening to release the information unless "hush money" is paid.

> The hacker Maxim allegedly broke into CD Universe and stole 300,000 credit card numbers.[76] He threatened to post the credit card numbers online unless he was paid $100,000. When CD Universe refused, he did post 25,000 of the stolen credit card numbers, generating massive unfavorable publicity for the firm.

TEST YOUR UNDERSTANDING

13. a. What is fraud? Be specific.
    b. What is click fraud?
    c. How do criminals engage in online extortion?

---

[73] U.S. Department of Justice, "Manhattan Paralegal Sentenced for Theft of Litigation Trial Plan," January 30, 2002. http://www.cybercrime.gov/farrajSentence.htm.

[74] Fran Foo, "Thugs Turn to Corporate e-Blackmail," *ZDNet Australia*, June 28, 2004. http://news.zdnet.com/2100-9595_22-5286999.html.

[75] Sandeep Junnarkar, "Online Banks: Prime Target for Attacks," *Znet.com*, May 1, 2002. http://techupdate.zdnet.com/techupdate/stories/main/0,14179,2863266-1,00.html.

[76] Canoe, "Hijacked Web Site Regroups After Infamous Attack," February 29, 2000. http://www.fan590.com/HackerAttack/feb29_apreshack.html.

Stealing Sensitive Data about Customers and Employees

Criminals tend to seek out "soft targets" that produce high gains for little effort. This often means targeting individual people instead of corporations. We will look at a number of attacks on individuals, in order of increasing severity.

CARDING   Probably the most common criminal attack on individuals is **credit card number theft**—a practice known as **carding**. Carders "hit the jackpot" if they can learn the credit card number, the card owner's name, and the three-digit card verification number. Once the thief has the information that he or she needs, the thief can make purchases until the card is invalidated. Fortunately, if carding victims report credit card number fraud promptly, they are only liable for $50 by law in the United States, and most credit card vendors waive even that liability.

BANK ACCOUNT THEFT   If the thief steals the authentication information required to engage in online transactions on behalf of the victim, however, the thief can drain the victim's bank account. **Bank account theft** is more serious than credit card number theft.

ONLINE STOCK ACCOUNT THEFT   In 2006, criminals surged into the theft of online stock accounts due to security weaknesses in online stock trading sites. Instead of stealing a few hundred dollars using stolen credit cards, stock account thefts often reached thousands of dollars.

IDENTITY THEFT   If the thief can steal even more information, he or she can engage in **identity theft**, in which the thief impersonates the victim sufficiently well to engage in large financial transactions, such as taking out large loans and making large purchases in the name of the victim. Victims of identity theft may suffer massive damages, and some have even been arrested for the actions of identity thieves.[77] Identity theft is far more serious than credit card number theft.

Criminals have long stolen consumer identity information without using computers. For example, carders have traditionally recorded credit card numbers during retail store purchases. With computers and networks, however, thieves have been able to steal consumer identity information for hundreds, thousands, and even millions of victims. Most commonly, hackers break into poorly protected corporate computers to steal this information. However, lost or stolen laptops and backup tapes also are gold mines for consumer information thieves. Furthermore, dishonest insiders are often involved.

Patrice Williams and Makeebrah Turner, employees at Chase Financial Corporation, were able to obtain customer information, including credit card numbers, for a number of accounts. They gave this information to outside conspirators. Williams and Turner were each sentenced to a year and a day in federal prison.[78]

---

[77] Unfortunately, the Federal Trade Commission, which publishes widely cited data on identity theft, defines identity theft very broadly, to include simple credit card number theft, not just more serious identity theft.

[78] U.S. Department of Justice, "Former Chase Financial Corp. Employees Sentenced for Scheme to Defraud Chase Manhattan Bank and Chase Financial Corporation," February 19, 2002. http://www.usdoj.gov/criminal/cybercrime/williams_turnerSent.htm.

In 2006, Gartner surveyed 5,000 U.S. bank customers. Based on the survey data, Gartner estimated that three million Americans had been victims of online scams during the past six years and that they lost an average of $900 each. Another study found an average loss of almost $4,000, found that victims spent an average of 81 hours trying to resolve their cases, and found that a quarter never fully recovered.[79] Some losses can be much worse, for instance, if an identity thief transfers title to a victim's home to himself or herself and then sells the house.

THE CORPORATE CONNECTION   Carding, bank account theft, and identity theft are not just consumer problems. They also are corporate problems. When companies report that their customer databases have been broken into and that thousands or millions of individuals have had their identity information compromised, the backlash from customers and investors can be substantial. In addition, firms can face government sanctions. In the United States, for instance, the Federal Trade Commission has extensive power to fine firms that fail to implement customer data protections appropriately. The Commission also can mandate expensive independent audits of a firm's handling of private information for ten or more years after a problem. Finally, major breaches often involve the firing of functional managers responsible for breached systems.

CORPORATE IDENTITY THEFT   Although identity theft occurs most often to individuals, it can also happen to corporations. By collecting information about a company on the Internet, corporate identity thieves can apply for, get, and use corporate credit cards in the name of the victim company. They can also accept credit card orders in the name of the victim company. They can even file documents to change the legal address of the victim company and change the name of the person in charge of the company.

> Software maker T-Data does not accept credit cards. However, $15,000 in credit card purchases was supposedly accepted by T-Data. A corporate identity thief had set up a false company claiming to be T-Data and received approval to accept credit card purchases. Nearly all of the purchases were made with stolen credit card numbers. In effect, identity theft provided a way to exploit stolen credit card numbers—a form of money laundering. The thieves worked hard to avoid fraud detection programs at credit card processing firms by keeping purchases small. They also avoided detection by being associated with several different processing firms and only making a few purchases with each processing firm. T-Data was not their only victim. They conducted corporate identity theft against at least 50 firms.[80]

TEST YOUR UNDERSTANDING

14. **a.** What is carding?
    b. Describe bank account theft and online stock account theft.
    c. Distinguish between credit card theft and identity theft.

---

[79] TechWeb News, "One in Four Identity Theft Victims Never Fully Recover," July 28, 2005. http://www. techweb.com/wire/security/166402606.

[80] Bob Sullivan, "Real Companies, Fake Money," *MSNBC.com*, October 7, 2004. http://www.msnbc.msn. com/id/6175738/.

d. Why is identity theft more serious than credit card number theft?

e. How do criminals usually get the information they need for credit card theft and identity theft?

f. How can companies be harmed if they allow personal information in their control to be stolen?

g. What is corporate identity theft?

COMPETITOR THREATS

Corporate competitors can also be attackers. They can engage in many types of attacks. We will focus on attacks on confidentiality and attacks on availability.

Commercial Espionage

In **public intelligence gathering**, a competitor will look at a company's website and other public information to find information that the victim company itself divulges. The competitor may also check Facebook pages for employees and other public information.

There have been few court cases to test the legality of such actions, but by definition, trade secrets are only protected by law if a company makes a reasonable effort to keep them secret. Note that Herculean efforts are not necessary—only reasonable efforts, which reflect the sensitivity of the asset and security practices in the industry.

Trade secrets are only protected by law if a company makes a reasonable effort to keep them secret.

> **Commercial Espionage**
> Attacks on confidentiality
> Public information gathering
> > Company website and public documents
> > Facebook pages of employees, etc.
> Trade secret espionage
> > May only be litigated if a company has provided reasonable protection for those secrets
> > Reasonableness reflects the sensitivity of the secret and industry security practices
> Trade secret theft
> > Theft through interception, hacking, and other traditional cybercrimes
> > Bribe an employee
> > Hire your ex-employee and soliciting or accept trade secrets
> National intelligence agencies engage in commercial espionage
>
> **Denial-of-Service Attacks**
> Attacks on availability
> Rare but can be devastating

FIGURE 1-14 Competitor Threats (Study Figure)

A frequent goal of corporate attackers is to *illegally* steal a company's trade secrets—a practice called **trade secret espionage**. In its most blatant form, a competitor will intercept a victim company's communication, hack its servers, or bribe an employee at the victim company to steal information. Or, it may hire one of your ex-employees and solicit or accept your trade secrets from that person.

Yan Ming Shan was an employee of a Chinese firm. He was sent to the United States for training on the proprietary software of 3DGeo Development. While there, he gained unauthorized access to 3DGeo's computer systems in an attempt to steal the software, including the original source code. This software would have been extremely valuable to his Chinese employer.[81]

Commercial espionage is not limited to corporate competitors. Since the end of the cold war, many national intelligence agencies have reportedly moved into commercial espionage. Robert Gates, director of the CIA from 1991 to 1993, reported that government economic espionage is widespread.[82] He specifically cited France, Russia, China, South Korea, Germany, Israel, India, and Pakistan as being engaged in intense corporate espionage. In 2007, the U.S.–China Economic and Security Review Commission's annual report to Congress said that "Chinese espionage activities in the US are so extensive that they comprise the single greatest risk to the security of American technologies."[83]

Denial-of-Service Attacks

Competitors can also engage in various other types of attacks against your firm, such as DoS attacks. Although these attacks on availability are rare, they can be devastating.

TEST YOUR UNDERSTANDING

15. a. Distinguish between public intelligence gathering and trade secret espionage.
    b. What must a company do to its trade secrets if it wishes to be able to prosecute people or companies who steal it?
    c. How strong do those protections have to be?
    d. Who is likely to engage in espionage against a firm?

CYBERWAR AND CYBERTERROR

Today, criminal attackers are raising the risk level for corporations. However, there also are nightmare scenarios that have levels of damage far greater than those caused by criminal attacks. These are attacks by organized terrorist groups and even by national governments. These attacks could have unprecedented scale that few corporate security plans today are prepared for.

---

[81] U.S. Department of Justice, "China Citizen Pleads Guilty to Unauthorized Access of a Software Company with Intent to Defraud," July 7, 2004. http://www.cybercrime.gov/shanPlea.htm.

[82] Margret Johnson, "Business Spy Threat is Real, Former CIA Chief Says," *NetworkWorldFusion*, October 17, 2000. http://www.nwfusion.com/news.1017spythreat.html.

[83] This report is available at http://www.uscc.gov/.

Nightmare Threats
  Potential for far greater attacks than those caused by criminal attackers

Cyberwar
  Computer-based attacks by national governments
  Espionage
  Cyber-only attacks to damage financial and communication infrastructure
  To augment conventional physical attacks
      Attack IT infrastructure along with physical attacks (or in place of physical attacks)
      Paralyze enemy command and control
      Engage in propaganda attacks

Cyberterror
  Attacks by terrorists or terrorist groups
  May attack IT resources directly
  Use the Internet for recruitment and coordination
  Use the Internet to augment physical attacks
      Disrupt communication among first responders
      Use cyberattacks to increase terror in physical attacks
  Turn to computer crime to fund their attacks

FIGURE 1-15   Cyberwar and Cyberterror (Study Figure)

Cyberwar

Today, when countries go to war, they use guns and bombs. However, they can also do extreme damage using computers. **Cyberwar** consists of computer-based attacks made by national governments.

Cyberwar consists of computer-based attacks made by national governments.

- Before physical hostilities commence, combatants can engage in computer espionage to learn their adversaries' secrets. China is particularly active in cyberwar espionage.[84] Cyberespionage from China has been a serious problem since 1999.[85]
- When physical hostilities do occur, countries can use cyberwar attacks to do massive damage to one another's financial infrastructures, to disrupt one another's communication infrastructures, and to damage the country's IT infrastructure.

---

[84] Dawn S. Onley and Patience Wait, "Red Storm Rising," *GCN.com*, August 21, 2006. Keith Epstein, "China Stealing U.S. Computer Data, Says Commission," *Business Week*, November 21, 2008. http://www.businessweek.com/bwdaily/dnflash/content/nov2008/db20081121_440892.htm.

[85] Daniel Verton and L. Scott Tillett, "DOD Confirms Cyberattack 'Something New'," *Cnn.com*, March 6, 1999. http://www.cnn.com/TECH/computing/9903/06/dod.hacker.update.idg/index.html.

- Cyberwar attacks during a conventional (non-cyber) attack may also include propaganda attacks. During the U.S. attacks on Serbia, owners of key industries were warned via e-mail that their companies would be targeted for bombing unless they forced the government to resign.
- In fact, cyberwar attacks can be made without engaging in physical hostilities, doing tremendous damage.

Cyberterror

Another nightmare scenario is **cyberterror**, in which the attacker is a terrorist or group of terrorists.[86]

- Of course, cyberterrorists can attack information technology resources directly. They can damage a country's financial, communication, and utilities infrastructure.[87]
- Most commonly, cyberterrorists use the Internet as a recruitment tool through websites and to coordinate their activities.[88]
- They can also use cyberterror in conjunction with physical attacks, say by disrupting the communication systems of first responders or disrupting electricity to cause traffic jams in order to compound terror.
- More subtly, but equally dangerously, many terrorist organizations turn to computer crime to fund their terrorist activities, just as they turn to slave prostitution and other physical crimes.[89]

TEST YOUR UNDERSTANDING

16. **a.** Distinguish between cyberwar and cyberterror.
    b. How can countries use cyberwar attacks?
    c. How can terrorists use IT?

A CONSTANTLY CHANGING THREAT ENVIRONMENT

This chapter has looked at the threat environment that existed at the time of this writing. However, the threat environment is changing rapidly. Every year or two, a radically new type of attack appears and grows explosively. Security professionals constantly have to reassess the threat environment.

---

[86] Although organized terrorist groups are very serious threats, a related group of attackers is somewhat dangerous. These are hacktivists, who attack based on political beliefs. During tense periods between the United States and China, for instance, hacktivists on both sides have attacked the IT resources of the other country.

[87] In 2008, the CIA revealed that attacks over the Internet had cut off electrical power in several cities. Robert McMillan, PC World, January 19, 2008. http://www.pcworld.com/article/id,141564/article.htm?tk=nl_dnxnws.

[88] According to one Saudi Arabian researcher, there were 5,600 websites linked to Al-Qaida in 2007, and that 900 more were appearing annually. Reuters, "Researcher: Al-Qaida-Linked Web Sites Number 5,600," December 4, 2007.

[89] David Talbot, "Terror's Server," *TechnologyReview.com*, February 14, 2005. http://www.technologyreview.com/articles/05/02/issue/feature_terror.asp.

In addition, every time victims create countermeasures, attackers analyze those countermeasures and often find ways to get around them. Security does not deal with programming error; it deals with intelligent adversaries who constantly adapt to corporate efforts.

Finally, attacks always grow more sophisticated and severe. In the National Security Agency, people frequently cite the dictum, "Attacks always get better; they never get worse."[90]

TEST YOUR UNDERSTANDING

17. In what three broad ways is the threat environment likely to change in the future?

Synopsis

We began this chapter by looking at several important pieces of security terminology. We first looked at the three security goals: confidentiality, integrity, and availability. We then defined the term *incidents* (also *called* breaches or *compromises*). Finally, we defined *countermeasures* (also called *safeguards* or *controls*). Controls generally are classified as preventive, detective, and corrective. This introduction ended with an important case example—the break-ins at TJX—which illustrates the complexity of real security situations.

Although many people envision attacks arriving over the Internet when they think about IT security, many security professionals believe that employees and ex-employees are the biggest threat facing corporations and that IT security professionals represent the biggest threat of all. Employees engage in a broad range of attacks ranging from spending too much time on personal websurfing to sabotage, financial theft, and the theft of IP.

Malware is a generic name for evil software. Numerically, the most frequent compromises are malware compromises, including viruses, worms, blended threats, mobile code, and Trojan horses. Nearly every firm has multiple malware compromises each year. Many malware attacks use social engineering, in which the victim is tricked into doing something against security policies, such as opening an e-mail attachment containing malware because the e-mail subject line and body make opening the attachment seem sensible or enticing.

People tend to envision attackers as being Hollywood movie hackers who can break into computers almost instantly. In reality, hackers—people who intentionally access computer resources without authorization or in excess of authorization—often take a long time to break into computers. They first tend to send probe packets into a network to identify potential host victims and the applications running on computers. Once the hacker understands the network, he or she uses an exploit program to achieve the hack (break-in). The hacker can then do damage at leisure. Hackers also use social engineering. Attackers sometimes execute denial-of-service (DoS) attacks. In addition to highly skilled hackers, the vast community of script kiddies constitutes a serious threat to corporations.

---

[90] Bruce Schneier, "An American Idol for Crypto Geeks," *Wired News*, February 8, 2007. http://www.wired.com/politics/security/commentary/securitymatters/2007/02/72657.

One fact that surprises many people is that traditional external attackers motivated by reputation and thrills have largely been replaced with career criminals, who use IT to engage in traditional criminal attacks, such as financial theft, the theft of intellectual property (IP), extortion, carding, bank account theft, identity theft, and espionage. Career criminals often create and use large botnets to execute their attacks.

Corporations face many other emerging security concerns, including employee theft and abuse, espionage by competitors and national intelligence agencies, and the nightmare scenarios of cyberwar and cyberterror. In addition, the threat environment is changing rapidly—always in the direction of more sophisticated and severe attacks.

Thought Questions

1. If an attacker breaks into a corporate database and deletes critical files, against what security goal is this attack aimed?
2. How can detective countermeasures act as preventive countermeasures? (The answer is not in the text.)
3. a) If you accidentally find someone's password and use it to get into a system, is this hacking? Explain. b) Someone sends you a "game." When you run it, it logs you into an IRS server. Is this hacking? Explain. c) Could you be prosecuted for doing this? d) You have access to your home page on a server. By accident, you discover that if you hit a certain key, you can get into someone else's files. You spend just a few minutes looking around. Is this hacking? Explain.
4. Addamark Technologies found that its webservers had been accessed without authorization by an employee of competitor Arcsight.[91] Arcsight's vice president for marketing dismissed the hacking, saying, "It's simply a screen that asked for a username and password. The employee didn't feel like he did anything illicit." The VP went on to say the employee would not be disciplined. Comment on the Arcsight VP's defense.
5. The Senate Judiciary Committee in 2004 suspected that two Republican aides took Democratic computer files on strategies for blocking judicial nominations.[92] The Senate Sergeant-at-Arms, William Pickle, investigated the case and reported that the two aides had tapped into 4,670 files between 2001 and 2003, most of them in the directories for Democratic staffers. Manuel Miranda, one of the aides identified by Pickle, resigned. Miranda argued that the Democratic messages regarded Democratic collusion with liberal groups and so were illicit activity, making them fair game. Comment on Miranda's defense.
6. Give three examples of social engineering not listed in the text.
7. Why do you think DoS attackers use zombies to attack victims instead of sending attack packets directly to victims? Come up with two reasons.
8. Why would using a script created by a hacker not give you the experience of expert hacking?
9. What do you think are the pros and cons of paying off extortionists?
10. A competitor goes to your public website and discovers that they can get into a directory that you did not know could be reached. There, they find a list of customer and use the list to their advantage. Have they hacked your webserver? What problem may you encounter in suing them for the theft of trade secrets?

---

[91] Addamark Technologies, "Even Security Firms at Risk for Break In," *E-week*, February 17, 2003.
[92] Helen Dewar, *Washington Post*, March 12, 2004, A21.

Internet Exercise

1. Look up information on recent rates of attacks. One source is Message Labs (http://www.messagelabs.com). Message Labs has daily information. Another source is Webroot (http://webroot.com); Webroot has periodic reports on attack frequencies.

Project

1. Look up the PCI-DSS control objectives on the Internet. Give its URL. Which ones did TJX violate? Justify your list.

Perspective Questions

1. What was the most surprising thing for you in this chapter?

2. What was the most difficult thing for you in this chapter?

Chapter 2

Planning

Security is a process, not a product.[1]

BRUCE SCHNEIER, BT

LEARNING OBJECTIVES:
By the end of this chapter, you should be able to explain the following:

- The need for formal management processes.
- The plan–protect–respond security management cycle.
- Compliance laws and regulations.
- Organizational issues.
- Risk analysis.
- The technical security infrastructure.
- Policy-driven implementation.
- Governance frameworks.

INTRODUCTION

Defense

Chapter 1 was a snapshot of threats facing corporations today. The chapter ended with a dark view of the future—threats will increase in number, and threats will get ever more dangerous. The rest of this book describes how corporations can respond to threats to their sensitive resources. To borrow from the Hogwarts curriculum, this book could have the title *Defense against the Dark Arts*.

Note that this is not a book about how to attack corporations. It is about defense. Defense is an IT security professional's main job, and defense is extremely complex. After you master the principles and practices of defense well, a detailed

---

[1] Bruce Schneier, "Computer Security: Will We Ever Learn?" *Crypto-Gram Newsletter*, May 15, 2000. http://www.schneier.com/crypto-gram-0005.html.

understanding of attacks will help you. But this is a book for people who are new to IT security. To focus heavily on attacks, while exciting, would push out the content that students need to prepare them for their real job, defense.

TEST YOUR UNDERSTANDING

1. Why does the book focus on defense instead of offense?

Management Processes

Bruce Schneier is one of the deepest thinkers in IT security today. His quote at the beginning of this chapter has become a standard teaching point in IT security. It emphasizes that it is a mistake to focus too heavily on security technology compared to security management.

MANAGEMENT IS THE HARD PART   One reason why people tend to focus on technology is that it is easier to think about technology than about management. Technology is visible, and there are many things that we can say about security technologies. Most of these technology concepts, furthermore, are well defined and are therefore easy to discuss.

Management, in contrast, is abstract. You cannot show pictures of devices or talk in terms of detailed concepts or software algorithms. There are fewer general principles to discuss, and most of these principles cannot be put into practice without well-defined and complex processes.

Security management, however, is far more important than security technology. One official from the U.S. federal General Services Administration talked about helping a series of federal agencies reorganize their security technologies. In every case, the agencies enjoyed good security immediately. Then security decayed rapidly. These agencies had the technology, but they lacked the management ability to make security work for the long term.

COMPREHENSIVE SECURITY   It is not surprising that these agencies failed. For one thing, attackers only need to find a single way to get into the corporation. In contrast, Figure 2-2 shows that organizations need **comprehensive security**—closing all routes of attack to their systems to attackers. Comprehensive security does not come by accident.

Technology is Concrete
   Can visualize devices and transmission lines
   Can understand device and software operation

Management is Abstract

Management is More Important
   Security is a process, not a product (Bruce Schneier)

FIGURE 2-1   Management Is the Hard Part (Study Figure)

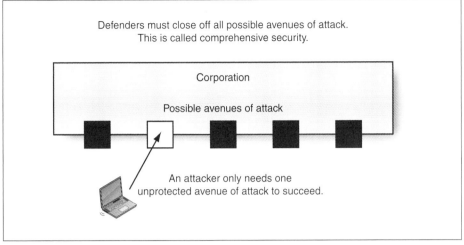

FIGURE 2-2 The Need for Comprehensive Security

WEAKEST LINKS FAILURES Another reason why security management is difficult is that some protections have many components that must all work for the countermeasure to succeed. Figure 2-3 gives an example. Here, the firewall administrator draws up filtering rules. The firewall then examines all packets passing through it. It drops provable attack packets and stores information about dropped packets in a log file. The firewall administrator should check the log file daily.

   If there is any failure in this process, the firewall becomes useless. If an important filtering rule is omitted, provable attack packets will get through. Or, if the administrator fails to read log files daily, a problem may go undetected for weeks or months.

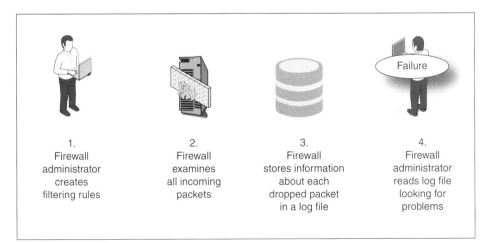

FIGURE 2-3 Weakest Link Failure

In chains of activities within a single countermeasure, *everything* must be done well. If even one step is not implemented well, security may seem good, but there will be no real protection. If the failure of a single element of a system will ruin security, this is called a **weakest link** failure. In many cases, human actions are the weakest links in security protections.

> *If the failure of a single element of a system will ruin security, this is a weakest link failure.*

THE NEED TO PROTECT MANY RESOURCES   A third reason why security management is difficult is that companies need to protect many resources. Some of these are relatively well-defined assets, such as databases and servers. Others are broad organizational processes, such as financial reporting and new product development. All are changing rapidly. As discussed later in this chapter, companies need to identify all of their resources and develop a security program for each one. This is a Herculean effort.

TEST YOUR UNDERSTANDING

2. **a.** For what reasons is security management hard?
   b. What is comprehensive security, and why is it needed?
   c. What are weakest link failures?

The Need for a Disciplined Security Management Process

Schneier's use of the term *process* in the quotation at the beginning of this chapter is particularly important. Security is too complicated to be managed informally. Companies must develop and follow formal **processes** (planned series of actions) in security management, for instance, processes for annual planning and processes for planning and developing individual countermeasures.

> *Processes are planned series of actions.*

Complex
   Cannot be managed informally

Need Formal Processes
   Planned series of actions in security management
   Annual planning
   Processes for planning and developing individual countermeasures

   . . .

A Continuous Process
   Fail if let up

Compliance Regulations
   Add to the need to adopt disciplined security management processes

---

FIGURE 2-4   Security Management Is a Disciplined Process (Study Figure)

Business strategists have long said that quality improvement is a never-ending process, not a one-time effort. One football coach noted that recruiting is like shaving; you miss one day, and you look like a bum. Security management is also a never-ending process.[2]

One external factor that is motivating firms to formalize their security processes is a growing number of compliance laws and regulations. Many compliance regimes require firms to adopt specific formal governance frameworks to drive security planning and operational management. We will look at several of these governance frameworks later in this chapter.

TEST YOUR UNDERSTANDING

3. **a.** Why are processes necessary in security management?
   b. What is driving firms to use formal governance frameworks to guide their security processes?

The Plan–Protect–Respond Cycle

If security processes must be managed comprehensively, we need a formal top-level security management process. Most firms today protect against threats by using a highest-level security management process called the **plan–protect–respond cycle**, which Figure 2-5 illustrates.

PLANNING   The cycle begins with planning. Without an excellent plan, you will never have comprehensive security. Of course, once plans are implemented, the results will feed back into planning. New threats and business conditions will also force companies to return to planning. Although the figure seems to indicate a neat and sequential process among the stages, all three activities take place simultaneously

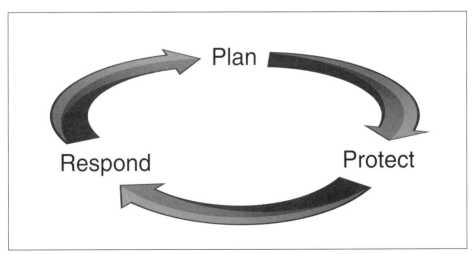

FIGURE 2-5   The Plan–Protect–Respond Cycle for Security Management

---

[2] Technically, then, security management is a death march.

and constantly feed into one another. Chapter 2 discusses planning in detail. We will also return to planning frequently throughout the book.

PROTECTION   Protection is the plan-based creation and operation of countermeasures. Most of the security professional's day will be spent in the protection phase, so it is no surprise that nearly all of this book is devoted to the creation and operation of controls.

> *Protection is the plan-based creation and operation of countermeasures.*

- Chapters 3 and 4 deal with cryptographic protections, which are used alone or as components of many other countermeasures. Given their use in other controls, we will look at them first. Before covering these chapters, many teachers will cover Appendix A, which reviews networking concepts.
- Chapter 5 deals with access control and site security. Attackers who cannot reach your resources cannot harm them.
- Chapter 6 deals with a particular family of access controls—firewalls. Although firewalls are not magic bullets for protection, they are enormously important (and complicated). It is important for IT security people to understand firewalls thoroughly.
- Chapter 7 deals with host and data security. This will look at host software up to the operating system. It then looks at how to protect the data on host computers, including the three most important data protections—backup, backup, and backup.
- Chapter 8 looks at application security. Most hackers today succeed by compromising application programs. If the attacker compromises an application, the attacker inherits the permissions of the application program. In many cases, these permissions give the attacker complete control of the computer.

For each type of protection, we need to manage the *systems development life cycle (SDLC)*, which runs from initial planning through implementation. Information systems professionals often focus on the SDLC (see Figure 2-6). However, most of a

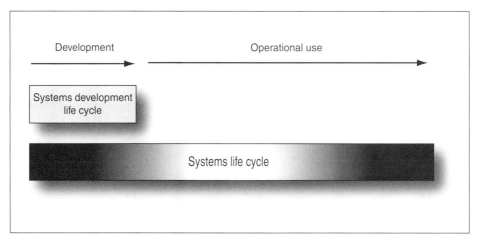

FIGURE 2-6 Systems Life Cycle

countermeasure's life consists of the operational stage *after* development. To teach security students to focus on the SDLC would be like training doctors in prenatal care and teaching them nothing about health care after birth. This book focuses on the management of controls through the entire **systems life cycle**, and this means focusing heavily on ongoing management after creation.

RESPONSE   Even with the great planning and meticulous protection, some attacks will succeed. Chapter 9 deals with incident response. Response is complex because incidents vary in severity from false alarms through disasters and because different levels of attack severity require different response approaches.

Response is recovery according to plan—a definition that emphasizes that if response is not carefully planned in advance, it will take too long and be only partially effective. Speed and accuracy of response are of the essence, and the way to achieve both is to rehearse the incident response plan frequently before compromises occur.

Response is recovery according to plan.

TEST YOUR UNDERSTANDING

4. **a.** List the three stages in the plan–protect–respond cycle.
   b. Is there a sequential flow between the stages?
   c. What stage consumes the most time?
   d. How does this book define protection?
   e. How does the book define response?

Vision in Planning

IT security's vision about its role with respect to your company, its employees, and the outside world drives everything else.

VIEWING SECURITY AS AN ENABLER   For security, there are two essential elements of vision. The first is the need to see security as an *enabler* rather than as a source of frustration. If a firm has poor security, many innovations are closed to it because they would be too dangerous. However, if a firm has strong security, this will enable it to do many things. For instance, a firm with strong security can engage in interorganizational systems with other firms. This can open new markets, bring better information flows, and lead to lower operational costs.

Our security vision must focus on security as an enabler rather than as a preventer.

To give another example, the Simple Network Management Protocol (SNMP) gives organizations the ability to manage hundreds or thousands of remote network devices from a single management console. Nearly all firms use the SNMP Get command, which asks a managed device to send back certain data about the device's status and operation. This is very useful in diagnosing problems. In turn, the SNMP Set command allows the

Vision

Your understanding about your role with respect to your company, its employees, and the outside world drives everything else

Security as an Enabler

Security is often thought of as a preventer

But security is also an enabler

If have good security, can do things otherwise impossible

Engage in interorganizational systems with other firms

Can use SNMP Set commands to manage their systems remotely

Must get in early on projects to reduce inconvenience

Positive Vision of Users

Must not view users as malicious or stupid

Stupid means poorly trained, and that is security's fault

Must have zero tolerance for negative views of users

Should Not View Security as Police or Military Force

Creates a negative view of users

Police merely punish; do not prevent crime; security must prevent attacks

Military can use fatal force; security cannot even punish (HR does that)

Need New Vision

Mother nurturing inexperienced offspring

. . .

Cannot be Effective Unless Users Will Work with You

Consultation, consultation, consultation

FIGURE 2-7   Vision (Study Figure)

manager to reconfigure devices remotely, for instance, by telling a switch to turn off a certain port or to put a port in testing mode. This kind of remote reconfiguration can save a great deal of network management labor cost by avoiding the need for network personnel to travel to the remote device to fix problems. It also reduces the time needed to get systems back into operation. However, many firms with weak security turn off the Set command because of the threat caused by attackers who might impersonate the SNMP manager and send malicious Set commands to cause chaos in the network. In contrast, firms that manage security well can confidently use Set and reap the benefits.

One key to making security an enabler is to get security involved early in all projects. Early in a project's life, security usually can be added relatively inexpensively and without making the final system inflexible. If security is brought in too late, then security retrofits are likely to be expensive and are likely to reduce system usability. In addition, of course, if a project cannot be undertaken because of unacceptable security risks, it is better to find this out earlier rather than later.[3]

---

[3] Every new aircraft engine must face the "chicken test," in which dead fowl are shot into the running engine. If there is too much damage, the engine must be redesigned. A common adage in aircraft engine manufacturing is "Face your chicken test early." Similarly if an IT project will have security problems, it is best to know that before you invest too much money.

DEVELOPING POSITIVE VISIONS OF USERS   Another key aspect of vision is to view users positively. One cynical security professional said, "there are two kinds of users—those who do bad things because they are malicious and those who do bad things because they are stupid." While it might be possible to sympathize with this viewpoint, viewing users as the enemy is corrosive.

Instead, we should view users as resources. For example, security needs to recruit and train users to be the front line of the firm's security defenses. Users often are the first to see security problems, and if they feel that they are part of the security team, they can give early warnings to the security staff. Also, users need to be trained in security self-defense so that they can protect their own assets from threats. If "stupid" means "poorly trained," this is the security department's fault.

In airline travel, a steward or stewardess who refers to passengers as "cattle" is likely to be fired. Security departments should do the same thing to security professionals who refer to employees in general in derogatory ways. There should be zero tolerance for user disrespect.

One problem in developing a positive vision of users is the frequent use of police or military imagery when talking about users. This has attractions, because it helps security professionals ask how the police or the military would deal with particular situations involving willful misbehavior. However, the police[4] tend to view suspects with a jaundiced eye, and soldiers are taught to hate the enemy. In the end, these are stupid ways to view the role of IT security.

There are other ways to view security's relationship to employees. For instance, one image is security as mother. Good mothers set limits, spend a great deal of time explaining those limits, and, more importantly, help their children mature so that they are safe in hazardous situations. It is also possible to view the security staff as teachers, personal coaches, and problem solvers.

Overall, if employees place wreaths of garlic around their necks and chant warding spells every time a security staff member approaches, security will not be effective in that company. In contrast, when a highly successful security head was asked about the three most important things about security, he said, "Consultation, consultation, and consultation."

TEST YOUR UNDERSTANDING

5. **a.** How can good security be an enabler?
   b. What is the key to being an enabler?
   c. Why is a negative view of users bad?
   d. Why is viewing the security function as a police force or military organization a bad idea?

Strategic IT Security Planning

Strategic IT security planning looks at the big picture. It first assesses the company's current security. It then considers factors that will be driving changes—including the increasingly complex and virulent threat environment, the growth of compliance

---

[4] For security professionals to see themselves as cops is particularly stupid. As most police officers will tell you, their job is to catch criminals, not to *prevent* crime. In contrast, an IT security professional's job *is* to prevent attacks, and catching the attacker is rare.

Current IT Security Gaps

Driving Forces
  The threat environment
  Compliance laws and regulations
  Corporate structure changes, such as mergers

Resources
  Enumerate all resources
  Rate each by sensitivity

Develop Remediation Plans
  Develop a remediation plan for all security gaps
  Develop a remediation plan for every resource unless it is well protected

Develop an Investment Portfolio
  You cannot close all gaps immediately
  Choose projects that will provide the largest returns
  Implement these

FIGURE 2-8   Strategic IT Security Planning (Study Figure)

laws and regulations, changes in the corporate structure, mergers, and anything else that will change conditions in the future.

Next, it must develop a census of all of its resources to be protected by IT security. These may be corporate databases, webservers, and even spreadsheets. You cannot protect something unless you know that you have it. After you enumerate all of your resources, you must classify them by sensitivity.

Once this preliminary work is done, you will identify many gaps in security. It must then develop a remediation plan for each. In particular, you will need remediation plans for all resources unless they are already well protected.

It would be nice if you could close all security gaps immediately. However, you almost certainly lack the resources to do so, and even if you had the resources, companies only have the ability to absorb so much at any given time. Investors have portfolios of investments, and they evaluate the payoffs from these investments. They carefully invest to maximize their returns at a certain level of risk. IT security also needs to prioritize its remediation projects, focusing on those that will bring the biggest gains.

TEST YOUR UNDERSTANDING

6. **a.** In developing an IT security plan, what should a company do first?
   b. What are the major categories of driving forces that a company must consider for the future?
   c. What should the company do for each resource?
   d. For what should a company develop remediation plans?
   e. How should the IT security staff view its list of possible remediation plans as a portfolio?

Compliance Laws and Regulations

Driving Forces

Many companies have relatively good security plans, protections, and response capabilities. To plan for the future, however, even these companies need to understand the **driving forces** that will require it to change its security planning, protections, and response.

Driving forces are things that require a firm to change its security planning, protections, and response.

Perhaps the most important set of driving forces for firms today are **compliance laws and regulations,** which create requirements for corporate security. In many cases, firms must substantially improve their security to be in compliance with these laws and regulations. This is especially true in the areas of documentation and identity management. These improvements can be very expensive. Another problem for corporate security is that there are so many compliance laws and regulations.

Compliance laws and regulations create requirements to which corporate security must respond.

TEST YOUR UNDERSTANDING

7. **a.** What are driving forces?
   b. What do compliance laws do?
   c. Why can compliance laws and regulations be expensive for IT security?

Sarbanes–Oxley

Around the year 2000, there were several massive financial frauds that cost billions of dollars and depressed the stock market. Congress responded by creating the **Sarbanes–Oxley Act of 2002**. This act produced the greatest change in financial reporting requirements since the Great Depression.

Under Sarbanes–Oxley, companies must report whether they have any material control deficiencies in their financial reporting process. Companies that report material control deficiencies are likely to take a hit in their stock price, and most chief financial officers in these companies are gone within a few months. If there was deception by the chief executive officer (CEO) or chief financial officer, they can go to jail.

In a *material* control deficiency, there is "a material deficiency, or combination of significant deficiencies, that results in more than a remote likelihood that a material misstatement in the annual or interim financial statements will not be prevented or detected." Vorhies[5] indicates that a 5 percent error in revenues is the usual threshold for labeling a financial reporting deficiency as material. Avoiding material control deficiencies obviously is very difficult.

(Continued)

---

[5] Vorhies, J. B., "The New Importance of Materiality," *Journal of Accountancy*, online. May 2005. http://www.aicpa.org/pubs/jofa/may2005/vorhies.htm.

Compliance Laws and Regulations   (Continued)

Compliance Laws and Regulations
Compliance laws and regulations create requirements for corporate security
    Documentation requirements are strong
    Identity management requirements tend to be strong
Compliance can be expensive
There are many compliance laws and regulations, and the number is increasing rapidly

Sarbanes–Oxley Act of 2002
Massive corporate financial frauds in 2002
Act requires firm to report material deficiencies in financial reporting processes
Material deficiency a significant deficiency, or combination of significant deficiencies,
that results in more than a remote likelihood that a material misstatement of the annual
or interim financial statements will not be prevented or detected
Material is a mere 5% deviation
If report material deficiencies, stock loses value, chief financial officer may lose job

Privacy Protection Laws
The European Union (E.U.) Data Protection Directive of 2002
Many other nations have strong commercial data privacy laws
The U.S. Gramm–Leach–Bliley Act (GLBA)
The U.S. Health Information Portability and Accountability Act (HIPAA) for private data
in health care organizations

Data Breach Notification Laws
California's SB 1386

Federal Trade Commission (FTC)
Can punish companies that fail to protect private information
Fines and required external auditing for several years

Industry Accreditation
For hospitals, etc.
Often have to security requirements

PCS-DSS
Payment Card Industry–Data Security Standards
Applies to all firms that accept credit cards
Has 12 general requirements, each with specific subrequirements

FISMA
Federal Information Security Management Act of 2002
Processes for all information systems used or operated by a U.S. Government federal
agencies
Also by any contractor or other organization on behalf of a U.S. Government agency
Certification, followed by accreditation
Continuous monitoring
Criticized for focusing on documentation instead of protection

FIGURE 2-9 Legal Driving Forces (Study Figure)

Under Sarbanes–Oxley, companies have had to take a detailed look at their financial reporting processes. In doing so, they uncovered many security weaknesses, and in many cases, they realized that these security weaknesses extended to other parts of the firm. Given the importance of Sarbanes–Oxley compliance, most firms were forced to increase their security efforts.

TEST YOUR UNDERSTANDING

8. **a.** In Sarbanes–Oxley, what is a material control deficiency?
   b. Why was Sarbanes–Oxley important for IT security?

Privacy Protection Laws

Several other laws have affected requirements for privacy and for the protection of private information. These include the following, among many others:

- The **European Union (E.U.) Data Protection Directive** of 2002 is a broad set of rules ensuring privacy rights in Europe.
- Although the E.U. Data Protection Directive is the most important international privacy rule, many other nations with which U.S. firms do business are also developing strong commercial data privacy laws.
- The U.S. **Gramm–Leach–Bliley Act (GLBA)** of 1999 requires strong protection for personal data in financial institutions.
- The U.S. **Health Insurance Portability and Accountability Act (HIPAA)** of 1996 requires strong protection for private data in health care organizations.

These laws have forced companies to look at how they protect personal information, including where this information is stored and how they control access to it. In many cases, they have discovered that this information is stored in many places, including word processing documents and spreadsheets. They also discovered that access controls and other protections often are either weak or nonexistent.

TEST YOUR UNDERSTANDING

9. **a.** What have privacy protection laws forced companies to do?
   b. What did they find when they did so?
   c. What institutions are subject to the Gramm-Leach-Bliley Act?
   d. What institutions are subject to HIPAA?

Data Breach Notification Laws

Beginning with California's 2002 data breach notification law (**SB 1386**), there has been a growing number of laws that require companies to notify affected people if sensitive personally identifiable information (PII) is stolen or even lost. Given the repercussions of data breaches, companies have been rethinking their security protections for data in central systems and end user applications.

TEST YOUR UNDERSTANDING

10. **a.** What do data breach notification laws require?
    b. Why has this caused companies to think more about security?

(Continued)

Compliance Laws and Regulations   (Continued)

The Federal Trade Commission

In the United States, the **Federal Trade Commission (FTC)** has powers to prosecute firms that fail to take reasonable precautions to protect private information. Although there are limitations on the FTC's powers, the FTC has imposed hefty fines on firms. It also has the power to require firms to pay to be audited annually by an external firm for many years and to be responsive to these audits.

TEST YOUR UNDERSTANDING

11. **a.** When can the Federal Trade Commission act against companies?
    b. What financial burdens can the FTC place on companies that fail to take reasonable precautions to protect private information?

Industry Accreditation

Many industries have their own accreditation standards for their members. In many cases, companies must demonstrate a certain level of security to be accredited. The hospital industry is a notable example of this.

TEST YOUR UNDERSTANDING

12. Besides HIPAA, what external compliance rules must hospitals consider when planning their security?

PCI-DSS

We have seen that Sarbanes–Oxley is important for all publicly traded companies and that the FTC also has broad jurisdiction. In addition, most companies accept credit card payments. All companies that do are subject to a set of requirements called the Payment Card Industry–Data Security Standard, which is almost always abbreviated as **PCI-DSS**. These standards were created by a consortium of the major credit card companies. Unfortunately, PCI-DSS compliance has lagged in many firms. This is what happened in the TJX data breach discussed at the beginning of Chapter 1.

TEST YOUR UNDERSTANDING

13. What companies does PCI-DSS affect?

FISMA

The Federal Information Security Management Act of 2002 (**FISMA**) was enacted to bolster computer and network security within the federal government and affiliated parties (such as government contractors) by mandating yearly audits.

FISMA mandates a set of processes for all information systems used or operated by a U.S. Government federal agency or by a contractor or other organization on behalf of a U.S. Government agency. These processes must follow a combination of Federal Information Processing Standards (FIPS) documents, the special publications SP-800 series issued by the National Institute of Standards and Technology (NIST), and other legislation pertinent to federal information systems.

FISMA has two stages. The first is a **certification** of the system by the organization itself or by an outside party. The latter is necessary if the risk category of the system is higher than a certain threshold.

Once a system has been certified, the security documentation package is reviewed by an accrediting official. If this official is satisfied with the certification, he or she **accredits** the system by issuing an authorization to operate (ATO).

All accredited systems are required to monitor a selected set of security controls for efficacy, and the system documentation is updated to reflect changes and modifications to the system. Significant changes to the security profile of the system should trigger an updated risk assessment, and controls that are significantly modified may need to be recertified.

FISMA has been heavily criticized for focusing on documentation instead of protection. At the time this book is being written, FISMA is under review.

TEST YOUR UNDERSTANDING

14. a. Who is subject to FISMA?
   b. Distinguish between certification and accreditation in FISMA.
   c. For what has FISMA been criticized?

ORGANIZATION

Comprehensive security is impossible unless corporations organize their security staffs, place them effectively in the organizational structure, and specify their relationships to other organizational units. Consequently, planning must begin with the placement of the security function in the firm.

Chief Security Officers (CSOs)

Different organizations give their security department heads different titles. The usual title is **chief security officer (CSO)**. Another is *chief information security officer (CISO)*. We will use CSO in this book.

TEST YOUR UNDERSTANDING

15. a. What is the manager of the security department usually called?
   b. What is another title for this person?

Should You Place Security within IT?

A first step for a corporation in managing security is to decide where the security function will sit on the firm's organization chart. There are no magic answers for the question of to whom the CSO and his or her security department should report. However, one common issue is whether to place the security department inside the corporate IT unit or outside of IT.

LOCATING SECURITY WITHIN IT   Placing the **IT security department** within the information technology (IT) department is attractive because security and IT share many of the same technological skills. Managers outside of IT might not understand technology issues well enough to manage the security function.

Another benefit is that if IT security reports to the firm's chief information officer (CIO), it is likely to be easier for security to get IT to implement security. If security is under the CIO, then the CIO will be accountable for security breaches. The CIO is likely to back the security department in its efforts to create a safe IT infrastructure.

Chief Security Officer (CSO)
Also called chief information security officer (CISO)

Where to Locate IT Security?
Within IT
Compatible technical skills
CIO will be responsible for security
Outside of IT
Gives independence
Hard to blow the whistle on IT and the CIO
This is the most commonly advised choice
Hybrid
Place planning, policy making, and auditing outside of IT
Place operational aspects such as firewall operation within IT

Top Management Support
Budget
Support in conflicts
Setting personal examples

Relationships with Other Departments
Special relationships
Ethics, compliance, and privacy officers
Human resources (training, hiring, terminations, sanction violators)
Legal department
Auditing departments
IT auditing, internal auditing, financial auditing
Might place security auditing under one of these
This would give independence from the security function
Facilities (buildings) management
Uniformed security
All corporate departments
Cannot merely toss policies over the wall
Business partners
Must link IT corporate systems together
Before doing so, must exercise due diligence in assessing their security

Outsourcing IT Security
Only e-mail or webservice (Figure 2-11)
Managed Security Service Providers (MSSPs) (Figure 2-12)
Independence from even IT security
MSSPs have expertise and practice-based expertise
Usually do not get control over policies and planning

FIGURE 2-10 Organizational Issues (Study Figure)

PLACING SECURITY OUTSIDE IT   Although placing security within IT has several benefits, it also has one serious negative consequence; security has no **independence** from IT. Chapter 1 noted that a large fraction of all corporate security attacks come from the IT staff itself—sometimes from senior IT managers. If security reports to the CIO, how can it enforce security over the CIO's actions? Reporting your boss for breaching corporate security is likely to be a "career limiting move."

In addition, while security must deal heavily with IT, IT security is much broader than IT. Locating IT security outside of IT can make it easier to deal with other departments that are critical for security success.

However, when security is outside IT, there are inevitable difficulties in getting the IT function, including the CIO, to accept the "mere advice" of an external security staff department. Even if security reports to a senior executive, it may be difficult to marshal support for security within the IT department, especially if IT's reporting line goes through a different senior executive.

The fundamental problem with making IT security a staff department outside IT is that separation reduces accountability. A staff department can only recommend. No single person in a line department becomes accountable for corporate security except the firm's top executives, who already have a broad range of concerns. To twist Harry Truman's classic statement, "The buck stops nowhere."

Despite problems that arise in placing security outside of IT, most analysts recommend doing so. The need for independence from IT is too important to consider placing security within IT.

A HYBRID SOLUTION   Some firms try to balance the closeness of IT and IT security with the need for independence. They do so by placing operational aspects of IT such as maintaining firewalls within IT while placing planning, policy-making, and auditing functions outside of IT.

TEST YOUR UNDERSTANDING

16. **a.** What are the advantages of placing security within IT?
    b. What are the disadvantages of placing security within IT?
    c. What do most IT security analysts recommend about placing or not placing IT security within IT?
    d. How are security roles allocated in the hybrid solution to placing IT security inside or outside of the IT department?

Top Management Support

Few firms have the CSO report directly to the firm's CEO. However, top management support is crucial to the success of any security program. Few efforts as pervasive as IT security succeed unless top management gives strong and consistent support. The proof of top management support comes in subsequent actions.

- If top management will not ensure that security has an adequate budget, any policy statement will be only lip service.
- Top management must support security when there are conflicts between the needs of security and the needs of other business functions—for instance, if a new system with inadequate security is being rushed into place.

- Subtly, but importantly, top managers have to follow security procedures themselves, for instance when they work from home and remotely access corporate resources. Everything that senior management does is symbolically important.

TEST YOUR UNDERSTANDING

17. **a.** Why is top management support important?
    b. What three things must top management do to demonstrate support?

Relationships with Other Departments

To be successful, the IT security department must develop productive relationships with other departments within the firm.

SPECIAL RELATIONSHIPS   Several organizational units in the firm are of special importance to the IT security department.

- **Ethics, Compliance, and Privacy Officers**. In addition to CSOs, most companies have directors of ethics, compliance, and privacy. If these positions are not in the IT security department, then coordination is obviously essential. Many firms do combine ethics, compliance, privacy, and security into a single umbrella department. If this is done, it requires the department manager to have knowledge of all areas.
- **Human Resource (HR) Departments**. HR departments have rich and complicated relationships with security departments. The human resources department is responsible for training, including security training. In addition, the human resources department handles the critical processes of hiring and terminating employees. IT security must work with Human Resources on hiring and termination procedures to ensure that security issues are taken into account. HR is *always* involved in sanctions when employees break security rules.
- **The Legal Department**. To ensure that security policies are legally sound, the security department must coordinate with the legal department. The legal department also becomes involved when there are major security incidents.
- **Auditing Departments**. Most corporations already have three auditing departments. The **internal auditing** department examines organizational units for efficiency, effectiveness, and adequate controls. **Financial auditing** does the same for financial processes. The **IT auditing** department, finally, examines the efficiency and effectiveness, and controls of processes involving information technology. Some firms place IT security auditing (but not security itself) under one of these departments in order to bring more independence to security auditing. This allows IT security auditing to blow the whistle on the IT security department or even the CSO if necessary.
- **Facilities Management**. Operating and maintaining buildings is the job of facilities management. For security cameras, building entry control, and similar matters, security must work closely with facilities management.
- **Uniformed Security**. The company's uniformed security staff, of course, will execute policies about building access. The uniformed security staff also is needed to seize computers that IT security to be involved in financial crime or abuse. In the other direction, IT security can help uniformed security with surveillance cameras and the forensics analysis of equipment that may have been used to commit a crime.

ALL CORPORATE DEPARTMENTS   Beyond these special relationships, the security department needs to have good relationships with all other business functions. IT security cannot merely "lob policies over the wall" and expect them to be followed.

IT security is almost always mistrusted by other departments because of security's potential to make life harder. Although IT security personnel cannot always be buddies with personnel in other departments, security professionals do have to learn to speak the languages of other departments and understand their situations. Security should accompany policies with financial benefits analyses and realistic business impact statements. Security is indeed about management more than technology, and knowledge of business and management often is more important than technological knowledge.

BUSINESS PARTNERS   Planning for firewalls and a number of other security controls tends to assume that a border exists between the corporation and the outside world. However, one of the biggest trends in recent years has been close but wary integration between firms and their business partners, including buyer organizations, customer organizations, service organizations, and even competitors.

For close cooperation, it often is necessary for external firms to access internal systems. This means poking holes through firewalls, giving access permissions on internal hosts, and taking other potentially risky actions. Firms must exercise **due diligence** before dealing with external companies, meaning that they should investigate the IT security implications of these partnerships closely before beginning them.

TEST YOUR UNDERSTANDING

18. **a.** Why is the human resources department important to IT security?
    b. Distinguish between the three main types of corporate auditing units.
    c. What is the advantage of placing IT security auditing in one of these three auditing departments?
    d. What relationships can the IT security have to the corporation's uniformed security staff?
    e. What can the security staff do to get along better with other departments in the firm?
    f. What are business partners?
    g. Why are they dangerous?
    h. What is due diligence?

Outsourcing IT Security

One option is to outsource some or all of the IT security. Complete outsourcing is rare because companies are wary of losing control over their security. However, the partial outsourcing of IT security is common.

E-MAIL OUTSOURCING   The most common IT security outsourcing is done for e-mail. As Figure 2-11 shows, e-mail connections to and from the Internet are routed through the outsourcer. (In some cases, the Internet or e-mail outsourcer will place its equipment on the customer's premises but control the equipment remotely.)

The outsourcer provides both inbound and outbound filtering. This filtering includes such things as spam and malware in attachments and scripts in e-mail bodies.

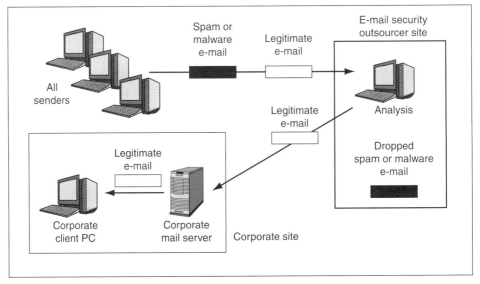

FIGURE 2-11 E-Mail Outsourcing

Outsourcing e-mail filtering is attractive because filtering is becoming a highly specialized field that relies on rapid responses to new threats. New malware is appearing constantly, and lists of dangerous e-mail sources are updated hourly or even more rapidly.

MANAGED SECURITY SERVICE PROVIDER   Another outsourcing alternative is to delegate even more controls to an outside firm called a **managed security service provider (MSSP)**. As Figure 2-12 shows, an MSSP watches over your firm. It places a central logging server on your network. This server uploads the firm's event log data to the MSSP site. There, scanning programs and security experts look through the log data, classifying events by severity level and throwing out false positives.

If the MSSP is doing its job, it will examine several hundred suspicious events each day. It will quickly identify most as obvious false positives. Still others will be classified as threats but negligible ones, such as minor scanning attacks. On a typical day, only one or two apparently serious threats may be brought to the attention of the client via pager or e-mail alerts, depending on their potential severity. By distilling the flood of suspicious incidents into a handful of important events requiring client action each day, MSSPs free the security staff to work on other matters.

Why should a company use an MSSP? As Bruce Schneier has said on many occasions, outsourcing security is done for the same reasons that companies "out-source" firefighting to the government. Internal corporate fire departments would be idle nearly all the time. This would make them enormously expensive per fire. Worse yet, when this internal firefighting force would be called upon, it would be

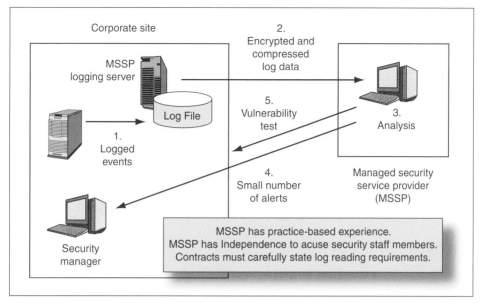

FIGURE 2-12   Managed Security Service Provider (MSSP)

inexperienced because it would not have had the daily firefighting experience that municipal fire workers have.

Another advantage of using an MSSP is **independence**. If MSSP employees see the client firm's CIO or CSO doing something that seems to be against the client firm's policy, the MSSP will notify a higher-level official in the firm. Members of the IT staff and even the IT security staff cannot do harm under the assumption that they are trusted and so will not be stopped. In Figure 2-12, the MSSP also does vulnerability testing.

Typically, firms do not outsource all controls to MSSPs. Policy and planning are too crucial to be outsourced to the MSSP, although the MSSP must be well aware of policies and procedures created by the firm.

Although MSSPs can be a great help, they sometimes do a poor job. If a contract specifies that the MSSP will look at logs but is not more specific, the outsourcing firm might simply scan log files in a cursory way every week or so. One firm reported that in the first six months of service, not a single alert was sent to it by the MSSP. The company believed that this indicated total neglect on the part of the outsourcing firm.

TEST YOUR UNDERSTANDING

19. a. What is an MSSP?
  b. What are the two main benefits of using an MSSP?
  c. Why are MSSPs likely to do a better job than IT security department employees?
  d. What security functions typically are outsourced?
  e. What security functions usually are not outsourced?
  f. What should a firm look for when selecting an MSSP?

RISK ANALYSIS

IT security planning always focuses on risk. Most people think that IT security professionals try to eliminate risk. This view is even captured in the term *information assurance*. But in business, it is never possible to eliminate risks and so to assure information. The goal is to *manage* risks. This requires a way of thinking about risk called risk analysis.

Risk analysis compares probable losses with the costs of security protections. It makes no sense to pay a million dollars to guard a $2,000 laptop that contains no sensitive information. That example is simplistic, of course. In real protections, of course, comparing costs and benefits is much more complex.

> *Risk analysis compares probable losses with the costs of security protections.*

Reasonable Risk

The term *information assurance* lies by saying that a company can guarantee its information's confidentiality, integrity, and availability. That is nonsense. After all, robbery has existed since the dawn of time, and no society has eliminated it. Absolute IT security protection is equally impossible. Rather, companies must think in terms of **reasonable risk** based on risk analysis thinking.

Although security can reduce the risk of attacks, security has negative side effects. Most obviously, security tends to impede functionality. Living in a high-security environment is always unpleasant and is usually inefficient. If you live in a quiet and safe neighborhood, putting bars on your windows would create a lock-down feeling, and requiring you to remember a long password to get into your house would slow you down every time you went into your house.

Besides these psychic and productivity costs, security is never free and seldom cheap. Security devices are expensive, and the labor to implement and operate them is far more expensive.

TEST YOUR UNDERSTANDING

20. **a.** Why is information assurance a poor name for IT security?
    b. Why is reasonable risk the goal of IT security?
    c. What are some negative consequences of IT security?

Realities
   Can never eliminate risk
   "Information assurance" is impossible

Risk Analysis
   Goal is reasonable risk
   Risk analysis weighs the probable cost of compromises against the costs of countermeasures
   Also, security has negative side effects that must be weighed

---

FIGURE 2-13   Risk Analysis (Study Figure)

Classic Risk Analysis Calculations

Some certification exams test a simple process for computing probable losses, for computing how countermeasures will alter the likelihood of losses, and for deciding whether those countermeasures produce benefits that exceed their costs. We will call this the **classic risk analysis calculation**. It is illustrated in Figure 2-14.

ASSET VALUE   The first line gives value of the asset to be protected. In Figure 2-14, the *asset value* is $100,000.

EXPOSURE FACTOR   The *exposure factor* is the percentage of the asset's value that would be lost in a breach. In the figure, the exposure factor is 80 percent. This means that 80 percent of asset's value would be lost in a compromise.

SINGLE LOSS EXPECTANCY   The *single loss expectancy* is the amount of damage that would be sustained in a single breach. The single loss expectancy is the asset value times the exposure factor. In the figure, this is $80,000 ($100,000 times 80%).

ANNUALIZED PROBABILITY OF OCCURRENCE   Now that we know how much damage would result from a single breach, the next issue is how frequently breaches will occur. This normally is done on an annualized basis. In Figure 2-14, the *annualized probability of occurrence* is 50 percent. This means that an attack is expected to succeed about once every two years.

ANNUALIZED LOSS EXPECTANCY (ALE)   The annualized probability of occurrence times the single loss expectancy gives the *annualized loss expectancy (ALE)*—the yearly average loss expected from this type of compromise for this asset. In the figure, the ALE is $40,000 ($80,000 times 50%).

COUNTERMEASURE IMPACT   The next step is to assess the benefits of a countermeasure. In Figure 2-14, Countermeasure A would reduce the exposure factor by 75 percent— from $80,000 in the base case to $20,000 with the countermeasure. This would reduce the annualized loss expectancy to $10,000. This would be a savings of $30,000.

| | Base Case | Countermeasure | |
		A	B
Asset Value (AV)	$100,000	$100,000	$100,000
Exposure Factor (EF)	80%	20%	80%
Single Loss Expectancy (SLE): = AV*EF	$80,000	$20,000	$80,000
Annualized Rate of Occurrence (ARO)	50%	50%	25%
Annualized Loss Expectancy (ALE): = SLE*ARO	$40,000	$10,000	$20,000
ALE Reduction for Countermeasure	NA	$30,000	$20,000
Annualized Countermeasure Cost	NA	$17,000	$4,000
Annualized Net Countermeasure Value	NA	$13,000	$16,000

FIGURE 2-14 Classic Risk Analysis Calculation

Countermeasure B has a different effect. It reduces the annual probability of occurrence from once every two years to once every four years. This countermeasure would reduce the ALE from $40,000 to $20,000. This is a savings of $20,000.

ANNUALIZED COUNTERMEASURE COST AND NET VALUE   So far, Countermeasure A looks better than Countermeasure B, saving an additional $10,000 per year. However, countermeasures are never free. Figure 2-14 shows that it is important to consider the cost of the countermeasure. In order to compare this cost with annualized countermeasure value, the cost must be an *annualized countermeasure cost.*

To compute the annualized countermeasure cost, it is important to consider both purchase costs and operation costs. Figure 2-14 shows that while Countermeasure A saves $30,000 per year, it costs $17,000 per year. So the annual net countermeasure value is only $13,000 per year.

Countermeasure B only produces an annual benefit of $20,000, but it is inexpensive, costing only $4,000 per year. So Countermeasure B's annualized net countermeasure value is $16,000 per year.

Overall, while Countermeasure B does not reduce the annualized loss expectancy as much as Countermeasure A, Countermeasure B's lower cost makes it the preferred option.

It is important to consider all countermeasure costs, including those outside of security. If a countermeasure reduces system functionality enough to have a serious impact on user productivity, this cost needs to be considered as part of the total countermeasure costs.

TEST YOUR UNDERSTANDING

21. a. Why do we annualize costs and benefits in risk analysis computations?
  b. How do you compute the ALE?

22. An asset has a value of $1,000,000. In an attack, it is expected to lose 60 percent of its value. Countermeasure X will cut the loss by two-thirds. Both countermeasures will cost $20,000 per year. Countermeasure Y will cut the loss by half. An attack is likely to be successful once in ten years. Both countermeasures can cut the occurrence rate in half. Do an analysis of these countermeasures and then give your recommendation.

Problems with Classic Risk Analysis Calculations

Although classic risk analysis calculations are widely taught, they are difficult or impossible to use in practice.

UNEVEN MULTIYEAR CASH FLOWS   One problem with classic risk analysis is that it assumes that countermeasure benefits and costs will be the same each year. In practice, the countermeasure cost often is highest in its first year and falls to a lower level afterwards. In turn, benefits often increase over time as the countermeasure becomes more familiar and so is likely to be used more effectively. Later, as a countermeasure ages, the cost may rise and the benefits may fall.

When there are uneven cash flows over a number of years, decision makers turn to discounted cash flow analysis, which is also called **return on investment (ROI)**

Uneven Multiyear Cash Flows
  For both attack costs and defense costs
  Must compute the return on investment (ROI) using discounted cash flows
  Net present value (NPV) or internal rate of return (IRR)

Total Cost of Incident (TCI)
  Exposure factor in classic risk analysis assumes that a percentage of the asset is lost
  In most cases, damage does not come from asset loss
  For instance, if personally identifiable information is stolen, the cost is enormous but the asset remains
  Must compute the total cost of incident (TCI)
  Include the cost of repairs, lawsuits, and many other factors

Many-to-Many Relationships between Countermeasures and Resources
  Classic risk analysis assumes that one countermeasure protects one resource
  Single countermeasures, such as a firewall, often protect many resources
  Single resources, such as data on a server, are often protected by multiple countermeasures
  Extending classic risk analysis is difficult

Impossibility of Knowing the Annualized Rate of Occurrence
  There simply is no way to estimate this
  This is the worst problem with classic risk analysis
  As a consequence, firms often merely rate their resources by risk level

Problems with "Hard Headed Thinking"
  Security benefits are difficult to quantify
  If only support "hard numbers" may under-invest in security

Perspective
  Impossible to do perfectly
  Must be done as well as possible
  Identifies key considerations
  Works if countermeasure value is very large or very negative
  But never take classic risk analysis seriously

FIGURE 2-15 Problems with Classic Risk Analysis Calculations (Study Figure)

analysis. This requires the computation of either the net present value (NPV) or the internal rate of return (IRR).

TOTAL COST OF INCIDENT (TCI)   A serious but easily cured problem with classic risk analysis is its measure for damage—the loss of asset value. This is absurd because damage can occur in many ways. For example, if customer information is stolen for use in identity theft, the value of the asset is not reduced at all. Yet the cost of the breach can be enormous.

   The simple way to address this problem without strongly disrupting classic risk analysis calculations is to replace the single loss expectancy calculation with a total cost of incident (TCI) value that gives estimates the complete cost of a compromise, including the cost of repairs, lawsuits, and many other factors.

MANY-TO-MANY RELATIONSHIPS BETWEEN COUNTERMEASURES AND RESOURCES A more difficult problem is that the classic approach assumes a one-to-one relationship between countermeasures and resources. This is rarely the case. A border firewall, for example, protects all of the servers and clients behind it. In cases like this, the simple classic calculation breaks down completely.

THE IMPOSSIBILITY OF COMPUTING ANNUALIZED RATES OF OCCURRENCE The worst problem with classic risk analysis is that it is rarely possible to estimate the annualized rate of occurrence for threats. Where can a planner find such probabilities? The simple fact is that there is not even a half-way good source of information about the frequency of attacks of various types, much less the percentage of such attacks that will succeed. Quite simply, it is impossible to compute the annualized probability of occurrence, and therefore it is impossible to compare countermeasure costs with their benefits.

There is no source of attack possibility data, so it is impossible to compute the annualized loss expectancy.

An alternative is to do damage analysis at a more coarse level. For instance, it might be possible to classify the dangers to resources as critical, significant, or minor. This will allow a company to prioritize risks and focus on the highest-priority risks. Then the security staff can plan countermeasures for these major risks.

THE PROBLEM WITH "HARD-HEADED THINKING" Although hard numbers are reassuring and should be used where possible, operations researchers also caution that "numbers drive out thinking." Critical considerations that are not as easily quantified can be ignored or strongly downplayed.

When Maria Lopez took over her father's Papa Lopez line of Mexican foods, she met with the company's chief information officer (CIO) to go over the firm's plans for a customer relationship management application, a wireless network proposal, and a security proposal.[6] Being a graduate of the Wharton School of Business, Maria requested return on investment (ROI) analyses of the three proposals. The ROI analyses clearly showed strong net positive benefits for the customer relationship management application and wireless network. The security project's benefits, in contrast, were impossible to quantify. The company invested minimally in security.

Soon, the company's database was hacked, and sensitive personal information on customers was stolen. No response plan was in place, so it took weeks to fix the security vulnerability that allowed the break-in. In addition, the family's secret salsa recipe was stolen, and a blackmailer demanded money to avoid its release. Worse yet, the California Attorney General's office notified the company that it could be subject to criminal prosecution for being negligent in protecting customer information.

[6] Dr. Larry Ponemon, "Security and the Secret Sauce," *Darwin Magazine*, August 2003. http://www.darwinmag.com/read/080103/sauce.html.

To accentuate the problem, sales quickly fell by 50 percent. ROI is a great tool where it can be used, but numbers should never drive out thinking.

This case is hardly unique. For the reasons we saw earlier, ROI is very difficult to measure for security investments and probably impossible. This fact creates great problems for companies that use ROI blindly.

PERSPECTIVE Paradoxically, although classic risk analysis is impossible to do, companies need to try doing it or something close to it. It imposes general discipline for thinking about risks and countermeasures. It identifies key considerations, even if they cannot be perfectly quantified. In addition, when countermeasure value greatly exceeds countermeasure cost (or when the opposite occurs), problems in quantifying some values are irrelevant. In any case, companies should *never* take classic risk analysis calculations at face value.

TEST YOUR UNDERSTANDING

23. **a.** Why is it a problem if benefits and costs both occur over several years?
    b. Why should the total cost of an incident (TCI) be used in place of exposure factors and asset values?
    c. Why is it not possible to use classic risk analysis calculations for firewalls?
    d. What is the worst problem with the classic approach?
    e. Why is hard-headed thinking about security ROI dangerous?

Responding to Risk

We have been discussing responses to risks in a single way so far—installing countermeasures. However, there are four logical possible responses to risk.

Risk Reduction
  The approach most people consider
  Install countermeasures to reduce harm
  Makes sense if risk analysis justifies the countermeasure

Risk Acceptance
  If protecting against a loss would be too expensive, accept losses when they occur
  Good for small losses

Risk Transference
  Buy insurance against security-related losses
  Especially good for rare but extremely damaging attacks
  Does not mean a company can avoid working on IT security
  If bad security, will not be insurable
  With better security, will pay lower premiums

Risk Avoidance
  Not to take a risky action
  Lose the benefits of the action
  May cause anger against IT security

FIGURE 2-16 Responding to Risk (Study Figure)

RISK REDUCTION   The most obvious response to risk is **risk reduction**—adopting active countermeasures such as installing firewalls. This will be our focus throughout the book. However, it is not always the best approach.

RISK ACCEPTANCE   However, if the impact of a compromise would be small, and if the cost of countermeasures would exceed the probable harm of a breach, then it makes sense to choose **risk acceptance**—implementing no countermeasures and absorbing any damages that occur. Not armoring your roof against meteorite strikes is an example of personal risk acceptance.

RISK TRANSFERENCE (INSURANCE)   The third alternative is **risk transference**—having someone else absorb the risk. The most common example of risk transference is **insurance**, in which an insurance company charges an annual premium, in return for which it will pay if damages occur. Insurance (and risk transference in general) is especially good for attacks that are rare but enormously damaging. This is why homeowners purchase fire and flood insurance.

Insurance companies often require customers to install reasonable countermeasures before they will provide coverage, so insurance cannot be used as a way of totally neglecting security. Also, insurance will have far high deductibles if a company's protections are not as strong as they should be.

One specific issue is what threats an insurance policy covers or does not cover. Damages resulting from natural disasters, cyberterror, and cyberwar often are specifically excluded from coverage.

RISK AVOIDANCE   The final choice is **risk avoidance**, which means not taking an action that is too risky. For instance, if it is too risky to use an outsourcer to store private customer or employee data, a company will simply not do it. While risk avoidance is good from the viewpoint of risk, it is means that a company has to forego an innovation that would be attractive had security problems not "killed" it. This does not endear IT security to the rest of the firm.

> *Risk avoidance means not taking the action that is risky.*

TEST YOUR UNDERSTANDING

24. **a.** What are the four ways of responding to risk?
    b. Which involves doing nothing?
    c. Which involves insurance?
    d. Why is insurance not a way to not deal with security?
    e. What is risk avoidance?
    f. Why does risk avoidance not endear IT security to the rest of the firm?

THE TECHNICAL SECURITY ARCHITECTURE

You would never build a house without having an architect first create a broad design for the house's rooms and the ways they will interact to provide a full living experience. This broad design is called an architecture.

Technical Security Architectures

In the same way, companies should not install technical countermeasures without having an overall plan. This plan is a company's **technical security architecture**, which includes all of a company's technical countermeasures—including firewalls, hardened hosts, intrusion detection systems, and other tools—and how these countermeasures are organized into a complete system of protection.

> *A firm's technical security architecture includes all of the company's technical countermeasures and how these countermeasures are organized into a complete system of protection.*

ARCHITECTURAL DECISIONS   The term *architecture* indicates that a firm's security systems should not simply evolve in an uncoordinated series of individual security investment decisions. Rather, a coherent architectural plan should be in place that allows a company to know that technical security protections are well matched to corporate asset protection needs and external threats. A major goal is to create a comprehensive wall with no holes for attackers to walk through.

DEALING WITH LEGACY SECURITY TECHNOLOGY   Security architectures usually must consider the firm's **legacy security technologies**, which are the security technologies that a company implemented in the past but that now are at least somewhat ineffective. No company can afford to replace its legacy security technologies all at once. If a legacy technology seriously impairs security, it must be replaced. However, unless the upgrade benefits exceed the upgrade costs, companies have to work around legacy security technology, adding strengths in other areas to compensate for the limits of the legacy security technology.

> *Legacy security technologies are the security technologies that a company implemented in the past and that now are at least somewhat ineffective.*

TEST YOUR UNDERSTANDING

25. **a.** What is a firm's technical security architecture?
    b. Why is a technical security architecture needed?
    c. When is the best time to create one?
    d. Why do firms not simply replace their legacy security technologies immediately?

Principles

Although creating a security architecture requires many decisions to be made on the basis of complex situational information, some general principles should guide the security architecture's design.

Technical Security Architectures
  Definition
      All of the company's technical countermeasures
      And how these countermeasures are organized
      Into a complete system of protection
  Architectural Decisions
      Must be well planned to provide strong security with few weaknesses
  Dealing with Legacy Technologies
      Technologies put in place previously
      Too expensive to upgrade all legacy technologies immediately
      Must upgrade if seriously impairs security
      Upgrades must justify their costs

Principles
  Defense in depth
      Resource is guarded by several countermeasures in series
      Attacker must breach them all, in series, to succeed
      If one countermeasure fails, the resource remains safe
  Defense in depth versus weakest links
      Defense in depth: multiple independent countermeasures that must be defeated in series
      Weakest link: a single countermeasure with multiple interdependent components that must all succeed for the countermeasure to succeed
  Avoiding single points of vulnerability
      Failure at a single point can have drastic consequences
      DNS servers, central security management servers, etc.
  Minimizing security burdens
  Realistic goals
      Cannot change a company's protection level overnight
      Mature as quickly as possible

Elements of a Technical Security Architecture
  Border management
  Internal site management
  Management of remote connections
  Interorganizational systems with other firms
  Centralized security management
      Increases the speed of actions
      Reduces the cost of actions

FIGURE 2-17 Corporate Technical Security Architecture (Study Figure)

DEFENSE IN DEPTH The first principle is **defense in depth**. With defense in depth, an attacker has to break through multiple countermeasures to succeed. For instance, to attack a server, an attacker might have to break through a border firewall, through an internal firewall, and finally through the defenses of a hardened application on a hardened server.

The reason for defense in depth is simple. Vulnerability reporters find problems in nearly every security countermeasure once or more per year. While a vulnerability in one defensive element is being fixed, others in the line of defense will remain effective, thwarting the attacker.

DEFENSE IN DEPTH VERSUS WEAKEST LINKS   You may be confused by the distinction between defense in depth and weakest links. In defense in depth, there are *multiple independent countermeasures placed in series.* If one countermeasure fails, the others remain in place.

In contrast, in weakest link failures, there is a *single countermeasure* composed of multiple interdependent components. Interdependence means that if one fails, they all fail.

SINGLE POINTS OF VULNERABILITY   At the opposite extreme from defense in depth lies the **single point of vulnerability**—an element of the architecture at which an attacker can do a great deal of damage by compromising a single system. During the terrorist attacks of September 11, 2001, for instance, it was discovered that most New York City telecommunications carriers brought their transmission lines together under the World Trade Center. The collapse of the towers did not bring the Internet to its knees, but it did degrade Internet traffic significantly. Single points of vulnerability often exist in a firm's DNS server (unless it has several), the central manager for the firm's network management program, and individual firewalls.

Not all single points of failure can be eliminated. Any security architecture whose devices are not controlled centrally might implement inconsistent policies, and many actions taken to thwart an ongoing attack require a systemic response that can work only through a central point of control. As central management of security resources grows, it will become ever more important to secure **central security management consoles** and their communication with a firm's security devices.

MINIMIZING SECURITY BURDENS   Another core principle is **minimizing security burdens** on functional departments. To some extent, security inevitably reduces productivity and may slow down the pace of innovation by requiring that security issues be addressed before innovations are rolled out. It is important to choose security architectures and elements that minimize lost productivity and slowed innovation.

In fact, in firms that are highly innovative, security might be the only factor retarding growth. The common complaint of functional managers, "You don't get it," often is correct. The value of growth compared to the value of security protection must be weighed carefully.

However, many actions can greatly reduce user burdens, such as moving to single sign-on authentication so that each individual will have to remember only one password to use all internal systems.

REALISTIC GOALS   Although it would be nice to be able to remove all vulnerabilities overnight, it is important to have realistic goals for improvements. For instance, in 1999, NASA developed a list of its most serious vulnerabilities—a list that it has continued to update.[7] Beginning in 2000, all network-connected systems were tested for these flaws. NASA created a goal of decreasing the ratio of vulnerabilities to computers from 1:1 to 1:4. In 2002, the ratio fell to 1: 0. By creating a spirit of competition, NASA was able to achieve strong gains while spending only $2 million to $3 million per year ($30 per computer).

TEST YOUR UNDERSTANDING

26. **a.** Why is defense in depth important?
    b. Distinguish between defense in depth and weakest link problems.
    c. Why are central security management consoles dangerous?
    d. Why are they desirable?
    e. Why is it important to minimize the burdens that security places on functional units in the firm?
    f. Why do you think it is important to have realistic goals for reducing vulnerabilities?

Elements of a Technical Security Architecture

In this book, we will look in detail at many of a firm's technical controls and at the way these controls are organized. At this point, we will merely list a few classes of technical countermeasures used by firms.

BORDER MANAGEMENT   Traditionally, companies have maintained a border between their (relatively trusted) internal networks and untrusted external networks, most commonly the Internet. Firewalls have been the staples of border management and should continue to remain so.

INTERNAL SITE SECURITY MANAGEMENT   Internal management of the trusted internal network is also crucial. For prevention, internal firewalls, hardened clients and servers, intrusion detection systems, and the other tools must be used.

MANAGEMENT OF REMOTE CONNECTIONS   Beyond the border, remote connections are needed between corporate sites, to individual remote employees, and to business partners. Virtual private network technologies have been central to the management of communication between trusted users and sites across untrusted networks, such as the Internet.

Individual employees working from their homes and hotel rooms represent a special problem, especially when employees put personal software on their remote access computers. In fact, they often use their own home computers to access corporate sites. The general lack of security discipline among home users can be mitigated by the management of remote access technology.

INTERORGANIZATIONAL SYSTEMS   In **interorganizational systems** two companies link some of their IT assets. In interorganizational systems, neither organization can directly enforce security in the other. In fact, they often cannot even learn the details of security in the other company.

---

[7] Megan Lisagor, "NASA Cyber Program Bears Fruit," *Federal Computer Week*, October 14, 2002. http://www.fcw.com/fcw/articles/2002/1014/mgt-nasa-10-14-02.asp.

In interorganizational systems, two companies link some of their IT assets.

CENTRALIZED SECURITY MANAGEMENT   An important goal in security architectures is **centralized security management**—being able to manage security technologies from a single security management console or at least from a relatively few security management consoles that each manages a cluster of security technologies. Centralized security management enforces policies directly on a firm's devices, bringing consistency to security. It also lowers the cost of security management by reducing travel, and it allows security management actions to affect devices immediately.

TEST YOUR UNDERSTANDING

27. **a.** Why is border management important?
    b. Why isn't it a complete security solution?
    c. Why are remote connections from home especially dangerous?
    d. Why are interorganizational systems dangerous?
    e. Why is central security management attractive?

POLICY-DRIVEN IMPLEMENTATION

Having good technology and a good plan are important, but it is important to implement controls carefully and maintain countermeasures throughout their lives. To do this, companies depend on the creation, implementation, and oversight of policies.

Policies

WHAT ARE POLICIES?   **Policies** are statements of what *should be done* under specific circumstances. For example, a policy may require a thorough background check for every new employee.

WHAT, NOT HOW   Note that policies are statements of *what* should be done, not *how* they should be done. Figure 2-19 shows that policies are separate from implementation. Over time, various jobs in the firm will change in sensitivity, and what constitutes a thorough background check will change as well. Policies set goals and vision, but they do not wrongly constrain future implementation changes as conditions change.

Policies are statements of **what** *should be done, not* **how** *it should be done.*

CLARITY   Focusing on what must be done instead of how it should be done does not mean that policies are irrelevant to implementers. On the contrary, when making design decisions, implementers constantly turn to policies for guidance. To continue our example, if there are two alternatives for doing background checks, implementers ask themselves if the alternatives fit the intent of the policy. By focusing on policy goals (and sometimes on rationales for these goals), policies bring clarity about what should be done. Implementers do not get lost in the details.

Policies
   Statements of what is to be done
   Not in detail how it is to be done
   Provides clarity and direction
   Allows the best possible implementation at any time
   Vary widely in length

Tiers of Security Policies
   Brief corporate security policy to drive everything
   Major policies
      E-mail
      Hiring and firing
      Personally identifiable information
      . . .
   Acceptable use policy
      Summarizes key points of special importance for users
      Typically, must be signed by users
   Policies for specific countermeasures
      Again, separates security goals from implementation

Writing Policies
   For important policies, IT security cannot act alone
   There should be policy-writing teams for each policy
   For broad policies, teams must include IT security, management in affected departments,
   the legal department, and so forth
   The team approach gives authority to policies
   It also prevents mistakes because of IT security's limited viewpoint

FIGURE 2-18 Policies (Study Figure)

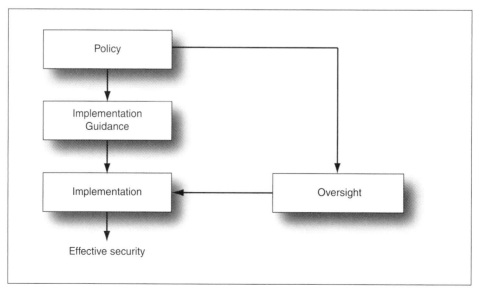

FIGURE 2-19 Policies, Implementation, and Oversight

TEST YOUR UNDERSTANDING

28. **a.** What are policies?
    b. Distinguish between policies and implementation.
    c. Why should policies not specify implementation in detail?

Categories Security Policies

CORPORATE SECURITY POLICY   A company needs several categories of security policies. At the top is the **corporate security policy**. As we have just noted, its goal is to emphasize a firm's commitment to strong security. It is brief and to the point.

A corporate security policy's goal is to emphasize a firm's commitment to strong security.

MAJOR POLICIES   Under the umbrella of the brief corporate security policy, companies need specific policies about major concerns. These major policies are much more detailed than the corporate security policy.

- E-mail policies exist in almost all firms. E-mail policies specify what the IT staff should do about e-mail and also what e-mail users should do.
- Hiring and termination policies are needed because hiring and termination are dangerous periods of time. The company needs strong policies for background checks and other matters at the time of hiring as well as termination policies for different types of terminations (voluntary, lay-offs, termination for cause, and so forth).
- Personally Identifiable Information (PII) policies specify protections for sensitive personal information. These policies must specify access controls, encryption, and other matters that can reduce the threat of revealing sensitive personal information.

ACCEPTABLE USE POLICY (AUP)   Users cannot be expected to read many detailed policies. For users, corporations create an **acceptable use policy (AUP)** that summarizes key points of special importance to users. For example, an AUP will note that the resources are company property and are not for personal use, that there should be no presumed right to privacy in e-mail or other uses, and that specific types of behavior will not be tolerated.

Typically, companies require users to read and sign the AUP. This provides legal protection so that the user cannot say that he or she never knew company policies. Of equal importance, signing creates a sense of ceremony that is memorable. Required signing also emphasizes the company's commitment to IT security.

POLICIES FOR SPECIFIC COUNTERMEASURES OR RESOURCES   At the most detailed level, major policies are not sufficiently detailed for specific countermeasures, such as a single firewall, or for specific resources, such as the payroll database. Countermeasure and resource policies provide this additional specificity. Again, the goal is to separate security goals from implementation.

TEST YOUR UNDERSTANDING

29. a. Distinguish between the corporate security policy and major security policies.
  b. Distinguish between major security policies and the acceptable use policies.
  c. What are the purposes of requiring users to sign the AUP?
  d. Why are policies for individual countermeasures and resources needed?

Policy-Writing Teams

For broad policies, the IT security staff cannot do development in isolation. For each policy, the company should create a team to create the policy. While IT security will be an important member of the team, it may not even chair the team.

For example, consider a policy for terminating employees in case of a specific crime. Obviously, the legal department should be on the team. So should any affected department, such as human resources, which would have to implement the policy.

Team-written policies carry much more weight with employees than policies written only by IT security. They are also more likely to be effective because they are not based on IT security's limited viewpoint.

TEST YOUR UNDERSTANDING

30. Why is it important to have corporate teams write policies?

Implementation Guidance

Although policies are and should be broad statements of vision and goals, Figure 2-19 shows that companies often develop **implementation guidance** for policies. Implementation guidance limits the discretion of implementers, in order to simplify implementation decisions, to avoid bad choices in interpreting policies, and to give consistency in implementation.

> *Implementation guidance limits the discretion of implementers, in order to simplify implementation decisions and to avoid bad choices in interpreting policies.*

Implementation guidance is distinct from the policy it addresses. Policies state security goals and vision to drive implementation. Implementation guidance constrains implementation choice to an appropriate degree. Policies rarely change. Implementation guidance, while generally stable, is likely to change faster than policies.

We now have three levels in Figure 2-19. Policies govern the what, and implementation determines the how. In between, implementation guidance forms an optional intermediate step of control.

NONE If a company can trust implementers to act wisely, then it should not create implementation guidance. Providing no implementation guidance frees implementers to develop what they see as the best possible policy implementation. It also avoids a lock-down feeling. This often is a good trade-off with the increased risk that not providing implementation guidance creates.

Implementation Guidance
Limits the discretion of implementers, in order to simplify implementation decisions and to avoid bad choices in interpreting policies

None
Implementer is only guided by the policy itself

Standards versus Guidelines
Standards are mandatory directives
Guidelines are not mandatory but must be considered

Types of Implementation Guidance
Can be either standards or guidelines
Procedures: *detailed* specification of how something should be done
  Segregation of duties: two people are required to complete sensitive tasks
    In movie theaters, one sells tickets and the other takes tickets
    No individual can do damage, although
  Request/authorization control
    Limit the number of people who may make requests on sensitive matters
    Allow even fewer to be able to authorize requests
    Authorizer must never be the requester
  Mandatory vacations to uncover schemes that require constant maintenance
  Job rotation to uncover schemes that require constant maintenance
Processes: less detailed specifications of what actions should be taken
  Necessary in managerial and professional business function
Baselines: checklists of what should be done
Best practices: Most appropriate actions in other companies
Recommended practices: normative guidance
Accountability
  Owner of resource is accountable
  Implementing the policy can be delegated to a trustee, but accountability cannot be delegated
Codes of ethics

FIGURE 2-20 Implementation Guidance (Study Figure)

STANDARDS AND GUIDELINES   It is common to divide implementation guidance into standards and guidelines. **Standards** are *mandatory* implementation guidance, meaning that employees subject to them—including managers—do not have the option of not following them. It is important to audit adherence to standards. Thanks to the mandatory nature of standards, it should be relatively straightforward for auditors to decide whether or not a standard is being followed in a particular situation.

In contrast to standards, which are mandatory, **guidelines** are discretionary. For instance, to continue an earlier example, a company might have a guideline that each new employee should have a background check.

Although it is mandatory for a decision maker to *consider* guidelines, it is not mandatory to *follow* guidelines if there are good reasons for not doing so. For instance, suppose that a guideline specifies fingerprint scanning for access control. Further suppose that a construction worker's fingerprints are too abraded to read. In this case, the person in charge of authentication may approve a different authentication method. Guidelines are appropriate in complex and uncertain situations for which rigid standards cannot be specified.

TEST YOUR UNDERSTANDING

31. a. Distinguish between standards and guidelines.
   b. For guidelines, what is mandatory?
   c. When are guidelines appropriate?

Types of Implementation Guidance

There are several types of standards and guidelines to implement policies. Companies should use each as appropriate.

PROCEDURES At the most detailed level, **procedures** specify the detailed actions that must be taken by specific employees. The operative word here is *detailed*. For instance, in a movie theater, one employee sells tickets and another takes the ticket to let the customer into the theater. If the ticket seller also allowed the customer in, the ticket seller might take the money and let the customer in without ringing up the sale, then pocket the money. Only if the sale is recorded is the ticket printed so that the person may enter the theater. Unless there is collusion between the ticket seller and the ticket taker, this security procedure is effective.

Procedures specify the detailed actions that must be taken by specific employees.

This theater example illustrates one of the most important principles in procedure design. In the **segregation of duties**, a complete act should require two people to complete. This prevents one person from acting alone to do harm. As noted in the example, collusion can defeat the segregation of duties, but at least the segregation of duties makes the communication of harmful conduct less likely.

Another example of the segregation of duties comes when there must be an authorization for something that is potentially risky. In this case, it is important to limit the number of people who may request an approval, and the number of people capable of authorizing the request must be even smaller. Most importantly, the person who authorizes the request must *never* be the made the request. This is called **request/authorization control**.

There should also be rules for vacation and job rotation. If someone is implementing an unapproved practice, they often need to be present constantly to make it work. Vacations should be mandatory to create a period under which a person cannot take action. Job rotations serve the same function if job rotations are feasible.

PROCESSES   For clerical work and other well-defined work, procedures may be appropriate. However, for managerial and professional work, guidance has to be looser because situations typically are not as cut and dried. However, even for managerial and professional work, companies follow **processes**, which are high-level descriptions of what should be done. For instance, new product development needs a broad process to operate well. The process would specify how to nominate new product ideas, who should do an initial feasibility analysis, and who should get promising new products of different types. In managerial and professional work, it is rarely possible to reduce each step in a process—including the feasibility analysis—to low-level procedures. However, processes must be clear enough to reduce risks.

Processes are broad descriptions of what should be done.

BASELINES   Procedures and processes describe steps in implementation. In contrast, baselines are like aircraft check lists. **Baselines** describe the details of what is to be achieved without specifically describing how to do them. For instance, if a systems administrator needs to harden a webserver against threats, he or she will turn to a corporate baseline that specifies such things as applying strong passwords to replace specific default passwords. The baseline does not describe how to do so, however, as a procedure or process would.

Baselines describe the details of what is to be achieved without specifically describing how to do them.

Baselines must be tailored to specific situations. For instance, a company would need different baselines for hardening Windows Server 2003, Windows Server 2008, Red Hat LINUX, and so forth. Without baselines, a systems administrator can easily forget to change a specific default password or to turn on event logging.

BEST PRACTICES AND RECOMMENDED PRACTICES   Although companies work hard on their policies and implementation guidance, they often want to look outside themselves. **Best practices** are descriptions of what the best firms in the industry are doing about security. Best practices usually are put together by consulting firms, but trade associations and even governments are beginning to develop them.

Best practices are descriptions of what the best firms in the industry are doing about security.

Best practices are different from **recommended practices**, which are prescriptive statements about what companies *should* do. Recommended practices usually are put together by trade associations and government agencies. Perhaps the most widely known set of recommended practices is the ISO 27000 family of standards discussed later.

> *Recommended practices are prescriptive statements about what companies should do.*

ACCOUNTABILITY   A final control that falls roughly into the area of implementation guidance is the assignment of **accountability**, which means liability for sanctions of implementation is not done properly. One person should be designated the **owner** for each resource and control. If something goes wrong, the owner will be held accountable. If a person knows that he or she will be held accountable, this is a powerful inducement to faithfully implementing the policy.

Often, the owner will delegate the job of implementing the policy to someone else, a **trustee**. Typically, a trustee has more technical skills or a better understanding of the detailed situation than the owner. However, while the work of implementation can be delegated to a trustee, accountability cannot be delegated.

ETHICS   In complex situations, hard-and-fast guidance is impossible. Decisions need to be made on the basis of **ethics**, which is a person's system of values. Consequently, different people of good will can make different ethical decisions in the same situation.

To make ethical decision making more predictable, most corporations have codes of ethics that provide some specific guidance. These codes of ethics tend to include statements on the following matters (among many others):

- It is important to have good ethics because good corporations with poor security are poor places to work and because any lapse in ethics can severely damage a firm's reputation, which can lead to lost sales and profits.
- The code of ethics applies to everyone, including part-time employees and senior managers. (In fact, most firms have additional codes of ethics for corporate boards and officers.)
- Ethical behavior is not optional; improper ethical behavior can lead to termination or lesser disciplines. If there is an ethical concern, it must be discussed with the person's superior or the corporate ethics officer.
- If an employee observes unethical behavior, he or she must report it to the corporate ethics officer or to the firm's audit committee.
- An employee must avoid conflicts of interest meaning that he or she must never exploit his or her position for personal gain. This includes preferential dealings with relatives, investing in competitors, and competing with the company while still employed by the company.
- An employee must never take bribes or kickbacks, including any nontrivial "gift." Bribes are monetary gifts to induce an employee to favor a supplier or other party. A kickback specifically is a payment made by a supplier to a corporate buyer when a purchase is made. Typically, the buyer requires the supplier to provide the kickback if the supplier wishes to continue doing business with the company.
- Employees must only use business assets for business use, not for personal use.
- An employee must never divulge confidential information, private information, or trade secrets.

Ethics

 A person's system of values

 Needed in complex situations

 Different people may make different decisions in the same situation

 Companies create codes of ethics to give guidance in ethical decisions

Code of Ethics: Typical Contents (Partial List)

Importance of good ethics to have a good workplace and to avoid damaging a firm's reputation

The code of ethics applies to everybody

 Senior managers usually have additional requirements

Improper ethics can result in sanctions, up to termination

An employee must report observed ethical behavior

An employee must involve conflicts of interest

 Never exploit one's position for personal gain

 No preferential treatment of relatives

 No investing in competitors

 No competing with the company while still employed by the firm

No bribes or kickbacks

 Bribes are given by outside parties to get preferential treatment

 Kickbacks are given by sellers when they place an order to secure this or future orders

Employees must only use business assets for business use, not personal use

An employee may never divulge

 Confidential information

 Private information

 Trade secrets

FIGURE 2-21   Ethics (Study Figure)

TEST YOUR UNDERSTANDING

32. **a.** Distinguish between procedures and processes.
  b. When would each be used?
  c. What is the segregation of duties, and what is its purpose?
  d. When someone requests to take an action that is potentially dangerous, what protections should be put into place?
  e. Why is it important to enforce mandatory vacations or job rotation?
  f. How do guidelines differ from procedures and processes?
  g. Distinguish between best practices and recommended practices.
  h. Distinguish between resource owners and trustees in terms of accountability.
  i. What can the owner delegate to the trustee?
  j. What can the owner not delegate to the trustee?
  k. Are the implementation guidance techniques involved in this set of test your understanding questions standards, guidelines, or either?

33. **a.** Why is ethics unpredictable?
  b. Why do companies create codes of ethics?

    c. Why is good ethics important in a firm?
    d. To whom do codes of ethics apply?
    e. Do senior officers often get an additional code of ethics?
    f. If an employee has an ethical concern, what must he or she do?
    g. What must an employee do if he or she observes unethical behavior?
    h. What examples of conflicts of interest were given?
    i. Give one not listed in the text.
    j. Why are bribes and kickbacks bad?
    k. Distinguish between bribes and kickbacks.
    l. What types of information should an employee not reveal?

Exception Handling

It would be nice if implementation would never require exceptions from policies or implementation guidance, but occasional exceptions are almost always necessary. This requires implementation guidance specifications to include guidance on **exception handling**. Guidance is critical because exceptions are dangerous, so they must be tightly controlled and documented.

- First, only some people should be allowed to request exceptions.
- Second, even fewer people should be allowed to authorize exceptions.
- Third, the person who requests an exception must never be the same person who authorizes the exception.
- Fourth, each exception must be carefully documented in terms of specifically what was done and who did each action.
- Fifth, special attention should be given to exceptions in periodic auditing.
- Sixth, exceptions above a particular danger level should be brought to the attention of the IT security department and the authorizer's direct manager.

TEST YOUR UNDERSTANDING

34. a. Why shouldn't exceptions be absolutely forbidden?
    b. Why is implementation guidance for exception handling necessary?

Exceptions Are Always Required

Limiting Exceptions
    Only some people should be allowed to request exceptions
    Fewer people should be allowed to authorize exceptions
    The person who requests an exception must never be authorizer

Exception Must Be Carefully Documented
    Specifically what was done and who did each action

Special Attention Should Be Given to Exceptions in Periodic Auditing

Exceptions Above a Particular Danger Level Should Be Brought to the Attention of
    The IT security department and the authorizer's direct manager

---

FIGURE 2-22   Exception Handling (Study Figure)

c. What are the first three rules for exceptions?
d. The fourth?
e. The fifth and sixth?

Oversight

Ideally, policies would be implemented faithfully under the constraints of applicable implementation guidance. Sadly, that is not always the case. In late 2007, the Ponemon Institute surveyed 890 IT professionals.[8] More than half said that they had personally copied personal information onto a USB memory stick, although 87 percent admitted that they knew of a policy forbidding them from doing so. The report was filled with similar admissions of policy violations by these IT professionals. In addition, many reported that their companies lacked policies for some sensitive IT security matters— or at least said that they did not know of such policies. Why were these violations so common? The respondents attributed their security breaches to convenience and a lack of policy enforcement. Oversight is a term for a group of tools to improve policy enforcement. There are many types of oversight.

Oversight is a term for a group of tools to improve policy enforcement.

POLICIES AND OVERSIGHT   Figure 2-19 shows that policy and oversight are related. Just as a policy drives implementation, the same policy drives oversight. The staff members involved in oversight must develop oversight plans appropriate for a specific policy.

PROMULGATION   The first job of security management after creating policies is to promulgate them. If users do not know or understand policies, they cannot follow them. It is important to market policies actively and to underscore the vision behind specific policies.

The need for promulgation down to the lowest affected levels in the organization is illustrated with an example of what happens when this is not done. During the 1970s, a young Marine second lieutenant was put ashore with his platoon in a certain country. He was told that that there was a revolution underway but little else. Almost immediately, his platoon took fire from both sides. It suddenly dawned on him that he had not been told which side he was supposed to support.

As noted earlier in this chapter, it is useful to have affected users sign policies. This brings a sense of security that heightens awareness.

One controversial way to publicize policies is to conduct stings of employees. In these stings, employees are asked to do something against a policy. For example, the State of South Carolina sent phishing e-mail to 100 state employees. Within

[8] Jaikumar Vijayan, "Security Policies? Workers Ignore Them, Survey Says," *Networkworld.com*, December 6, 2007. http://www.networkworld.com/news/2007/120607-security-policies-workers-ignore-them.html.

Oversight
  Oversight is a term for a group of tools for policy enforcement
  Policy drives oversight, just as it drives implementation

Promulgation
  Communicate vision
  Training
  Stinging employees?

Electronic Monitoring
  Electronically collected information on behavior
  Widely done in firms and used to terminate employees
  Warn subjects and explain the reasons for monitoring

Security Metrics
  Indicators of compliance that are measured periodically
  Percentage of passwords on a server that are crackable, etc.
  Periodic measurement indicates progress in implementing a policy

Auditing
  Samples information to develop an opinion about the adequacy of controls
  Database information in log files and prose documentation
  Extensive recording is required in most performance regimes
  Avoidance of compliance is a particularly important finding
  Internal and external auditing may be done
  Periodic auditing gives trends
  Unscheduled audits trip up people who plan their actions around periodic audits

Anonymous Protected Hotline
  Often, employees are the first to detect a serious problem
  A hotline allows them to call it in
  Must be anonymous and guarantee protection against reprisals
  Offer incentives for heavily damaging activities such as fraud?

Behavioral Awareness
  Misbehavior often occurs before serious security breaches
  The fraud triangle indicates motive (see Figure 2-24)

Vulnerability Tests
  Attack your own systems to find vulnerabilities
  Free and commercial software
  Never test without a contract specifying the exact tests, signed by your superior
  The contract should hold you blameless in case of damage
  External vulnerability testing firms have expertise and experience
  They should have insurance against accidental harm and employee misbehavior
  They should not have hackers or former hackers
  Should end with a list of recommended fixes
  Follow-up should be done on whether these fixed occurred

Sanctions
  If people are not punished when they are caught, nothing else matters

FIGURE 2-23 Oversight (Study Figure)

20 minutes, 30 replied.[9] This result was widely publicized in the state employee newsletter.

Conducting stings is good for raising awareness. Stings can also be used as a ploy to increase IT security awareness training money. If specific stings are repeated annually, they can also be used to indicate positive trends.

Stings are controversial because they will generate resentment if they are not handled properly. To avoid problems, the identities of the stung employees should never be revealed. In addition, they should only be used as teaching situations and never for punishment.

ELECTRONIC MONITORING   In many cases, it will be able to electronically monitor compliance behavior automatically. In 2007, for example, an American Management Association survey found that 66 percent of the respondent firms said that they monitor internet connections. In addition, over half said that they had fired workers for e-mail abuse or other network abuse.[10] If there will be electronic monitoring, it is important to inform employees about it ahead of time, including explaining why it is being done.

SECURITY METRICS   Monitoring gives details. Another way to measure compliance is to create **security metrics**, which are a few well-chosen measurable indicators of security success or failure that are measured periodically. Examples are the percentage of user PCs left on at night, the percentage of crackable passwords on a server, and the percentage of critical patches applied to webservers. Measuring these metrics periodically indicates whether a company is doing better or worse in implementing its policies.

Security metrics are measurable indicators of security success or failure.

AUDITING   All publicly traded companies must have their financial statements audited. Auditing firms do not look at every piece of information that goes into financial statements. Rather, they purposefully sample specific pieces of financial data. On the basis of the sample data, they develop an opinion on how well the financial reporting process is controlled. The purpose of auditing is to develop opinions on the health of controls, not to find punishable instances of noncompliance.

The purpose of auditing is to develop opinions on the health of controls, not to find punishable instances of noncompliance.

Auditing is only possible if information is recorded. Consequently, most compliance laws and regulations require the extensive recording of information. If the

---

[9] Amy Joyce, "It's the Boss Fooling You—For Safety's Sake," *Washingtonpost.com*, May 20, 2007.

[10] Nancy Gohring, "Over 50% of Companies have Fired Workers for E-mail, Net Abuse," *Computerworld.com*, February 28, 2008. http://www.computerworld.com/action/article.do?command=viewArticleBasic&articleId=9065659.

information is recorded in database form, it is called logged information. If the information is recorded on forms or memos, the information is called documentation.

Auditing takes a sample of logged and documented information. In some cases, the auditing will measure the number of times there was noncompliance, for example, if an exception was not authorized. In other cases, the auditor develops metrics, such as the percentage of actions in a certain category that were in violation of the policy.

One key principle is to measure noncompliance events carefully but to focus intensively on every instance in which there is *active avoidance of compliance*. Avoidance of compliance indicates a deliberate circumvention of security, and always calls for follow-up investigation.

Internal audits are done by the organization itself. External audits are done by an outside firm. In financial auditing, firms are required to have both internal and external auditing. The same is advisable for IT security auditing.

Audits should be scheduled frequently enough to warn of growing dangers. Many firms do IT security auditing quarterly with more rigorous audits once per year. Regularly spaced audits are attractive because they allow a company to compare results over time. However, regularly scheduled audits can work to the advantage of people who are avoiding security. Unscheduled audits therefore are also desirable.

ANONYMOUS PROTECTED HOTLINE   In fraud, companies have long known that the best way to detect frauds and other serious abuse has been to create an anonymous protected hotline. Often it is a coworker who first discovers a security violation.

After Hurricane Katrina, for example, 22 people working for a Red Cross contractor in Bakersfield were indicted for filing false claims. They benefited from weak controls that were in place because of the urgent need to get assistance out to people. They were only caught when a Western Union manager saw the same person come in three times to collect money. She contracted authorities, and this broke the fraud.[11]

Employees who see misbehavior may be reluctant to speak for fear of reprisals. By having an anonymous hotline for people to call, and by guaranteeing protection against reprisals, companies can maximize participation from employees. Some firms even require employees who detect serious misconduct to use the hotline. All publicly traded companies must have a hotline for Sarbanes–Oxley compliance. They can broaden its scope to consider all serious misbehavior.

One option is to offer payment for information as an incentive. This is built into a number of compliance laws, including HIPAA. Few companies offer payments, but it may be wise to do so for frauds and other heavily damaging activities.

BEHAVIORAL AWARENESS   One oversight control is to be aware of human behavior. Any serious abusive employee behavior should be taken as a red flag because in many cases of serious security violations, the perpetrator had a history of violence, threats, or other unacceptable overt behavior. Not paying attention to such behaviors is serious negligence.

---

[11] *CNN.com*, "Dozens indicted in alleged Katrina scam," December 29, 2005. http://www.cnn.com/2005/LAW/12/28/katrina.fraud/index.html.

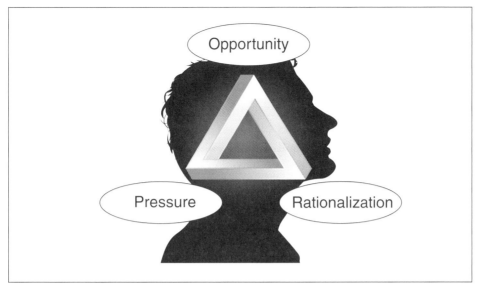

FIGURE 2-24   Fraud and Abuse Triangle

In fraud, writers have long discussed the fraud triangle, which is used to understand fraudulent behavior. It also seems applicable to general security misbehavior. Consequently, we will refer to it as the **fraud and abuse triangle**. Figure 2-24 shows that the triangle considers three aspects of human motivation that usually are in place before misbehavior occurs. By being sensitive to these aspects of motivation, a firm may be able to spot a problem before it occurs or at least have a realistic understanding of why security abusers do so.

The first tip of the triangle is opportunity. Obviously, if there is little opportunity to commit the abuse, or if the perpetrator is likely to be caught, the abuse is not likely to occur. Reducing opportunities to succeed and increasing detection are the normal roads toward achieving security.

However, the psychology of the perpetrator is equally important. Obviously, few people who have the opportunity to commit serious security abuse actually do so. Opportunity is not enough. Another factor is pressure. This pressure pushes the person to commit abuse. Money pressure and greed are obvious examples, but there are many other types of pressure, including the desire to hide poor performance that would jeopardize the employee's job. Perhaps the most common form of pressure is unreasonable performance expectations.

Even with pressure and opportunity, employees are not likely to act unless they can rationalize their action in their own heads. For instance, they may talk themselves into believing that an act is justified because the company has unrealistic performance expectations or that they will pay back embezzled money. The goal of rationalization is to allow perpetrators to think of themselves as good people. The moral for companies are that excessive performance expectations can backfire by making rationalization easier. It is important not to underestimate rationalization or dismiss the possibility from attacks by good people.

VULNERABILITY TESTS   One way to tell if a security policy is succeeding is to attack the system yourself to see if you can find vulnerabilities before attackers do. This is called vulnerability testing.

> *Vulnerability testing is attacking the system yourself to see if you can find vulnerabilities before attackers do.*

There are many pieces of software for vulnerability testing. Hacker software usually is available for free, while commercial vulnerability testing programs are less likely to do harm as a side effect.

If vulnerability testing is to be done internally, the employee doing the vulnerability test should insist on a vulnerability test contract signed by his or her superior. Vulnerability tests look exactly like actual attacks, and even if vulnerability testing is in a person's list of written responsibilities, uncontracted vulnerability tests can easily get an IT security professional fired or worse.

The vulnerability testing contract should specify what will be done in detail and when it will be done. During the test, there should be no deviation from the contract. In addition, vulnerability tests occasionally crash systems or do other damage. The contract must hold the internal vulnerability tester blameless if such damage occurs.

External vulnerability testing companies provide more independence and probably more expertise and experience. Specific tests plans are also important, and the testing company should have insurance against possible damage. Most importantly, the testing company should not employ current or former hackers because the testers will develop very detailed knowledge of your systems.

After a vulnerability testing study, the tester should create a specific list of recommended fixes, and the tester's superior should sign it. There should also be follow-up later to confirm that the fixes were made.

SANCTIONS   An old saying is that you get what you enforce. If employees break security protocols, they should be **sanctioned** (disciplined) appropriately. If this does not happen, the firm's lack of intention to follow up on security quickly becomes well known.

Often, firms are very reluctant to sanction senior staff. In one case, an intern for the Ohio Department of Administrative Services took home a backup tape device with a backup tape. This $10 per hour intern had been told to do so by a more experienced intern. The supervisor never discussed procedures for keeping backup tapes safe overnight. On one occasion, the intern's car was broken into, and the device was stolen. The tape had data on all 64,467 state employees, 19,388 former employees, and 47,245 Ohio taxpayers. The data breach was expected to cost the state upwards of $3 million. The intern was harshly interrogated and forced to resign. His supervisor merely lost one week of vacation time.[12]

---

[12] Brian Fonseca, "Ohio Official Loses a Week's Vacation for Theft of Tape," *Computerworld*, October 10, 2007, http://www.computerworld.com/action/article.do?command=viewArticleBasic&taxonomyName=storage&articleId=9042001&taxonomyId=19&intsrc=kc_top.

TEST YOUR UNDERSTANDING

35. a. What is oversight?
    b. How is oversight related to policy?
    c. What is promulgation?
    d. What is stinging employees?
    e. What are its benefits?
    f. What are its problems?
    g. Is electronic monitoring widely done?
    h. What should you tell employees before your begin monitoring?
    i. What are security metrics?
    j. Why is periodic measurement beneficial?

36. a. What is the purpose of auditing?
    b. Distinguish between log files and documentation.
    c. Why is the avoidance of compliance a serious red flag?
    d. Distinguish between internal and external auditing.
    e. Why is regularly scheduled auditing good?
    f. Why are unscheduled audits done?

37. a. Why should companies install anonymous protected hotlines?
    b. Why are anonymity and protection against reprisals importance when hotlines are used?
    c. Why should general employee misbehavior be a concern?
    d. What are the three elements in the fraud and abuse triangle?
    e. Give an example of pressure not discussed in the text.
    f. Why are rationalizations important?
    g. Give two examples of rationalization not given in the text.

38. a. What is a vulnerability test?
    b. Why should you never engage in a vulnerability test without a signed contract?
    c. What should be in the contract?
    d. What should you look for in an external vulnerability testing company?
    e. Why is follow-up needed on recommended fixes?

39. Why is it important to sanction violators?

GOVERNANCE FRAMEWORKS

Earlier, we saw guidelines, which are checklists for policy implementation. Many companies struggling with security planning would like something like a baseline to guide them. In fact, Figure 2-25 shows that there are several of **governance frameworks** that specify how to do security planning and implementation. However, the fact that several exist means making the selection of one or more governance frameworks to follow a complex decision. The figure shows that these governance frameworks focus on somewhat different areas. For example, **CobiT** focuses specifically on controlling the entire IT function, while **COSO** focuses more broadly on corporate internal and financial controls. The **ISO/IEC 27000** family of standards specifically addresses IT security.

Governance frameworks specify how to do security planning and implementation.

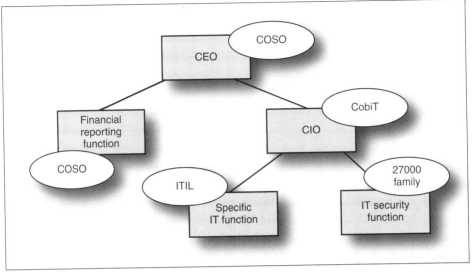

FIGURE 2-25   Governance Frameworks

TEST YOUR UNDERSTANDING

40. a. What is a governance framework?
  b. Compare the focus of COSO with that of CobiT.
  c. Compare the focus of CobiT with that of the ISO/IEC 27000 family of standards.

COSO

Sarbanes–Oxley implementation explicitly requires corporations to use a well-developed comprehensive control framework. Although this implementation requirement does not require corporations to use a specific framework, it has specifically listed only a single framework as acceptable, and most companies are using this framework to implement Sarbanes–Oxley. This is the COSO framework.

THE COSO FRAMEWORK   Although COSO is universally known by its acronym, the COSO framework actually is a document called *Internal Control—Internal Framework* (COSO, 1994). The acronym COSO comes from the organization that created the document, the Committee of Sponsoring Organizations of the Treadway Commission (http://www.coso.org).

OBJECTIVES   Control frameworks require objectives. In the COSO framework, there are three objectives.

- *Operations.* The firm wishes to operate effectively and efficiently. It is necessary for the firm to control its general internal operations to do this.
- *Financial Reporting.* The firm must create accurate financial reports. This, of course, is the focus of Sarbanes–Oxley.
- *Compliance.* The firm wishes to be in compliance with external regulations. In this chapter, we are only directly concerned with SOX compliance.

Focus

    Corporate operations, financial controls, and compliance

    Effectively required for Sarbanes–Oxley compliance

    Goal is reasonable assurance that goals will be met

Origins

    Committee of Sponsoring Organizations of the Treadway Commission (http://www. coso.org)

Components

    Control Environment

        General security culture

        Includes "tone at the top"

        If strong, weak specific controls may be effective

        If weak, strong controls may fail

        Major insight of COSO

    Risk Assessment

        Ongoing preoccupation

    Control Activities

        General policy plus specific procedures

    Monitoring

        Both human vigilance and technology

    Information and Communication

        Must ensure that the company has the right information for controls

        Must ensure communication across all levels in the corporation

FIGURE 2-26   COSO (Study Figure)

REASONABLE ASSURANCE   Good controls cannot completely guarantee that goals will be met. However, an effective control environment will give *reasonable* assurance that goals will be met.

COSO FRAMEWORK COMPONENTS   The COSO framework has five components. These are components rather than phases because there is no time ordering among them. All must occur simultaneously, and each feeds into others constantly.

- *Control Environment.* The component at the base of the COSO framework is the corporation's control environment. This is the company's overall control culture. It includes the "tone at the top" set by top management, the company's commitment to training employees in the importance of control, the punishment of employees (including senior managers) who violate control rules, attention by the board of directors, and other broad matters. If the broad control environment is weak, other control elements are not likely to be effective.
- *Risk Assessment.* More specifically, a company needs to assess the risks that it faces. Without systematic risk analysis, it is impossible to understand what level of controls to apply to individual assets. Risk assessment must be an

ongoing preoccupation for the firm because the risk environment constantly changes.

- *Control Activities.* An organization will spend most of its control effort on the control activities that actually implement and maintain controls. This includes approvals and authorization, IT security, the separation of duties, and many other matters. Controls usually have two elements. One is a general policy, which tells what must be done. The other is a set of procedures, which tell how to do it.
- *Monitoring.* Having controls in place means nothing if organizations do not monitor and enforce them. Monitoring includes both human vigilance and audit trails in IT. It is essential to have an independent monitoring function that is free to report on problems even if these problems deal with senior management.
- *Information and Communication.* For the control environment, risk assessment, control activities, and monitoring to work well, the company needs to ensure that it has the required information and communication across all levels of the corporations.

TEST YOUR UNDERSTANDING

41. a. What are the three objectives of COSO?
   b. List COSO's five components.
   c. What is the control environment, and why is it important?

CobiT

COSO is a general control planning and assessment tool for corporations. For IT controls, there is a more specific framework, CobiT (*Control Objectives for Information and Related Technologies*). In addition to creating the broad control objectives framework, the IT Governance Institute also has developed detailed guidance for implementing the CobiT framework.

THE COBIT FRAMEWORK   Figure 2-28 illustrates the CobiT framework. This framework has four major domains, which follow the general systems development life cycle:

- *Planning and Organization.* The planning and organization domain has 11 high-level control objectives that cover everything from strategic IT planning and the creation of a corporate information architecture to the management of specific projects.
- *Acquisition and Implementation.* After planning, companies need to acquire and implement information systems. This domain has six high-level control objectives.
- *Delivery and Support.* Most of an IT project's life takes place after implementation. Consequently, the CobiT framework has 13 high-level control objectives for delivery and support. This is more than any other domain.
- *Monitoring.* Finally, firms must monitor their processes, assess the adequacy of internal controls, obtain independent assurance, and provide for independent auditing. These are four control objectives.

CobiT

Control Objectives for Information and Related Technologies

Many documents that help organizations understand how to implement the framework

The CobiT Framework

Four major domains (Figure 2-28)

34 high-level control objectives

Planning and organization (11)

Acquisition and implementation (60)

Delivery and support (13)

Monitoring (4)

More than 300 detailed control objectives

Dominance in the United States

Created by the IT governance institute

Which is part of the Information Systems Audit and Control Association (ISACA)

ISACA is the main professional accrediting body of IT auditing

Certified information systems auditor (CISA) certification

FIGURE 2-27   CobiT (Study Figure)

Beneath the four of CobiT, then, there are 34 high-level control objectives. Beneath these are more than 300 detailed control objectives. CobiT also includes many documents that help organizations understand how to implement the framework.

DOMINANCE IN THE UNITED STATES   The IT Governance Institute was created by the Information Systems Audit and Control Association (ISACA). ISACA, in turn, is the primary professional association for IT audit professionals in the

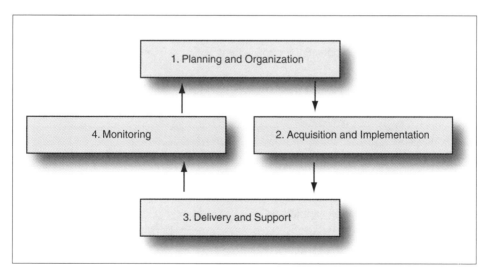

FIGURE 2-28   CobiT

United States. The Association's certified information systems auditor (CISA) certification is the dominant certification for U.S. IT auditors, so it is not surprising that CobiT has become the dominant framework for auditing IT controls in the United States.

TEST YOUR UNDERSTANDING

42. **a.** Distinguish between the focuses of COSO and CobiT.
    b. List the four CobiT domains.
    c. How many high-level control objectives does CobiT have?
    d. Which domain has the most control objectives?
    e. How many detailed control objectives does CobiT have?
    f. Why is CobiT strongly preferred by U.S. IT auditors?

The ISO/IEC 27000 Family

While CobiT focuses on the governance of the IT function broadly, the ISO/IEC 27000 family of standards focuses specifically and in detail on IT security.

ISO/IEC 27000
    Family of IT security standards

ISO/IEC 27002
    Originally called ISO/IEC 17799
    Eleven broad areas
        Security policy
        Organization of information security
        Asset management
        Human resources security
        Physical and environmental security
        Communications and operations management
        Access control
        Information systems acquisition, development, and maintenance
        Information security incident management
        Business continuity management
        Compliance

ISO/IEC 27001
    Created in 2005, long after ISO/IEC 27002
    Specifies certification by a third party
        COSO and CobiT do self-certification

Other 27000 Standards
    Many more standards are under preparation

FIGURE 2-29   The ISO/IEC 27000 Family of Security Standards (Study Figure)

ISO/IEC 27002   The first standard in this series was originally called ISO/IEC 17799. When it was decided to have all security standards begin with 27000, this standard was renamed ISO/IEC 27002. This standard divides security into 11 broad areas, which are subdivided into many more specific elements:

- security policy;
- organization of information security;
- asset management;
- human resources security;
- physical and environmental security;
- communications and operations management;
- access control;
- information systems acquisition, development, and maintenance;
- information security incident management;
- business continuity management; and
- compliance.

ISO/IEC 27001   In 2005, ISO and the IEC released ISO/IEC 27001. This standard specifies how to certify organizations as being compliant with ISO/IEC 27002. This is important because by demonstrating compliance, companies can assure business partners (and their management) that the company's security is well managed. In other frameworks, including COSO and CobiT, companies certify themselves, sometimes with the concurrence of an external auditor. They lack ISO/IEC 27001's third-party certification process, which external parties may value highly.

However, certification does not necessarily perfect security—only that the IT security management function follows ISO/IEC 27002. IT security, as noted at the beginning of this chapter, cannot guarantee that no security breaches will occur.

OTHER 27000 STANDARDS   ISO and IEC are working on a number of other standards for the 27000 family. The ISO/IEC 27004 standard will define how to measure security metrics, ISO/IEC 27005 will be a proposed standard for risk management, and ISO/IEC 27007 will focus on auditing.

TEST YOUR UNDERSTANDING

43. **a.** In the 27000 standards family, what is the function of ISO/IEC 27001?
    b. In the 27000 standards family, what is the function of ISO/IEC 27002?
    c. List the 11 broad areas in 27002.
    d. Why is ISO/IEC 27000 certification more attractive to firms than COSO or CobiT certification?

CONCLUSION

Synopsis

The chapter began with a quote stressing the importance of security management compared with security technology. Following that, we looked at some of the many complexities of IT security management. We will continue to see aspects of IT security management throughout the book, in the context of various security protections.

Thought Questions

1. List the 12 PCI-DSS control objectives. You will have to look this up on the Internet.
2. The chapter discussed three ways to view the IT security function—as a police force, as a military organization, and as a loving mother. Name another view and describe why it is good.
3. A company has a resource XYZ. If there is a breach of security, the company may face a fine of $100,000 and pay another $20,000 to clean up the breach. The company believes that an attack is likely to be successful about once in five years. A proposed countermeasure should cut the frequency of occurrence in half. How much should the company be willing to pay for the countermeasure?

Perspective Questions

1. What was the most surprising thing you learned in this chapter?
2. What was the most difficult material in this chapter for you?

Chapter 3

The Elements of Cryptography

LEARNING OBJECTIVES:

By the end of this chapter, you should be able to discuss the following:

- The concept of cryptography.
- Symmetric key encryption for confidentiality, including the importance of key length and the major symmetric key encryption standards (RC4, DES, 3DES, and AES).
- If you read the boxes, substitution and transposition ciphers and the difference between ciphers and codes.
- Cryptographic systems.
- The negotiation stage.
- Initial authentication, including MS-CHAP.
- Keying, including public key encryption for confidentiality and Diffie–Hellman key agreement.
- Electronic signatures, including digital signatures, digital certificates, and key-hashed message authentication codes (HMACs).
- Public key encryption for authentication.
- If you read the box, nonrepudiation and replay attacks and defenses.
- Quantum security.

Caution: This chapter contains difficult material. The individual topics require close attention, so go slowly. Also, this chapter contains many concepts that are similar to one another. As you study, be careful to distinguish between similar concepts.

WHAT IS CRYPTOGRAPHY?

Although most people think of security as a recent issue, security threats and countermeasures have existed for thousands of years. Early military commanders needed to send orders securely, and merchant princes of the Renaissance had to keep their commercial messages secret. Today, businesses and governments have the same need for secrecy. For this, they turn to **cryptography**, which is the use of mathematical operations to protect messages traveling between parties or stored on a computer.

> *Cryptography is the use of mathematical operations to protect messages traveling between parties or stored on a computer.*

In the 1960s, many believed that cryptography would be the main counter-measure for attacks. Although that view has proven to be too limited, cryptography remains a very important security countermeasure. Additionally, cryptography is a part of many other countermeasures, so we begin the discussion of countermeasure technology with cryptography in this chapter and the next.

ENCRYPTION FOR CONFIDENTIALITY

A common security goal is **confidentiality**,[1] which means that people who intercept messages cannot read them. Figure 3-1 shows that confidentiality requires a type of cryptography called **encryption for confidentiality**. Encryption for confidentiality was the original purpose of cryptography.[2]

> *Confidentiality means that people who intercept messages cannot read them.*

Terminology

PLAINTEXT   Figure 3-1 shows that the original message is called the **plaintext**. This name seems to suggest that cryptography only works with text messages. This was true when the term *plaintext* was coined. Today, however, plaintext messages can be images, sounds, videos, or a combination of several data formats. The original name stuck, however, so any original message is called *plaintext*.

ENCRYPTION AND CIPHERTEXT   **Encryption** is a cryptographic process that turns the plaintext into a seemingly random stream of bits called the **ciphertext**. The sender sends this ciphertext to the receiver. **Eavesdroppers** will not be able to make sense of the ciphertext if they do intercept it. However, the receiver will be able to **decrypt** the ciphertext, turning it back into the original plaintext.

---

[1] Historically, confidentiality was also called *privacy*. However, in the last few years, *privacy* has come to mean personal privacy.

[2] In fact, "cryptography" comes from the Greek words *kryptos* (hidden) and *graphos* (writing). The meaning of the writing (message) is hidden from everyone except the intended receiver.

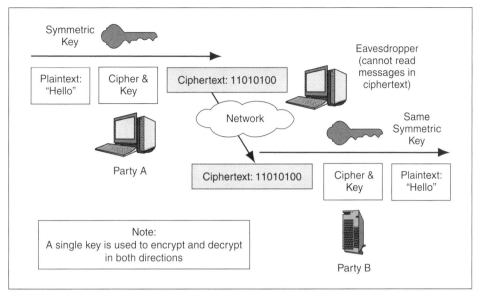

FIGURE 3-1 Symmetric Key Encryption for Confidentiality

CIPHER Figure 3-1 shows that encryption and decryption require two things. The first is a **cipher**, which is a specific mathematical process used in encryption and decryption. There are many ciphers, and they all operate differently. Both sides must use the *same* cipher for the receiver to be able to decrypt the message.

A cipher is a specific mathematical process used in encryption and decryption.

KEY The second thing that encryption and decryption require is a **key**, which is a random string of 40 to 4,000 bits (ones and zeros). (Longer keys are harder to guess and so give stronger confidentiality.) For a given cipher, different keys will generate different ciphertexts from the same plaintext.

A key is a random string of bits (ones and zeros).

KEEPING THE KEY SECRET Mathematician Auguste Kerckhoffs argued that it is impossible in practice to keep a cipher secret. There are only a few well-tested ciphers, and it usually is easy to determine which cipher is being used. Fortunately, Kerckhoffs proved that as long as the *key* is kept secret, the two parties will still have confidentiality. **Kerckhoffs' Law** says that keeping keys secret is the recipe for secure encryption.[3]

---

[3] Auguste Kerckhoffs, "La Cryptographie Militaire," *Journal des Sciences Militaires*, Vol. IX, January 1883, pp. 5–83 and February 1883, pp. 161–191.

> *Kerckhoffs' Law says that, in order to have confidentiality, communication partners only need to keep the key secret, not the cipher.*

The Simple Cipher

Figure 3-2 illustrates a simple cipher. This cipher works on letters of the alphabet. The figure has three columns.

- The first column has the rather banal plaintext, *nowisthetime*. Removing capitalization and spaces was done to simplify the example.
- The second column has the key. This key is a series of numbers between 1 and 26.
- The third column is the ciphertext to be transmitted.

In this cipher, the plaintext letter is changed to the letter N places later in the alphabet, where N is the number in the key for that letter. So if a plaintext letter is *b* and the key value is 2, the ciphertext symbol is *d*.

- The first letter in the example's plaintext is *n*, and the key value is 4. Four places beyond *n* in the alphabet is *r*, so *r* is the ciphertext symbol for the first character.
- The next plaintext letter is *o*. The key value for this is 8 this time. Consequently, the ciphertext is *w*.
- The third letter in the plaintext is *w*, and the key value is 15. Fifteen steps goes beyond the end of the alphabet and begins again at *a*. The final ciphertext symbol is *l*.

So far, we have the ciphertext *rwl*. As you might suspect, the lazy textbook writer wants you to do the rest of the work in a Test Your Understanding question.

If you have watched the television game show Wheel of Fortune, you know that the most common letter in the alphabet is *e*. This letter appears twice in this simple

Plaintext	Key	Ciphertext
n	4	r
o	8	w
w	15	l
i	16	. . .
s	23	. . .
t	16	. . .
h	3	. . .
e	9	. . .
t	12	. . .
i	20	. . .
m	6	. . .
e	25	. . .

FIGURE 3-2 Example of Symmetric Key Cipher

message. However, it has different key values each time—9 and 25. By using a random key, this cipher can make it impossible to analyze the text by letter frequency.

This example has used letters of the alphabet for the plaintext. However, almost all computer information is encoded as a set of bits. Keys are also strings of ones and zeros. In addition, real ciphers use multiple rounds of computations. By the time encryption is finished, the ciphertext resembles a purely random string of ones and zeros.

Cryptanalysis

A **cryptanalyst** is someone who cracks encryption. This simplest type of cryptanalysis is **brute force key cracking**—trying all possible keys until the cryptanalyst finds the right key. However, as we will see later in this chapter, if keys are long, brute force key cracking will take too long to be useful.

In some cases, cryptanalysts can guess at least part of the message. In World War II, for instance, Japanese naval reports often began with the same standardized opening salutation. When such regularities occur, a cryptanalyst may be able to learn at least part of the key fairly quickly.

In addition, the implementation of a cipher may be poor, allowing part of the key to "leak" out with each message. The 802.11 wireless LAN transmission standard initially used a security method called Wired Equivalent Privacy (WEP). WEP used a leaky implementation of the RC4 encryption cipher. Today, WEP keys can be broken in two or three minutes.

TEST YOUR UNDERSTANDING

1. **a.** Define cryptography.
   b. What is confidentiality?
   c. Distinguish between plaintext and ciphertext.
   d. Which is transmitted across the network—the plaintext or the ciphertext?
   e. What is a cipher?
   f. What is a key?
   g. What must be kept secret in encryption for confidentiality?
   h. What is a cryptanalyst?

2. Complete the enciphering in Figure 3-2.

Substitution and Transposition Ciphers

The specific mathematical processes in ciphers today are extremely complex. However, most use variations of two basic mathematical processes—substitution and transposition.

Substitution Ciphers

In **substitution ciphers**, one character is substituted for another, but the order of characters is not changed. If this sounds like the cipher discussed in the body of the text (Figure 3-2), it should. The example cipher is a very simple substitution cipher. Each letter is substituted for another letter in the alphabet. However, the position of each letter is the same. So *n-o-w* becomes *r-w-l*.

(Continued)

Substitution and Transposition Ciphers   (Continued)

In substitution ciphers, one character is substituted for another.

Transposition Ciphers

In **transposition ciphers**, in turn, the letters are moved around within a message, based on their initial positions in the message. The letters themselves are not changed, as they are in substitution ciphers, but their position in the message does.

Figure 3-3 shows a simple transposition cipher. First, the plaintext (*nowisthet*) is written in a three-by-three matrix—or as much of the message as will fit in the matrix. The key has six numbers—the first part consists of a number on each column, the second of a number on each row.

The cipher determines how the letters are taken out of the transposition box. The first letter out will have column key value 1 and row key value 1. This is the first column and the third row. The letter there is *h*. So *h* is the first ciphertext character.

The second letter out will have column key value 1 and row key value 2. This is the first column and the first row. The letter there is *n*. So *n* is the second ciphertext character. We now have *hn* at the beginning of the ciphertext. And yes, the mean textbook writer will expect you to do the rest of the work.

Real Encryption

In substitution ciphers, letters are changed but their position is not. In transposition ciphers, the letters are not changed, but their position in the ciphertext is changed. Real ciphers are much more complex than our examples have indicated. First, encryption is done on bits, not on letters of the alphabet. In addition, real-world ciphers mix several rounds of both transposition and substitution to give good randomness. Fortunately, working security professionals in organizations do not have to understand the specific workings of real encryption ciphers.

TEST YOUR UNDERSTANDING

3. **a.** Which leaves letters unchanged—transposition or substitution ciphers?
   b. Which leaves letters in their original positions—transposition or substitution ciphers?

4. Complete the enciphering in Figure 3-3.

Key (Part 2)	Key (Part 1) 1	3	2
2	n	o	w
3	i	s	t
1	h	e	t

FIGURE 3-3 Transposition Cipher   Key = 132 231

Ciphers and Codes

When you read this chapter, you may have been expecting to see the term *code* instead of *cipher*. However, a cipher is a general way to encrypt information, while codes are limited.

In a cipher, an individual letter is replaced by another letter, or a string of bits of fixed length is replaced by a different string of bits of fixed length. The two sides only need to know the key. If they do, they can transmit anything they wish. The trade-off is that the encryption may be subject to cryptanalysis.

Whereas ciphers work on individual characters, **codes** use **code symbols** that represent complete words or phrases. In World War II, the Japanese JN-25 naval operational code was a code. Figure 3-4 shows a simplified version of JN-25.

For each word or punctuation symbol, there is a five-digit code word. This code word is sent instead of the word or other symbol. To encode a message, the sender looks up the word or symbol and writes down the five-digit code. He or she then goes on to the next word or symbol. To begin, he or she looks up "from" and sees that the code is 17434. The sender begins the ciphertext with 17434.

For common words or symbols, the code book would have several code numbers. For instance, STOP appears three times in the message. The first time, it is encoded as 34058. The next time, it is encoded as 26733. The third time, it is encoded as 61552. Having multiple codes for common words and symbols makes it more difficult for cryptanalysts to crack the code.[4]

Message	Code
From	17434
Akagi	63717
To	83971
Truk	11131
STOP	**34058**
ETA	53764
6 PM	73104
STOP	**26733**
Require	29798
B	72135
N	54678
STOP	**61552**

FIGURE 3-4   Japanese Naval Operational Code JN-25 (Simplified)

(Continued)

---

[4] The figure shows one other feature of the JN-25 code. The ship (the Akagi) will arrive at the Truk naval base at 6 pm. It will need some servicing at the base. Instead of stating the exact service, it refers to *BN*. What does this mean? The JN-25 code does not say. In effect, BN is a code within a code. Even if the JN-25 code is completely cracked, this would not tell cryptanalysts what *BN* means. The full JN-25 code had many other subtleties. Also, after the encoded message is created, the JN-25 used a limited form of ciphering to frustrate cryptanalysis further.

Ciphers and Codes   (Continued)

Codes are attractive because people can do encoding and decoding manually, without a computer. On the negative side of the balance sheet, code books must be distributed ahead of time, and if one code book is intercepted, all confidentiality is lost.

Additionally, even common terms only have a limited number of possible codes. Consequently, it is relatively straightforward for cryptanalysts who have intercepted a lot of traffic to learn the code book. In contrast, ciphers can encrypt anything, and if the cipher key is long enough (and if proper steps are taken to ensure that people do not do something that lessens protection), then ciphers are extremely strong. The fact that ciphers are computationally complex is no longer an impediment to their use, thanks to the high-speed processing available even in mobile telephones.

TEST YOUR UNDERSTANDING

5. a. In codes, what do code symbols represent?
   b. What is the advantage of codes?
   c. What are the disadvantages?

6. Finish encoding the message in Figure 3-4.

Symmetric Key Encryption

The cipher we have been discussing is called a **symmetric key encryption** cipher because both parties encrypt and decrypt with the same key. In two-way communication with symmetric key encryption, the two parties only use a single key for encryption and decryption in both directions.

> *In symmetric key encryption, a single key is used for encryption and decryption in both directions.*

Symmetric key encryption is very fast, placing only a small processing burden on computers. As a result, even personal computers and handheld devices have sufficient processing power to encrypt with symmetric key encryption. Due to this low processing burden, file transfers, instant messaging, and other popular applications use symmetric key encryption in encryption for confidentiality. In fact, all but a tiny fraction of encryption for confidentiality uses symmetric key encryption.

> *Nearly all encryption for confidentiality uses symmetric key encryption.*

KEY LENGTH   We have seen that only the key needs to be kept secret for successful confidentiality. One way for an attacker to learn the key is doing an **exhaustive search**—trying *all possible keys* until he or she finds the correct one. The easiest way to thwart exhaustive searches is simply to make the key so long that the time needed for attackers to crack the key is far too long for practicality.

If there is a key length of N bits, there are 2^N possible keys. On average, the cryptographer will have to try half of all keys before succeeding, so it should take about $(2^N/2)$ tries to crack the key. For instance, if a key is only 8 bits long, there are only 256 (2^8) possible keys. It will take the cryptanalyst an average of only 128 tries to find the correct key.

As Figure 3-5 shows, each additional bit in the key *doubles* the time it will take to crack the key. So increasing a key's length from 8 to 16 bits will require the cryptanalyst to try half of 65,536 keys instead of half of 256. This is 256 times as many required attempts (65,536/256) for the doubling of key length. To give a more impressive example, increasing key length from 56 to 112 bits increases exhaustive search time 72 quadrillion times!

Each additional bit in the key **doubles** *the time it will take to crack the key.*

Some countries have restricted symmetric key lengths in exported products to 40 bits in order to preserve the ability of government agencies to crack keys when they need to do so. Today, 40-bit keys can be cracked very quickly. In the 1970s, **strong symmetric keys** (that is, keys that are prohibitively time-consuming to crack) only had to be about 56 bits long for symmetric key encryption. Today, symmetric keys

Key Length in Bits	Number of Possible Keys
1	2
2	4
4	16
8	256
16	65,536
40	1,099,511,627,776
56	72,057,594,037,927,900
112	5,192,296,858,534,830,000,000,000,000,000,000
112	5.1923E+33
168	3.74144E+50
256	1.15792E+77
512	1.3408E+154

Notes:

Adding one bit to the key doubles the amount of time a cryptanalyst will take to crack the key.

Shaded keys, with lengths of 100 bits or more, are considered strong symmetric keys today.

Keys, with lengths less than 100 bits, are considered weak symmetric keys today.

Public key/private key pairs (discussed later in the chapter) must be much longer to be considered to be strong because of the disastrous consequences if a private key is cracked and because private keys cannot be changed frequently. Public keys and private keys must be at least 512 to 1,024 bits long.

FIGURE 3-5 Key Length and Exhaustive Search Time

need to be at least 100 bits long to be considered strong in symmetric key encryption. In the future, as the power of cryptanalysts' computers continues to grow, even longer symmetric keys will be needed for strong encryption.

Today a symmetric key that is 100 bits long or longer is considered a strong symmetric key.

TEST YOUR UNDERSTANDING

7. **a.** Why is the word *symmetric* used in symmetric key encryption?
   b. When two parties communicate with each other using symmetric key encryption, how many keys are used in total?
   c. What type of encryption cipher is almost always used in encryption for confidentiality?

8. **a.** What is the best way to thwart exhaustive searches by cryptanalysts?
   b. If a key is 43 bits long, how much longer will it take to crack it by exhaustive search if it is extended to 45 bits?
   c. If it is extended to 50 bits?
   d. If a key is 40 bits long, how many keys must be tried, on average, to crack it?
   e. How long must a symmetric encryption key be to be considered strong today?

Human Issues in Cryptography

With sufficiently long keys and a well-tested cipher, symmetric key encryption for confidentiality is impractical to crack from a technical standpoint. However, if the sender or receiver fails to keep the key secret, the eavesdropper may learn the key and read every message.

More broadly, poor communication discipline in general can defeat the strongest cipher and longest key. In World War II, for instance, the Japanese Navy often sent messages when there was little need, giving Allied cryptologists a large base of messages to examine. This made the jobs of cryptanalysts much easier than if the Japanese had used better communication discipline. In addition, as noted earlier in this chapter, Japanese Naval reports often began with a standard flowery introduction that was several sentences long. This "known plaintext" situation was invaluable in cracking Japanese codebooks. Also helpful was the fact that transmissions often followed a set format for common types of situations such as reporting a ship's speed and compass bearing.

Communicating partners can even have a false sense of security because they will think that the cracked encryption method is still protecting them. In World War II, the Germans had an encryption machine called Enigma, which was very advanced technically. However, the Polish military captured a copy of the machine and reverse-engineered it to reveal how it worked. After Poland fell to Germany, the Poles passed their results to the English, who continued the work. Eventually, the English could read a large percentage of German messages encrypted with Enigma. The overconfident Germans sent vast amounts of very sensitive traffic thinking that they were completely safe. The Japanese also sent large amounts of encrypted traffic due to overconfidence.

The reality of cryptography is that it is not an automatic protection. It only works if companies have and enforce organizational processes that do not compromise the technical strengths of cryptography.

TEST YOUR UNDERSTANDING

9. Why is cryptography not an automatic protection?

SYMMETRIC KEY ENCRYPTION CIPHERS

Symmetric key encryption uses many specific ciphers that work in the same general way but that function very differently in their details. Communication partners must choose a specific symmetric key encryption cipher if they wish to communicate securely. Only a few common symmetric key encryption ciphers have been well tested, and it is important to select from these few. We will look at the most common well-tested ciphers: RC4, DES, 3DES, and AES. Figure 3-6 compares these ciphers.

RC4

The weakest cipher in common use today is **RC4**, which is usually pronounced as "ARK FOUR." RC4 has two advantages over other popular encryption algorithms.

First, RC4 is extremely fast and uses only a small amount of RAM.[5] This means that it is ideal for small handheld devices and was viable for even the earliest 802.11 wireless access points. Consequently, RC4 became the basis for the notorious WEP encryption system for wireless LANs, which we will see in Chapter 4.

	RC4	DES	3DES	AES
Key length (bits)	40 bits or more	56	112 or 168	128, 192, or 256
Key strength	Very weak at 40 bits	Weak	Strong	Strong
Processing requirements	Low	Moderate	High	Low
RAM requirements	Low	Moderate	Moderate	Low
Remarks	Can use keys of variable lengths	Created in the 1970s	Applies DES three times with 2 or 3 keys	Today's gold standard, likely to be dominant in the future

FIGURE 3-6   Major Symmetric Key Encryption Ciphers

---

[5] One way to see why RC4 is fast is to note that RC4 can be implemented in only about 50 lines of code. In contrast, the gold-standard AES algorithm requires 350 lines of code (http://www.informit.com). More lines of code generally correspond to longer processing time per key.

Second, RC4 can use a broad range of key lengths. For most ciphers, longer key length is better. However, RC4 was widely used primarily because its shortest optional key length is 40 bits. As noted earlier in this chapter, national export restrictions in many countries once limited commercial products to 40-bit encryption. Consequently, 40-bit RC4 became the standard key length for WEP.

Unfortunately, RC4 is a dangerous cipher to use. If it is not implemented perfectly, its protection is minimal. Poor RC4 implementation is what made WEP such a weak protection system for wireless LANs.

TEST YOUR UNDERSTANDING

10. **a.** What are the two advantages of RC4?
    b. Why is an RC4 key length of 40 bits commonly used?
    c. Is this a strong key?

The Data Encryption Standard (DES)

In 1977, the U.S. National Bureau of Standards, which is now the National Institute of Standards and Technology (NIST), created the **Data Encryption Standard (DES)**. DES quickly became the most widely used symmetric key encryption method.

DES is still widely used because it has survived everything except brute-force exhaustive search attacks, because it is widely available, and because it is supported by hardware accelerators.

56-BIT KEY SIZE   The DES key is 56 bits long. It comes in a block of 64 bits, of which 56 bits represent the key. The other 8 bits are redundant in the sense that you can compute them if you know the other 56 bits. This redundancy allows parties to detect incorrect keys.

Today, a 56-bit key size is too short for major business transactions and highly sensitive trade secrets.[6] However, it is sufficient for most residential consumer applications, and, as we will see next, cryptographers have extended DES to 3DES for industrial-strength security. Even 56-bit DES consumes a moderate amount of RAM and is only moderately fast.

BLOCK ENCRYPTION   Figure 3-7 shows that DES is a **block encryption** standard. DES encrypts messages 64 bits at a time. The inputs for the encryption are the key and the 64-bit block of plaintext. The output is a 64-bit block of ciphertext.[7]

TEST YOUR UNDERSTANDING

11. **a.** How long is a DES key?
    b. Is this a strong length?
    c. Describe block encryption with DES.

---

[6] In fairness to NIST, DES was only designed to be used for about ten years—until the mid 1980s. During that period, a 56-bit key was a fairly strong key.

[7] In block encryption, the specific way that the encryption is done is called a mode. Figure 3-7 specifically shows *electronic codebook mode*, which is the simplest DES block encryption mode. More complex DES modes offer better protection.

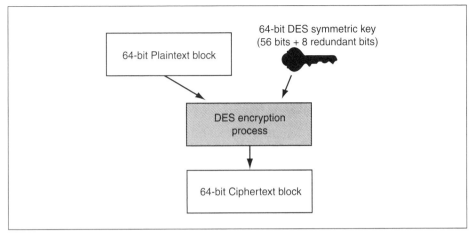

FIGURE 3-7 DES Block Encryption

Triple DES (3DES)

Where firms need stronger encryption than DES provides, they can turn to **triple DES (3DES)**, which extends the effective key size of DES in a simple but painfully slow way that uses a moderate amount of RAM.

168-BIT 3DES OPERATION   The 3DES algorithm simply applies DES three times in a row for extra strength.[8] Normally, this is done with three different DES keys. This gives an effective key length of 168 bits (3 times 56). This is very strong.

112-BIT 3DES   A variant of 3DES uses only two keys. In this approach, the third operation of the sender is to encrypt the output of the second stage with the *first* key—the key it used in the first step. This effectively gives 112-bit[9] encryption, which is strong, and only requires the secure distribution of two DES keys.

PERSPECTIVE ON 3DES   From a security standpoint, 3DES gives strong symmetric key encryption. However, from a practical point of view, DES is slow, and having to apply DES three times is extremely slow and therefore extremely expensive in terms of processing cost. 3DES is prohibitively slow for use on personal computers.

---

[8] Actually, 3DES encrypts the plaintext block with the first key, *decrypts* the output of the first step with the second key, and then encrypts the output of the second step with the third key. Does the pattern of encrypting, decrypting, and then encrypting again seem odd? The reason for this algorithm is that it works even if the two parties only share a single DES key. Encrypting plaintext with a DES key and then decrypting the output of the first step with the same key returns the original plaintext. The third encryption, then, is equivalent to traditional single DES. This means that 3DES software can handle both 3DES and DES. In addition, a receiver that implements only DES is able to work with a 3DES sender and vice versa by using a single key. Of course, the effective key length is only 56 bits when only a single key is used.

[9] Some people call this type of encryption 128-bit DES. As we saw earlier, although DES keys only have 56-bit key strength, they are 64 bits long.

TEST YOUR UNDERSTANDING

12. **a.** How does 3DES work?
    b. What are the two common effective key lengths in 3DES?
    c. Are these lengths strong enough for communication in corporations?
    d. What is the disadvantage of 3DES?

Advanced Encryption Standard (AES)

In response to the weak key length of DES and the processing burden of 3DES, NIST released the **Advanced Encryption Standard (AES)** in 2001. AES is efficient enough in terms of processing power and RAM requirements to be used on a wide variety of devices—even cellular telephones and personal digital assistants (PDAs).[10]

AES offers three alternative key lengths: 128 bits, 192 bits, and 256 bits. Even the 128-bit key length is strong. A brute-force code-breaking system that could defeat 56-bit DES in a second would take over 100 trillion years to crack 128-bit AES. The longer key lengths are sufficiently strong even for material that must be kept secret for many years. Many cryptographic systems now support AES, and AES should dominate encryption for confidentiality in the near future.

TEST YOUR UNDERSTANDING

13. **a.** What is the big advantage of AES over 3DES?
    b. What are the three key lengths offered by AES?
    c. Which strong symmetric key encryption cipher can be used with small mobile devices?
    d. Which symmetric key encryption cipher probably will dominate symmetric key encryption in the near future?

Other Symmetric Key Encryption Ciphers

There are many other symmetric key encryption ciphers. However, only a few of these other ciphers have survived years of extensive cryptanalysis. Among those that have done so and that see significant use are IDEA (especially in Europe), SEED (in South Korea), GOST (in Russia), and Camellia (in Japan).

Unfortunately, many companies proudly advertise "new and proprietary" encryption ciphers. They argue that because attackers will not know the cipher's algorithm, they will not be able to break the encryption. However, security professionals deride this as **security through obscurity** because it relies on attackers not to obtain learnable information that would result in a catastrophic loss of security if known.

> *Security through obscurity is the principle of relying on attackers not to obtain learnable information that would result in a catastrophic loss of security if known.*

---

[10] 3DES requires 48 rounds of processing for encryption. AES requires only 9–13 rounds, depending on key length. Although the rounds in 3DES and AES are not completely comparable, this comparison gives you a feeling for why AES is so much faster than 3DES.

In practice, ciphertext encrypted with proprietary algorithms typically is cracked quickly, *even if the attacker does not know the detailed cipher.* Creating a vulnerability-free encryption cipher is extremely difficult, even for professionals in the field. This is why only extremely well-tested ciphers should be used in organizations. In security classes in computer science departments, students usually learn how to design new encryption ciphers. In contrast, information systems security classes teach students *never* to create their own encryption algorithms.

> *In security classes in computer science departments, students usually learn how to design new encryption ciphers. In contrast, information systems security classes teach students never to create their own encryption algorithms.*

TEST YOUR UNDERSTANDING

14. a. It is claimed that new and proprietary encryption ciphers are good because cryptanalysts will not know them. Comment on this.
   b. What is security through obscurity, and why is it bad?

CRYPTOGRAPHIC SYSTEMS

Cryptographic Systems

Until fairly recently, confidentiality was the major goal of cryptography. However, cryptography has matured to the point where military and business organizations know that encryption for confidentiality is only one of the several cryptographic protections needed in message exchanges. In practice, these protections are provided by a **cryptographic system**, which is a *packaged set* of cryptographic countermeasures for protecting dialogues.

> *A cryptographic system is a* packaged set *of cryptographic countermeasures for protecting dialogues.*

Cryptographic System Standards

When two parties communicate using a cryptographic system, they need to use a specific **cryptographic system standard**. This standard specifies both the protections to be applied and the mathematical processes that will be used to provide protections. Popular cryptographic system standards include SSL/TLS and IPsec. We will see these and other cryptographic system standards in the next chapter and in subsequent chapters.

Initial Handshaking Stages

When two parties (devices or programs) begin to communicate via a cryptographic system standard, they go through three **handshaking stages**, as Figure 3-8 illustrates.

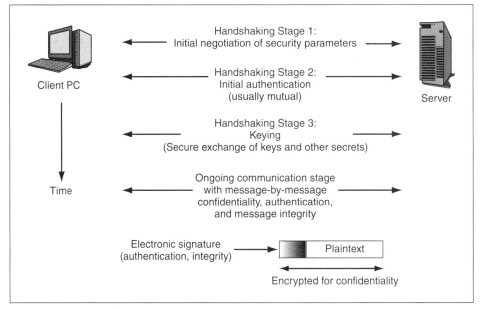

FIGURE 3-8 Cryptographic System Stages

NEGOTIATION Nearly all cryptographic system standards offer multiple crypto-graphic methods for use in communication, and nearly all cryptographic methods have multiple options. Consequently, the first handshaking stage is the negotiation of cryptographic methods and options to be used in the communication. A specific set of options in SSL/TLS is called a **cipher suite**. Before the two parties in an SSL/TLS connection do anything else, they must negotiate a specific cipher suite for the communication session. (Other cryptographic system standards use different names for combinations of methods and options.)

> *A cipher suite is a specific set of options for a particular cryptographic system standard.*

INITIAL AUTHENTICATION The second handshaking stage is **initial authentication**. Messages can be sent by **impostors**, so before two parties begin communication, they need to **authenticate** each other, that is, test the identity of their communication partner. This is called initial authentication because it is done before communication begins. As noted later in this section, there may also be subsequent message-by-message authentication for each message the two parties send.

When both parties authenticate themselves, this is **mutual authentication**. Sometimes, however, authentication is only done by one party. When you log into a server, for instance, you must authenticate yourself to the server, but the server usually does not authenticate itself to you.

> *In authentication, communication partners prove their identities to each other.*

Note that initial authentication takes place *after* the negotiation stage. The reason for this is very simple. Until the two parties negotiate authentication methods and options within these methods, they cannot begin authentication.

KEYING   The third stage is keying. As noted earlier, confidentiality ciphers require keys. As we will see later, authentication requires **secrets**. Both keys and secrets are simply long strings of bits that must be kept secret between the two parties. In most cases, keys and secrets must be sent securely. Sending keys or secrets securely is generically called **keying**. We will see two keying methods later in this chapter.

Note that keying comes *after* authentication. This is necessary because a number of keying methods are vulnerable to key stealing by third parties unless authentication is done first.

Ongoing Communication

After the two sides have authenticated each other and keys have been exchanged, the handshaking stages are over and the ongoing communication stage begins. In the ongoing communication stage, the two parties typically send many messages back and forth. The two parties usually apply several cryptographic protections during ongoing communication on a message-by-message basis.

- First, the sender adds an **electronic signature** to each message. This allows the receiver to authenticate each message. **Message-by-message authentication** thwarts efforts by impostors to insert messages into the dialogue stream.
- Second, all good electronic signature technologies also provide **message integrity**, which means that if an attacker captures and alters a message (for example, changing a customer's bank balance amount), the authentication process will reject the message.
- Third, the sender encrypts the combined message and electronic signature for confidentiality.

TEST YOUR UNDERSTANDING

15. **a.** Distinguish between cryptography and cryptographic systems.
    b. Distinguish between cryptographic systems and cryptographic system standards.
    c. Why is the first handshaking stage the negotiation of security methods and options?
    d. What is an impostor?
    e. What is authentication?
    f. What is mutual authentication?
    g. Why is a secure keying phase necessary?

16. **a.** What three protections do cryptographic systems provide on a message-by-message basis?
    b. What is an electronic signature?
    c. What two protections do electronic signatures usually provide?
    d. Distinguish between the handshaking stages and ongoing communication.

THE NEGOTIATION STAGE

We have gone fairly quickly through the four stages involved in cryptographic systems. Now, we will go through each of these stages in more detail, beginning with the negotiation stage.

Cipher Suite Options

As discussed earlier in this chapter, a cipher suite is a specific set of security methods and options for a particular cryptographic system standard, SSL/TLS. A cipher suite includes a specific set of methods and options for initial authentication, key exchange, and ongoing message confidentiality, authentication, and integrity.

Figure 3-9 shows a small subset of optional cipher suites offered by the popular SSL/TLS standards that we will see in Chapter 4. They are shown in order of increasing cryptographic strength. We will see most of the specific cryptographic methods shown in the figure later in this chapter and in other chapters.

Cipher Suite Policies

The weakest cipher suites in a cryptographic system standard often provide very little protection or none at all. For instance, the first cipher suite in Figure 3-9 provides no security at all. The second only uses export-grade encryption, and so, while stronger, it is still quite weak. The last cipher suite is very strong.

Due to wide variation in the strengths of SSL/TLS cipher suites, companies must develop risk-based policies for the selection of cipher suites, only allowing cipher suites with suitable strength for the risks facing the application. The IPsec cryptographic system standard (which we will see in Chapter 4) can set policies for security methods and options centrally and impose these policies on all communicating partners.

Cipher Suite	Key Negotiation	Digital Signature Method	Symmetric Key Encryption Method	Hashing Method for HMAC	Strength
NULL_WITH_NULL_NULL	None	None	None	None	None
RSA_EXPORT_WITH_ RC4_40_MD5	RSA export strength (40 bits)	RSA export strength (40 bits)	RC4 (40-bit key)	MD5	Weak
RSA_WITH_DES_CBC_ SHA	RSA	RSA	DES_CBC	SHA-1	Stronger but not very strong
DH_DSS_WITH_3DES_ EDE_CBC_SHA	Diffie– Hellman	Digital signature standard	3DES_ EDE_CBC	SHA-1	Strong
RSA_WITH_AES_256_ CBC_SHA256	RSA	RSA	AES 256 bits	SHA-256	Very strong

FIGURE 3-9 Selected SSL/TLS Cipher Suites

TEST YOUR UNDERSTANDING

17. **a.** In SSL/TLS, what is a cipher suite?
    b. Why do companies wish to create policies for which sets of security methods and options two parties may use for a particular application?

INITIAL AUTHENTICATION STAGE

Once the security negotiation stage is finished, the next handshaking stage in establishing a cryptographic system dialogue is authentication. There are several initial authentication methods. We will only look at one, MS-CHAP, which is based on password authentication on servers.

Authentication Terminology

In authentication, the party trying to prove its identity to the other is called the **supplicant**. The other party is the **verifier**. The supplicant sends **credentials** (proofs of identity) to the verifier (Figure 3-10). In mutual authentication, the two parties take turns being supplicants and verifiers.

TEST YOUR UNDERSTANDING

18. **a.** In authentication, distinguish between the supplicant and the verifier.
    b. What are credentials?
    c. How many supplicants and verifiers are there in mutual authentication between two parties? Explain.

Hashing

When most people think of cryptography, they think of encryption. However, cryptography also uses a very different process, hashing, which we need to look at before considering MS-CHAP initial authentication (Figure 3-11).

A simplistic way to think about hashing is to treat the message's bits as a very large binary number and divide it by a smaller number. The *remainder* can be the hash. For instance, to put things in decimal, if the message is 6,457 and the hash number is 236, the hash value will go into the message number 27 times with a remainder of 85. This remainder, 85, is the hash. Real hashing is more complex than this, but this example gives you the flavor of hashing.

FIGURE 3-10   Authentication: Supplicant, Verifier, and Credentials

Hashing
  A hashing algorithm is applied to a bit string of any length
  The result of the calculation is called the hash
  For a given hashing algorithm, all hashes are the same short length

Hashing versus Encryption

Characteristic	Encryption	Hashing
Result length	About the same length as the plaintext	Short fixed length regardless of message length
Reversible?	Yes. Decryption	No. There is no way to get from the short hash back to the long original message

Hashing Algorithms
  MD5 (128-bit hashes)
  SHA-1 (160-bit hashes)
  SHA-224, SHA-256, SHA-384, and SHA-512 (name gives hash length in bits)

Note: MD5 and SHA-1 should not be used because have been shown to be unsecure

FIGURE 3-11 Hashing

When **hashing** is applied to a binary message, the result (called the **hash**) is far shorter than the original message—typically only 128 to 512 bits long. In contrast, encryption produces ciphertext that is about as long as the plaintext.

Unlike encryption, which can be reversed by decryption, hashing is **irreversible**. There is no "dehashing" algorithm. You cannot begin with a message of several thousand bits, create a hash of a few hundred bits, and expect to be able to recover the whole original message. In the previous example, if someone tells you that the hash is 87, there is no way for you to compute that the original value was 6,457. Another way to remember irreversibility is that you cannot turn a hamburger back into a cow.

Hashing is also repeatable. If two different people apply the same hashing algorithm to the same bit string, they always get exactly the same hash.

The most widely used hashing method today probably is **MD5**, which produces 128-bit hashes. In addition, there is a family of **Secure Hash Algorithm (SHA)** variants of increasing strength, including SHA-1, SHA-224, SHA-256, SHA-384, and SHA-512. SHA-1 produces a hash of 160 bits, while other versions of SHA have their hash length (in bits) in their names. Unfortunately, cryptanalysts have recently found weaknesses in both MD5 and SHA-1. Only stronger versions of SHA should be used today, and MD5 should not be used at all.[11]

[11] The National Institute of Standards and Technology (NIST) is currently working to define a new family of SHA standards.

TEST YOUR UNDERSTANDING

19. **a.** In hashing, what is the hash?
    b. Is encryption reversible?
    c. Is hashing reversible?
    d. Is hashing repeatable?
    e. When a hashing algorithm is applied, does the hash have a fixed length or a variable length?
    f. What is the hash size of MD5?
    g. What is the hash size of SHA-1?
    h. What is the hash size of SHA-256?
    i. Which hashing algorithms should not be used because they have been found to be vulnerable?

Initial Authentication with MS-CHAP

We will look at one initial authentication method, MS-CHAP, which is used by servers to authenticate clients by means of reusable passwords. With password authentication, it is important not to send passwords in the clear, that is, without cryptographic protection. If the password is sent in the clear, then an attacker can intercept it and use the password to hack into the user's account later.

Figure 3-12 illustrates the **Microsoft Challenge–Handshake Authentication Protocol (MS-CHAP)**.[12] MS-CHAP is widely used when users log into a server running the Microsoft Windows Server operating system. The password becomes a shared secret known by both the supplicant (the user) and the verifier (the server). The supplicant authenticates himself or herself by proving that he or she knows the password for a particular account.

ON THE SUPPLICANT'S MACHINE: HASHING In MS-CHAP, the server (1) sends the supplicant's PC a **challenge message** (2), which is simply a random bit string. The server sends this message in the clear, without encryption for confidentiality.

The supplicant's PC then *appends* the applicant's password to this challenge message, producing a longer bit stream. The supplicant's PC then hashes this bit stream to produce the **response message** (3). The supplicant's PC sends this response message to the server, again in the clear (4).

ON THE VERIFIER SERVER To test the response message, the server repeats the client's actions. The server takes the challenge message it sent to the user, appends the user's password, which it also knows, and applies the same hashing algorithm the supplicant used (5). (Recall that hashing is repeatable.) If the server's hash is identical to the response message, then the user must know the account's password (6).[13] The server logs in the authenticated user.

---

[12] This is the Microsoft (MS) version of the IETF Challenge Handshake Authentication Protocol (CHAP).

[13] Users may have their PCs remember their passwords. If so, anyone taking control of a computer could impersonate the user.

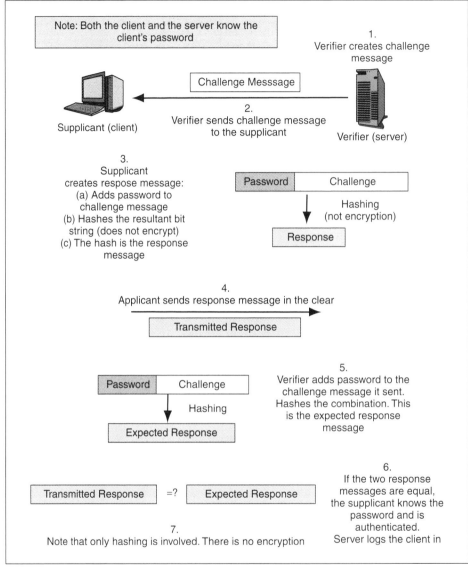

FIGURE 3-12 MS-CHAP Challenge-Challenge Authentication Protocol

TEST YOUR UNDERSTANDING

20. **a.** Is MS-CHAP used for initial authentication or message-by-message authentication?
    b. How does the supplicant create the response message?
    c. How does the verifier check the response message?
    d. What type of encryption does MS-CHAP use? (This is a trick question but an important one.)
    e. In MS-CHAP, does the server authenticate itself to the client?

THE KEYING STAGE

Session Keys

After the authentication stage, the two partners must exchange one or more symmetric keys for confidentially. These keys are called **session keys** because they are only used for a single communication session. If the two parties communicate again, they will exchange a different session key. We will look at two keying methods that are widely used in organizations.

Public Key Encryption for Confidentiality

One of these keying methods uses public key encryption for confidentiality. Although symmetric key encryption dominates encryption for confidentiality, another family of ciphers is sometimes used for confidentiality. These are **public key encryption** ciphers, also called **asymmetric key encryption** ciphers. Public key encryption can be used in key exchange for symmetric session keys (and other secrets).

TWO KEYS   In public key encryption, each party has two keys—a **private key** and a **public key**. Each party keeps its private key secret, but the public keys can be learned by anyone without creating problems. Figure 3-13 shows how these two types of keys are used for confidentiality.

PROCESS   In Figure 3-13, Bob[14] wishes to send a message securely to Carol. Bob encrypts the plaintext with *Carol's public key.* At the otzarol decrypts the ciphertext

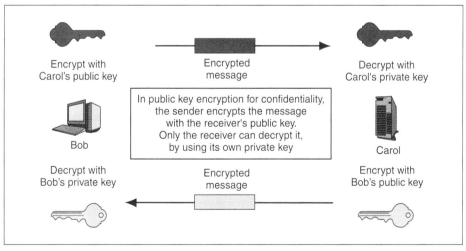

FIGURE 3-13   Public Key Encryption for Confidentiality

---

[14] Many writings on cryptography use partners named Bob and Carol. These names were introduced by Diffie and Hellman in their seminal work that produced public key encryption. W. Diffie and M. E. Hellman, "New Directions in Cryptography," *IEEE Transaction on Information Theory*, Vol. IT-22, November 1976, pp. 644–654.

using *her own private key.* Note that we cannot simply say, "the public key," and "the private key," because each side has a public key and a private key.

Note also that the sender encrypts with the receiver's public key, which is widely known, and the receiver decrypts the message with his or her own private key, which only he or she knows. Anyone can encrypt a message to a party using the party's nonsecret public key. There is no need for prior secure key exchange as there is in symmetric key encryption.

HIGH COST AND SHORT MESSAGE LENGTHS   Symmetric key is fast and inexpensive, but it requires the secure distribution of session keys. Public key encryption is the opposite. We have just seen that in public key encryption there is no need to distribute keys secretly before encryption for confidentiality. No prior keying is necessary. This is highly desirable.

However, public key encryption ciphers are extremely complex and therefore slow and expensive to use. (Typically, public key encryption takes 100 to 1,000 times longer than symmetric key encryption to encrypt a message of a given length.) Consequently, cryptography only uses public key encryption to encrypt very short messages for confidentiality.

RSA AND ECC   There are only two widely used public key encryption ciphers. The first is the **RSA** cipher, which dominates public key encryption. However, the more efficient **elliptic curve cryptography (ECC)** public key cipher is seeing increasing use.

KEY LENGTH   While symmetric key encryption relies on briefly used session keys, public–private key pairs are rarely changed. For instance, to be able to receive encrypted messages, the receiver needs to protect a private key for weeks, months, or even years. As the duration of key use increases, so does traffic volume, and so must key length for a given degree of security. While session keys of 100 bits are strong in symmetric key encryption, public keys need to be far longer. For RSA public key encryption, a recommended minimum key length for a strong key is 1,024 bits. For the more efficient ECC cipher, 512-bit keys give equivalent strength. Longer key length requires more processing time during encipherment, and long key length is one of the reasons why public key encryption is so slow and expensive to implement.

TEST YOUR UNDERSTANDING

21. **a.** When Carol sends a message to Bob, what key will she use to encrypt the message?
    b. Why is "the public key" not a good answer to Question 21a?
    c. What key will Bob use to decrypt the message?
    d. Why is "the private key" not a good answer to Question 21c?
    e. In a classroom with 30 students and a teacher, how many public keys will there be?
    f. How many private keys?

22. **a.** What is the main drawback to public key encryption?
    b. What is the most popular public key encryption cipher?
    c. What is the other commonly used public key encryption cipher?

   d. Which need to be longer—symmetric keys or public keys? Justify your answer.
   e. How long are strong RSA keys?
   f. How long are strong ECC keys?

23. Julia encrypts a message to David using public key encryption for confidentiality. After encrypting the message, can Julia decrypt it?

Symmetric Key Keying Using Public Key Encryption

Although public key encryption and symmetric key encryption may seem like rivals, they actually are complementary. For example, public key encryption can deliver symmetric session keys securely, as Figure 3-14 illustrates.

- First, one side (Party A) generates a random bit string that will be used as a symmetric session key.
- Second, Party A encrypts this symmetric session key with the public key of the other party (Party B). Because this key is public, there is no need for a prior secret key distribution as there is with symmetric key encryption for confidentiality.
- Third, Party A sends this encrypted session key to Party B.
- Fourth, Party B decrypts the encrypted session key with Party B's own private key. It can now read the original plaintext, which is the symmetric session key generated by the other party.
- Fifth, now that the keying is complete, both sides have the symmetric session key and will use it to send messages confidentially using symmetric key encryption.

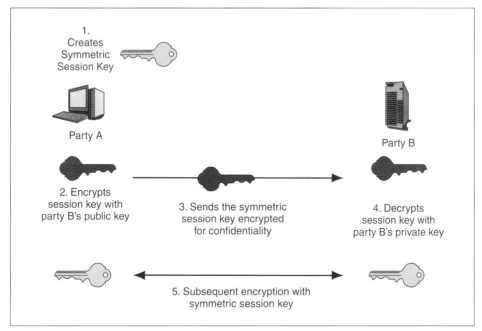

FIGURE 3-14 Public Key Keying for Symmetric Session Keys

TEST YOUR UNDERSTANDING

24. Explain how public key encryption can facilitate symmetric session key exchange.

Symmetric Key Keying Using Diffie–Hellman Key Agreement

Although the use of public key encryption to do keying is widespread, public key encryption is extremely slow. Another popular keying method, **Diffie–Hellman key agreement**, is much faster. This technique is named for the two creators of public key encryption, who also created this keying method. Figure 3-15 briefly illustrates how Diffie–Hellman key agreement does keying.

The figure shows that the two sides exchange keying information in the first two exchanges (Steps 1 and 4). If you are mathematically inclined, you can follow the process in detail, but we will only look at the most important highlights.

Using this keying information plus information that each side *does not* transmit (random numbers x and y), the two sides each compute the same symmetric key ($g^{xy} \bmod p$). They then use this key as a session key for subsequent symmetric key encryption (Step 6).

The two sides send their keying information in the clear. However, an eavesdropper listening to these exchanges cannot learn the random numbers x and y that

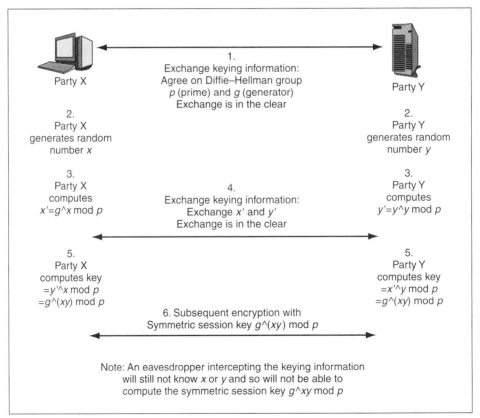

FIGURE 3-15 Keying Using Diffie–Hellman Key Agreement

Parties A and B generate but do not transmit. Consequently, the eavesdropper cannot compute the key by reading the transmitted keying information alone.[15]

TEST YOUR UNDERSTANDING

25. **a.** What is the purpose of Diffie–Hellman key agreement?
    b. Can an attacker who captures the exchanged keying information compute the symmetric session key?

MESSAGE-BY-MESSAGE AUTHENTICATION

After two parties exchange session keys, the initial security negotiation stage is complete. The partners then begin sending many messages back and forth in the ongoing communication stage.

Electronic Signatures

For message-by-message authentication, each message must contain an **electronic signature**, as noted earlier in this chapter. This electronic signature provides both authentication and message integrity. There are two common types of electronic signatures—digital signatures and key-hashed message authentication codes (HMACs).[16] Although digital signatures are widely discussed in textbooks, they actually are used much less frequently than HMACs in practice.

Public Key Encryption for Authentication

Earlier, we saw that public key encryption can be used for *confidentiality*. The sending party encrypts with the public key of the receiving party. The receiving party then decrypts the arriving ciphertext with its own private key, which only it knows. Interceptors cannot read the message at all.

   Public key encryption can also be used for *authentication*. Earlier in this chapter, we saw that the supplicant in authentication must prove his or her identity by sending credentials to the verifier. Only if these credentials are verified as belonging to the **true party**—the person the supplicant claims to be—will the verifier accept the sender as the true party. (Given the possibility of impersonation, the supplicant may not be the true party.)

> *In authentication, the true party is the person the supplicant claims to be.*

   In public key encryption for authentication, the supplicant must prove that it knows something nobody else should know—*the true party's private key.* By proving

---

[15] However, it is mandatory for the two parties to do mutual authentication before using Diffie–Hellman key agreement because a man-in-the-middle attacker can defeat it if it can impersonate itself to the two parties.

[16] Why don't we call them KHMACs, including a K for the key? When the author talked to one of the creators of the HMAC method, the answer was, "There's no need because key-hashed message authentication codes *always* use a key."

that it knows the true party's private key, the supplicant can authenticate itself as the true party. To do this, the supplicant encrypts something with its private key. If the server can decrypt the resultant ciphertext with the true party's public key, then the sender must know the true party's private key and therefore must be the true party.

TEST YOUR UNDERSTANDING

26. **a.** In public key encryption for authentication, which key does the supplicant use to encrypt?
    b. Does the verifier decrypt the ciphertext with the supplicant's public key? (If not, explain what key it does use.)
    c. Who is the true party?
    d. What does the sender attempt to prove it knows that only the true party should know?

Message-by-Message Authentication with Digital Signatures

Public key encryption for confidentiality is used in one common electronic signature method, digital signatures.

Note to the reader: Slow way down when you read this section. Be sure you understand the overall flow in Figure 3-16 and that you understand each step well.

DIGITAL SIGNATURES   Figure 3-16 shows how to create a **digital signature**, which authenticates a single message with public key encryption. The process is roughly analogous to the way human signatures authenticate documents.

HASHING TO PRODUCE THE MESSAGE DIGEST   To create the digital signature, the sender (who is the supplicant) first hashes the plaintext message. (Note that the sender does not add anything to the plaintext before hashing it, as happens in MS-CHAP.) The resulting hash is called the **message digest**. This hash is short enough to be encrypted by public key encryption.

SIGNING THE MESSAGE DIGEST TO PRODUCE THE DIGITAL SIGNATURE   Next, the sender encrypts the message digest with the sender's own private key. This step creates the **digital signature**. *Note that the message digest is not the digital signature; it is only used to produce the digital signature.*

Note that the message digest is not the digital signature; it is only used to produce the digital signature.

When a party encrypts a message digest with its own private key, this is called **signing** a message digest. The sender proves his or her identity like a person signing a letter. The sender "signs" the message digest with his or her private key to create the digital signature.

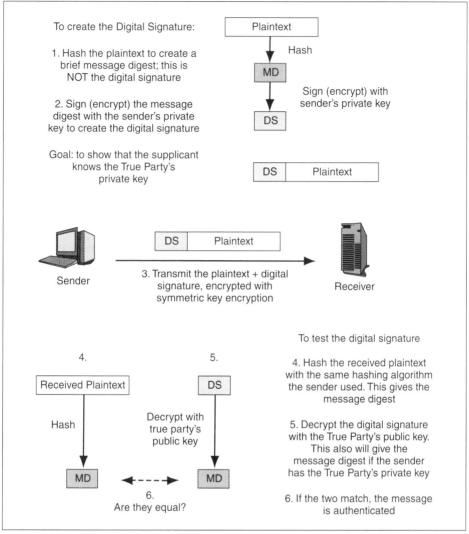

FIGURE 3-16 Digital Signature for Message-by-Message Authentication

Signing *a message digest means encrypting it with the sender's private key.*

SENDING THE MESSAGE WITH CONFIDENTIALITY The message that the sender wishes to send, then, consists of the original plaintext message plus the digital signature. If confidentiality is not an issue, the sender can simply send the combined message in the clear. However, confidentiality normally *is* important, so the sender usually encrypts the combined original message and digital signature for confidentiality. The combined message is likely to be long, so the sender must use symmetric key encryption.

At the other end, the receiver (verifier) decrypts the entire message with the symmetric key used for confidentiality. Again, this step is for confidentiality and has nothing to do with authentication.

VERIFYING THE SUPPLICANT   Again, the true party is the person (or software process) the supplicant claims to be. If the sender is the true party, the sender will be authenticated. Otherwise, the sender is an impostor and should not be authenticated.

To begin the verification process, the receiver first decrypts the digital signature with the *true party's* public key, which is widely known. This will produce the original message digest if the supplicant/sender has signed the message digest with the true party's private key.

Note again that verification requires knowing the *true party's* public key. The verifier does not use the *sender's* public key because the sender may be an impostor. If the sender's public key is used for testing, then the sender's public key will *always* "prove" that the sender is the true party by decrypting the digital signature.

In the next step, the verifier hashes the original plaintext message with the same hashing algorithm the supplicant used. This also should produce the message digest.

Third, if the message digests produced in these two different ways match, then the sender must have the true party's private key, which only the true party should know. The message is authenticated as coming from the true party.[17]

MESSAGE INTEGRITY   If someone has changed the message in transit, the two message digests will not match. Therefore, digital signatures also give **message integrity**—the ability to reject an altered message. All real-world message-by-message authentication methods provide message integrity as a byproduct.

PUBLIC KEY ENCRYPTION FOR CONFIDENTIALITY AND AUTHENTICATION   In this chapter, we have seen that public key encryption is used for both confidentiality and authentication. A frequent source of confusion for students is that public key encryption uses different keys for these two goals. Figure 3-17 illustrates these differences.

In public key encryption for confidentiality, the sender encrypts with the *receiver's public key.* The receiver decrypts with the *receiver's private key*, which only the receiver knows.

In public key encryption for authentication, however, the sender (supplicant) is attempting to prove that he or she knows the true party's secret private key. The *sender encrypts something with its own private key.* The receiver (verifier) then decrypts the message with the *true party's public key.* Note again that the verifier does *not* use the sender's public key to decrypt the message because the sender may be an impostor.

---

[17] This digital signature process is widely used, but it is not the only way to create a digital signature with public key authentication. Another approach, which is used by the U.S. Federal Government, is the Digital Signature Standard (DSS), which uses the Digital Signature Algorithm (DSA). National Institute of Standards and Technology, "Digital Signature Standard (DSS)," Federal Information Processing Standards Publication (FIPS PUB) 186, May 19, 1994. http://www.itl.nist.gov/fipspubs/fip186.htm.

Encryption Goal	Sender Encrypts with	Receiver Decrypts with
Public key encryption for confidentiality	The receiver's public key	The receiver's private key
Public key encryption for authentication	The sender's private key	The True Party's public key (not the sender's public key)

FIGURE 3-17   Public Key Encryption for Confidentiality and Authentication

TEST YOUR UNDERSTANDING

27. **a.** In public key authentication, what must the sender know that an impostor should not be able to learn?
   b. For what type of authentication is a digital signature used—initial authentication or message-by-message authentication?
   c. How does the supplicant create a message digest?
   d. How does the supplicant create a digital signature?
   e. In public key encryption, what is "signing?"
   f. What combined message does the supplicant send?
   g. How is the combined message encrypted for confidentiality?
   h. How does the verifier check the digital signature?
   i. Does the verifier use the sender's public key or the true party's public key to test the digital signature?

28. **a.** Besides authentication, what security benefit does a digital signature provide?
   b. Explain what this benefit means.
   c. Do most message-by-message authentication methods provide message integrity as a byproduct?

29. **a.** Contrast the key the sender uses for encryption in public key encryption for confidentiality and public key encryption for authentication.
   b. Contrast the key the receiver uses for decryption in public key encryption for confidentiality and public key encryption for authentication. (Careful!)

Digital Certificates

CERTIFICATE AUTHORITIES   Public keys are not secret, but you must get the true party's public key from a trusted source if you are to use it confidently in authentication. The source normally is a **certificate authority (CA)**,[18] which is an independent and trusted source of information about the public keys of true parties. Unfortunately, few countries regulate CAs, so the verifier must only accept digital certificates from certificate authorities it trusts by reputation.

By the way, a common misconception is that certificate authorities vouch for the honesty of the party named in the certificate. They do not! They merely vouch for the named party's public key. Although customers who misbehave may have

---

[18] PGP uses a different method to get public keys. This method is called circles of trust. If I trust people, I place my list of trusted people and their public keys on a list and make this list available to others. This avoids the need to have a certificate authority. However, if one person is duped into placing an impostor on their list, this misplaced trust may spread quickly to other people.

their certificates revoked, CAs rarely give strong warranties about the trustworthiness of their certificate holders. That is not their job. Their job is to associate a public key with a name.

> *When a CA gives a digital certificate to a person or organization, this does not mean that the CA vouches for the honesty of the party named in the certificate. It merely asserts that a certain party has a certain public key.*

DIGITAL CERTIFICATE The CA will send the verifier a digital certificate. Digital certificates follow the **X.509** syntax. A **digital certificate** contains a number of fields, which are shown in Figure 3-18. Most importantly, the digital certificate contains the *name of the true party* (in the Subject field) and the *true party's public key* (in the Public Key field). The verifier looks up the digital certificate of the true party, then uses this public key in the digital certificate to test the digital signature of the supplicant.

VERIFYING THE DIGITAL CERTIFICATE How does the verifier know that the digital certificate is legitimate? The answer is that the verifier must take three steps.

Field	Description
Version Number	Version number of the X.509 standard. Most certificates follow Version 3. Different versions have different fields. This figure reflects the Version 3 standard.
Issuer	Name of the certificate authority (CA).
Serial Number	Unique serial number for the certificate, set by the CA.
Subject	The name of the person, organization, computer, or program to which the certificate has been issued. This is the true party.
Public Key	The public key of the subject (the true party).
Public Key Algorithm	The algorithm the subject uses to sign messages with digital signatures.
Valid Period	The period before which and after which the certificate should not be used. Note: Certificate may be revoked before the end of this period.
Digital Signature	The digital signature of the certificate, signed by the CA with the CA's own private key. For testing certificate authentication and integrity. User must know the CA's public key independently.
Signature Algorithm Identifier	The digital signature algorithm the CA uses to sign its certificates.
Other Fields	. . .

FIGURE 3-18 X.509 Digital Certificate Fields

Testing the Digital Signature
  The digital certificate has a digital signature of its own
  Signed with the Certificate Authority's (CA's) private key
  Must be tested with the CA's well-known public key
  If the test works, the certificate is authentic and unmodified

Checking the Valid Period
  Certificate is only valid during the valid period in the digital certificate

Checking for Revocation
  Certificates may be revoked for improper behavior or other reasons
  Revocation must be tested
  Verifier may download the entire certificate revocation list from the CA
      See if the serial number is on the certificate revocation list
      If so, do not accept the certificate
  Or, the verifier may send a query to the CA
      Requires the CA to support the Online Certificate Status Protocol

FIGURE 3-19   Verifying the Digital Certificate (Study Figure)

Testing the Certificate's Own Digital Signature   First, the verifier must check that the digital certificate is authentic and has not been modified. Every digital certificate contains its own digital signature, which is signed by the certificate authority with the CA's private key. The verifier can use the CA's well-known public key to test the digital certificate's digital signature. If test works, then the digital certificate must be authentic and unmodified. All browsers have built-in lists of the public keys of popular CAs.[19]

Valid Period   Second, each digital certificate has dates before which and after which it is not valid. The receiver must check whether the digital certificate is in its **valid period**.

Checking for Revocation   Third, even during a digital certificate's valid period, a CA may **revoke** a digital certificate, for instance, if there is misbehavior on the part of the certificate subject. Receivers should not accept revoked certificates.

To check for revocation, the verifier can download the certificate authority's **certificate revocation list**. If the serial number of the certificate is in the list, then the CA has revoked the digital certificate.

Although downloading the certificate revocation lists work, the revocation lists of large CAs are quite long. Downloading and checking a long certificate revocation list can significantly delay the start of communication. Fortunately, most CAs offer a more streamlined way to check for revocations. This is the **Online Certificate Status Protocol**. Using this protocol, a program can simply send in the serial number of a digital certificate to the CA. The CA will send back a response saying whether the serial number is good, revoked, or unknown.

---

[19] Actually, there often is a hierarchy of certificate authorities. If you must deal with a new certificate authority, you must go up the hierarchy until you find a CA you trust. At each step in the hierarchy, the higher-level CA's relationship to the lower-level CA is verified.

THE ROLES OF THE DIGITAL CERTIFICATE AND DIGITAL SIGNATURE   Note that a digital certificate does not, by itself, authenticate a supplicant. As Figure 3-20 shows, certificates merely provide the public key of the true party for the verifier to use to make the authentication. Anyone can have the true party's digital certificate without being the true party, so just having the digital certificate does not authenticate the person or process having the certification.

Similarly, with a digital signature alone, the verifier has no proven way to know the true party's public key. Therefore, a digital signature alone cannot be tested and so does not authenticate the applicant.

Overall, then, digital certificates and digital signatures must be used together in public key authentication. Neither by itself provides authentication. Specifically, the digital certificate provides the public key that authentication methods (such as digital signatures) use to authenticate the applicant.

The digital certificate provides the public key that authentication methods (such as digital signatures) use to authenticate the applicant.

TEST YOUR UNDERSTANDING

30. **a.** From what kind of organization can a verifier receive digital certificates?
    b. Are most CAs regulated?
    c. Does a digital certificate indicate that the person or firm named in the certificate is trustworthy? Explain.

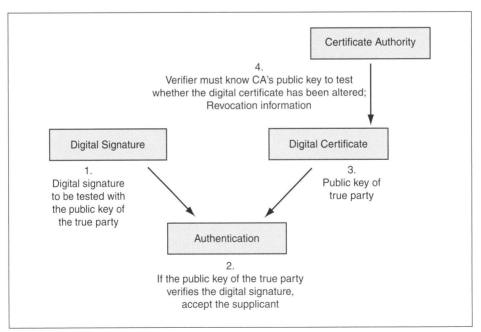

FIGURE 3-20   Digital Signature and Digital Certificate in Authentication

31. **a.** What are the two most critical fields in the digital certificate?
    b. What field in a digital certificate allows the receiver of a certificate to determine if the certificate has been altered?
    c. What three things must the receiver of a digital certificate check to ensure that a digital certificate is valid?
    d. What are the two ways to check a certificate's revocation status?

32. **a.** Does a digital signature by itself provide authentication? Explain why or why not.
    b. Does a digital certificate by itself provide authentication? Explain why or why not.
    c. How are digital signatures and digital certificates used together in authentication?

Key-Hashed Message Authentication Codes (HMACs)

THE PROBLEM WITH DIGITAL SIGNATURES   We have just seen how digital signatures provide message-by-message authentication and message integrity. Unfortunately, although digital signatures provide very strong security, they also consume extensive processing power. In addition, setting up a public key infrastructure to distribute private keys and digital certificates is extremely difficult and expensive.

Consequently, cryptographic systems normally use a different technique for message-by-message authentication and message integrity. This is the key-hashed message authentication code (HMAC).

CREATING AND TESTING THE HMAC   The HMAC uses a key exchanged during the initial negotiation phase. However, it does not use this key for symmetric key encryption. Rather, as Figure 3-21 shows, the sender adds the key to each outgoing message, then hashes the combined message and key (2). This hash is the **key-hashed method authentication code (HMAC)**. The sender adds the HMAC to the message (3), and then encrypts this combined bit stream with symmetric key encryption (4).

The receiver decrypts the transmitted bit string for confidentiality. Then it tests the HMAC. It does this by adding the key (which it also knows) to the message and then hashing the combined message and key with the same hashing algorithm the sender used (5). This computed HMAC should match the transmitted HMAC. If it does, the sender is authenticated (6). Like digital signatures, HMACs also provide message integrity.

Hashing is much faster and therefore less expensive than public key encryption. This is very important given the large number of messages exchanged in a session. In addition, no digital certificate is necessary. Consequently, HMACs are used much more than digital signatures for message-by-message authentication and integrity in cryptographic systems.

TEST YOUR UNDERSTANDING

33. **a.** What two cryptographic protections does an HMAC provide?
    b. Do HMACs use symmetric key encryption, public key encryption, or hashing?
    c. What is the benefit of HMACs over digital signatures?

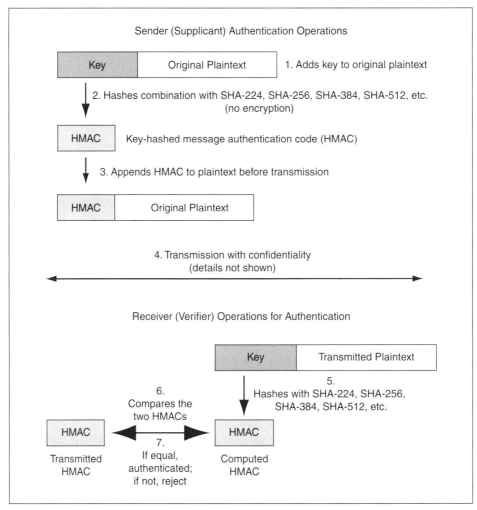

FIGURE 3-21 Key-Hashed Message Authentication Code (HMAC)

Nonrepudiation

Although HMACs are very fast and take little processing power, they have one limitation that is sometimes serious. One possible goal of electronic signatures is **nonrepudiation**, which means that the sender cannot send an important message, such as a contract, and later claim that he or she did not send it.

HMACs fail to give nonrepudiation because the sender and receiver *both* know the secret key. Consequently, the alleged sender could argue in court that the receiver could have forged the HMAC on the message; so the HMAC did not prove that the sender in fact sent it.

In contrast, digital signatures *do* give nonrepudiation. No impostor, including the receiver, can create a message with a valid digital signature because only the true party should know his or her private key. If the true party's private key is used to create a digital signature, only the true party could have sent the message. (Of course, this mechanism breaks down if the true party does not protect its private key.)

A practical way to overcome the limits of HMACs is to use them to authenticate individual packets at the internet layer. Then, public key authentication can be used on the application document. This way, although the individual packet could be repudiated, the application document—such as a contract—cannot be repudiated.

TEST YOUR UNDERSTANDING

34. a. Why can't HMACs provide nonrepudiation?
   b. Why is it usually not a problem that HMACs fail to provide nonrepudiation?

Replay Attacks and Defenses

Replay Attacks

One attack that we did not look at in the body of the chapter is the **replay attack**, in which an adversary intercepts an encrypted message and transmits it again later. In the Arabian Nights tale, Ali Baba overhears robbers say, "Open, Sesame." Although he does not understand the meaning of the phrase, he repeats it and is admitted to the treasure cave. Similarly, in poorly designed cryptographic systems, an attacker can record an encrypted set of commands to log in or do something else, then play them back to create the same response. Note that this works even if the message is encrypted for confidentiality and if the attacker cannot read it.

Thwarting Replay Attacks

Replay attacks can be thwarted in several ways.

Time Stamps

One defense is to ensure "freshness" by including a **time stamp** in each message. If an attacker retransmits a message that is older than a preset cutoff value, the receiver rejects it. If attackers can act quickly, the cutoff value must be very short.

Replay Attacks
   Capture and then retransmit an encrypted message later
   May have a desired effect
   Even if the attacker cannot read the message

Thwarting Replay Attacks
   Time stamps to ensure freshness of each message
   Sequence numbers so that repeated messages can be detected
   Nonces
      Unique randomly generated number placed in each request message
      Reflected in the response message
      If a request arrives with a previously used nonce, it is rejected

---

FIGURE 3-22 Replay Attacks and Defenses (Study Figure)

(Continued)

Replay Attacks and Defenses   (Continued)

Sequence Numbers

Another approach is to place a **sequence number** in each encrypted message. By examining sequence numbers, the receiver can detect a retransmitted message. The replayed message will have the sequence number of the earlier original message.

Nonces

A third approach, used in client/server processing, is to include a **nonce** (randomly generated number created for the occasion[20]) in each client request. The client never uses the same nonce twice. The response from the server includes the same nonce sent in the request.

By comparing a nonce in a request with previous request nonces, the server can ensure that the request is not a repeat of an earlier one. The client, in turn, can ensure that the response is not a repeat of a previous response.

Nonces work well because even fast attackers cannot exploit them. However, they only work in applications that rely entirely (or almost entirely) on request–response client/server interactions.

TEST YOUR UNDERSTANDING

35. **a.** What is a replay attack?
    b. Can the attacker read the contents of the replayed message?
    c. Why are replay attacks attempted?
    d. What are the three ways to thwart replay attacks?
    e. How do time stamps thwart replay attacks?
    f. How do sequence numbers thwart replay attacks?
    g. How do nonces thwart replay attacks?
    h. In what types of applications can nonces be used?

QUANTUM SECURITY

At the level of fundamental particles, physics becomes unbelievably complex and even weird. At the same time, quantum mechanics, which governs small-scale interactions, can be used to perform actions that are impossible at the level of normal devices and circuits. These differences have two important implications for security.

First, we have seen keying using Diffie–Hellman key agreement and public key encryption for confidentiality. Quantum mechanics offers a new method, **quantum key distribution**, which can deliver enormously long keys to communication partners. With such long keys, traditional forms of key cracking become useless. Quantum key distribution creates a **one-time key** that is as long as the entire message. A message encrypted with a one-time key as long as itself is not susceptibility to cryptanalysis.

---

[20] This is related to the Shakespearean expression "for the nonce" (for the moment).

Quantum Mechanics

    Describes the behavior of fundamental particles

    Complex and even weird results

Quantum Key Distribution

    Transmits a very long key as long as the message

    This is a one-time key

    A one-time key as long as a message cannot be cracked by cryptanalysis

    If an interceptor reads part of the key in transit, this will be immediately apparent

Quantum Key Cracking

    Tests many keys simultaneously

    If becomes capable of working on long keys, today's strong key lengths will offer no protection

---

FIGURE 3-23 Quantum Security (Study Figure)

In addition, if an eavesdropper attempts to intercept the keying information, this action will be immediately apparent, and the two legitimate parties will discard the compromised key instead of using it. Quantum key distribution products already exist, but traditional keying methods are sufficient for almost all applications.

Second, **quantum key cracking** can be used to crack keys quickly by trying dozens, hundreds, or potentially thousands of keys at once. Today, quantum computers can only crack keys that are a handful of bits long, but if quantum computers become much more capable, many traditional cryptographic methods will no longer be secure with key lengths considered to be strong today.

TEST YOUR UNDERSTANDING

36. **a.** What is quantum key distribution?
    b. What are the two advantages of quantum key distribution?
    c. Why is quantum key cracking a major threat to many traditional cryptographic methods?

CONCLUSION

Synopsis

In this chapter, we looked at the core concepts that every IT security professional needs to know to about cryptography and cryptographic systems.

One common cryptographic protection is encryption for confidentiality, in which the original plaintext message is encrypted with a cipher (encryption/decryption method) and a key. This produces ciphertext that cannot be read by anyone intercepting it. The receiver applies the cipher in reverse with the same key or another key (depending on the cipher) to recover the original plaintext message. A box discussed two operations commonly used in ciphers—substitution and transposition. Another box discussed the difference between ciphers and codes.

In symmetric key encryption for confidentiality, the sender and receiver use the same key in both directions. In public key encryption, each party has a public key and a private key. In public key encryption for confidentiality, the sender encrypts with the public key of the receiver. The receiver decrypts with its own private key.

For strong security, keys need to be very long to thwart cracking through exhaustive search. Symmetric key encryption ciphers need keys that are at least 100 bits long in order to be strong today. Public and private keys must be even longer to be strong. RSA keys need to be at least 1,024 bits long, and ECC keys need to be at least 512 bits long.

Another important cryptographic protection is authentication, in which a supplicant (such as a client PC) attempts to prove its identity to a verifier (typically a server) by sending credentials. Authentication typically is done both at the beginning of a communication session and also when each message is sent.

We referred frequently to three core cryptographic processes: symmetric key encryption, public key encryption, and hashing. These are easy to confuse with each other. Figure 3-24 compares how the three processes are used for confidentiality and authentication.

- Note that only public key encryption is used for both confidentiality *and* authentication and that public–private key pairs are used *differently* in these processes.
- In contrast, symmetric key encryption is only used for confidentiality.
- Hashing, in turn, is only used for authentication. Although hashing for authentication does use a key, this does not make it symmetric key encryption, which is an entirely different process.

Cryptographic protections are rarely used alone. Rather, they are almost always packaged in cryptographic systems, which secure dialogues with a full range of protections. Cryptographic systems begin with three initial handshaking stages, then move into an ongoing communication stage.

The handshaking stages begin with the negotiation of sets of security methods and options that the communication partners will use subsequently. Corporate policies

	Confidentiality	Authentication
Symmetric key encryption	Applicable. Sender encrypts with key shared with the receiver.	Not applicable.
Public key encryption	Applicable. Sender encrypts with *receiver's public key.* Receiver decrypts with the *receiver's own private key.*	Applicable. Sender (supplicant) encrypts with *own private key.* Receiver (verifier) decrypts with the *public key of the true party*, usually obtained from the true party's digital certificate.
Hashing	Not applicable.	Applicable. Used in MS-CHAP for initial authentication and in HMACs for message-by-message authentication.

FIGURE 3-24 Core Cryptographic Processes

may limit which sets of methods and options can be used in order to prevent communicating partners from using weak methods and options.

Next, the two parties do initial authentication—usually mutual authentication. We specifically looked at MS-CHAP authentication, which is for users logging into Microsoft servers. MS-CHAP protects the user's login password with confidentiality. Normally, two communication partners do mutual authentication. However, MS-CHAP only authenticates the user. MS-CHAP does not use encryption. Rather, it uses hashing. Due to its use of reusable passwords as secrets and its lack of mutual authentication, MS-CHAP is a weak initial cryptographic method. Although we did not discuss it in the chapter, initial challenge–response authentication can also use public key authentication. This is very strong.

Finally, in the keying handshaking stage, the two parties must exchange symmetric session keys (and other secrets) securely. Session keys are only used for a single communication session. We saw how to do keying using public key distribution and Diffie–Hellman key agreement. This ends the handshaking stages.

In the ongoing communication stage, the two partners exchange many messages securely. Each message gets an electronic signature for message-by-message authentication and message integrity. There are two types of electronic signatures—HMACs and digital signatures. HMACs use hashing and a key (really, a shared secret). HMACs are inexpensive to implement and are the most widely used electronic signatures. Digital signatures use public key encryption. The sender encrypts a message digest hash with the sender's own private key. The receiver (verifier) decrypts the message with the true party's public key—the party the supplicant claims to be.

Digital signatures give extremely strong authentication. However, digital signatures use public key encryption, which is extremely slow and therefore expensive. In addition, public key encryption for authentication normally is tested using information in the true party's digital certificate. This requires a system of trusted certificate authorities. The digital certificate gives the true party's public key, which must be used to test that the digital signature was created with the true party's private key.

During the ongoing communication stage, cryptographic systems also use symmetric key encryption to encrypt each message for confidentiality.

The chapter closed with boxes on nonrepudiation and replay attacks and a brief section on quantum key distribution and quantum key cracking.

Thought Questions

1. The total processing speed of microprocessors (based on clock rate and number of circuits) is doubling roughly every year. Today, a symmetric session key needs to be 100 bits long to be considered strong. How long will a symmetric session key have to be in 30 years to be considered strong? (Hint: consider how much longer decryption takes if the key length is increased by a single bit.)

2. Longer keys are more difficult to crack. Most symmetric keys today are 100–300 bits long. Why don't systems use far longer symmetric keys—say, 1,000 bit keys?

3. Brute force is used to crack a 100-bit key. The key is cracked in only 5,000 tries. How can this be?

4. In practice, public key authentication is used heavily for initial authentication but rarely

for message-by-message authentication. Given the intense processing power required for public key authentication and the fact that public key authentication gives the strongest authentication, explain these two usage patterns.

5. Did we see symmetric key encryption used for authentication in this chapter? If so, how was it used?

6. a) Describe the entries in the second row of Figure 3-9. Comment on the strengths of the choices it uses. b) For the second-to-last row of Figure 3-9, comment on the strengths of its symmetric encryption cipher and of its hashing algorithm. c) Describe the entries in the last row of Figure 3-9. Comment on the strengths of the choices it uses.

7. How are digital certificates and drivers' licenses similar, and how are they different?

8. How are digital certificates and passports similar, and how are they different?

9. How are digital certificates and university diplomas similar, and how are they different?

10. How are digital certificates and movie tickets similar, and how are they different?

Harder Thought Questions

1. Identify potential security threats associated with authentication via digital signatures and digital certificates. Explain each and describe how you would address each threat.

2. The book described how public key authentication is used for message-by-message authentication in digital signatures. However, public key authentication is widely used for *initial* authentication. Describe the processes that the supplicant and verifier would use if public key encryption were used in initial challenge–response authentication. Draw heavily on your understanding of digital signatures, but put this information in challenge–response context.

3. If a supplicant gives you a digital certificate, should you accept it? Explain. (Think about this carefully. The answer is not obvious.)

4. Pretty good privacy uses public key encryption *and* symmetric key encryption to encrypt long documents. How might this be possible?

Perspective Questions

1. What was the most difficult section for you in this chapter?

2. What was the most surprising thing you learned in this chapter?

Chapter 4

Cryptographic System Standards

LEARNING OBJECTIVES:

By the end of this chapter, you should be able to discuss the following:

- Virtual private network standards, including SSL/TLS VPNs; IPsec VPNs.
- Commercial WANs and MPLS VPNs.
- Wired LAN security standards.
- Wireless LAN (WLAN) security standards.

INTRODUCTION

In Chapter 3, we looked at the bits and pieces of cryptographic protections, including confidentiality, authentication, and integrity. In this chapter, we will see how these cryptographic elements are combined into complete cryptographic systems that protect dialogues from attackers without users having to know about the details about how these cryptographic systems work. Figure 4-1 illustrates the operation of a typical cryptographic system.

The first task in establishing a cryptographic system is selecting a **cryptographic system standard** for the dialogue. Thanks to cryptographic system standards, companies do not have to invent their own mixes of cryptographic protections. In this chapter, we will look at the several of the most important cryptographic system standards, including Secure Sockets Layer (SSL)/Transport Layer Security (TLS), IP security (IPsec), and core wireless LAN (WLAN) security standards. In the next chapter, we will see Kerberos. There are several other cryptographic system standards that we do not have the time to cover. When two parties begin communicating using the cryptographic system standard they have selected, they initially engage in three **handshaking stages**.

- First, the two parties negotiate which security methods and options they will use in the dialogue. Most cryptographic system standards offer multiple cryptographic methods and various options within individual cryptographic methods. (In Chapter 3, we saw several SSL/TLS cipher suites that combine methods and options to these methods.) These choices can greatly affect the security of the ongoing dialogue. Companies need to create and enforce policies against the use of weak security methods and options.

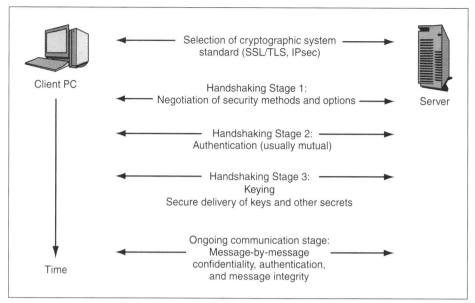

FIGURE 4-1 Cryptographic System

- Second, the two parties perform authentication based on the authentication method and options they selected in the first stage. Authentication usually is mutual, meaning that both parties authenticate themselves to the other. However, one-way authentication is also common, for instance, when a user logs into a server with a reusable password.
- Third, the two parties do keying, which is the secure delivery of keys and other secrets to be used during the ongoing dialogue. Secure keying means that eavesdroppers cannot learn anything from keying messages.

After the two parties have done this initial handshaking work, they enter the ongoing communication stage. Every message they send usually has an electronic signature to provide message-by-message authentication and integrity. In addition, they usually encrypt every message with symmetric key encryption for confidentiality so that an eavesdropper cannot read it. They may also add other protections to dialogues.

TEST YOUR UNDERSTANDING

1. **a.** What must partners do before beginning the handshaking stages of a connection?
   b. What are the three handshaking stages?
   c. What happens in the first handshaking stage?
   d. Distinguish between mutual authentication and one-way authentication.
   e. What is keying?
   f. What protections are provided during the ongoing communication stage?

VIRTUAL PRIVATE NETWORKS (VPNs)

A common type of cryptographic system is a virtual private network. Figure 4-2 shows that a **virtual private network (VPN)** is a cryptographic system that provides secure communication over an untrusted network (the Internet, a wireless LAN, and so forth).

> *A virtual private network (VPN) is a cryptographic system that provides secure communication over an untrusted network (the Internet, a wireless LAN, and so forth).*

Why VPNs?

Why bother to transmit over untrusted networks at all? In the case of Internet VPNs, the answer is simple economics: Internet transmission is far less expensive per bit transmitted than commercial wide area networks (WANs) such as Frame Relay. The Internet's enormous size brings large economies of scale.

VPNs on wireless LANs, in turn, allow a company to enjoy the benefits of mobility despite the questionable security of many WLANs—especially those in wireless hot spots. Later in this chapter, we will see how VPNs can defeat "evil twin" attacks on wireless clients.

Host-to-Host VPNs

Figure 4-2 illustrates three types of VPNs. The simplest type is the host-to-host VPN. As exemplified by VPN 1, a **host-to-host VPN** connects a single client over an

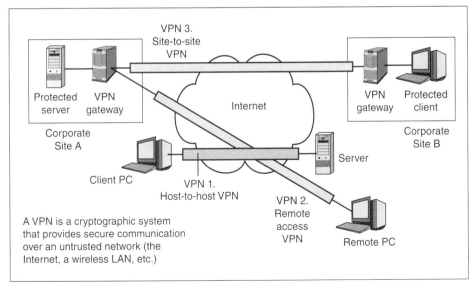

FIGURE 4-2   Virtual Private Networks (VPNs)

untrusted network to a single server. When you connect to an e-commerce server on the Internet, the server usually creates a host-to-host VPN between itself and your browser before you begin entering sensitive information such as credit card numbers.

> *A host-to-host VPN connects a single client over an untrusted network to a single server.*

Remote Access VPNs

In turn, a **remote access VPN** connects a single remote PC over an untrusted network to a site network (see VPN 2 in the figure). Remote access VPNs provide access to individual employees working at home or traveling, to selected customers, to selected supplier representatives, and to other approved communication partners coming in as individuals.

Remote access users connect to a **VPN gateway**, which authenticates them and gives them access to authorized resources within the site. Note that this gateway gives remote users access to *multiple* computers within the site, while a host-to-host VPN only gives you access to a *single* computer.

> *A remote access VPN connects a single remote PC over an untrusted network to a site network.*

Site-to-Site VPNs

Finally, **site-to-site VPNs** (see VPN 3 in Figure 4-2) protect all traffic flowing over an untrusted network between a pair of sites. These may be two corporate sites or a corporate site and either a customer site or a supplier site. The site-to-site connection cryptographically protects the traffic of many simultaneous conversations taking place between various computers in the two sites. In site-to-site VPNs, sending VPN gateways encrypt outgoing messages. Receiving VPN gateways then decrypt incoming messages and pass these messages to the correct destination hosts in the receiving site.[1]

> *Site-to-site VPNs protect all traffic flowing over an untrusted network between a pair of sites.*

---

[1] Although many companies build their own VPNs, quite a few outsource their VPNs to managed VPN providers. These providers, most of which are ISPs, install all necessary hardware at the customer's site, do configuration, and manage the customer's VPNs on an ongoing basis. Outsourcing reduces the skills a company's security staff must have and reduces internal security labor costs. It also gives predicable costs. Although outsourced VPNs are convenient, companies are often reluctant to use them because customer companies lose control over their VPN security.

TEST YOUR UNDERSTANDING

2. **a.** What is the definition of a VPN?
   b. Why do companies transmit over the Internet?
   c. Why do they transmit over untrusted wireless networks?
   d. Distinguish between the three types of VPNs.
   e. What does a VPN gateway do for a remote access VPN?
   f. What does a VPN gateway do for a site-to-site VPN?
   g. Which types of VPNs use VPN gateways?

SSL/TLS

Having looked at VPNs in general, we will now begin looking at specific VPN standards. We will begin looking at the simplest popular VPN standard today, SSL/TLS. This cryptographic system standard is widely used for host-to-host VPNs and remote access VPNs.

Introduction

When you make a purchase over the Internet, your sensitive traffic is almost always protected by a cryptographic system standard that was originally called **Secure Sockets Layer (SSL)** when the Netscape Corporation created it. Netscape passed the standardization effort to the Internet Engineering Task Force (IETF), which renamed the standard **Transport Layer Security (TLS)** to emphasize that it works at the transport layer.[2] We will refer to it as SSL/TLS, but in actual practice, people simply call it SSL or TLS. Figure 4-3 shows how an SSL/TLS host-to-host VPN operates.

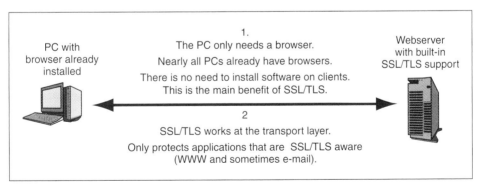

FIGURE 4-3 Host-to-Host SSL/TLS VPN

---

[2] SSL/TLS also can be viewed as working at an extra layer above the normal transport layer but below the application layer. Netscape called this the *sockets layer*. However, the IETF viewed the standard as merely working in a sublayer of the transport layer, so the IETF changed the standard's name to Transport Layer Security (TLS).

Although SSL/TLS began as a host-to-host VPN standard, it has recently become a remote access VPN, thanks to the emergence of SSL/TLS gateways. However, we will see that SSL/TLS is limited for both of these VPN roles.

TEST YOUR UNDERSTANDING

3. **a.** Distinguish between SSL and TLS.
   b. For what type of VPN was SSL/TLS developed?
   c. For what type of VPN is SSL/TLS increasingly being used?

Non-Transparent Protection

Because SSL/TLS works at the transport layer, it can protect application layer traffic encapsulated in transport layer messages. We will see this pattern of a cryptographic system at one layer protecting higher-layer communication again when we discuss IPsec.

However, SSL/TLS's protection of application-layer messages is not **transparent**, meaning that it does not *automatically* protect all higher-layer messages. It only protects applications that are **SSL/TLS-aware**, meaning that these applications have been specifically written or rewritten to work with SSL/TLS. Although all browsers and webserver application programs are SSL/TLS-aware, and while many e-mail programs offer SSL/TLS as optional protection, few other applications can work with SSL/TLS.

Inexpensive Operation

The biggest attraction of SSL/TLS is that every computer today has a browser, and all browsers know how to act as clients for SSL/TLS. This means that SSL/TLS requires no setup on clients. In addition, all webservers and most mail servers know how to work with SSL/TLS. Consequently, using SSL/TLS is nearly free (apart from the processing power needed to implement SSL/TLS).

TEST YOUR UNDERSTANDING

4. **a.** At what layer does SSL/TLS operate?
   b. What types of applications can SSL/TLS protect?
   c. What are the two commonly SSL/TLS-aware applications?
   d. Why is SSL/TLS popular?

SSL/TLS Gateways and Remote Access VPNs

So far, we have looked at host-to-host SSL/TLS VPNs. As Figure 4-5 shows, to convert SSL/TLS from a host-to-host VPN into a remote access VPN, firms place an **SSL/TLS gateway** at the border of each site (1). The remote client's browser (2) establishes a single SSL/TLS connection with the SSL/TLS gateway (3), rather than with individual hosts within the site.

SSL/TLS Operation

Step	Sender	Name of Message	Semantics (Meaning)
1	Client	Client Hello	Client requests secure connection. Client lists cipher suites it supports.
2	Server	Server Hello	Server indicates willingness to proceed. Selects a cipher suite to use in the session.
3	Server	Certificate	Server sends its digital certificate containing its public key. (Client should check the certificate's validity.)
4	Server	ServerHelloDone	Server indicates that its part in the initial introduction is finished.
5	Client	ClientKeyExchange	Client generates a random symmetric session key. Encrypts it with the server's public key. It sends this encrypted key to the server. Only the server can decrypt the key, using the server's own private key. The server decrypts the session key. Both sides now have the session key.
6	Client	ChangeCipherSpec*	Client changes selected cipher suite from pending to active.
7	Client	Finish	Client indicates that its part in the initial introduction is finished.
8	Server	ChangeCipherSpec*	Server changes selected cipher suite from pending to active.
9	Server	Finish	Server indicates that its role in selecting options is finished.
10	Ongoing communication stage begins		

*Not cipher suite.

FIGURE 4-4 SSL/TLS Handshaking Phase

Figure 4-1 showed the three general handshaking phases for cryptographic systems. Figure 4-4 shows the details of how SSL/TLS executes these phases for a host-to-host VPN. (The phases are the same for remote access VPNs.) After this handshaking process, the two sides engage in the protected transmission of data.

Client Initialization and Cipher Suites

The handshaking phase begins when a client's browser sends a **ClientHello** message to the webserver. This message requests a secure connection and lists the cryptographic cipher suites the browser supports.

(Continued)

SSL/TLS Operation   (Continued)

Recall from Chapter 3 that a cipher suite is a specific set of protocols that SSL/TLS will use to provide protection. In Chapter 3, we saw a few of the many cipher suites that SSL/TLS can use. Note that there is no way to answer the question, "What type of symmetric key encryption does SSL/TLS use for confidentiality?" SSL/TLS can use several forms of symmetric key encryption, including no symmetric key encryption at all.

Server Reponses

In Figure 4-4, the server responds with three messages.

- The **ServerHello** message indicates that the server is willing to proceed. It also lists the *single* cipher suite that it has selected from the client's list of proposed cipher suites.[3]
- Next, the server sends a **Certificate** message. As the name of the message indicates, this message contains the server's digital certificate. In SSL/TLS, the server MUST have a digital certificate. Note that the client gets the server's digital certificate directly from the server. This may seem dangerous, but it is safe because the digital certificate has a digital signature of its own, signed by the certificate authority. If the browser checks the certificate for validity in the ways we saw in Chapter 3, accepting the digital certificate from the server is safe.
- Finally, the server sends a **ServerHelloDone** message to indicate that it is finished replying to the ClientHello message.

Final Client Handshaking Transmission

After checking the validity of the digital certificate, the client sends two messages.

- The **ClientKeyExchange** message handles the exchange of a symmetric session key. The specific keying method will depend on the selected cipher suite. In this case, the client generates a random symmetric session key. The client then encrypts the symmetric session key with the public key of the server (provided by the digital certificate). Only the server can decrypt the message, using its private key. So only the server named in the digital certificate can learn the symmetric key.
- The client then sends a **ChangeCipherSpec** (not ChangeCipher*Suite*) message. This changes the cipher suite specified by the server from *pending* to *active*. From now on, the client will communicate using this cipher suite, using the exchanged key.
- Finally, the client sends a **Finish** message. This message tells the server that the client has concluded its part of the handshaking negotiation.

Final Server Handshaking Transmission

The server completes its role in the negotiation phase by sending two final messages.

- By sending its own ChangeCipherSpec message, the server affirms that it will now use the selected cipher suite and exchanged key in all future communication with the client.
- The Finish message indicates that the server's role in the initial handshaking phase is complete. The handshaking stages are over.

---

[3] If the server cannot or will not use any of the browser's suggested cipher suites, the server terminates the connection-opening attempt.

Perspective

Now that the handshaking negotiations are finished, SSL/TLS can protect all subsequent application messages.

Variations

There are many possible variations in this initial handshaking process. For example, in this interaction, the server authenticates itself to the client, but the client does not authenticate itself to the server. This is normal in e-commerce because restricting business to clients who have digital certificates would leave e-commerce sites with population too small for profitability. However, businesses often require client certificate-based authentication as well.

Server Authentication

If you have been following closely, you may be asking yourself, "Hey, when did authentication take place?" The answer is that authenticated took place *implicitly*. The server began the authentication process by sending its digital certificate to the client. By itself, this is not authentication.

The client then generates a random symmetric session key and encrypts the session key with the public key contained in the digital certificate. It then sends this encrypted session key to the server. This is the keying stage.

What will happen if the server is an impostor? Suppose that an impostor server claims to be server XYZ, which is the server the client expects to communicate with? In this case, when the impostor sends a digital certificate, it must send the digital certificate for XYZ, or the client will break off communication immediately because the digital certificate is not for Server XYZ. Later, when the client browser encrypts the session key with the public key of XYZ found in the digital certificate, the impostor server will not be able to decrypt the symmetric session key because it does not know Server XYZ's private key. Therefore, the impostor will not be able to read encrypted messages from the client or send properly encrypted messages to the client. Before any damage is done, the browser will terminate the connection.

Of course, if the server really is Server XYZ, then it will be able to decrypt the symmetric session key and use the session key correctly in subsequent message exchanges during the session.

Overall, while there is no explicit authentication, communication with impostors is blocked, and communication with true parties is facilitated. This is effective authentication, if not explicit authentication.

TEST YOUR UNDERSTANDING

5. a. What is a cipher suite?
   b. In the handshaking process, what are the commands in the security method negotiation process?
   c. In the handshaking process, what commands are part of the key exchange or key negotiation process?
   d. Which party created the symmetric session key in this example?

6. a. Does SSL/TLS require mutual authentication?
   b. Why does it make sense for SSL/TLS not to use client authentication for consumer e-commerce?
   c. When would companies require SSL/TLS client authentication?
   d. In SSL/TLS, is server authentication explicit or implicit? Explain briefly.
   e. Why will impostors not be able to act in the ongoing communication phase?

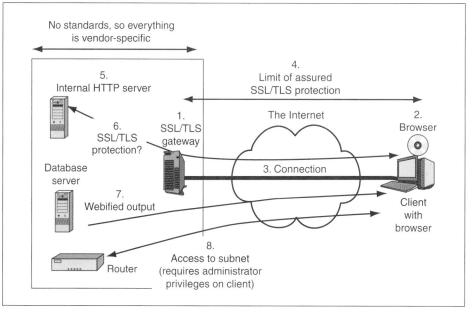

FIGURE 4-5 SSL/TLS and Remote Access VPN Using a Gateway

The remote client's browser establishes a single SSL/TLS connection with the SSL/TLS gateway, rather than with individual hosts within the site.

VPN GATEWAY STANDARDS   The situation with SSL/TLS gateway standards is very simple. There are none. SSL/TLS merely governs the link between the client and the SSL/TLS gateway (3), and SSL/TLS only definitely protects traffic traveling between the client and the gateway (4). In effect, an SSL/TLS gateway is simply a webserver as far as SSL/TLS is concerned. There is no need to add anything to the SSL/TLS standard.

An SSL/TLS gateway is simply a webserver as far as SSL/TLS is concerned. There is no need to add anything to the SSL/TLS standard.

Beyond the gateway, in the customer site, everything is vendor specific. This makes it difficult to talk in general about VPN gateway operation and services. However, SSL/TLS gateways tend to have several common features.

AUTHENTICATION   First, the SSL/TLS gateway always authenticates itself to the client, using public key authentication. This is mandatory in SSL/TLS gateways. After SSL/TLS protection is complete, the gateway then requires the user to authenticate itself, usually using a username and password. The client authentication is outside of the SSL/TLS process.

CONNECTING THE CLIENT PC TO AUTHORIZED RESOURCES   If authentication succeeds, the SSL/TLS gateway allows the user to connect to selected resources within the site.

- In many cases, the SSL/TLS gateway allows the client PC to connect to multiple internal webservers (5). Usually, the gateway merely opens a connection to the site and ignores traffic going beyond it.
- In other cases, the VPN gateway connects the client PC to a database server or other server that does not know how to work with browsers as clients (7). When the client transmits, the VPN gateway converts the webpage into a database query or some other query. The VPN gateway then intercepts replies from the server. The VPN gateway "**webifies**" these messages (converts them into webpages) for the browser to present to the user. VPN gateways vary widely in the number of applications they can handle this way and the way they handle these applications.
- In still other cases, the SSL/TLS gateway connects the client PC to an entire subnet of the site network (8). The client can then connect to any server on the subnet.

SECURITY FOR SERVICES   As just noted, SSL/TLS provides protection between the client and the SSL/TLS gateway (4). However, there may or may not be security between the SSL/TLS gateway and resources *within* the network (6). It is all up to the gateway vendor's design choices. For instance, if an internal webserver will serve the external client, the SSL/TLS gateway may maintain two secure connections—one between the internal webserver and the gateway and another between the gateway and the external client. Or, there may be no security at all between the VPN gateway and the internal webserver.

BROWSER ON THE CLIENT   What does the client need to have to use SSL/TLS? For basic operation, it needs no additional software. Consequently, SSL/TLS can work with any client PC connected to the Internet, including those at work, in hotels, in Internet cafes, and at customer or supplier sites. This makes SSL/TLS extremely attractive as a remote access VPN.

ADVANCED SERVICES REQUIRE ADMINISTRATOR PRIVILEGES ON PCs   However, to allow a client to get transparent access to a subnet (8) and to provide some other services, the SSL/TLS gateway must download a plug-in module for the client PC's browser. Unfortunately, installing the add-in requires the client user to have administrator privileges on the client PC. Internet cafes and other public computers are not likely to give users this level of permissions. Nor are most other places the user may be visiting.

Furthermore, using SSL/TLS for either remote access or host-to-host connections to a webserver is dangerous because SSL/TLS leaves information on the client PC's hard drive after the user finishes an SSL/TLS session. This is a serious security risk for people working at public computers. Many SSL/TLS gateways permit the downloading of plug-ins that erase all traces of a user's session. Again, however, places that a user visits are not likely to grant the administrative status that installing a session information removal add-in requires. In other words, wiping your traces is rarely possible when you need it the most—when you are not using your own computer.

PERSPECTIVE   Although Netscape designed SSL/TLS for a single purpose—to protect browser–webserver communication, VPN gateways have substantially extended its use. An SSL/TLS gateway can provide remote access to almost any PC without modification or configuration.

This makes SSL/TLS a very attractive remote access VPN technology. However, implementation has a tendency to be limited and clumsy. In addition, SSL/TLS gateways are completely unstandardized and vary widely in the services they offer. Using SSL/TLS for remote access VPNs requires strong due diligence in needs assessment and product analysis. It also tends to require a good deal of operational handholding by the network staff.

In addition, SSL/TLS is *not* able to create site-to-site VPNs. In most corporations, site-to-site VPNs will carry far more traffic than remote access VPNs. Still, not having to add any software to a user's remote computer is so compelling that SSL/TLS gateways are growing very rapidly in importance.

TEST YOUR UNDERSTANDING

7. **a.** SSL/TLS was created for host-to-host (browser–webserver) communication. What device can turn SSL/TLS into a remote access VPN?
   b. In SSL/TLS remote access VPNs, to what device does the client authenticate itself?
   c. When a remote client transmits in an SSL/TLS VPN, how far does confidential transmission definitely extend?
   d. What three services do SSL/TLS gateways commonly provide?
   e. What is webification?
   f. What software does the client need for basic SSL/TLS VPN operation?
   g. For what purposes may the client need additional downloaded software?
   h. Why may installing the additional downloaded software on the browser be problematic?
   i. Why is SSL/TLS attractive as a remote access VPN technology?
   j. What problems do companies face if they use it as a remote access VPN technology?
   k. Which of the three types of VPNs can SSL/TLS support?

IPsec

Firms that require the strongest VPN security use a family of IETF cryptographic security standards collectively called **IPsec (IP security)**.[4] IP is the Internet Protocol, and *sec* is short for security. These standards, in other words, secure the IP (including everything in an IP packet's data field).

Attractions of IPsec

Figure 4-6 compares IPsec with the SSL/TLS cryptographic security standard we have just seen. IPsec is more complex and therefore more expensive to introduce than SSL/TLS, but IPsec is the gold standard in VPN security. It offers the strongest protections and supports centralized corporate control over all IPsec operation on all devices.

SSL/TLS GIVES NON-TRANSPARENT TRANSPORT LAYER SECURITY   Earlier, we saw that SSL/TLS, which operates at the transport layer, can only protect applications that are SSL/TLS-aware—primarily HTTP webservice and some e-mail systems. We also saw that SSL/TLS gateways extends the standard to handle remote access, albeit awkwardly.

---

[4] The pronunciation is eye'-pee'-sek', with roughly equal emphasis on all syllables.

	SSL/TLS	IPsec
Cryptographic security standard	Yes	Yes
Cryptographic security protections	Good	Gold Standard
Supports central management	No	Yes
Complexity and expense	Lower	Higher
Layer of operation	Transport	Internet
Transparently protects all higher-layer traffic	No	Yes
Works with IPv4 and IPv6	NA	Yes
Modes of operation	NA	Transport, Tunnel

FIGURE 4-6   IP Security (IPsec) versus SSL/TLS

IPsec: TRANSPARENT INTERNET LAYER SECURITY   In contrast, IPsec operates at the internet layer. It protects the IP packet and everything in an IP packet's data field, including ICMP, TCP, and UDP messages and including all applications, period.

> *IPsec works at the internet layer.*

In IPsec, furthermore, protection at the higher layers is completely **transparent**. There is no need to modify applications or transport layer protocols to work with IPsec. In fact, transport layer protocols and application protocols are not even aware of IPsec's presence when IPsec is used.

In comparison, the webification and other kludges in SSL/TLS VPNs tend to create substantial installation and operation costs. Although IPsec is more complex to set up than SSL/TLS, transparent protection reduces implementation and operating costs, although it does not completely offset the higher cost of IPsec.

> *SSL/TLS works at the transport layer and does not give transparent protection to application layer messages.*
>
> *IPsec works at the internet layer and gives transparent protection to transport layer and application layer messages.*

IPsec IN BOTH IPv4 AND IPv6   The IETF designed IPsec originally for the newest version of the Internet Protocol, IP Version 6 (IPv6). However, when it was created, IPsec also was written to work with currently dominant version of IP—IP Version 4 (IPv4). In other words, no matter which version of IP a network uses, IPsec will protect it.

TEST YOUR UNDERSTANDING

8. **a.** At what layer does IPsec operate?
   b. What layers does IPsec protect?

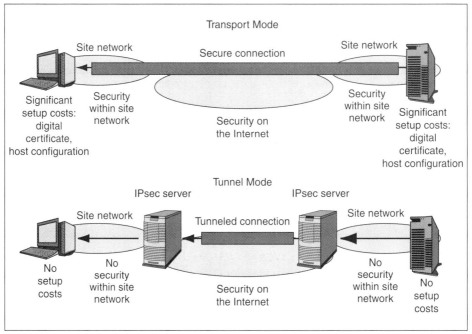

FIGURE 4-7　IPsec Operation: Tunnel and Transport Modes

    c. Compare the amount of cryptographic security in IPsec with that in SSL/TLS.
    d. Compare centralized management in IPsec and SSL/TLS.
    e. Why is IPsec's transparent protection attractive compared with SSL/TLS' non-transparent protection?
    f. Which versions of IP can use IPsec?

IPsec Transport Mode

In IPsec, there are two operating modes. These are the transport mode and the tunnel mode. Figure 4-7 illustrates how these two modes work. Figure 4-8 compares their characteristics in a table.

HOST-TO-HOST SECURITY　**IPsec Transport mode** gives host-to-host security. In other words, it implements host-to-host VPNs. Transport mode allows two hosts to communicate securely without regard to what else is happening on the network.

END-TO-END PROTECTION　Transport mode is attractive because it provides security when packets travel over internal site networks as well as across the Internet. This provides end-to-end security even if the internal networks of the sender and receiver are not trusted.

COST OF SETUP　On the negative side, transport mode IPsec requires the firm to set up IPsec explicitly on every client and server. This involves generating a private key–digital certificate pair, placing a private key on each computer, and then managing the digital

Characteristic	Transport Mode	Tunnel Mode
Uses an IPsec VPN gateway?	No	Yes
Cryptographic protection	All the way from the source host to the destination host, including the Internet and the two site networks.	Only over the Internet between the IPsec gateways. Not within the two site networks.
Setup costs	High. Setup requires the creation of a digital certificate for each client and significant configuration work.	Low. Only the IPsec gateways must implement IPsec, so only they need digital certificates and need to be configured.
Firewall friendliness	Bad. A firewall at the border to a site cannot filter packets because the content is encrypted.	Good. Each packet is decrypted by the IPsec gateway. A border firewall after the IPsec gateway can filter the decrypted packet.
The "bottom line"	End-to-end security at high cost.	Low cost and protects the packet over the most dangerous part of its journey.

FIGURE 4-8 Comparing IPsec Transport and Tunnel Modes

certificate over its life cycle. In addition, although all recent client PC operating systems can implement IPsec, configuring them to use it usually involves manual configuration labor. Although the labor cost per client and server is modest, the total cost of transport mode installation labor can be daunting in a firm that has many clients and servers.

IPsec IN TRANSPORT MODE AND FIREWALLS   Although IPsec transport mode provides high security to dialogues, it reduces the effectiveness of another security countermeasure, the border firewall. The border firewall should investigate each packet passing through it, looking for indications of unacceptable content. For encrypted IP packets, however, firewalls are useless because they cannot read a packet's plaintext content to filter it. If the source host sends an attack packet to a destination host via IPsec transport mode, the firewall cannot stop the attack packet.

IPsec Tunnel Mode

In contrast, Figure 4-7 shows that **IPsec tunnel mode** only protects traffic between two **IPsec gateways** at different sites.[5] These gateways send traffic securely through the Internet between themselves. Tunnel mode creates a site-to-site VPN.

---

[5] Many people are taught that the name *tunnel mode* means that IPsec creates a secure tunnel through the nonsecure Internet or a nonsecure wireless LAN. This is good if it helps you remember what IPsec does, but that is not really why the name tunnel mode came about. In network standards, *tunneling* simply means placing a message inside another message. In IPsec tunnel mode, the entire original packet is encapsulated in the data field of a new packet that is sent between the two IPsec gateways. In other words, the original packet is tunneled in a new packet. In transport mode, in contrast, protections extend to parts of the original packet, but there is no placing the original packet inside another packet, that is, no tunneling.

PROTECTION IS PROVIDED BY IPsec GATEWAYS   The source IPsec gateway receives original (unencrypted) IP packets from its site hosts, encrypts them, and sends them to the other IPsec gateway. The receiving IPsec gateway decrypts IP packets and sends them in the clear to the destination host.

LESS EXPENSIVE THAN TRANSPORT MODE   The major advantage of tunnel mode operation is cost. All of the cryptographic work is done on the IPsec gateway servers. Clients and servers merely transmit and receive their packets in the clear. The company does not need to make any changes to their clients and servers, as it must do in transport mode. Not needing to create and manage digital certificates for all of its clients and servers makes tunnel mode much less expensive than transport mode.

FIREWALL-FRIENDLY PROTECTION   In addition, IPsec transport mode is firewall friendly. Packets are only encrypted between the two IPsec gateways, so after a packet arrives, it can be filtered by a firewall placed after the IPsec gateway at each site.

NO PROTECTION WITHIN THE TWO SITES   The disadvantage of tunnel mode is that it gives absolutely no protection at all to IP packets when they are traveling *within* the site networks at the two sites. This leaves packets open to attack within site networks. However, transmission within site networks generally is safer than transmission over the Internet, so the loss of protection within sites is often considered a good trade-off for the lower cost of tunnel mode IPsec tunnel mode operation and for IPsec's firewall friendliness.

TEST YOUR UNDERSTANDING

  9. **a.** Distinguish between transport and tunnel modes in IPsec in terms of packet protection.
     b. What are the attractions of each?
     c. What are the problematic issues of each?

IPsec Security Associations (SAs)

Before two hosts or IPsec gateways communicate, they first must establish security associations. A **security association (SA)** is an agreement about what IPsec security methods and options two hosts or two IPsec gateways will use. An SA in IPsec is reminiscent of an SSL/TLS cipher suite.

> *A security association (SA) is an agreement about what IPsec security methods and options two hosts or two IPsec gateways will use.*

SEPARATE SAs IN THE TWO DIRECTIONS   Figure 4-9 illustrates how communicating partners negotiate security associations. Note that when two parties communicate, they must establish *two* SAs—one in each direction. If Sal and Julia communicate, there must be an SA for Sal to follow when sending to Julia and a separate SA for Julia to follow when sending to Sal. This use of two SAs allows a different level of protection in each direction if that is desirable.

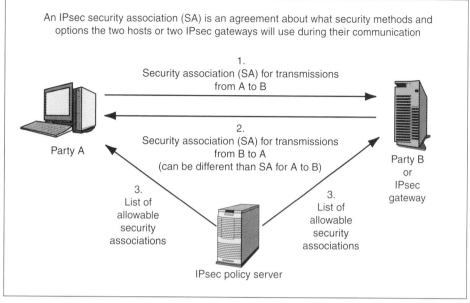

An IPsec security association (SA) is an agreement about what security methods and options the two hosts or two IPsec gateways will use during their communication

1.
Security association (SA) for transmissions
from A to B

Party A

2.
Security association (SA) for transmissions
from B to A
(can be different than SA for A to B)

Party B
or
IPsec
gateway

3.
List of
allowable
security
associations

3.
List of
allowable
security
associations

IPsec policy server

FIGURE 4-9 IPsec Security Associations

POLICY-BASED SAs   As noted earlier, some allowable security methods and options in cryptographic security standards may be inadequate for a company's security needs. A company would like to set policies for acceptable security methods and options and enforce these policies on all devices that implement the standard.

SSL/TLS has no way to set and enforce policies centrally, but IPsec does. As Figure 4-9 shows, IPsec supports the use of **IPsec policy servers,** which push a list of suitable policies to individual IPsec gateway servers or hosts. From the viewpoint of security management, this is a critical capability.

TEST YOUR UNDERSTANDING

10. **a.** What does an SA specify? (Do not just spell SA out.)
    b. When two parties want to communicate in both directions with security, how many IPsec SAs are necessary?
    c. May there be different SAs in the two directions?
    d. What is the advantage of this?
    e. Why do companies wish to create policies for SAs?
    f. Can they do so in SSL/TLS?
    g. How does IPsec set and enforce policies?

COMMERCIAL WAN CARRIER SECURITY

Although the use of Internet VPNs is increasing as a way to reduce the cost per bit transmitted, firms still use commercial wide area networks (WANs), including traditional Layer 2 WAN services such as Frame Relay and ATM and new Layer 3 IP carrier services using Multiprotocol Label Switching.

◈ IPsec Details

This box looks at some advanced aspects of IPsec.

The Encapsulating Security Payload Header and Trailer

Figure 4-10 shows IPsec's **encapsulating security payload (ESP)** header and trailer. The sender adds the ESP header and trailer to every packet during ongoing communication. This header and trailer provide confidentiality, message authentication, and message integrity.[6]

More specifically, the figure shows that ESP extends confidentiality to everything following the ESP header and to part of the ESP trailer, as well. The figure also shows that ESP provides authentication and message integrity to the entire IPsec header and to part of the ESP trailer.

The figure shows that ESP works in both transport and tunnel modes but works somewhat differently in the two modes.

- In tunnel mode, IPsec protects the entire original IP packet. It encrypts the packet and places it inside a new IP packet.
- In transport mode, the information between the ESP header and ESP trailer is the protected transport header and application message. Transport mode cannot protect the IP header because information in the IP header must be readable by routers along the packet's route.

TEST YOUR UNDERSTANDING

11. a. What protections do the encapsulating security payload header and trailer provide to the part of the packet that lies between them?

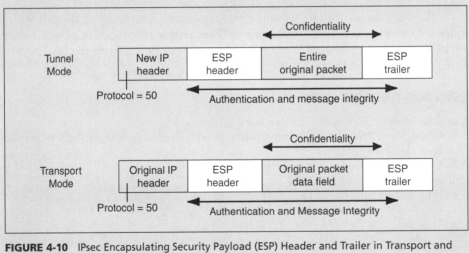

FIGURE 4-10 IPsec Encapsulating Security Payload (ESP) Header and Trailer in Transport and Tunnel Modes

---

[6] IPsec also offers a second type of IPsec header. This is the authentication header. The authentication header only implements authentication (and message integrity as a byproduct). It specifically *does not* support encryption for confidentiality. The authentication header typically is only used when encryption is forbidden by law. This is rare today.

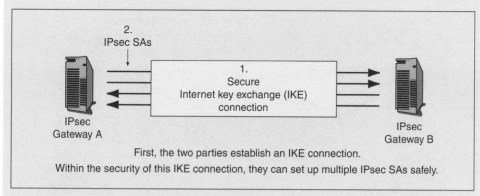

FIGURE 4-11   Establishing IPsec Security Associations Using IKE

   b. Does ESP work in transport mode, tunnel mode, or both?
   c. What part of the original IP packet does ESP protect in tunnel mode?
   d. What part of the original IP packet does ESP protect in tunnel mode?

Establishing Security Associations

Establishing IPsec security associations is a two-phase process, as Figure 4-11 illustrates.

Establishing Internet Key Exchange (IKE) Protection

In the first phase, the two parties create a secure connection between themselves using the **Internet Key Exchange (IKE)** standard. IKE is a general protocol for protecting the establishment of security associations in cryptographic systems. It is not limited to creating IPsec SAs.

Establishing IPsec Security Associations within IKE Protection

Once the IKE connection is in place, the two parties can negotiate one or more IPsec SAs with confidence that attackers will not be able to disrupt or learn anything during this IPsec SA creation process. This is particularly important for site-to-site IPsec gateways, which may need to establish dozens or hundreds of SAs for different types of traffic.

TEST YOUR UNDERSTANDING

   12. a. Is IKE limited to protecting IPsec security associations?
   b. How does IKE protect the negotiation of IPsec SAs?
   c. How many SAs is a pair of site-to-site VPN gateways likely to implement within IKE's protection?

Traditional Security in Commercial WAN Carriers

Traditionally, companies have used commercial carriers such as telephone companies for their site-to-site transmission needs. Figure 4-12 illustrates a commercial WAN, which is called a **public switched data network (PSDN)** because it is a switched data network offered to the public (customers). The figure depicts the WAN as a cloud because the internal operation of the WAN is irrelevant to **subscribers** (corporate users). Subscribers only need to buy or lease data communication termination equipment required by the WAN carrier and obtain a leased line to the PSDN's nearest connection point.

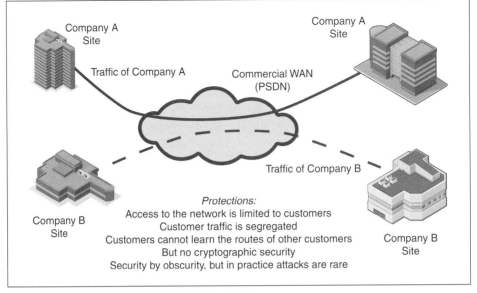

FIGURE 4-12 Protections in a Commercial WAN

REDUCING RISKS FOR COMMERCIAL WANs Commercial WANs rarely offer cryptographic protections for subscriber transmissions. However, most companies feel reasonably safe transmitting their data in the clear when dealing with commercial WANs.

First, commercial WANs restrict who attaches to them. Commercial WANs are not open-to-all services like the global Internet. They are more like private clubs. This alone dramatically reduces risks. Of course, if a hacker breaks into one of a customer's hosts, the hacker may then have access to the commercial WAN.

Second, commercial WANs do not give customers access to information about traffic routes within the WAN or to supervisory functions. A wire tapper would not know what lines within the WAN lines to tap, and even if a customer had a computer compromised by a hacker, the hacker would not be able to pick out a firm's traffic within the WAN or use the commercial WAN's supervisory commands to do mischief.

IS THIS ENOUGH? In essence, commercial WANs provide "security through obscurity." They try to be secure merely by keeping attackers out and keeping secrets from adversaries—specifically how to access routes and how to access supervisory commands.

Security by obscurity is never a great strategy. If attackers compromise hosts and do learn how to obtain route information or supervisory communication, there is no security left at all.

Of course, the most vulnerable point in commercial WANs transmission is not the core of the WAN but rather the leased access line between a corporate site and the WAN. If an attacker can tap the access line, none of the WAN's internal protections matter if customers send traffic in the clear.

TEST YOUR UNDERSTANDING

13. a. What two types of security do commercial WANs provide?
   b. Is this strong security?
   c. Have there been many successful attacks on commercial WANs?
   d. Why is this not reassuring?
   e. What is the most vulnerable point in WAN communication?

Multiprotocol Label Switching (MPLS) VPN Services

Traditional PSDNs were Layer 2 switched services. Today, many carriers offer Layer 3 WAN service based on the TCP/IP standards. As noted in Module A, routers tend to do a great deal of work for every packet they receive. Whenever a packet arrives, the router must compare it with all possible routes, and then find the best-matching route. If another packet going the same destination arrives next, the router will again do all of the work needed to find the best route. This is very expensive.

Due to the amount of work involved in packet-by-packet decision making, the Internet Engineering Task Force created a standard to set up a best route beforehand, and then use this prearranged decision for every packet that arrives during a session. This requires some setup time, but this initial setup time is small compared with the time saved during transmission because of simpler handling for each packet.

This standard is called **MultiProtocol Label Switching (MPLS)**. As Figure 4-13 shows, the source host's MPLS label-switching router adds a label (2) that specifies the predetermined label-switched route to be followed by the packet (3).

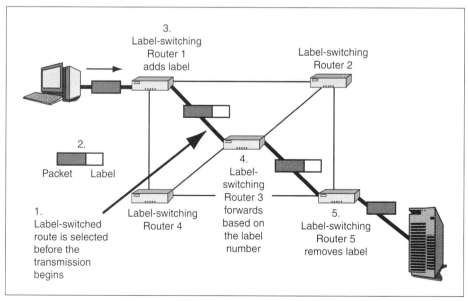

FIGURE 4-13   Multiprotocol Label Switching (MPLS) VPN

Each label-switching router along the way forwards the packet on the basis of the label (4). The final label-switching router (5) removes the label and passes the packet to the destination host.

MPLS reduces transmission cost. However, is it a security protocol? The answer is that an MPLS IP carrier can restrict access, hide internal label-switched routes, and prevent access to supervisory functions. In other word, MPLS, like traditional PSDN WAN transmission, only offers "security through obscurity."

TEST YOUR UNDERSTANDING

14. a. What is the main business benefit of MPLS?
    b. What security protections does MPLS provide?
    c. Is this strong security?

Routed VPNs versus Cryptographic VPNs

As Figure 4-14 shows, there are two types of VPN. **Cryptographic VPNs** provide all of the cryptographic protections described in the last chapter. These protections are delivered in the context of a cryptographic system.

In turn, **routed VPNs** provide protection by confining transmissions to routes whose details are not accessible to hosts attached to the network. However, if the routing information is compromised, there are no cryptographic protections to protect customer transmission.

Of course, nothing prevents subscribers from establishing their own site-to-site cryptographic protections on top of a routed carrier service. However, this adds complexity. It would be better if more MPLS VPN carriers offered cryptographic protections as an option.

TEST YOUR UNDERSTANDING

15. Distinguish between cryptographic and routed VPNs in terms of the security each provides.

	Cryptographic VPNs	Routed VPNs
Examples	SSL/TLS IPsec	Carrier PSDNs Carrier TCP/IP MPLS VPNs
Cryptographic protections	Confidentiality, integrity, authentication, etc.	None
Other protections		Limiting customer access Limiting access to routing supervisory protocols
Customer actions to improve protection		Create a cryptographic VPN to run over carrier services

FIGURE 4-14 Cryptographic versus Routed VPNs

ACCESS CONTROL FOR WIRED AND WIRELESS LANs

Virtual private networks emerged to protect wide area networking—specifically communication over the Internet. SSL/TLS was created to protect Internet e-commerce. IPsec, in turn, is a general VPN protocol for IP networks, of which the Internet is the most prominent. However, LANs within individual corporate sites also have security issues and need cryptographic system protections.

LAN Connections

Figure 4-15 illustrates a LAN at a corporate site. Computers connect to the LAN through Ethernet switches. Some do so via 4-pair UTP cords connected to a wall jacks.

Although all-wireless LANs are possible, most wireless communication in LANs is used to link wireless clients to the firm's wired Ethernet network. The wireless client communicates by radio with an 802.11 wireless access point, which in turn connects via 4-pair UTP to an Ethernet switch.

Why does the client need to connect to the wired LAN? Quite simply, the servers that a wireless client needs are on the wired LAN, and so is the Internet access router that a wireless client needs to reach the Internet.

Access Threats

Traditionally, Ethernet LANs offered no access security. Any intruder who entered a corporate building could walk up to any wall jack and plug in a notebook computer. The intruder would then have unfettered access to the LAN's computers, bypassing the site's border firewall. This was a complete breakdown in access control.

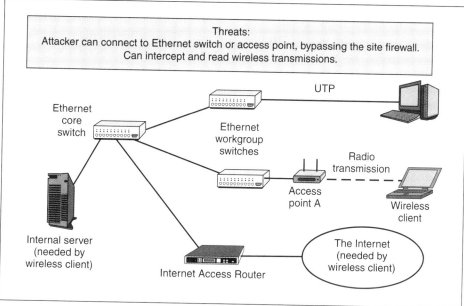

FIGURE 4-15   Corporate LAN

Wireless LANs have even deeper access threats. As in the case of Ethernet LANs, an intruder can connect by radio to an unprotected wireless access point. This again gets the attacker into the network, bypassing the border firewall. The wireless intruder does not even have to enter the building. A **drive-by hacker** can sit in a car outside the corporate walls. With a high-gain antenna, in fact, the intruder can be far enough away to be invisible from the building.

Eavesdropping Threats

For both wired LANs and wireless LANs, once intruders gain access, they can intercept and read legitimate traffic. On Ethernet LANs, encryption is rare, but it is difficult to get physical access to Ethernet wires or wall jacks.

On wireless LANs, however, radio transmission makes eavesdropping trivial unless the traffic is strongly encrypted. Unfortunately, as we will see in this chapter, wireless traffic often is encrypted in ways that is childishly easy to crack with hacker software that is readily downloadable from the Internet. In some cases, there is no encryption at all.

TEST YOUR UNDERSTANDING

16. **a.** What is the main access threat to Ethernet LANs?
    b. What is the main access threat to 802.11 wireless LANs?
    c. Why is the access threat to WLANs more severe?
    d. Is eavesdropping usually a concern for wired LANs, wireless LANs, or both?

ETHERNET SECURITY

Ethernet and 802.1X

We will begin looking at the specifics of LAN security with Ethernet and 802.1X. The **802.1X** standard provides access control to prevent illegitimate clients from associating with a network. We will begin with Ethernet because 802.1X is relatively easy to implement in wired LANs.

Figure 4-16 illustrates the main elements of Ethernet and 802.1X security. 802.1X makes the Ethernet workgroup switch[7] (3) the gateway to the network. The user's computer connects via UTP to a wall jack or directly to the switch. Speaking more precisely, the computer connects to a specific *port* on the workgroup switch. That port is the real point of access control. Not surprisingly, the name of the 802.1X standard is **Port-Based Access Control**.

The 802.1X standard provides access control to prevent illegitimate clients from associating with a network.

---

[7] A workgroup switch is the switch to which a client connects. In contrast, core switches connect switches to other switches. Workgroup switches provide access to the network, so placing access control in workgroup switches is an obvious choice.

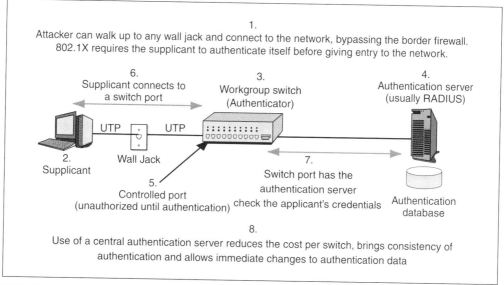

1.
Attacker can walk up to any wall jack and connect to the network, bypassing the border firewall.
802.1X requires the supplicant to authenticate itself before giving entry to the network.

6.
Supplicant connects to
a switch port

3.
Workgroup switch
(Authenticator)

4.
Authentication server
(usually RADIUS)

UTP   UTP

2.
Supplicant

Wall Jack

7.
Switch port has the
authentication server

5.
Controlled port
(unauthorized until authentication) check the applicant's credentials

Authentication
database

8.
Use of a central authentication server reduces the cost per switch, brings consistency of
authentication and allows immediate changes to authentication data

FIGURE 4-16   Ethernet and 802.1X

When the computer first connects, the port is in an *unauthorized* state (5). It will not permit the user to communicate over the network. The port remains unauthorized until the computer authenticates itself. After authentication, the port changes to the *authorized* state, and the computer has unimpeded access to the network.

Although the switch port is the primary point of control, the switch is not burdened with having to do heavy authentication work. For that, the switches rely on a **central authentication server** (4). This server has credentials-checking authentication data and the processing power needed to check passwords, biometrics scans, and other access credentials.

There are three advantages in using a central authentication server instead of having each workgroup switch do all the work:

- First, as just noted, this reduces the *cost* of each workgroup switch. If a firm has many workgroup switches spread throughout the building, not having to do heavy authentication processing and not having to maintain an authentication database on each switch is very important.
- Second, using a central authentication server brings *consistency* in authentication. Credential checking is always done the same way, no matter what workgroup switch the attacker connects to. The attacker cannot try different workgroup switches until he or she finds a switch with an incorrect authentication database that allows the attacker in.
- Third, central authentication servers bring immediate access control changes. For instance, if you fire an employee, you can immediately suspend his or her access to the network on the central authentication server instead of having to reconfigure credential checking on all workgroup switches.

In 802.1X, there are three devices involved in authentication. The computer seeking access obviously is the supplicant (2), but what device is the verifier? Is it the workgroup switch or the central authentication server? Obviously, the verification function is spread across the two devices. Rather than calling either device the verifier, 802.1X calls the workgroup switch the **authenticator** (3). The central authentication server is simply called the central authentication server (4).

TEST YOUR UNDERSTANDING

17. a. Why is 802.1X called Port-Based Access Control?
   b. Where is the heavy authentication work done?
   c. What are the three benefits of using a central authentication server?
   d. Which device is the verifier? Explain. (Trick question.)
   e. Which device is called the authenticator?

The Extensible Authentication Protocol (EAP)

Figure 4-17 shows that 802.1X relies on another protocol, the **Extensible Authentication Protocol (EAP)**, to govern the specifics of authentication interactions. The figure shows a simple authentication dialogue using EAP.

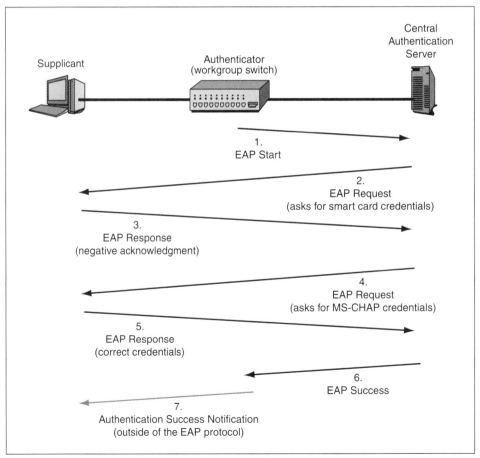

FIGURE 4-17 The Extensible Authentication Protocol (EAP)

EAP OPERATION   Ethernet switches can sense when a host connects to one of its ports. When a switch senses a connection, it sends an *EAP Start* message to the RADIUS server (1). This begins the EAP session.

The central authentication server sends an *EAP Request* message to the client. This message contains a field indicating that this EAP Request message requires smart card credentials (2). The supplicant cannot use smart card authentication, so it sends back an *EAP Response* message that contains a negative acknowledgement (3).

These messages go between the authentication server and the supplicant. The authenticator switch merely passes the message through. This is called **pass-through operation**.

After the failure of the first EAP request, the central authentication server sends another EAP Request message, this time with a code indicating that it wishes MS-CHAP credentials (4). This request message contains the challenge message that MS-CHAP uses, as we saw in Chapter 3. This time, the supplicant complies with the request. It sends back an EAP Response message containing the MS-CHAP response string (5). Again, the authenticator switch merely passes the message through.

The central authentication server evaluates the string and sends back an *EAP Success* message if the supplicant is authenticated or an *EAP Failure* message if the supplicant is not authenticated (6). This message goes to the authenticator instead of directly to the supplicant. How the authenticator notifies the client (7) is outside the scope of EAP.

EXTENSIBILITY   EAP is called **extensible** because it is easy to add new authentication methods to EAP. The structure of EAP messages does not change at all when a new authentication method is added. A new option code is simply added to the list of methods.

When a new authentication code is defined, the supplicant and verifier must implement the new method before they can use it. However, the operation of authenticator does not change. The authenticator merely passes through the EAP Request and EAP Response messages dealing with the new authentication mode. Pass-through operation means that once the firm's many workgroup switches implement EAP, there is no need to upgrade them whenever new authentication methods appear and others become obsolete. A company has many workgroup switches, so these cost savings for authenticators are very important.

TEST YOUR UNDERSTANDING

18. **a.** How does an EAP session start?
    b. What types of messages carry requests for authentication information and responses to these requests?
    c. Describe how the central authentication server tells the authenticator that the supplicant is acceptable.
    d. How does the authenticator pass this information on to the supplicant?
    e. In what sense is EAP *extensible*?
    f. When a new authentication method is added, what device software must be changed to use the new method?
    g. Why is there no need to change the operation of the authenticator when a new EAP authentication method is added or an old EAP authentication mode is dropped?
    h. Why is this freedom from the need to make changes in the switch beneficial?

RADIUS Servers

Most central authentication servers are governed by the **RADIUS** standard. RADIUS is a client/server protocol, with the authenticator being the client and the central authentication being the server. Figure 4-18 illustrates the relationship between EAP and RADIUS.

RADIUS AND EAP   The RADIUS protocol provides authentication, but it goes beyond that. It also provides authorizations, meaning that it can specify limits on such matters as what servers the authenticated supplicant may connect to, what directories the supplicant may access on those servers, and what users can do in these directories (read files, modify files, etc.). RADIUS also provides optional auditing of connections so that a company can check later what workgroup switches a particular computer connected to and how long it was connected.

Although RADIUS has its own methods for authentication communication, Figure 4-18 shows that EAP over RADIUS specifies how to use EAP instead for native RADIUS authentication when RADIUS governs communication between an authenticator and the central authentication server. In other words, EAP is only used in the first A in AAA.

TEST YOUR UNDERSTANDING

19. a. What standard do most central authentication servers follow?
   b. How are EAP and RADIUS related in terms of functionality?
   c. What authentication method does RADIUS use?

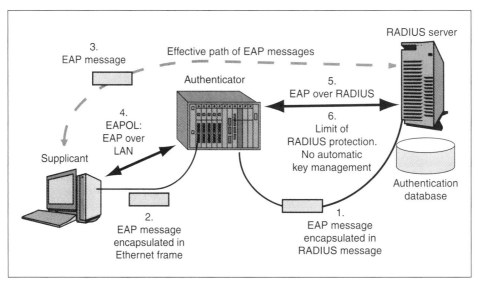

FIGURE 4-18   EAPOL and EAP over RADIUS

WIRELESS SECURITY

As noted earlier in this chapter, Ethernet LANs are not the only LANs that require access control. In fact, 802.11 wireless LANs have more serious security issues than wired LANs because drive-by hackers do not even have to enter the building to plug a computer into a wall to get access to the LAN.

Wireless LAN Security with 802.11i

For reasons we will discuss, 802.1X cannot be applied directly to 802.11 wireless LANs. It had to be extended, and this extension was called 802.11i. Figure 4-19 illustrates both 802.1X on a wired LAN and 802.11i for an 802.11 connection. For the 802.11i connection, you still see the familiar central authentication server. You also see the supplicant, which is a wireless computer. The authenticator has changed from a switch port to the wireless access point (5), but that is not a fundamental modification.

EAP's NEED FOR SECURITY The difference comes in the communication between the access point and the wireless client. EAP is a great protocol, but it has a serious security limitation. It assumes that the connection between the supplicant and the authenticator is secure. Of course, there is no explicit security in the UTP connection between a computer and an Ethernet switch, but the practical risk of someone tapping a line between a wall jack and the switch is small, so the need of EAP for security can be ignored (3).

In wireless LANs, however, Figure 4-19 shows that radio transmission makes EAP's need for security critical. Thanks to the inherent lack of security in wireless transmission (7), there *has* to be added security between the wireless client and the access point, or EAP authentication can be easily attacked. To provide this security, the 802.11 Working Group enhanced the 802.1X standard to work over wireless LANs. This enhanced standard is **802.11i**.

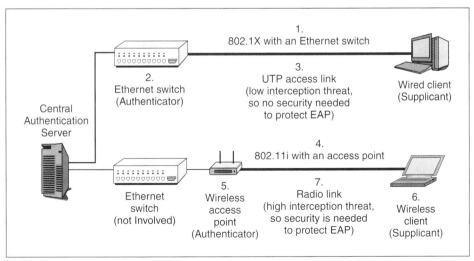

FIGURE 4-19 802.11i or WPA Wireless LAN Access Control in 802.1X Mode

EAP assumes that the connection between the supplicant and the authenticator is secure. Additional security is needed between the supplicant and the access point in 802.11 WLANs.

ADDING SECURITY TO EAP   The enhancement comes through **extending EAP standards** to add security. All extended EAP standards begin the same way. As Figure 4-20 shows, the authenticator first establishes an SSL/TLS secure connection between the authenticator and the wireless client. In this **outer authentication**, the access point has a digital certificate that it uses to authenticate itself to the wireless client.

Once outer authentication is implemented, security is established between wireless client and the access point, and EAP can be used for the rest of the authentication. Digital certificate-based authentication is very strong. It requires the installation of a digital certificate on each access point, but a company has a limited number of access points, so the cost of installing digital certificates is not prohibitive.

The next step is **inner authentication**, in which the wireless client authenticates itself via EAP. For inner authentication, the client supplicant uses EAP within the protection of outer authentication to communicate with the central authentication server in EAP exchanges.

EAP-TLS AND PEAP   Two extended EAP standards are common in the marketplace today. The first is **EAP-TLS**. In this standard, the inner authentication also uses TLS. This requires the supplicant to have a digital certificate. This is very secure, but implementing a digital certificate on each client and server is expensive.

The second popular extended EAP standard is **Protected EAP (PEAP)**. For inner authentication using PEAP, the client can use any method specified in the EAP standard, ranging from passwords through digital certificates. PEAP has been successful in the marketplace because it is favored by Microsoft and strongly supported by Cisco systems. In addition, companies like it because they can apply whatever level of client authentication is appropriate.

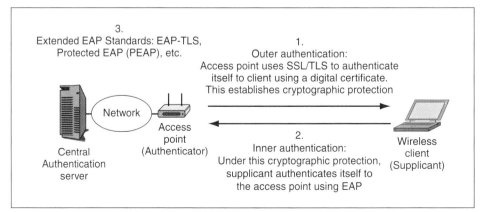

FIGURE 4-20   Extended EAP Protocols

TEST YOUR UNDERSTANDING

20. a. Why is it impossible to extend 802.1X operation using EAP directly to WLANs?
   b. What standard did the 802.3 Working Group create to extend 802.1X operation to WLANs with security for EAP?
   c. For 802.11i, distinguish between outer and inner authentication.
   d. What authentication method or methods does outer authentication use?
   e. What two extended EAP protocols are popular today?
   f. Distinguish between their options for inner authentication.
   g. Is 802.11i security strong? Explain.

Core Security Protocols

For 802.11 wireless LANs, Figure 4-21 shows that **core security protocols** protect communication between the wireless client and the access point. They do not provide protection all the way to the server the client wishes to reach. The 802.11i standard is a core security protocol, but it is not the only core security protocol. In fact, it was the third to be created.

WIRED EQUIVALENT PROTECTION (WEP)   When the 802.11 committee created the first versions of its standards in 1997, it created the **Wired**[8] **Equivalent Protection (WEP)** standard to provide basic security between wireless access points and wireless clients. By the late 1990s, it became obvious that WEP was fatally flawed. With WEP-cracking software readily downloadable from the Internet, attackers could crack WEP security within minutes. (Today, WEP cracking is even faster.) Using WEP is arguably worse than no security because companies that implement WEP may think they are protected when they are not.

> The TJX security breach that we saw in Chapter 1 was made possible by TJX deciding not to upgrade their WEP core security standard. The company consciously decided not to upgrade to WPA or 802.11i because it believed that attacks probably would not happen.

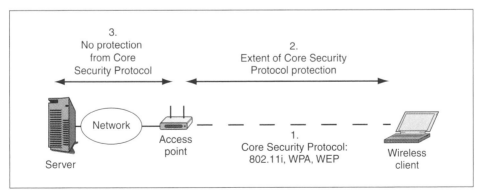

FIGURE 4-21   802.11 Core Security Protocol

---

[8] Not wireless. The idea was to provide security as strong as Ethernet LANs offered on wired hubs. WEP failed even in this unchallenging goal.

WI-FI PROTECTED ACCESS (WPA™)   The failure of WEP sent the nascent WLAN industry into turmoil. Many corporations froze WLAN deployment or even turned off their existing WLANs. This led to the 802.11 Working Group's effort to create the 802.11i standard. However, the slow pace of the development effort frustrated manufacturers. They turned to the **Wi-Fi Alliance**, which normally only certifies operability between 802.11 equipment. If equipment is sold with the Wi-Fi label on the box, it has passed Wi-Fi Alliance interoperability certification.

The Wi-Fi Alliance took an early draft of the 802.11i standard and created its own standard, which it called **Wi-Fi Protected Access (WPA™)**. To get the standard out quickly and to make WPA suitable for early equipment, which had limited processing power and RAM, the Wi-Fi Alliance selected relatively weak security methods. As Figure 4-22 shows, WPA uses the relatively weak RC4[9] cipher in encryption for confidentiality and uses the only moderately strong Temporal Key Integrity Protocol (TKIP) for keying and rekeying. Although there have been no published cracks for WPA as a whole, at least at the time of this writing, TKIP has been partially cracked, and security professionals are uncomfortable with WPA's security methods.

Although WPA kept the WLAN industry growing, the 802.11 Working Group completed the 802.11i standard in 2002. The Wi-Fi Alliance called this new standard **WPA2™** for purposes of interoperability testing.

Today, nearly all wireless access points and wireless network interface cards can support 802.11i with its far stronger security methods. However, many firms continue to use WPA to avoid the cost of reconfiguring all of their access points and wireless clients to support 802.11i.

Cryptographic Characteristic	WEP	WPA	802.11i (WPA2)
Cipher for confidentiality	RC4 with a flawed implementation	RC4 with 48-bit initialization vector (IV)	AES with 128-bit keys
Automatic rekeying	None	Temporal Key Integrity Protocol (TKIP), which has been partially cracked	AES-CCMP mode
Overall cryptographic strength	Negligible	Weaker but no complete crack to date	Extremely strong
Operates in 802.1X (enterprise) mode?	No	Yes	Yes
Operates in pre-shared key (personal) mode?	No	Yes	Yes

FIGURE 4-22   Core Security Standards for 802.11 LANs

[9] The deprecated WEP standard also used RC4, but WPA has a stronger implementation.

TEST YOUR UNDERSTANDING

21. a. What prompted the Wi-Fi Alliance to create WPA?
  b. Compare WPA and 802.11i security.
  c. What does the Wi-Fi Alliance call 802.11i?
  d. Despite its relatively security weaknesses, why do many companies continue to use WPA instead of 802.11i?

Pre-Shared Key (PSK) Mode

For large firms, using 802.11i or WPA to implement 802.1X mode with its expensive central authentication server is necessary. For very small businesses and individual households, however, using a central authentication server would be overkill. Consequently, 802.11i and WPA both offer a non-802.1X mode called **pre-shared key (PSK)** mode. WPA, which is based on an early draft of 802.11i, also includes this mode but calls it **personal mode**. Specifically, PSK/personal mode was created for homes or small businesses that only have a single access point.

PSK/personal mode was created for homes or small businesses that only have a single access point.

Figure 4-23 shows that all wireless clients being authenticate themselves to the access point using a **shared initial key** used by all clients. Shared keys generally are bad for security because people tend to view them as nonsecret and give them to unauthorized people. In addition, if someone leaves or is fired, a new secret key must be installed on the access point and all clients. In large corporations, these problems tend to be insurmountable. However, in small firms and homes, shared keys can be kept secret.

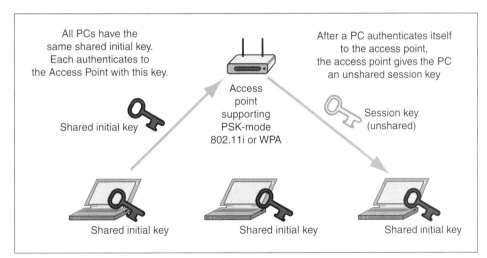

FIGURE 4-23 Pre-Shared Key (PSK)/Personal Mode for 802.11i and EAP

Using a shared key generally means that there will be a great deal of traffic encrypted with the same key. This makes it far easier for cryptanalysis programs to crack the key. Once the key is cracked, then all security is gone.

To address this concern, 802.11i and WPA in PSK/personal mode only use the shared initial key very briefly—when a client first authenticates itself to the access point. After authentication, the access point sends the client an **unshared session key** for use during the session. With only a few messages transmitted using the shared initial key, cryptanalysis to discover the shared initial key is effectively impossible.

However, PSK/personal mode has one serious operational security issue. Unless the shared initial key is complex, cryptanalysis of the initial key will not only be possible, it will be easy. In practice, the administrator or user has to type a **passphrase** into every wireless client and the access point. The equipment generates the key from this passphrase. Long passphrases produce strong keys, but if the passphrase is too short, then 802.11i or WPA in PSK/personal mode will have very weak security. Passphrases must be at least 20 characters long, and longer passphrases are better.

In 802.11i or WPA in PSK/personal mode, passphrases must be at least 20 characters long.

TEST YOUR UNDERSTANDING

22. a. Why is 802.1X mode unsuitable for homes and small offices?
  b. What mode was created for homes or very small businesses with a single access point?
  c. How do users in this mode authenticate themselves to the access point?
  d. Why is using a shared initial key not dangerous?
  e. How are PSK/personal keys generated?
  f. How long must passphrases be for adequate security?

Evil Twin Access Points

Although 802.11i and WPA offer strong security, they are susceptible to man-in-the-middle attacks that intercept messages during and after security setup. In wireless LANs, man-in-the-middle attacks use **evil twin access points**. An evil twin access point is simply a PC that has software to allow it to masquerade as an access point.

As Figure 4-24 shows, the attacker sets up an evil twin access point outside the company's premises. The attacker sets transmission power high because clients often associate with the access point that has the strongest signal. If the victim wireless client is such a client, it will associate with the evil twin access point instead of with its legitimate access point (4).

The evil twin will then associate with the legitimate access point within the corporate walls, pretending to be the supplicant user. This effectively puts it between the wireless client and the legitimate access point. It is ready to execute the man-in-the middle attack.

The evil twin access point intercepts all traffic passing through it, then passes the traffic on (5). Initially, it captures credentials transmissions and keys. Afterward, when

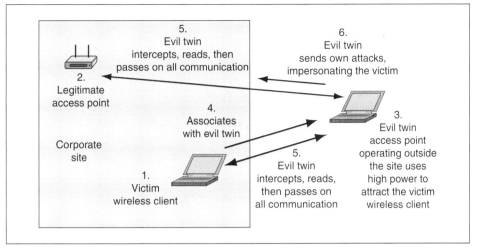

FIGURE 4-24   Evil Twin Access Point Man-in-the-Middle Attack

an encrypted message arrives, it can decrypt it, read it, encrypt it again, and passes it on. The evil twin can also send attack packets of its own, impersonating the victim client (6).

Evil twin access point attacks are quite common, especially in public hot spots.[10] The protections offered by WPA and 802.11i are meaningless when a man-in-the-middle attack is executed properly by an evil twin.

To address this threat, some companies require clients coming in via remote access establish a VPN connection as well. This is illustrated in Figure 4-25. A VPN uses

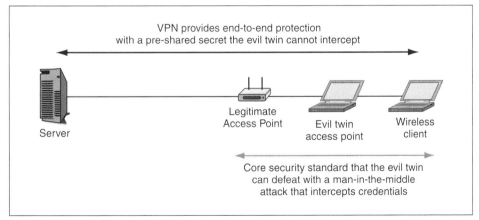

FIGURE 4-25   VPN Protection against Evil Twin Access Point Attacks

---

[10] The danger of getting hit with an evil twin attack in a public hot spot can be reduced by being astute about deciding which access point to use within a hot spot. Instead of associating with the strongest signal, check on the SSIDs (access point identifiers) of the available access points. Then ask a knowledgeable party for the SSID of the official access point. Only associate with that access point.

a pre-shared secret that the client and server exchanged beforehand. This secret therefore cannot be intercepted by the evil twin.

TEST YOUR UNDERSTANDING

23. a. What man-in-the-middle attack is a danger for 802.11 WLANs?
   b. Physically, what is an evil twin access point?
   c. What happens when the legitimate supplicant sends credentials to the legitimate access point?
   d. In what two types of attacks can the evil twin engage?
   e. Are evil twin attacks frequent?
   f. Where are they the most frequently encountered?
   g. How can the danger of evil twin attacks be addressed?

Wireless Intrusion Detection Systems

Companies that have central management for their many access points can purchase **centralized wireless intrusion detection system** software. As Figure 4-26 illustrates, each access point becomes a wireless IDS agent, sending appropriate information to the central wireless IDS console. The console transfers the data to an IDS database. It also sorts through data in the database to find indications of problems.

There is a good chance that a centralized wireless IDS can identify evil twin access points. Centralized wireless IDSs are also good at finding **rogue access points**, which are unauthorized access points set up by individuals or departments. Rogue access points are dangerous because they often have no security at all or use the discredited WEP security method. Rogue access points give a drive-by hacker a clean shot into the network, bypassing a firm's carefully developed wireless security in legitimate access points.

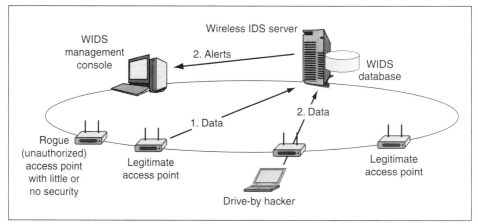

FIGURE 4-26 Centralized Wireless Intrusion Detection System

Rogue access points are unauthorized access points set up by individuals or departments.

There are two alternatives to using a centralized wireless IDS. The first is simply not to worry about intrusion detection. Given the commonness of wireless attacks, this is hardly wise. The second alternative is to walk around the building frequently with a laptop that has wireless IDS software. This is likely to require a prohibitive amount of labor, and it cannot catch threats that appear after the wireless security administrator has checked a part of the site for threats. Nor is this approach likely to catch evil twin access points, which only operate occasionally and so may not be operating when the wireless administrator is sweeping the building for concerns.

TEST YOUR UNDERSTANDING

24. a. What is the purpose of a wireless IDS?
   b. How do wireless IDSs get their data?
   c. What is a rogue access point?
   d. What are the two alternative to using a centralized wireless IDS?
   e. Why are they not attractive?

Wired Equivalent Privacy (WEP)

The 802.11 Working Group's initial core WLAN security standard in 1997 was **wired equivalent privacy (WEP)**. This standard had fatal security vulnerabilities.

Shared Keys and Operational Security

First, WEP mandates **shared keys**, meaning that the access point and all stations using it use *the same* shared key for all cryptographic protections. The shared key provides de facto authentication. If a station knows the shared key, it is assumed to be legitimate and so is accepted into the network. The single shared key also encrypts messages for confidentiality.

Obviously, if an attacker learns the key, all security is lost. This suggests that firms should change the shared key frequently. However, WEP offered no automated rekeying. In large firms that have many access points sharing the same WEP key, the practical difficulties in changing everyone's key mean that shared keys are almost never changed. In addition, because "everybody knows" the key, people share the key freely even when they are told not to.

Worst of all, suppose that a company fires a disgruntled employee. To be safe, the company must change the key on every access point for which the employee knows the key. This will also require all clients to use the updated key on each access point. This is difficult even if the key is only used at one access point. If the key is used at multiple access points or even all access points, then changing the key will be prohibitively expensive and will inconvenience many workers.

Software Attacks

To find the WEP key, hackers can use automated WEP-cracking software readily available on the Internet. WEP specifies the RC4 cipher for symmetric key encryption. We saw RC4

(Continued)

Wired Equivalent Privacy (WEP)   (Continued)

Origin of WEP

Original core security standard in 802.11, created in 1997

Uses a Shared Key

Each station using the access point uses the same (shared) key

The key is supposed to be secret, so knowing it "authenticates" the user

Encryption uses this key

Problem with Shared Keys

If the shared key is learned, an attacker near an access point can read *all* traffic

Shared keys should at least be changed frequently

> But WEP had no way to do automatic rekeying
>
> Manual rekeying is expensive if there are many users
>
> Manual rekeying is operationally next to impossible if many or all stations use the same shared key because of the work involved in rekeying many or all corporate clients

Because "everybody knows" the key, employees often give it out to strangers

If a dangerous employee is fired, the necessary rekeying may be impossible or close to it

RC4 Initialization Vectors (IV)

WEP uses RC4 for fast and therefore cheap encryption

But if two frames are encrypted with the same RC4 key, the attacker can learn the key

To solve this, WEP encrypts with a *per-frame key* that is the shared WEP key *plus* an initialization vector (IV)

However, many frames "leak" a few bits of the key

With high traffic, an attacker using readily available software can crack a shared key in two or three minutes

(WPA uses RC4 but with a 48-bit IV that makes key bit leakage negligible)

Conclusion

Corporations should never use WEP for security

FIGURE 4-27   Wired Equivalent Privacy (WEP) (Study Figure)

briefly in Chapter 3. RC4 is very efficient and so worked even on the earliest access points and wireless NICs.

Unfortunately, if an attacker reads two messages encrypted with the same key using RC4, the attacker can find the key immediately. Consequently, WEP actually encrypts each frame with a **per-frame key** that consists of the shared RC4 key *plus* a 24-bit **initialization vector (IV)** that is different for each frame. The sender randomly generates the IV. The sender also transmits the IV in the clear in the frame header so that the receiver can learn it. The receiver decrypts the frame with the known shared key plus the frame-specific initialization vector.

Also unfortunately, 24-bit IVs are too short. With a 24-bit IV, many frames will "leak" a few bits of the secret key. If a company encrypts a large enough volume of traffic with the same secret key, the attacker can often compute the entire secret key in two or three minutes.

By the way, WPA extends the security of RC4 primarily by increasing the IV from 24 bits to 48 bits. This extension vastly reduces leakage and so makes RC4 much harder to crack, giving WPA good security for confidentiality.

Perspective

Given how easily and quickly WEP can be cracked, it makes no sense for corporations to use WEP today. In fact, it only gives a false sense of security, and this may be worse than no security at all.

TEST YOUR UNDERSTANDING

25. **a.** What was the first core wireless security standard?
    b. What encryption algorithm does it use?
    c. Why are permanent shared keys undesirable?
    d. What per-frame key does a WEP computer or access point use to encrypt when it transmits?
    e. What mistake did the 802.11 Working Group make in selecting the length of the IV?
    f. How long may WEP take to crack today?
    g. Should corporations today use WEP for security today?

False 802.11 Security

Many magazine articles about 802.11 security give advice that is now widely seen as offering only a false sense of security. They are what my grandfather called whiskey cures. He said that of all the things that fail to cure the common cold, whiskey is the most popular.

The actions deprecated in this section for corporate use may be enough to keep out nosy neighbors. However, drive-by hackers with good hacking software increasingly roam neighborhoods to get free Internet access and look through residential computers. In addition, these poor "protections" take as much effort or more to set up as full WPA or 802.11i security.

Spread Spectrum Operation and Security

All 802.11 wireless LAN standards use **spread spectrum transmission**, which spreads the signal over a wide range of frequencies. Many people have heard that the military uses spread spectrum transmission for security. However, the types of spread spectrum transmission used in 802.11 offer no security; in fact, spread spectrum modes of operation for 802.11 WLANs specifically make it *easy* for stations to find and hear one another.[11] Users should not dismiss hackers because "My system uses spreads spectrum transmission, which can't be intercepted."

Turning off SSID Broadcasting

To work with an access point, a station must know the access point's **Service Set Identifier (SSID)**. To make it easy for stations to find access points, access points broadcast their SSIDs frequently. Turning off **SSID broadcasting** would seem to offer security. However,

(Continued)

---

[11] Spread spectrum transmission is mandated by law for the 2.4 GHz and 5 GHz unlicensed radio bands in which 802.11 operates in order to *reduce propagation problems.* Many propagation difficulties are frequency dependent, and using a broad spectrum of frequencies reduces the damage of frequency-specific problems. Again, spread spectrum is *not* mandated for security.

False 802.11 Security   (Continued)

Spread Spectrum Operation and Security
  Signal is spread over a wide range of frequencies
  NOT done for security, as in military spread spectrum transmission

Turning off SSID Broadcasting
  Service set identifier (SSID) is an identifier for an access point
  Users must know the SSID to use the access point
  Drive-by hacker needs to know the SSID to break in
  Access points frequently broadcast their SSIDs
  Some writers favor turning off of this broadcasting
  But turning off SSID broadcasting can make access more difficult for ordinary users
  Will not deter the attacker because he or she can read the SSID, which is transmitted in the clear in each transmitted frame

MAC Access Control Lists
  Access points can be configured with MAC access control lists
  Only permit access by stations with NICs having MAC addresses on the list
  But MAC addresses are sent in the clear in frames, so attackers can learn them
  Attacker can then spoof one of these addresses

Perspective
  These "false" methods, however, may be sufficient to keep out nosy neighbors
  But drive-by hackers hit even residential users
  Simply applying WPA or 802.11i provides much stronger security and is easier to do

FIGURE 4-28   False 802.11 Security (Study Figure)

even if SSID broadcasting is turned off, the SSID will still be transmitted in the clear in the header of each transmitted frame. Sniffer programs have no trouble reading SSIDs in frame headers. Quite simply, there is nothing a firm can do to hide SSIDs from an attacker who has even minimum hacking software.

MAC Access Control Lists

Each network interface card has a **MAC address**. It is possible to configure most access points to serve only stations on a pre-approved list of MAC addresses. The wireless access point ignores other stations. However, MAC addresses must be transmitted in the clear in every frame, so drive-by hackers can easily learn them and send frames that appear to come from one of the approved stations. Managing MAC access control lists is a good deal of work and provides no effective security.

Implementing 802.11i i or WPA is Easier

Turning off SSID broadcasting and creating MAC access control lists are not just ineffective. They are time consuming. Turning on 802.11i or WPA not only gives full security (aside from evil twin access points). It is also less work.

TEST YOUR UNDERSTANDING

26. **a.** Does the use of spread spectrum transmission in 802.11 create security?
   b. What are SSIDs?
   c. Does turning off SSID broadcasting offer real security? Explain.
   d. What are MAC access control lists?
   e. Do they offer real security? Explain.

CONCLUSION

Synopsis

Chapter 3 introduced the elements of cryptographic security. In this chapter, we looked at how these elements are packaged into cryptographic systems, which provide the elements of security in a single integrated package. Specific cryptographic systems use cryptographic security standards. In this chapter, we looked at some of the major cryptographic security standards.

We first looked at virtual private network (VPN) standards. A virtual private network (VPN) is a cryptographic system that provides secure communication over an untrusted network (the Internet, a wireless LAN, etc.). There are host-to-host, remote access, and site-to-site VPNs.

One widely used VPN standard is SSL/TLS. SSL/TLS is very popular because the client only needs a browser, and all client computers today have browsers. We saw how SSL/TLS was created for host-to-host VPNs—specifically browser–webserver VPNs. All browsers and webservers know how to set up SSL/TLS VPNs, so using them is inexpensive. We then saw how SSL/VPN gateways can turn SSL/TLS into a remote access VPN technology. However, SSL/TLS does not provide transparent protection to all applications, and setting up SSL/TLS gateways for remote access can be clumsy.

The gold standard for VPNs is IPsec. IPsec offers extremely strong security, including the requirement that both communication partners authenticate themselves using public key authentication with digital certificates. In addition, IPsec has strong policy control capabilities so that communicating partners cannot select weak security options. This policy management is centralized and therefore easy to administer. IPsec can be used for all three types of VPNs.

IPsec operates in two modes. In transport mode, IPsec provides security all the way between the source and destination host. However, IPsec transport mode is expensive because of setup requirements on all clients and servers and the management of digital certificates over their life cycles. Transport mode also makes firewall filtering impossible or at least difficult. In tunnel mode, IPsec only provides security between IPsec gateways at each site. This eliminates computer setup requirements and allows firewall filtering. On the down side, tunnel mode does not provide any security within sites.

A box provided additional information about IPsec. This included what the ESP header and trailer protect in tunnel and transport modes. It also included information on the establishment of security associations using IKE.

We also looked at noncryptographic VPNs that provide security of a sort by hiding routing information. Commercial WANs have long been routed VPNs, and new

IP networks that use MPLS are also routed VPNs. Hiding routing information is security by obscurity. This is dangerous. So far, attacks on commercial WANs, including IP/MPLS VPNs, have been rare. However, if attackers learn how to find routes, this situation could become very dangerous very quickly.

We next looked at security for wired LANs, which almost always use Ethernet technology from the 802.3 Working Group, and then at wireless LANs, which use standards from the 802.11 Working Group. Another working group, 802.1, developed the 802.1X standard to prevent intruders from simply plugging laptops into wall jacks to get access to the network.

In 802.1X mode, there are three devices. The client or server PC connecting to the network is the supplicant. A central authentication server does credential checking. This central authentication server is usually governed by the RADIUS standard. The Ethernet workgroup switch to which the client or server PC connects is called the authenticator. Until the PC is authenticated, the port to which it connects is unauthorized and will only pass authentication information.

Authentication interactions are governed by the Extensible Authentication Protocol (EAP). We looked at the EAP interactions required for a computer connected to a workgroup switch port to authenticate itself. For most interactions, the workgroup switch authenticator merely passes EAP interactions between the connected computer and the central authentication server. Consequently, when new authentication methods are added, the authenticator does not have to be changed at all.

The situation in wireless networking is more complicated because of higher security risks. Initially, the 802.11 Working Group created the WEP core security standard for security traffic flowing between wireless computers and the wireless access point. This standard was a disaster. WEP is old news and has long been superseded by better access control standards. In 2002, the 802.11 Working Group finished the 802.11i standard, which describes how to use 802.1X security, including EAP, in wireless LANs. The key innovation in 802.11i was providing security between the wireless client and the access point before EAP interactions begin. This is necessary because EAP is easy to defeat in a nonsecure environment. Another organization, the Wi-Fi Alliance, produced a stop-gap standard before the 802.11i standard was finished. Based on an early draft of 802.11i, the Alliance created the Wi-Fi Protected Access (WPA) standard. Although 802.11i has now been available for several years and uses stronger cryptographic methods than WPA, and although WPA has been partially cracked, many companies that invested early in WPA security are reluctant to reconfigure their many access points and wireless computers to use 802.11i.

Even if a firm implements 802.11i or WPA, security problems remain. The most serious is that evil twin access points (notebook computers with software to make them act as access points) can conduct man-in-the-middle attacks that 802.11i and WPA cannot stop. The best way to handle the evil twin access point threat is to establish a VPN between the wireless client and the server it ultimately wishes to work with. This VPN can use a pre-shared secret between the wireless computer and the computer it wishes to reach. The evil twin access point cannot intercept pre-shared secrets because these secrets are never transmitted.

Companies are beginning to manage all of their access points from a central management console. Companies that do this can use wireless intrusion detection systems to locate problems such as evil twin access points and rogue access points, which are set up by individuals and departments and that usually have little or no security.

We closed the chapter with two boxes. The first dealt with the details of the obsolete and deprecated WEP standard. The second dealt with false security measures that require work to set up but that offer no real security against drive-by hackers who have readily downloadable attack software.

Thought Questions

1. Distinguish between EAP and RADIUS in terms of functionality.
2. Why would it be desirable to protect all of a corporation's IP traffic by IPsec? Give multiple reasons.
3. What wireless LAN security threats do 802.11i and WPA *not* address?
4. Given the weakness of commercial WAN security, why do you think companies continue to use WAN technology without added cryptographic protections?
5. What could a company do if it was using a commercial WAN and a vulnerability appeared that allowed attackers to easily find routing information and therefore be able to eavesdrop on corporate transmissions?
6. The 802.1X standard today is being applied primarily to wireless LANs rather than to wired LANs. Why do you think that is?

Project

1. Create a two-page memorandum advising a business with about 200 users about major wireless LAN threats and how to achieve adequate wireless LAN security.

Perspective Questions

1. What was the most surprising thing you learned in this chapter?
2. What part was the most difficult for you?

Chapter 5

Access Control

LEARNING OBJECTIVES:

By the end of this chapter, you should be able to discuss the following:

- Basic access control terminology.
- Physical building and computer security.
- Reusable passwords.
- Access cards and tokens.
- Biometric authentication, including verification and identification.
- Authorizations.
- Auditing.
- Central authentication servers.
- Directory servers.
- Toward full identity management.

INTRODUCTION

Access Control

We saw in Chapter 2 that a firm must develop a security plan for each sensitive resource. Part of this security plan will focus on access control. Attackers who cannot get to your resources cannot harm them. Companies need to plan access controls, implement the required controls, and respond when the controls fail.

Formally defined, **access control** is the policy-driven control of access to systems, data, and dialogues. There are many ways to control access, including physical barriers, passwords, and biometrics. Many of these access control mechanisms use cryptographic protections, so we have covered cryptography before covering access control. However, many access control techniques do not use cryptography at all, and others use cryptography only tangentially. Access control is not just cryptography.

Access control is the policy-driven control of access to systems, data, and dialogues.

The key concept is *policy*. As Chapter 2 discussed, all security begins with the development of security policies for individual resources. Policies, when properly created, coordinate everyone and guide implementation and oversight.

Authentication, Authorizations, and Auditing

Access controls have three functions, which are known collectively as **AAA** (authentication, authorization, and auditing).

Access Controls
  Firms must limit access to physical and electronic resources
  Access control is the policy-driven control of access to systems, data, and dialogues

Cryptography
  Many access control tools use cryptography to some extent
  However, cryptography is only part of what they do and how they work

The AAA Protections
  Authentication—supplicant sends credentials to verifier to authenticate the supplicant
  Authorization—what permissions the authenticated user will have
      What resources he or she can get to at all
      What he or she can do with these resources
  Auditing—recording what people do in log files
      Detecting attacks
      Identifying breakdowns in implementation

Credentials Are Based on
  What you know (e.g., a password)
  What you have (e.g., an access card)
  What you are, or (e.g., your fingerprint)
  What you do (e.g., speaking a passphrase)

Two-Factor Authentication
  Use two forms of authentication for defense in depth
  Example: access card and personal identification number (PIN)
  Multifactor authentication: two or more types of authentication
  But this can be defeated by a Trojan horse on the user's PC
  It can also be defeated by a man-in-the-middle attack by a fake website

Individual and Role-Based Access Control
  Individual access control—base access rules on individual accounts
  Role-based access control (RBAC)
      Base access rules on organizational roles (buyer, member of a team, etc.)
      Assign individual accounts to roles to give them access to the role's resources
      Cheaper and less error-prone than basing access rules on individual accounts

Human and Organizational Controls
  People and organizational forces may circumvent access protections

---

FIGURE 5-1 Access Control (Study Figure)

- **Authentication** is the process of assessing the identity of each individual claiming to have permission to use a resource. The person or process requesting access is the supplicant. The person or process providing admission is the verifier. The supplicant authenticates himself, herself, or itself to the verifier by sending credentials (a password, a fingerprint scan, etc.).
- **Authorizations** are specific **permissions** that a particular authenticated user should have, given his or her authenticated identity. For example, Bob may have permission to read a file but not to change it or delete it. Carol may not even have permission to see the file's name.
- **Auditing** consists of collecting information about the activities of each individual in log files for immediate and later analysis. Without auditing, violations of authentication and authorization policies are likely to be rampant.

Authentication

Most of this chapter focuses on authentication, which is the most complex part of AAA access controls. To be authenticated, you must show a verifier credentials that are based on one of the following:

- What you know (a password or a private key),
- What you have (a physical key or a smart card),
- Who you are (your fingerprint), or
- What you do (how you specifically pronounce a passphrase).

Beyond Passwords

Once, simple passwords were sufficient for most authentication needs. Today, however, companies find that they must use a growing variety of authentication technologies, including access cards and tokens, biometric authentication, and cryptographic authentication (which we saw in Chapters 3 and 4). This diversity of authentication method allows us to choose one of appropriate strengths for the risks associated with each resource.

Two-Factor Authentication

An increasingly important principle in authentication is **two-factor authentication**, in which two different forms of authentication must be used for access. Two-factor authentication provides defense in depth, which we saw was a basic principle of security planning in Chapter 2. Some systems even use **multifactor authentication**, which uses more than two forms of authentication.

However, two-factor authentication may provide far weaker authentication than it first appears to offer. Bruce Schneier[1] has noted that Trojan horses and man-in-the middle attacks can negate the strength of two-factor authentication.

- First, if a client PC is infected with a Trojan horse, the Trojan horse can send transactions when a user has already authenticated himself or herself to an e-commerce site. If a user's computer is compromised, two-factor authentication means nothing.

---

[1] Bruce Schneier, "Two-Factor Authentication: Too Little, Too Late," *Communications of the ACM*, 48(4), April 2005, p. 36.

• Second, two-factor authentication often can be defeated with a man-in-the-middle attack. If a user logs into a fake banking website, the fake site can act as a silent go-between to the real banking website. After the user successfully authenticates, the fake website can execute transactions of its own on the real website.

Individual and Role-Based Access Control

We normally think of access control rules that apply to individual users and devices. However, whenever possible, firms try to use **role-based access control (RBAC)**, which is based on organizational roles rather than individual people. One role might be *buyer*. Several people might be assigned this role. Although they would log into resources using their own accounts, access control would be based on their roles as buyers.

• Creating access control rules based on roles is cheaper than assigning access control rules separately to the individual accounts of buyers because there are fewer assignments to be made.
• Creating access control rules based on roles also lessens the number of opportunity for errors.
• Finally, once a person is no longer a buyer, he or she can simply be dropped from the buyer's group. This is much cheaper and less likely to create errors than looking at each person's permissions and deciding which should be removed when he or she is no longer a buyer.

ORGANIZATIONAL AND HUMAN CONTROLS

Many of the access control technologies we will see in this chapter offer extremely strong security. However, these technologies are always embedded in an organizational and human context. This creates many opportunities to bypass technology. For instance, if a lax or untrained worker gives an impostor a private key to use in authentication, then the strength of public key authentication means nothing. To give another example, if a company places trust in a business partner, and if this trust is misplaced, technological access control tools again mean nothing.

TEST YOUR UNDERSTANDING

1. a. List the AAA access controls.
   b. Explain each in a sentence.
   c. What are the four bases for authentication credentials?
   d. What is two-factor authentication's promise?
   e. How can a Trojan horse defeat this promise?
   f. How can a man-in-the-middle attack defeat this promise?
   g. What is RBAC? (Do not just spell it out).
   h. Why is RBAC less expensive than access control based on individual accounts?
   i. Why is it less error-prone? (The answer is not specifically in the text.)
   j. Why may technologically strong access controls not provide strong access control in real organizations?

Military and National Security Organization Access Controls

This is a book on corporate security. In the military and in national security organizations, additional access control considerations appear.

Mandatory and Discretionary Access Control

Corporations normally use either individual access controls or role-based access controls. In the military and national security organizations, two other forms of access control are common.

In **mandatory access control**, departments have no ability to alter access control rules set by higher authorities. In principle, this offers very strong security. In practice, this is difficult to sustain because some flexibility is almost always needed.

Consequently, organizations typically are allowed to use **discretionary access control**, in which the department has discretion over giving access to individuals, within policy standards set by higher authorities.

Multilevel Security

Documents and other resources vary in sensitivity. Typically, military and national security organizations have a **multilevel security** system that rate documents by sensitivity. Some documents will be completely public, while others will be sensitive but unclassified (SBU). Beyond this, there are several levels of classifications, such as secret and top secret.

Mandatory and Discretionary Access Control

Mandatory access control (MAC)

   No departmental or personal ability to alter access control rules set by higher authorities

Discretionary access control (DAC)

   Departmental or personal ability to alter access control rules set by higher authorities

MAC gives stronger security but is very difficult to implement

Multilevel Security

Resources are rated by security level

   Public

   Sensitive but unclassified

   Secret

   Top secret, etc.

People are given the same clearance level

Some rules are simple

   People with a secret clearance cannot read top-secret documents

Some rules are complex

   What if a paragraph from a top-secret document is placed in a secret document?

Access control models have been created to address multilevel security

   Will not discuss because not pertinent to corporations

FIGURE 5-2   Military and National Security Organization Access Controls (Study Figure)

(Continued)

Military and National Security Organization Access Controls (Continued)

Giving access to classified information requires careful thought. Obviously, if someone does not have a security clearance, he or she should not be allowed to read a top secret document. Other issues require more thought. For instance, what if a single paragraph from a classified document is copied into a sensitive but unclassified document? To cope with such issues, organizations that use multilevel security must follow complex **access control models** to determine how to deal with various access situations. This book is written for corporate security, where traditional multilevel security does not work for many reasons. Consequently, we will not discuss access control models.

TEST YOUR UNDERSTANDING

2. a. Distinguish between mandatory access controls and discretionary access controls.
   b. What is multilevel security?
   c. What are SBU documents?
   d. Do they need to be considered in access controls?
   e. Why are access control models needed?

PHYSICAL ACCESS AND SECURITY

Although many attacks take place over networks, attackers can sometimes walk into a building, walk up to a computer, and steal or hack it. Although network access control is crucial, IT security professionals need to understand physical access control for buildings, high-security zones within buildings, and individual computers. We will base this section on ISO/IEC 27002's[2] Security Clause 9, **Physical and Environmental Security**.

Risk Analysis

Security Clause 9 assumes that risk analysis has already been done. IT security professionals need to begin with an understanding of risks that exist at the levels of buildings, secure zones within buildings, and computers. A bank obviously needs far stronger perimeter security than a university; and a server room needs stronger security than an ordinary office area.

ISO/IEC 9.1: Secure Areas

Security Clause 9 has two main security categories. The first is 9.1, **Secure Areas**, which is concerned with securing physical areas, including entire buildings, equipment rooms, office areas, delivery and shipping areas, and general public areas. Main Security Category 9.1 has six controls.

---

[2] The current version is ISO/IEC 27002:2005. The 2005 is the date of the last update. Until 2007, ISO/IEC 27002:2005 was known as ISO/IEC 17799:2005. The renumbering was done as part of a comprehensive program to develop new security standards under the 27000 heading.

ISO/IEC 27002's Security Clause 9, Physical and Environmental Security
Risk Analysis Must Be Done First
ISO/IEC 9.1: Secure Areas
   Securing the building's physical perimeter (single point of entry, etc.)
   Implementing physical entry controls
      Access should be justified, authorized, logged, and monitored
   Securing public access, delivery, and loading areas
   Securing offices, rooms, and facilities
   Protecting against external and environmental threats
   Creating rules for working in secure areas
      Limit unsupervised work, forbid data recording devices, etc.

9.2 Equipment Security
   Equipment siting and protection
      Siting means locating or placing (same root as *site*)
   Supporting utilities (electricity, water, HVAC)
      Uninterruptible power supplies, electrical generators
      Frequent testing
   Cabling security (conduits, underground wiring, etc.)
   Security during off-site equipment maintenance
      Permission for removal of sensitive information if taken off-site
   Security of equipment off-premises
      Constant attendance except when locked securely
      Insurance
   Secure disposal or reuse of equipment
      Removal of all sensitive information
   Rules for the removal of property

FIGURE 5-3   ISO/IEC 27002:2005 Physical and Environmental Security (Study Figure)

PHYSICAL SECURITY PERIMETER   It is important to control building entry points. Ideally, there will be a **single point of entry**. In addition, the walls that separate the building from the outside should be sound, and there should be no gaps through which people can enter. If security requirements call for a staffed reception area, it should be staffed constantly.

Although a single point of entry facilitates control, every building has **emergency exits** that can be opened for egress whenever justified. If the intruder has a confederate in the building, the confederate can open one of these doors to let in the attacker. Consequently, emergency exits should be alarmed, monitored (preferably with cameras), and tested frequently.

In all cases, security provisions must be compatible with fire codes. Most importantly, it is illegal to lock fire exits to bar egress.

PHYSICAL ENTRY CONTROLS   Operationally, all physical access must be authorized. (In the terminology of CobiT, entry must be justified, authorized, logged, and monitored—including in emergencies.) Access authorizations should be reviewed and updated frequently.

Visitors should be logged in and out and should be supervised at all times while inside the building. Everyone inside should wear identification badges.

PUBLIC ACCESS, DELIVERY, AND LOADING AREAS   Delivery and loading areas are sensitive zones in a building. Internal people should have limited access to delivery and loading areas, and delivery and pickup people should have no access to the building beyond the delivery and loading dock. Incoming shipments should be inspected and logged. Outgoing shipments should be separated from incoming shipments to reduce the risk of theft.

SECURING OFFICES, ROOMS, AND FACILITIES   Certain areas of a building will be especially sensitive. They should be given extra security, but this security must be consistent with health and safety standards. Sensitive areas should have locks with keys, access cards, or other limited entry mechanisms.[3]

Secure areas should be located away from public access and should be as unobtrusive as possible. Internal room directories and telephone directories that list these areas should not be available to the public.

PROTECTING AGAINST EXTERNAL AND ENVIRONMENTAL THREATS   Although IT security is primarily concerned with human intruders, building safety and security is inextricably concerned with nonhuman threats as well. Hazardous and combustible material should be located away from sensitive areas, and there should be adequate equipment for fire fighting. Disaster response facilities and backup media should be located safely away from the building.

RULES FOR WORKING IN SECURE AREAS   The company should have special rules for people working in secure areas. Most importantly, unsupervised work should be avoided. When no one is in a secure area, it should be locked and checked periodically.

In most cases, photographic equipment will be forbidden, including cameras in mobile phones. Data recording media, such as writable disks and USB RAM and hard drives, should be forbidden as well. These media now allow a physical penetration attacker to steal gigabytes worth of information. Of course, unauthorized PCs, intelligent mobile phones, and other computing devices should be excluded in many cases as well.

There should be inspections of people arriving and leaving in order to ensure that rules against recording devices, media, and other prohibited devices are effective. People must be notified that these searches will occur, and searches must be conducted in compliance with company policy, laws, and union contracts.[4]

Needless to say, restrictions on devices and recording media are extremely difficult to put into practice, although companies can use technology to prevent recording devices from being attached to computers or the network.

---

[3] Locks and other physical mechanisms actually are discussed in 9.1.2.

[4] Such searches actually are not discussed until 9.2.7.

TEST YOUR UNDERSTANDING

3. a. Why is having a single point of building entry important?
  b. Why are emergency exits important?
  c. What should be done about them?
  d. List the four elements of entry authorization in CobiT.
  e. Why is loading dock security important?
  f. What access control rules should be applied to loading docks?
  g. What steps should be taken to reduce the danger of environmental damage?
  h. List rules for working in secure areas.

9.2 Equipment Security

Main Security[5] Category 9.1 deals with site security. Main Security Category 9.2, in turn, focuses on **equipment security**. It has seven controls.

EQUIPMENT SITING AND PROTECTION   Sensitive equipment should be **sited** (placed) in secure areas to minimize access. These areas should not be subject to damage from smoke, water supply failure, vandalism, and other threats.

Siting is a synonym for locating or placing. It is from the root site.

Equipment should be positioned so that unauthorized people cannot read information on screens. There should also be eating and drinking guidelines and well-monitored controls for temperature and humidity, which can be damaging to equipment and media.

SUPPORTING UTILITIES   People and equipment need electricity, water, and **HVAC** (heating, ventilation, and air conditioning). These utilities must be supplied to an adequate level and should be inspected and tested regularly.

Special attention must be given to the electrical supply because a loss of electric power can cause loss of availability or even permanent damage. An **uninterruptible power supply (UPS)** has a battery that can supply equipment with power for a brief period of time after an outage. UPSs allow orderly shutdown during power failures. For longer-duration outages, companies can maintain backup **electrical generators**, which run on gasoline. Both UPSs and backup generators should be inspected and tested regularly. For backup generators, inspections should include the adequacy of the fuel supply.

CABLING SECURITY   If electrical or network cables are cut, the company will lose service. If network cables are tapped, an intruder can read the contents of packets. Where possible, wiring should run underground or within walls. Where this is not possible, wires should be run through **conduits** (preferably armored conduits) and should not be run through public areas. **Wiring closets**, where various wiring bundles are interconnected, should be locked and monitored.

---

[5] The author's wife is an archivist. The archive is located on the ground floor of a building that will be flooded in case of a hurricane or a very serious storm. At least it is not in a basement like many archives.

SECURITY DURING OFFSITE EQUIPMENT MAINTENANCE   Equipment maintenance is easy to overlook but crucial for availability. Equipment should be maintained according to the supplier's specification. If maintenance involves taking the equipment offsite, even temporarily, only authorized people should be allowed to remove the equipment. The equipment must be logged out and logged back in. In addition, when equipment is to be taken offsite, all sensitive information must be removed.

SECURITY OF EQUIPMENT OFF-PREMISES   When equipment is taken **off-premises** for maintenance or use, special care must be taken because of theft or loss, which not only deprive the firm of the physical computer asset but also may expose sensitive data. Off-site equipment should never be left unattended. If the equipment is for home use, there should be lockable filing cabinets, and all paperwork should be locked away when not in active use. Preferably, the equipment will be locked as well. Given the importance of portable device theft and loss, insurance is desirable.

SECURE DISPOSAL OR REUSE OF EQUIPMENT   When equipment is to be discarded, sensitive data must be removed before equipment **disposal**. This is true even if the equipment is to be reused within the firm. If the equipment is not to be reused, the hard drive should be physically destroyed or erased with **drive-wiping programs** that do not permit data to be recovered. (Reformatting a drive is not sufficient.)

REMOVAL OF PROPERTY   When property is removed for off-site use or disposal, this should only be done with proper authorization. In addition, there should be limits on who can provide this authorization. Typically, there will be time limits for off-site use. When equipment is taken in or out, in addition, this should be logged. Removal policies are often violated, so periodic spot checks are important.

TEST YOUR UNDERSTANDING

4. a. What is siting?
   b. Distinguish between UPSs and electrical generators.
   c. If wiring cannot be run through walls, what should be done to protect the wiring?
   d. What should be done to protect laptops taken off premises?
   e. What controls should be applied to off-site equipment maintenance?
   f. What controls should be applied to equipment disposal or reuse?
   g. What controls should be placed over employees taking equipment off-site?

Other Physical Security Issues

Although ISO/IEC 27002 Security Clause 9 is very comprehensive, there are several areas in which additional concern is needed.

TERRORISM   Due to increasing threats from terrorism, terrorist attacks must be considered in all matters of physical security. For instance, new buildings should be set back from streets and protected with rolling hill landscaping. In appropriate situations, guards may be armed. Bullet-proof doors may also be needed to guard sensitive areas.

Terrorism
  Building setback from street
  Armed guards
  Bullet-proof glass

Piggybacking
  Following an authorized user through a door
  Also called tailgating
  Psychologically difficult to prevent
  But can and should be done

Monitoring Equipment
  CCTV
  Tapes wear out
  High-resolution cameras are expensive and consume a great deal of disk space
  Low-resolution cameras may be insufficient for recognition needs

Dumpster[TM] Diving
  Protect trash that may contain sensitive information
  Maintain trash inside the corporate premises and monitor until removed

Desktop PC Security
  Locks that connect the computer to an immovable object
  Login screens and screen saver with strong passwords

FIGURE 5-4   Other Physical Security Issues (Study Figure)

PIGGYBACKING   Enforcing entrance controls is very difficult because of a social engineering trick called **piggybacking**. (It is also called **tailgating**.) When an authorized user opens a door with an access device, an intruder may follow the authorized user through. (Often, the intruder will approach a door with his or her arms loaded with papers and reach ineffectually in his or her pocket to get a key.)

   To not allow someone to piggyback after you seems very rude to most people, so the prohibition of piggybacking is difficult to enforce. However, unless piggybacking is eliminated, physical access security is nearly impossible. Although eliminating piggybacking is difficult, it is possible with effort. The author spent an hour in the entrance hall of one large computer firm and watched employees enter. Not one piggybacked on another. It simply was not done or tolerated by other employees.

MONITORING EQUIPMENT   ISO/IEC 27002 frequently refers to monitoring. Typically, this involves remote sensors that are connected by wire to a central security center. Typically, this security center is staffed by uniformed guards. If a sensor is activated, an alarm goes off in the security center. If a wire to a sensor is disabled, this should also set off an alarm.

   Sometimes monitoring involves **closed-circuit television (CCTV)**, which allows the security staff to see an area visually. CCTV systems must be selected very carefully. The firm should not use a system that uses videotape because videotape quality degrades rapidly with tape reuse.

In turn, digital CCTV systems, which store information on hard drives and digital backup tapes, vary widely in **image resolution**, which is the number of picture elements on the screen. Most digital security cameras have extremely low resolution, making subject identification questionable. High-resolution cameras exist, but they are expensive. In addition, high-resolution cameras require more storage capacity for recordings than low-resolution cameras.

To reduce storage burdens, many systems only record the video feed if there is motion. Some go beyond simple **motion detection** and only record the video feed when there is a *specific type* of motion, say when an object larger than a bird moves across the screen from left to right.

DUMPSTER™ DIVING   A final common building-related threat is **Dumpster™ diving**, in which an attacker goes through a firm's trash bins looking for documents, backup tapes, floppy disks, and other information-carrying media. The term *Dumpster* is trademarked, so we will use the term *building trash bins*. Building trash bins should be located in a secure and lighted area, preferably under CCTV surveillance. This area must be *on the company premises*, because once building trash bins are moved beyond the company premises, their contents usually are considered to be abandoned and have no legal protection.

DESKTOP PC SECURITY   To reduce the danger of theft, individual desktop PCs in ordinary office areas can be locked onto their desks with a cable—provided that there is something on the desk to wrap the cable around. In addition, each PC should have a login screen that requires a complex password and a screen saver so that an intruder cannot simply walk up to it and use it.

NOTEBOOK SECURITY   Security for notebooks that are taken off-site is a complex topic. We will wait until Chapter 7 to discuss it.

TEST YOUR UNDERSTANDING

5. **a.** What special controls are required by terrorism threats?
   b. Why is it necessary to prevent piggybacking?
   c. What advice would you give a company about CCTV?
   d. What is Dumpster™ diving?
   e. How should trash bins be protected?
   f. What can be done to reduce the dangers of desktop PC theft and unauthorized use?

REUSABLE PASSWORDS

There are many technologies for access control. Undoubtedly the most common is the password. To log onto a server, for instance, you normally need to know your account name (which is not secret) and its secret password. This is called a **reusable password** because it is used for weeks or months at a time. By contrast, a **one-time password** is only used once.

Password-Cracking Programs

Over a network, an attacker could try to log in repeatedly with different possible account names and passwords. However, such an attacker will almost always be locked out after a few attempts. Lockouts might frustrate users who cannot get into their locked-out accounts, but lockouts will not give attackers access to their resources.

If the attacker can physically enter a site, however, he or she has a much more effective way to crack passwords—installing a **password-cracking program**

Reusable Passwords
  A password that is used multiple times
  Almost all passwords are reusable passwords

Difficulty of Cracking Passwords by Guessing Remotely
  Account is usually locked after a few login failures

Password-Cracking Programs
  Password-cracking programs exist
      Run on a computer to crack its passwords or
      Run on a downloaded password file
  Brute-force password guessing
      Try all possible passwords of Length 1, Length 2, etc.
      Thwarted by passwords that are long and complex (using all keyboard characters)
          N is the password length, in characters
          Alphabet, no case: N^{26} possible passwords
          Alphabet, upper and lower case (N^{52})
          Alphanumeric (letters and digits) (N^{62})
          All keyboard characters ($\sim N^{80}$)
      With complexity, password length is very powerful (Figure 5-6)
  Dictionary attacks
      However, many people do not choose random passwords
      Dictionary attacks on common word passwords are almost instantaneous
          Names of people and pets
          Names of ports teams, etc.
      Hybrid dictionary attacks on common word variants (e.g., Processing1)

Other Password Threats
  Keystroke capture software
      Trojan horse displays a fake login screen, reports its finding to attackers
  Shoulder surfing
      Attacker watches as the victim types a password
      Even partial information can be useful
          Part of the password: P_ _sw_ _d
          Length of the password (reduces time to do brute-force cracking)

FIGURE 5-5 Server Password Cracking (Study Figure)

on a server. These programs try thousands of possible account name/password combinations per second until one works.

Another way to exploit a machine with physical access is to copy the password file and crack it later on another machine. This is less obtrusive than taking the time to run a password-cracking program on a server during an intrusion.

TEST YOUR UNDERSTANDING

6. **a.** What are reusable passwords?
   b. Why is password cracking over a network difficult to do?
   c. In what two ways can password-cracking programs be used?
   d. Which is safer for the cracker? Why?

Password Cracking Techniques

Password-cracking programs generally allow the attacker to use three cracking methods. These are brute-force guessing, dictionary attacks, and hybrid dictionary attacks.

BRUTE-FORCE GUESSING   The obvious approach to password cracking is to try all possible passwords on all (or selected) accounts. This **brute-force** approach tries all possible single-character passwords, and then all possible two-character passwords, and so forth.

The attacker can limit **brute-force guessing** to the 26 letters of the alphabet, to the 52 uppercase and lowercase letters, to the 62 alphanumeric characters (letters and the digits from 0 to 9), or to the approximately 75 characters that can be typed on a keyboard.

Broader character sets require the cracker to try many more combinations per character. If a password is N characters long, 26^N possible combinations must be tried if simple lowercase (or uppercase) letters are used. Using both uppercase and lowercase letters in passwords increases the number of combinations for N characters to 52^N. Using alphanumeric characters (both letters and numbers) increases this to 62^N, and using all keyboard characters increases the number of possible combinations to about 75^N. Passwords that use several types of keyboard characters are called **complex passwords**.

Passwords that use several types of keyboard characters are called complex passwords.

In addition to password complexity, **password length** is important to defend against brute-force attacks. Longer passwords require the cracking program to try more combinations to succeed. Figure 5-6 shows how password length is related to the number of possible passwords through which a password cracker has to search. Even in the simple situation of case-insensitive alphabetic passwords, the number of possibilities grows rapidly with password length. For two-character passwords, 676 possibilities exist with lowercase-only passwords. Increasing password length to four characters increases the number of possibilities to more than 400,000. With six characters, more

Password Length in Characters	Low Complexity: Alphabetic, No Case (N=26)	Alphabetic, Case-Sensitive (N=52)	Alphanumeric: Letters and Digits (N=62)	High Complexity: All Keyboard Characters (N=80)
1	26	52	62	80
2	676	2,704	3,844	6,400
4	456,976	7,311,616	14,776,336	40,960,000
6	308,915,776	19,770,609,664	56,800,235,584	2.62144E+11
8	2.08827E+11	5.34597E+13	2.1834E+14	1.67772E+15
10	1.41167E+14	1.44555E+17	8.39299E+17	1.07374E+19

Note: On average, an attacker will have to try half of all combinations.

FIGURE 5-6 Password Complexity and Length

than 300 million possibilities exist. Given the speed of the computers that can be used in password cracking, however, passwords today must be at least eight characters long, even if passwords vary by case and have digits and special characters.

> *Increasing password length exponentially increases brute-force password cracking time.*

On average, an attacker will have to try half of all possible combinations before finding the correct one. Due to randomness, however, brute-force guessing sometimes finds a password after only a small number of attempts.

DICTIONARY ATTACKS ON COMMON WORD PASSWORDS Few people have passwords that are true random combinations of letters, digits, and other keyboard characters. Instead, many users create **common word passwords**, such as *gasoline*. They may also use the names of relatives or pets. They may even use the dumbest password of all, *password.*

A Pentasafe Security Technologies survey of 15,000 staff members in 600 organizations in the United States and Europe found that 25 percent used common dictionary words. Fifty percent used the names of family members, friends, or pets. Thirty percent use the names of pop idols or sports heroes. Ten percent based their passwords on fictional characters. Only 10 percent used complex difficult-to-break passwords.[6]

Although there are millions of random combinations of characters that are at least eight characters long, there are only a few thousand common words in any language. **Dictionary attacks** compare passwords to lists of common words. If a user chooses a common word password, cracking it usually will take only a few seconds.

---

[6] The total exceeds 100 percent because some respondents gave multiple answers. Andrew Brown, "UK Study: Passwords Often Easy to Crack," CNN.com, March 13, 2002. http://www.cnn.com/2002/TECH/ptech/03/13/dangerous.passwords/index.html.

Adding lists of sports teams or celebrities to the dictionary will catch many other simple passwords.

Some users create long passwords by using phrases, such as *Nowisthetime*. Dictionary attacks also search for such common phrases.

HYBRID DICTIONARY ATTACKS   Many users try to modify common word passwords in simple ways, such as putting a single digit at the end of the word or capitalizing only the first letter. An example would be *Processing1*. **Hybrid dictionary attacks** try such simple modifications of common words.

OTHER PASSWORD THREATS

Keystroke Capture and Password-Stealing Programs   A **keystroke capture program** steals passwords as the user types them in and sends the keystrokes to the attacker. The attacker can then mine the keystroke data for account names and passwords. More directly, **password-stealing programs** present the user with a fake login screen and ask the person to log in again. It will then send this information to the attacker.[7]

Shoulder Surfing   There should be a policy that employees should never let someone watch as they enter a password—a practice known as **shoulder surfing**. An attacker may even benefit from getting partial information, such as the length of the password (which would greatly reduce the time needed for brute-force guessing) or partial information about the keys pressed (such as p*ss***d, where the stars indicate letters that could not be read). Shoulder surfers often talk to their victims during the password entry process because this slows typing time, making the letters easier to read.

TEST YOUR UNDERSTANDING

7. a. What is brute-force password guessing?
   b. Why is it important to not simply use all lowercase letters in passwords?
   c. What are complex passwords?
   d. Why is password length important?
   e. What is a dictionary attack?
   f. Why are dictionary attacks faster than brute-force guessing?
   g. What are hybrid dictionary attacks?

8. a. What do Trojan horse password capture programs do?
   b. What is shoulder surfing?
   c. Does the shoulder surfer have to read the entire password to be successful? Explain.

Password Policies

Given the large number of threats that face reusable passwords, companies need to have strong password policies.

---

[7] Password-stealing programs are necessary for operating system logins in which the data are only saved in an area of memory inaccessible to user programs (including keystroke capture programs). Most current operating systems have this protection. Of course, physical keystroke capture programs that plug into the keyboard cord do not benefit from this protection.

Password Strength Policies

Password policies must be long and complex

At least 8 characters long

Change of case, not at beginning

Digit (0–9), not at end

Other keyboard character, not at end

Example: tri6#Vial

Completely random passwords are best but usually are written down

Testing and enforcing passwords

Other Password Policies

Not using the same password at multiple sites

Password duration policies

Shared password policies (makes auditing impossible)

Disabling passwords that are no longer valid

Lost passwords (password resets)

Opportunities for social engineering attacks

Automated password resets use secret questions (Where were you born?)

Many can be guessed with a little research, rendering passwords useless

The End of Passwords?

Many firms want to eliminate passwords because of their weaknesses

Quite a few firms have already largely phased them out

FIGURE 5-7 Password Policies (Study Figure)

PASSWORD STRENGTH   It is important for corporations to have policies that require strong passwords. For example, a corporate policy might require that passwords have the following length and complexity characteristics:

- Be at least eight characters long.
- Have at least one change of case, not at the start of the password.
- Have at least one digit (0 through 9), not at the end of the password.
- Have at least one non-alphanumeric character, not at the end of the password.

An example of a password that fits all of these rules is tri6#Vial. It is nine characters long. Although it uses mostly lowercase letters, lowercase brute-force cracking will not work because of the digit (6), the special symbol (#), and the capital letter (V).

It may also be useful to create passwords from long phrases with complex character mixes. For instance, "In 1492, Columbus sailed the ocean blue" could give the password, "i1492,Cstob" (if a comma is allowed).

TRULY RANDOM PASSWORDS   Although tri6#Vial is a reasonably strong password, the best passwords are long and truly random strings of uppercase letters, lowercase letters, digits, and special characters. Unfortunately, such passwords are almost impossible to memorize, and few users will even try to memorize them. Instead, users will write them down next to their computer or even on the edge of the display. This may be even more dangerous than using a somewhat meaningful string that users actually will memorize, such as is tri6#Vial.

For extremely important accounts, such as super user accounts, however, very long random passwords are a must. These passwords should be written down and then locked away securely.

TESTING AND ENFORCING THE STRENGTH OF PASSWORDS   Systems administrators can run a password-cracking program against their own servers to check for policy violations in password length and complexity. In addition, most operating systems can now be set up to enforce the selection of relatively strong passwords by users.

Password testing using cracking programs should *never* be done without written permission from the tester's superior. Even if testing is implicit or explicit in the tester's job description, the tester risks being fired or even prosecuted if the company suspects that the tester is doing a specific test for illicit purposes.

TEST YOUR UNDERSTANDING

9. a. What is the book's recommended password policy for length and complexity?
   b. How can password-cracking programs be used to enforce password strength policy?
   c. Before you run a password cracking program on your company's computers to check for weak passwords, what should you do?

Other Password Policies

Although creating strong passwords is important, a company needs other password use and management policies.

NOT USING THE SAME PASSWORD AT MULTIPLE SITES   People often use the same password at multiple sites. For instance, a 2005 study by Cyota found that 44 percent of people surveyed used the same password at multiple sites, and 37 percent of online banking customers used the same password at less secure sites. When passwords are used at multiple sites, if a password is compromised at one site, it is compromised at all sites. In fact, attackers sometimes invite someone to an attractive site and let them pick their own username and password. The attackers then try that username and password at other sites the victim is likely to use.

Having a policy that users must use different passwords at different sites is important, but it is very difficult to enforce. For users to remember different passwords at different sites is very difficult. Using different passwords is even difficult if the passwords are written in a password book.

To address this difficulty of use, there are **password management programs** that manage multiple passwords automatically. These programs automatically generate strong passwords for each site and remember these passwords. Unfortunately, these promising programs are somewhat cumbersome to use, especially if the user has several different computers and must share password information across these computers.

PASSWORD DURATION POLICIES   Password policies also should require the frequent changing of passwords. User passwords should be changed perhaps every 90 days. This way, if an attacker learns a password, he or she will only be able to use it for a limited time. Crucial passwords should be changed more frequently. In addition, users should be forbidden from reusing an older password for the account to prevent a user from cycling through a handful of passwords.

POLICIES PROHIBITING SHARED ACCOUNTS   One especially dangerous password practice is having several people in a group share a single account. Each person will log in with the same account name and password. Shared account names and passwords are bad for three reasons:

- First, shared passwords are rarely changed because of the number of people who must be coordinated. The longer a password goes unchanged, the longer a hacker can use the password if he or she has cracked it.
- Second, because "everybody knows" the shared password, users are likely to give it out freely to people who should not have it.
- Third, and most seriously, if the account is used inappropriately, it will be impossible to tell from audit logs which member of the group committed the attack because any member of the group could have committed the infraction.

Overall, companies should have clear policies that prohibit shared accounts. All operating systems and secure application programs allow systems administrators to create **groups** from a list of individual accounts. If the systems administrator assigns access permissions to the group, the accounts of individual members of the group automatically inherit those permissions. The individuals can then log in with their own account names and passwords. This way, there is no loss of individual identity in logins and subsequent audits.

DISABLING PASSWORDS THAT ARE NO LONGER VALID   Many accounts and passwords in corporations are inappropriate because the owner has left the firm, because the owner has a different position in the firm, because the account was a temporary one for a contractor, and for other reasons. The International Data Corporation has estimated that 30 percent to 60 percent of all accounts in large corporations are inappropriate. Strong policies and effective procedures should be in place for disabling accounts that become inappropriate.

Unfortunately, it is difficult to keep accounts updated. While special action is almost always needed to create accounts, if no action is taken afterward, accounts normally continue to exist eternally. Although the firm-wide identity management systems discussed later in this chapter can cancel all accounts when someone leaves the firm, there usually are no similar protections when someone leaves a project team or takes a different position in the firm.

One option is to assign someone to be the owner of logical groups of accounts and require this person to confirm the suitability of accounts frequently. At the very least, they can be required to review lists of accounts that have not been used recently.

LOST PASSWORDS   Lost passwords prompt roughly a quarter to a third[8] of all calls to help desks. Therefore, handling lost passwords is a large problem. At the same time, dealing with lost passwords is dangerous.

Password Resets   Help desk employees cannot read existing passwords, but they normally have the ability to create a new password for an account. This action is called, not entirely accurately, a **password reset**. Usually, this password is temporary. The next time the user logs in, he or she must change the password.

The Danger of "Lost Password" Social Engineering Attacks   A major social engineering danger is that an attacker will call the help desk claiming to be the owner of an account and request a password reset, usually expressing extreme urgency and authority. A harried help desk employee might yield to pressure and reset the account password. Afterward, the attacker effectively would control the account. In addition, the proper account owner would be locked out.

Automating Password Resets   Password resets are very expensive. For example, the Wellpoint company received 14,000 calls each month from employees who had lost their passwords.[9] The company's help desk labor cost for a reset was at least $25 and could range up to $200 if the employee had access to multiple systems.

To reduce the cost of password resets, Wellpoint and many firms now use **automated password reset systems**. To use such a system, an employee logs into the password reset system and types his or her account name. He or she is then asked "Where were you born?" or another question that the employee answered when he or she first received the account. If the employee answers correctly, he or she is allowed to create a new password for the account.

Although the idea is simple, it is difficult to create good password reset questions for people to answer.

- Some questions are themselves security violations. For instance, some questions ask for sensitive information, such as social security number or mother's maiden name (which many banks still use to identify people).
- Some questions can be answered by an attacker who has done a little research, such as "In what city were you born?" or "What is your pet's name?"
- For some questions, the subject will not be able to remember their answer. For instance, in the question, "Who was your favorite teacher in high school?" remembering the answer originally given might be difficult for someone who had several favorite teachers in high school.
- For some questions, spelling might be a problem, for instance, in "What was the name of your favorite teacher in high school?"

In general, it is good to provide several reasonable questions that do not ask for sensitive information and that could not be answered with research about the party, and then have the person select one or more questions to answer.

---

[8] These are widely quoted percentages. For specific data, see David Lewis, "Bank Cuts Help Desk Costs," *Internetweek*, October 22, 2001. http://www.internetweek.com/netresults01/net102201.htm.

[9] Alexander Salkever, "Software That Asks 'Who Goes There?'" *SecurityFocus*, February 26, 2002. Online.security.focus.com/news/339.

Are Password Resets Secure?   Although password resets are a fact of corporate life, they are a serious security threat. A chain of security is only as strong as its weakest link, and the password reset is potentially the weakest link in the use of passwords—especially the self-service password reset.

One controversial way to strengthen password security is to eliminate self-service password resets completely for higher-security accounts. This will add to help desk costs, but the reduction in risk may be well justified.

In fact, for high-risk accounts, help desk password resets over the phone might be banned. If you lose your ATM PIN, you usually are required to go into a bank branch and show identification before you get a new PIN. In addition, you may have to wait a few days while the bank's central headquarters okays the revised PIN.

Convenience is good, but it may need to be limited in password resets when security risks are high.

TEST YOUR UNDERSTANDING

10. **a.** Why is it a problem to use the same password at multiple sites?
    b. Why is it difficult to enforce a policy of using a different password at each site?
    c. Why are password duration policies important?
    d. What are password resets?
    e. Why are password resets dangerous?
    f. How can password resets be automated?
    g. Why are password reset questions difficult to create?
    h. How may password resets be handled in high-risk environments?

The End of Passwords?

Although passwords are widely used, there is nearly total agreement among security professionals that passwords are no longer safe. Growing computer power has made simple passwords so fast to crack that only the longest and most complex passwords are safe. However, when users are forced to use very long and complex passwords, they usually write them down or circumvent their strength in other ways. Passwords are likely to be phased out in the fairly near future. Quite a few firms have already largely phased them out, and many others will soon do so. We will now begin to look at alternative authentication technologies for companies to use in the post-password world.

TEST YOUR UNDERSTANDING

11. What is the likely future of passwords?

ACCESS CARDS AND TOKENS

One approach to replacing reusable passwords is to have people carry small physical devices to authenticate them. These physical devices usually are divided into two categories—access cards and tokens.

Access Cards

  Magnetic stripe cards

  Smart cards

    Have a microprocessor and RAM

    Can implement public key encryption for challenge/response authentication

  In selection decision, must consider cost and availability of card readers

Tokens

  Constantly changing password devices for one-time passwords

  USB plug-in tokens

Proximity Access Tokens

  Use Radio Frequency ID (RFID) technology

  Supplicant only has to be near a door or computer to be recognized

Addressing Loss and Theft

  Both are frequent

  Card cancellation

    Requires a wired network for cancellation speed

    Must cancel quickly if risks are considerable

Two-Factor Authentication Needed because of Ease of Loss and Theft

  PINs (Personal Identification Numbers) for the second factor

    Short: 4 to 6 digits

    Can be short because attempts are manual

    Should not choose obvious combinations (1111, 1234) or important dates

  Other forms of two-factor authentication

    Store fingerprint template on device; check supplicant with a fingerprint reader

---

FIGURE 5-8 Access Cards and Tokens (Study Figure)

Access Cards

Figure 5-9 shows that an **access card** is a plastic card that usually is the size of a credit or debit card. Normally, the person wishing access to a door or a computer slides the access card through a reader or pushes it into a reader. This is exactly what you do when you use a credit or debit card at a retail store.

MAGNETIC STRIPE CARDS The simplest access cards use magnetic stripes like the ones on your credit cards. Magnetic stripes can store authentication data about the individual. If you have traveled recently, you know that **magnetic stripe cards** are often used for hotel room access.

SMART CARDS A **smart card** looks like a magnetic stripe card but has a built-in microprocessor and memory. This allows smart cards to do processing for more sophisticated authentication. For instance, it could do public key encryption for challenge/response authentication, encrypting the challenge message with the user's private key. Smart cards can also give out information differentially to

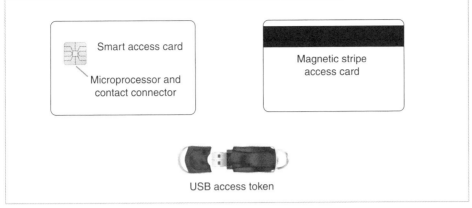

FIGURE 5-9 Access Cards and Tokens

different applications. While magnetic stripe cards are passive, only containing data, smart cards are active.

CARD READER COSTS   A problem with both magnetic stripe access cards and smart card access cards is the cost and availability of the **card readers**. Although individual readers are not expensive, installing many of them is collectively very expensive. In addition, if someone needs to use a computer that does not have a card reader, he or she cannot do so if access card authentication is mandatory.

Tokens

To play a slot machine, you insert a token into the coin slot. The token represents a coin. In general, a token is something that represents something else. An authentication **token** represents the person wishing to be authenticated.

> *A token is something that represents something else. An authentication token represents the person wishing to be authenticated.*

ONE-TIME-PASSWORD TOKENS   A **one-time-password token** is a small device with a display that has a number that changes frequently. Users must type the current number into key locks or into their computers. Using a one-time password avoids the need for reusable passwords, which, as we saw earlier, often are easy to defeat.

USB TOKENS   A USB token is simpler. A **USB token** is simply a small device that plugs into a computer's USB port to identify the owner. USB tokens give many of the protections of smart cards without requiring the cost of a smart card reader on each PC.

Proximity Access Tokens

One problem with both access cards and USB tokens is the need to make physical contact with a reader or USB port. A new alternative is the **proximity access token**, which contains a small **radio frequency ID (RFID)** tag. When a supplicant nears a computer or door, a radio transmitter at the computer or door sends out a radio signal. This radio signal's power is partially absorbed by the RFID tag, which uses this power to transmit identification information contained in the tag. With a proximity token, a person can simply walk up to a computer or door and be admitted.[10]

Addressing Loss and Theft

Although physical access devices can enhance security, they need to be managed carefully due to their frequent loss and theft. The finder or thief may be able to use the access device to gain unauthorized entry.

PHYSICAL DEVICE CANCELLATION   One response to theft and loss is to disable compromised devices. For instance, in hotels, if you lose your room access card, a front desk employee will disable the old card's access to all locks. The employee will then give you a new card for your room. The new card will have a new access code.

Cancellation requires installing wiring from the security center to individual verification devices. However, access device loss is so common that dealing actively with lost access devices is mandatory. (Access device security usually also requires connections to log access events for auditing purposes.)

How fast must cancellation be? This is a matter for risk analysis that balances the cost of faster cancellation against the cost of break-ins that are likely to occur during the time before cancellation.

TWO-FACTOR AUTHENTICATION   Two-factor authentication, which we saw briefly earlier in this chapter, requires the use of two different authentication methods. The access device would only be one of these methods. As noted at the beginning of this chapter, two-factor authentication has limitations, but it is still useful in many cases.

PINs   Some firms require employees to type **personal identification numbers (PINs)** when they use physical access devices. Typically, these PINs are only four to six digits. Passwords need to be long because attackers can try millions of comparisons per second. However, people must enter PINs manually, so attackers can only enter a PIN every second or two. In addition, someone standing over an access door trying many PIN codes would be highly conspicuous and therefore vulnerable to detection. Still, the company should ban easily guessed PINs such as 1111, 2222, 1234, the last four digits of the user's social security number, or an important personal date in month/day format, such as the supplicant's birthday or wedding anniversary.

Companies should aggressively ban the recording of the PIN on the card or in the wallet a person uses to carry the card. Such practices negate the benefits of two-factor authentication.

---

[10] Passive RFID tags can only be read over a very small range. One half-way measure is to have the person tap the reader with his or her proximity card. This is less work than swiping a card and is likely to work more reliably. However, this is more work than merely walking up to a door or computer. In particular, tapping may require the person to wear it on a stretchable lanyard around the neck or may require the user to tap a wallet containing the access token against the reader. Active RFID tags have their own batteries and can be read over a longer range. However, active RFID tags are more expensive, and if the battery dies, the active RFID tag is useless.

Other Forms of Two-Factor Authentication   There are many other ways to do two-factor authentication. For instance, a smart card can contain the access device owner's fingerprint. The person using the physical access device would also have to run a finger over a fingerprint scanner to verify that he or she is the legitimate user of the devices.

TEST YOUR UNDERSTANDING

12. **a.** Distinguish between magnetic stripe cards and smart cards.
    b. What are one-time-password tokens?
    c. What are USB tokens?
    d. What is the advantage of USB tokens compared to cards?
    e. What is the attraction of proximity tokens?

13. **a.** Why is it important to disable lost or stolen access devices?
    b. Give an example of two-factor authentication not mentioned in the text.
    c. What is a PIN?
    d. Why can PINs be short—only four to six digits—while passwords must be much longer?

BIOMETRIC AUTHENTICATION

Biometrics

We forget passwords. We lose access cards. Yet despite jokes about leaving our heads at home, we always take our bodies with us. This allows **biometric authentication**, which is based on biological (bio) measurements (metrics). Biometric authentication is based on something you are (your fingerprint, iris pattern, face, hand geometry, and so forth) or something you do (write, type, and so forth). The major promise of biometrics is to make reusable passwords obsolete.

Biometric Authentication
Authentication based on biological (bio) measurements (metrics)
    Biometric authentication is based on something you are (your fingerprint, iris pattern, face, hand geometry, and so forth)
    Or something you do (write, type, and so forth)
A major promise of biometrics is to make reusable passwords obsolete

Biometric Systems (Figure 5-11)
Enrollment (enrollment scan, process for key features, store template)
    Scan data are variable (scan fingerprint differently each time)
    Key features extracted from the scan should be nearly the same
Later access attempts provide access data, which will be turned into key feature data for comparison with the template
Biometric access key features will never be exactly the same as the template
There must be configurable decision criteria for deciding how close a match (match index) to require
    Requiring an overly exact match index will cause many false rejections
    Requiring too loose a match index will cause more false acceptances

---

FIGURE 5-10 Biometric Authentication (Study Figure)

The major promise of biometrics is to make reusable passwords obsolete.

TEST YOUR UNDERSTANDING

14. **a.** What is biometric authentication?
    b. On what two things about you is biometric authentication based?
    c. What is the major promise of biometrics?

Biometric Systems

ENROLLMENT   Figure 5-11 shows a biometric authentication system. Each user must first be **enrolled** in the system. Enrollment has three steps:

- The reader **scans** each person's biometric data. This **enrollment scan** creates far too much data to use. In addition, the scan data will be different each time the user is scanned.
- The reader then processes the enrollment scan data to extract a few **key features** from the mass of scanned data. These few key features, not the entire set of scanned data, will be used to identify or verify the user in the future.
- The reader finally sends the key feature data to the database, which stores the key feature data as the user's **template**.

Why not use entire scans instead of key features? The problem is that entire scans are not very useful in raw form. If a person swipes his or her finger at different angles, raw scan files will be very different, but key features such as the relative locations of loops and whorls in fingerprints will be the same or almost the same no matter how a finger is scanned.

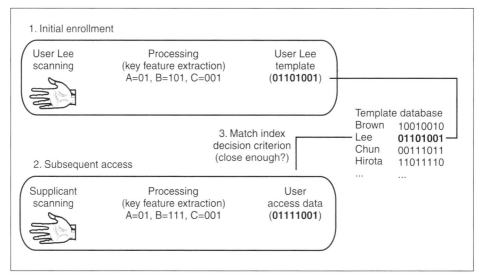

FIGURE 5-11   Biometric Authentication System

LATER ACCESS ATTEMPTS   When users later wish to be authenticated, they are scanned again. The reader processes this **supplicant scanning** information to create key features. These key features become the **user access data**. The central system matches the user access data against the person's template in the database.

ACCEPTANCE OR REJECTION   When a system receives access data, it computes a **match index**, which is the difference between the scan's key features and the template. There is never a perfect match, because scanning never works exactly the same way twice. If the error is smaller than a value called the **decision criterion**, the supplicant is accepted as a match. If not, the supplicant is rejected as a match.

TEST YOUR UNDERSTANDING

15. **a.** Describe the three scanner actions in the enrollment process.
    b. What are key features?
    c. Why are they necessary?
    d. What does the server do with the key features created by the enrollment scan?
    e. What is a template?
    f. What is user access data?
    g. What are match indices, and how are they related to decision criteria?

Biometric Errors

Access control requires high accuracy. Unfortunately, there are many questions about the reliability of various types of biometric authentication. One issue is **error rate**, which refers to accuracy when the supplicant is *not* trying to deceive the system. The other accuracy issue is the **deception rate**, which is the likelihood that an impostor will be able to deceive the system if he or she tries. For now, we will focus on error rates.

Caution: The following material is difficult to learn because there are several related concepts that are easy to confuse. Slow way down as you study this section, and keep comparing what you are reading with what you have already read.

FALSE ACCEPTANCE RATE (FAR)   An acceptance means that the person is matched to a particular template. As we have just seen, a **false acceptance** is a match to a template that should not be made. The rate of false acceptances as a percentage of total access attempts is called the **false acceptance rate (FAR)**.

An acceptance means that the person is matched to a particular template.
   A false acceptance is a match to a template that should not be made.
      The rate of false acceptances as a percentage of total access attempts is called the false acceptance rate (FAR).

False acceptances have different implications for different uses, for instance, in door or computer access versus terrorist watch lists.

- For access to a computer or a door, a false acceptance means an impostor is matched with a legitimate template and therefore should be given access. As a consequence, an impostor can get in (even without attempting deception). This is a serious security violation.
- For terrorist watch list matching, in contrast, a false acceptance means incorrectly matching a person to the list—in other words, marking an innocent person as a terrorist. This will inconvenience the person falsely matched, but it is not a security breakdown. If there are too many false acceptances, however, complaints may force the system to be discontinued.
- For watch list access to an equipment room, in turn, false acceptances are security problems, while false rejections are merely inconvenient.

FALSE REJECTION RATE (FRR) In a **false rejection**, in turn, the supplicant is incorrectly rejected as a match to a template when the applicant should be accepted as a match. The **false rejection rate (FRR)**, then, is the probability that the system will reject a person who should be matched to a template.

> *The false rejection rate (FRR) is the probability that the system will reject a person who should be matched to a template.*

Note that false rejections, like false acceptances, have different implications for different uses—door or computer access versus terrorist watch lists.

- For instance, in access to a computer, a false rejection means that a legitimate user is denied access. Although not necessarily bad from a security viewpoint, a high FRR for computer or door access can lead to a great deal of user dissatisfaction, and this can kill the system.
- For watch lists, false rejection means that a person who should be identified as being on a watch list is not. If this is a terrorist watch list, this means that a terrorist goes unidentified. This is a serious security violation. If it is a door access watch list for an equipment room, then it is merely an inconvenience.

WHICH IS WORSE? Which is worse, then—a false acceptance or a false rejection? It obviously depends on the context. In door or server access, a false acceptance allows an attacker in and is a serious violation. A false rejection is simply an inconvenience. For terrorist watch list matching, however, a false rejection (a failure to match an attacker to a watch list template) is a major security violation. A false acceptance, in turn, is only a nuisance.

VENDOR CLAIMS Unfortunately, vendor claims for FARs and FRRs often are misleading. They usually are based on highly idealized situations that are not representative of real-world conditions. For instance, we have seen that the false acceptance rate increases as the number of templates increases because there is a small false acceptance probability for each template. To take advantage of this, many vendors base FAR estimates on databases with only a few templates.

In addition, vendors enroll users under ideal circumstances and have ideal situations for the access attempt. For instance, in face recognition, their test subjects might be very well lit and looking straight forward for both enrollment and access attempts—conditions that are not likely to occur in the real world. This can make a vendor's reported false rejection rate lower than it would be in practice.

FAILURE TO ENROLL (FTE) There is another type of error, **failure to enroll (FTE)**. This occurs if the system will not enroll. For instance, in the case of fingerprint authentication, some people do not have well-defined fingerprints due to age, years of construction labor, long clerical paper handling, or other reasons. In some cases, this can make a fingerprint authentication system useless.

TEST YOUR UNDERSTANDING

16. **a.** In biometrics, what is a match?
    b. Distinguish between false acceptances and false rejections.
    c. What are false acceptance rates (FARs) and false rejection rates (FRRs)?
    d. For computer access, why is a false acceptance bad?
    e. Why is a false rejection bad?
    f. Which is worse from a security viewpoint?
    g. Which is worse from a user acceptance viewpoint?

17. **a.** For watch lists of criminals, what is a false acceptance?
    b. For watch lists of criminals, which is worse from a security viewpoint, a false acceptance or a false rejection? Explain.
    c. For watch lists of people who should be allowed to enter a room, what is a false acceptance?
    d. For watch lists of people who should be allowed to enter a room, which is worse from a security viewpoint, a false acceptance or a false rejection? Explain.

18. What is failure to enroll?

Verification, Identification, and Watch Lists

VERIFICATION Biometric authentication has one of three possible goals. In **verification**, a supplicant claims to be a particular person, and the challenge is to measure the supplicant's biometric access data against the template of the person he or she claims to be. When you log into a server with a username and password, this is verification.

> *In verification, the verifier determines whether the supplicant is a particular person.*

Every time a match is attempted, there is a danger of a false match, meaning that the template data may match the applicant's access data when there should not be a match. This danger usually is small, and because verification only matches the access data to a single template, there is only one chance of a false match.

To give an example, if the probability of a false acceptance is one in a thousand, then probability of a false acceptance is one in a thousand because only one match is attempted. There is a false acceptance rate (FAR) of 0.1 percent.

Verification

Supplicant claims to be a particular person

Is the supplicant who he or she claims to be?

Compare access data to a single template (the claimed experiment)

Verification is good to replace passwords in logins

If the probability of a false acceptance (false match) probability is 1/1,000 per template match,

    the probability of a false acceptance is 1/1,000 (0.1%)

Identification

Supplicant does not state his or her identity

System must compare their data to *all* templates to find the correct template

If the probability of a false acceptance (false match) probability is 1/1,000 per template match,

    and if there are 500 templates in the database, then

    the probability of a false acceptance is 500 * 1/1,000 (50%)

Identification is good for door access and other situations where entering a name would be difficult

Watch Lists

Subset of identification

Goal is to identify members of a group:

    Terrorists

    People who should be given access to an equipment room

More comparisons than validation but fewer than identification, so the risk of a false acceptance is intermediate

If the probability of a false acceptance (false match) probability is 1/1,000 per template match,

    and if there are 10 templates in the watch list, then

    the probability of a false acceptance is 10 * 1/1,000 (1%)

FIGURE 5-12 Biometric Verification, Identification, and Watch Lists (Study Figure)

IDENTIFICATION In **identification**, in contrast, the supplicant does not claim to be a particular person. It is the job of the system to identify the supplicant, that is, to determine who he or she is.

In identification, the verifier determines the identity of the supplicant.

In identification, the supplicant's biometric access data must be matched against the templates of *everyone whose template is stored in the system*. If the system finds no matches, it rejects the supplicant.

In identification, the system makes many matches between the applicant's access data and the templates in the system. With each match, there is a small danger of a false match (false acceptance). Given the many matches required in identification compared with the single match required in verification, the chance of a false match is much higher in identification than it is in verification.

For example, suppose that the probability of a false match per template is 1/1000. Suppose also that there are 500 templates in the database. Then there will be 500 match attempts, and the FAR will be 1/1000 times 500 or 50 percent. This is 500 times the false acceptance rate for verification.

On the positive side, identification frees users from the need to type their names or account names. Identification is best for door access control and other situations in which identity claims cannot be made by the supplicant.

WATCH LISTS A limited but increasingly important form of identification is the **watch list**, which identifies a person as being a member of a group. For instance, the matches may be made against the templates of people on a terrorist watch list. Or, matches may be made against the members of a repair team who should be allowed to enter a room. Watch list matching makes more access data–template comparisons than verification and so is more prone to false acceptances. However, watch list matching makes fewer comparisons than full identification and so is less susceptible to false acceptances.

TEST YOUR UNDERSTANDING

19. **a.** Distinguish between verification and identification.
    b. Which requires more matches against templates?
    c. Which is more likely to generate a false acceptance? Why?
    d. Compare identification with watch list matching.
    e. Which is more likely to generate a false match? Why?

20. Suppose that the probability of a false acceptance is one in a million, that there are 10,000 identities in the database, and that there is a watch list with 100 people.

    a. What will be the FAR for verification?
    b. For identification?
    c. For the watch list?

Biometric Deception

Although errors are a serious concern, deception is even more troublesome. A biometric system with low error rates is useless if it can be deceived effectively with reasonable effort.

In **deception**, an attacker deliberately attempts to fool the system. For instance, many fingerprint scanners can be fooled if the adversary lifts a latent (invisible) fingerprint from a glass, puts it on a gelatin finger, and places the fake finger on the fingerprint scanner.

In deception, an attacker deliberately attempts to fool the system.

In watch list matching with a surveillance camera system at an airport, an attacker may walk into an airport and keep his or her head down and wear a brimmed hat to deceive the matching algorithm.

Errors versus Deception

False Acceptance Rates (FARs)

Percentage of people who are identified or verified as matched to a template but should not be

False Rejection Rates (FRRs)

Percentage of people who should be identified or verified as matches to a template but are not

Can be reduced by allowing multiple access attempts

Which Is Worse?

Situation	False acceptance	False rejection
Identification for computer access	Security Violation	Inconvenience
Verification for computer access	Security Violation	Inconvenience
Watch list for door access	Security Violation	Inconvenience
Watch list for terrorists	Inconvenience	Security Violation

Vendor Claims for FARs and FRRs

Tend to be exaggerated through tests under ideal conditions

Failure to Enroll (FTE)

Subject cannot enroll in system

(poor fingerprints due to construction work, clerical work, age, etc.)

Deception

Errors: when subject is not trying to fool the system

Deception: when subject is trying to fool the system

Hide face from cameras used for face identification

Impersonate someone by using a gelatin finger on a fingerprint scanner

Etc.

Many biometric methods are highly vulnerable to deception

Fingerprint scanners should only be used where the threat of deception is very low

Fingerprint scanners are better than passwords because there is nothing to forget

Fingerprint scanners are good for convenience rather than security

FIGURE 5-13 Biometric Errors and Deception (Study Figure)

Deception rates are largely unknown, except for fingerprint scanners, for which deception *frequently* works—often, unsophisticated deception.

Fortunately, for many assets, deception is *not* a critical issue. For instance, an ordinary person without sensitive information on a notebook computer is not likely to face a sophisticated attacker. In the case of notebooks without sensitive information, fingerprint readers mainly exist to eliminate passwords, which are too frequently weak and are too frequently written down by users.

TEST YOUR UNDERSTANDING

21. **a.** Distinguish between error rates and deception in biometrics.
    b. Why may fingerprint scanning, which is often deceived, be acceptable for entry into a supplies cabinet?
    c. When may it not be sufficient?

Biometric Methods

FINGERPRINT RECOGNITION   Thanks to crime movies, almost everyone is familiar with fingerprint recognition. **Fingerprint recognition** technology is well developed and inexpensive. Fingerprint scanners are cheap enough to be added to computers and even small hand-held devices. Due to their low cost, fingerprint scanners account for most of the total biometrics market.

Unfortunately, as just noted, fingerprint recognition technology often is easy to deceive. In 2002, researchers were able to defeat 80 percent of fingerprint recognition systems by creating a gelatin finger from a **latent print** (that is, an invisible print left

---

Fingerprint Recognition

Simple, inexpensive, well proven

Most biometrics today is fingerprint recognition

Often can be defeated with latent fingerprints on glasses copied to gelatin fingers

However, fingerprint recognition can take the place of reusable passwords for low-risk applications

Iris Recognition

Pattern in colored part of eye

Uses a camera (no light is shined into eye, as in Hollywood movies)

Very low FARs

Very expensive

Face Recognition

Surreptitious (without the person's knowledge) identification is possible (in airports, etc.)

High error rates, even without deception

Hand Geometry for Door Access

Shape of hand

Reader is very large, so usually used for door access

Voice Recognition

High error rates

Easily deceived by recordings

Other Forms of Biometric Authentication

Veins in the hand

Keystroke recognition (pace in typing password)

Signature recognition (hand-written signature)

Gait (way the person walks) recognition

FIGURE 5-14   Biometric Methods (Study Figure)

on a glass or other object).[11] Fingerprint readers that can better detect deception use measures such as measuring skin capacitance and even pulse rates. However, these types of fingerprint readers are expensive and so are less widely used.

Given that fingerprint scanners can be deceived, we have noted that they should only be used in applications for which there is little danger of serious deception. An example would be logging into a personal computer that does not hold sensitive information.

IRIS RECOGNITION   The iris is the colored part of your eye. Irises are far more complex and individual than fingerprints. In fact, **iris recognition** is the most precise form of biometric authentication, with very low FARs. In general, iris scanning is the gold standard in biometric authentication today. Unfortunately, like gold, it is expensive.

Iris scanners can read iris patterns from several centimeters to a meter or so away.[12] In movies, iris scanning typically is shown shining a red laser beam shining into the supplicant's eye. This is complete nonsense. With iris scanners, people simply look into ordinary cameras. There is typically a small TV monitor to help the supplicant ensure that he or she is looking directly into the camera.

FACE RECOGNITION   Facial features can be read from several meters away. This makes **face recognition** useful for door access control. However, face recognition is highly sensitive to lighting differences between the scanned image stored on the computer and the situation in which the scan is taken. It also is moderately sensitive to changes in facial features such as facial hair, and it is often very sensitive to deception by people turning their faces away from the camera.

The only major benefit of face recognition is that it can be used **surreptitiously**, that is, without the subject's knowledge. This makes it seem to be good for surveillance cameras searching for criminals and terrorists. However, its high error rates and the ease with which it can be deceived make its use for criminal and terrorist watch lists highly suspect.

HAND GEOMETRY   Human **hand geometry**, including finger length, finger width, palm width, and other characteristics, is fairly easy to measure and is used mostly in door access control because of the size of hand geometry scanners. The user simply places his or her hand on a scanner the size of a textbook.

VOICE RECOGNITION   Fingerprint, iris, face, hand geometry, and vein recognition are examples of something you *are*. **Voice recognition**, in contrast, is based on something you *do*, namely speak. Unfortunately, voice recognition is easily deceived by recordings. In addition, high false rejection rates make voice recognition frustrating to users.

---

[11] "Doubt Cast on Fingerprint Security," BBC News, May 17, 2002. http://news.bbc.co.uk/hi/english/sci/tech/newsid_1991000/1991517.stm.

[12] In contrast, retinal scanning, which is based on patterns in the retina at the back of the eyeball, requires users to press their eye sockets against a reader; many users will not do this. Although movies frequently mention retinal scanning, it is rare in practice—*Biometrics, Identity.*

OTHER FORMS OF BIOMETRIC AUTHENTICATION There are many other forms of biometric authentication—the recognition of veins in the hand, keystroke recognition (typing pace between levels), written signature recognition, and the recognition of gait (way of walking), to name just a few. However, fingerprint, iris, face, and hand geometry are the most widely used types of biometric authentication today, and fingerprint recognition is dominant.

TEST YOUR UNDERSTANDING

22. **a.** What is the advantage of fingerprint recognition?
    b. What are the disadvantages?
    c. For what type of use is fingerprint recognition sufficient?
    d. What is the advantage of iris recognition?
    e. What are the disadvantages?
    f. Does iris scanning shoot light into your eye?

23. **a.** What is the advantage of face recognition?
    b. What does surreptitious mean?
    c. Where is hand geometry recognition used?
    d. What are the disadvantages of voiceprint recognition?
    e. What are the most widely used forms of biometric authentication?
    f. What is the most widely used form of biometrics?

CRYPTOGRAPHIC AUTHENTICATION

Key Points from Chapters 3

In Chapter 3, we looked at cryptographic authentication in the context of cryptographic systems. Cryptographic authentication is the gold standard in authentication. It is the most secure form of authentication if it is implemented properly. Like gold, it also is the most expensive form of authentication. Chapter 3 made several key points:

- In cryptographic systems, there are two forms of authentication—initial authentication at the beginning of the dialogues and message-by-message authentication with electronic signatures for all messages in the dialogue.
- We looked at MS-CHAP for initial authentication using passwords.
- We then looked at two forms of electronic signatures. Key-hashed message authentication codes (HMACs) are fast and inexpensive, but they lack nonrepudiation.
- Digital signatures use public key encryption and digital certificates to give extremely strong but slow authentication.
- Although Chapter 3 did not discuss it, public key authentication with digital certificates is also useful for initial authentication.[13]

Public Key Infrastructures (PKIs)

Using public key authentication with digital certificates requires the organization to establish a **public key infrastructure (PKI)** to create and manage public key–private key pairs and digital certificates. Figure 5-16 illustrates the functions of a PKI.

---

[13] More precisely, this was left to a thought question.

Key Points from Chapter 3

Cryptographic systems have initial and message-by-message authentication

MS-CHAP uses passwords for initial authentication

Electronic signatures provide message-by-message authentication

> Key-Hashed Message Authentication Codes (HMACs) are fast and inexpensive

> Digital signatures with digital certificates are extremely strong but slow

Chapter 3 did not mention that digital certificates are also good for initial authentication

Public Key Infrastructures (PKIs) (Figure 5-16)

Firms can be their own certificate authorities (CAs)

But this requires a great deal of labor

Provisioning

> Giving the user access credentials

> Human registration is often the weakest link

>> If an impostor can deceive the provisioning authority, the system breaks down

>> Controlling the giving of access credentials is the prime authentication problem

>> If an impostor is given credentials, no technology access controls will work

>> Limit who can submit names for registration

>> Limit who can authorize registration

>> Have rules for exceptions

> Must have effective terminating procedures

> Supervisors and Human Resources department must assist

FIGURE 5-15 Cryptographic Authentication (Study Figure)

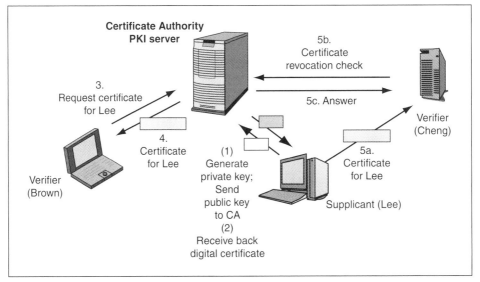

FIGURE 5-16 Functions of a Public Key Infrastructure

THE FIRM AS A CERTIFICATE AUTHORITY (CA)   As Chapter 3 noted, certificate authorities (CAs) manage digital certificates. The chapter also noted that CAs are not regulated, and this creates questions of trust. However, if firms act as their own CAs, they have control of trust in their entire public key infrastructure. On the negative side, being a certificate authority is quite expensive because of the labor involved.

CREATING PUBLIC KEY–PRIVATE KEY PAIRS   First, a PKI needs a way to generate public key–private key pairs for non-PKI servers and clients. This is typically done by the client or non-PKI server rather than by the PKI server. The client or server generates a private key–public key pair,[14] and then sends the public key to the CA. This transmission can be done in the clear because public keys are not secret. The private key, which *is* secret, is not transmitted at all.

DISTRIBUTING DIGITAL CERTIFICATES   Obviously, the PKI infrastructure must be able to distribute public keys in digital certificates.

ACCEPTING DIGITAL CERTIFICATES   The figure also shows that a supplicant can send the true party's digital certificate to the verifier. This might seem suspicious, but recall that digital certificates have their own digital signatures signed (encrypted) by the private key of the PKI server. Digital signatures give message integrity as well as authentication. Consequently, an impostor cannot change the true party's name and replace it with his or her own name.

> It is safe to accept a digital certificate from a supplicant, even if the supplicant is an impostor. The digital certificate has its own digital signature, which gives integrity. This means that the sender cannot change it.

CERTIFICATE REVOCATION STATUS   As discussed in Chapter 3, digital certificates may be revoked before the termination date listed in the digital certificate. Consequently, PKI servers must support the downloading of certificate revocation lists (CRLs) and must respond to Online Certificate Status Protocol (OCSP) queries.

PROVISIONING   We have been focusing on the technology of PKIs. Even more expensive is the labor cost involved in **provisioning**—the accepting of public keys and the providing of new digital certificates to users.

   At the other end of a digital certificate's life cycle, the staff must have good procedures for terminating digital certificates, and employee supervisors and the human resources department also must handle the termination of digital certificates properly and faithfully.

---

[14] It is easy to create public key–private key pairs. However, computing a private key if you know a public key is almost impossible.

THE PRIME AUTHENTICATION PROBLEM   Although technology can be very effective, good technology means nothing unless the entire system is well managed. There have to be strong procedures in place, and these procedures must be enforced and audited.

The most serious issue is the **prime authentication problem**, which says that unless individuals are carefully vetted before being allowed into the system, impostors can simply enroll through social engineering. Provisioning is the riskiest aspect of public key infrastructures because if an impostor can trick the PKI staff into registering him or her, all technical protections are automatically bypassed. There needs to be strong procedures for who may submit someone for inclusion, who may approve it (always someone else), what identification is required, and how to handle exceptions. These procedures must be carefully enforced and audited.

TEST YOUR UNDERSTANDING

24. a. What is the strongest form of authentication?
   b. List the functions of a PKI.
   c. Can a firm be its own certificate authority?
   d. What is the advantage of doing so?
   e. Who creates a computer's private key/public key pair?
   f. How do CAs distribute public keys?
   g. What is provisioning?
   h. What is the prime authentication problem?
   i. What can be done to reduce this risk?

AUTHORIZATION

Access control has three elements that we have called AAA—authentication, authorization, and auditing. So far, we have only looked at authentication. However, knowing the identity of the communication partner is not enough. The specific authorizations (**permissions**) of the communicating party also need to be defined. Not everyone who is authenticated may be allowed to do anything he or she wishes in every directory. (To give an analogy, you probably would not let some of the people you know drive your car.)

The Principle of Least Permissions

In planning authorizations, it is important to follow the **principle of least permissions**. This means that each person should only get the permissions that he or she absolutely needs to do his or her job. If the initial assignment of permissions is too narrow, additional permissions can be granted as needed.

> *The principle of least permissions is that each person should only get the permissions that he or she absolutely needs to do his or her job.*

To give an example, suppose that the system has permissions A, B, C, D, E, and F and that a person needs permissions A, C, and E. Suppose the person is only given the permissions that he or she needs. Then the person will be given A, C, and E. What if a mistake is made, and the person only receives A and C? The answer is that E can be added later. The person will be inconvenienced until E is provided, but security is not violated. Assigning least permissions means that system tends to **fail safely**, not giving each user too many permissions if an error is made.

The opposite approach is to give each user either full permissions or extensive permissions. This way, the user will always or almost always have the permissions they need to do his or her job. It is then possible to take away privileges that the user does not need. However, it is very easy to forget to take away a permission that allows the user to take actions that cause serious damage. To continue the example in the previous paragraph, suppose that a person is given permissions A through F and that B and D are taken away. Here, an error has been made. Permission F has not been removed. Until the error is discovered and fixed, the person will have permission F and may be able to take actions contrary to security. This is a security violation.

Quite simply, beginning with least permissions with the option of adding more later if necessary will rarely cause security problems, while beginning with a extensive permissions and then reducing them has a much higher chance of creating a serious security vulnerability.

Authentication versus Authorizations

    Authentication: Proving a supplicant's identity

    Authorizations: The assignment of permissions (specific authorizations) to individuals or roles

    Just because you are authenticated does not mean that you should be able to do everything

Principle of Least Permissions

    Initially give people only the permissions a person absolutely needs to do his or her job

    If assignment is too narrow, additional permissions may be given

        If assignment is too narrow, the system fails safely

    System has permissions A, B, C, D, E, and F

        Person needs A, B, and E

        If only given A and B, can add E later although user will be inconvenienced

        Errors tend not to create security problems

    This will frustrate users somewhat

Giving Extensive or Full Permissions initially Is Bad

    User will almost always have the permissions to do its job

    System has permissions A, B, C, D, E, and F

        Person needs A, B, and E

        If only given all and take away C and D, still has F

        Errors tend to create security problems

    Assignments can be taken away, but this is subject to errors

    Such errors could give excessive permissions to the user

    This could allow the user to take actions contrary to security policy

    Giving all or extensive permissions and taking some away does not fail safely

FIGURE 5-17   Principle of Least Permissions (Study Figure)

TEST YOUR UNDERSTANDING

25. **a.** Why are authorizations needed after a person is authenticated?
    b. What is another name for authorizations?
    c. What is the principle of least permissions?
    d. Why is it a good way to assign initial permissions?
    e. What is bad about assigning all permissions and then taking away the permissions a user does not need?
    f. What does failing safely mean in a security system?

AUDITING

The third *A* in AAA is auditing. The first A, *authentication*, identifies the person or program. The second A, *authorizations*, specifies what that person or program is permitted to do. Finally, **auditing** records and analyzes what the person or program *actually did*. Unless authentication and authorization activities are audited frequently, improper behavior can go on for a very long time.

> *Authorizations specify what that person or program is* permitted to do. *Auditing records and analyzes what the person or program* actually did.

Logging

Security cameras record visual images of what people do. In a similar way, **logging** records the actions that an account owner takes on a resource. To give just a few examples, a server's logging system on a server might collect data on such events as successful logins, unsuccessful logins, file deletions, file creations, file printings, and so forth. This information is stored in a **log file**, along with the identity of the person or process that took the action. Later, the systems administrator can read the log file to look for suspicious patterns or to learn who committed an act they should not have.

Auditing
    Authentication: Who a person is
    Authorization: What a person may do with a resource
    Auditing: What the person *actually did*

Logging
    Events
    On a server, logins, failed login attempts, file deletions, and so forth
    Events are stored in a log file

Log Reading
    Regular log reading is crucial or the log becomes a useless write-only memory
    Periodic external audits of log file entries and reading practices
    Automatic alerts for strong threats

FIGURE 5-18 Auditing (Study Figure)

Log Reading

Unless logs are studied, they are useless. Log files become a form of "write-only memory." Unfortunately, reading log files is difficult and time consuming. Consequently, it often is ignored.

REGULAR LOG READING   It is important to read log files regularly. Depending on the sensitivity of the events that the file logs, this can mean daily or even several times a day.

PERIODIC EXTERNAL AUDITS OF LOG FILE ENTRIES   In addition to regular reading, log files should be externally audited periodically. An external audit examines randomly selected log entries and determines whether the log reading has been done adequately.

AUTOMATIC ALERTS   Reading log files only tells you about the past. Ideally, logging systems should have active log-reading functions that send the security administrator real-time alerts for certain types of events.

TEST YOUR UNDERSTANDING

26. **a.** What is auditing?
    b. Why is it necessary?
    c. Why is log reading important?
    d. What are the three types of actions that should be taken on log files?
    e. Why are automatic alerts desirable?

CENTRAL AUTHENTICATION SERVERS

The Need for Centralized Authentication

Most firms have hundreds or thousands of servers. Individual employees may need access and authorizations for a dozen or more servers. As we saw in Chapter 4, companies address this need by using central authentication servers. Central authentication servers reduce costs, give consistency in authentication no matter where a user or attacker comes into the network, and allow company-wide changes to be made instantly.

As we also saw in Chapter 4, the most widely used standard for central authentication servers is RADIUS. Figure 5-19 recaps the basic elements in RADIUS central authentication. When a central authentication server is used, the device to which the supplicant connects is called the authenticator. When a supplicant sends credentials to any authenticator, the authenticator passes the credentials on to the central authentication server. The authentication server checks the credentials and sends a message back to the authenticator. This message tells the authenticator whether or not the supplicant's credentials were verified. Based on this information, the authenticator will either accept or reject the supplicant.

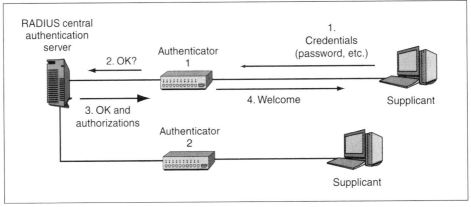

FIGURE 5-19 RADIUS Central Authentication Server

TEST YOUR UNDERSTANDING

27. a. What are the three devices in central authentication using RADIUS servers?
   b. What is the role of the authenticator?
   c. What is the role of the central authentication server?

Kerberos

Although RADIUS is arguably the most popular central authentication server standard, Kerberos[15] is also important, in large part because Microsoft uses it to link hosts together, as we will see in the next section. Actually, Kerberos is more than a central authentication server. It also provides keying information to parties that need to communicate with one another, and it can provide authorization information as well. (RADIUS can also do this.)

Figure 5-20 shows that when a host wishes to connect to another host, it first logs into a Kerberos server. If it succeeds in logging in, it gets a **Ticket Granting Ticket**. This is like getting a wrist bracelet when you enter a concert or sports event. It gets you back in later without having to show your original authentication credentials.

Next, the authenticated supplicant (S) wishes to communicate with a verifier host (V). Figure 5-21 shows that S contacts the Kerberos server. In the process, S sends its Ticket Granting Ticket to the Kerberos server to prove that it has already been authenticated. If the Kerberos server permits the connection to the verifier, it sends a **Service Ticket** to S, which sends the Service Ticket on to V. The verifier has a symmetric key that it only shares with the Kerberos server. It uses this shared key to decrypt the Service Ticket sent by the Kerberos server. The decrypted Service Ticket contains a session key for S to use to talk to V. It may also list permissions that S should have on V.

---

[15] Kerberos got its name from Kerberos (or Cerberus), the three-headed dog in Greek mythology that guards the gate leading to the afterlife. (Yes, sort of like "Fluffy" in *Harry Potter and the Philosopher's/Sorcerer's Stone*.) In the Kerberos myth, if a person approaching the gate is dead, Kerberos allows the person to pass. If a person approaches the gate is still living, Kerberos removes the "still living" impediment. (Talk about tough authentication.) The name Kerberos was chosen because Kerberos authentication involves three devices—the two hosts and the Kerberos server.

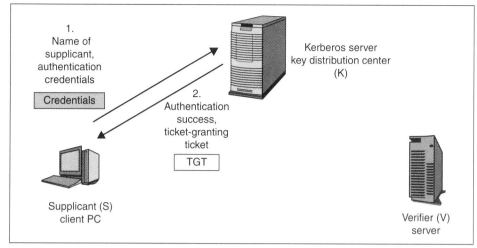

FIGURE 5-20   Kerberos Initial Login

When the Kerberos server sends the Service Ticket to S, it also sends the session key with V encrypted with a key that only the supplicant and the Kerberos server share. S uses this shared key to decrypt the symmetric session key with V.

Now that both hosts have the same symmetric session key, they can begin communicating back and forth, encrypting their transmission for confidentiality with the session key.

If you have been following this closely, you undoubtedly asked, "Hey, how does V know that S is not an impostor?" The answer is that if another host, say X, intercepts the Service Ticket and sends it to V, X will not know the symmetric session key. It will not be able to communicate with V using this key. Consequently, there is no need to inform V explicitly that S is authenticated and has permissions for the

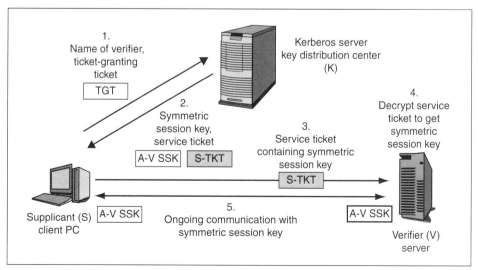

FIGURE 5-21   Kerberos Ticket Granting Service

conversation. V simply acts as if this was the case, and if it is not, the communication will break down. In other words, the system fails safely.

TEST YOUR UNDERSTANDING

28. **a.** In Kerberos, distinguish between the Ticket Granting Ticket and the Service Ticket.
    b. What information does the Service Ticket give the verifier?
    c. How does the supplicant get the symmetric session key?
    d. Is the verifier notified explicitly that the supplicant has been authenticated? Explain.

DIRECTORY SERVERS

RADIUS, Kerberos, and other central authentication servers improve centralization, but two problems remain in most large firms.

- First, most large firms find themselves with multiple RADIUS, Kerberos, and other central authentication servers.
- In addition, most large companies have made a strategic decision to use directory servers as their place to store data centrally in the firm.

What Are Directory Servers?

Directory servers are central repositories for information about people, equipment, software, and databases. Directory servers store authentication, authorization, and auditing information required for security. However, directory servers are not limited to security information. They store information about host configurations, employee contact information such as telephone numbers, and a great deal of general information.

Security information is only one aspect of directory server information.

Hierarchical Data Organization

Database courses usually focus on relational databases. Relational databases are good when there are about an equal numbers of accesses and updates. However, when there are many more accesses than updates, as there are with directory servers, a **hierarchical database organization** may be better. As Figure 5-22 illustrates, directory servers use a hierarchical database organization. The directory server database schema is a hierarchical collection of **objects (nodes)**.

- The top level object is the *organization (O)*. This is the name of the organization. In the figure, this is the University of Waikiki. The *common name (CN)* is a shortcut way of referring to this node.
- Below the organization level are several *organizational unit (OU)* objects. In the figure, the three organizational units are Astronomy, Business, and Computer Science. There probably are several more OUs not shown in the figure.

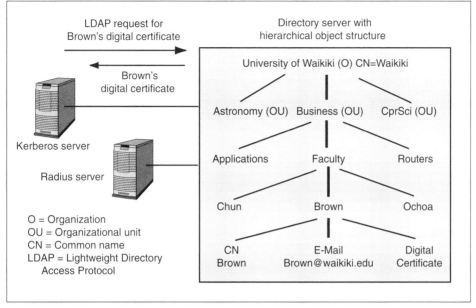

FIGURE 5-22 Directory Server Organization

Usually, the management of the OU's data is at least partially delegated to the organization unit.

- There may be several levels of organizational units in the hierarchical structure, but this directory server only has one level of OU.
- The next level consists of more nodes. In this case, the nodes are applications, faculty members, and routers. This emphasizes that directory servers are not limited to information about people.
- Under faculty, there are many people objects. One of those is for Brown. Brown has subnodes for common name (Charlene Brown), e-mail address, and digital certificate.

TEST YOUR UNDERSTANDING

29. **a.** How is information in directory servers organized?
    b. What are the top two levels of the organization?
    c. Do directory servers only hold information about people?

Lightweight Data Access Protocol (LDAP)

Authentication servers communicate with directory servers using the **Lightweight Directory Access Protocol (LDAP)**. Mostly, LDAP is used to retrieve data from the directory server. However, it can also be used to update information in the directory server. Nearly all directory servers support LDAP. Note that LDAP does not govern the internal operations of the directory server—only communication between directory servers and other devices, including authentication servers.

TEST YOUR UNDERSTANDING

30. What is LDAP's purpose?

Use by Authentication Servers

In security, directory servers are important because they are used by central authentication servers such as RADIUS servers and Kerberos servers. Figure 5-23 shows that a directory server can provide authentication information to many authentication servers. Just as authentication servers are valuable because they centralize authentication information, directories provide a higher level of centralization for firms that have many central authentication servers.

TEST YOUR UNDERSTANDING

31. a. How do central authentication servers often get their authentication information?
   b. What is the advantage of this?

Active Directory

Microsoft's directory server product is **Active Directory (AD)**. Given the widespread use of Microsoft products in corporations, security professionals should understand AD. Figure 5-24 shows a firm with several Active Directory servers.

ACTIVE DIRECTORY DOMAINS   As Figure 5-24, shows, companies usually divide their resources into multiple **Active Directory domains**. AD domains usually are organizational units. For instance, in a university, an individual school or college

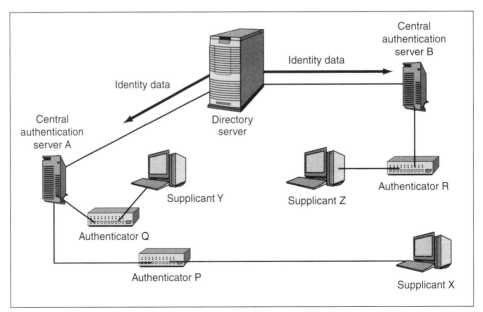

FIGURE 5-23   Using a Directory Server to Centralize Authentication Information

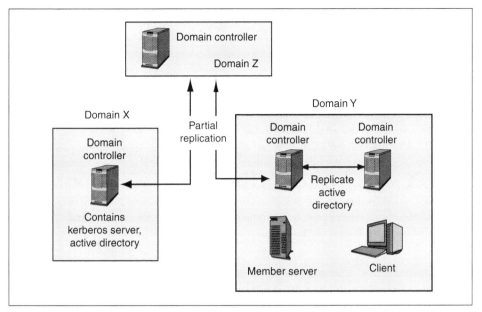

FIGURE 5-24   Active Directory Domains and Tree

may be a domain. The resources of the domain typically are managed by the organizational unit. AD domains may correspond to DNS domains, but they do not have to.

Domain Controllers   In Figure 5-24, Domain X has a single **domain controller** server, which controls the resources in the domain. The domain controller has both an active directory database and a Kerberos authentication server program. Consequently, it handles authentication within the domain and handles AD searches within the domain.

Domains with Multiple Controllers   Domain Y has *two* domain controllers. The two servers have their AD databases synchronized, so either can handle any Active Directory LDAP requests. Having two (or more) domain controllers gives reliability in case one crashes or is successfully attacked.

Trees   Figure 5-24 shows that AD domains can be organized into hierarchies called **trees**. The hierarchy in the figure only has two levels, but some trees have many levels of domains.

Forests   Figure 5-24 shows a simple tree with multiple domains. Some companies also have multiple trees. They can connect their multiple trees together into a **forest**.

Replication   Within a domain, there is total replication between domain controllers. What about replication in trees? The answer is that domain controllers often replicate some of their AD database to domain controllers at the next higher level, but they usually do not replicate all data. Replication across domains at the same level and between forests usually is even more selective.

Fortunately, AD is rich in tools for specifying replication across specific domains. Of course, this same richness requires strong policy control to avoid chaos and Swiss-cheese security.

TEST YOUR UNDERSTANDING

32. **a.** What is Microsoft's directory server product?
    b. What is the smallest organizational unit in Active Directory?
    c. What two things does a domain controller contain?
    d. Can a domain have multiple domain controllers?
    e. What is the advantage of having multiple domain controllers?
    f. Into what larger structures are domains organized?
    g. Into what larger structure can trees be organized?
    h. Describe replication among domain controllers within a single AD domain.
    i. Describe replication between a domain controller in one domain and the domain controller in the parent domain.

Trust

Trust means that one directory server will accept information from another. Several types of trust are possible.

Trust means that one directory server will accept information from another.

- Trust may be **mutual** (bi-directional). However, **one-way** trust is also possible, in which one directory server trusts another, but this trust is not reciprocated.
- Sometimes, trust is **transitive**. This means that if Directory Server X trusts Directory Server Y, and if Directory Server Y trusts Server Z, then Directory Server X will automatically trust Directory Server Z.

```
Trust Directionality
    Mutual
        A trusts B and B trusts A
    One-Way
        A trusts B or B trusts A, but not both
Trust Transitivity
    Transitive Trust
        If A trusts B
            and B trusts C,
                then A trusts C automatically
    Intransitive Trust
        If A trusts B
            and B trusts C,
                this does NOT mean that A trusts C automatically
```

FIGURE 5-25 Trust Directionality and Transitivity (Study Figure)

- In contrast, if Directory Server X trusts Directory Server Y, and Directory Server Y trusts Directory Server Z, but Directory Server X does not automatically trust Directory Server Z, then trust is **intransitive**.

By controlling trust directionality and transitivity, a company can create appropriate trust relationships between its directory servers. However, there are many possible trust relationships, so setting trust relationships is a difficult task, and mistakes can lead to security vulnerabilities. An important principle governing the assignment of trusts is that it is safer to give too little trust initially than too much trust.

TEST YOUR UNDERSTANDING

33. a. Distinguish between mutual and one-way trust among AD domains.
   b. Distinguish between transitive and intransitive trust.
   c. What principle should companies follow in making trust assignments?

TOWARD FULL IDENTITY MANAGEMENT

Central authentication servers and directory servers are only two steps that organizations take to manage the identities of their users and technical resources.

Other Directory Servers and Metadirectories

In an ideal world, a company would only have a single family of directory servers. Instead, companies typically have several types of directory servers, as Figure 5-26 shows. Other common types of directory servers are Novell eDirectory and Sun ONE directory servers for Solaris (Sun's version of Unix).

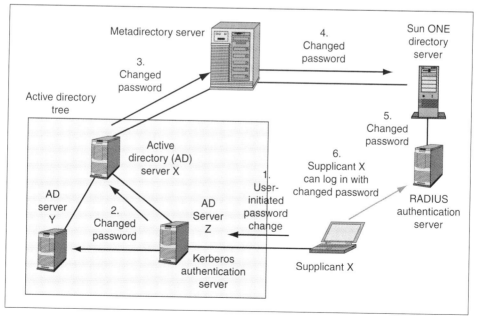

FIGURE 5-26   Multiple Directory Servers and Metadirectory Server

To connect these disparate directory servers together, the company in the figure has a **metadirectory server**. The metadirectory server gets the directory servers to exchange information and to synchronize services in a variety of ways. Unfortunately, these exchanges and synchronizations are limited today. Most commonly, when a user resets a password on one directory servers, the metadirectory server passes the password reset to other directory servers.

TEST YOUR UNDERSTANDING

34. **a.** Why are metadirectory servers needed?
    b. What do metadirectory servers do?

Federated Identity Management

Within companies, trust is complex. The situation is even more complex between companies. Between companies, we talk about federated authentication, authorization, and auditing or, more commonly, **federated identity management**.[16] Figure 5-27 illustrates federated identity management.

In this case, Employee Dave first logs into Firm A's identity management server and is authenticated in the process. Employee Dave is a buyer in Firm A. He has a $10,000 purchase limit. Dave asks the federated identity management server in firm A to contact the sales server in firm B so that he can purchase supplies from firm B.

The federated identity management server in Firm A sends an assertion to its counterpart in Firm B. An **assertion** is a statement that Firm B should accept as true if Firm B trusts Firm A. The assertion may have three major elements.

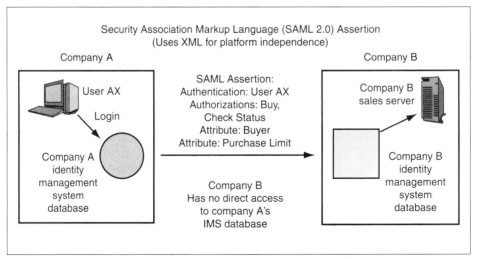

FIGURE 5-27   Federated Identity Management

---

[16] To federate means to join together as equals.

An assertion is a statement that Firm B should accept as true if Firm B trusts Firm A.

- First, the assertion may contain **authenticity** information, namely that Dave is an employee by that name and has been authenticated at Firm A.
- The assertion may also contain an **authorization**, in this case that Firm B should allow Dave to access Firm B's sales server.
- Third, the assertion may contain **attributes** that describe the party being described, for instance, stating that Dave is a buyer and that Employee AX has a maximum purchase limit of $10,000.

Note that Firm B is not allowed to query Firm A's identity management database. This is good for Firm A's security because it keeps Firm B from potentially learning other identity information, such as Dave's employee's salary and commission level. Firm B only knows what is in the assertion, and this is all that Firm B needs to know for a transaction.

At the same time, Firm B must trust Dave to have access to its sales server to make a purchase. This requires that Firm B has already agreed to a trust relationship with Firm A so that Firm B will accept Firm A's assertions. This normally will require a contract that protects Firm B if Firm A sends an assertion that is not true.

This might seem to put Firm B at a disadvantage, but sellers have long had to trust buyers to do business. Assertions actually reduce the risk to Firm B compared to traditional trust methods such as, "Oh, yes, I recognize Jennifer's from Firm A's voice; we have been doing business with her for years." In addition, Firm B can specify that it will only accept certain attributes in assertions and in fact will *require* certain attributes, such as a maximum purchase amount. This way, it will be protected if Jennifer's purchase limit has been lowered or if Jennifer has left the buyer's firm and wishes to do mischief.

THE SECURITY ASSERTION MARKUP LANGUAGE (SAML) The dominant standard for sending security assertions today is the **Security Assertion Markup Language (SAML)**. This standard uses XML to structure messages. Consequently, the interacting identity management systems do not have to use the same software technology. Thanks to XML, SAML is **platform-independent**. It does not matter what programming language the two partners use to program their systems. This is the key to SAML interoperability across firms.

PERSPECTIVE Creating federated identity management systems is extremely difficult, especially with today's relatively undeveloped standards. However, given the flexibility and potential for cost savings that federated identity management can bring, business partners have already begun to implement federated identity management on a limited basis.

TEST YOUR UNDERSTANDING

35. **a.** In federated identity management, do firms query one another's identity management databases?
   b. What do they do instead?
   c. What risk does this method avoid for the firm sending the security assertion?

   d. How are risks to Firm B reduced?
   e. What is a security assertion?
   f. What three things may it contain?
   g. What is the main standard for one firm to send security assertion to another firm?
   h. What is the major benefit of using XML?

Identity Management

We began this discussion with authentication, authorizations, and auditing. As we moved to more sophisticated topics, the term *identity management* began to appear. It is now time to be more precise in talking about identity management. Formally, **identity management** is the policy-based management of all information required for access to corporate systems by people, machines, programs, or other resources.

> *Identity management is the centralized policy-based management of all informa-tion required for access to corporate systems by people, machines, programs, or other resources.*

Definition

   Identity management is the centralized policy-based management of all information required for access to corporate systems by a person, machine, program, or other resource

Benefits of Identity Management

   Reduction in the redundant work needed to manage identity information

   Consistency in information

   Rapid changes

   Central auditing

   Single sign-on

   Increasingly required to meet compliance requirements

   At least reduced sign-on when SSO is impossible

Identity

   The set of attributes about a person or nonhuman resource that must be revealed *in a particular context*

   Principle of minimum identity data: only reveal the information necessary

Identity Lifecycle Management

   Initial credential checking

   Defining identities (pieces of information to be divulged)

   Managing trust relationships

   Provisioning, reprovisioning if changes, and deprovisioning

   Implementing controlled decentralization

      Do as much administration as possible locally

      This requires tight policy controls to avoid problems

   Providing self-service functions (password reset)

FIGURE 5-28   Identity Management (Study Figure)

BENEFITS OF IDENTITY MANAGEMENT   Identity management can reduce costs by reducing the amount of redundant work needed to manage user access, including provisioning, deprovisioning, password resets, and many other tasks. Identity management enforces consistency by permitting a single change on an identity management server to add, change, or remove an employee's access permissions on all servers in an organization. In addition, an identity management system allows the centralized auditing of all of an employee's access permissions across the firm.

A potential benefit of identity management is **single sign-on (SSO)**. In SSO, a user will authenticate himself or herself to the identity management system once. Thereafter, whenever the user asks for access to a specific server, there is no need for additional logins.

Unfortunately, complete SSO across an entire firm is almost impossible. Although SSO is a good long-term objective, *reduced* sign-on is all that companies can accomplish today. In **reduced sign-on**, an employee can log in once and receive service from several servers but not from all servers. Typically, reduced sign-on will give the typical user access to e-mail and most other services he or she will need, so logging into other servers usually is not too burdensome.

Another reason for identity management's growing importance is that many compliance regimes (discussed in Chapter 2) require strong access control that is only likely to be effective with strong identity management.

WHAT IS IDENTITY?   Although *identity* may seem like a simple concept, in practice it is highly contextual. We all have family identities, work identities, and identities at school. Each identity involves some information about us but does not include other information. Due to these factors, we will define an **identity** as the set of attributes about a person or nonhuman resource that must be revealed in a particular context. We say, "must be" because a core principle is **minimum identity data**—not revealing more information about a person or resource than is necessary for a particular purpose. Otherwise, attackers may be able to get information than they should not.

> An identity is the set of attributes about a person or nonhuman resource that must be revealed in a particular context.

IDENTITY MANAGEMENT   We have looked primarily at identity management technologies, but labor and management are the most complex aspects of identity management. We will list only a few aspects of **identity management**, which manages identities from their creations to their deletions.

- *Initial credential checking*. Recall the prime authentication problem from earlier in the chapter. Unless employee credentials are checked very thoroughly at the beginning of employment, subsequent security measures will be meaningless.
- *Defining identities*. As just discussed, the amount of information that should be given out in a particular circumstance should be limited. Designing identities carefully for each situation is critical for security.

- *Trust relationships*. We saw earlier that there are many types of trust relationship. The proper trust relationships are also necessary for good security.
- *Provisioning*. Authorizations and authentication must be provisioned carefully and then changed whenever roles or other conditions change. This can be an enormous task. The account may need to be reprovisioned when there are changes and finally deprovisioned when it is no longer appropriate.
- *Decentralization*. Ideally, identities should be managed by people closest to the situation. Of course, proper separation and policies must be maintained; so decentralization has to be planned and managed carefully.
- *Self-service functions*. For nonsensitive information, people can do their own updating. For instance, if someone changes their marital status, and if this does not have security implications, they should be able to do so themselves in the identity management system, preferably through a web portal.

TEST YOUR UNDERSTANDING

36. **a.** What is identity management?
    b. What are the benefits of identity management?
    c. What is SSO?
    d. Why is full SSO generally impossible?
    e. What is reduced sign-on?
    f. What is an identity?
    g. Why is providing minimum identity data an important principle?

37. **a.** In identity management, what are provisioning, reprovisioning, and deprovisioning?
    b. Why is decentralized management desirable?
    c. Why are self-service functions desirable?
    d. What changes should be made through self-service functions?

Trust and Risk

Many people are uncomfortable with the idea of trust. Consequently, it is often more useful to think in terms of risk instead of trust. Whenever we deal with others, there is risk involved. However, we must accept that risk if we are to work with others. As Chapter 2 noted, security is really about managing risk. The purpose of security is to reduce risk to an acceptable level, not to completely eliminating risk. Identity management in its varying levels of strength brings varying degrees of risk reduction. A company must balance these risk reductions with the amount of money that identity management will cost to implement over their entire life cycle.

In considering risks, a company must consider possible future endeavors, not just current ones. One factor to consider when thinking about identity management and risk is that a strong identity management system may allow new endeavors that would be too risky without strong identity management.

TEST YOUR UNDERSTANDING

38. **a.** In what sense is identity management really just another form of risk management?
    b. How can identity management reduce risk?
    c. How much should companies spend on identity management?

CONCLUSION

Synopsis

Access control is the policy-driven control of access to systems, data, and dialogues. Access security begins with physical building security. It is important to control access and entry points to the building with guards and monitoring devices. It is also important to have control over internal doors leading to sensitive parts of the building. It is important to have control over disposal so that attackers cannot do Dumpster™ diving looking for information. Physical security has to extend all the way down to computer equipment rooms, desktop PC, and mobile devices, and even removable storage media.

Reusable passwords provide a weak level of authentication but are familiar to people and are built into computer operating systems. If attackers can steal the password file, they can run a password-cracking program against the file. If they crack the root account password or can elevate their privileges to that of the root account, attackers will "own" the machine. Firms need strong password policies to ensure that passwords are long (at least eight characters) and complex (including letters with case, digits, and other keyboard characters). They specifically should not be common words or slight variations on common words. The company also needs to develop a password reset system for lost passwords. To reduce cost, a company may use automated password resets, but this must be done very carefully.

Access cards and physical tokens limit access to people who have physical devices. Proximity access tokens can even be read at a distance, as the person approaches a resource. Physical devices can be lost or stolen, so most companies require two-factor authentication, in which the user must enter a PIN or use some other type of authentication along with the physical device.

Biometric authentication uses body measurement or actions to authenticate people. A user must enroll in a system initially. From his or her enrollment scan's data, a few key features are extracted from the scan and stored in an authentication database as the person's template. For later access attempts, each access scan's data is again reduced to a few key features, and these access key features are compared with the user's template. Biometric authentication holds the promise of eliminating the use of reusable passwords.

Unfortunately, uncertain error rates and susceptibility to deception remain major concerns. In a false acceptance, the person is incorrectly declared a match to a template in the authentication database. In a false rejection, a person who should be declared a match to a template is not considered to be a match. Another set of important distinction in biometrics is the differences between verification (authenticating someone who claims a particular identity), identification (determining the person's identity), and watch list membership.

Fingerprint scanning dominates biometrics use today; it provides inexpensive but low-security authentication. Iris scanning dominates for high-security applications. Face scanning is controversial. It permits surreptitious identification but has very high error rates and deception rates.

Cryptographic authentication uses the digital certificates we saw in Chapter 3. Cryptographic authentication requires the company to create a public key infrastructure (PKI). Most companies become their own certificate authority.

Authorizations are the permissions that should be accorded to authenticated subjects. Authorization should follow the principle of least permissions—giving each subject the minimum permissions the subject needs to work.

Auditing is necessary to detect actions counter to policy. Key access events should be logged and should be read regularly. There should also be periodic external audits, and real-time alerts are also desirable.

Companies have many users and servers, and most users need access permissions on multiple servers. If permissions are assigned independently on different servers, this can cause many problems. Identity management centralizes access permissions. No company has full identity management, but companies are moving towards it. As Figure 5-29 shows, the first step is to use centralized authentication servers. The next steps are to use directory servers and multiple types of directories linked by metadirectory servers. We looked in some detail at Active Directory, which is Microsoft's directory server product. Finally, federated identity management allows different companies that trust each other to exchange identity assertions about employees to each other but not to look at each others' identification databases.

Identities are complex things. An identity is the set of attributes about a person or nonhuman resource that must be revealed in a particular context. For security, it is

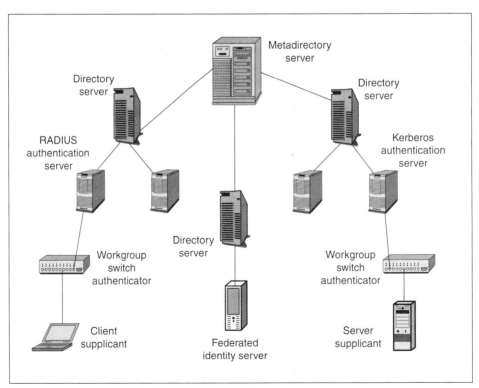

FIGURE 5-29 Authentication and Identity Management Servers

important to limit the information revealed to the minimum required in a context. Employees will have many different identities as they deal with different contexts, but there will be only one set of identity data for each person in a centralized identity management database.

One potential benefit of identity management is single sign-on, which allows anyone to work with any resource after signing in first with a central authentication server. In practice, companies can only provide reduced sign-on in which an initial authentication can give access to a limited group of resources.

Although security professionals usually speak of AAA protections in terms of trust, keep in mind that trust is just another way to look at risk analysis. Better AAA protections reduce the risk of dealing with a person or organization. In addition, very strong AAA protections may allow a firm to engage in certain activities that would be too risky without very strong AAA protections. At the same time, the benefits of risk reduction must be weighed against the cost of the AAA protections needed to bring these benefits.

Thought Questions

1. Reusable passwords offer poor security. What do you think is holding back their replacement with other approaches?
2. What password-cracking method would be used for each of the following password? a) *swordfish*, b) *Lt6^*, c) *Processing1*, and d) *nitt4aGm^*.
3. Critique the safety of each of the following passwords, giving your specific reasoning. a) *swordfish*, b) *Lt6^*, c) *Processing1*, and d) *nitt4aGm^*.
4. Create two good password reset questions. For each, explain why you think it is a good question.
5. Someone says that they wish to protect their desktop PC from a walk-up attacker with a password or passwords. Give them advice and reasons for your advice. This is not very short answer.
6. a) Give two situations in which the risk of deception is high. b) Give two situations in which the risk of deception is low.
7. Your friend wants to secure his or her desktop PC with fingerprint scanning or password access protection. Give your friend the information that he or she should know to make the decision. Consider alternatives. This is not very short answer.

8. What do FRRs mean when fingerprint scanning is used to secure a PC against walk-up attacks? What might produce high FRRs? Can you think of a way that this problem could be reduced in fingerprint scanning?
9. Some airports are installing face recognition systems to identify terrorists and criminals. About one in a million people passing through the airport is a terrorist. Suppose the FAR is about 1 percent. The FRR is about 30 percent. Is this system likely to be workable? Explain using a spreadsheet analysis with reasonable assumptions. Cut and paste the spreadsheet analysis into your homework file instead of handing it in separately. Give a short paragraph giving your conclusion.
10. Centralizing authentication and authorization reduces cost, improves consistency, and permits rapid provisioning and changes. List the technologies on the way toward greater centralization, beginning with stand-alone authenticators through corporate metadirectory servers.
11. Suppose that the probability of a false acceptance is 0.0001 per match attempt. Suppose that there are 1,000 templates in the database. What is the probability of a false acceptance

in the case of verification? What is the probability of a false acceptance in the case of identification? What is the probability of a false acceptance if there is a watch list of 50 people who should be given access to a system?

12. List at least six identities for yourself that require different authentication and authorizations.

Troubleshooting Question

1. Your company installs a face recognition system for door access. a) Its FRR is much worse than the vendor's claims. What might be causing this? b) The system's FRR increases over time. What might be causing this?

Perspective Questions

1. What information in this chapter was the most surprising for you?

2. What material in this chapter was the most difficult for you?

Chapter 6

Firewalls

LEARNING OBJECTIVES:

By the end of this chapter, you should be able to discuss the following:

- Firewalls in general (basic operation, architecture, the problem of overload).
- Static packet filtering.
- Stateful packet inspection (SPI) for main border firewalls.
- Network address translation (NAT).
- Application proxy firewalls and application content filtering in SPI firewalls.
- Intrusion detection systems (IDSs) and intrusion prevention systems (IPSs).
- Antivirus filtering and firewalls.
- (In a box) Denial-of-service (DoS) protection.
- Firewall architectures.
- Firewall management (defining policies, implementing policies, reading log files).
- Difficult problems for firewalls.

INTRODUCTION

Basic Firewall Operation

Figure 6-1 shows that a firewall examines each packet passing through it. If the packet is a **provable attack packet**, the firewall drops the packet. If the packet is *not* a provable attack packet, the firewall passes the packet on to its destination. In firewalls, this is called a **pass/deny decision**.

Note that a firewall passes all packets that are not provable attack packets. This means that it will pass any true attack packet that is not a *provable* attack packet. This will allow attack packets to get through to their targets. Consequently, it is important to harden hosts to protect them against attack packets that the firewall does not drop. Hardening involves a series of protections that we will see in Chapters 7 and 8.

In addition to dropping provable attack packets, firewalls usually record information about each dropped packet in a **log file**. This process is called **logging**. The firewall

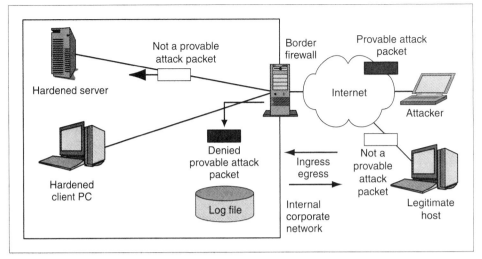

FIGURE 6-1 Basic Firewall Operation

administrator should look through this log file daily or even more frequently to understand the types of attacks that the firm is experiencing. Even if the firewall is dropping many packets from a particular attacker, it may not be dropping them all. The firewall administrator may reconfigure the firewall to drop all packets from an attacker's IP address or may take other actions.

The firewall shown in Figure 6-1 is a **border firewall**. It sits at the boundary between the corporate site and the external Internet. We will see later that many firms also have **internal firewalls**, which filter traffic passing between different parts of the site's internal network.

In **ingress filtering**, the firewall examines packets *entering the network from the outside*, typically from the Internet. The purpose of ingress filtering is to stop attack packets from entering the firm's internal network. Ingress filtering is what most people think of when they hear the term "firewall filtering."

In **egress filtering**, in turn, the firewall filters packets when they are *leaving the network*. This prevents replies to probe packets from leaving the network. (We discussed probe packets in Chapter 1.) It also prevents a firm's infected hosts from attacking other firms. (This makes the firm a good neighbor; it may also prevent lawsuits.) Egress filtering may even prevent employees and compromised hosts from sending files containing the firm's intellectual property out of the firm.

TEST YOUR UNDERSTANDING

1. **a.** What is a pass/deny decision?
   b. What type of packet does a firewall drop and log?
   c. What does the firewall do about packets that it suspects (but cannot prove) are attack packets?
   d. Why does the firewall log information about dropped packets?
   e. Distinguish between border firewalls and internal firewalls.
   f. Distinguish between ingress and egress filtering.

The Danger of Traffic Overload

What if traffic becomes so high that a firewall lacks the capacity to examine all arriving packets? Will the firewall pass the packets it cannot examine, or will it drop them?

The answer is that an overloaded firewall *drops* all packets that it cannot process. This is the most secure approach, because it will not allow attack packets through. The firewall fails safely.

If a firewall becomes overloaded with traffic, it **drops** *packets it cannot process.*

However, dropping packets that a firewall cannot process effectively creates a self-inflicted denial-of-service attack against the firm. It is critical for firms to purchase firewalls with sufficient processing power to handle the traffic they will have to examine.

Even if a firewall can handle the traffic when a firm purchases it, the firewall may run out of capacity later.

The Problem

If a firewall cannot filter all of the traffic passing through it, it *drops* packets it cannot process

This is secure because it prevents attack packets from getting through

But it creates a self-inflicted denial-of-service attack by dropping legitimate traffic

Firewall Capacity

Firewalls must have the capacity to handle the incoming traffic volume

Some can handle normal traffic but cannot handle traffic during heavy attacks!

They must be able to handle incoming traffic at wire speed—the maximum speed of data coming into each port

Processing Power Is Increasing Rapidly

As processing power increases, more sophisticating filtering methods should become possible

We can even have unified threat management (UTM), in which a single firewall can use many forms of filtering, including antivirus filtering and even spam filtering. (Traditional firewalls do not do these types of application-level malware filtering)

However, increasing traffic is soaking up much of this increasing processing power

Firewall Filtering Mechanisms

There are many types

We will focus most heavily on the most important firewall filtering method, stateful packet inspection (SPI)

Single firewalls can use multiple filtering mechanisms, most commonly, SPI with other secondary filtering mechanisms

---

FIGURE 6-2 The Danger of Traffic Overload (Study Figure)

- Most obviously, traffic is likely to grow.
- Also, as new threats appear, the firewall administer must write more filtering rules, and processing these additional rules will require more firewall processing work per packet.[1]
- Worse yet, during DoS attacks and heavy scanning attacks, traffic can increase dramatically. If a firewall works fine at normal traffic levels but cannot deal with traffic surges during major attacks, it is a very poor firewall. Firewalls must be able to filter traffic at **wire speed**—the maximum speed of the lines that connect to it.

As firewall processing power increases, firewalls will be able to do ever more sophisticated processing. For example, we will see later in this chapter that intrusion prevention systems (IPSs) can stop some very subtle attacks by examining all layers in each packet and by examining complex relationships within streams of packets.

More importantly, we are likely to see the growth of unified threat management (UTM) firewalls, which handle traditional firewall processing but which also do antivirus filtering and even spam filtering. (As we will discuss later, traditional firewalls do *not* do antivirus filtering and other application-level malware filtering.)

Of course, traffic is also continuing to grow, and this will use up at least some of firewalls' increasing processing power.

TEST YOUR UNDERSTANDING

2. **a.** What does a firewall do if it cannot keep up with the traffic volume?
   b. Why is this action good?
   c. Why is this action bad?
   d. Why can a firewall keep up with traffic in general but fail to do so during a major attack?
   e. As processing power increases in the future, what will this mean for firewall filtering?
   f. What is unified threat management (UTM)?
   g. What does it mean that a firewall should operate at wire speed?

Firewall Filtering Mechanisms

We have used the term "filtering" without defining it specifically. The reason for this lack of precision is that there are several **filtering methods** for examining packets. These methods include stateful packet inspection filtering, static packet filtering, network address translation, application proxy filtering, intrusion prevention system filtering, and antivirus filtering. We will look at these filtering methods in this chapter.

Although it is important to understand all of these mechanisms, it is also important to understand that nearly all main border firewalls use stateful packet inspection (SPI) as their primary inspection mechanism. However, they use some of the other filtering mechanisms we will see as secondary filtering mechanisms to supplement SPI.

---

[1] This is another reason why firewall administrators should read their firewall logs daily. If more than about 1 percent of all packets are dropped because of limited capacity, then the firewall is running out of capacity and needs to be upgraded or replaced.

> *Nearly all main border firewalls use stateful packet inspection (SPI) as their primary inspection mechanism.*

TEST YOUR UNDERSTANDING

3. **a.** Is there only one firewall filtering mechanism?
   b. What filtering mechanisms do almost all main border firewalls use?
   c. Do SPI firewalls only do stateful packet inspection?

STATIC PACKET FILTERING

The earliest border firewalls used **static packet filtering**, which is extremely limited. Today, static packet filtering is no longer used by main border firewalls as their primary filtering mechanism, but some use it as a secondary mechanism to supplement stateful packet inspection.

Looking at Packets One at a Time

Static packet filtering looks at packets one at a time, in isolation. This is a serious limitation because many attacks can only be stopped by understanding a packet's place in a stream of packets.

For example, if an internal host sends a TCP SYN segment to an outside host, the outside host will respond with a legitimate TCP SYN/ACK segment. Then what happens if a static packet filtering firewall receives a TCP SYN/ACK segment coming into the site from the outside? This may be a legitimate response to an internal host's TCP SYN segment. However, it might also be part of an externally initiated attack. An external attacker may send a TCP SYN/ACK segment in hopes of receiving an RST segment in response. The RST segment will confirm that there is a host at the IP address to which the attacker sent the TCP SYN/ACK segment.

Static packet filtering, not knowing the context of the packet, cannot tell the difference. By default, it will have to pass all packets containing SYN/ACK segments because dropping such segments would cut off all internally initiated communication. This is only one example of how examining packets in isolation means that certain attacks cannot be stopped by static packet filtering.

Looking Only at Some Fields in the Internet and Transport Headers

In addition to only looking at packets in isolation, static packet filter firewalls only look at the internet and transport headers, and they usually only look at some fields in these headers. This also means that they cannot stop all attacks, including attacks that require the filtering of application messages or the filtering of header fields that static packet filtering does not examine.

Usefulness of Static Packet Filtering

Although there are many attacks that static packet filtering cannot stop, there are many attacks that it can stop, and it can stop many of these attacks very efficiently. For instance, a static packet filter firewall can stop Internet Control Message

Static Packet Filtering

This was the earliest firewall filtering mechanism

Limitation 1: Inspects Packets One at a Time, in Isolation

Cannot stop many attacks

If it receives a packet containing a SYN/ACK segment, this may be a legitimate response to an internally initiated SYN segment

> The firewall must pass packets containing these segments, or internally initiated communications cannot exist

However, this SYN/ACK segment could be an external attack

> It could be sent to elicit an RST segment confirming that there is a victim at the IP address to which the SYN/ACK segment is sent

> A static packet-filtering firewall cannot stop this attack

There are many other attacks that static packet-filtering firewalls cannot stop because they only filter single packets in isolation

Limitation 2: Only Looks at Some Fields in the Internet and Transport Layer Headers

Never reads the application layer message

This also means that certain attacks cannot be stopped

However, Static Packet Filtering Can Stop Certain Attacks Very Efficiently

Incoming ICMP Echo packets and other scanning probe packets

Outgoing responses to scanning probe packets

Packets with spoofed IP addresses (e.g., incoming packets with the source IP addresses of hosts inside the firm)

Packets that have nonsensical field settings—such as a TCP segment with both the SYN and FIN bits set

Market Status

No longer used as the main filtering mechanism for border firewalls

May be used as a secondary filtering mechanism on main border firewalls

Also may be implemented in border routers, which lie between the Internet and the firewall

> Stops simple, high-volume attacks to reduce the load on the main border firewall

FIGURE 6-3 Static Packet Filtering (Study Figure)

Protocol (ICMP) echo messages from coming into the site from the outside because hackers use these messages as scanning probes. In addition, a static packet filter firewall can stop all ICMP echo reply packets in case the firewall missed any incoming echo messages.

A static packet filtering firewall can also stop incoming packets with spoofed source IP addresses. The attacker may send a packet from the outside with a source IP address that should only be used by hosts *within* a site. Internal hosts might trust such addresses because they are "local." In addition, if a host within the site sends an outgoing packet with a spoofed source IP address, the sending host may be an infected computer that is part of a botnet.

To give another example, an attacker may set both the SYN and FIN bits in the TCP header. This means that the packet simultaneously asks to open and close a connection. This makes no sense. If the target host's operating system was not tested for this odd condition, this packet may crash the target host or cause the host to send back an RST segment in a packet containing the target host's source IP address.

Perspective

Due to the limitations of filtering individual packets in isolation and only looking at some fields in the internet and transport layer headers, static packet filtering proved to be a dead end as a main filtering mechanism for border firewalls. This limited static packet filtering to two peripheral uses.

- Most importantly, many main border firewalls use static packet filtering as a secondary filtering mechanism because of static packet filtering's ability to stop some specific attacks that are more difficult and therefore more expensive to stop in other ways.
- In addition, Figure 6-4 shows that some firms turn their border *routers* into static packet filtering firewalls by adding software (and sometimes RAM).[2] These filtering routers can stop many high-volume but simple incoming attacks in order to lighten the load on the main border firewall. These filtering routers can also ensure that outgoing ICMP echo reply messages and other probe responses do not get out to people probing the network.

TEST YOUR UNDERSTANDING

4. **a.** What are the two limitations of static packet filtering? Explain why each limitation is bad.
   b. For what two reasons do companies not use static packet filtering as the main filtering mechanism in border firewalls today?
   c. In what two secondary ways do corporations sometimes use static packet filtering?

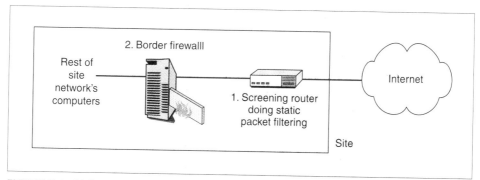

FIGURE 6-4 Main Border Firewall and Screening Router that Uses Static Packet Filtering

---

[2] Border routers from *some* vendors require expensive upgrades in software and RAM to be used as static packet filtering firewalls. For other vendors, upgrades are relatively inexpensive or even unnecessary.

STATEFUL PACKET INSPECTION (SPI)

Basic Operation

We have just seen that static packet filtering is not used as a main border firewall filtering mechanism. In contrast, *nearly all* corporate border firewalls today use the **stateful packet inspection (SPI)** filtering method. Consequently, we will look at SPI filtering in the most depth in this chapter.

CONNECTIONS SPI focuses on **connections**, which are persistent conversations between different programs on different computers. To give an analogy, a connection is like a telephone call between two people.

STATES When you call someone on the telephone, there are implicit rules of conduct that should be observed in different periods of the conversation. When a called party answers, it is polite to ask if they are free to talk. At the end of the conversation, it is rude to merely hang up. During the main phase of the conversation, it is rude to monopolize the conversation.

Instead of talking about time periods, phases, or stages, computer scientists use the term **state** to describe a particular temporal period during a connection. In human conversations, then, there is an opening state, an ongoing communication state, and an ending state.

The concept of states is central to SPI filtering. Figure 6-5 illustrates a simple connection in which there are only two states.[3]

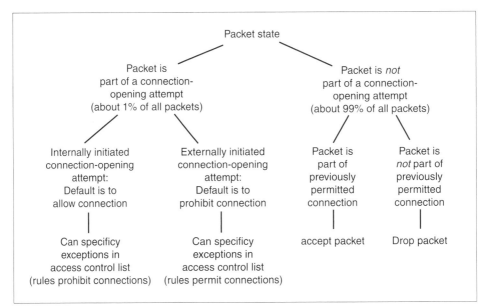

FIGURE 6-5 States in a Connection

---

[3] For some protocols, there are more than two states. For instance, there may be a distinct session closing state at the end of the communication.

A state is a distinct phase in a connection between two applications.

- First, there is an opening state, when the two applications agree to open a connection.
- Afterward, the two applications enter the ongoing communication state. For most connections, traffic is dominated by exchanges during the ongoing communication state. The two applications communicate back and forth using the same port numbers and other conditions.

STATEFUL PACKET INSPECTION WITH TWO STATES   The concept of states is important because it is appropriate to check for different things during different states. Stateful inspection does precisely that: It changes its specific examination method depending on the state.

Stateful packet inspection (SPI) uses different specific examination methods depending on the state of the connection.

Figure 6-5 shows that when a packet arrives, the firewall first determines whether the packet is part of a connection-opening attempt. For example, if the packet contains a TCP segment, it is only attempting to open a connection if the SYN bit is set.

The figure shows that different rules apply to packets that are part of connection-opening attempts and those that are not.

The vast majority of packets are *not* part of connection-opening attempts. Note in the figure that stateful packet inspection is simple for packets that do not attempt to open a connection. Consequently, nearly all packets are handled quickly, simply, and therefore inexpensively.

For the few packets that do attempt to open connections, the processing of stateful packet inspection firewalls is more complex. Fortunately, because few packets attempt to open connections, connection-opening packets do not place a heavy burden on SPI firewalls.

REPRESENTING CONNECTIONS   SPI focuses on connections between programs on different hosts. In networking, a connection is represented by its **socket**, which designates a specific program (designated by a port number) on a specific computer (IP address). A socket is written as an IP address, a colon, and a port number—for example, 10.3.47.16:4400. As Figure 6-6 shows, a **connection** is a link between programs on different machines. It consists of two sockets—an internal socket and an external socket.

TEST YOUR UNDERSTANDING

5. **a.** What is a state?
   b. Are most packets part of the connection opening state or the ongoing communication state?
   c. Why is the answer to part b important for stateful packet inspection's efficiency?
   d. What is a connection?
   e. How is a connection between two programs on different computers represented?

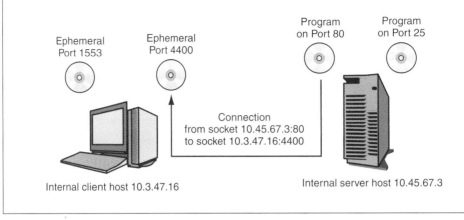

FIGURE 6-6   Connection and Socket

Packets that Do Not Attempt to Open Connections

In stateful packet inspection, as Figure 6-5 shows, when a packet arrives that does not attempt to open a connection, an SPI firewall checks if it is part of a previously approved connection.

- If it is part of an existing connection in the connection table, the packet is passed, usually without further filtering.
- If it is *not* part of an existing connection in the connection table, it is dropped and logged.

TCP CONNECTIONS   For example, suppose that a packet arriving from the outside does not attempt to open a connection (Step 1 in Figure 6-7). The packet has IP source address 123.80.5.34, TCP source port number 80, IP destination address 60.55.33.12, and TCP destination port number 4400. This matches the connection in the first row. Therefore, the packet is part of an approved connection. The firewall passes the packet.

UDP AND ICMP CONNECTIONS   Although ICMP and UDP are connectionless, SPI firewalls can handle ICMP and UDP. For ICMP, for instance, there are echo–echo reply interactions. If an ICMP echo message arrives, this is viewed as a connection-opening attempt. An echo reply message would not. Some UDP interactions can also be handled in a similar way. Figure 6-7 shows a row that represents a UDP connection. It will pass subsequent packets matching this connection.

ATTACK ATTEMPTS   Suppose that an attacker's host sends a packet with the IP source address 10.5.3.4 (a spoofed IP address) and the TCP destination port 80. This is not a connection-opening attempt. (The SYN flag is not set in the TCP segment.) In Figure 6-8, we see that this packet does not match any row in the connection table. The firewall drops and logs the packet.

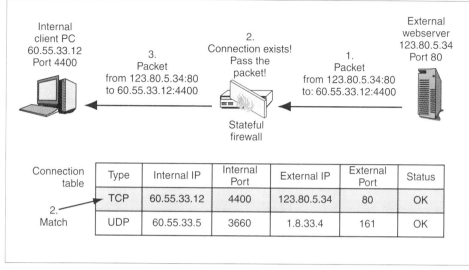

FIGURE 6-7 Stateful Packet Inspection for a Packet that Does Not Attempt to Open a Connection I

PERSPECTIVE We have seen that for packets that do not attempt to open a connection and therefore appear to be part of the ongoing communication state, SPI processing is very simple. If the connection is in the connection table, pass the packet; if not, drop the packet.

Although basic SPI processing for ongoing communication is this simple, it is also possible to build additional filtering into the processing. Additional filtering increases the work and therefore the cost of the SPI firewall. However, it is justified for some applications.

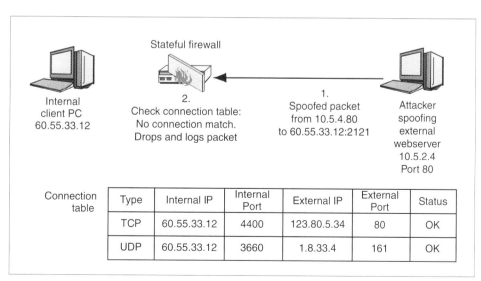

FIGURE 6-8 Stateful Packet Inspection for a Packet that Does Not Attempt to Open a Connection II

TEST YOUR UNDERSTANDING

6. **a.** Give the simple stateful packet inspection firewall rule for packets that do not attempt to open connections.
   b. Is SPI filtering for packets that are part of ongoing communications usually simple and inexpensive? Explain.
   c. UDP is connectionless. How is it possible for an SPI firewall to handle UDP connections?

Packets that Do Attempt to Open a Connection

So far, we have looked at how SPI firewalls handle packets that *do not* attempt to open a connection. Figure 6-5 shows that stateful inspection firewalls also have a simple default behavior for deciding whether to pass packets that *do* try to open connections. (In general, the **default** is what you get if you do not specify something else explicitly.)

- By default, SPI firewalls permit all attempts to open a connection from an internal host to an external host. This makes sense because it generally is acceptable for internal clients to open connections to external servers. When an internal host tries to open a connection to an external host, the firewall by default adds an appropriate row to the state table.
- By default, the SPI firewall stops all external hosts from opening connections to internal hosts. This makes sense because few external clients should be able to reach internal servers. This defaults stops attackers from connecting to internal servers (or clients).

TEST YOUR UNDERSTANDING

7. Give the two simple default SPI firewall rules for packets that attempt to open connections.

Access Control Lists (ACLs) for Connection-Opening Attempts

Although the default behavior of stateful packet inspection firewalls works most of the time for connection-opening attempts, organizations need to have exceptions. For exceptions, the default behavior will need to be superseded.

- For example, firms may need to permit some externally initiated connections. For example, external clients will need access to the firm's internal e-commerce server.
- To give another example, firms may need to prevent some internally initiated connections to the outside world. For instance, the firewall may need to prevent internal clients from connecting to known phishing sites. It may also need to prevent malware on internal compromised hosts from attacking external hosts or from sending sensitive information out of the site.

To specify exceptions to default rules, SPI firewalls have access control lists for both internal and external connection-opening attempts.

Access control lists (ACLs) consist of a series of rules that are exceptions to the default behavior.

> *Access control lists (ACLs) consist of a series of rules that are exceptions to the default behavior.*

- For internally initiated connection-opening attempts, the default rule is to allow all connections. Therefore, ACLs for internally initiated connection-opening attempts specify conditions under which internally initiated connections should be prevented.[4]
- For externally initiated connection-opening attempts, the default rule is to prevent all connection openings. Therefore, ACLs for externally initiated connection-opening attempts specify conditions under which certain externally initiated connection-opening attempts should be allowed.

WELL-KNOWN PORT NUMBERS   ACL rules typically involve TCP or UDP port numbers. Servers have **well-known port numbers**, which designate specific applications running on the server. For example, Port 80 is the well-known port number for HTTP. To prevent access to servers, SPI firewalls by default block incoming TCP and UDP connections to well-known port numbers. Figure 6-9 shows some of the well-known port numbers that are frequently referred to in ACLs. You will have to use this figure extensively in this and following chapters. Well-known port numbers range from 1 to 1023.

Port	Primary Protocol*	Application
20	TCP	FTP Data Traffic
21	TCP	FTP Supervisory Connection
22	TCP	Secure Shell (SSH)
23	TCP	Telnet
25	TCP	Simple Mail Transfer Protocol (SMTP)
53	TCP	Domain Name System (DNS)
69	UDP	Trivial File Transfer Protocol (TFTP)
80	TCP	Hypertext Transfer Protocol (HTTP)
110	TCP	Post Office Protocol (POP)
135–139	TCP	NETBIOS service for peer-to-peer file sharing in older versions of Windows
143	TCP	Internet Message Access Protocol (IMAP)
161	UDP	Simple Network Management Protocol (SNMP)
443	TCP	HTTP over SSL/TLS

*In many cases, both TCP and UDP can be used by an application. In such cases, the same port number is used for both. Typically, however, the use of either TCP or UDP will be predominant.

FIGURE 6-9   Well-Known Port Numbers

---

[4] As we will see later, there is an exception to the statement that ACL rules are exceptions. The last rule specifies the default behavior instead of an exception.

ACCESS CONTROL LISTS (ACLs) FOR INGRESS FILTERING   Figure 6-10 illustrates a simple ACL for ingress filtering (which examines externally initiated connection-opening attempts). Recall that in ingress filtering, the default behavior is to automatically deny external connection-opening attempts. Consequently, a typical ingress ACL rule *permits* a specific externally originated connection (say to an internal webserver).

IF-THEN FORMAT   Rules in the figure follow an **if-then** format. If certain of the packet's field values match certain criteria values, then we say that the packet matches the rule. Based on the "then" part of the rule, the firewall will either allow or disallow the connection-opening attempt.

- If the packet matches the rule, the firewall takes the indicated action.
- However, if the packet does not match the rule, the firewall does not take action based on that rule and goes on to the next rule.
- The final rule does not have an if-then format. If the firewall reaches the last rule in the ACL, it will follow that rule.

Access Control List Operation

An ACL is a series of rules for allowing or disallowing connections

The rules are executed in order, beginning with the first

If a rule DOES NOT apply to the connection-opening attempt,
     the firewall goes to the next ACL rule

If the rule DOES apply, the firewall follows the rule,
     no further rules are executed

If the firewall reaches the last rule in the ACL, it follows that rule

Ingress ACL's Purpose

The default behavior is to drop all attempts to open a connection from the outside

All ACL rules except for the last give exceptions to the default behavior under specified circumstances

The last rule applies the default behavior to all connection-opening attempts that are not allowed by earlier rules are executed by this last rule

Simple Ingress ACL with Three Rules

1. If TCP destination port = 80 or TCP destination port = 443, then Allow Connection
    [Permits connection to ALL internal webservers]
2. If TCP destination port = 25 AND IP destination address = 60.47.3.35, then Allow Connection
    [Permits connections to A SINGLE internal mail server]
3. Disallow ALL Connections
    [Disallows all other externally initiated connections; this is the default behavior]

FIGURE 6-10   Ingress Access Control List (ACL) in a Stateful Packet Inspection Firewall (Study Figure)

PORTS AND SERVER ACCESS In Figure 6-10, Rule 1 permits externally initiated connections if the TCP destination port number is 80 (HTTP) or 443 (SSL/TLS over HTTP). This permits access to *all* internal webservers.

In turn, Rule 2 permits externally initiated connections if the TCP destination port is 25 (which is the well-known destination port for mail servers). However, it *only* permits Port 25 connections to a single mail server, 60.47.3.35. This obviously is safer than allowing connections to *any* internal mail server, as is done in Rule 1.

Comparing the security of Rules 1 and 2 illustrates a crucial point. There often are multiple ways to implement a policy. The firewall administrator should always choose the ACL rule that implements the policy but also minimizes openings through the firewall. If possible, this means only permitting connections to a single internal server or at most a few internal servers.

> *The firewall administrator should always choose the ACL rule that implements the policy but also minimizes openings through the firewall.*

DISALLOW ALL CONNECTIONS The final rule, Rule 3, is Disallow ALL Connections. This rule implements the SPI firewall's default behavior for externally initiated connections. All connections that are not specifically permitted by earlier ACL rules are specifically denied.

Note that while ACL rules in general specify exceptions to the default behavior, the last rule specifies the default behavior. If a packet is not subject to an exception and reaches the final rule, the default behavior is implemented.

In this discussion, we have noted that (1) there is the default behavior and that (2) access control lists permit exceptions. This may have sounded like there were two processes involved. In fact, there is only one. The SPI firewall simply *always* executes the ACL. Initially, there is only a single rule, which specifies the default behavior, so the default behavior is automatically executed. Later, the firewall administrator will add exception rules.

TEST YOUR UNDERSTANDING

8. **a.** For stateful packet inspection firewalls, what do ingress ACLs permit in general?
   b. What do egress ACLs disallow in general in SPI firewalls?
   c. What do well-known port numbers designate?
   d. Is Figure 6-10 an ACL for ingress filtering or egress filtering?
   e. Why is Rule 2 in Figure 6-10 safer than Rule 1?
   f. Which rule in the ACL in Figure 6-10 represents the default behavior of SPI firewalls for ingress connection-opening attempts?

9. Given the ACL in Figure 6-10, what would the firewall do with an incoming ICMP echo message? (This will require some thought. Think about how ICMP messages are encapsulated and what field in the IP header indicates that the packet's data field contains an ICMP message.)

10. Redo the ACL in Figure 6-10 to add rules for the following conditions. After Rule 1, create a rule that permits all connections to internal DNS servers. After the original Rule 2, create rules that permit connections to all Trivial File Transfer Protocol (TFTP) servers and that

permit access to FTP Server 60.33.17.1. (Hint: only allow an FTP supervisory connection; the SPI firewall will later open data connections automatically as needed.)

11. **a.** In ingress and egress filtering, does an SPI firewall always consider its ACL rules when a new packet arrives that attempts to open a connection?
   b. In ingress and egress filtering, does an SPI firewall always consider its ACL rules when a new packet arrives that does not attempt to open a connection? (The answer was not specifically in this section.)

Perspective on SPI Firewalls

LOW COST   Although deciding whether to allow connections is somewhat complex, we saw in Figure 6-5 that most packets are not connection-opening attempts. Rather, they are subsequent packets in a recognized connection. For the vast majority of packets, then, the stateful packet inspection firewall does a simple table lookup and decides immediately whether to pass or drop the packet. (There is no need to consider ACL rules as there is for connection-opening attempts.) This is fast and therefore inexpensive.

SAFETY   The absence of sophisticated examination beyond checking if a packet is part of a connection might seem like a serious limitation. However, in practice, attacks other than application layer attacks rarely get through an SPI firewall unless the administrator creates an incorrect ACL. In addition, as we noted earlier, SPI firewalls *can* go beyond stateful inspection and implement other protections.

DOMINANCE   The combination of high safety and low cost makes SPI firewalls extremely popular. In fact, we noted earlier that nearly all main border firewalls today use stateful packet inspection.

TEST YOUR UNDERSTANDING

12. **a.** Why are stateful packet inspection firewalls inexpensive?
   b. In practice, are they fairly safe?
   c. Are SPI firewalls limited to SPI filtering?
   d. What firewall inspection mechanism do nearly all main border firewalls today use?

Low Cost
   Most packets are not part of packet-opening attempts
   These can be handled very simply and therefore inexpensively
   Connection-opening attempt packets are more expensive process but are rare

Safety
   Attacks other than application-level attacks usually fail to get through SPI firewalls
   In addition, SPI firewalls can use other forms of filtering when needed

Dominance
   The combination of high safety and low cost makes SPI firewalls extremely popular
   Nearly all main border firewalls today use stateful packet inspection

---

FIGURE 6-11   Perspective on SPI Firewalls (Study Figure)

NETWORK ADDRESS TRANSLATION (NAT)

In this chapter, we look at several filtering methods that firewalls use to make pass/deny decisions about arriving packets. However, there is one technique used in several types of firewalls that does not actually filter packets but that effectively provides a great deal of protection. This is **network address translation (NAT)**. It is used in firewalls that use various types of examination methods as a second type of protection.[5]

Sniffers

Figure 6-12 shows that hackers sometimes can place **sniffers** outside of corporate networks. As packets from these corporate networks pass through the sniffer, the sniffer captures them and notes source IP addresses and port numbers. This allows the attacker to learn about the network's host IP addresses and open port numbers on servers without sending probe packets. The sniffer will be able to send attack packets to these IP addresses and port numbers.

NAT Operation

Figure 6-12 illustrates how a process called network address translation (NAT) can thwart sniffers.

PACKET CREATION First, the internal client sends a packet to an external server. This packet contains the client's real IP address, 192.168.5.7. The UDP datagram or TCP segment it carries has the ephemeral port number 3333. (In Windows, clients use *ephemeral port numbers*, which range from 1024 to 4999.) This is the source socket 192.168.5.7:3333.

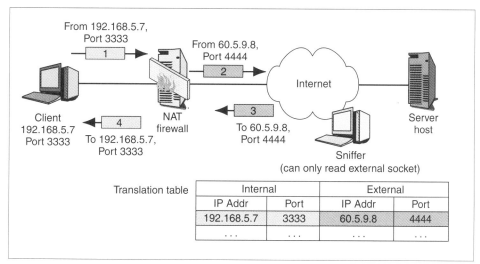

FIGURE 6-12 Network Address Translation (NAT)

---

[5] It is also done on all household Internet access routers as part of their basic operation. NAT allows several PCs to share a single IP address given to the household. It provides security as a byproduct.

NETWORK AND PORT ADDRESS TRANSLATION   The NAT firewall intercepts all outgoing traffic and replaces source IP addresses and source port numbers with external (stand-in) IP addresses and port numbers. In this case, the external IP address is 60.5.9.8, and the stand-in port number is 4444. So the stand-in socket in the outgoing packet is 60.5.9.8:4444. The NAT firewall then sends the packet to the external server.

TRANSLATION TABLE   The NAT firewall also places the internal socket and the external socket in the translation table.

RESPONSE PACKET   When the server replies, it will send a packet to destination IP address 60.5.9.8 and destination Port 4444.

RESTORATION   The NAT firewall notes that the socket 60.5.9.8:4444 exists in its translation table. It replaces the external destination IP address and port number with 192.168.5.7 and 3333. The firewall sends this packet to the client PC.

PROTECTION   The sniffer cannot learn internal IP addresses or port numbers, so it cannot use this information to make attacks (unless it can act immediately, which is rare). In addition, network scanning probes are automatically rejected because the IP addresses and port numbers will not be in the translation table.

Perspective on NAT

NAT/PAT   Although the firewalls we are discussing are called NAT firewalls, they translate both network addresses (IP addresses) and port addresses. Therefore, it would seem appropriate to call them NAT/PAT firewalls. This is seldom done, but it is important to understand that NAT does not only translate network IP addresses but port numbers as well.

TRANSPARENCY   NAT is transparent to both the internal and the external hosts. Neither the client nor the server knows that NAT is being done. They do not have to change their way of operating at all.

NAT TRAVERSAL   Unfortunately, certain protocols have problems with NAT. These include such widely used applications as VoIP and such important security protocols as IPsec. VoIP creates a new port number for a conversation after an administrative connection is made, and IPsec requires true internal IP addresses. Although **NAT traversal**—allowing applications that were not designed to work with NAT—is possible, there are several NAT traversal methods, and all have limitations. Selecting and using them can be complex.

TEST YOUR UNDERSTANDING

13. **a.** When NAT is used, why can sniffers not learn anything about the internal IP addresses of internal hosts?
    b. Why does NAT stop scanning probes?
    c. Why is NAT traversal necessary?
    d. Is a NAT traversal method easy to select?

APPLICATION PROXY FIREWALLS AND APPLICATION CONTENT FILTERING

Neither static packet filter firewalls nor stateful packet inspection firewalls examine application messages.[6] This is unfortunate because application messages contain information that is valuable for detecting many types of attacks. **Application proxy firewalls** remedy this oversight by explicitly filtering application messages.

Application Proxy Firewall Operation

OPERATIONAL DETAILS Figure 6-13 looks at application proxy firewall operation. Note that the application proxy firewall inspects application content in all traffic between clients and servers. In this case, the client is internal and the server is external. This is an HTTP interaction, so an HTTP proxy program on the application proxy firewall does the filtering.

In order to do this, the HTTP proxy program establishes HTTP connections to both the client and the webserver. To the client, the proxy program acts like a webserver. To the webserver, the HTTP proxy program acts like a browser client.

Whenever a packet arrives, the application proxy firewall inspects its application layer content. More specifically, it collects all of the segments of an application message if the application message is fragmented, and then inspects the

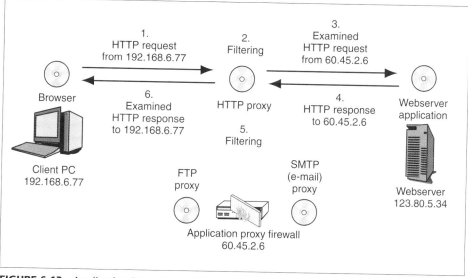

FIGURE 6-13 Application Proxy Firewall Operation

---

[6] Actually, SPI firewalls do look at some application message content, but only in limited ways. For example, in voice over IP and several other applications, after two application programs initially connect, one side tells the other to use a different port number for subsequent communication. This is called port switching. Port switching notifications come inside application messages. Stateful inspection firewalls, then, read application messages to look for port switching notifications so that the firewall can modify the connection's port number or port numbers in the connection table or add a new connection to the connection table. This is a very limited reading of application messages, however.

content. If there is no problem, the application proxy firewall passes the application message on.

APPLICATION PROXY PROGRAMS VERSUS APPLICATION PROXY FIREWALLS Application proxies use application-specific relaying, in which they act as both a client and a host when packets arrive. Consequently, the firewall needs a separate application proxy program for each application protocol, as Figure 6-13 illustrates.

PROCESSING-INTENSIVE OPERATION Maintaining two connections for each client/server pair is highly processing-intensive. For this reason, application proxy firewalls can only handle a limited number of client/server pairs. Consequently, application proxy firewalls cannot be used as main border firewalls. They simply could not handle the traffic load.

ONLY A FEW APPLICATIONS CAN BE PROXIED In addition to their slow operation per packet handled, application proxy firewalls have another serious limitation. Only a few applications can be effectively proxied. For most applications, there are no specific patterns that can be filtered or protocols that can be enforced. Most application proxy firewalls, in fact, support either HTTP or SMTP.

TWO COMMON USES Once, application proxy firewalls were used as main border firewalls. For reasons we just seen, they require too much processing power to serve in that role today. However, application proxy firewalls never disappeared. Figure 6-14 shows that there are two common uses of application proxy firewalls today.

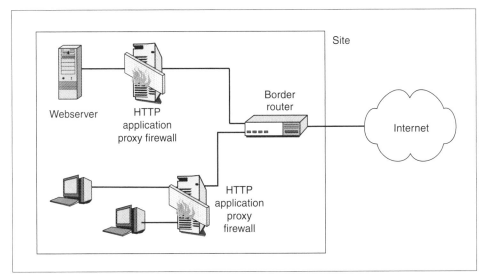

FIGURE 6-14 Roles for Application Proxy Firewalls Today

The first role is to protect internal clients from malicious external servers. All client connections to external servers are proxied through a single application proxy firewall. This firewall examines the application content of all packets coming in from the external servers. If the firewall detects dangerous content, it drops the packet.

The second role for application proxy firewalls today is to sit between an internal server and external clients. In such cases, the application proxy firewall protects a single server. It examines the application layer content of all incoming client requests for dangerous behavior.

TEST YOUR UNDERSTANDING

14. a. What distinguishes an application proxy firewall from static packet filtering firewalls and SPI firewalls?
  b. Distinguish between proxy programs and application proxy firewalls.
  c. If you will proxy four different applications, how many proxy programs will you need?
  d. How many application proxy firewalls will you need at a minimum?
  e. Can nearly all applications be proxied?
  f. Why is application proxy firewall operation processing-intensive?
  g. Why do firms not use application proxy firewalls as main border firewalls?
  h. What are the two main roles of application proxy server firewalls today?

Application Content Filtering in Stateful Packet Inspection Firewalls

Application proxy firewalls are not the only firewalls that can provide application content filtering. As Figure 6-15 notes, most stateful packet firewalls can also do application content filtering—often the same types of application content filtering that application proxy firewalls do.

Topic	Application proxy firewalls	Stateful packet inspection firewalls	Remarks
Can examine application layer content	Always	As an extra feature	
Capabilities for application layer content filtering	Somewhat more	Somewhat less	
Uses relay operation with two connections per client/server pair?	Yes	No	Maintaining two connections is highly processing intensive. Cannot support many client/server pairs. Consequently, application proxy firewalls cannot be used as main border firewalls
Speed	Slow	Fast	

FIGURE 6-15 Application Content Filtering in Application Proxy Firewalls and Stateful Packet Inspection Firewalls

Stateful packet inspection firewalls do not have to implement relay operation as application firewalls do. This permits SPI firewalls to add application content filtering more economically.

However, SPI firewall application inspection lacks some of the protections offered by application proxy firewalls, which are discussed in the box "Application Proxy Firewall Protections." Most importantly, SPI application inspection does not provide the important automatic protections offered by application proxy firewalls—the hiding of internal IP addresses, header destruction, and protocol fidelity.

Overall, the ability to do application content filtering considerably expands the usefulness of SPI firewalls, further cementing their position as the main type of corporate firewall today.

TEST YOUR UNDERSTANDING

15. **a.** Do stateful packet inspection firewalls automatically do application content filtering? Explain.
    b. Do they have the slow speed of relay operation?
    c. What three advantages do application proxy firewalls have in protection that SPI firewalls with content inspection not have?
    d. Why are SPI content filtering firewalls faster than application proxy firewalls?

Application Proxy Firewall Protections

Application Content Filtering for HTTP

We have noted that application proxy firewalls filter the content of application messages. The specifics of this filtering vary by application. We will only mention a few filtering actions that HTTP application proxies can take. There are other filtering actions for HTTP, SMTP, and other types of applications.

Client Protections

As noted earlier, many firms use application proxy firewalls to protect internal clients from malicious external servers. For HTTP, proxy programs can do several types of filtering. We will only list three:

- The proxy can inspect the URL and compare it with a table of black-listed URLs that are known phishing sites, pornography sites, or recreational sites.
- The proxy can inspect scripts in downloaded webpages, dropping these webpages if the scripts appear to be malicious or if policies prohibit either certain types of scripts or all scripts.
- The proxy can inspect the MIME type in an HTTP response message. The MIME type describes the type of file downloaded in the message. Files with certain MIME types of files might be allowed or dropped by policy.

The HTTP proxy can also examine outgoing packets from the internal client to the external webserver to detect client misbehavior. For example, the proxy can inspect the method in the URL header. The HTTP GET method is generally safe because it is used to retrieve files. However, the POST method can send files out of the firm. Many firms drop any HTTP request message that uses the POST method in order to provide extrusion prevention.

Protections for Internal Clients against Malicious Webservers

URL blacklists for known attack sites

Protection against some or all scripts in webpages

The disallowing of HTTP response messages with prohibited MIME types that indicate malware

Protections against Misbehaving Internal Clients

Disallowing the HTTP POST method, which can be use to send out sensitive files

Protections for Internal Webservers against Malicious Clients

Disallow HTTP POST methods, which could allow malware files to be placed on the server

Indications of SQL injection attacks

Automatic Protections

The hiding of internal host IP addresses from sniffers

  Packets to the server have the firewall's IP address as the source IP address

Header destruction

  In operation, the firewall removes incoming application messages from packets

  Any attack using the header fields will automatically fail

Protocol fidelity

  If the client or server does not follow the protocol that should be used with the specified port number, communication with the firewall will automatically break down

FIGURE 6-16   Application Proxy Firewall Protections (Study Figure)

Server Protections

For servers, the HTTP proxy program attempts to protect the server from malicious clients.

- As just noted, the proxy can inspect the method in the URL header. The POST method will allow clients to upload files to the webserver. This might be disallowed by policy to prevent clients from uploading malware, pornography, or any other type of unimproved content.
- The HTTP proxy might also filter out HTTP request messages that appear to contain SQL injection attacks. (We will learn about this type of attack in Chapter 8.)

Other Protections

While filtering the content of the application layer message is important, there are three other protections that application proxy firewalls offer automatically by the very way in which they work.

- **Internal IP address hiding**. Like NAT, application proxy firewalls hide the IP addresses of internal hosts. Packets that leave the firm have as their source IP addresses the IP address of the application proxy firewall, not the IP addresses of the internal hosts. This thwarts sniffers.
- **Header destruction**. Recall that when a packet arrives at an application proxy firewall, the proxy program examines the application layer message. To do this, the

(Continued)

Application Proxy Firewall Protections   (Continued)

proxy program decapsulates the application message. In doing so, it discards the internet and transport layer headers in the arriving packet. If the attacker has manipulated the fields in the internet or transport layer headers to cause problems, header destruction automatically defeats these attack methods. If the application proxy firewall passes the application layer message, it places the message in a new transport message and a new internet packet. The attacker has no way of affecting the contents of fields in these new headers.

- **Protocol fidelity**. In operation, the application proxy program acts like a server to the client and like a client to the server. Suppose the client and the server attempt to get around firewalls by using Port 80—the well-known port for HTTP—to handle a different program, such as an instant messaging program that the company has forbidden. In such cases, the connections to the application proxy firewall will fail because the HTTP proxy program will be expecting HTTP interactions and will not receive them. The connections will automatically be broken.[7]

TEST YOUR UNDERSTANDING

16. **a.** What filtering actions were listed to protect clients from malicious webservers?
    b. What filtering action was mentioned to prevent internal client misbehavior in HTTP?
    c. What two filtering actions were mentioned for protecting webservers from malicious clients?
    d. What three automatic protections do application proxy firewalls provide simply because of the way in which they operate?

INTRUSION DETECTION SYSTEMS (IDSs) AND INTRUSION PREVENTION SYSTEMS (IPSs)

As noted at the beginning of this chapter, firewall filtering sophistication is limited by the processing power of firewalls. The earliest firewalls could only do simple static packet filtering. As processing power increased, stateful packet inspection became possible and then became dominant.

Today, SPI is beginning to be challenged by a new type of filtering, which is called intrusion prevention system filtering (IPS). This new filtering method is capable of detecting and stopping attacks that are more sophisticated than earlier forms of filtering, including SPI, could address. Only time will tell if IPS filtering is capable of becoming a dominant filtering method for border firewalls.

Intrusion Detection Systems (IDSs)

Intrusion prevention system filtering grew out of an earlier technology—intrusion detection systems. Many homes and cars have burglar alarms that sound off if there is suspicious movement. Similarly, many corporations install **intrusion detection**

---

[7] Some rogue applications get around this problem by using HTTP to carry their messages in HTTP bodies. This is called HTTP tunneling. An HTTP proxy program should look for indications of HTTP tunneling during its filtering process.

Perspective
 Growing processing power made stateful packet inspection possible:
 Now, growing processing power is making a new firewall filtering method attractive
 Intrusion prevention systems (IPSs)

Intrusion Detection Systems (IDSs)
 Firewalls drop provable attack packets only
 Intrusion detection systems (IDSs) look for *suspicious* traffic
  Cannot drop because the packet is merely suspicious
 Sends an alarm message if the attack appears to be serious
 Problem: Too many false positives (false alarms)
  Alarms are ignored or the system is discontinued
  Can reduce false positives by tuning the IDSs
   Eliminate inapplicable rules, such as a Unix rule in an all-Windows company
   Reduce the number of rules allowed to generate alarms
   Most alarms will still be false alarms
 Problem: Heavy processing requirements because of sophisticated filtering
  Deep packet inspection:
   Looks at application content and transport and internet headers
  Packet stream analysis
   Looks at patterns across a series of packets
   Often, patterns cannot be seen unless many packets are examined

Intrusion Prevention Systems (IPSs)
 Use IDS filtering mechanisms
 Application-specific integrated circuits (ASICs) provide the needed processing power
 Attack confidence identification spectrum
  Somewhat likely
  Very likely
  Provable
 Allowed to stop traffic at the high end of the attack confidence spectrum
 Firm decides which attacks to stop

Possible Actions
 Drop packets
  Risky for suspicious traffic even with high confidence
 Bandwidth limitation for certain types of traffic
  Limit to a certain percentage of all traffic
  Less risky than dropping packets
  Useful when confidence is lower

FIGURE 6-17 Intrusion Detection Systems (IDSs) and Intrusion Prevention Systems (IPSs) (Study Figure)

systems (IDSs), which examine streams of packets to look for suspicious activities that indicate possible attacks. If an IDS detects an apparently serious attack, it may send an alarm message to the security administrator. (If the attack does not seem too serious, the IDS will merely log it.)

FIREWALLS VERSUS IDSs Traditionally, there was a strong distinction between firewalls and IDSs. Firewalls *stop provable* attack packets. If a packet is not a provable attack packet, the firewall cannot drop it. IDSs, in turn, *identify suspicious* packets that may or may not be parts of attacks. To give an analogy, a police officer may only arrest someone if the officer has probable cause (a relatively high standard of proof). If someone is behaving suspiciously, a police officer may only investigate them.

> *Firewalls* **stop** provable *attack packets. If a packet is not a provable attack packet, the firewall cannot drop it. IDSs, in turn,* **identify suspicious** *packets that may or may not be parts of attacks.*

FALSE POSITIVES (FALSE ALARMS) We will look at intrusion detection systems in more detail in Chapter 9. Our focus in this chapter is two serious limitations of IDSs. The first is that, like many home and car alarms, IDSs tend to generate far too many **false alarms**, which, in IDS-speak, are **false positives**. Like the little boy who cried wolf too many times, IDSs tend to be ignored after exhausted security staff members receive too many false alarms.

It is possible to **tune** IDSs to reduce the number of false positives to a bearable degree. Many rules make no sense in a particular organization. For instance, if a rule identifies a packet that would be dangerous if sent to a specific type of Unix server, and if an organization has no Unix servers of that type, the rule can be deleted to eliminate the alarms it would generate. However, tuning requires a great deal of labor.

IDSs log all suspicious activity but only create alarms for some suspicious activities. In addition to removing nonsensical rules, tuning may reduce the number of attack signatures that generate alarms. However, while this reduces alarms, it also creates greater urgency for security administrators to read log files regularly to catch attacks that are no longer alarmed.

There are many rules, and each must be considered very carefully. Consequently, tuning is so expensive and resource-draining that few organizations implement fully.

HEAVY PROCESSING REQUIREMENTS Another problem is that IDS methodologies are highly processing-intensive. This limits the traffic volume that IDSs can filter.

Deep Packet Inspection One reason for IDS's processing intensiveness is that IDSs do not merely look at a few fields in a packet. They use **deep packet inspection**, which looks at all fields in the packet, including the IP header, the TCP or UDP header, and the application message. Many attacks cannot be stopped if a firewall only looks at application content or only at internet and transport layer headers.

Packet Stream Analysis IDSs also need to filter **packet streams**, rather than individual packets. Many attacks are not apparent from individual packets. For instance, a single ICMP echo message is not very diagnostic, but a stream of ICMP echo messages trying different IP addresses is a very strong sign that the company is experiencing a systematic scan. More subtly, application content will be spread over quite a few packets. To analyze application content, an IDS will have to reassemble original application messages—sometimes, a succession of application messages. Examining packet streams instead of just individual packets for dangerous patterns is very processing-intensive.

TEST YOUR UNDERSTANDING

17. **a.** Distinguish between firewalls and IDSs.
    b. Why are IDS alarms often a problem?
    c. What is a false positive?
    d. What two types of filtering do IDSs use?
    e. Why is deep packet inspection important?
    f. Why is deep packet inspection processing intensive?
    g. Why is packet stream analysis important?
    h. Why does packet stream analysis place a heavy load on IDSs?

Intrusion Prevention Systems (IPSs)

As just noted, intrusion prevention systems grew out of IDS processing. However, although they use IDS filtering methods, **intrusion prevention systems (IPSs)** actually stop some kinds of attacks instead of merely identifying them and generating alarms, as IDSs do. This is why they are called intrusion *prevention* systems.[8]

> *Although they use IDS filtering methods, intrusion prevention systems (IPSs) actually stop some kinds of attacks instead of merely identifying them and generating alarms, as IDSs do.*

ASICs FOR FASTER PROCESSING Also as noted earlier, IDS/IPS filtering is very processing-intensive. The most important development leading to IPSs has been the emergence of **application-specific integrated circuits (ASICs)**,[9] which can do filtering in hardware. Hardware filtering is much faster than software filtering, allowing IPSs to be used even when traffic volume is high.

---

[8] Of course, all firewalls are intrusion prevention systems, aren't they? Another triumph of marketing over reality.

[9] Usually, a firewall has a general purpose CPU and application software to execute functions. ASICs, in contrast, execute most or all functions with custom-designed hardware. This is far faster than executing them as software. As the name application-specific integrated circuit indicates, specific integrated circuits have to be created for an application's functionality if functions are to be execute in hardware. This used to be prohibitively expensive, but the cost of ASICs has fallen greatly in recent years.

THE ATTACK IDENTIFICATION CONFIDENCE SPECTRUM When experienced security professionals who have worked with IDSs hear about IPSs, they usually cringe at first. Given the number of false positives that IDSs generate, the thought of allowing these unreliable filtering mechanisms to actually stop traffic is deeply disturbing.

In practice, however, there always is a spectrum of **attack identification confidence** in intrusion detection. Some attacks, especially DoS attacks, can be identified with a very high degree of confidence. In fact, many border firewalls today *already* identify and stop DoS attacks regardless of their main filtering technology. Other attacks cannot be identified with such high confidence.[10]

TEST YOUR UNDERSTANDING

18. **a.** Distinguish between IDSs and IPSs.
    b. Why is the attack identification confidence spectrum important in deciding whether to allow IPSs to stop specific attacks?

IPS Actions

What do IPSs do when they detect suspicious traffic at the high end of the attack identification confidence spectrum?

DROPPING PACKETS In many cases, the IPS will drop attack packets, acting like a traditional firewall. This is dangerous but highly effective.

LIMITING TRAFFIC In other cases, the IPS limits suspicious traffic to a certain percentage of the total bandwidth. **Bandwidth limitation** can ensure that even if peer-to-peer file sharing traffic and other illegitimate traffic cannot be identified with precision and dropped, this undesirable traffic at least will not result in an overloaded network.

TEST YOUR UNDERSTANDING

19. **a.** What two actions can IPSs take when they identify an attack?
    b. Which can be the most effective?
    c. Which can do the most damage?

ANTIVIRUS FILTERING AND UNIFIED THREAT MANAGEMENT (UTM)

Firewalls normally do not do antivirus filtering. However, firewalls and antivirus filtering servers work together closely. All major firewall vendors have protocols for working with antivirus servers. Figure 6-18 illustrates this dynamic.

When a packet arrives at a firewall, the firewall decides what to do with it. (Actually, the firewall may have to assemble many packets into an e-mail message, webpage, or image before deciding what to do with them.) To decide, the firewall

---

[10] When organizations install IPSs, they typically do not use them to prevent attacks immediately. Rather, companies have them record what they *would* have stopped had they been allowed to stop them. If this experience builds confidence, companies usually have their IPSs stop attacks at the high-confidence end of the attack identification confidence spectrum. In time, they may even move to having their IPS stop attacks for which identification confidence is not quite so high.

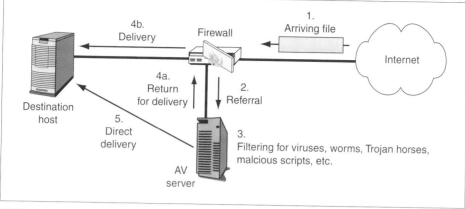

FIGURE 6-18   Firewalls and Antivirus Servers

will check its policy rules base. If the rule for this type of object is to pass the object to an antivirus server, the firewall will do so.

The antivirus server will examine the object. This filtering goes beyond viruses. It also searches for worms, Trojan horses, spam, phishing, rootkits, malicious scripts, and other malware. After filtering, if the antivirus server does not drop the object, it returns the object to the firewall to be passed on, or the antivirus server passes on the object to the receiver by itself.

Some firewalls do embrace both traditional firewall filtering methods and antivirus filtering. As noted briefly at the start of the chapter, these are called **unified threat management (UTM) firewalls**. Although UTM products do exist, the ones sold today tend to be good in one area and inadequate in others. In addition, given the need to do both firewall and antivirus filtering, most UTM products only have the processing power to be used in smaller firms or branch offices of larger firms.

TEST YOUR UNDERSTANDING

20. a. How do firewalls and antivirus servers work together?
  b. Are antivirus servers limited to looking for viruses? Explain.
  c. What may the antivirus server do after it performs filtering?
  d. What type of firewall does both traditional firewall filtering and antivirus filtering?

Traditional Firewalls
  Do not do antivirus filtering
Unified Threat Management (UTM) Firewalls
  SPI
  Antivirus Filtering
  VPNs
  DoS Protection
  NAT
  . . .

FIGURE 6-19   Unified Threat Management (UTM) (Study Figure)

Denial-of-Service (DoS) Protection

Although we have not talked about denial-of-service (DoS) filtering as a separate filtering method, almost all main border firewalls also do DoS filtering. Most DoS attacks are easy to detect, although many are very difficult to stop even if they are detected.

One popular DoS attack is the half-open TCP attack, in which the attacker sends a large number of TCP SYN segments to the victim server. Each SYN begins a TCP session opening process on the server. The server sets aside RAM and other resources for the connection. The server then sends back a SYN/ACK segment. The attacker never completes the connection opening by sending a final ACK. As the attacker sends more SYN segments, the victim host keeps setting aside resources until it crashes or refuses to provide any more connections, even to legitimate users. Either way, the attacker wins.

Some firewalls address TCP SYN attacks by creating **false opens**. Whenever a SYN segment arrives, the firewall itself sends back a SYN/ACK segment, without passing the SYN segment on to the target server. Only when the firewall gets back an ACK, which only happens in legitimate connections, does the firewall send the original SYN segment on to the server for which the original SYN segment was intended. The firewall does not set aside resources for a connection when a SYN segment arrives, so handling a large number of false SYN segments is only a small burden.

Perspective

    Done by most main border firewalls

    DOS attacks are easy to detect but difficult to stop because their traffic looks like legitimate packets

TCP Half-Opening Attacks

    Attacks

        Attacker sends a TCP SYN segment to a port

        The application program sends back a SYN/ACK segment and sets aside resources

        The attacker never sends back an ACK, so the victim keeps the resources reserved

        The victim soon runs out of resources and crashes or can no longer serve legitimate traffic

    Defenses

        Firewall intercepts the SYN from an external host

        Firewall sends back an SYN/ACK without passing the segment on to the target host

        Only if the firewall receives a timely ACK does it send the original SYN the destination host

Rate Limiting

    Set a limit on all traffic to a server—both legitimate and DoS packets

    Keeps the entire network from being overloaded

    Not perfect—does not protect the target server or allow legitimate traffic

DoS Protection Is a Community Problem

    If an organization's access line to the Internet becomes overloaded, it cannot solve the problem itself

    Its ISP or other upstream agencies must help

FIGURE 6-20 Stopping Denial-of-Service (DoS) Attacks (Study Figure)

Many DoS attacks cannot be stopped this simply. For more subtle DoS attacks, DoS filtering often uses rate limiting—reducing a certain type of traffic that may be DoS traffic to a reasonable amount. This is good if an attack aims at a single server because it keeps transmission lines at least partially open for other communication. However, rate limiting frustrates both attackers and legitimate users. It helps, but it does not solve the problem.

Most troublingly, once DoS traffic clogs the site's access line going to the Internet, there is nothing a border firewall can do to alleviate the situation. In general, DoS attacks are community problems that can only be stopped with the help of ISPs and organizations whose computers are taken over as bots and used to attack other firms.

TEST YOUR UNDERSTANDING

21. a. Why do half-open (SYN flooding) DoS attacks cause problems for servers?
    b. What can be done to stop half-open Dos attacks?
    c. Why is rate limiting good as a way to reduce the damage of some DoS attacks?
    d. Why is it limited in effectiveness?
    e. Why is DoS protection a community problem, not just a problem for individual victim firms to solve?

FIREWALL ARCHITECTURES

Most firms have multiple firewalls, each serving different purposes. Figure 6-21 shows a representative firewall architecture for a single large corporate site.

Types of Firewalls

MAIN BORDER FIREWALLS   As expected, the figure shows a main border firewall (2) at the point where the corporate network connects to the Internet. However, it also shows several other firewalls.

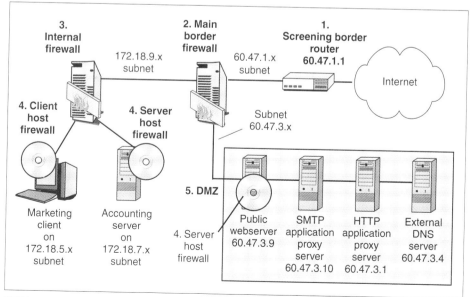

FIGURE 6-21   Firewall Architecture

SCREENING BORDER ROUTERS   Between the border firewall and the Internet is the site's border router (1). As noted earlier in the chapter, some companies put static packet filtering software on the router and make it a **screening border router**. This screening border router stops simple high-volume attacks and ensures that responses to external scanning probes cannot reach an external attacker. It economically reduces the load on the main border firewall.

INTERNAL FIREWALLS   In addition, the figure shows an internal firewall (3) that controls traffic flowing between different parts of the firm's internal network. For example, computers in the accounting department might be allowed to send packets to the accounting server, but packets from people in other departments to the accounting server should be stopped. Although Figure 6-21 only shows a single internal firewall, many sites have several internal firewalls to separate parts of the network according to different trust relationships.

HOST FIREWALLS   Individual hosts—both clients and servers—may have firewalls. Border firewalls and internal firewalls are complex to set up because they must protect a large number of client–server connections with different filtering needs. It is easy to make an error when creating an ACL rule under these circumstances.

In contrast, a typical server only has a single application or at most a handful of applications. It is much easier to create appropriate ACL rules under these circumstances. A webserver host firewall, for instance, normally only needs to allow external access on TCP Ports 80 (HTTP) and 443 (HTTP over SSL/TLS).

DEFENSE IN DEPTH   Using border, internal, and host firewalls has another advantage. It creates defense in depth. If the main firewall or an internal firewall has an ACL configuration error, individual hosts will still be protected.

TEST YOUR UNDERSTANDING

22. **a.** Why are screening routers used in a firewall architecture?
    b. Why are internal firewalls desirable?
    c. Why is it easier to create appropriate ACL rules for server host firewalls than for border firewalls?
    d. How does the use of border, internal, and host firewalls provide defense in depth?

The Demilitarized Zone (DMZ)

DMZs   In Figure 6-21, the border firewall is **tri-homed**, meaning that it connects to three subnets. One subnet leads only to the screening firewall router. (This is the 60.47.1.x subnet.) Another subnet (172.18.9.x) leads to the firm's internal network.

The third subnet (60.47.3.x) is the **demilitarized zone (DMZ)**.[11] The DMZ is a subnet that contains all of the servers and application proxy firewalls that must be

---

[11] The term "demilitarized zone" stems from the Korean War in the early 1950s. After the armistice was signed, a narrow buffer zone was established in which neither side could station its forces. However, both sides realized that future attacks would have to come through the DMZ. Consequently, both sides placed heavy troop concentrations at the edges of the DMZ. Instead of being the intended place of peace, the DMZ became the likely focal point of future struggles. Similarly, hosts placed in firewall DMZs are assumed to be major targets for attacks.

Demilitarized Zone (DMZ)

Subnet for servers and application proxy firewalls accessible via the Internet (Figure 6-22)

Hosts in the DMZ must be especially hardened because they will be accessible to attackers on the Internet

DMZs Use Tri-Homed Main Firewalls

One subnet to the border router

One subnet to the DMZ (accessible to the outside world)

One subnet to the internal network

    Access from the internal subnet to the Internet is nonexistent or minimal

    Access from the internal subnet to the DMZ is also strongly controlled

Hosts in the DMZ

Public servers (public webservers, FTP servers, etc.)

Application proxy firewalls to require all Internet traffic to pass through the DMZ

External DNS server that knows only host names in the DMZ

FIGURE 6-22 The Demilitarized Zone (DMZ) (Study Figure)

accessible to the outside world. Because these hosts are accessible to attackers on the Internet, they will face constant attack. Consequently, they must be especially hardened against attack.

> *The demilitarized zone (DMZ) is a subnet that contains all of the servers and application proxy firewalls that must be accessible to the outside world.*

SECURITY IMPLICATIONS Tri-homing allows the border firewall to create separate access rules for the DMZ and the internal subnet. The firewall should make access to the DMZ relatively easy for external Internet users. However, it should not permit any externally initiated connections from the Internet directly to internal clients or servers on the internal subnet. Only externally initiated connections to hosts in the DMZ make any sense, so only they are allowed.

What about connections between the DMZ and the internal subnet? Some DMZ servers do need to connect to internal servers. For instance, e-commerce application servers in the DMZ may have to connect to internal databases. To give another example, the HTTP proxy application server in the DMZ will need to connect to an internal browser. All connections between the DMZ and the internal subnet are dangerous. Companies limit them in numbers and tightly control the few that are allowed.

Overall, tri-homing makes it easier to develop rules to control access to public-facing hosts and internal hosts.

HOSTS IN THE DMZ In general, DMZs have three kinds of hosts.

Public Servers In Figure 6-21, the DMZ has a public webserver (60.47.3.9). If it had a public FTP server or another public server, it would also place them in the DMZ. Public servers must be accessible to clients on the Internet, and placing them in the DMZ reduces risks.

Application Proxy Firewalls   In addition to being a good place for public servers, the DMZ is a good place for application proxy firewalls, which also must be connected to the outside world. Application proxy firewalls placed in the DMZ can be used to enforce a policy that all communication with the outside world must pass through the DMZ. In the figure, there are two application proxy firewalls in the DMZ—an HTTP proxy firewall and an SMTP relay proxy firewall.

Of course, it is possible to run both the HTTP and SMTP proxy programs on the same server. However, putting the proxy programs on different servers increases security. If attackers take over one server, only that application proxy program is compromised.

External DNS Server   The DMZ in Figure 6-21 contains an **external DNS server**, 60.47.3.4, which is created to be accessed by the outside world. This allows the firm to give servers in the DMZ host names. However, this external DNS server in the DMZ only knows the host names and IP addresses of hosts in the DMZ. This way, outside attackers cannot use the DNS server in the DMZ to learn about host IP addresses on the firm's internal protected network.

TEST YOUR UNDERSTANDING

23. **a.** What is a tri-homed router?
    b. What is a DMZ?
    c. Why do companies use DMZs?
    d. What three types of hosts are placed in the DMZ?
    e. Why do companies put public servers in the DMZ?
    f. Why do companies put application proxy firewalls in the DMZ?
    g. What host names does the external DNS server know?
    h. Why do all hosts in the DMZ have to be hardened stringently?

FIREWALL MANAGEMENT

Firewalls do not work automatically. They require careful planning, implementation, and day-to-day management. Without a great deal of initial and continuing management labor, firewalls look impressive physically but provide little protection.

Defining Firewall Polices

Chapter 2 discussed strategic security planning and asset security planning. These should lead to the creation of **firewall policies**, which are high-level statements to guide firewall implementers. For example, a firewall policy may require that any HTTP connection coming from the Internet can only be made to a server in the DMZ.

WHY USE POLICIES?   Each firewall policy must be translated into an ACL rule (or multiple rules) that the firewall can understand. An access control list with many rules can be difficult to understand. However, a list of firewall policies is comparatively easy to understand.

Firewalls Are Ineffective Without Planning and Ongoing Management

Defining Firewall Policies

Policies are high-level statements about what to do

E.g., HTTP connections from the Internet may only go to servers in the DMZ

Policies are more comprehensible than actual firewall rules

There may be multiple ways to implement a policy

Defining policies instead of specific rules gives implementers freedom to choose the best way to implement a policy

Implementation

Firewall hardening

Firewall appliances are hardened at the factory

Vendors sell software plus a server with a pre-hardened operating system

Firewall software on a general-purpose computer requires the most on-site hardening

Central firewall management systems (Figure 6-24)

Creates a policy database

Changes policies into ACL rules

Sends ACLs out to individual firewalls

Vulnerability testing after configuration

There *will* be problems

Tests, like firewall configuration, should be based on policies

Change authorization and management

Limit the number of people who can make change requests

Limit the number of authorizers even more

Require requesters and authorizers to be different people

Implement the rule in the most restrictive way possible—to pass the least number of packets

Document all changes carefully

Do vulnerability testing after every change

The change should work

All previous behaviors should still work (regression testing)

Audit changes frequently

Focus especially on asking if each change opens the firewall in the most restrictive way possible

Reading the Firewall Logs

Should be done daily or more frequently

The most labor-intensive part of firewall management

Strategy is to find unusual traffic patterns

Top ten source IP addresses whose packets were dropped

Number of DNS failures today versus in an average day

Attackers can be black holed (have their packets dropped)

FIGURE 6-23   Firewall Management (Study Figure)

In addition, there may be multiple ways to satisfy the policy. If implementation methods were specified instead of the broad policy, then implementers would not be free to choose the best approach to reaching the underlying goal that a policy would state.

EXAMPLES OF POLICIES   The following is a list of some possible firewall polices that a firm might use.

- The company will permit all access by internal clients to external webservers except for webservers on a black list of sites that deal with pornography and other problem topics.
- Only people in marketing should have access to a server containing corporate sales data.
- All individuals must authenticate themselves before they are allowed to use a server in Human Resources server.
- All traffic to an engineering server must be logged, and
- An alert should be sent to the security administrator whenever five authentication attempts fail.

TEST YOUR UNDERSTANDING

24. **a.** Distinguish between firewall policies and ACL rules.
    b. Why is creating firewall policies desirable compared to just creating a list of ACL rules?
    c. Create three firewall policies not listed in the text.

Implementation

After planning is finished, it is time to implement the firm's policies on individual firewalls.

FIREWALL HARDENING   It is important to protect firewalls themselves against attacks because if an attacker takes over a firewall, he or she can do massive damage.

- **Firewall appliances** are pre-packaged firewalls. A firm simply installs the appliance between its Internet access router and its internal network. Operation is largely automatic. Firewall appliances are hardened at the factory.
- In addition, firewall vendors often sell firewall computers that have pre-hardened versions of UNIX or Windows. These limit the ability of organizations to make mistakes in hardening the operating system.
- If a firm purchases a general-purpose computer and installs the firewall software itself, however, strong actions must be taken to harden the firewall computer. General computer hardening is discussed in the next two chapters.

CENTRAL FIREWALL MANAGEMENT SYSTEMS   If a company has many firewalls, it probably will use a **central firewall management system**. Figure 6-24 shows that the heart of this system is the **firewall policy management server**, which has a firewall policy database holding the firm's firewall policies.

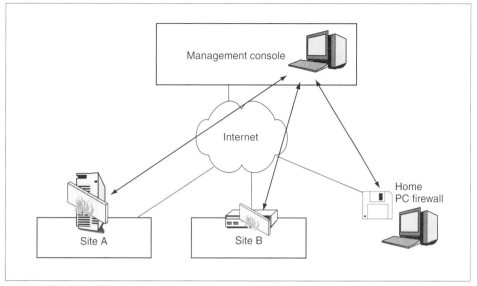

FIGURE 6-24 Central Firewall Management System

- Working from client PCs, firewall administrators create policies and send them to the firewall policy management server.
- Second, the administrator selects firewalls that should be governed by the policies. Often, a rule will govern many firewalls.
- Based on policies, the central configuration system sends appropriate ACL rules based on these policies to the individual firewalls. There is no need for an administrator to manually install the rules on each firewall.

FIREWALL POLICY DATABASE Figure 6-25 shows a somewhat typical **firewall policy database**. It shows that each policy has a number of fields.

Policy number	Source	Destination	Service	Action	Track	Firewalls
1	Internal	DNS servers	UDP dns	Pass	None	All
2	External	Internal	TCP http	Drop	Log	All
3	External	DMZ webserver	TCP http	Pass	None	Border
4	Internal	External	TCP http	Pass	Log	Border
5	Internal	External	ICMP	Drop	None	Border
6	Internal	Mail server	TCP smtp	Authenticate	Log if fail	Central
7	Marketing	Plans server	TCP http	Authenticate	Alert if fail	Marketing
8	Any	Plans server	TCP http	Drop	Log	Marketing
9	Any	Any	Any	Drop	Log	All

FIGURE 6-25 Firewall Policy Database

- The **policy number** field has a unique number for each policy. Policies can therefore be referred to by number.
- The **source** field and **destination** field are fairly explanatory. These can be host names, or they can be groups of IP addresses. Some groups, such as *Any*, are defined automatically by the system. The firewall administrator must define other groups manually.
- The **service** field describes the service to be filtered. Often, this will be TCP or UDP, plus the port number or name of an application. It may also be ICMP[12] or some other type of service defined by the number in the IP header's protocol field
- The **action** field says what firewalls should do with this service. The most obvious actions are *Pass* and *Drop*. Another possible action is *Authenticate*, which tells the firewall to authenticate the user. Other special-handling actions can be defined depending on the firm's specific policy.
- The **track** field describes what the firewall should do after taking its action. This may be nothing ("none"), logging the information in a log file, or alerting someone.
- The **firewalls** field tells the firewall management server what firewalls or routers should be sent ACLs based upon this policy.

The firewall policy database in Figure 6-25 has only nine rules. Most policy databases are much longer.

Policy 1 permits all internal hosts to reach the firm's DNS servers. The service is DNS over UDP, all packets are passed, and nothing is tracked. This policy is installed on all firewalls. Policies 2 through 4 handle HTTP traffic flowing between external hosts, hosts in the DMZ, and hosts in the internal network.

VULNERABILITY TESTING AFTER CONFIGURATION   Given the complexity of firewall policies, the complexity of translating firewall policies into specific sets of ACL rules, and the complexity of writing individual ACL rules, firewall ACL rule errors are inevitable during installation. It is important to conduct **vulnerability testing** after installation in order to detect these errors.

Just as policies govern implementation, they also govern vulnerability testing. For instance, in the case of client black listing, a vulnerability testing plan would have the tester try to reach several black-listed websites from each of several clients in different parts of the site or firm.

CHANGE AUTHORIZATION AND MANAGEMENT   Assets and threats change constantly. It is important to keep the policy database up-to-date. Although updates are inevitable, companies must make them in a disciplined way. There is a tendency for firewalls to be very strong initially but then to have holes punched through them until they resemble slices of Swiss cheese.

---

[12] Services are defined by values in the IP header protocol field.

- First, only certain people should be allowed to *request* changes, and fewer people should be allowed to *authorize* changes. Most importantly, the change requester should always be different from the change authorizer.
- Second, the firewall administrator should implement the change in the most restrictive way—the way that will pass the smallest number of packets. For example, instead of opening a port completely, the staff should only open it to a particular host if possible.
- Third, the firewall administrator should document the change carefully. Unless every change is documented very well, the firewall will become impossible to understand, and future changes may have unintended consequences. In addition, many compliance regulations *require* extensive documentation.
- Fourth, the firewall should be vulnerability tested after every change to make sure that the change works and that all of the previous behaviors still work. Testing that all previous behaviors work is called regression testing.
- Fifth, the company should audit the whole process frequently to ensure compliance with these procedures. This is especially important to ensure that the firewall administrator opened the firewall as little as possible to implement the changed policy.

READING FIREWALL LOGS   One crucial way to develop an understanding of the changing threat environment is to read firewall log files daily or even several times each day. Overall, reading firewall logs is the most time-consuming part of firewall administration.

Reading firewall logs is the most time-consuming part of firewall administration.

The basic strategy of log file reading is to determine what traffic is unusual. For example, one firewall administrator looks hourly at his log file to see the ten IP addresses that have been responsible for the most dropped packets. In a scanning attack, the attacker's IP address will appear on the "top ten" list.

The basic strategy of log file reading is to determine what traffic is unusual.

If the attack does not look too serious, the administrator **black holes** the IP address, meaning that a rule is added to the firewall (at least temporarily) to block all traffic from that IP address. If the attack appears to be more serious, the administrator may log all packets from the IP address whether these packets are attack packets or not.

Another useful approach is to develop historical data and then divide the number of events occurring on a particular day in a category by the average number of events. For example, if the number of failed DNS queries is a hundred times its usual value, this is a strong indicator that the firewall administrator should look at DNS queries in more depth. Overall, there is no one set of rules or strategies for reading firewall logs.

TEST YOUR UNDERSTANDING

25. a. Compare firewall hardening needs for firewall appliances, vendor-provided systems, and firewalls built on general-purpose computers.
   b. List what centralized firewall management systems do.
   c. What columns does the firewall policy database described in the text contain? Be able to describe each and what options it offers.
   d. Why is vulnerability testing necessary?
   e. Why should firewall policies govern both configuration and testing?
   f. What are the steps in firewall change management?
   g. On what should change auditing focus?
   h. Why is reading firewall logs important?
   i. What is the most time-consuming part of firewall management?

Reading Firewall Logs

As noted at the beginning of this chapter, it is important for firewall administrators to read their log files daily or even more often. In this section, we will look at some strategies administrators use to scan their log files.

Log Files

To help you understand the reading of firewall log files, Figure 6-26 shows a snippet of an ingress log file for a border firewall. The log file contains selected data for each packet that was dropped. This simplified log file contains six pieces of information for each packet:

- The first field is the identification number. In a real log file, there is no ID number. However, an ID number makes it easier for us to talk about entries in the log file.
- The second field gives the time the packet arrived at the firewall, in thousandths of a second.
- The third field is the rule that caused the packet to be dropped. In Figure 6-25, rules were not given names. Figure 6-26 uses names for rules, again to make reading the figure easier.
- The fourth and fifth fields give the source and destination IP addresses of the packet.
- The final field in the table is the service being requested. In this table, the services include ICMP, FTP, and HTTP.

Sorting the Log File by Rule

There is no firm set of rules for reading log files. The only general advice that most firewall administrators cite is "Look for something different from normal patterns."

One way to look for unusual patterns is to sort the file on the various fields in the form. For example, in Figure 6-26, the firewall administrator might sort on the Rule column, sorting from the most frequently used rule to the least frequently used rule. Then, administrator counts the number of events for each rule.

Echo Probes

In the figure, the most frequently used rule stops incoming ICMP echo probes, which are used in IP address scanning. This rule was applied eight times. If the host at the destination IP address responds by sending back an ICMP echo reply message, the attacker knows that there

ID	Time	Rule	Source IP	Destination IP	Service
1	15:34:005	Echo probe	14.17.3.139	60.3.87.6	ICMP
2	15:34:007	Echo probe	14.17.3.139	60.3.87.7	ICMP
3	15:34:008	Forbidden webserver access	128.171.17.3	60.17.14.8	HTTP
4	15:34:012	External access to internal FTP server	14.8.23.96	60.8.123.56	FTP
5	15:34:015	Echo probe	14.17.3.139	60.3.87.8	ICMP
6	15:34:020	External access to internal FTP server	128.171.17.34	60.19.8.20	FTP
7	15:34:021	Echo probe	1.124.82.6	60.14.42.68	ICMP
8	15:34:023	External access to internal FTP server	14.17.3.139	24.65.56.97	FTP
9	15:34:040	External access to internal FTP server	14.17.3.139	60.8.123.56	FTP
10	15:34:047	Forbidden webserver access	128.171.17.3	60.17.14.8	HTTP
11	15:34:048	Echo probe	14.17.3.139	60.3.87.9	ICMP
12	15:34:057	Echo probe	1.30.7.45	60.32.29.102	ICMP
13	15:34:061	External packet with private IP source address	10.17.3.139	60.32.29.102	ICMP
14	15:34:061	External access to internal FTP server	1.32.6.18	60.8.123.56	FTP
15	15:34:062	Echo probe	14.17.3.139	60.3.87.10	ICMP
16	15:34:063	Insufficient capacity	1.32.23.8	60.3.12.47	DNS
17	15:34:064	Echo probe	14.17.3.139	60.3.87.11	ICMP
18	15:34:065	Forbidden webserver access	128.171.17.3	60.17.14.8	HTTP

FIGURE 6-26   Ingress Firewall Log File

is a host at the ICMP echo's original destination IP address. Dropping incoming packets with ICMP echo messages ensures that no ICMP echo replies are sent out. All ICMP echo messages were sent from the same source IP address, 14.17.3.139. The first echo message went to 60.3.87.6. Subsequent ICMP echo messages increased the host part number by 1 each time.

Overall, this is just a classic scanning probe attack. In fact, it is the least sophisticated scanning probe attack. Given its lack of sophistication and normal frequency, these packets do not cause

(Continued)

Reading Firewall Logs   (Continued)

concern. The firewall administrator might black hole address 14.17.3.139 (drop all incoming packets from it) to prevent the noise of attacks from this unsophisticated attacker (and to stop the attacker from sending different types of attacks that might be more dangerous).

External Access to All Internal FTP Servers

During the very brief period covered by the log file, the rule prohibiting external access to internal FTP servers was applied five times. These packets came from multiple source IP address, and they went to multiple FTP servers. If this normally is a rare attack, and if there are multiple attacks from multiple sources to multiple destination FTP servers, this might indicate that the attacks are trying to exploit a newly discovered vulnerability in one or all FTP server programs. The fact that the attacks are coming from different IP addresses may indicate a sophisticated attack. This bears further investigation. If the firm has some FTP servers that are available from the outside, say in the DMZ, they should be checked at once. In addition, the firm's internal FTP servers may be vulnerable from internal attackers.

Attempted Access to Internal Webservers

There were three attempts to access a webserver to which access was forbidden. All were from the same source IP address. They came very quickly in time, so this was an automated attack. This probably is a common attack, and if there were only three attempts, this probably does not constitute a problem. However, the log file only covers a very brief period of time, so we cannot tell whether this is part of an ongoing attack based on attempted webserver access.

Incoming Packet with a Private IP Source Address

One incoming packet was dropped because its source IP address was in an IP address range for private IP addresses—those that should only be used *within* companies and should never be sent over the Internet. This is a clumsy attack, and it is not repeated during the logging period. Consequently, it probably does not constitute a threat.

Lack of Capacity

Finally, one packet was dropped because the firewall lacked sufficient capacity to process it. As we saw at the beginning of this chapter, if a firewall does not have the capacity to process a packet, it drops the packet in case it might be an attack packet. In this small sample of 18 packets, one packet was dropped because of a lack of capacity. If anything like this ratio holds for a longer period of time, it is imperative to upgrade the firewall's capacity immediately.

Perspective

Overall, only the attacks on FTP servers seem to constitute a threat worth further investigation. Although it would be nice to be able to investigate all attacks, this is impossible in practice.

Sizes of Log Files

The log file in Figure 6-26 is very brief, representing attacks dropped over the course of only 60 milliseconds. Of course, real log files cover much longer periods of time. Ideally, the time covered by log files should be extremely long, so that attacks that are spaced out in time can be detected. It would be possible to see if the three illegal attempts to access prohibited servers were isolated or part of a larger attack. Quite simply, it is difficult to detect attacks that span the boundaries of log files.

Long log files require a great deal of disk capacity. In addition, as time goes on, traffic usually increases, so disk capacity that was sufficient for reasonable log files will require the shortening of log file periods over time. Sizing the firewall's disk drives is extremely important—as is ensuring that there is enough archival capacity to store older log files so that they can be used to understand attacks that occurred during a previous period.

Logging All Packets

Normally, firewalls are configured to only log packets that they drop. However, many firewalls can be configured to *log all packets*, whether the packets are dropped or passed. The downside of this approach is that it vastly increases the number of entries that must be recorded per period of time. This inevitably shortens the period of time that each log file can cover, even with very large disk drives to store the log files.

Then why do some companies log *all* packets? The answer is that they can ask deeper questions about the traffic passing through the firewall. In the example given earlier, Host 14.17.3.139 sent a number of unsophisticated echo probes into the firm. The firewall easily stopped those echo probes. However, what if Host 14.17.3.139 then switched to more sophisticated probes and hacking attacks that the firewall could not stop? If the firm logged all packets, it could then look at all packets sent from Host 14.17.3.139 to see if the attacker succeeded in sending packets into the network that the firewall did not drop.

In essence, logging only dropped packets shows you only the packets the firewall succeeded in stopping. Far more dangerous are the packets the firewall did not stop, and these packets are not logged if only dropped packets are logged.

TEST YOUR UNDERSTANDING

26. **a.** What packets are usually logged in log files?
    b. What are the fields in the log file shown in Figure 6-26?
    c. In the examples given, by what field was the log file sorted?
    d. From the log file, what could we infer about the echo probe attack?
    e. Did this attack seem to be serious? Explain.
    f. From the log file, what could we infer about the FTP attack?
    g. Did this attack seem to be serious? Explain.
    h. Why was the dropping of a single packet because of lack of firewall capacity a cause for concern?
    i. What cannot be determined if log files cover too short a period of time?
    j. Why is it difficult for a log file to cover a long period of time?
    k. What is the advantage of logging *all* packets passing through a firewall?
    l. Why is logging all packets problematic?

DIFFICULT PROBLEMS FOR FIREWALL FILTERING

We will end our discussion of firewalls with three difficult problems that may create long-term challenges for firewalls.

The Death of the Perimeter

For border firewalls to be effective, there must be a single point of connection between a site network and the outside world. However, in real firms, a single point of entry is impossible to maintain.

Protecting the Perimeter is No Longer Possible

There are too many ways to get through the perimeter

Avoiding the Border Firewall

Internal attackers are inside the firewall already

Compromised internal hosts are inside the firewall

Wireless LAN drive-by hackers enter through access points that are inside the site

Home notebooks, mobile phones, and media brought into the site

Internal firewalls can address some of these threats

Extending the Perimeter

Remote employees must be given access

Consultants, outsourcers, customers, suppliers, and other subsidiaries must be given access

Essentially, all of these tend to use VPNs to make external parties "internal" to your site

---

FIGURE 6-27 The Death of the Perimeter (Study Figure)

AVOIDING THE BORDER FIREWALL   Many attackers can avoid firewall filtering by avoiding the border firewall entirely.

Internal Attackers   Most fundamentally, many attackers are internal to the firm. By various accounts, something like 30 to 70 percent of all misbehavior is done by employees working within a site. Border firewalls have no ability at all to stop such internal attacks.

Compromised Internal Hosts   Even if the person using an internal computer is honest, his or her PC may be compromised and may be attacking internal hosts not protected by the border firewall.

Wireless LAN Hackers   Also, as we saw in Chapter 4, wireless LANs may allow drive-by hackers to enter the site network through an access point. This will allow the attacker to bypass the border firewall entirely.

Home Notebooks, Mobile Phones, and Media Brought Into the Site   Users often bring their home notebook computers, mobile phones, and other portable devices into the firm and plug them into wall outlets or connect them to the wireless LAN through an access point. If the device contains a virus or worm, it may spread the infection within the site. The border firewall would have no chance of stopping it. Optical disks and USB RAM drives can also bring damaging software into the firm or take trade secret information out of the firm.

Internal Firewalls   As noted earlier, internal firewalls prevent attacks between subnets within a site. The ease with which many threats can bypass border firewalls will make internal firewalls increasingly necessary.

EXTENDING THE PERIMETER   Another problem with border firewalls is that outside users and locations may have to be allowed through the firewall so that they can do their work. If these external users are not careful, they may inadvertently send worms, viruses, and other harmful files into the network.

Remote Employees Remote access by employees on the road or at home is one of the biggest problems with perimeter thinking. Communication with the remote computer is passed through the firewall, effectively placing the employee's home or hotel room "inside" the site's perimeter. If a remote PC is compromised, this is as bad as if an internal site PC is compromised.

Consultants, Outsourcers, Customers, Suppliers, and Subsidiaries In addition, firms constantly deal with consultants, IT outsourcing firms, customers, suppliers, and even other subsidiaries of the firm. Often, the sites of these outside parties use VPNs to become extensions of the internal network. Their sites effectively are brought within the site's border.

PERSPECTIVE Although border firewalls will not disappear in the near future, they are no longer acceptable as a firm's only line of defense, and in truth they never were. In addition to implementing internal firewalls, companies have to assume that an increasing number of attacks will reach their internal clients and servers. Consequently, it will be increasingly important to harden internal hosts against attacks. The next two chapters discuss how to harden clients and servers.

TEST YOUR UNDERSTANDING

27. **a.** How can attackers avoid the border firewall?
    b. How has the perimeter extended outside the site?
    c. How can firms react to this decline in the effectiveness of border firewall filtering?

Attack Signatures versus Anomaly Detection

In the access control lists shown earlier in this chapter, each rule detected an attack on the basis of an **attack signature**, which is a pattern in the traffic data. (Antivirus filtering also uses signatures to detect viruses, worms, and Trojan horses.) When new threats appear, their signatures are identified and added to the firewall rule base.

Most Filtering Methods Use Attack Signature Detection
Each attack has a signature
This attack signature is discovered
The attack signature is added to the firewall

Problem
Zero-day attacks are attacks without warning, before a signature is developed
Signature defense cannot defend against zero-day attacks

Anomaly Detection
Detects an unusual pattern indicating a possible attack
This is difficult, so there are many false positives
Shrinking time needed to define signatures
Anomaly detection is necessary in today's firewalls

FIGURE 6-28 Signature versus Anomaly Detection (Study Figure)

ZERO-DAY ATTACKS   Of course, new attacks that have not been seen before do not have signatures for firewalls and antivirus programs to use. New attacks that are made before signatures are defined are called **zero-day attacks**. Until the attack's signature is defined and added to the firewall rule base, a signature-based firewall cannot stop the attack.

ANOMALY DETECTION   One way to address threats for which no signature exists is to use **anomaly detection**, which looks at traffic patterns that indicate that some kind of attack is underway. For example, if a host that always acts like a client begins to act like an FTP server, this suggests that it is a client that has been compromised and is being used as an FTP server, perhaps as a way to store identity information that the attacker wishes to sell. Anomaly detection can stop new attacks that have no well-defined signatures.

ACCURACY   Unfortunately, anomaly detection today is less accurate than signature-based detection. Traffic patterns vary for many legitimate reasons. As in IDSs, anomaly detection tends to generate so many false positives that many companies will not use it. However, given the speed with which vulnerability exploits, worms, and viruses are beginning to spread, anomaly detection is essential in firewalls today.

TEST YOUR UNDERSTANDING

28. **a.** Distinguish between signature detection and anomaly detection.
    b. What is a zero-day attack?
    c. Why are zero-day attacks impossible to stop with attack signatures?
    d. What is the promise of anomaly detection?
    e. Why is anomaly detection becoming critical for firewalls?

CONCLUSION

Synopsis

Firewalls stand like guards at the electronic gates to site networks. Although they do not provide total protection, they remain one of the prime elements in any company's security. Traditionally, firewalls provided ingress filtering to stop attack packets from getting into the firm. Today, they also do egress filtering to prevent outgoing attacks by infected computers, responses to probe attacks, and the theft of intellectual property. Internal firewalls provide protection to sensitive servers from internal attacks, and host firewalls protect both clients and servers directly. Companies must carefully plan their firewall architectures (how they arrange their firewalls to provide maximum protection). Firewalls typically log dropped attack packets, and the security staff should look through these logs frequently.

There are many firewall filtering mechanisms. The first firewalls used static packet inspection, which only looks at single packets in isolation. Static packet inspection is unable to stop many attacks, so it is now used only as a secondary filtering mechanism or on a screening router—if it is used at all.

Most border firewalls today use stateful packet inspection (SPI) as their main filtering mechanism. SPI has different rules for packets that attempt to open connections and for other types of packets. For packets that attempt to open connections (such as packets carrying TCP SYN segments), internally initiated connections are opened by default, while externally initiated connections are prevented by default. Access control lists (ACLs) modify these default behaviors as appropriate for the firm's firewall policies. All other packets (that is, packets that do not attempt to open connections) are passed if they are part of an approved connection and dropped if they are not. SPI firewalls are fast and therefore inexpensive because most packets are processed simply, and they provide a large amount of protection.

Many routers provide network address translation (NAT). NAT hides the internal IP addresses and port numbers used by internal hosts. Consequently, sniffers cannot learn these IP addresses and port numbers used. NAT does no actual filtering, but networks with NAT protection tend to be very difficult to attack.

Application proxy firewalls provide protection at the application layer. They relay packets between an internal host and an external host, examining the application content as they do so. (Specific protections are discussed in a box.) Application proxy firewalls provide extremely strong security, but a separate proxy program is needed for each application to be protected, and only a few types of application programs are suitable for application proxy protection. Worst of all, application proxy firewalls are very slow. It is most common to see an application proxy firewall placed between a single server and the clients that attempt to reach it or between internal clients and external webservers.

Firms have long used intrusion detection systems (IDSs), which provide deep packet inspection and examine streams of packets instead of just individual packets. The goal of an IDS is to look for suspicious packets and report them—but not stop them. New firewalls that use IDS methods to actually drop packets are called intrusion prevention systems (IPSs). IPSs use ASIC hardware to provide the speed needed to analyze traffic in real time (which is necessary to drop packets). In addition, IPSs only drop packets if they are highly certain that they are seeing an actual attack instead of just suspicious activities. If IPSs are less sure that a stream of packets is an attack, they may limit that traffic to a certain percent of total bandwidth in order to minimize damage.

Firewalls rarely do antivirus filtering directly. However, there usually are strong connections between firewalls and antivirus servers. When information needing antivirus checking arrives at a firewall, the firewall will pass it to an antivirus server. If the antivirus server does not drop the information, it either delivers the information to the destination host or returns it to the firewall for delivery (and probably additional filtering). A few firewalls, called unified threat management (UTM) firewalls, do antivirus filtering as well as traditional filtering, but these are not common today.

(In a box) Most main border firewalls also can detect and stop denial-of-service (DoS) attacks. DoS attacks are difficult to stop because DoS packets have the same form as legitimate packets. Border firewalls often address DoS attacks by limiting the rate of suspected DoS traffic and by protecting internal servers against half-open DoS attacks with false opens. However, if the volume of attack traffic is high, the firm's link to the Internet will be saturated, and there will be nothing the firm can do. ISPs need to help prevent DoS attacks, and companies that own infected computers must stop these computers from sending out DoS attack packets.

Typically, a border router is tri-homed, which means that it connects to three subnets. One is the subnet leading to the Internet. The second is a subnet leading to the firm's internal network. The third subnet is called the demilitarized zone (DMZ). The firm puts all servers that must be accessible from the Internet in the DMZ subnet. Hosts found in DMZs include public webservers, application proxy servers, and a DNS server that only knows the host names and IP addresses of hosts within the DMZ. Firms must harden hosts in the DMZ aggressively because these hosts will face constant attacks from attackers on the Internet.

Firewall technology is useless without strong management. Firms must define policies for firewalls very carefully, and these policies must drive both configuration and vulnerability testing to ensure that the firewall is operating properly. The firm must update firewall policies and ACLs constantly, and they must read the firewall log files very frequently. Many firms use central firewall management systems, which actively manage firewalls from a single computer. This reduces management costs.

The chapter closed with two difficult problems that will face firewall administrators in the future. One is the death of the perimeter. Border firewalls are only useful if attackers must come in through the Internet border router. However, not all attackers have to do so today. Internal attackers and attackers coming in through access points are already inside the site, as are employees who bring in malware on removable media. In addition, VPNs bring remote works, consultants, outsourcers, and other parties into the network—essentially extending their borders.

The second is that firewalls have long used signature detection. Attacks are discovered and analyzed. Then their signatures are put into the firewall's filtering rule base. However, attacks now come soon after they are first discovered. In zero-day attacks, they come before any prior discovery. Without signatures, companies are extremely vulnerable to such attacks. Anomaly detection works a different way, by detecting the changes that attacks make in traffic. Anomaly detection can stop even previously unseen attacks automatically. Unfortunately, anomaly detection is imprecise, but the speed of attacks makes the development of effective anomaly detection mandatory in firewalls today.

Thought Questions

1. Modify the ACL in Figure 6-10 to permit externally initiated connections to an SNMP network management server, 60.47.3.103, and to allow both regular and SSL/TLS connections to the internal webserver 60.47.3.137 but not to other webservers.

2. The ACL in Figure 6-10 is in effect. A packet containing a TCP SYN segment reaches a stateful packet inspection firewall from the outside. What actions will the SPI firewall take?

3. The ACL in Figure 6-10 is in effect. A packet containing a TCP ACK segment reaches a stateful packet inspection firewall from the outside. What actions will the SPI firewall take? Explain.

4. Create an egress ACL for an SPI firewall if policy only forbids connections to external FTP servers.

5. Contrast what sniffers can learn if a company being attacked uses NAT or an application proxy server.

6. Most IP addresses are public, in the sense that they can appear on the public Internet. However, a few IP addresses have been designated as private IP addresses. One private IP address range is 172.16.0.0 to 172.31.255.255. Private IP addresses can only appear within a firm. In Figure 6-21, internal hosts have private IP addresses except for those in the DMZ, which use public IP addresses. Explain this discrepancy if you can.

7. a) Describe the Policy 5 in the firewall policy database shown in. b) Repeat for Policy 6. c) Repeat for Policy 7. d) Repeat for Policy 8. e) Repeat for Policy 9.

8. (If you read the box "Reading Firewall Logs") Sort the log file in Figure 6-26 by source IP address. What do you conclude from the analysis? This is not a trivial question.

Design Question

1. A firm has the following firewall policy: Employee access to Internet servers should be unrestricted and external clients should only be able to access the firm's public webserver, http://www.pukanui.com. The firm also has a finance server that should only be accessible to people in the finance department. The server and the finance departments are all on the internal subnet 10.5.4.3. The firm has a single large site. How would you implement this policy? Create both a firewall architecture and ACLs for the border firewall for both internal and external connection-opening attempts.

Troubleshooting Question

1. A stateful packet inspection border firewall contains a rule that permits external connections to an internal public webserver, http://www.pukanui.com. However, the firewall does not permit access to this server. Come up with at least two hypotheses for the cause of the problem. Describe how you would test each hypothesis.

Perspective Questions

1. What material was most surprising for you in this chapter?

2. What material was most difficult for you in this chapter?

Chapter 7

Host and Data Security

LEARNING OBJECTIVES:

By the end of this chapter, you should be able to discuss the following:

- The elements of host hardening, security baselines and images, and systems Administration.
- Important server operating systems.
- Vulnerabilities and patches.
- Managing users and groups.
- Managing permissions.
- Testing for vulnerabilities.
- Windows client PC security, including centralized PC security management.
- Testing for vulnerabilities.
- Data protection: backup.
- Other data protections: encryption, data destructions, and document restrictions.

INTRODUCTION

Although firewalls stop most Internet-based attacks, they never stop all. Consequently, protecting individual servers and other hosts is critical. In fact, if you install a server "out of the box," that is, using the operating system's installation media and installation defaults and then connect the server to the Internet, a hacker is likely to "own" it within minutes or even seconds.[1]

What Is a Host?

In networking, any device with an IP address is a host. That simple definition works in security as well because any device with an IP address can be over a network. Consequently, the

---

[1] *The Register*, "Unpatched Windows PCs Own3d in Less than Four Minutes," July 15, 2008. http://theregister.co.uk/2008/07/15/unpatched_pc_survival_drops/print.html.

The Problem

    Some attacks inevitably reach host computers

    Servers installed out of the box have vulnerabilities

    Hackers can take them over quickly

    So servers and other hosts must be hardened—a complex process that requires a diverse set protections to be implemented on each host

What Is a Host?

    Anything with an IP address is a host (because it can be attacked)

    Servers

    Clients (including mobile telephones)

    Routers (including home access routers) and sometimes switches

    Firewalls

FIGURE 7-1   Threats to Hosts (Study Figure)

term *host* includes servers, clients, routers, firewalls, and even many mobile phones. Although we do not usually think of firewalls and routers as hosts, think of the damage a hacker could do if he or she took over a firewall or router.

Any device with an IP address is a host.

The Elements of Host Hardening

The process of protecting a host against attacks is called **host hardening**. Hardening is not a single protection but rather a number of protections that often have little in common with each other. Among these protections are the following:

- Back up the host regularly. Without this, nothing else matters.
- Restrict physical access to the host (discussed in Chapter 5).

1. Backup
2. Backup
3. Backup
4. Restrict physical access to hosts (see Chapter 5)
5. Install the operating system with secure configuration options
6. Minimize the applications that run on the host
7. Harden all remaining applications on the host (see Chapter 8)
8. Download and install patches for vulnerabilities
9. Manage users and groups securely
10. Manage access permissions for users and groups securely
11. Encrypt data if appropriate
12. Add a host firewall
13. Read operating system log files regularly for suspicious activity
14. Run vulnerability tests frequently

FIGURE 7-2   The Elements of Host Hardening (Study Figure)

- Install the operating system with secure configuration options. In particular, be sure that all default passwords are replaced by strong passwords. Adversaries know every default password. If you fail to change even one, they can use it to get into your system immediately.
- Minimize the applications and operating system services that run on the host to reduce the ability of hackers to take over the host by compromising an application or service. Minimizing the number of running programs reduces the "attack surface" of hosts.
- Harden all remaining applications on the host. (This is the focus of Chapter 8.)
- Download and install patches for known operating system vulnerabilities.
- Manage users and groups (adds, changes, deletions, etc.).
- Manage access permissions for users and groups securely.
- Encrypt data if appropriate.
- Add a host firewall.
- Read operating system logs regularly to look for suspicious activities.
- Run vulnerability tests against the system regularly to identify security weaknesses that were not caught in the normal course of installation or operation.

Security Baselines and Image

In a long and complex set of actions, it is easy to overlook something. Consequently, firms adopt standard **security baselines**—sets of specific actions to be taken to harden all hosts of a particular type (Red Hat Linux PC servers, Windows Server 2008 servers, etc.) and of particular versions within each type.[2] You also need baselines for servers with

---

Security Baselines Guide the Hardening Effort

Security baselines are specifications for how hardening should be done

Needed because it is easy to forget a step

    It is like a pilot's checklist

Different baselines for different operating systems and versions

Different baselines for servers with different functions (webservers, mail servers, etc.)

Disk Images

    Can also create a well-tested secure implementation for each operating system versions and server function

    Save as a disk image

    Load the new disk image on new servers

Server Administrators Are Called Systems Administrators

Administer one or more servers

Implement security baseline actions

Larger firms have many systems administrators

    Security baselines help ensure uniformity in hardening

Systems administrators usually *not* responsible for network administration

---

FIGURE 7-3   Security Baselines and Systems Administrators (Study Figure)

---

[2] There are many places to get security baselines. Many vendors offer them for their own products. A good general source of baselines is the U.S. National Institute of Standards and Technology's Security Configuration Checklists Repository (http://checklists.nist.gov/).

different functions, such as webservers and FTP servers. Security baselines are like pilot checklists for aircraft. Even experienced pilots make mistakes if they do not follow the checklist before takeoff.

Some companies go beyond baselines by creating a few secure software installations and testing them extensively. These companies then save **disk images** (full copies) of these installations. When a new computer of that type must be installed, the company downloads the operating system image directly into the new computer. This saves money on each installation. It also ensures that each server is properly configured according to the firm's security baselines and general security policies.

Systems Administrators

IT employees who manage individual hosts or groups of hosts are called **systems administrators**. (No, the name is not very descriptive.) Typically, it is the job of the systems administrator of a particular server to conduct the hardening effort. Larger firms have many systems administrators, and security baselines help ensure uniformity across the hardening efforts of systems administrators. Systems administrators do not, in general, administer the network.

> *IT employees who manage individual hosts or groups of hosts are called systems administrators. Systems administrators do not, in general, administer the network.*

TEST YOUR UNDERSTANDING

1. **a.** What is our definition of a host?
   b. Why is host hardening necessary?
   c. What major categories of hosts did this section mention?
   d. What specific things can an attacker do if he or she takes over a firewall? The answer was not explained in the text.
   e. What specific things can an attacker do if he or she takes over a router? The answer was not explained in the text.
   f. List the elements of host hardening.
   g. Why is it important to replace default passwords during configuration?
   h. What is a security baseline, and why is it important?
   i. Why is the downloading of disk images of the operating system desirable compared to configuring each host individually?
   j. What does a systems administrator manage?
   k. Does a systems administrator generally manage the network?

IMPORTANT SERVER OPERATING SYSTEMS

In the previous section, we looked at several types of hosts, including servers, client PCs, routers, and firewalls. We will now look at these categories in more depth, focusing first on servers, which are frequent targets of attack, and focusing on operating systems, which are frequent attack vectors for server hackers.

Windows Server Operating Systems

Microsoft's server operating system is **Windows Server**. Early versions, such as Windows Server NT, had poor security. The latest versions of Windows Server, such as Windows Server 2008, are much more secure. They intelligently minimize the number of running applications and utilities by asking the installer questions about how the server will be used. They also make the installation of vulnerability patches very simple and usually automatic. They include server software firewalls, the ability to encrypt data, and many other security enhancements.

These protections are not perfect. Most annoyingly, several security vulnerabilities need patches each month. However, other operating systems also have this problem.

THE WINDOWS SERVER USER INTERFACE   All recent versions of Windows Server have user interfaces that look like the interfaces in client versions of Windows. This makes learning Windows Server relatively easy. As Figure 7-5 shows, Windows Server 2008 uses Internet Explorer for downloads and other Internet operations. It also uses My Computer for file management, and it has a Start menu with most choices being familiar to desktop users. You can even run standard client software on Windows Server.[3]

Windows Server

    The Microsoft Windows Server operating system

    Windows NT, 2003, and 2008

Windows Server Security

    Has improved over time

    Intelligently minimize the number of running programs and utilities by asking questions during installation

    Simple (and usually automatic) to get updates

    Many other improvements

    Still many patches to apply, but this is true of other operating systems

Graphical User Interface (GUI)

    Looks like client versions of Windows for easy learning and use (Figure 7-5)

    Most administrative tools under Start / Programs / Administrative Tools

Microsoft Management Consoles (MMCs)

    Used by systems administrators to manage a server

    Standardized organization for ease of learning and use (Figure 7-6)

    Can add snap-ins for specific functionality

    Usually located under Programs, Administrative Tools

FIGURE 7-4   Windows Server Operating Systems (Study Figure)

---

[3] To do the Windows Server screenshots for this chapter, I installed Adobe Illustrator—a popular drawing program for Windows client machines—on the server. I couldn't find anything on capturing screen images in the Windows 2003 help system, so I simply tried Alt-PrintScreen, which captures window images in client versions of Windows. It worked. I pasted the PrintScreen images into Adobe Illustrator documents for annotation.

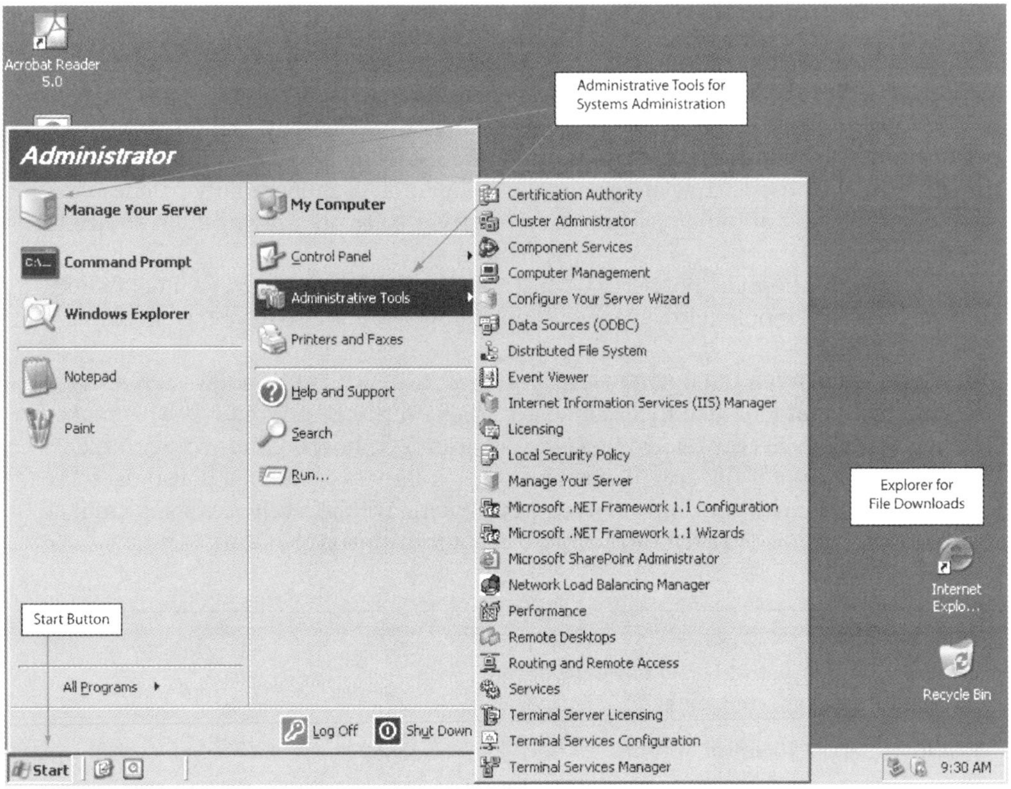

FIGURE 7-5   Windows 2008 Server User Interface

START → PROGRAMS → ADMINISTRATIVE TOOLS   As Figure 7-5 shows, Windows Server places most management tools on the **Administrative Tools** choice on the Programs menu of the Start menu. This makes it easier for systems administrators to guess where to find the tools they will need.

MICROSOFT MANAGEMENT CONSOLES (MMCS)   Most administrative tools in Windows Server come in the same general format, called the **Microsoft Management Console (MMC)**. Figure 7-6 shows the organization of an important MMC, *Computer Management*.

- First, there is the icon bar. When a user selects an object in one of the two lower panes, the icons specify actions that the administrator can take on the selected object. One of the most important choices is Action, which is specific to the selected object.
- Second, there is a tree of administrative applications in the lower-left pane (the **tree pane**).
- The individual applications on the tree pane are called **snap-ins** because they can be added or dropped from the tree list easily. This allows systems administrators to tailor MMCs easily to their particular needs. In the figure, the snap-in *Services* is selected.
- There are sub-objects for the selected tool (*Services*) in the lower-right pane. In this case, the *RunAs Service* is selected.

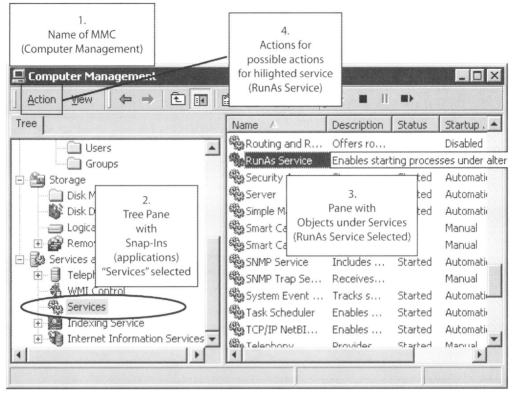

FIGURE 7-6 Computer Management Microsoft Management Console

All MMCs have this same general organization, with an icon bar, a tree pane, and the sub-objects pane. The actions that the administrator can take on a selected object are displayed by clicking the *Action* icon. This consistent user interface makes it fairly easy to learn how to use new MMCs and new snap-ins.

TEST YOUR UNDERSTANDING

2. **a.** What is the name of Microsoft's server operating system?
   b. What security protections do recent versions of this operating system offer?
   c. Why is Microsoft Windows Server easy to learn?
   d. What are MMCs? (Do not just spell out the acronym.)
   e. On what object does an icon bar icon operate?
   f. What is in the tree pane?
   g. To what things do items in the sub-object pane refer?
   h. What is a snap-in?
   i. Why are snap-ins called that?
   j. Why is the standardized layout of MMCs beneficial?
   k. How does the systems administrator get to most administrative tool MMCs?
   l. What does selecting *Action* do?

UNIX (Including LINUX) Servers

UNIX is a popular operating system for the largest servers. It is also used on some individual PCs.

Many Versions of UNIX

There are many commercial versions of UNIX for large servers

Compatible in the kernel (core part) of the operating system

Can generally run the same applications

But may run many different management utilities, making cross-learning difficult

LINUX is a version of UNIX created for PCs

Many different LINUX distributions

Distributions include the LINUX kernel plus application and programs, usually from the GNU project

Each distribution and version needs a different baseline to guide hardening

Cost

Attractive because LINUX is free (or at least inexpensive compared with commercial operating systems)

Buy one copy and install it on many servers

But may take more labor to administer, making it economically unattractive

Has moved beyond PC, to use on servers and some desktops

User Can Select the User Interface

Multiple user interfaces are available (unlike Windows)

Graphical user interfaces (GUIs)

Users spend most time working on a GUI interface

Many UNIX vendors have proprietary GUIs

LINUX has multiple standard GUIs (Gnome, KDE, etc.)

Command line interfaces (CLIs)

At prompts, users type commands

Unix CLIs are called shells (Bourne, BASH, etc.)

Command line interfaces are picky syntax and spacing

However, they place a low processing burden on the computer

Sets of commands can be stored as a script and replayed when needed

FIGURE 7-7 UNIX Operating Systems (Study Figure)

UNIX was created many years ago. This long history has given it broad functionality and high reliability. In some cases, however, the fact that its basic architecture is very old shows itself in some limitations and archaic modes of interaction with users.

MANY VERSIONS It is difficult to talk about UNIX security broadly because UNIX is not a single operating system like Windows. Instead, many different versions of UNIX exist. The major vendors, including IBM, SUN, and Hewlett-Packard, all have their own commercial versions of UNIX. A company does not just purchase UNIX; it purchases a specific version of UNIX.

A company does not just purchase UNIX; it purchases a specific version of UNIX.

These different versions of UNIX tend to be interoperable at the **kernel** level (the core part of the operating system). Kernel compatibility allows them to run most of the same applications.

However, the kernel is only part of the operating system. Different versions of UNIX usually have different management tools, including security tools. This can make UNIX administration difficult if a company uses several different types of UNIX.

LINUX[4]   For UNIX on PCs, the situation is even more chaotic. The most popular version of UNIX for PCs is **LINUX**. However, LINUX is only the operating system kernel. What LINUX vendors actually offer are **distributions** that combine this kernel with other software—usually software from the GNU project. For most functions, GNU offers several alternative programs. Consequently, LINUX distributions tend to be rather different, especially in management and security.[5] In many cases, departments purchase PC versions of LINUX without overall coordination by the firm.

> LINUX is a version of UNIX that runs on ordinary PCs. Actually, LINUX is only the kernel of the operating system. Actual LINUX packages are distributions that contain the kernel and many other programs—mostly commonly programs from the GNU project.

LINUX is popular because it is free, although "free" must be taken with several grains of salt. First, most LINUX vendors charge fees to use their versions of LINUX, whether they call this a sales price or not. Even so, LINUX is much less expensive to purchase than commercial server operating systems, and a single copy of LINUX may be installable on multiple servers without additional cost. This is certainly not the case with Microsoft Windows Server or version of UNIX created by server vendors.

However, purchase price is only one factor in the total cost of ownership (TCO). Many firms find that LINUX is rather expensive to administer, especially if they have many distributions in use from multiple LINUX vendors.

The fact that many different distributions of LINUX exist makes hardening a LINUX system difficult. It is important to have a good security baseline for the particular version of the particular UNIX distribution you are using.

Although LINUX was created originally for personal computers, many large servers now run LINUX. Server purchasing usually is centralized, so the variety of LINUX distributions on corporate servers can be controlled.

UNIX USER INTERFACES   Even within a specific version of UNIX, the operating system software may come with several alternative user interfaces. Some of these interfaces will be graphical user interfaces (GUIs) similar to the interface of Microsoft Windows. On LINUX, there are two popular GUIs: Gnome and KDE.

---

[4] The GNU project's management programs and application programs can run on most versions of UNIX. However, LINUX vendors use GNU programs almost exclusively above the LINUX kernel. Some GNU project members are understandably a bit miffed that these distributions, which predominantly use GNU programs, are called LINUX distributions instead of GNU distributions.

[5] There are other versions of UNIX for PCs, including FreeBSD and OpenBSD.

Other interfaces will be **command-line interfaces (CLIs)**, which UNIX calls **shells**. In CLIs, the user types a command and hits Enter. For instance, to see files in a directory, a user might type "list –ls[Enter]" at the command prompt. Command shells tend to have picky syntax in general, and in UNIX, case is critically important.[6]

On the positive side, CLI shells use fewer system resources than GUIs. In addition, any process that involves a sequence of commands can be combined into a script, which can be run whenever this sequence of actions must be executed.

Many security tools only work at CLIs, so UNIX security specialists tend to find themselves typing complex, syntax-picky commands to do security work. Even when a GUI is used, UNIX systems administrators frequently drop down to the command line for specific tasks.

There are several popular shells in use. The **Bourne shell** was one of the first original popular shells. The current market leader probably is the **Bourne Again Shell (BASH)**.[7]

TEST YOUR UNDERSTANDING

3. **a.** Why is UNIX systems security difficult to describe generally?
   b. Distinguish between UNIX and LINUX.
   c. What is the LINUX kernel?
   d. What is a LINUX distribution?
   e. Comment on the cost of LINUX.
   f. Does a particular version of UNIX have a single user interface?
   g. What are UNIX CLIs called?
   h. How are CLIs beneficial?
   i. Why are CLIs difficult to use?

VULNERABILITIES AND PATCHES

Vulnerabilities and Exploits

The arms race between operating system vendors and hackers is an endless battle. Vulnerability finders constantly discover new **vulnerabilities**, which are security weaknesses that open a program to attack.

Vulnerabilities are security weaknesses that open a program to attack.

Most vulnerability finders notify software vendors, so that vendors can develop fixes for these vulnerabilities. However, some vulnerability finders sell their vulnerabilities to hackers, who quickly develop **exploits**—programs that take advantage of the vulnerability.

Software vendors create fixes when vulnerabilities are reported to them. However, hacker attacks may come before these fixes are created. Attacks that come before fixes are released are called **zero-day attacks**.

---

[6] This is why unix people tend to write everything in lower case.
[7] Yep, more UNIX "humor."

Vulnerabilities
Vulnerabilities are security weaknesses that open a program to attack
Vulnerabilities are common
An exploit takes advantage of a vulnerability
Vendors develop fixes
Zero-day exploits: exploits that occur before fixes are released
Exploits often follow the vendor release of fixes within days or even hours
It is important to apply fixes quickly for critical vulnerabilities

Fixes
Work-arounds
    A series of manual actions to be taken; no new software
    Labor-intensive and therefore expensive and error-prone
Patches
    Small programs that fix vulnerabilities
    Usually easy to download and install
Service packs
    Collections of patches and improvements (Microsoft Windows)
Upgrading to a new version of the program
    Often, security vulnerabilities are fixed in new versions
    If a version is too old, the vendor may even stop offering fixes

FIGURE 7-8 Vulnerabilities and Exploits (Study Figure)

Attacks that come before fixes are released are called zero-day attacks.

Ironically, the most dangerous period usually comes immediately *after* a fix is released by a vendor. Attackers reverse engineer the fix to learn about the underlying vulnerability. Reengineering-based exploits typically appear in a day or two, and they sometimes occur within hours. Companies must not delay in applying newly released fixes for critical vulnerabilities.

TEST YOUR UNDERSTANDING

4. **a.** What is a vulnerability?
   b. What is an exploit?
   c. What is a zero-day attack?
   d. Why is the quick application of critical fixes important?

Fixes

We have seen than when vendors discover that they have vulnerabilities, they create **fixes**. There are four types of fixes.

WORK-AROUNDS The least satisfactory fix is a **work-around**, which is a series of manual steps the systems administrator must take to ameliorate the problem.

No new software is involved. Work-arounds tend to be highly labor intensive. In addition, it is easy to make a mistake when doing complex manual fixes; this can have disastrous results, even if no attacks occur.

PATCHES It is better when vendors create a **patch**, which is a small program that fixes a particular vulnerability. A systems administrator must download, install, and run the patch.

A patch is a small program that fixes a particular vulnerability.

SERVICE PACKS Periodically, vendors typically put vulnerability fixes and sometimes functionality improvements together into a single large update. In Windows, these are called **service packs**. A systems administrator can install new service packs with some confidence that his or her host will be up to date after installation.

VERSION UPGRADES Often the best fix is to upgrade the software to the newest version. Often, security problems are corrected in newer versions, and in general each newer version of an operating system has improved security. In addition, if a version is too old, the vendor will stop creating fixes for it.[8]

TEST YOUR UNDERSTANDING

5. **a.** List the four types of fixes for vulnerabilities.
   b. Distinguish between work-arounds and patches.
   c. What is a service pack in Microsoft Windows?
   d. Why is upgrading to a new version of an operating system usually good for security?

The Mechanics of Patch Installation

MICROSOFT WINDOWS SERVER In Microsoft Windows Server, installing patches is simple. Since Windows Server 2003, servers can be programmed to check for updates automatically. Even in Windows Server 2000, the administrator merely had to choose the first item on the Start menu.

LINUX RPM PROGRAM Each UNIX vendor has its own patch download approach. LINUX vendors also use different approaches, although many LINUX vendors follow the **rpm**[9] method created by Red Hat, which is the leading LINUX vendor. This method is named after the rpm command used to initiate a download.

TEST YOUR UNDERSTANDING

6. **a.** In Windows Server 2003 and 2008, how automatic can patching be?
   b. What patch downloading method is commonly used in LINUX?

---

[8] At the same time, it may be useful to wait on the upgrade decision for a new version until the first release of bug fixes, including security fixes. Until then, the vulnerability level may be too high to make the transition unless the firm is forced to do so.

[9] Originally called Red Hat Package Manager, it is now usually called RPM package manager.

Mechanics of Patching
Microsoft Windows Server looks for updates (patches) automatically
  It also can install updates automatically
LINUX distributions often use rpm

Problems with Patching
Companies get overwhelmed by number of patches
  Use many programs; vendors release many patches per product
  Especially a problem for a firm's many application programs
Cost of patch installation
  Each patch takes some time and adds to labor costs
  Mitigated by patch management servers that find vulnerabilities and patches and then distribute patches to general servers
Prioritization
  Often lack the resources to apply all; must be selective
  Prioritize patches by criticality
  May not apply all patches, if risk analysis does not justify them
Patch management servers reduce costs
  Download patches from software vendors
  Find vulnerable computers in the firm automatically and push patches out to them
Risks of patch installation
  Reduced functionality
  Freeze machines, do other damage—sometimes with no uninstall possible
  Should test on a test system before deployment on servers

FIGURE 7-9 Applying Patching (Study Figure)

Problems with Patching

Although patching is critical, many firms fail to patch some of their servers, and patching clients is even less common. What can account for this neglect?

THE NUMBER OF PATCHES The main problem is the sheer number of patches generated annually by vendors. Companies typically use several different operating system vendors, each of which releases many vulnerability reports and patches each year. In addition, companies use many application programs, and most applications need frequent patching. Attackers often can use application program exploits to take over the computer, as Chapter 8 discusses.

To put numbers on these matters, the Computer Emergency Response Team/Coordination Center (CERT/CC) counted 1,090 vulnerabilities in 2000. In 2007, this number had risen to 7,236.[10] As far back as 2001, Activities estimated that a security manager in a company with only eight firewalls and nine servers would have to apply an average of five patches per day.[11] Today, this situation is far worse.

---

[10] http://www.cert.org/stats/fullstats.html.
[11] Dan Vernon, "Study: Constant Security Fixes Overwhelming IT Managers," *Computerworld.com*, November 30, 2001. http://www.computerworld.com/securitytopics/security/story/0,10801,66215,00.html.

COST OF PATCH INSTALLATION   Although patches themselves are free, the labor needed to learn of their existence, download them, and install them is expensive. Given the overwhelming number of patches released each year, the total cost of patch management can be enormous.

PRIORITIZING PATCHES   For most firms, the cost of installing all patches is prohibitive. Many firms sort patches by priority. Critical vulnerabilities that will open the firm to very serious attacks are the first to be patched, of course. How deeply the firm goes down the priority list of vulnerabilities and patches depends on risk analysis—balancing costs against threats.

PATCH MANAGEMENT SERVERS   Faced with overwhelming patching loads, many companies now use internal patch management servers. **Patch management servers** learn what software is running on the firm's servers. Patch management servers then actively assess what programs on each host need to be patched and push patches out to the servers. Patch management servers can greatly reduce patching costs.

THE RISKS OF PATCH INSTALLATION   Installing patches is not without its own risks. First, added security often comes at the cost of reduced functionality, which might not be justified given the degree of added safety offered by a patch.

Second, some patches actually freeze machines or do other damage. This is particularly bad if a patch has no uninstall option. Firms typically download a patch on a test system and examine the effects of the patch thoroughly before rolling the patch out to all servers or clients. If a company has a standard security baseline for various types of hosts, chances are good that experiences on the test system will mirror those on other hosts.[12]

TEST YOUR UNDERSTANDING

7. **a.** Why do firms have a difficult time applying patches?
   b. Why do many firms prioritize patches?
   c. How do patch management servers help?
   d. What two risks does patching raise?

MANAGING USERS AND GROUPS

The Importance of Groups in Security Management

The next aspect of host hardening we will discuss is creating and managing user accounts and groups. Every user must have an account. In addition, it is common to create groups and then add individual users to these groups. When security measures,

---

[12] Patching is especially troublesome for mission-critical production servers that the firm cannot allow to fail because of patch problems. Some firms never patch mission-critical production servers despite the fact that leaving them unpatched could allow a hacker to damage them.

In addition, some application program vendors will not certify their programs for working on operating systems with new patches. In some cases, it takes application program vendors several months to certify their applications for specific patches.

Accounts

Every user must have an account

Groups

Individual accounts can be consolidated into groups

Can assign security measures to groups

Inherited by each group's individual members

Why Assign Security Measures to Groups?

Reduces labor costs compared to assigning security measures to individual accounts

Assigning permissions to groups reduces errors

Because group permissions are more obvious than individual permissions

---

FIGURE 7-10   Managing Users and Groups (Study Figure)

such as requiring long and complex passwords, are applied to groups, then all users in these groups are automatically subjected to these measures. Applying security measures to groups obviously requires much less labor than applying these measures to accounts individually.

Applying measures to groups also tends to reduce errors because most groups have well-defined roles that lead to clear security requirements. Individuals, in contrast, may have multiple roles with different security requirements, making it difficult to assign proper security settings to individual accounts.

TEST YOUR UNDERSTANDING

8. Give two reasons why assigning security measures to groups is better than assigning security measures to individuals within groups.

Creating and Managing Users and Groups in Windows

For stand-alone Windows servers, a administrator can turn to the Computer Management MMC. As Figure 7-11 shows, there is a **Local Users and Groups** snap-in with two subcategories—Users and Groups. The Users category is selected.

In the right pane, a list of users is shown. The *Administrator* user is selected. If the systems administrator selects the *Action* menu choice or right clicks any account, he or she will be able to rename the account, delete it, change its security properties, or take other actions.

THE ADMINISTRATOR ACCOUNT   Each operating system has a **super user account** that has total control over the computer. In Windows, the super user account is **Administrator**. In UNIX, it is the **root** account.

Anyone logging into the super user account has total control of the computer. He or she can see everything and change anything. Consequently, the main goal of hackers is to take over the super user account. Because hacking began on UNIX computers, taking over the super user account on any computer is called **hacking root**.

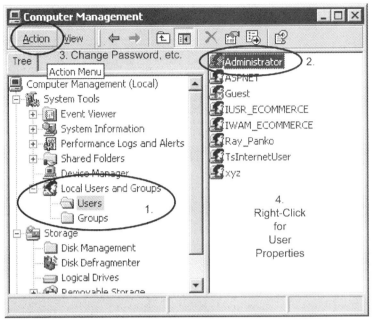

FIGURE 7-11   Users and Groups in Windows

To minimize dangers, systems administrators should use the super user account as little as possible. Whenever they do not require super user powers, they should work with individual personal accounts that have few privileges. Only when they need super user permissions should they log into the super user account. In Windows Server, the **RunAs** command allows them to switch between

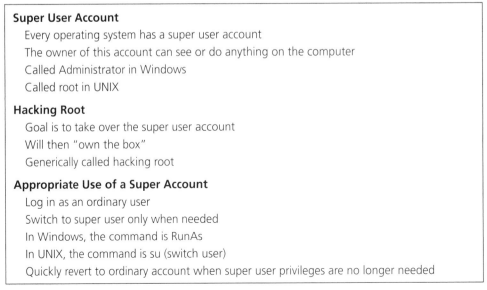

FIGURE 7-12   The Super User Account (Study Figure)

running as Administrator and working with their normal account. In UNIX, the **su** (switch user[13]) command can switch the systems administrator between the root account and his or her limited personal accounts.[14]

MANAGING ACCOUNTS   Figure 7-13 shows what happens if the systems administrator right-clicks on an account (in this case, the Administrator account) and selects *Properties*. This action will take the user to the dialog box shown in the figure. The *General* tab (shown) allows the systems administrator to place password restrictions on the user. Another tab allows the systems administrator to add the user account to multiple groups.

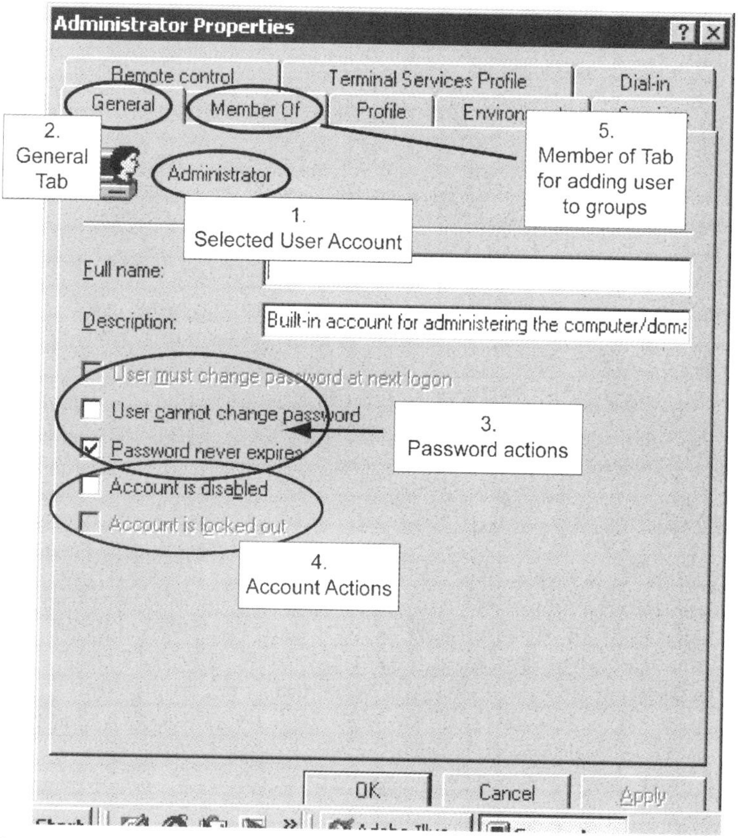

FIGURE 7-13   Windows User Account Properties

---

[13] Not super user as is sometimes said. The su command can switch the user to *any* other account.

[14] One additional protection in Windows is to rename the Administrator account to something else, say David. David is now the super user account. Next, someone working with David privileges can create a new Administrator account and give it few, if any, privileges. Afterward, if hackers do succeed in taking over the new Administrator account, they will not get super user privileges.

At the other end of the privileges spectrum, most operating systems have a *Guest* account with few privileges. People can use the Guest account even if they cannot log into a normal account. This is dangerous because in some cases, privilege escalation attacks allow someone logging into the Guest account to gain higher privileges, sometimes even super user privileges. During configuration, the Guest account should be deleted or disabled.

CREATING USERS The Action command in Figure 7-11 allows new user accounts to be created. To create a new account, the systems administrator will enter an account name, a password, and other information about the account.

WINDOWS GROUPS In Figure 7-11, selecting the Groups choice instead of Users will show a list of groups. The systems administrator will be able to look at each group to see its members, then add to or delete members from the group.

TEST YOUR UNDERSTANDING

9. **a.** What Windows snap-in is used to manage users and groups?
   b. On which MMC is this snap-in available?
   c. In this snap-in, if the administrator clicks on an account, what may he or she do?
   d. How does the administrator create a new account?
   e. How does an administrator add an account to a group?
   f. How does the administrator create a new group?

10. **a.** What privileges does the super user account have?
    b. What is the super user account in Windows?
    c. What is the super user account in UNIX?
    d. What is hacking root, and why is it desirable to hackers?
    e. When should a Windows systems administrators use the Administrator account?
    f. How does the administrator get to the super user account in Windows?
    g. In UNIX?

MANAGING PERMISSIONS

Permissions

Just because someone logs in correctly does not mean that they should have free reign to do anything they wish on the server. To each account and group, systems administrators assign **permissions**, which specify what the user or group can do and not do to files, directories, and subdirectories. Permissions can range from not even being able to see a directory to being allowed to do everything to it.

Permissions

Permissions specify what the user or group can do to files, directories, and subdirectories—if anything at all

Assigning Permissions in Windows (Figure 7-15)

Right click on file or directory in My Computer or Windows Explorer

Select Properties, then Security tab

Select a user or group

Click on or off the 6 standard permissions (permit or deny)

For more fine-grained control, 13 special permissions collectively give the standard 6

FIGURE 7-14 Managing Permissions in Windows (Study Figure)

Permissions specify what the user or group can do or not do to files, directories, and subdirectories.

Assigning Permissions in Windows

DIRECTORY PERMISSIONS To assign permission in Windows, the systems administrator can right click on a directory (folder) or file under My Computer or Windows Explorer. In Figure 7-15, the systems administrator has done this for the My Music directory and has selected *Properties* from the pop-up menu. The systems administrator has then selected the *Security* tab.

Note that the top pane shows all of the users and groups that have been assigned permissions for this directory. The *Power Users* group has been selected.

WINDOWS PERMISSIONS The lower pane shows the six **standard permissions** in Windows and shows which of these permissions have been assigned to the Power Users group. If another group or user were selected, different permissions would appear.

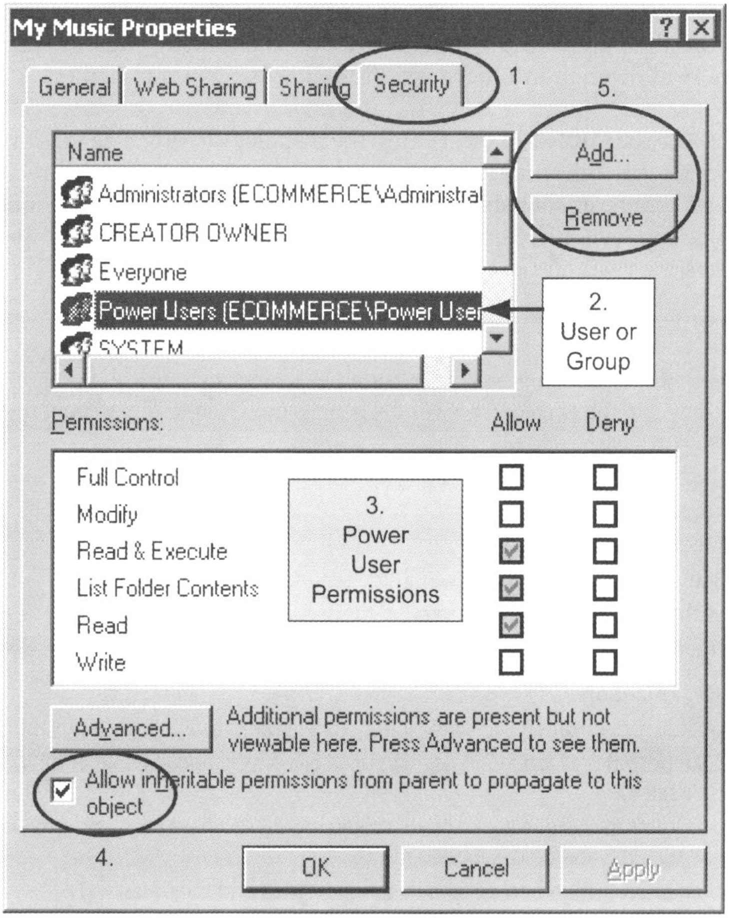

FIGURE 7-15 Assigning Permissions in Windows

Although these standard permissions give a good range of options, sometimes more detailed permissions are needed. The advanced button on the Security tab allows permissions to be assigned in more detail if necessary. This button leads to 13 specialized permissions from which the 6 standard permissions are built.

ADDING USERS AND GROUPS   Note that there are buttons for adding new users or groups and for removing users and groups that have been assigned permissions. There is no limit to how many users and groups can be assigned permissions to a directory. Each user and group, furthermore, can be assigned a different set of permissions in the directory.

INHERITANCE   In Windows, **inheritance** means that a directory receives permissions from the parent directory. This means that the child directory has exactly the same permissions as the parent directory for each user and group. Note that the *Allow inheritable permissions from parent to propagate to this object* box in Figure 7-15 must be checked to allow permissions to be inherited from the parent directory. This is the default.

An individual's or group's effective permissions are the permissions that are inherited from the parent (if the inheritance box is checked), plus permissions that are specifically allowed, minus permissions that are specifically denied.

DIRECTORY ORGANIZATION   In most cases, the installer can organize top-level directories to make simple inheritance the normal process in almost all directories. For instance, if all programs that should be available to all logged-in users are grouped under a single top-level directory, *public programs*, the installer can give the group *all logged-in users* the read and execute permission in the *public programs* directory. By

---

Inheritance

If the *Allow inheritable permissions from parent to propagate to this object box* is checked in the security tab, the directory receives the permissions given to this account or group in the parent directory.

This box is checked by default, so inheritance from the parent is the default

Total permissions include

Inherited permissions (if any)

Plus the Allow permissions checked in the security tab

Minus the Deny permissions checked in the security tab

The result is the permissions level for a directory or file

Directory Organization

Proper directory organization can make inheritance a great tool for avoiding labor

Example: Suppose the *all logged-in user group* is given read and execute in the *public programs* directory,

Then all programs in this directory and its subdirectories will have read and execute permissions for everyone who is logged in.

There is no need to assign permissions to subdirectories and their files

---

FIGURE 7-16   The Inheritance of Permission (Study Figure)

default, read and execute will be inherited for all programs in all subdirectories. Only if this default needs to be overruled do the Allow and Deny boxes need to be checked.

TEST YOUR UNDERSTANDING

11. **a.** How are permissions applied to a directory in Windows?
    b. List each standard Windows privilege and explain it briefly.
    c. To how many accounts and groups can different permissions be applied in Windows?
    d. How can inheritance reduce labor costs in assigning permissions?
    e. How can inheritance be modified?
    f. How are a user's effective permissions calculated for a directory?
    g. How would you set up a top-level directory for a firm's public policy documents, which should be readable by all logged-in users?

Assigning Groups and Permissions in UNIX

Compared with access permissions in Windows, access permissions in UNIX are limited. This is one of the most serious problems associated with security in UNIX computers. Some versions of UNIX assign permissions more granularly than the standard, but the standard is the normal behavior of UNIX. Figure 7-17 compares the assignment of permissions in Windows and UNIX.

NUMBER OF PERMISSIONS   As just noted, Windows has six different permissions that can be assigned to users and groups. If finer granularity is needed, Windows has 13 specialized permissions to assign.

In contrast, UNIX only has three permissions to assign. **Read** is read-only access. **Write** allows the account or group to make changes. **Execute** permits the execution of programs. These permissions are usually written as **rwx** (with execute being denoted by the x).

NUMBER OF ACCOUNTS OR GROUPS   Also as just noted, Windows can assign different permissions to many accounts and groups. In a directory (folder) for a project team, for instance, different members and subgroups within the team probably should be given different access permissions.

UNIX, however, historically can only assign different permissions to three entities. One entity is the account that owns the file or directory. The second is a

Category	Windows	UNIX
Number of permissions	6 standard, 13 specialized if needed	Only 3: read (read only), write (make changes), and execute (for programs). Referred to as rwx
For a file or directory, different permissions can be assigned to	Any number of individual accounts and groups	The account owner A single group, and All other accounts

FIGURE 7-17   Assigning Permissions in Windows and UNIX

single group associated with the directory. The third is everyone else. There is no way to assign different permissions to multiple accounts or groups. This is very limiting.

Although UNIX generally has good security, its inflexibility in handling permissions is a serious issue. Even UNIX evangelists touting the security strengths of UNIX will say, "Oh yeah, that," when asked about permissions in UNIX.

TEST YOUR UNDERSTANDING

12. **a.** What are the three UNIX permissions?
    b. Briefly characterize each.
    c. Compare the number of UNIX directory and file permissions with that of Windows.
    d. To which three individual accounts or groups can permissions be assigned for a particular directory in UNIX?
    e. How does the number of accounts or groups to which permissions can be assigned in UNIX compare with that of Windows?

TESTING FOR VULNERABILITIES

Even if companies attempt to be diligent about implementing protections, planners and implementers inevitably make mistakes due to the complexities of the many protections they need to implement. **Vulnerability testing** attempts to find any weaknesses in a firm's protection suite before attackers do, letting the systems administrator know what work still needs to be done.

To do vulnerability testing, a security administrator installs **vulnerability testing software** on his or her PC, and then runs it against the servers within the security administrator's realm of concern. These programs run a battery of attacks against the servers, and then generate reports detailing the security vulnerabilities it found on the

---

Mistakes Will be Made in Hardening
   So do vulnerability testing

Run Vulnerability Testing Software on Another Computer
   Run the software against the hosts to be tested
   Interpret the reports about problems found on the server
      This requires extensive security expertise
   Fix them

Get Permission to Do Vulnerability Testing First
   Can be fired for vulnerability testing
      Looks like an internal attack
   Vulnerability testing plan
      Tester should prepare an exact list of testing activities
      Supervisor must approve in writing to cover the tester
      Supervisor must agree, in writing, to hold the tester blameless if there is damage
      Tester must not diverge from the plan

FIGURE 7-18   Vulnerability Testing (Study Figure)

servers.[15] While vulnerability testing software is easy to run, it is meaningless unless the vulnerability tester has a solid understanding of the attacks it is running and what the vulnerability reports mean. These are not tools for brainless operation.

Vulnerability testing must be managed very carefully to protect the careers of vulnerability testers. Attackers also use vulnerability testing tools, and a number of security administrators have "gone over to the dark side," using vulnerability testing software to help them attack their own companies. There have been several cases of security administrators who lost their jobs and even went to jail for doing vulnerability testing without proper authorization. Arguing that these security administrators were doing vulnerability testing as part of their job descriptions did not work in the corporation or in courts.

Before doing vulnerability testing, it is important to create a **vulnerability testing plan** containing a detailed description of what will be done. The plan should also warn that vulnerability testing occasionally crashes computers and does other damage. It is then important to have the tester's superior sign the plan to give approval and to acknowledge that damage may be done. Vulnerability testers call these signed plans their "get out of jail" cards. The final thing to know about testing plans is that diverging from the agreed-upon plan removes all protections.

TEST YOUR UNDERSTANDING

13. **a.** Why is vulnerability testing desirable?
    b. What two things does vulnerability testing software do?
    c. Why is it important to get approval in writing before conducting a vulnerability test?
    d. What two things should this written approval specifically mention?
    e. Why is it important never to diverge from the test plan when running the tests?

WINDOWS CLIENT PC SECURITY

So far in this chapter, we have focused on servers. Of course, corporations also need to secure their client PCs, which are far more numerous. We will focus on Windows client PC security because of Windows' dominance in the client market.

Client PC Security Baselines

To protect clients, companies need security baselines for each operating system version. For example, a company needs security baselines for Windows XP, Vista, and Windows 7.[16] In this section, we will only look at Microsoft Windows clients because of Windows' dominance of the desktop and notebook markets. However, a firm also needs security baselines for its Macintosh and UNIX desktop computers. In addition, for each client operating system, a firm may have multiple baselines, such as for desktop versus laptop computers, for in-site versus external computers, and for regular clients versus computers with especially high-security needs.

---

[15] For UNIX servers, *Nessus* is the most popular vulnerability testing tool.

[16] At the time of this writing, Windows 7 has not been released, so we will not discuss it in this chapter.

Client PC Security Baselines

For each version of each operating system

Within an operating system, for different types of computers (desktop versus notebook, in-site versus external, high-risk versus normal risk, and so forth)

Windows Security Center in Vista (Figure 7-20)

The Windows Security Center is the control panel for most Windows Client security features

Called the Action Center in Windows 7

Automatic Updates for Security Vulnerabilities

Completely automatic updating is the only reasonable policy

Antivirus and Antispyware Protection

Important to know the status of antivirus protection

Users turn off deliberately

Users turn off automatic updating for virus signatures

Users do not pay the annual subscription and so get no more updates

Windows Firewall

Stateful inspection firewall

Since Windows SP Service Pack 2

Accessed through the Security Center (or Action Center)

FIGURE 7-19 Windows Client PC Security (Study Figure)

TEST YOUR UNDERSTANDING

14. What different baselines does a company need for its client PCs?

The Windows Security Center

Windows XP Service Pack 2 (SP2) introduced the **Windows Security Center** to give the user a quick status check of the PC's main security posture settings. Windows Vista extended the Windows Security Center to embrace more security options. Figure 7-20 shows the Windows Security Center in Vista. In Windows 7, the Windows Security Center is being replaced by a broader Windows Action Center.

TEST YOUR UNDERSTANDING

15. How can you quickly assess the security posture of your Windows PC?

Automatic Updates

The user can set up **Automatic Updates** to download and install operating system updates (patches) automatically. The user also has other options, including notifying the user of downloads and letting the user decide when to install them. Because of the shortening time between the release of patches and the widespread use of exploits that take advantage of the patched vulnerability, completely automatic operation is the only thing that makes sense for PCs in corporations.

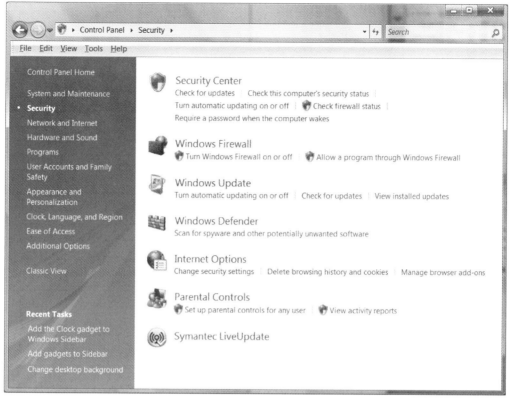

FIGURE 7-20   Windows Security Center

TEST YOUR UNDERSTANDING

16. Why should updating be done completely automatically on client PCs?

Antivirus and Spyware Protection

Antivirus protection is critical, but it is easy to make antivirus programs ineffective.

- The user may turn off the antivirus program because it slows down the computer (and it does) or because it will not allow the user to download something or open an attachment (probably wisely).
- More subtly, the user may have turned off automatic downloads for new virus signatures or schedule the updates for the middle of the night when the computer is turned off. This is bad because the user still thinks that he or she is protected.
- Finally, the user may not pay the annual fee; this is insidious because although the antivirus protection appears to be working fine, there will be no updates for viruses and other malware after the contract ends.

The Windows Security Center indicates whether the antivirus program is operating effectively. However, the information it presents varies somewhat between vendors.

TEST YOUR UNDERSTANDING

17. What can go wrong with antivirus protection?

Windows Firewall

Windows XP SP2 introduced the **Windows Firewall**. This stateful packet inspection (SPI) firewall has been included in all subsequent client versions of Windows. The Security Center (or Action Center) lets users check the status of their Windows Firewall installations.

TEST YOUR UNDERSTANDING

18. What SPI firewall has come with client version of Windows since Windows XP SP2?

Protecting Notebook Computers

Notebook computers need special protection because so many are lost[17] or stolen each year.

THREATS   Each notebook represents a significant capital investment. More importantly, all data that had not been backed up will be lost. In theft, the hardware is expensive, but the value of lost data usually is far larger. A third consideration is that the computer may contain sensitive data, including private customer data or intellectual property; this is a worst-case situation.

BACKUP   Few stolen (or even lost) computers are recovered. Backup is critical to protect the loss of working data and documents that will have to be recreated. The notebook should be backed up before being taken off-site. If it is taken off site for more than a few hours, it should be backed up frequently while off-site.

POLICIES FOR SENSITIVE DATA   For sensitive data, the company must develop strong policies, and it must strongly enforce these policies.

- Most important, policies should strongly limit what sensitive data can be stored on mobile PCs at all. Sensitive data should be permitted on mobile PCs only after careful thought and preferably with the signed approval of the person's superior. There may even be a specific policy for the type of information that may not be taken off-site at all or only with very high-level authorization.
- A second policy is to require encryption on all mobile computers regardless of what information they contain. Encryption will reduce the threat of losing trade secrets or private information. In many states, a loss of personal information requires the notification of all people whose private information was released. Typically, however, this notification is *not* required if the private information is properly encrypted.

---

[17] Laptop losses probably far exceed laptop thefts. In 2008, the Ponemon Institute studied laptop losses at 106 U.S. airports. The study found that over 12,000 laptops were lost each *week* at these airports. Larry Ponemon, Airport Insecurity: The Case of Missing & Lost Laptops, Ponemon Institute, LLC., June 30, 2008. http://www.dell.com/downloads/global/services/dell_lost_laptop_study.pdf.

Threats

    Loss or theft

    Loss of capital investment

    Loss of data that were not backed up

    Loss of trade secrets

    Loss of private information, leading to lawsuits

Backup

    Before taking the notebook out

    Frequently during use outside the firm

Use a Strong Password

    If attackers bypass the operating system password, they get open access to encrypted data

    The loss of login passwords is a major concern

Policies for Sensitive Data

    Four main policies:

    1. Limit what sensitive data can be stored on all mobile devices

    2. Require data encryption for all data

        Notification may not be required if private information that is lost or stolen is encrypted

    3. Protect the notebook with a strong login password

    4. Audit for the previous two policies

    Apply these four policies to all mobile data on disk drives: USB RAM drives, MP3 players that store data, and even mobile phones that can store data

Other Measures

    Teach users loss and theft protection techniques

    Use notebook recovery software

        Contacts the recovery company the next time the computer connects to the Internet

        The recover company contacts local police to recover the software

FIGURE 7-21 Protecting Notebook Computers (Study Figure)

- A third good policy is to require the device to be protected by strong passwords or by biometrics. This way, if a person takes possession of a computer, he or she cannot use it. Most encryption is transparent to logged-in users, meaning that anyone who has the login password for the computer will not even know that the data are encrypted. Of course, if an attacker cannot log in, he or she cannot read the encrypted data.
- A good fourth policy is to require the auditing of the first three policies.

These four policies should be applied to all mobile data on notebook disk drives, USB RAM drives, MP3 players, and even mobile phones that can store data.

TRAINING Another protection is to teach people with portable devices the dangers that mobile devices create and how to avoid theft and loss (for instance, when checking in at a hotel, place the portable device on the counter, not at your feet.)

COMPUTER RECOVERY SOFTWARE   It is also possible to install computer recovery software on notebook computers to allow the recovery of some lost or stolen notebook. When the notebook next connects to the Internet, the computer recovery software reports its IP address to a recovery company. The recovery software company works with local police to recover the notebook.

TEST YOUR UNDERSTANDING

19. **a.** What are the three dangers created by notebook computer loss or theft?
    b. When should backup be done for mobile computers?
    c. What four policies are necessary to protect sensitive information?
    d. To what should these policies be applied?
    e. What training should be provided?
    f. What does computer recovery software do?

Centralized PC Security Management

Trained systems administrators manage servers, but ordinary users typically manage their own client PCs. Lacking training on host security and corporate PC security policies, users often make mistakes in configuring and using their PCs. In some cases, they knowingly violate corporate PC security policies. Companies must be able to manage client PCs centrally to ensure compliance with good practice and corporate policies. In addition, centralized PC security management often has automation tools that can reduce the labor involved in enforcing security. We will look at three major approaches to centralized PC security management.

STANDARD CONFIGURATIONS   One strategy for centrally managing client PCs is to mandate standard configurations for clients. **Standard configurations** detail how client PCs should be configured, including important options, application programs, and, sometimes, the entire user interface. Users cannot add unauthorized programs or reduce security settings. Overall, standard configurations enforce corporate security policies, reducing opportunities for user errors and violations.

In addition, standard configurations greatly simplify PC troubleshooting and general maintenance. Without standard configurations, troubleshooters often must cope with unfamiliar problems that involve subtle interactions between different application programs and between application programs and the computer's operating system configuration. With standard configurations, these interactions are well known.

> The U.S. Federal government mandates that all U.S. government PCs running Windows XP or Windows Vista must conform to a standard configuration called the Federal Desktop Core Configuration.

NETWORK ACCESS CONTROL (NAC)   In most cases, initial access control is meaningless if client PCs are compromised. The exploit program will have all of the legitimate user's access permissions. The emerging solution is to install **network access control (NAC)** software on PCs that will connect over a network.

Importance

Ordinary users lack the knowledge to manage security on their PCs

They sometimes knowingly violate security policies

Also, centralized management often can reduce costs through automation

Standard Configurations for PCs

May restrict applications, configuration settings, and even the user interface

Ensure that the software is configured safely

Enforce policies

More generally, reduce maintenance costs by making it easier to diagnose errors

Network Access Control (NAC)

Goal is to reduce the danger created by computers with malware

Stage 1: Initial Health Check

Checks the "health" of the computer before allowing it into the network

For Windows clients, retrieves data from the Windows Security Center or Action Center

If health appears to be good, admits the client to the network

If health does not appear to be good, two options

Reject: Do not admit

Quarantine: Give access only to a single remediation server

Recheck health after remediation

Stage 2: Ongoing Traffic Monitoring

If traffic after admission indicates malware on the client, drop or remediate

Not all NAC systems do this

Windows Group Policy Objects (GPOs)

Windows GPOs are policy sets governing a particular class of computers (e.g., on-site, normal-risk desktops)

Domain controller pushes GPOs out to target computers (Figure 7-23)

Target computers obey the policy set

FIGURE 7-22 Centralized PC Security Management (Study Figure)

As the term *access control* suggests, NAC focuses primarily on controlling initial access to the network. Just as visitors to a country may be screened for health problems before entering a country, NAC analyzes the security health of a client PC before giving it access to the network. Primarily, it does this by querying the PC for the information presented in the Windows Security Center or Action Center. This ensures that the client PC has automated updating installed, has an up-to-date antivirus program, and so forth.

If a client PC fails the initial NAC inspection, there are two alternatives. One is simply to forbid access to the network until the user fixes the problem. More commonly, the user is given access to a single **remediation server**. From the remediation server, the user can download updates that are needed and then try again to be accepted by the NAC control point.

Although NAC once looked only at the initial health assessment, most NAC software today also monitors the client PC's traffic *after* initial access. If the PC begins sending traffic created by malware, the central NAC server can cut off the PC or send it back for remediation.

WINDOWS GROUP POLICY OBJECTS (GPOS)   As Figure 7-23 shows, Microsoft Windows domain controllers can transmit sets of policies, called **group policy objects (GPOs)**, to groups of client PCs. GPOs allow a firm to enforce finely grained policies for controlling distinct classes of individual PCs, such as general client PCs, high-risk client PCs, and notebook computers.

GPOs are very powerful. For example they can lock down a client's desktop so that it cannot be changed. In addition, they can prevent the attachment of removable media, such as DVDs and USB flash drives. In general GPOs are very good for enforcing standard configurations and other important policies.

> *The Federal Desktop Core Configuration standard for Windows XP and Vista can be configured almost entirely through GPOs.*

TEST YOUR UNDERSTANDING

20. **a.** Why is central PC security management desirable?
   b. Why are standard configurations attractive?
   c. What does NAC do when a computer attempts to connect to the network?
   d. If a PC fails its initial health assessment, what are a NAC system's two options?
   e. Does NAC control usually stop after access is granted?
   f. What things can Windows GPOs restrict?
   g. Why are Windows GPOs powerful tools for managing security on individual Windows PCs?

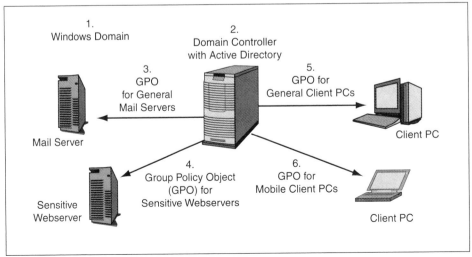

FIGURE 7-23 Windows Group Policy Objects (GPOs)

DATA PROTECTION: BACKUP

The Importance of Backup

So far in the chapter, we have focused on hardening server and client operating systems. We only looked in passing at the protection of data stored on hosts. This omission was not done to downplay the importance of data protection. Rather, it was done to wait until data could be given special emphasis, and this required covering operating system hardening first.

In this first section on data security, we will look at backup—ensuring that copies of data files are stored safely and securely and will survive even if the data on the host are lost or damaged. Backup is critical because other protections will inevitably break down, and your backup practices will determine how much you lose. In many ways, the three most important parts of host hardening are backup, backup, and backup.

> *Backup is ensuring that copies of data files are stored safely and securely and will survive even if the data on the host are lost, stolen, or damaged.*

TEST YOUR UNDERSTANDING

21. Why is backup critical?

Threats

There are many ways to lose data. Mechanical hard drive failures occur frequently, and fires and floods can destroy data on many computers. In addition to these non-security threats, malware can delete or change data, and mobile devices can be stolen or lost.

However data are lost, the only recourse for the firm is to restore the data from the last backup. Backup specifically protects the availability security goal. If backed up data are lost on a host, it will still be available, although with more work, on backup media.

TEST YOUR UNDERSTANDING

22. List the ways in which data can be lost, adding some of your own if you can.

Importance
  In an incident, you may lose all data that are not backed up

Threats that Are Addressed by Backup
  Mechanical hard drive failure or damage in a fire or flood
    Not a security issue but very important
  Data on lost or stolen computers are not available to the organization
  Malware can reformat the hard drive or do other data destruction

---

FIGURE 7-24 Data Protection: Backup (Study Figure)

Scope of Backup

Backup scope is the fraction of information on a hard drive that is backed up. These three degrees of completeness are image backup of the entire hard drive, only data files and directories, and single files. Each is appropriate under different circumstances.

FILE/DIRECTORY DATA BACKUP The most common type of backup is **file/directory data backup**. As the name suggests, this approach only backs up data on the computer—not programs, registry settings, and other customization information. In fact, it may not even backup all data. It may only backup data in certain directories. In terms of backup scope, it is in the middle of the three approaches.

On a Windows computer, a common directory/file backup approach is to back up Documents (or My Documents) and other high-level directories, such as Music and Pictures. This is relatively simple to set up. However, many users store active data files on their desktops and in other locations, and they must be sure to back these up because these often are a user's most current files.

Which data directories should users and systems administrators back up? When patients ask dentists which teeth they should floss, the common riposte is "Only the ones you want to keep." The advice is also good for data files. Given that even a single data file will take hours or days to rebuild from scratch, if it can be rebuilt at all, requiring the backing up of *all* data files is good corporate policies.

Scope of Backup
  Fraction of information on the hard drive that is backed up

File/Directory Data Backup
  Select data files and directories to be backed up
      (Do not forget items on the desktop!)
  Not good for programs

Image Backup
  Everything, including programs and settings
      Can be restored to a different computer if necessary
  Image backup is very slow
  Data files change the most rapidly, so doing several file/directory data backups for each image backup may be appropriate

Shadowing
  Whenever the user saves a file, the backup software saves a copy to a USB flash drive or another storage location
  But the shadow device usually only has limited storage capacity
      When the capacity is exceeded, the oldest files are deleted first
      Consequently, shadowing should only supplement file/directory data backup, image backup, or both

---

FIGURE 7-25 Scope of Backup (Study Figure)

IMAGE BACKUP   In **image backup**, the entire contents of the hard drive are copied to backup media. This includes programs, data, personalization settings, and other matters. (In other words, "everything" means everything.) Even if the entire hard drive is lost, its contents can be restored onto the same machine or a different machine. File and directory data backup cannot provide this degree of loss protection.

However, image backup is the slowest form of backup. Due to this slowness, most companies do image backup less frequently than file/directory data backup. This also makes sense because data usually change far more rapidly than programs and configuration settings.

Of course, before installing a new program or modifying the configuration or another program, doing an image backup is always prudent.

SHADOWING   A third scope of backup is shadowing. In **shadowing**, a backup copy of each file being worked on is written every few minutes to the hard drive or to another location, such as a USB flash drive.[18] This is important because with file/directory data backup or image backup, everything since the last backup is lost. This is a window of loss ranging from several hours to several days and sometimes longer. With shadowing, the time window of data loss is very brief.

> *In shadowing, a backup copy of each file being worked on is written every few minutes to the hard drive or to another location, such as a USB flash drive.*

Typically, the shadow storage space is very limited. When it is exceeded, the oldest files are deleted to make room for the newest. This usually is not too bad because most restorations from the shadow area are done within minutes or days. Having enough shadow backup space for a few days is sufficient—as long as a firm also does regular file/directory data backup, image backup, or both more frequently than the shadow backup discards files.

TEST YOUR UNDERSTANDING

23. **a.** Distinguish between file/directory data backup and image backup.
    b. Why is file/directory backup attractive compared with image backup?
    c. Why is image backup attractive compared with file/directory data backup?
    d. What is shadowing?
    e. What is the advantage of shadowing over file/directory data backup?
    f. How is shadowing limited?

Full versus Incremental Backups

In file/directory data backup, **full backups**, which record up all the data on the computer, can take a long time. Consequently, most companies only do a full backup once a week or so. They then do daily **incremental backups**, which only save the data changed since the most recent backup (either full or incremental). For instance,

---

[18] Some shadowing systems even make each save a new version of the file each time. This lets a user to roll back to an earlier version, even after several minutes or even hours of work.

if the full backup takes place on Sunday, Monday's incremental backup will only save information changed since Sunday's full backup. Tuesday's backup, in turn, will only save data changed since Monday's incremental backup. Wednesday's incremental backup will save data changed since Tuesday's incremental backup. On the following Sunday, a full backup will be done again.

Full backups record all data on the computer. Incremental backups only save the data changed since the most recent backup (either full or incremental).

The advantage of doing periodic full backups and then more frequent incremental backups is simply that incremental backups take less time to do. For large hard drives with many data directories, daily backup speed is very important. Therefore, almost all companies mix full and incremental backups.

However, with incremental backups, restoration must be done carefully. In the example, suppose that the hard drive fails on a Wednesday. The restorer *must* first restore Sunday's full backup, then Monday's incremental backup, then Tuesday's incremental backup. In other words, backups must be restored in the order in which they were created. Otherwise, newer files may be overwritten by older files.

Full and incremental backups must be restored in the order in which they were created.

Usually, several generations of full backups will be kept, so that files that were accidentally changed some time ago can be retrieved. In the case of weekly backup, this means keeping several weeks or even months of full backups. Incremental backups, however, usually are discarded after the next full backup.

Full backups
    All files and directories
    Slow, so it is typically done weekly

Incremental Backups
    Only records changes since the last backup
    Fast, so usually done daily
    Do incremental backups until the next full backup

Restoration Order
    Restore the full backup first
    Then restore incremental backups in the order created
    (Otherwise, newer files will be overwritten)

Generations
    Save several generations of full backups
    Usually do not save incremental backups after the next full backup

---

FIGURE 7-26 Full versus Incremental Backup (Study Figure)

TEST YOUR UNDERSTANDING

24. **a.** Why don't most companies do full backup every night?
    b. What is incremental backup (be precise)?
    c. A company does a full backup one night. Call this backup *Cardiff*. On three successive nights, it does incremental backups, which it labels *Greenwich*, *Dublin*, and *Paris*. In restoration, what backups must be restored first and second?

Backup Technologies

There are several common technologies for doing backup, and more are on the horizon.

LOCAL BACKUP   Traditionally, companies did **local backup**, meaning that each computer was backed up individually. With local backup, there usually is no way to enforce policy. Also, there is no way to know which computers were backed up in compliance with backup policy, how backups were done, or how data were protected.

Local Backup

   On individual computers

   No way to enforce backup policies

   Difficult to audit backup compliance

Centralized Backup (Figure 7-28)

   Central backup console collects data from each device over the network

   Stores on console's backup hardware

   It is economical to use expensive backup hardware on a single console compared to giving each host a backup device

   Easy to audit compliance

   Generally results in a well-maintained repository of backup media

Continuous Data Protection (CDP)

   Used when a firm has two server locations

   Each location backs up the other in real time

   Other site can take over very quickly in case of a disaster, with little data loss

   Requires expensive high-speed transmission link between the sites

Internet Backup Services

   Backup to a commercial backup service's site, over the Internet

   Convenient but very slow

   Lose security over data

Mesh Backup (Figure 7-29)

   Peer-to-peer backup onto other client computers

   Sends backup data in parcels to many other client PCs

   Stores data redundantly so if a PC is offline, all data are still available

   Security must be considered carefully

FIGURE 7-27   Backup Technologies (Study Figure)

CENTRALIZED BACKUP   To avoid these problems, many firms use **centralized backup**. As Figure 7-28 shows, backup is done over the network, from a central **backup console**. This console usually is a PC. The central backup console has magnetic tape or other storage hardware.

At a preset time, the central backup console "pulls" the data to be backed up from each server (and sometimes each client) for which it is responsible.

Centralized backup means that only one or two computers must have backup hardware. This makes it economical to buy very good backup equipment.

Centralized backup makes it easier to determine if backup policies are being followed. Centralized backup also tends to bring the benefits of a single, well-organized, and well-maintained repository for backup media.

CONTINUOUS DATA PROTECTION   An option available to companies that have two server sites is **continuous data protection (CDP)**, in which each site backs up the other site. Furthermore, as *continuous* in the name indicates, CDP does backup in real time. If one site fails, the second site can take over the processing load immediately, with little or no loss of data. For disaster recovery, CDP is becoming viewed as mandatory. Of course, CDP requires a very high speed (and therefore expensive) data transmission link between the two sites.

INTERNET BACKUP SERVICE   A number of backup vendors now offer backup service over the Internet. This is relatively convenient for client PC users who might not otherwise back up their PCs. However, Internet access speeds are slow compared with network transmission speeds, so sending large sections of a hard drive over the Internet to the storage provider will require a long time. In addition, there is the concern that the company owning the PC loses control over its data, which can be disastrous.

MESH BACKUP   An emerging option for client PCs is **mesh backup**, in which the client PCs in an organization back up each other. As Figure 7-29 shows, mesh backup is a peer-to-peer application. Each PC sends parcels of its backup files to several other client PCs. Of course, the client shown sending its backup parcel to other PCs will also receive backup parcels from other PCs.

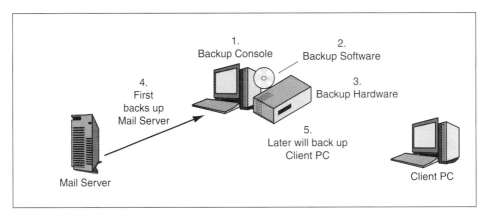

FIGURE 7-28   Centralized Backup

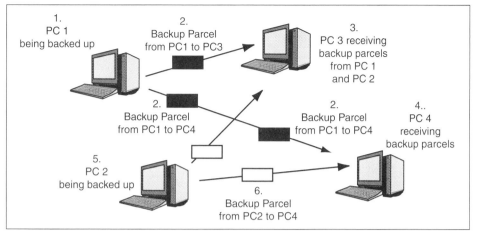

FIGURE 7-29 Mesh Backup

Mesh backup presents formidable technical problems. First, mesh backup operation must not slow down the computer on which packets are being written or from which packets are being retrieved. Second, specific client PCs are not always available for packet retrieval, so parcels need to be sent out redundantly. The most difficult technical problem is security. When a client PC receives a backup parcel, its user must not be able to read, modify, or delete it.

Despite these problems, mesh backup is desirable. Most organizations have had little success in getting users to back up their PCs. Mesh backup could make client PC backup automatic and so eliminate user failures to do backup regularly.

TEST YOUR UNDERSTANDING

25. **a.** What are the advantages of centralized backup compared with local backup?
    b. What is CDP (do not just spell out the acronym)?
    c. Why is CDP attractive?
    d. Why is it expensive?
    e. Why is backup over the Internet to a backup storage provider attractive for client PC users?
    f. What security risk does it create?
    g. What is mesh backup?
    h. What are its technical challenges?
    i. Why is mesh backup desirable?

Backup Media

Backed-up data must be physically stored on something. Physical storage options are called **backup media**.

MAGNETIC TAPE The traditional backup medium has been **magnetic tape**. (If you have seen an old music or VHS cassette, you have an idea of what magnetic tape looks like.) Magnetic tape can store vast amounts of data at the lowest cost per bit of all backup media.

Servers Normally Use Magnetic Tape

Slow but inexpensive per bit stored

Second hard drive on computer

    Very fast backup

    But lost if computer is stolen or damaged in a fire

    Backup up on tape occasionally for archival (long-term storage)

Clients Normally Use Optical Disks (DVDs)

Attraction is that almost all users have optical disk burners

Dual-layer DVDs offer about 8 GB of capacity

    This often is not enough

    User may have to insert additional disks to do backup

Backup up to a second client PC hard drive; then occasionally back up onto optical disks

The life of information on optical disks is unknown

FIGURE 7-30 Backup Media (Study Figure)

However, magnetic tape recording and read back are excruciatingly slow. This means that tape backups usually are done overnight. Although tape backup speeds keep improving, so does the amount of information being saved each time.

Given the desirability of faster backup, it is becoming popular to store backups on other hard drives. This slashes backup time, but hard drives are too expensive for long-term storage. Consequently, many companies use two-tier backup, storing information on disk for as long as possible and then **archiving** (storing backed-up data for extended periods) onto tape.

CLIENT PC BACKUP Client PC users typically save backups on DVDs. The main advantage of using optical disks for storage is that almost all PCs have optical disk burners. However, even with dual-layer (or double-layer) DVDs, which store about 8 GB of data, many users need multiple disks for a single backup.

Many PC users now use a second hard drive on their systems for backup. This is much faster than optical disk backup, but hard drives, as just noted, are not good for long-term archival storage. In addition, if a PC is stolen or lost in a fire, both drives are lost. Consequently, even users who do backup on a second hard drive need to do periodic backup onto DVDs.

How long do CDs and DVDs last before their data begin degrading? For short-term use, they appear to be fine, but some research suggests that even storage longer than two years may be problematic.

TEST YOUR UNDERSTANDING

26. **a.** Why is magnetic tape desirable as a backup medium?
    b. Why is tape not desirable?
    c. Why is backup onto another hard drive attractive?
    d. Why is it not a complete backup solution?
    e. How can this limitation be addressed?
    f. How much data can be stored on a dual-layer DVD?
    g. What is the advantage of burning backup data onto optical disks?
    h. Is storing backups on optical disks for several years likely to be safe?

Backup Management Policies

The best technology is worthless without good management, and policies are essential to good management.

BACKUP CREATION POLICIES   Like everything else in security, good management is critical to success in backup. Management begins with an understanding of the current system and future needs. It then creates policies for different types of data and different types of computers. Policies should address what data should be backed up, how frequently it should be backed up, how frequently restorations should be tested, and so forth.

RESTORATION POLICIES   The nightmare scenario is to have a failure, attempt to do a restoration, and then discover that restoration will not work. Backup policies should mandate frequent restoration tests, and audits should include sample restorations.

MEDIA STORAGE LOCATION POLICIES   Backup management requires some sophisticated policies regarding media storage location. The first is where to store the backup media. The most important thing is to require that the backup media are moved to

---

Backup Creation Policies
  Understand current system and future needs
  Create policies for different types of data and computer
  What should be backed up, how frequently, how frequently to test restorations, etc.

Restoration Policies
  Do restoration tests frequently

Media Storage Location Policies
  Store media at a different site
  Store backup media in a fireproof and waterproof safe until it can be moved offsite

Encryption Policies
  Encrypt backup media before moving them so that confidential information will not be exposed if the tape is stolen or lost

Strongly Access Control Policies for Backup Media
  Checkouts are rare and therefore suspicious
  Checking out media can result in their loss and the damages that come with this loss
  The manager of the person requesting the checkout should approve the checkout

Data Retention Policies
  There are strong legal requirements for how long certain types of data must be kept
  The legal department must get involved in retention policies

Auditing Policy Compliance
  All policies should be audited
  Includes tracing what happened in samples of data

FIGURE 7-31   Backup Management Policies (Study Figure)

another site. This way, if there is computer theft, a fire, or flood at the main site, the backup tapes will still be safe.

It normally takes a few hours or even a day to move backup media off-site. Policies should mandate that backup media should be stored in a fireproof and waterproof safe until they are shipped from the site.

ENCRYPTION POLICIES   When media are moved from their creation locations to their storage locations, loss and theft can result in the release of critical data. Consequently, policies should mandate that all media should be encrypted. This will make backup times longer, but there have been many cases of backup data loss that have required companies to notify customers and other affected people that sensitive personal information about them may be available to identity thieves.

ACCESS CONTROL POLICIES   Another storage policy should be to limit who may access backup media in storage. The data on the tape typically are very sensitive. In addition, if the backup media are stolen, the company will have no protection against data loss. Also, there have been cases of systems administrators stealing backup tapes, erasing them, and then deleting the data on the original hard drive. This makes restoration impossible.

Consequently, every checkout should require the written permission of the *manager* of the person wishing to access tapes. This permission should specify the particular media to be retrieved and the reason for retrieving them. Retrieval is rare, so checkouts should be suspicious. Of course, if the original system fails, rapid recovery is essential. Still, given the dangers involved in checkout, control must be maintained even in emergency restorations.

RETENTION POLICIES   Backup data will not be kept forever. Firms need strong and clear policies for how long data will be retained. **Retention** decisions cannot be made simply on the basis of how much storage space a company has. There are many business and legal requirements on the retention of certain types of data, so business units and the legal department must be active in the creation of retention policies.

AUDITING POLICY COMPLIANCE   Of course, having policies is one thing. Ensuring that they are implemented is another. There should be periodic audits for compliance, including tracing what happened to samples of data that should have been backed up.

TEST YOUR UNDERSTANDING

27. **a.** What should backup creation policies specify?
    b. Why are restoration tests needed?
    c. Where should backup media be stored for the long term?
    d. What should be done about backup media until they are moved?
    e. Why is the encryption of backup media critical?
    f. What three dangers require control over access to backup material?
    g. If Person A wishes to check out backup media, who should approve this?
    h. Why are checkouts of backup media suspicious?
    i. Why should business units and the legal department be involved in creating retention policies?
    j. What should backup audits include?

OTHER DATA PROTECTIONS

Encryption

In Chapter 3, we saw that encryption for confidentiality makes information unreadable to attackers but readable to authorized people who possess the key that must be used to decrypt it.

Encryption is growing in importance. The release of sensitive trade secrets or private information can produce massive damages. Not encrypting sensitive data is almost impossible to justify today. On the positive side, as we have seen, if encrypted data are lost or stolen, laws that govern the reporting of lost or stolen sensitive information often do not require notification because the finder or thief presumably cannot read the encrypted data.

KEY ESCROW   If you forget your password, it is a mere inconvenience. The help desk staff simply resets the password and tells you the reset password.

Encryption

Makes data unreadable to someone who does not have the key

Prevents theft of private or trade secret information

May reduce legal liability if lost or stolen data are encrypted

Key Escrow

Loss of the key is disastrous

　　Not like losing a password that can be reset

Key escrow stores a copy of the key in a safe place

Bad if managed by user

　　May not do it

　　May not be able to find it

　　If fired, may refuse to give it, locking up all data on the computer

Central key escrow on a corporate server is better

　　May be quite expensive

What to Encrypt

Files and directories

The entire disk

Strong Login Authentication Is Needed

Encryption is transparent to logged in users

　　Once a user is logged in, he or she can see all encrypted data

Protect with strong password or biometrics

　　Ensure that the password is not lost

File-Sharing Problems

File sharing may be more difficult because files usually have to be decrypted before sending them to another computer

---

FIGURE 7-32   Data Protection: Encryption (Study Figure)

Key loss in encryption is far more serious. If encryption is done so that attackers cannot get the information without the key, then people with legitimate access needs also will be equally locked out if the key is lost. If encryption is done well, then the answer to the question "How can I find my key?" will be "You can't." If you can get the key back, so could an attacker.

In fact, some organizations forbid encryption in most circumstances, fearing that the risk of key loss is far more serious than the risk of attackers reading unencrypted information.

The solution to the key loss problem is **key escrow**, which automatically saves the key so that it can be stored off the computer. If a problem occurs, the escrowed key can be retrieved and used to decrypt the information. The escrowed key should be locked away securely, and access to the key should be restricted.[19]

Key escrow should never be left to individual users. First, individual users are not likely to comply with key escrow policies. Second, if only individual users know their encryption keys, they can blackmail the company by refusing to decrypt critical data. The use of an automatic central key escrow server is better.[20]

FILE/DIRECTORY ENCRYPTION VERSUS WHOLE-DISK ENCRYPTION   When encrypting information on a disk, there are two general options—**file/directory encryption** and **whole-disk encryption**. The names are self-explanatory. File/directory encryption only encrypts the specific files and directories you tell it to encrypt, while whole-disk encryption encrypts an entire disk drive. If a user knows the directories containing sensitive data, he or she can use file/directory encryption confidently. However, whole-disk encryption ensures that sensitive data are protected even if a user overlooks an important directory.

PROTECTING ACCESS TO THE COMPUTER   Encryption usually is fully transparent to the PC user. As long as you know the password for your computer, you can work with encrypted directories and files exactly as you do with unencrypted directories and files. In fact, you usually do not even know if information is encrypted. Of course, anyone knowing the password for your computer gets the same easy access. Consequently, encryption typically is only as strong as your login password, and login password practices tend to be poor.

DIFFICULTIES IN FILE SHARING   Although encryption is very desirable, it makes sharing more difficult. Files usually have to be decrypted if they are moved to another computer.

TEST YOUR UNDERSTANDING

28. a. Why is encryption usually attractive for sensitive data from a legal standpoint?
 b. How long must an encryption key be to be considered strong today?

---

[19] One option is *n of M* access, in which the escrowed key is encrypted with another key. Parts of the decryption key are given redundantly to *M* people. Any subset of *n* of these *M* people can combine their key parts to decrypt the escrowed key. This prevents any single person from retrieving the key, and as *n* grows, collusion has to be broader. At the same time, allowing any *n* people to retrieve the key provides some flexibility in retrieving keys using the staff on hand at any time.

[20] Do not confuse file/folder versus whole-disk encryption with image versus file/folder data backup.

c. What happens if the encryption key is lost?
d. How do companies address this risk?
e. Why is entrusting users to do key escrow risky?
f. In what sense is encryption usually transparent to the user?
g. Why is this attractive?
h. Why is this dangerous?
i. What must users do to address this danger?
j. How does encryption make file sharing more difficult?

Data Destruction

At some point, data destruction becomes necessary. First, companies must securely destroy backup media that are no longer needed. Second, data destruction is necessary when a computer is discarded or transferred to another user. There are many horror stories of people buying computers on eBay or in flea markets that contain sensitive personal, corporate, or even national security data.

Simply deleting files or even reformatting a hard drive does not really destroy data. Forensics examiners (and thieves) can still restore most of the deleted file or most of the data on the reformatted hard drive.[21]

For media, the best approach seems to be shredding the media physically. Many office shredders can now shred optical disks as well as paper. Companies should have a policy that before any optical disk is discarded, it must be shredded.

For hard drives, physical destruction is sometimes recommended, but anyone who has tried to do this develops great respect for the ruggedness of hard drives. In practice, companies use **drive-wiping software**, which overwrites every sector on the drive many times with different bit patterns. After this, even forensics examiners cannot retrieve data from the drive.

Data Destruction Is Necessary
Backup media are not needed beyond their retention dates
If a computer is to be discarded
If the computer is to be sold or given to another user

Approaches
Deleted files and reformatted hard drives can still be partially or almost fully recovered
For media (optical disks), office shredders should be used
For hard drives, use drive wiping software
Rewrites all sectors on the drive many times with different patterns of data
Wiped data cannot be read

FIGURE 7-33 Data Destruction (Study Figure)

---

[21] A file is stored in a chain of sectors on the disk. Each sector in the chain points to the next sector. In normal file deletion, only the first sector in the chain is deleted, including its pointer to the second sector. A computer forensics examiner can find the next sector and so retrieve the rest of the file. Reformatting a hard drive also merely deletes pointers to information on the hard drive. The information itself is left intact.

TEST YOUR UNDERSTANDING

29. **a.** Why is it important to destroy data on backup media and PCs before discarding them or transferring them to someone else?
    b. How can optical disks be destroyed?
    c. How can data on hard drives be destroyed?

Document Restrictions

A final set of protections is embryonic at this time. *Document restrictions* attempt to limit what users can do to documents, in order to reduce security threats.

Document Restrictions
  Attempt to restrict what users can do to documents, in order to reduce security threats
  Embryonic

Digital Rights Management (DRM)
  Prevent unauthorized copying, etc.
  Used mostly by music and video publishers to thwart piracy
      Most of these technologies have been defeated
  For office documents, DRM can
      Prevent saving, printing, and other actions
      Often thwarted simply by capturing whatever appears on the screen and then saving the capture
      Some things can be prevented. For instance, in a spreadsheet,
          Hidden information can remain unreadable
          Even visible parts of a spreadsheet may not be accessible

Data Extrusion Management
  Attempts to prevent restricted data files from leaving the firm without permission
  Watermark with invisible restriction indicators
      Can be notified if sent via e-mail attachments or FTP
      If each document is given a different watermark, can forensically the source of a document leak
  Traffic analysis to look for unusually large numbers of outgoing files sent by a user

Removable Media Controls
  Forbid the attachment of USB RAM drives and other portable media
  Malware on USB RAM drives can autorun automatically when you insert the stick
  Must enforce technologically

Perspective
  Document restrictions have proven difficult to enforce
  Also, often reduce functionality in uncomfortable ways
  Companies have been reluctant to use them

FIGURE 7-34 Document Restrictions (Study Figure)

DIGITAL RIGHTS MANAGEMENT (DRM) The first of these protections is **Digital rights management (DRM)**, which restricts what people can do with data. In fact, a better term might be digital *restrictions* management. For corporations, DRM is desirable to protect trade secrets and sensitive personal data.

> *Digital rights management (DRM) restricts what people can do with data.*

In the past, DRM has been used mostly by music and video publishers to keep people from pirating copyright material. Of course, this also made it impossible for users to move files between their devices. The only good thing to come from publisher DRM has been the realization that almost all technical DRM protections can be beaten by attackers. There is a growing trend among publishers to make nonprotected versions available at a slightly higher price.

In business, DRM usually limits what people can do to documents of various types. For instance, a person may be able to download a spreadsheet file or word processing document but may not be able to save it locally, print it, change it, or take other actions. Many of these restrictions can be bypassed simply by taking screen shots of what appears on the monitor. Other restrictions are more successful. For instance, a person viewing a spreadsheet file probably can be kept from viewing hidden information and even visible portions of the spreadsheet.[22]

DATA EXTRUSION MANAGEMENT Another document protection is **data extrusion management**, which attempts to prevent restricted data files from leaving the firm without permission. While DRM builds restrictions into document files, data extrusion management applies filtering whenever an attempt is made to send a file outside the firm.

One way to restrict the transmission of files is to use a **watermark**, which is invisible information stored in files. Files can be watermarked for internal use only, and these files can be filtered out if attempts are made via e-mail attachments, FTP, or other means to send them outside the firm.

In addition, each copy of a file can be given a different watermark. If a file is extruded to the outside world and then found again, the file can be traced back to its first receiver through the file's specific watermark.

Another approach is **traffic analysis**, which measures the amount of traffic of a particular type from one party to another. The goal is to raise red flags if someone is downloading an unusually large number of sensitive documents or sending an unusually large number of documents out of the firm.

REMOVABLE MEDIA CONTROLS A final strategy for restricting document transmission is to forbid the use of removable media such as floppy disk disks, optical disks, and USB static RAM drives. Such a policy is only likely to be successful if technological restrictions are placed on individual computers. Relying on user behavior alone is a prescription for failure.

---

[22] Microsoft Excel Services does this for Excel spreadsheets.

USB RAM drives are particularly dangerous because Windows by default implements **autorun** on these drives. This means that if you insert a USB RAM stick in your computer, and if the stick has malware set for autorun, then the malware will execute as soon as you insert the drive.

PERSPECTIVE   So far, attempts to reduce document transmission have proven difficult to enforce. In addition, they usually restrict functionality in uncomfortable ways. Most companies are reluctant to use DRM today.

TEST YOUR UNDERSTANDING

30. **a.** What is DRM? (Do not just spell out the acronym.)
    b. Why is DRM desirable?
    c. Give some examples of use restrictions that a company may wish to impose on a document.
    d. How can many DRM protections against unauthorized printing be circumvented?
    e. What is the purpose of data extrusion management?
    f. What is watermarking?
    g. In what two ways can watermarking be used in data extrusion management?
    h. Why is it desirable to prevent a computer from working with removable media?
    i. Why should restrictions on removable media be enforced technologically?
    j. Why have document protections not been used heavily in organizations?

CONCLUSION

The host is the last line of defense for thwarting attacks. A host is any device with an IP address, and it is important to harden all hosts. This is especially true for servers, routers, and firewalls, but it is also true for client PCs and even mobile phones. An attacker can use a compromised client PC to circumvent firewalls and all other defenses. Hardening is a large set of diverse protections that should be applied to reduce risks if the host is attacked. Given the complexity of host hardening, it is important to follow a security baseline for the particular version of the operating system the host is running, although it is also possible to save images of well-tested hosts and then download these disk images to other computers.

We looked at Microsoft's Windows Server operating systems for servers. Recent versions of Microsoft Windows Server have graphical user interfaces (GUIs) that look like the user interfaces on client versions of Windows. We looked at many elements of Windows security, which uses GUI tools, especially Microsoft management consoles (MMCs).

It is difficult to talk generally about UNIX hardening because several versions of UNIX exist, and they offer different systems administration tools, including security tools. On PCs, LINUX is a family of UNIX versions; although all versions of LINUX use the same LINUX kernel, they are offered as "distributions" that use many other programs, and these programs vary among distributions. Although UNIX versions (including LINUX) offer some GUIs, many security tools must be run from command-line shells.

We looked at the important topic of vulnerabilities and fixes (especially patches). Given the large number of patches that are released each year, companies have a difficult time patching vulnerabilities and often have to prioritize the patches they will apply. For servers, it is important to test patches on test machines before installing them on production servers. Patch management servers automate some of the work of finding patches and pushing these patches out to servers that require them.

We looked at how recent versions of Microsoft Windows Server create and manage user and group accounts. We also saw how permissions can be assigned to users and groups in directories and individual files. Microsoft Windows offers 6 standard permissions, which can be divided into 13 finer permissions. In a file or directory, Windows can assign different permissions to many different users and groups. In contrast, UNIX only has three permissions, and it can only assign them to an owner, a single group, and the rest of the world.

Permissions in all operating systems are inherited from higher level directories, so intelligently selecting a hard drive's top-level directory structure to take advantage of inheritance can greatly reduce the work of assigning permissions. Assigning permissions to groups instead of to individuals also simplifies the assignment of permissions and has the added benefit of reducing errors.

We briefly looked at Windows Client PC security, focusing on the Windows Security Center/Action Center, which is a dashboard for various security settings on the computer.

We looked specifically at protecting notebook computers when they are off-site, and we looked at centralized PC security management, which can enforce policies on many computers. Centralized PC security management includes the use of standard configurations, network access control (NAC), and Windows group policy objects (GPOs).

We finished with a discussion of data protection. We began with backup, which is a company's first line of defense against devastating attacks. We looked at the difference between file/directory data backup, image backup, and shadowing. We looked at full and incremental backup for file/directory data backups. We also contrasted local backup (on a single computer) with network backup systems, including centralized backup, continuous data protection (CDP) for servers, Internet backup services for clients, and mesh backup for clients. We looked at backup media and backup management policies, including specifying which data must be backed up on which schedule, requiring restoration testing, limiting media storage, specifying retention, and auditing the implementation of all policies.

For data, we also looked at encryption, including key escrow and the distinction between file/directory encryption and whole-disk encryption. We looked at data destruction, including shredding optical disks and using a drive-wiping program instead of deleting files or reformatting the hard drive. We finished by looking briefly at the embryonic field of document restrictions, including digital rights management (DRM), data extrusion management, and restrictions on removable media.

One aspect of host hardening that was not considered in this chapter is application security. If attackers can take over an application, they usually can execute commands with the permission of the compromised application—often super user privileges. Application hardening is perhaps the most crucial aspect of host hardening today. For this reason, it has its own chapter, which we will look at next.

Thought Questions

1. Why do you think companies often fail to harden their servers adequately?
2. Why do you think companies often fail to harden their clients adequately?
3. a) How is the diversity of UNIX offerings bad? b) How is it good?
4. Why do you think UNIX has such a limited ability to assign permissions compared with Windows?
5. a) Directory DunLaoghaire has several subdirectories. Each of these subdirectories has very sensitive information that should only be accessible to a single user. What permissions would you give in the top-level DunLaoghaire directory to the group *all logged-in users* if you do not want to change the *Allow inheritable permissions from parent to propagate to this object* box default in subdirectories? b) What would you then do in each subdirectory?

Research Project

1. On the Internet, use a search engine to find a security baseline for Microsoft Windows Vista. List the title, the organization, and the URL. Briefly describe what is in the baseline. Note: Not all sources use the term "baseline."
2. The National Institute of Standards and Technology of the U.S. Department of Commerce has a special publications series on IT security. The webpage listing these 800 series publication is http://csrc.nist.gov/publications/PubsSPs.htmlcon. Read Special Publication 800-123 Guide to General Server Security. List recommendations that are in the publication but that were not listed in this chapter.

Applying Your Knowledge

1. In their purest form, **netbooks** are PCs designed to have little or no software stored on them. Instead, they are designed to use cloud computing, in which the software and data are both stored on Internet servers. Netbooks in this pure form can only work when they have an Internet connection. Based on what you learned in this chapter, discuss security implications for netbooks, both pro and con?

Perspective Questions

1. What material was most surprising for you in this chapter?
2. What material was most difficult for you in this chapter?

Chapter 8

Application Security

LEARNING OBJECTIVES:

By the end of this chapter, you should be able to discuss the following:

- Why attackers increasingly focus on applications.
- The main steps in securing applications.
- Securing WWW service and e-commerce service.
- Securing e-mail.
- (In a box) Securing voice over IP (VoIP).
- (In a box) The Skype VoIP Service.
- Securing other user applications.
- Securing TCP/IP supervisory applications.

GENERAL APPLICATION SECURITY ISSUES

In Chapter 7, we looked at host security, focusing on the operating system, and data. However, it is equally important to harden applications running on the host. Applications security actually requires more work than operating system hardening because clients and servers run many applications and because each application is about as difficult to harden as an operating system.

Executing Commands with the Privileges of a Compromised Application

If an attacker takes over an application, the attacker usually can execute commands with the access permissions of the compromised application. Many applications run with root (super user privileges), so taking them over gives the attacker total control of the host.

Often, attackers can take over an application with a single message, so gaining root tends to be far easier through application exploits than through traditionally difficult attacks on the operating system. Although hackers still attack operating systems, breaking in by taking over applications is the dominant hacking vector today.

Executing Commands with the Privileges of a Compromised Application

If an attacker takes over an application, the attacker can execute commands with the privileges of that application

Many applications run with super user (root) privileges

Buffer Overflow Attacks

From Chapter 7: Vulnerabilities, exploits, fixes (patches, manual work-arounds, or upgrades)

Buffers are places where data are stored temporarily

If an attacker sends too much data, a buffer might overflow, overwriting an adjacent section of RAM

If that section is retrieved, various problems can occur

    Read as data, read as program instructions, illegal values that cause a crash

Stacks are used to hold information temporarily on subprograms

Stack overflows might allow an attacker to execute any command (Figure 8-2)

An example: The IIS IPP Buffer Overflow Attack: Host variable is overflowed

Few Operating Systems but Many Applications

Application hardening is more total work than operating system hardening

FIGURE 8-1 Application Security Threats (Study Figure)

TEST YOUR UNDERSTANDING

1. **a.** What can hackers gain by taking over application programs?
   b. What is the most popular way for hackers to take over hosts?

Buffer Overflow Attacks

As discussed in Chapter 7, when vulnerabilities are found in application programs, attackers create exploit software. Vendors offer fixes—manual work-arounds, software patches, or updates. It is important to have reasonably up-to-date application software and to apply all patches.

BUFFERS AND OVERFLOWS Among the most widespread vulnerabilities in application programs are buffer overflow vulnerabilities. Programs often store information temporarily in areas of RAM called **buffers**. If the attacker sends a message with more bytes than the programmer had allocated for a buffer, the attacker's information will spill over into other areas of RAM. This is a **buffer overflow**. The impact of a buffer overflow can range from nothing to the crashing of the server or the ability to execute any command on the server.

STACKS We will look in more detail at a common type of buffer overflow, the **stack overflow**. Often, operating systems run several programs. Whenever the operating system must put a program on hold to run another, it writes information about the suspended program in a **stack entry**. Figure 8-2 shows a single stack entry.

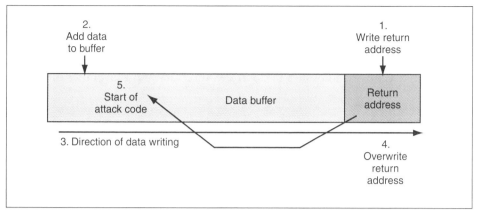

FIGURE 8-2   Stack Entry and Buffer Overflow

RETURN ADDRESS   The stack entry's **return address** (1) points to the location in RAM that holds the address of the next command to be executed in the suspended program. (Programs are stored in RAM when they execute.) When the entry is retrieved from (popped off of) the stack, the program that placed the entry there will pass control to the command at the location indicated in the return address. The return address is written into the stack entry before data is written into the buffer.

THE BUFFER AND BUFFER OVERFLOW   The operating system then adds data to the stack's **data buffer** (2). It writes this information from the bottom of the data buffer to the top (3). If the operating system writes too much information to the buffer, this will create a **buffer overflow**, overwriting the return address (1).

EXECUTING ATTACK CODE   When the entry is popped off the stack, the program that called the entry will pass control to the return address for that entry. If the attacker has skillfully overwritten the return address, the return address will point back to "data" in the buffer (5). If this data really is program code, this attack code will be executed instead of the legitimate program's code.

AN EXAMPLE: THE IIS IPP BUFFER OVERFLOW ATTACK   Microsoft's webserver software is the **Internet Information Server (IIS)**. IIS offers a number of services, including an Internet Printing Protocol (IPP) service. Although few users ever use this service, it was turned on by default in early versions of IIS.

Vulnerability reporters discovered that IPP was vulnerable to a buffer overflow attack. Not long after, an attacker created the jill.c program to exploit this vulnerability. This exploit was written in the C programming language.

At its heart, jill.c sends the following HTTP request message to IIS. HTTP requests begin with a line indicating what should be done—in this case, executing a printing request. The next line indicates the host to which the request should go. The host name is replaced with a 420-character string that causes a buffer overflow.

```
GET /NULL.printer HTTP/1.0
Host: 420-character input to launch command shell
```

The next line, shown below, is the response from the webserver. The attack code executed when the request arrived has caused Windows to create a new command shell—what used to be called a DOS prompt. The attacker is now in a sensitive directory. In addition, the attacker has SYSTEM privileges, which means that he or she can do anything that he or she wishes to do in this directory and most other directories.

```
C:\WINNT\system32\>
```

TEST YOUR UNDERSTANDING

2. **a.** What is a buffer?
   b. What is a buffer overflow attack?
   c. What impacts can buffer overflows have?
   d. In a stack overflow, what is overwritten by the overflow?
   e. To where does the overwritten return address point?
   f. In the IIS IPP buffer overflow attack, what buffer is overflowed?

Few Operating Systems, Many Applications

Although the mechanics of vulnerabilities, exploits, patches, and work-arounds are not fundamentally different for operating systems and applications, what is different is the small number of operating systems that most firms support versus the large number of applications they typically use.

For operating systems, most firms have to deal with only vulnerability reports, patches, and work-arounds from a handful of vendors. However, firms might run application programs from dozens of application software vendors. In most firms, the lion's share of all vulnerabilities and fixes relate to application programs.

Just finding information about vulnerabilities and fixes can be a maddening chore because each vendor releases information about its products' vulnerabilities and fixes in its own way. Although various vulnerability tracking services help (especially BugTraq at SecurityFocus.com), server administrators have to visit their application vendors' websites frequently.

After the firm finds patches, it must download and install the patches. Adding to the confusion, each vendor has different mechanisms for downloading and installing patches.

TEST YOUR UNDERSTANDING

3. Why is patching applications more time consuming than patching operating systems?

Hardening Applications

How can companies harden applications so that they are difficult to attack? The answer is that firms must take several actions to protect their applications.

UNDERSTAND THE SERVER'S ROLE AND THREAT ENVIRONMENT   The first task in security is to understand the environment to be protected. If a service such as e-mail runs on a single computer, for instance, then the systems administrator can rigorously cut out everything that does not deal directly with e-mail and perhaps with remote administration. However, if a server must support multiple applications, cutting out services will be a less viable option.

Understanding the Server's Role and Threat Environment
If it runs only one or a few services, easy to disallow irrelevant things

Basics
Physical Security
Backup
Harden the Operating System
Etc.

Minimize Applications
Main applications
Subsidiary applications
Be guided by security baselines

Create Secure Application Program Configurations
Use baselines to go beyond default installation configurations for high-value targets
Avoid blank passwords or well-known default passwords
Etc.

Install Patches for All Applications

Minimize the Permissions of Applications
If an attack compromises an application with low permissions, will not own the computer

Add Application Layer Authentication, Authorizations, and Auditing
More specific to the needs of the application than general operating system logins
Can lead to different permissions for different users

Implement Cryptographic Systems
For communication with users

FIGURE 8-3   Hardening Applications (Study Figure)

The threat environment is also important. If the threat environment is very dangerous, even remote administration might have to be cut off.

THE BASICS   As discussed in Chapter 5, servers and clients must be protected with physical security. As we saw in Chapter 7, they also need to be backed up properly, and their operating systems need to be hardened with patches and high-security configuration settings.

MINIMIZE APPLICATIONS
Minimize Main Applications   As noted in Chapter 7, firms should minimize the applications a host runs. Fewer applications mean fewer opportunities to take over the computer.

Minimize Subsidiary Applications   Hackers often attack obscure programs that are started automatically when the operating system is installed with default settings or when a complex application depends on subsidiary applications, as all webserver programs do.

For example, when users of many older versions of Windows 2000 started the IIS webserver, the operating system also started the Gopher service automatically under the default installation. Never heard of Gopher? Join the club. Gopher was a service that showed great promise for information retrieval just before the World Wide Web tidal wave hit. Today, nobody uses it. However, when attackers found a problem with the obscure Gopher program, they made almost every IIS implementation immediately vulnerable to attack until it the company installed a patch.

Security Baselines for Application Minimization   Again, our old friend from Chapter 7, the security baseline, should guide us. The installer must know which optional helper programs to install for a given application and which are installed automatically that should be deleted after installation.

CREATE A SECURE CONFIGURATION   Baselines will describe how to create a secure configuration in general. Most importantly, an application should never lack a password or have a well-known default password.

INSTALL APPLICATION PATCHES AND UPDATES   Most importantly, the installer should ensure to install all application patches. As noted earlier, this usually involves tracking vulnerability and fix reports from many application vendors.

In addition, the company should install a recent version of the software, updating the software if necessary. Newer versions of applications, once beyond the initial "teething period," usually are much safer than older versions.

MINIMIZE THE PERMISSIONS OF APPLICATIONS   As noted earlier, if attackers can take over an application, they can execute commands with the privileges of the program. Some programs must run with root privileges, but many can run with lower levels of privileges and should be run with the minimum privileges possible for them to do their job.

ADD APPLICATION-LEVEL AUTHENTICATION, AUTHORIZATIONS, AND AUDITING   One way to stymie attackers is to disregard input from anyone who has not been authenticated properly. To compromise a system, then, the attacker would have to have both an exploit and authenticated access to the system.

The operating system account password system provides some protection, but many applications also provide their own authentication. Instead of broad access to a computer, application authentication can be specific to the application program's needs, for instance, only accepting people on an access control list specific to the application and giving different people permissions that are relevant to the application.

The application program can require its own password—one with strong complexity. Or, the application program might require a smart card or some other form of strong authentication such as public key authentication. Two-factor authentication is even better.

Although adding application-level authentication is difficult and sometimes impossible, firms should do it wherever possible. This is especially true for highly sensitive applications, such as human resource databases and customer information databases.

IMPLEMENT CRYPTOGRAPHIC SYSTEMS   In Chapter 4, we saw the strong protections offered by cryptographic systems such as SSL/TLS and IPsec. Cryptographic system protections should always be used between the user and the application.

TEST YOUR UNDERSTANDING

4. **a.** Why must you know a server's role to know how to protect it?
   b. Why is it important to minimize both main applications and subsidiary applications?
   c. Why are security baselines needed for installing applications?
   d. Why is it important to minimize permissions for application programs?
   e. Why is application-level authentication superior to operating system authentication?
   f. Why should cryptographic protections be used?

Securing Custom Applications

Commercial off-the-shelf software is likely to have been written with some care, including checking for security vulnerabilities. However, custom applications built within a firm for its own use and the use of its customers are rarely constructed so carefully. The problem is that ordinary programmers are not likely to have been well trained in secure coding in general or in the good security practices necessary for given programming languages.

NEVER TRUST USER INPUT   For all applications, a basic rule is "Never trust user input." If a user is expected to enter text, check that the input really is text and ensure that it is

---

Custom Applications
  Written by a firm's programmers
  Not likely to be well trained in secure coding

The Key Principle
  Never trust user input
  Filter user input for inappropriate content

Buffer Overflow Attacks
  In some languages, specific actions are needed
  In other languages, not a major problem

Login Screen Bypass Attacks
  Website user gets to a login screen
  Instead of logging in, enters a URL for a page that should only be accessible to authorized users

Cross-Site Scripting (XSS) Attacks
  One user's input can go to another user's webpage
  An example
    Usually caused if a website sends back information sent to it without checking for data type, scripts, etc.

FIGURE 8-4   Securing Custom Applications (Study Figure)

> Example, If you type your username, it may include something like, "Hello username" in the webpage it sends you
>
> Example of an XSS attack
>
> > Attacker sends the intended victim an e-mail message with a link to a legitimate site
> >
> > However, the link includes a script that is not visible in the browser window because it is beyond the end of the window
> >
> > The intended victim clicks on the link and is taken to the legitimate webpage
> >
> > The URL's script is sent to the webserver with the HTTP GET command to retrieve the legitimate webpage
> >
> > The webserver sends back a webpage including the script
> >
> > The script is invisible to the user (browsers do not display scripts)
> >
> > But the script executes
> >
> > The script may exploit a vulnerability in the browser or another part of the user's software
>
> Many other examples exist
>
> **SQL Injection Attacks**
>
> For database access
>
> Programmer expects an input value—a text string, number, etc.
>
> > May use it as part of an SQL query or operation against the database
> >
> > Say to accept a last name as input and return the person's telephone number
>
> Attacker enters an unexpected string
>
> > For example: a last name followed by a full SQL query string
> >
> > The program may execute both the telephone number lookup command and the extra SQL query
> >
> > This may look up information that should not be available to the attacker
> >
> > It may even delete an entire table
>
> There are many other SQL injection attacks
>
> **Must Require Strong Secure Programming Training**
>
> General principles
>
> Programming-language-specific information
>
> Application-specific threats and countermeasures

FIGURE 8-4 (Continued)

not too long, does not contain an improper URL, does not contain a script, does not contain an SQL statement or part of an SQL statement, and so forth. Later in this chapter, we will look at how attackers can use improper input to do damage or hack a computer.

Never trust user input.

BUFFER OVERFLOW ATTACKS From the discussion above, one obvious concern with user input is buffer overflow attacks against the program. In some languages, such as C, one protection is only to use input functions that do length checking on the input.

LOGIN SCREEN BYPASS ATTACKS   For website access programs, potential problems abound. For example, in **login screen bypass**, the attacker types a URL to a page beyond the login screen when the login screen appears. If the application is not programmed correctly, the bypass will work, giving an unauthenticated user access to information that should only be accessed by authenticated users.

CROSS-SITE SCRIPTING (XSS) ATTACKS   Another danger of website programming is accidentally allowing **cross-site scripting (XSS)**, in which one user's input can appear on the page of another user. This is a danger in any webpage that reflects back a user's input. For instance, reflection exists if you type a username and the next webpage contains, "Hello, username."

Consider the following example. The attacker sends the intended victim an e-mail message. The message contains a link to a legitimate website that does reflection. The link is long and extends past the URL window. In the part that the user cannot see because it is beyond the URL window, the URL has a script. When the user clicks on the URL, the GET request including the script goes to the legitimate website. The legitimate website reflects back legitimate information *plus the script*. The script will execute without user intervention. If the intended victim's browser has the vulnerability that the script is designed to exploit, the intended victim becomes an actual victim.

This is only one example of an XSS attack. Any time a webpage reflects user input, an XSS attack is likely to be possible. Consequently, HTML user input must be filtered to ensure that it does not contain scripts.

SQL INJECTION ATTACKS   When database access is being implemented, the user may be asked for certain information, such as a username, password, or account code. In many cases, that input will be tested with an SQL query. For instance, if you type your last name, the string you type, $name, may be input into an SQL query to find your telephone number.

If input checking is not done or poorly done, an attacker may be able to enter a string that includes both the user's name and another SQL query. When the program enters the input string in the SQL query, it may unwittingly execute both the telephone number lookup query and the query entered by the user. This second query can look up information that should not be available to the attacker.

There are many types of SQL injection attacks. In some cases, the "input" may even contain a full SQL statement that will be executed to do whatever the attacker wishes.

TRAINING IN SECURE COMPUTING   Validating user input can only thwart some attacks. Programmers who create custom programs need to be trained in secure programming in general and for their particular programming language and application.

TEST YOUR UNDERSTANDING

5. a. What is a login screen bypass attack?
   b. What is a cross-site scripting (XSS) attack?
   c. What is an SQL injection attack?
   d. What attitude should programmers have about user input?
   e. What training should programmers who do custom programming have?

WWW AND E-COMMERCE SECURITY

The Importance of WWW and E-Commerce Security

Companies are justly concerned with the security of their webservers and e-commerce security. Attacks can disrupt service, harm a company's reputation, and expose private information with heavy repercussions to the firm. It can also enable customer fraud against the firm to succeed more effectively.

TEST YOUR UNDERSTANDING

6. What risks do webservice and e-commerce service create for corporations?

WWW Service versus E-Commerce Service

Some confusion occurs over the terms *WWW service* and *e-commerce*. Figure 8-6 shows the distinction between them.

WWW SERVICE   We will use the term **WWW service** for the basic functionality of HTTP webservers, including the retrieval of static files (fixed webpages) and the creation of dynamic webpages (webpages created in response to a specific query) using software on the webserver.

In Microsoft Windows, the native webserver program is Internet Information Server (**IIS**). This software dominates webserver use on Windows Server hosts—in part because it is part of the core Windows Server software and therefore free. On LINUX and UNIX hosts, the dominant software is the freeware Apache webserver program. Many more webservers use Apache than IIS, although among commercial webservers, IIS probably has a much larger market share. Large UNIX vendors, such as SUN, offer their own webserver software.

Webserver programs, as Figure 8-6 shows, often have components that come from different companies. For instance, the PHP application development software is built into many webservers. In 2002, a serious PHP vulnerability threatened software from *almost all* webserver vendors.

E-COMMERCE SERVICE   We will use the term **e-commerce service** to refer to the additional software needed for buying and selling, including online catalogs,

---

Importance of WWW Service and E-Commerce Security
  Cost of disruptions, harm to reputation, and market capitalization
  Customer fraud
  Exposure of sensitive private information

Webservice versus E-Commerce Service (Figure 8-6)
  WWW service provides basic user interactions
  Microsoft Internet Information Server (IIS), Apache on UNIX, other webserver programs
  E-commerce servers add functionality: Order entry, shopping cart, payment, etc.
  Links to internal corporate databases and external services (such as credit card checking)
  Custom programs written for special purposes

FIGURE 8-5   WWW and E-Commerce (Study Figure)

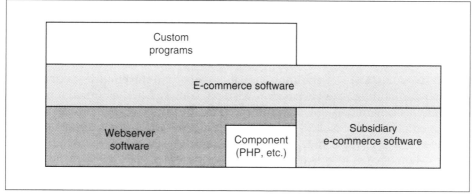

FIGURE 8-6   WWW Service versus E-Commerce Service

shopping carts, checkout functions, connections to back-end databases within the firm, and links to outside organizations, such as banks.

> *We will use the term e-commerce to refer to the additional software needed for buying and selling.*

EXTERNAL ACCESS   An e-commerce server needs to have network access to a number of systems external to itself, including servers within firms (for order entry, accounting, shipping, and so forth) and servers outside the firm in merchant banks and companies that check credit card numbers for validity. The webmaster or e-commerce administrator often has no control over the security of other systems.

CUSTOM PROGRAMS   Many companies that use e-commerce software write their own programs to supplement the capabilities of the packaged software they purchase. As noted earlier in this chapter, most firms do a poor job of overseeing the development of these custom programs. Consequently, attackers often can exploit vulnerabilities in custom programs or, even more insidiously, write their own custom programs that they can execute on the victim server to aid in their attacks.

Many firms believe that attackers will not know their custom software and so will have a difficult time hacking these programs. However, most programming languages produce programs that have common security failure modes that are well known by hackers. We saw an example of this earlier in the chapter, when we looked at cross-site scripting. The attacker only had to know that the site reflected user input. To learn this, the attacker only had to send input and see if it was reflected.

TEST YOUR UNDERSTANDING

7. **a.** Distinguish between WWW service and e-commerce service.
    b. What kinds of external access are needed for e-commerce?
    c. Does the webmaster or e-commerce administrator have control over the security of other servers?
    d. Why are custom programs especially vulnerable?

Some Webserver Attacks

How do attackers attack webservers? In this section, we will look at a number of webserver attacks.

WEBSITE DEFACEMENT   A common attack is **website defacement**—taking over a computer and putting up a hacker-produced page instead of the normal home page. Although this generally is only a nuisance,[1] it can be much worse. For instance, after a fatal airplane crash, hackers defaced the ValueJet website with the statement, "So we killed a few people." Even worse, hackers sometimes install "Out of Business" home pages to get customers to go away and stay away.

BUFFER OVERFLOW ATTACK TO LAUNCH A COMMAND SHELL   Earlier in this chapter, we discussed the IIS IPP buffer overflow vulnerability and the jill.c program used to exploit the vulnerability. We noted that the attacker gets a command shell and strong (SYSTEM) privileges. IIS has been subject to many other buffer overflow attacks with equally devastating impacts. So have other webserver programs.

DIRECTORY TRAVERSAL ATTACK   Sometimes, the attacker knows that a certain sensitive file, such as a password file, normally is stored in a particular directory under a particular name. The attacker would like to download many of these sensitive files.

   When users send a request for a file to be downloaded, the "root" is really a particular directory owned by the webserver. We will call this directory the **WWW root**. Figure 8-8 illustrates the WWW root. On this computer, the WWW root is one level down from the computer's true root. If the user types the path */Projects/Bak.doc*, the request does not go to the server's root and then go one level

---

Website Defacement

Numerous IIS Buffer Overflow Attacks
   Many of which take over the computer

IIS Directory Traversal Attacks (Figure 8-8)
   Normally, paths start at the WWW root directory
   Adding "../" might take the attacker up a level, out of the WWW root box
   If traverse to command prompt directory in Windows 2000 or NT, can execute any command with system privileges
   Companies filter out ".."
   Attackers respond with hexadecimal and UNICODE representations for ".." and ".."

FIGURE 8-7   Webserver Attacks (Study Figure)

---

[1] To give an example of a nondestructive defacement, USAToday.com's home page and six other USAToday.com pages were defaced in July 2002. Several news items were replaced with prankish entries, such as "Oops says the Pope/Christianity a Sham" and "Another shocking ruling from 9th Circuit Court—Pentagon unconstitutional?" The attack lasted only 15 minutes before the original pages were restored. Bob Sullivan, "USAToday.com Home Page Hacked," MSNBC.com, July 12, 2002. http://www.msnbc.com/news/779372.asp.

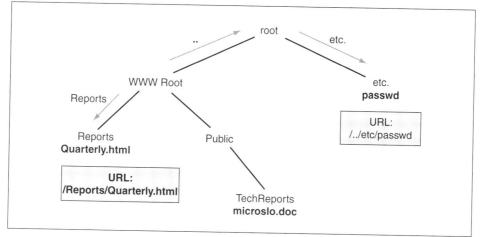

FIGURE 8-8 Directory Traversal

down to a *Projects* directory. Instead, it starts at the WWW root directory and goes one level down to the *Projects* subdirectory. It then retrieves the *Bak.doc* file stored in that directory.

However, attackers learned that if they began with "../" in their path, some webserver programs would allow them to break out of the WWW root box and get to the directory above the WWW root. In operating systems, ".." means go up one level. To go down one level, the command gives the name of the directory. For instance, to go up one level and down to the etc directory, the path would be "../etc".

Typing URLs with ".." in them can give access to sensitive directories, including the command prompt directory. This is the basic **directory traversal attack**. With directory traversal, the path ../etc/passwd would allow the attacker to download the passwd file in the etc directory (on a Unix computer).

THE DIRECTORY TRAVERSAL WITH HEXADECIMAL CHARACTER ESCAPES As usually happens, the vendors responded with a patch that rejected HTTP request messages containing a series of two dots.

Next, as often happens, attackers soon found a variant of the basic attack that would succeed against this countermeasure. For instance, IIS allows hexadecimal input, in which % is followed by two symbols between 0 and F. Each symbol represents four bits, so the two symbols together represent a byte.

Soon, attackers were sending HTTP directory traversal messages with two hexadecimal codes for dot. For a while, this **hexadecimal directory traversal attack** was successful. Then vendors issued a patch to stop it.

UNICODE DIRECTORY TRAVERSAL This cat and mouse game continued. For instance, the UNICODE coding system can represent non-English languages. Each character in each language is assigned a code sequence. Some of these code strings in various languages represent dots. Soon, attackers used several UNICODE representations to get around the hex patches. In turn, vendors created a patch for **UNICODE directory traversal attacks**.

TEST YOUR UNDERSTANDING

8. **a.** What is website defacement?
   b. Why is it damaging?
   c. In directory access commands and URLs, what does ".." represent?
   d. What are directory traversal attacks?
   e. Create a URL to retrieve the file aurigemma.htm under the rainbow directory on the host www.pukanui.com. The WWW root is three levels below the system's true root directory and the rainbow directory, which is under the projects directory, which is directly under the root directory. (Hint: Draw a picture.)
   f. In what two ways have attackers circumvented filtering designed to stop directory traversal attacks?

Patching the Webserver and E-Commerce Software and Its Components

E-COMMERCE SOFTWARE VULNERABILITIES   The webhosting company MindSpring suffered an embarrassment when it was found that its servers exposed the passwords of some of the websites they hosted.[2] The problem was tracked to a single website that used a commercial e-commerce program and failed to register it. The website's owners were not notified of an important patch because of the failure to register the product. Two years later, the vulnerable software was discovered by attackers.

Patching the WWW and E-Commerce Software and Their Components
  Patching the webserver software is not enough
  Also must patch e-commerce software
  E-commerce software might use third-party component software that must be patched

Other Website Protections
  Website vulnerability assessment tools, such as Whisker
  Reading website error logs
  Placing a webserver-specific application proxy server in front of the webserver

Controlling Deployment (Figure 8-10)
  Development Server
  Testing Server
      Developers have no authorizations to use this server
  Production Server
      Developers have no authorizations to use this server
      Testers have no authorizations to use this server

FIGURE 8-9 Webserver and E-Commerce Protections (Study Figure)

---

[2] Ann Harrison, "MindSpring Site Exposes Password Files: E-Commerce Application Opens Floodgates," Computerworld.com, October 23, 2000. http://www.computerworld.com/industrytopics/retail/story/0,10801,52714,00.html.

The website was one of several websites running on a single Sun Solaris (UNIX) server at the webhosting company. That server was configured incorrectly, and the vulnerability in the single website ended up opening access to password files on other websites hosted at the same machine.

This example underscores the importance of patching commercial e-commerce server software (and of configuring shared machines properly). E-commerce software is complex and has many subsystems. It would be foolish to assume that vulnerabilities will never be found in a firm's commercial e-commerce software, and much of this software runs as root, giving attackers open access to the entire server if they compromise the software components of WWW or E-commerce software.

Even when a webserver or e-commerce server produces clean code, some subsystems often are left open to attack by their vendors. Many webserver programs, for instance, support PHP programming. A series of flaws in PHP discovered in January 2002 allowed attackers to take over a website, sometimes easily. More PHP vulnerabilities were found later in the year as bug hunters increasingly turned their attention to PHP after initial disclosures. To give another example, a flaw in the OpenSSL component rendered most Apache webservers open to attack later in 2002.

Other Website Protections

WEBSITE VULNERABILITY ASSESSMENT TOOLS   Several webserver-specific vulnerability assessment tools have been developed, most prominently Whisker. Running a vulnerability assessment tool against the website frequently should be viewed as normal maintenance.

WEBSITE ERROR LOGS   In addition, websites usually log responses that contain error messages. Log reviews should be done frequently to look for signs of attacks. For instance, an excessive number of 500 error messages may indicate that an attacker is trying to send invalid data to the server. In turn, an excessive number of 404 errors might indicate that an attacker is searching blindly for files on your website.

WEBSERVER-SPECIFIC APPLICATION PROXY FIREWALLS   One protection is to use an application proxy firewall for a webserver. This firewall sits between the webserver and the rest of the network. It checks incoming request messages for signs of buffer overflow attacks and other problems. It also stops outgoing response messages that are inappropriate.

TEST YOUR UNDERSTANDING

9. **a.** What software must be patched on an e-commerce server?
   b. What three other webserver protections were mentioned in the text?
   c. Where is an application proxy firewall placed relative to the webserver?

Controlling Deployment

It is also critical to control the **deployment** of new server-side applications. As Figure 8-10 shows, firms with rigorous deployment policies use three types of servers: development servers, testing servers, and production servers.

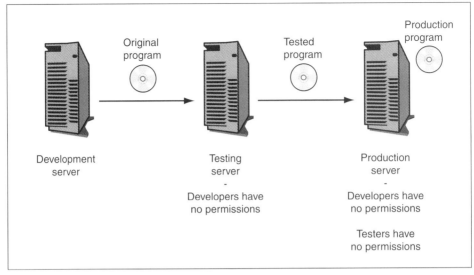

FIGURE 8-10 Staging Servers

DEVELOPMENT SERVERS Server-side programs should be created on **development servers** dedicated to that purpose. Developers need extensive permissions on these servers.

TESTING SERVERS After development, the program is moved to a **testing server** for testing. Developers should have no access permissions on this server. Only testers should have access permissions to make changes so that developers do not slip in back doors and last minute changes. ("It's just a few lines of code.")

PRODUCTION SERVERS After a program has been tested fully on the staging server, it should be moved to the **production server** that will serve users. On the production servers, even testers should be given no change permissions. Only the systems administrators needed to run the production server should have any permissions beyond reading and execution.

TEST YOUR UNDERSTANDING

10. **a.** In staged development, what three servers do companies use?
    b. What permissions does the developer have on the development server?
    c. On the testing server?
    d. On the production server?
    e. On what servers does the tester have access permissions?

Browser Attacks

Although many World Wide Web/e-commerce attacks focus on servers, browsers on clients are also popular targets. As many firms tighten their server security, browsers could become even more popular targets.

PCs Are Major Targets
  Have interesting information and can be attacked through the browser

Client-Side Scripting (Mobile Code)
  Java applets: Small Java programs
    Usually run in a "sandbox" that limits their access to most of the system
  Active-X from Microsoft; highly dangerous because it can do almost everything
  Scripting languages (not full programming languages)
    A script is a series of commands in a scripting language
    JavaScript (not scripted form of Java)
    VBScript (Visual Basic scripting from Microsoft)
    A script usually is invisible to users

Malicious Links
  User usually must click on them to execute (but not always)
  Tricking users to visit attacker websites
    Social engineering to persuade the victim to click on a link
    Choose domain names that are common misspellings of popular domain names

Other Client-Side Attacks
  File reading: turn the computer into an unintended file server
  Executing a single command
    The single command may open a command shell on the user's computer
    The attacker can now enter many commands
  Automatic redirection to unwanted webpage
    On compromised systems, the user may be automatically directed to a specific malicious website if they make any typing error
  Cookies
    Cookies are placed on user computer; can be retrieved by website
    Can be used to track users at a website
    Can contain private information
    Accepting cookies is necessary to use many websites

Enhancing Browser Security
  Patches and updates
  Set strong security configuration options (Figure 8-12) for Microsoft Internet Explorer
  Set strong privacy configuration options (Figure 8-13) for Microsoft Internet Explorer

FIGURE 8-11 Browser Attacks and Protections (Study Figure)

BROWSER THREATS   Browser security in the World Wide Web and e-commerce security is important because, as noted in Chapter 7, attackers might want to have data stored on the client and because attackers can use a compromised client to attack other systems for which the client has access credentials.

MOBILE CODE   Mobile code consists of commands written into a webpage. When the webpage is downloaded, the script can execute automatically. (The code is "mobile" because it travels from the webserver to user PCs.) Although mobile code can enhance the browser user's surfing experience, it also can poke large holes in the client's security.

Java Applets   Many languages are used in mobile code. **Java applets** (small Java programs) probably are the safest because many attack-related actions are disabled; however, this protection is far from perfect.

Active-X   Another major language for active webpage content is **Active-X**, a technology created by Microsoft. Active-X is powerful and can do almost anything on the client machine. This power, coupled with the fact that Active-X offers almost no protection against misuse, makes Active-X supremely dangerous. Unfortunately, many websites require users to have Active-X turned on.

Microsoft initially said that Active-X components are safe because they must be cryptographically signed by the developer, and if you can trust the developer, you should be able to trust its programs. However, users often do not know the developer, and even good developers can create products with vulnerabilities.

Scripting Languages: VBScript and JavaScript   Attackers also use **scripting languages**, which are easier to use than full programming languages like Java and Active-X. The most popular scripting languages for mobile code are **VBScript** and **JavaScript** (which is not a scripted version of Java despite its name). These scripting languages, although easier to use than Java, lack the protections of Java.

MALICIOUS LINKS   Browsers often are vulnerable to **malicious links** in webpages and in e-mail bodies. If the user clicks on a malicious link and downloads a webpage, an attack script in the downloaded page will execute. Sometimes, the script will activate even if the user does not click on it, depending on how the browser or e-mail program works.

How do attackers get users to go to websites that will deliver attack scripts? Sometimes they do so through social engineering. For instance, you may get an urgent message telling you that your computer is infected with a virus and that you should go immediately to a particular URL to learn how to get the virus out of your system. Sometimes, the social engineer tells you to go to a popular website, such as CNN.com. However, although the link says CNN.com on the screen, it may actually be a link to an attack website.

In addition, many attackers register domain names that are common misspellings for legitimate website domain names, for example, micosoft.com. In some cases, they merely find a ".org" nonprofit website and register the ".com" version of its name. (For many years, whitehouse.com was a pornography site.) Users who find themselves at these sites often find themselves reading pages with malicious scripts.

OTHER CLIENT-SIDE ATTACKS   Many other client-side attacks are possible. We will discuss just a few to give you a concept of the possibilities.

File Reading   In 2000, a Java applet delivered primarily via e-mail essentially turned the user's client PC into an unwilling file server, making all of its files easily accessible to the attacker.

Executing a Single Command   Worse yet, several common malicious script attacks allow attackers to execute any command they choose on the victim's computer.

Sometimes, the single command can be used to open a command shell; if so, the attacker will then be able to execute many commands within the command shell.

Automatically Redirecting Users to Unwanted Webpages   A number of scripts permanently change your browser settings and even your computer registry. The next time you use your computer, you might find that your default home page has been changed to a pornography site or to another site with content you do not want to see.

More subtly, when you make errors typing URLs, you might find you are taken to one of several unauthorized sites because the script has Trojanized your DNS error-handling routine.

Cookies   Some websites use **cookies**. A cookie is a small text string that the website owner can place on a client computer. The website owner can later retrieve cookies they have written (but not cookies written by other websites).

Cookies are valuable in transactions that require the exchange of several messages because they can keep track of where the user is in the process. Cookies also can remember your login name and password for easier access to websites that require authorization.

Unfortunately, cookies also can track where you have been at a website (and do other things that are against user desires). Users can turn off cookies to prevent tracking, but this makes the use of many websites impossible. Cookies can also contain highly private information that you would not want an attacker to learn if they compromise your computer. Antispyware programs can identify dangerous cookies.

TEST YOUR UNDERSTANDING

11. **a.** Why do hackers attack browsers?
    b. What is mobile code?
    c. Why is it called mobile code?
    d. What is a client-side script?
    e. What is a Java applet?
    f. Why is Active-X dangerous?
    g. How do scripting languages compare to full programming languages?
    h. Is JavaScript a scripted form of Java?

12. **a.** Why is it bad to go to a malicious website?
    b. How can social engineering be used to trick a victim to go to a malicious website?
    c. Why do attackers want to get domain names such as micosoft.com?
    d. Why may malware that allows an attacker to execute a single command on a user's computer not really be limited to executing a single command?
    e. What may happen on a compromised computer if a user mistypes the host name in a URL?
    f. What dangers do cookies create?

Enhancing Browser Security

PATCHING AND UPGRADING   All of the attacks just covered can be stopped by installing patches on Internet Explorer and other browsers. However, relatively few users patch their browsers, giving attackers long windows of opportunity. In fact, many users have versions that are so old that patches are not created for them when new vulnerabilities are found.

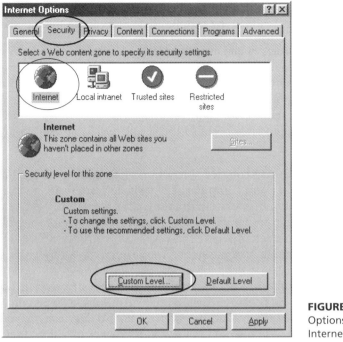

FIGURE 8-12 Internet Options Dialog Box in Internet Explorer

CONFIGURATION Stopping browser attacks also involves changing browser configuration settings to reduce the likelihood of damage. Unfortunately, different browsers do this differently, and even different versions of IE do it differently.

INTERNET OPTIONS In IE, users begin to change their settings by selecting Internet Options under the Tools menu. This opens the **Internet Options dialog box** shown in Figure 8-12.

SECURITY TAB The dialog box shows its *Security* tab. From this tab, the user can select security settings for general Internet websites, intranet websites, trusted websites, and restricted websites. All websites are initially in the Internet category. However, the user can place them in other categories—intranet for internal company sites, trusted websites for highly trusted websites, and restricted websites for questionable websites.

The defaults in each category generally are good choices for security, but the user can also select the *Custom Level* button to change the settings for the four types of websites to control content more finely.

For instance, in the general Internet zone, signed Active-X controls (Active-X controls with digital signatures) by default execute after a prompt that identifies the creator of the Active-X control. Employees might not have sufficient knowledge to understand the danger of using even signed Active-X controls. In addition, active scripting is enabled by default, including Java scripting. These are at least somewhat risky choices.

PRIVACY TAB In addition to the Security tab, there is the *Privacy* tab. The Privacy tab, which is shown in Figure 8-13, allows the user to control what information is released to websites, including how cookies are used. IE has a sliding scale that

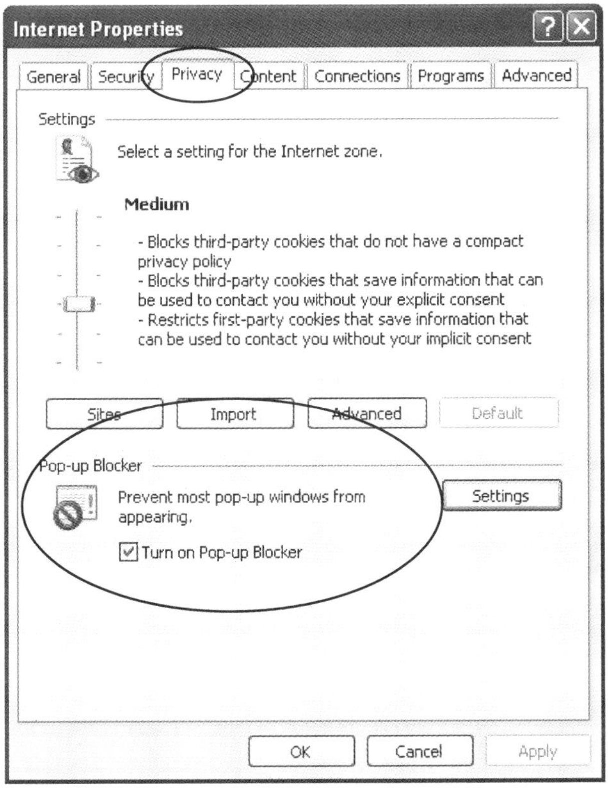

FIGURE 8-13 Internet Explorer Privacy Tab

the user can push up for greater privacy and down for reduced privacy. The default is medium privacy. An *Advanced* button allows more specific control over cookies.

The Privacy tab also controls the website's pop-up blocker, which is on by default. Under the Settings button, the user can set different pop-up defaults for individual websites.

TEST YOUR UNDERSTANDING

13. a. What can users do to enhance browser security?
  b. Under Internet Options in IE, what can the user do on the security tab?
  c. What are your computer's settings for the four zones?
  d. In which tab are cookies controlled?

E-MAIL SECURITY

We have been looking at WWW service/e-commerce security and browser security. Another big application on the Internet is **electronic mail (e-mail)**.

E-Mail Content Filtering

Many firms now filter incoming e-mail messages (and sometimes outgoing messages) for dangerous or inappropriate content.

Content Filtering
  Malicious code in attachments and HTML bodies (scripts)
  Spam: Unsolicited commercial e-mail
  Volume is growing rapidly: Slowing PCs and annoying users (porno and fraud)
  Filtering for spam also rejects some legitimate messages

Inappropriate Content
  Companies often filter for sexually or racially harassing messages
  Could be sued for not doing so

Extrusion Prevention for Intellectual Property (IP)

Stopping the Transmission of Sensitive Personally Identifiable Information (PII)

Where Do We Do E-Mail Filtering? (Figure 8-15)
  At the user PC (users often turn off antivirus protection or make it effective)
  At corporate e-mail servers
  At e-mail managed service providers

E-Mail Retention (Figure 8-16)

Employee Training
  E-mail is not private; company has right to read
  Your messages may be forwarded without permission
  Never to put anything in a message they would not want to see in court, printed in the newspapers, or read by their boss
  Never forward messages without permission

E-Mail Encryption (Figure 8-17)

FIGURE 8-14 E-Mail Security (Study Figure)

MALICIOUS CODE IN ATTACHMENTS AND HTML BODIES   As we saw in Chapter 1, e-mail attachments can contain viruses, worms, and other malicious code. In addition, now that many e-mail systems can show messages with HTML bodies, scripts in the bodies may execute malicious code, as we saw earlier in this chapter.

SPAM

   A Growing Problem   One of the most annoying aspects of e-mail is that most users are deluged by **spam**[3]—unsolicited commercial e-mail. Today, spam accounts for 60–90 percent of all Internet mail traffic on any given day. Spam clogs mailboxes, slows user computers, annoys users, and requires users to spend time deleting the unwanted messages.

   In addition, many spammers now use **image spam**, which presents their message as a graphical image. This frustrates most content filtering. It also makes each

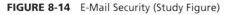

[3] Spam is a canned meat product (it is not an abbreviation for spongy pink animal matter). Hormel, which owns the name Spam, allows the use of the term *spam* in the e-mail context if spam is spelled in lowercase except at the beginning of a sentence.

spam message much larger, consuming even more bandwidth and disk storage space than traditional text spam.

     Filtering Spam   Given the large volume of spam today, most firms filter incoming mail to discard spam. However, firms that filter incoming spam sometimes find that they have **over-filtered** arriving mail. A growing number of legitimate messages are being rejected as spam, and few spam-filtering systems warn either the sender or the receiver if a message is rejected. Companies that filter spam should quarantine dropped messages to study them later and to address receiver and sender complaints about lost messages.

INAPPROPRIATE CONTENT   In some cases, employees send sexually or racially harassing or abusive e-mail to fellow workers. If the company does nothing to attempt to prevent this, it will be liable for lawsuits. Consequently, a growing number of firms scan all e-mail for indications of sexual, racial, or abusive content. Many already have fired employees for sending inappropriate e-mail.

EXTRUSION PREVENTION   Filtering can also be done to prevent employees from sending intellectual property out of the corporation. Extrusion prevention filtering begins with a simple search through documents looking for words like "confidential." In practice, it goes far beyond that.

PERSONALLY IDENTIFIABLE INFORMATION (PII)   Another goal is to stop the sending of **personally identifiable information (PII)**, such as private employee information and private customer information. In health care, PII must be protected by law. In general, the transmission of social security numbers and other sensitive personal information is likely to lead to lawsuits if it can potentially lead to credit card number theft or identity theft.

TEST YOUR UNDERSTANDING

14. **a.** Why are HTML bodies in e-mail messages dangerous?
    b. What is spam?
    c. What three problems does spam create?
    d. Why is spam filtering dangerous?
    e. For what legal reason should companies filter sexually or racially harassing message content?
    f. What is extrusion prevention?
    g. Why is extrusion prevention needed for intellectual property?
    h. What is PII, and why must it be prevented from leaving the firm?

Where to Do E-Mail Malware and Spam Filtering

One issue that companies face is where to do e-mail malware and spam filtering. Traditionally, this filtering was done on client PCs, as Figure 8-15 shows. Client filtering has several problems. Users often turn off their antivirus and antispam filters. They frequently fail to set up their systems properly for automatic downloading. They may even fail to maintain their subscription for receiving updates. If they do any of these things, they still will have antivirus and antispam software on their systems but no protection against new attacks.

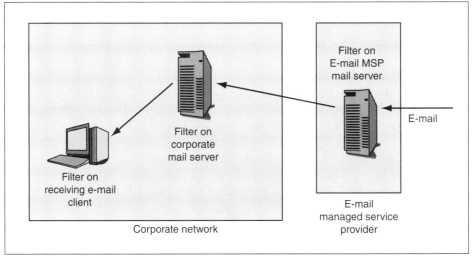

FIGURE 8-15 Possible E-Mail Filtering Locations

In light of problems with client-based filtering, most companies now use filtering at the corporate e-mail server as the primary line of defense for e-mail (see Figure 8-15). This relegates client filtering to secondary importance as a defense-in-depth measure. E-mail administrators have the discipline and knowledge needed to manage e-mail filtering. In fact, e-mail administrators usually spend most of their time on antivirus filtering, spam filtering, and other security issues.

Due to the labor burdens of e-mail security, some companies are moving filtering entirely out of the firm, to e-mail managed service providers. Managed service providers reduce labor costs. They also have expertise in e-mail filtering.

Many companies do filtering at all three locations to increase defense in depth. At their corporate e-mail server, they may use a different filtering program than their managed service providers use. Different antivirus and antispam programs catch somewhat different threats.

E-Mail Retention

Many mail servers store messages on their disk drives for some time, and then **archive** messages onto tape. The coordinated use of online storage and backup storage for messages is referred to as **retention**.

THE BENEFIT OF RETENTION On the positive side, retention allows users to go through their old mail to look for information. A great deal of a corporation's "organizational memory" and of an individual employee's working information is stored in online e-mail files and archives. Although most messages retrieved are recent ones, corporate projects can last a long time, and some retrievals must go back months or sometimes even years.

THE DANGERS OF RETENTION On the negative side, lawyers can use the legal **discovery process** in lawsuits to dredge up messages in which an employee has said

Benefits of Retention
- Major part of corporate memory
- Often need to retrieve old mail for current purposes

Dangers of Retention
- Legal discovery process
- Defendant must supply relevant e-mails
- Potentially very damaging information
- Always expensive
- Even if very expensive to retrieve, firms must pay whatever is necessary to do so

Accidental Retention
- Even if firms delete e-mail from mail servers
- May be stored on backup tapes
- Users will often store copies on their own computers

Legal Archiving Requirements
- Many laws require retention
    - Securities and Exchange Commission
    - Many labor laws
    - Involuntary terminations
    - Public information about job openings
    - Medical problem complaints that may relate to toxic chemicals
- Laws vary in duration of storage requirements
- Fines or summary judgments if fail to retain and produce required e-mails

U.S. Federal Rules of Civil Procedure
- Specify rules for all U.S. federal civil trials
- Specifically address electronically stored information
- Initial discovery meeting
    - Defendant must be able to specify what information is available
    - Comes shortly after a civil lawsuit begins
    - Unless carefully thought through before hand, will fail
- Holds on destruction
    - Must be put in place if it is foreseeable that a lawsuit will soon begin
    - Must have strong hold procedures to place holds on all electronically stored information

Message Authentication
- Spoofed messages can frame employees or the firm itself
- Need message authentication to prevent spoofed sender addresses

Archiving Policies and Processes
- Must have them
- Must reflect a firm's legal environment
- Must be drawn up with the firm's legal department

FIGURE 8-16 E-Mail Retention (Study Figure)

something embarrassing or even obviously illegal. In the Federal Microsoft antitrust lawsuit, for instance, e-mail messages from Bill Gates and other senior managers found during the discovery process were vivid and damaging to Microsoft.

In some cases, the e-mail messages will be very difficult to retrieve, turning the backup files into a "write-only memory." However, courts have consistently ruled that if such archives exist, companies under discovery orders must use their own money to create programs to sort through the accidental archives.

ACCIDENTAL RETENTION   Some firms have responded to the specter of discovery by refusing to archive e-mail at all or by keeping mail for only 30 days or some other short time period. However, mail servers are backed up routinely using magnetic tape, and information can stay on those tapes for long periods of time. Oliver North, the central figure in the Iran Contra scandal during the Reagan administration, deleted his e-mail messages, but the prosecution was able to find them on routine backup tapes.

In addition, even if mail is deleted from servers and backup tapes, employees may have retained messages on their client PCs. If discovery includes e-mail on client PCs, this may find embarrassing information that could have been legally discarded, and it certainly will be expensive.

LEGAL ARCHIVING REQUIREMENTS   In addition, in the financial services industry, companies are *required* to archive their communication, including e-mail. In 2002, the U.S. Securities and Exchange Commission fined six financial services firms a total of $10 million for failing to maintain good e-mail archives. Many government agencies are also required to retain e-mail messages as public documents, although transient communications usually are exempt from this rule.

All industries, in fact, are legally required to retain certain forms of communication, whether these are on e-mail or on paper. In such cases, deleting messages will not make a company immune from punishment. Examples include involuntary terminations, public information on job openings, and complaints about certain medical problems that might be caused by toxic chemicals. These requirements come from different laws, and these laws require different retention durations for different types of e-mail.

The failure to retain required e-mail can be very costly. In one court case, Sprint was fined in a patent lawsuit for failing to keep good e-mail records relevant to the patent.[4] The courts can even impose a summary judgment in a civil trial if a defendant has failed to retain e-mail.

U.S. FEDERAL RULES OF CIVIL PROCEDURE   In the U.S. federal court system, the **Federal Rules of Civil Procedure** specify processes that apply to lawyers and judges in civil cases. The most recent version, which took effect in 2006, had several implications for the handling of **electronically stored information** including both traditional databases and newer forms of information, such as e-mail and instant messaging.

One of the most important changes in the rules pertains to the **initial discovery meetings** between the plaintiff and defendant. In these initial discovery meetings, the

---

[4] Michael Osterman, "E-Mail Archiving," *Network World Fusion Focus: Michael Osterman on Messaging,* Electronic newsletter, August 4, 2000.

defendant *must* be able to specify what information is available for the legal discovery process. These initial meetings must take place shortly after the beginning of the lawsuit, so that once a lawsuit starts, it is already too late to begin preparing for lawsuits. Companies need to develop a clear understanding of all of their discoverable information, and they need to have clear plans for ways to provide the information if necessary.

One rule requires companies to take several actions if a lawsuit has begun or even if it is *foreseeable* that a lawsuit will soon begin. The most important action is to place a **hold** on all destruction of potentially relevant information. If a company does not have comprehensive policies and procedures for placing holds on all electronically stored information, it will find itself in violation of this rule.

MESSAGE AUTHENTICATION   It is embarrassingly easy to fabricate a message so that it appears to come from someone else. Networked e-mail was less than four years old when someone sent the first spoofed message over the ARPANET. This message, claiming to come from a DARPA official, announced an unpopular policy. It was broadcast widely to ARPANET users. Spoofed messages can be used to frame other employees and the firm itself, so a good archiving system—and indeed any good e-mail system—must have authentication protections built in.

DEVELOPING POLICIES AND PROCESSES   Overall, corporations need to develop archiving policies and processes for e-mail archiving, and these plans must reflect their legal environments. It is important to work with the firm's legal department in creating such archives.

TEST YOUR UNDERSTANDING

15. **a.** Why is retaining e-mail for a long period of time useful?
 b. Why is it dangerous?
 c. What is legal discovery?
 d. What are courts likely to do if it would be very expensive for a firm to discover all of its e-mail pertinent to a case?
 e. What can happen if a firm fails to retain required e-mail?
 f. What is accidental retention?
 g. Is there a specific law that specifies what information must be retained for legal purposes?
 h. What two requirements in the U.S. Rules of Civil Procedure are likely to cause problems for firms who do not have a good archiving process?
 i. Why is message authentication important in an archiving system?
 j. Comment on a corporate policy of deleting all e-mail after 30 days.

User Training

Although technology may help companies, the key to avoiding problems in the discovery process is to train users in what not to put into e-mail messages.

Users tend to think of e-mail messages as personal. However, the law does not view them that way. Discovery can dredge them up, they might be sent to the wrong party accidentally, and they can be forwarded to unintended parties. In addition, employers generally have the right to inspect e-mail messages and restrict messages to company business. Employees must be taught never to put anything in a message that they would not want to see in court, printed in the newspapers, or read by their boss.

Employees must be taught never to put anything in a message that they would not want to see in court, printed in the newspapers, or read by their boss.

Users also need to be taught not to forward messages unless specifically authorized to do so. Once messages are forwarded, all control is lost. Even the list of original receivers can be damaging information.

TEST YOUR UNDERSTANDING

16. **a.** Are e-mail messages sent by employees private?
    b. What should employees be trained not to put in e-mail messages?

E-Mail Encryption

E-mail is a perfect candidate for cryptographic protection. However, relatively few corporations have their employees encrypt e-mail for confidentiality, authenticity, message integrity, or replay protection. One reason for this is the difficulty of using end-to-end encryption methods.

TRANSMISSION ENCRYPTION Figure 8-17 shows cryptographic protections for e-mail. The figure shows that many companies encrypt transmission between an e-mail client and its mail server with SSL/TLS. However, unless SMTP servers also use transmission encryption when they send and receive e-mail, and unless the recipient also communicates securely with its mail server, there will not be end-to-end encryption.

MESSAGE ENCRYPTION For end-to-end security, the sender must encrypt the message, including the header, body, and attachments. Two popular standards for this end-to-end encryption are S/MIME and PGP (together with OpenPGP).

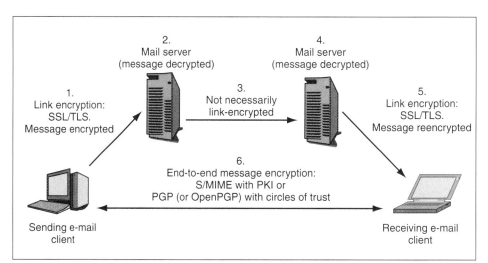

FIGURE 8-17 Cryptographic Protection for E-Mail

S/MIME and PGP encryption both use digital signatures, which require the receiver to know the sender's public key. S/MIME requires a traditional public key infrastructure with a central certificate authority and digital certificates.

Instead of a PKI, PGP uses **circles of trust**. If you trust Pat, and if Pat trusts Leo, then you may trust Leo. This is dangerous because if misplaced trust is present anywhere in the system, bogus public key/name pairs may circulate widely. PGP has had most success in person-to-person communication without corporate control.

TEST YOUR UNDERSTANDING

17. **a.** Is encryption widely used in e-mail?
    b. What part of the e-mail process does SSL/TLS usually secure?
    c. Is this end-to-end security? Explain.
    d. What standards provide end-to-end security?
    e. Compare PGP and S/MIME in terms of how applicants learn the true party's public key.
    f. Describe the advantages and disadvantages of each approach.

Voice over IP (VoIP) Security

Sending Voice between Phones

The idea of **voice over IP (VoIP)** is simple. Instead of calling someone else over the public switched telephone network, you call them over an IP internet. As Figure 8-18 shows, a VoIP user has either a dedicated **IP telephone** (1) or a **soft phone**—a PC with VoIP software (2). We will use the generic term *VoIP phone*.

When a person speaks, hardware or software called a **codec** in the VoIP phone converts the person's voice into a stream of digital bytes. The VoIP phone then puts these bytes into packets and sends these packets to the other telephone (3).

Each packet carrying digital voice data has an IP header, followed by a User Datagram Protocol (UDP) header, an RTP header (discussed next), and a group of voice octets. These packets go directly between the two phones.

VoIP voice transmission uses UDP to carry the digital voice data. In VoIP voice transmission, if a packet is lost, there is no time to wait for a retransmission to correct the loss. Consequently, there is no reason for TCP. The receiving codec merely inserts a packet's worth of false sound based on preceding sound.

RTP is the **Real Time Protocol**. It makes up for two of UDP's biggest weaknesses. First, the RTP header has a sequence number so that the receiver can place voice octets in order if their packets arrive out of order. Second, the RTP header contains a time stamp so that the receiver's codec plays the sounds in the packet at the right time compared to the previous packet's sounds.

TEST YOUR UNDERSTANDING

18. **a.** What is VoIP?
    b. Distinguish between IP telephones and soft phones.
    c. List, in order of appearance at the receiver, the headers and message of a packet carrying voice between phones.
    d. What does RTP add to compensate for the limitations of UDP?

(Continued)

Voice over IP (VoIP) Security   (Continued)

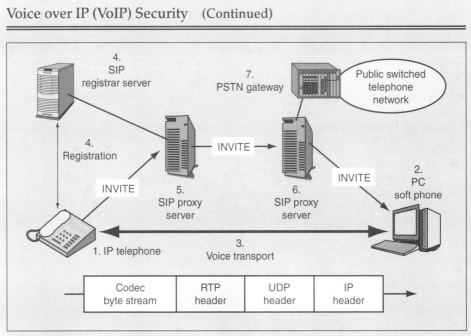

FIGURE 8-18   Voice over IP (VoIP)

Transport and Signaling

In telephony, it is important to understand the fundamental distinction between transport and signaling. **Transport** is the carriage of voice between the two parties. Quite simply, when you talk back and forth with someone, this is transport. In Figure 8-18, the transmission of RTP packets (3) is transport.

Transport is the carriage of voice between the two parties.

A telephone network must also provide **signaling**, which consists of communication to *manage* the network. When you dial another number on your ordinary telephone, this initiates a signaling process to locate the called party and cause their telephone to ring. In addition to call setup, signaling handles billing information, terminates the call cleanly, and does several other things.

Concept	Meaning
Transport	The carriage of voice between the two parties
Signaling	Communication to manage the network
	Call setup
	Call teardown
	Accounting
	Etc.

FIGURE 8-19   Transport versus Signaling

Signaling consists of communication to manage the network.

SIP and H.323

In voice over IP, there are two main signaling standards. Older systems usually follow the **H.323** OSI signaling standard. Newer systems usually follow the IETF **Session Initiation Protocol (SIP)** signaling standard. We will focus on SIP signaling, but threats to H.323 signaling are similar.

Registration

The bottom portion of Figure 8-18 represents the transport process. The remainder of the figure shows some of the complexities of SIP signaling. The first aspect of signaling consists of registration. The user's phone contacts a **registrar server** and presents the user's credentials (such as a password, a PIN, or something stronger). The registrar server then adds the user and his or her location to its registration database. Proxy servers, which we will see next, use registration information to route calls.

SIP Proxy Servers

The user at the IP telephone (1) in Figure 8-18 sends a SIP INVITE message to the PC soft phone (2) to request a connection. Of course, the calling phone does not know how to reach the called phone. Consequently, the IP telephone sends the INVITE message to the sender's **SIP proxy server** (5). This proxy server checks the IP telephone's registration information and then contacts a proxy server in the called party's network (6). That proxy server passes the INVITE message to the called soft phone. If the called VoIP phone sends back an OK message, SIP communication will continue until a session is established.

After a session is established, the two VoIP phones communicate directly with each other in transport mode using RTP packets. The SIP proxy servers are not involved in transport mode unless additional supervisory signaling is needed.

PSTN Gateway

What if an IP telephone or soft phone needs to call someone on the public switched telephone network (or vice versa)? VoIP and the PSTN use different codecs, transport technology, and signaling systems. Consequently, interconnection requires the use of a **PSTN gateway** that can translate between the different technologies.

TEST YOUR UNDERSTANDING

19. **a.** Distinguish between transport and signaling.
    b. In Figure 8-18, is the packet shown a transport packet or a signaling packet?
    c. What are the two main signaling standards in VoIP?
    d. What does the registrar server do? (Hint: Don't say, "It registers things.")
    e. What type of SIP message does a VoIP phone use when it wants to connect to another VoIP phone?
    f. How is this message routed to the called VoIP phone?
    g. Are SIP proxy servers involved during transport transmissions? Explain.
    h. What two types of communication does the media gateway translate between the VoIP network and the PSTN?

(Continued)

Voice over IP (VoIP) Security   (Continued)

Notes
  Highly sensitive to latency, jitter, packet loss, and reduced bandwidth
  Users are extremely intolerant of downtime
  VoIP generates extensive traffic that can overload a network

Eavesdropping

Denial-of-Service Attacks
  Even small increases in latency and jitter can be highly disruptive

Caller Impersonation
  Useful in social engineering
  Attacker can appear to be the president based on a falsified source address

Hacking and Malware Attacks
  Compromised clients can send attacks
  Compromised servers can do disruptive signaling

Toll Fraud
  Attacker uses corporate VoIP network to place free calls

Spam over IP Telephony (SPIT)
  Especially disruptive because it interrupts the called party in real time

New Threats Appear Constantly
  Injecting the attacker's voice into a conversation

FIGURE 8-20   VoIP Threats (Study Figure)

VoIP Threats

VoIP technology faces many threats because it is not a closed system like the Public Switched Telephone Network. Attackers typically can get to the VoIP network via the Internet and wireless LAN access points.

Eavesdropping

Listening to a voice call without permission is **eavesdropping**. This is very easy to do in traditional telephony. Telephone linemen with simple alligator clips can easily connect a handset to a physical telephone line and listen to calls. Eavesdropping is more difficult on VoIP networks. Interceptors usually must pick a particular call out of a large call stream and then decode the packets. However, technology is making this easier.

Denial-of-Service (DoS) Attacks

Adversaries may use denial-of-service (DoS) attacks against phones, proxy servers, registrar servers, PSTN gateways, and other elements in the VoIP network. DoS attacks tend to be very effective because even slight increases in latency (delay), jitter (variable delay between packets), or reduced bandwidth can make a call unintelligible. Latency is especially sensitive. If latency rises to only 150 ms to 250 ms, turn-taking in calls becomes almost impossible. Just when you think that the other person has stopped talking and you begin to talk, more of their voice comes through, interrupting you.

Caller Impersonation

On the telephone, a caller can claim to be someone they are not. On the PSTN, caller ID reduces this risk somewhat by giving you the actual number of a caller. **Caller impersonation** is also possible with IP telephones and soft phones. If fact, it can be more effective. If call identification in VoIP gives a person's name or organizational position as well as their IP telephone number, impersonation will seem even more legitimate. If the president of the company or the chief of security calls you, you are likely to do what they tell you to do.

Hacking and Malware Attacks

If an attacker hacks a VoIP telephone or VoIP server or successfully places malware on one, he or she will "own" the device. Additional attacks using the compromised device become trivial. For instance, the attacker can send SIP BYE commands to many phones, causing conversations to terminate.

Toll Fraud

So far, we have been looking at sophisticated attacks aimed at large malicious goals. A smaller but still important threat is toll fraud—breaking into a corporate VoIP system in order to place free long-distance and international telephone calls. Although this may seem like a trivial threat, a break-in followed by the sharing of the exploit with many attackers can lead to substantial dollar losses.

Spam over IP Telephony (SPIT)

One emerging threat is **spam over IP telephony (SPIT)**.[5] Corporations already spend a great deal of time and effort controlling e-mail spam. VoIP may be an even easier way to deliver spam, and SPIT would be much more interruptive than e-mail spam because a ringing telephone is difficult to ignore.

New Threats

We have looked at the main threats to VoIP today, but new threats are emerging constantly. For instance, a theoretical RTP exploit can allow a hacker to inject his or her voice into the stream reaching the receiver. Compounding the damage, the real speaker would not hear the additional voice reaching the receiver.

TEST YOUR UNDERSTANDING

20. **a.** What is eavesdropping?
    b. Why can DoS attacks be successful even if they only increase latency slightly?
    c. Why is caller impersonation especially dangerous in VoIP?
    d. Why are hacking and malware dangerous in VoIP?
    e. What is toll fraud?
    f. What is SPIT?
    g. Why is SPIT more disruptive than e-mail SPAM?

Implementing VoIP Security

Basic Corporate Security

The first step in creating VoIP security is to have good basic security. If the company's basic security is strong, adding VoIP security measures will be comparatively straightforward. If a company's basic security is weak, security VoIP will be nearly impossible.

(Continued)

---

[5] Honest. I *do not* make up these abbreviations!

Voice over IP (VoIP) Security   (Continued)

Basic Corporate Security Must be Strong

Authentication

SIP Identity (RFC 4474) provides strong authentication assurance between second-level domains

Encryption for Confidentiality

Can add to latency

Firewalls

Many short packets

Firewall must prioritize VoIP traffic

Must handle ports for signaling

   SIP uses Port 5060

   H.323 uses Ports 1719 and 1720

Must create an exception for each conversation, which is assigned a specific port

   Must close the transport port immediately after conversation ends

NAT Problems

NAT firewall must handle VoIP NAT traversal

NAT adds a small amount of latency

Separation: Anticonvergence

The convergence goal for data and voice

Virtual LANs (VLANs)

   Separate voice and data traffic on different VLANs

   Separate VoIP servers from VoIP phones on different VLANs

FIGURE 8-21   Implementing VoIP Security (Study Figure)

Authentication

The way to deal with impersonation threats is to require strong authentication. Internally, companies can implement their own authentication systems. For example, using an IP telephone or soft phone may require the user to enter a username and a password or PIN. Companies can also use stronger authentication.

What about VoIP calls going between companies? The IETF has developed SIP Identity (RFC 4474) for authentication across second-level domains. Proxy servers sign SIP messages (such as INVITE) with the servers' own private keys. Servers receiving SIP messages can ensure that they come from the second-level domain they claim to be from by checking the digital signature with the second-level domain's public key found in its digital certificate.

Encryption for Confidentiality

The obvious way to thwart eavesdropping is to encrypt both transport traffic and signaling messages. For instance, IP telephones and soft phones can encrypt traffic before sending it out. Alternatively, a company may only encrypt traffic passing over nonsecure links, such as the Internet. In that case, a company would then use a virtual private network.

Encryption always adds a small delay. For example, software encryption typically adds latency of 5 ms to 15 ms. This added latency can harm voice quality, so hardware encryption is desirable.

Firewalls

VoIP challenges firewall technology. Most obviously, VoIP traffic consists of many small packets. Firewalls often have a difficult time with this type of traffic. Firewalls also must be able to prioritize VoIP traffic to minimize latency. Most importantly, firewall filtering must not add appreciable latency to packet delivery. Some firms do little or no firewall filtering on transport packets, focusing instead on less frequent (but more dangerous) signaling packets.

VoIP presents challenges for port-based firewall filtering. Most obviously, the firewall must allow traffic arriving on signaling ports. For SIP, this is Port 5060. H.323, in contrast, uses Ports 1719 and 1720 for signaling. Signaling is complex, and the firewall should know the signaling protocol in order to detect threats, such as risky SIP commands that should be blocked.

For transport connections, VoIP requires the opening of a separate port for each transport connection between users. Firewalls must be able to read the SIP (and H.323) protocol to learn what port the signaling protocol assigns to each transport connection. It must then open that port for a very short time, closing the port as soon as the call terminates to reduce risks.

NAT problems

As noted in Chapter 6, NAT causes problem for some protocols. These protocols include Layer 3 IP addresses in their messages. If NAT changes the IP destination address, the protocol will no longer work properly. VoIP signaling has this kind of problem with NAT firewalls. In addition, NAT IP address and port number translation take a small amount of time that increases latency.

Separation: Anticonvergence

One goal of VoIP is to provide convergence—using a single IP network for both voice and data. However, security may require the limited separation of voice and data traffic.

The most important aspect of separation is the use of virtual LANs (VLANs). Placing voice and data on separate VLANs makes it difficult for attackers coming through the data side to attack VLAN services. Even within voice technology, it may be good to place servers on different VLANs than IP telephones and soft phones to reduce attacks on servers from phones, which are easier to compromise than servers. If a company uses Windows-based servers, it may even put all VoIP servers in a single Windows domain for management by a specially trained VoIP staff group.

TEST YOUR UNDERSTANDING

21. **a.** What authentication mechanisms are common on IP telephones?
    b. What does SIP Identity ensure?
    c. How can eavesdropping be thwarted?
    d. What sound quality problem may encryption create?
    e. Why do firewalls have problems with typical VoIP traffic?
    f. For SIP signaling, what port has to be opened on firewalls?
    g. Describe firewall port openings for VoIP transport.
    h. Why is NAT traversal problematic?
    i. How are VLANs useful in VoIP?

The Skype VoIP Service

The Skype public VoIP service currently offers free calling among Skype customers over the Internet and reduced-cost calling to and from Public Switched Telephone Network customers. Skype is extremely popular among consumers. However, many corporations ban Skype.

Skype uses proprietary software and protocols that have not been studied by security professionals. This causes security professionals to be concerned with the existence of vulnerabilities, backdoors, and other security threats.

Although Skype uses encryption for confidentiality, its method is unknown. Worse yet, Skype controls the encryption keys so that it can read traffic if it wants.

A particularly important point is that Skype does not provide adequate authentication. Although Skype authenticates users each time they enter the Skype network, initial registration is open and uncontrolled, so that user names mean nothing from a security standpoint. An attacker can register other people's names and impersonate them.

Another problem is that Skype is a peer-to-peer (P2P) service that is almost impossible to control at firewalls because the Skype protocol is unknown and changes frequently to avoid analysis. Skype uses its structure to help users communicate through NAT firewalls. This is good for the user but bad for corporate security.

Nor does Skype's file transfer mechanism work with antivirus products at the time of this writing.

Overall, although most of these Skype concerns are theoretical, the fact that Skype cannot be well controlled by corporate security policies makes it unacceptable in many firms.

TEST YOUR UNDERSTANDING

22. **a.** What is Skype?
    b. Why is Skype's use of proprietary software problematic?
    c. What problem is there with Skype's encryption for confidentiality?

Widely Used Public VoIP Service

Uses Proprietary Protocols and Code
   Vulnerabilities? Backdoors? Etc.
   Firewalls have a difficult time even recognizing Skype traffic

Encryption for Confidentiality
   Skype reportedly uses strong security
   However, Skype keep encryption keys, allowing it to do eavesdropping

Inadequate Authentication
   Uncontrolled user registration; can use someone else's name and so appear to be them

Peer-to-Peer (P2P) Service
   Uses this architecture and its proprietary (and rapidly changing) protocol to get through corporate firewalls

   Bad for corporate security control

File Sharing
   Does not work with antivirus programs

FIGURE 8-22 Skype Security Concerns (Study Figure)

d. Does Skype control who can register a particular person's name?
e. Why do firewalls have a difficult time controlling Skype?
f. Does Skype's file transfer generally work with antivirus programs?
g. Overall, what is the big problem with Skype?

OTHER USER APPLICATIONS

We have looked at several important corporate applications. However, there are many others. We will look at a few briefly.

Database

RELATIONAL DATABASES   Most databases are relational. They store their data in tables called relations. In these tables, rows hold data for individual people, transactions, and other "entities." Columns, in turn, are attributes of the entity. For instance, in a table containing data on employees, one column may represent salary.

Databases
   Often used in mission-critical applications
   Relational databases: Tables with rows (entities) and columns (attributes)
   As discussed earlier, avoid SQL injection attacks
   Restrict Access to Data
       Restrict users to certain columns (attributes) in each row
           For instance, deny access to salary column to most users
       Limit access control to rows
           For instance, only rows containing data about people in the user's own department
   Restrict Granularity
       Prevent access to individual data
       Allow trend analysts to deal only with sums and averages for aggregates such as departments

Instant Messaging (IM)
   Many companies only use presence servers to introduce the two users
       Communication afterward takes place directly between the two users
   For security, companies can use relay servers (Figure 8-24)
       All communication passes through the relay server
       This allows the firm to filter and retain all messages for legal purposes

Spreadsheet Security
   Spreadsheets are widely used and the subject of many compliance regulations
   Need for security testing
   Spreadsheet vault server to implement controls (Figure 8-25)

FIGURE 8-23   Other Applications (Study Figure)

LIMITING ACCESS TO ROWS AND ATTRIBUTES   Not every employee should even be able to see all of the information in the database. For example, only a few employees who have access to the database might be allowed to retrieve information in the salary column. Other employees could read other attributes but not salaries. Moving from columns to rows, access control may limit a user's access to certain rows, for example, to the rows containing information for the employees in another department.

LIMITING GRANULARITY   In addition, when a database is used for trend analysis and other functions, it may be desirable to reduce the **granularity** (level of detail) in queries. For instance, in analyzing data for personnel, privacy concerns may restrict searches to being no more detailed than sums and averages at the department level.

SQL INJECTION ATTACKS   As noted earlier in this chapter, users must be prevented from doing SQL injection attacks whenever they make queries or authenticate themselves.

TEST YOUR UNDERSTANDING

23. **a.** Why is it good for database applications and other applications to have their own passwords beyond the computer's login password?
    b. What access limitations do databases impose on what content a person can see?

Instant Messaging (IM)

Most people think of instant messaging (IM) as transient communication. However, most of the same laws that require e-mail retention also require the retention of instant messaging.

Figure 8-24 shows that different IM designers have choices for how they will use servers. Many IM systems only use presence servers. Presence servers allow the two parties to locate each other (much like SIP proxy servers in VoIP). Afterward, communication is peer-to-peer between the two IM users. Servers are no longer involved at all.

Another option is to use an IM relay server. All messages pass through the relay server. This allows the firm to filter IM for inappropriate content. This also allows the firm to satisfy legal retention and other compliance requirements. Consequently, corporate IM systems should use a relay server rather than a presence server.

TEST YOUR UNDERSTANDING

24. **a.** In IM, what does a presence server do?
    b. What does a relay server do?
    c. For corporate IM, what are the advantages of using a relay server instead of only a presence server?

Spreadsheets

In the past, IT security people (like IT people in general) have ignored spreadsheets. However, that is no longer a tenable position. Spreadsheets are at the focus of many compliance regimes, especially the Sarbanes–Oxley Act of 2002 and the 21 CFR Part 11 rules for pharmaceutical companies doing product testing.

Use of a presence server

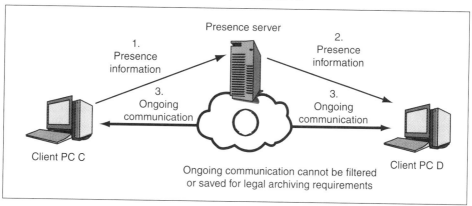

Use of a relay server

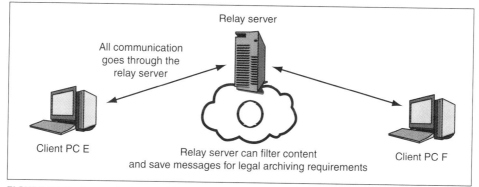

FIGURE 8-24   Servers in Instant Messaging (IM)

In general, companies are concerned with spreadsheet errors, spreadsheet fraud, and traditional security attacks targeted at private information, proprietary information, and other information in spreadsheets.

Two sets of controls are needed to reduce spreadsheet threats. The first is extensive testing for both errors and fraud indicators. The second is the use of **spreadsheet vault servers**. Figure 8-25 illustrates the protections offered by vault servers.

- The vault server provides strong access control, including authentication of suitable strength, authorizations, and auditing.
- Authorizations go beyond what a person can do with a file. They also limit what a user can even see on the spreadsheet. For instance, the firm could refuse data entry users permission to see the formulas that constitute extensive intellectual property. Report users, it turn, may be limited to seeing reports and not be allowed to see either the logic or data input portions of the spreadsheet. This may be easiest to implement with a Web-based interface read by a browser. This way, the information to which the user should not have access is never sent to the user at all.

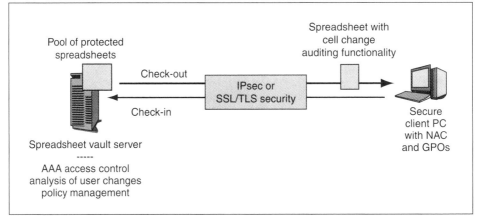

FIGURE 8-25 Spreadsheet Vault Server

- Auditing begins with check-out/check-in auditing but continues down to the level of individual cell changes. Downloaded spreadsheets come with an auditing module to record all cell changes. Later, the company can use these cell change logs in forensics analyses.
- The vault server will ensure that a user can only work with the most current version of the file. The vault server will also archive older versions of the file securely so that they fit the rules of evidence.
- Of course, the vault server will protect all transmissions between the PC user and the vault server cryptographically at an appropriate level of strength.
- There should be active detection tools that look for policy violations and that allow the administrator to read log files efficiently and effectively.
- Finally, there should be strong management tools that allow managers to state policies and automatically implements these policies.

TEST YOUR UNDERSTANDING

25. **a.** Why is spreadsheet security an IT security concern?
    b. What two protections should be applied to spreadsheets?
    c. Briefly list the functions of a vault server.
    d. Comment on vault server authorizations.
    e. Describe vault server auditing.

TCP/IP SUPERVISORY APPLICATIONS

TCP/IP has many supervisory protocols, including ARP, ICMP, DNS, DHCP, LDAP, RIP, OSPF, BGP, and SNMP, among many others. These supervisory protocols are favorite targets for attackers because disrupting supervisory protocols can disrupt the operation of an entire internet.

We only have the room to look at one supervisory protocol, but the IETF has a long-term program (called the Danvers Doctrine) to add strong security to all of its supervisory protocols and application protocols.

TCP/IP Supervisory Protocols
   Many supervisory protocols in TCP/IP
      ARP, ICMP, DNS, DHCP, LDAP, RIP, OSPF, BGP, SNMP, etc.
   The targets of many attacks
   The IETF has a program to improve security in all (the Danvers Doctrine)

Example
   Simple Network Management Protocol (SNMP)
   Messages
      GET messages to get information from a managed object
      SET messages to change the configuration of a managed object
      SET is often turned off because it is dangerous
   SNMP versions and security
      Version 1: No security
      Version 2: Weak authentication with a community string shared by the manager and managed devices
      Version 3: Pair-shared secrets, optional confidentiality, message integrity, and anti-replay protection
      Still needed: Public key authentication

IT Security People Must Work with the Networking Staff
   To ensure that appropriate security is being applied to supervisory protocols
   Not a traditional area for IT security in most firms

FIGURE 8-26   TCP/IP Supervisory Applications (Study Figure)

We will look at the Simple Network Management Protocol (SNMP), which allows a company to control many remote managed devices from a central manager. The SNMP GET command allows the manager to ask managed devices to send it information about their status. The SNMP SET command, in turn, allows the manager to tell remote managed devices to change their configurations. Due to the damage that attackers can do with the SET command if security is not excellent, many companies disable the SET command. In doing so, they lose the cost savings that follow from remote configuration instead of traveling to each managed device to change the configuration.

SNMP Version 1 had no security at all, making the protocol extremely dangerous given its power. SNMP Version 2 was supposed to add security, but an inability to settle differences within the IETF forestalled strong security. Version 2 did introduce the community string. This is a "secret" shared by the manager and all managed devices. Shared secrets rarely stay secret. In fact, SNMP V2 sends the shared secret in the clear in messages. Worst of all, most vendors use the default community string "public."

Version 3 finally added individual secrets shared between the manager and each managed device. SNMP V3 also offered confidentiality (optionally), message integrity, and time stamps to guard against replay attacks. Hopefully, a later version will add public key authentication.

The development of security in SNMP is being repeated in other TCP/IP supervisory protocols. IT security professionals need to work closely with the corporate networking staff to ensure that the company has appropriate security for its network supervisory protocol. IT security people traditionally have not been active in this area.

TEST YOUR UNDERSTANDING

26. **a.** What is the Danvers Doctrine?
    b. Distinguish between security in SNMP V1 and security in SNMP V2.
    c. Distinguish between security in SNMP V2 and security in SNMP V3.
    d. What still needs to be done for SNMP security?

CONCLUSION

In this chapter, we looked at the hardening of applications. At the beginning of this chapter, we looked at general principles for hardening applications. These included the following:

- Understanding the server's role and threat environment
- Basics: physical security, backup, harden the operating system
- Minimize applications
- Create secure configurations
- Install patches
- Minimize the permissions of applications
- Add application layer authentication, authorizations, and auditing
- Implement cryptographic systems
- Secure custom applications

The remainder of this chapter looked at how to apply these principles (and application-specific protections) to major applications, including the WWW, e-commerce, e-mail, and VoIP. However, there are many other applications, each with its special needs. We looked very briefly at databases, instant messaging, spreadsheets, and TCP/IP supervisory protocols.

Thought Questions

1. Do you think programmers should be allowed to develop server-side dynamic webpages, given the dangers that are involved in their doing so?
2. Client-side scripting attacks usually require the client to visit a webserver with malicious content. How do you think attackers get users to visit such webpages?
3. What three main topics would you select for a one-hour *user* training session on e-mail security? This question requires you to be selective. Do not create topics that are extremely broad to avoid being selective.
4. What three main topics would you select for a one-hour training session for *senior managers* on e-mail security? This question requires you to be selective. Do not create topics that are extremely broad to avoid being selective.

Troubleshooting Questions

1. An employee working at home complains that some of her messages to fellow employees at the firm's headquarters site are not getting through. What might be the problem?
2. A company is warned by its credit card companies that it will be classified as a high-risk firm unless it immediately reduces the number of fraudulent purchases made by its e-commerce clients. Come up with a plan to avoid this outcome.

Perspective Questions

1. What was the most surprising thing for you in this chapter?
2. What was the most difficult material in this chapter for you?

Chapter 9

Incident and Disaster Response

LEARNING OBJECTIVES:

By the end of this chapter, you should be able to discuss the following:

- The basics of disaster response.
- The intrusion response process for major incidents.
- In a box, legal considerations.
- Backup.
- Intrusion detection system (IDS) technology.
- Business continuity planning.
- IT disaster recovery.

INTRODUCTION

Wal-Mart and Hurricane Katrina

In 2005, Hurricane Katrina slammed into Louisiana and Mississippi, devastating New Orleans and many other cities along the U.S. Gulf Coast. Shortly afterward, the fourth-most intense Atlantic hurricane in history, Rita, added enormously to the destruction. The Federal Emergency Management Agency (FEMA) became notorious for its handling of the crisis, responding belatedly and acting ineptly when it did respond.

Many businesses collapsed because they were poorly prepared for the hurricanes. One company that *did* respond effectively was Wal-Mart.[1] In its Brookhaven, Mississippi

---

[1] Liza Featherstone, "Wal-Mart to the Rescue!" *The Nation*, September 26, 2005, http://www.thenation.com/doc/20050926/featherstone. Michael Barbaro and Justin Gillis, "Wal-Mart at Forefront of Hurricane Relief," Washington Post.com, September 6, 2005. http://www.washingtonpost.com/wp-dyn/content/article/2005/09/05/AR2005090501598.html. NewsMax.com, "Wal-Mart Praised for Hurricane Katrina Response Efforts," http://www.newsmax.com/archives/ic/2005/9/6/164525.shtml. Ann Zimmerman and Valerie Bauerlein, "At Wal-Mart, Emergency Plan has Big Payoff," *Wall Street Journal*, September 12, 2005, B1.

distribution center, the company had 45 trucks loaded and ready for delivery even before Katrina made landfall. The company soon supplied $20 million in cash donations, 100,000 free meals, and 1,900 truckloads full of diapers, toothbrushes, and other emergency supplies to relief centers. The company also supplied flashlights, batteries, ammunition, protective gear, and meals to police and relief workers.

The Situation
Wal-Mart is the largest retailer in the United States
Hurricane Katrina devastated New Orleans in 2005
    Followed shortly by Hurricane Rita
The U.S. Federal Emergency Management Administration (FEMA) botched the relief effort

Wal-Mart's Response
Supplied $20 million in cash
Supplied 100,000 free meals
1,900 truckloads full of diapers, toothbrushes, other emergency supplies
    45 trucks were rolling before the hurricane hit land
Provided police and relief workers with flashlight, batteries, ammunition, protective gear, and meals

Wall-Mart Business Continuity Center
A permanent department with a small core staff
Activated two days before Katrina hit
Soon, 50 managers and specialists were at work in the center
Before computer network went down, sent detailed orders to its distribution center in Mississippi
Recovery merchandise for stores: bleach and mops, etc.
40 power generators to supply stores with backup power
Sent loss-prevention employees to secure stores

Communication
Network communication failed
Relied on telephone to contact its stores and other key constituencies

Response
Stores came back to business within days
Engaged local law enforcement to preserve order in lines to get into stores

Preparation
Full-time director of business continuity
Detailed business continuity plans
Clear lines of responsibility

Multitasking
During all of this, were monitoring a hurricane off Japan

FIGURE 9-1 Wal-Mart and Hurricane Katrina (Study Figure)

Although the relief effort was impressive, it was merely the visible tip of Wal-Mart's disaster recovery program. Two days before Katrina hit, Wal-Mart activated its business continuity center. Soon, 50 managers and experts in specific areas such as trucking were hard at work. Just before the storm knocked out the company's computer network, the center ordered the Mississippi distribution center to send out recovery merchandise such as bleach and mops to its stores. The company also sent 40 generators to its stores so that stores that lost power could open to serve their customers. It also sent out many security employees to protect stores.

After computer networks failed, the company relied on the telephone to contact its stores and other key constituencies. Most stores came back immediately, and almost all stores were able to serve their customers within a few days. Lines of customers were long, and Wal-Mart engaged local law enforcement to help maintain order.

Wal-Mart was successful because of intensive preparation. The company has a full-time director of business continuity. It also has detailed business continuity plans and clear lines of responsibility. In fact, while the company was still responding to Katrina and Rita, it was monitoring a hurricane off Japan, preparing to take action there if necessary.

TEST YOUR UNDERSTANDING

1. **a.** Why was Wal-Mart able to respond quickly?
   b. List at least three actions that Wal-Mart took that you might not have thought of.

Incidents Happen

Previous chapters covered the planning and protection phases of the plan–protect–respond cycle. Well-executed planning and protection can greatly reduce the number of successful attacks, but protection is never perfect. According to the Federal Bureau of Investigation (FBI), about 1 percent of concentrated attacks are successful. Consequently, even companies with good security must be prepared to handle successful attacks (also known as security incidents, breaches, or compromises). In this chapter, we will look at different severity levels of security incidents and appropriate corporate responses.

TEST YOUR UNDERSTANDING

2. **a.** Can good planning and protection eliminate security incidents?
   b. What three things are successful attacks commonly called?

Incident Severity

Not all incidents are equally severe. Incidents range from situations mild enough to ignore to threats against the very continuity of the business. We will use a four-category incident severity threat scale in this chapter: false alarms, minor incidents, major incidents, and disasters.

Incidents Happen
Protections inevitably break down occasionally
Successful attacks are called security incidents, breaches, or compromises

Incident Severity
False alarms
  Apparent compromises are not real compromises
  Also called false positives
  Handled by the on-duty staff
  Waste time and may dull vigilance
Minor incidents
  Small virus outbreaks, etc.
  Can be handled by the on-duty staff
Major incidents
  Beyond the capabilities of the on-duty staff
  Must convene a Computer Security Incident Response Team (CSIRT)
  CSIRT needs participation beyond IT security
Disasters
  Fires, floods, hurricanes, major terrorist attacks
  Must assure business continuity
    Maintaining the day-to-day operations of the firm
    Need a business continuity group headed by a senior manager
    Core permanent staff will facilitate activities
IT disaster response is restoring IT services
    May be a subset of business continuity
    May be a stand-alone IT disaster

FIGURE 9-2   Incident Response (Study Figure)

FALSE ALARMS   **False alarms** are situations that seem to be incidents (or at least potential incidents) but turn out to be innocent activities.[2] The actions that attackers take often are similar to those that employees, systems administrators, or network managers routinely take in their work. Intrusion detection systems (IDSs) are likely to flag many legitimate activities as suspicious. In fact, in almost all IDSs, a large majority of suspicious activities turn out to be **false positives**, that is, false alarms.

False alarms, which are handled by the on-duty staff, waste a great deal of scarce and expensive security time. More subtly, if there are too many false alarms,

---

[2] In one case, an employee reported that someone had attempted to use the employee's PC several times, always at night. Although the attacker never got past the password, the computer stored sensitive information. Investigation revealed that a certain custodian had always been on duty when the incidents occurred. Further investigation revealed that the custodian was the only custodian who dusted keyboards as part of her cleaning process. Vince Tuesday, "The Strange Case of the Phantom Intruder," *Computerworld*, February 28, 2002. http://www.computerworld.com/action/article.do?command=viewArticleBasic&articleId=68546.

this may dull readiness to investigate each potential incident. This may allow real incidents to go unnoticed.

MINOR INCIDENTS   Moving up the severity scale, **minor incidents** are true breaches that the on-duty staff can handle and that do not have broader implications for the firm. An example of a minor incident is a virus infection involving a dozen or so computers. Minor incident response methods tend to be breach specific and so are difficult to talk about in general. We will not look at minor incidents in this chapter. Companies must cope with them, but they do not raise serious management or policy issues.

> *Minor incidents are breaches that the on-duty staff can handle and that do not have broader implications for the firm.*

MAJOR INCIDENTS   In contrast, **major incidents** have an impact too large for the on-duty IT staff to handle. For major incidents, many firms create **computer security incident response teams (CSIRTs)**.[3] In addition to having IT and IT security professionals, CSIRTs typically have members from the legal department, public relations, and senior management.

> *Major incidents have an impact too large to be handled by the on-duty IT staff and require action by a firm's staff members outside the IT department.*

    Major incidents can be serious profit hazard. Firms must handle these incidents quickly, efficiently, and effectively in order to contain losses. We will focus heavily on responses to major incidents in this chapter because of the importance and complexity of this type of incident response.

DISASTERS   Fires, floods, and other disasters are beyond even the abilities of CSIRTs. Disasters often threaten **business continuity**, which is the maintenance of the day-to-day revenue-generating operations of the firm. **Business continuity planning** aims at keeping a business running or getting it back in operation as quickly as possible. Businesses need strong business continuity plans and well-rehearsed **business continuity teams** headed by a senior manager.

TEST YOUR UNDERSTANDING

  3. **a.** What are the four severity levels of incidents?
     b. What is the purpose of a CSIRT?
     c. From what parts of the firm do its members come?
     d. What is business continuity?
     e. Who should head the business continuity team?

---

[3] Many firms use the term Computer Emergency Response Team (CERT), but this term has been copyrighted by the CERT Coordination Center and may only be used with the center's permission.

Speed and Accuracy are of the Essence

Speed of response can reduce damage

Attacker will have less time to do damage

The attacker cannot burrow as deeply into the system and become very difficult to detect

Speed is also necessary in recovery

Accuracy is equally important

Common mistake is to act on incorrect assumptions

If misdiagnose the problem or take the wrong approach, can make things much worse

Take your time quickly

Planning before an incident or disaster

Decide what to do ahead of time

Have time to consider matters thoroughly and without the time pressure of a crisis

(During an attack, human decision making skills degrade)

Incident response is reacting to incidents according to plan

Within the plan, need to have flexibility to adapt

Best to adapt within a plan than to improvise completely

Team members must rehearse the plan

Rehearsals find mistakes in the plan

Practice builds speed

Types of rehearsals

Walkthroughs (table-top exercises)

Live tests (actually doing planned actions) can find subtle problems but are expensive

---

FIGURE 9-3 Rehearsals for Speed and Accuracy (Study Figure)

Speed and Accuracy

SPEED IS OF THE ESSENCE Major security breaches and threats to business continuity always create severe time pressure. Attackers will continue to do damage until they are stopped. Attackers will also continue to take steps to make their actions more difficult to detect and analyze.

Even after the company stops the attacker, the need for speed continues. In many cases, important corporate systems will have failed, and their failure can cost the company a great deal of money each hour they are down. Rapid recovery is critical for reducing damage.

SO IS ACCURACY Accuracy is as important as speed. A common error that humans under pressure make is to respond hastily, acting before having a solid understanding of the problem. Hasty response may blind people to the real root cause of the problem, which remains invisible and allows the attacker to continue to do damage while the problem solver goes off trying to solve the wrong problem.

PLANNING   The way to respond both rapidly and correctly is to prepare ahead of time. Paradoxically, the actions taken *before* an incident usually are more critical than the actions taken after an incident begins.

Organizations have to plan in detail how they will respond to major incidents and disasters. Perhaps the best definition of incident response is reacting to incidents according to plan. A crisis is no time to begin thinking about how to respond. No plan will precisely fit an incident, and rigid adherence to a plan can be damaging. However, doing improvisation within a plan is far more effective than working without a plan.

Incident response is reacting to incidents according to plan.

REHEARSAL   Besides planning, another key to rapid and correct incident response is **rehearsal**. When a football team learns a play, it practices the play repeatedly, until its execution is effective and fluid. Minor incidents are sufficiently common for speed and accuracy to be normal. However, for rare major incidents and disasters, rehearsals are critical, and companies must execute them frequently.[4]

The simplest type of rehearsal is the **walkthrough**, in which managers and other key personnel get together and discuss, step by step, what each will do during an incident. For complex incidents, these walkthroughs (also called **table-top exercises**) are major undertakings because they involve people from many departments.

Walkthroughs often use a scenario exercise in which there is an initial scenario describing the incident or disaster. Frequently, the scenario manager will throw in complications during the execution of the exercise to make the situation as realistic as possible.

Occasional **live tests** for critical systems have the team actually take the actions instead of describing what they would do. Live tests reveal subtle flaws that walkthroughs cannot. For instance, one live test revealed that a critical password required at a backup site was in a safe at the damaged site. Chemical contamination due to a fire made that safe inaccessible. Live tests are also superior for training people. Of course, live tests are expensive, so firms usually do them less frequently than table-top exercises.

TEST YOUR UNDERSTANDING

4. **a.** Why is speed of response important?
   b. Why is accuracy of response important?
   c. Define incident response in terms of planning.
   d. Why are rehearsals important?
   e. What is a walkthrough or table-top exercise?
   f. Why is a live test better?
   g. What is the problem with live tests?

---

[4] It is often said that "Practice makes perfect." However, practice only makes *habit*. As musicians often say, "Perfect practice makes perfect."

THE INTRUSION RESPONSE PROCESS FOR MAJOR INCIDENTS

Incident response is responding according to plan. Typically, the plan will lay out processes for the firm to follow for different types of incident. We will look at a typical process for the breach of a single server that contains sensitive customer information. This is a major incident because the server contains sensitive customer information, so it has wider importance to the firm.

Process for Major Incidents

Detection, Analysis, and Escalation

   Must detect the incident through technology or people

        Need good intrusion detection technology

        All employees must know how to report incidents

Must analyze the incident enough to guide subsequent actions

        Confirm that the incident is real

        Determine its scope: Who is attacking; what are they doing; how sophisticated they are, etc.

If deemed severe enough, escalate to a major incident

        Pass to the CSIRT, the disaster response team, or the business continuity team

Containment

Disconnection of the system from the site network or the site network from the internet (damaging)

        Harmful, so must be done only with proper authorization

        This is a business decision, not a technical decision

Black-holing the attacker (only works for a short time)

Continue to collect data (allows harm to continue) to understand the situation

        Especially necessary if prosecution is desired

Recovery

Repair during continuing server operation

        Avoids lack of availability

        No loss of data

        Possibility of a rootkit not having been removed, etc.

Data

        Restoration from backup tapes

        Loses data since last trusted backup

Software

        Total software reinstallation of operating system and applications may be necessary for the system to be trustable

        Manual reinstallation of software

           Must have the installation media and product activation keys

           Must have good configuration documentation before the incident

---

FIGURE 9-4 The Incident Response Process: I (Study Figure)

Reinstallation from a disk image
    Can greatly reduce time and effort
    Requires a recent disk image

Apology
Acknowledge responsibility and harm without evasion or weasel words
Explain potential inconvenience and harm in detail
Explain what actions will be taken to compensate victims, if any

FIGURE 9-4 (Continued)

Detection, Analysis, and Escalation

There are three priorities at the beginning of an incident.

- The first is to learn quickly that an incident has occurred. This is detection.
- The second is to understand the incident to be sure that it is a real event, to determine its damage potential, and to gather information needed to begin planning for containment and recovery. This is analysis.
- The third is to handle the incident with the on-duty staff or to escalate handling to the CSIRT or business continuity team.

DETECTION   There are many ways to detect an attack. An IDS might alert the firm to an attack, or a security analyst might find suspicious event patterns while analyzing an IDS log file. More simply, an important system may fail.

Although technology may be able to detect many incidents, the company should never underestimate its human resources. Frequently, a nontechnical employee will be the first person to notice that a system has failed or appears to be malfunctioning. Consequently, whoever discovers an incident must know how to report it. Each telephone, for instance, should have a sticker giving the number of the IT security department, and employee training should encourage all employees to call even when in doubt. IT security staff members, in turn, must be trained to respond to calls respectfully.

ANALYSIS   Once an intrusion response begins, the security analyst must understand the situation before effective action can be taken. Initially, the security analyst will not even be sure whether the incident is a security problem, an equipment problem, a software glitch, or even normal operation.

Frequently, much of the intrusion analysis phase is done by reading through log files for the time period in which the incident probably began. The goal is to learn how the attack was undertaken, who perpetrated it, and what has happened since the beginning of the incident. Armed with this information, the company can proceed effectively.

ESCALATION   Major incidents must be **escalated** (passed) to the CSIRT or business continuity team.

TEST YOUR UNDERSTANDING

5. **a.** Distinguish between detection and analysis.
   b. Why is good analysis important for the later stages of handling an attack?
   c. What is escalation?

Containment

The next step is **containment**—stopping the damage.

DISCONNECTION   A radical way to contain the situation is to disconnect the server from the local network or even to disconnect the site's Internet connection. Although **disconnection** stops intrusions, it also prevents the server from serving its legitimate users. In effect, disconnection helps the attacker by making the server completely unavailable. The business impact can be severe if the server is an important one.

BLACK-HOLING THE ATTACKER   Another approach to containment is to cut off the attacker, say by **black-holing** the attacker's IP address, meaning that the company will drop all future packets from that IP address. However, attackers often can switch to different IP addresses quickly. In addition, black-holing definitively notifies hackers that they have been discovered. If the attackers come back in again, their next approach might be stealthier and more difficult to detect.

CONTINUING TO COLLECT DATA   If the damage is not too severe, a company might allow the hackers to continue working on the server. During this time, the company can observe what the attacker does. This information may aid in analysis and may be needed to collect evidence for prosecution.

However, not blocking attackers as soon as possible is risky. The longer attackers are in a system, the more invisible they become through the deletion of IDS logs, and the more backdoors and other damage the attackers can create.

Whether to stop the attack or let it continue is a business decision, not only an IT decision or an IT security decision. The disconnection of a business-critical system also is a business decision. There should always be a senior business executive available to make a critical security-related business decision. This executive should be as knowledgeable as possible through discussions of scenarios ahead of time.

TEST YOUR UNDERSTANDING

6. **a.** What is containment?
   b. Why is disconnection undesirable?
   c. What is black holing?
   d. Why may it only be a temporary containment solution?
   e. Why might a company allow an attacker to continue working in the system for a brief period of time?
   f. Why is this dangerous?
   g. Who should make decisions about letting an attack continue or disconnecting an important system?

Recovery

Once the attack is contained, the **recovery** stage begins. The attack undoubtedly left the server littered with backdoors and other problems. The staff must restore the system to operation.

In fact, the system needs to be *better* than before the attack, so that the attacker cannot come back in. Once an attacker has cracked a system, he or she often invites other attackers in to prove his or her skills. If the attack is stopped, other attackers will try to break in to show their superiority.

REPAIR DURING CONTINUING SERVER OPERATION   Ideally, the staff can repair the server while the computer is operating. For instance, if your antivirus program detects a virus, it can usually repair infected files while you continue working. Doing this on a server with a critical function keeps those services available to users. It also means that no data is lost because there is no need to resort to backup tapes, which only contain information since the last backup.

Unfortunately, it is very difficult to root out all of the Trojan horses, registry entries, rootkits, and other unpleasant surprises planted by an attacker. For a virus or worm attack, there sometimes are programs that remove the specific artifacts created by the specific attack. For handcrafted break-ins, however, there is no general detection program, and there always is a strong concern that "we may have missed one."

RESTORATION FROM BACKUP TAPES   If the attack occurred at a particular time, the staff may be able to restore program and data files from the last trusted backup tape. However, data collected since the last backup will be lost. Worse yet, if the attacker began the attack earlier than believed, the "trusted" backup tape might restore the attackers' Trojan horses and other artifacts.

TOTAL SOFTWARE REINSTALLATION   Unless firms are confident that they can find all rootkits and other malware, they usually do a complete reinstallation of the operating system and programs. This is an involved process and does not address the issue of data loss. To achieve it, furthermore, the company must retain and have ready its original installation media and product keys. It is also important to document the software's configuration options before an incident, so that the company can restore the configuration after reinstallation. To reduce problems, firms may take periodic images of the entire disk and simply restore this disk image when needed.

TEST YOUR UNDERSTANDING

7. **a.** What are the three major recovery options?
   b. For what two reasons is repair during continuing operation good?
   c. Why may it not work?
   d. Why is the restoration of *data* files from backup tapes undesirable?
   e. What are the potential problems with total software reinstallation?
   f. How does having a disk image reduce the problems of total software reinstallation?

Apology

If the attack has caused harm to customers or employees, it is important to give a prompt apology. Unfortunately, most apologies after leaks of personal information and other damaging incidents usually are filled with weasel words that cause more anger than they assuage.

- First, acknowledge responsibility and harm. Apologies that blame the hacker or that apologize conditionally by saying something like "if anyone was inconvenienced" understandably create ire when they are read. Apologize that the company let the attack succeed, and apologize simply for the inconvenience or other harm that the incident caused the addressee.
- Second, explain what happened. Technical details are not necessary. However, potential inconvenience and harm need to be explained in detail. The apology writer should consider what he or she would want to know if he or she had been the victim.
- Third, explain what action will be taken to compensate the person, if any.

Of course, different incidents require different apologies. Some do not require an apology at all, but more deserve apologies than get them. Explanations and actions to be taken may or may not be necessary.

TEST YOUR UNDERSTANDING

8. What are the three rules for apologies?

Punishment

Some companies focus entirely on recovery, ignoring the possibility of punishing the intruder. However, some firms will choose to try to punish intruders under certain circumstances.

Punishment

Punishing employees usually is fairly easy

    Most employees are at-will employees

    Companies usually have wide discretion in firing at-will employees

    This varies internationally

    Union agreements may limit sanctions or at least require more detailed processes

The decision to pursue criminal prosecution

    Must consider cost and effort

    Must consider probable success if pursue (often attackers are minors or foreign nationals)

    Loss of reputation because the incident becomes public

Collecting and managing evidence

    Forensics: Courts have strict rules for admitting evidence in court

---

FIGURE 9-5 The Incident Response Process: II (Study Figure)

Call the authorities and a forensics expert for help

Protecting evidence

　　Pull the plug on a server if possible

　　This is a business decision, not an IT decision

Document the chain of custody

　　Who held the evidence at all times

　　What they did to protect it

　　Document the chain of custody

Postmortem Evaluation

What should we do differently next time?

Organization of the CSIRT

Should be led by a senior manager

Should have members from affected line operations

The IT security staff may manage the CSIRT's operation on a day-to-day basis

Might need to communicate with the media; only do so via public relations

The corporate legal counsel must be involved to address legal issues

Human resources is necessary, especially if there are to be sanctions against employees

FIGURE 9-5   (Continued)

PUNISHING EMPLOYEES   Prosecuting an outside attacker is very complex. It is considerably easier to punish an employee who is attacking internally or from home. Although the courts require strong evidence for prosecution, the justification for reprimanding or terminating an employee usually can be much weaker. Consequently, most companies are far more likely to punish an employee than to try to prosecute an external hacker.[5] However, the human resources department and legal department will have to make the decision to punish an employee based on such factors as union rules and local labor laws.

THE DECISION TO PURSUE PROSECUTION   Pursuing the prosecution of an attacker is desirable for a number of reasons, but many firms are reluctant to do it.

　　Cost and Effort   One pair of reasons for not prosecuting attackers is the cost and effort that would be needed to find and prosecute the adversary. These are never trivial.

　　Probability of Success   In many cases, the intruder will turn out to be living in another country or a teenager who would get only a few months in a detention center. In such cases, prosecution is rarely worth the effort.

　　Loss of Reputation   Prosecution is a public process. The firm will be admitting publicly that it could not prevent an intrusion. This could hurt the firm's reputation,

---

[5] It may be good to do a good forensics analysis of the fired employee's computer as a defensive measure. If the employee wishes to bring a wrongful termination lawsuit, he or she may be dissuaded by the prospect of strong forensics evidence.

and this loss of reputation could cost the firm some of its customers. At the least, some customers will mentally put the firm on probation.

COLLECTING AND MANAGING EVIDENCE   The courts have stringent rules for how to collect and handle **forensics evidence** (evidence that is acceptable for court proceedings) after collection.

Forensics evidence is evidence that is acceptable for court proceedings.

The Police and the FBI   Before any attack, the IT security staff should become familiar with their local police cybercrime unit and the local Federal Bureau of Investigation cybercrime unit. Law enforcement officials tell the security staff who to call and what the security staff will need to do until law enforcement personnel arrive.

The FBI will investigate matters of interstate commerce and some other attacks. The police will investigate violations of local and state laws. During an incident, however, the security staff should call both the local police and the FBI because it is not always certain which agency has jurisdiction over a particular crime.

Forensics Expert   The police and FBI have their own computer forensics experts, but for torts (civil lawsuits), the company must use a certified forensics expert to collect data and interpret it in court. If it attempts to collect evidence on its own, the evidence probably will not be permissible in court.

Preserving Evidence   Although a company should call in the authorities as rapidly as possible, IT employees must understand the basic rules of evidence handling. For instance, it is critical to **preserve evidence**. The contents of a computer's disk change rapidly. If possible, employees should pull the plug (literally) on an affected server.[6]

Documenting the Chain of Custody   Another important principle is documenting what happens to the evidence after collection. The **chain of custody** is the history of all transfers of the evidence between people and of all actions taken to protect the evidence while in each person's possession. The chain of custody must be clear and well documented. Otherwise, a judge probably will disallow the evidence completely. Even if the evidence is admitted, the jury might not believe the evidence if significant custody problems were uncovered.

TEST YOUR UNDERSTANDING

9. **a.** Is it easier to punish employees or to prosecute outside attackers?
    b. Why do companies often not prosecute attackers?
    c. What is forensics evidence? Contrast what cybercrimes the FBI and local police investigate.
    d. Why should both be called?
    e. Under what conditions will you need to hire a forensics expert?

---

[6] They should pull the plug at the back of the server rather than at the wall power jack. This will kill the machine immediately even if it is protected by an uninterruptible power supply.

    f. Why should you hire a forensics expert rather than doing your own investigation?

    g. What is the chain of evidence, and why is documenting it important?

Postmortem Evaluation

During response, some things will inevitably not go well. It is important to do a postmortem evaluation of what went right or wrong after an attack and to implement any improvements needed in the response process. Unfortunately, this rather simple but important step is often skipped because the firm needs to catch up on actions that were postponed during the attack.

TEST YOUR UNDERSTANDING

10. Why should companies undertake a postmortem evaluation after an attack?

Organization of the CSIRT

Most of what we have been describing so far are the actions taken by the IT and IT security staffs. However, as noted earlier in this chapter, most firms use computer security incident response teams (CSIRTs) to manage major incidents. CSIRTs have broader participation, including the following:

- A senior manager should chair the CSIRT. All security decisions during a major incident are *business* decisions. Only senior managers can decide whether to take down an e-commerce server. Although the *manager* of the CSIRT is likely to be an IT security employee, his or her role has to be subordinate to business chair.
- The CSIRT should have members from affected line organizations. In the case of an e-commerce incident, for instance, someone from the e-commerce department should participate in the decision making, although they may not be permanent members of the CSIRT.
- The firm's public relations director should be a member of the CSIRT. The PR director *must* be the only voice that speaks for the corporation to the outside world during an incident. IT staff members and IT security staff members should never speak directly to the press or other outside parties. Even within a firm, the public relations director should handle communications.
- The firm's legal counsel should be a member of the team to place everything in the proper legal framework. The legal counsel may advise on the legal implications of various actions, including the wisdom of attempting to prosecute.
- The firm's human resources department should be a member to offer guidance on labor issues. In addition, if the perpetrator is an employee, the human resources department will implement sanctions.

TEST YOUR UNDERSTANDING

11. a. Why should a senior manager head the CSIRT?

    b. Why should members of affected line departments be on CSIRT?

    c. Who is the only person who should speak on behalf of the firm?

    d. Why should the firm's legal counsel be on the CSIRT?

    e. Why should a firm's human resource department be on the CSIRT?

Legal Considerations

If a company decides to pursue prosecution, it needs a strong understanding of the law. Although lawyers do the hard legal work, IT security people need a general understanding of legal processes if they hope to avoid making mistakes that invalidate their cases.

Also, a firm may find itself in the defendant's chair. It may fail to protect customer data, an employee may attack computers at another firm, or a compromised computer may attack other firm. In these cases, too, IT security needs a reasonable understanding of legal processes.

Criminal versus Civil Law

Perhaps the most fundamental distinction in law is the distinction between criminal law and civil law. Figure 9-6 shows that this distinction has several factors.

- Most importantly, **criminal law** deals with violations of **criminal statutes**, which are laws that specify proscribed behavior. In contrast, civil law deals with interpretations of rights and duties that companies or individuals have relative to each other.
- In terms of *punishment*, criminal cases may involve jail time and fines, while civil cases only result in monetary penalties or orders to the defendant to take or not take certain actions.
- Most visibly, criminal cases are brought by a **prosecutor** against a **defendant**, while in civil cases the **plaintiff** (the party that brings the tort) initiates the case against the defendant. Typically, a party being sued will bring a countersuit against the suing party. In such cases, both parties are plaintiffs and both are defendants.
- In criminal cases, the prosecutor is required to prove a defendant's guilt *beyond a reasonable doubt*. In a civil case, the plaintiff usually only has to prove a *preponderance of*

Dimension	Criminal Law	Civil Law
Deals with	Violations of criminal statutes	Interpretations of rights and duties that companies or individuals have relative to each other
Penalties	Jail time and fines	Monetary penalties and orders to parties to take or not take certain actions
Cases brought by	Prosecutors	Plaintiff is one of the two parties
Criterion for verdict	Beyond a reasonable doubt	Preponderance of the evidence (usually)
Requires *mens rea* (guilty mind)	Usually	Rarely, although may affect the imposed penalty
Applicable to IT security	Yes. To prosecute attackers and to avoid breaking the law	Yes. To avoid or minimize civil trials and judgments

FIGURE 9-6   Criminal Law versus Civil Law

the evidence (more than 50%) that the defendant is liable for damages. Preponderance of the evidence is a much lower standard of proof.[7]
- In criminal cases, the prosecutor usually must prove *mens rea*[8]—that the defendant was in a certain mental state, such as having the intention to commit the act. Mental state is a complex topic, and requirements to prove a particular mental state vary strongly across different types of crime. In U.S. federal hacking, for example, the prosecutor must prove that the defendant *intentionally* accessed resources without authorization or in excess of authorization. However, the prosecutor is not required to prove that the defendant intended to do damage if damage occurred.[9] In contrast, civil cases usually do not require the plaintiff to prove a certain mental state in the defendant.

IT security professionals need to understand both criminal and civil cases. If a company loses the personal information of its customers, for instance, it is likely to be the subject of a civil case. If a company wishes a computer criminal punished, however, it will have to convince a prosecutor to pursue a criminal trial.

Sometimes the same conduct may violate both criminal and civil laws. A defendant whose actions violate both criminal and civil rules may be criminally prosecuted by the state and later civilly sued by a victim for monetary damages. For instance, in 1995, O. J. Simpson was prosecuted for homicide and found not guilty. In an entirely separate case, Simpson was also sued civilly for "wrongful death" by the victims' families. At the close of the civil case, in 1997, Simpson was found "liable" for the victims' deaths and ordered to pay millions of dollars in damages.

TEST YOUR UNDERSTANDING

12. **a.** What different actions do criminal and civil law deal with?
    b. How do punishments differ in civil and criminal law?
    c. Who brings lawsuits in civil and criminal cases?
    d. What is the normal standard for deciding a case in civil and criminal trials?
    e. What is *mens rea*?
    f. In what type of trial is *mens rea* important?
    g. Can a person be tried separately in a criminal trial and later in a civil trial?

Jurisdictions

Different government bodies have different **jurisdictions**—areas of responsibility within which they can make and enforce laws but beyond which they cannot. These jurisdictions apply to **cyberlaw**, which is any law dealing with information technology.

Cyberlaw is any law dealing with information technology.

(Continued)

---

[7] If fraud is alleged, however, the level of proof in civil cases rises to *clear and convincing evidence*, which falls somewhere between the other two levels of proof.

[8] This term comes from the legal dictum *et actus non facit reum, nisi mens sit rea*, which means that "the act is not guilty unless the mind is guilty."

[9] In the *United States vs. Sablan* (1996), the United States District Court for the District of Guam denied an appeal. In the denial, the court ruled that access has to be intentional but that damage does not have to be intentional for a crime to be committed.

Legal Considerations   (Continued)

Cyberlaw

Cyberlaw is any law dealing with information technology

Jurisdictions

Areas of responsibility within which government bodies can make and enforce law but beyond which they cannot

The United States Federal Judicial System

U.S. District Courts

94 in the United States

Decisions in trials are only binding on the litigants

U.S. Circuit Courts of Appeal

13 in the United States

Do not conduct trials

Review district court decisions

Decisions are precedents only for the district courts under the circuit court of appeals making a decision

U.S. Supreme Court

Final arbiter of U.S. federal law

Only hears about 100 cases per year

Usually only reviews cases that involve conflicts between appellate court precedents or important constitutional issues

U.S. State and Local Law

In the United States, many powers are reserved for the states

This typically includes the prosecution of crimes taking place within a state or that do not affect interstate commerce

For most cybercrimes committed within a state, state law applies

State cybercrime laws vary widely

Local police usually investigate crimes under both local and state laws

International Law

Differences are wide and rapidly changing (generally improving)

Important to multinational firms

Also important to purely domestic firms

Suppliers and buyers may be in other countries

Attackers may be in other countries

Several treaties exist to harmonize laws and facilitate cross-border prosecution

Generally immature

FIGURE 9-7   Jurisdictions (Study Figure)

The United States Federal Judicial System

In the U.S. federal system, the U.S. Constitution is the source of constitutional law and Congress is the source of statutes. The federal court system is the source of **case law**, in which judicial decisions in individual cases set precedents for how laws will be interpreted in subsequent trials. Case law allows the courts to clarify the application of specific laws and clarify which laws take precedent when they conflict. The federal court system has three levels:

- At the lowest level, trials are held in **U.S. District Courts**. There are 94 districts in the United States. Decisions are only binding on the participants in individual trials, so the District Courts do not make case law.
- U.S. **Circuit Courts of Appeal** do not conduct trials. Instead, they selectively review decisions made by district court judges. Federal courts of appeals produce case law that is binding on all district courts within the appellate court's territory. It is possible for appellate courts in different regions to impose different case law on district courts. In the United States, there are 13 circuits.
- The **U.S. Supreme Court** is the final arbiter of law in the United States. The Supreme Court usually only reviews cases that involve conflicts between appellate court rulings or important constitutional issues. The Supreme Court typically only hears about 100 cases per year.

U.S. State and Local Laws

The U.S. Constitution recognizes that the states reserve many powers. Consequently, the federal government is limited in its ability to act in cases that do not involve litigants from different states or that do not involve interstate commerce. For instance, generally speaking, only the hacking of federal government computers or computers that affect interstate commerce is subject to federal statutes and courts.

For most crimes committed within a state, state laws apply. Consequently, most computer crimes are prosecuted under state statutes and in state courts. As you might suspect, state cybercrime laws vary widely. Consequently, it is important for security professionals to understand laws and prosecution in their own states or in the several states in which their company operates.

Like the federal government, most states have several levels of courts. In fact, they often have two "lowest" levels of courts—one level for minor violations and another for more serious violations. The federal court system does not require this because federal law rarely involves minor infractions. In addition, even when more serious infractions occur, federal prosecutors typically will not pursue the case unless damages are substantial.

Local laws for cities and other small jurisdictions within a state generally involve such local issues as zoning and traffic violations. However, the local police typically investigate crimes committed against both local and state laws.

International Law

Internationally, cybercrime laws also vary widely. For criminal and civil laws involving computers, the differences between countries often are large and rapidly changing (in most cases, getting tougher). International law is important for multinational companies and even for companies who only deal with customers or suppliers in other countries.

International law is also important because attackers often live in a different country than the victim. A number of treaties have been signed to promote international cooperation in harmonizing laws and in cross-border prosecution, but the general state of international cooperation at this stage is immature.

TEST YOUR UNDERSTANDING

13. **a.** What is case law?
    b. What are jurisdictions?
    c. What is cyberlaw?
    d. What are the three levels of U.S. federal courts?
    e. Which levels can create precedents?

(Continued)

Legal Considerations   (Continued)

f. Does federal jurisdiction typically extend to computer crimes that are committed entirely within a state and that do not have a bearing on interstate commerce?
g. Who is likely to investigate a cybercrime that takes place within a city?
h. Are international laws regarding cybercrime fairly uniform?
i. Why should companies that do business only within a country be concerned about international cyberlaw?

Evidence and Computer Forensics

In the courts, there are strong rules for what evidence will be **admissible** (allowed) into court. The goal is to protect the jury from hearing evidence that is unreliable. Quite simply, jurors are not trusted to be able to evaluate the reliability of evidence. Common law, for instance, has long been suspicious of hearsay evidence, which involves overhearing what someone said while not under oath. Only in very limited circumstances is hearsay evidence admissible.

In the U.S. federal court system, the rules for the admissibility of evidence are codified in the **Federal Rules of Evidence**. The Rules are updated every few years and now have strong rules for evaluating the admissibility of electronic evidence.

Given the strictness of federal evidence rules, as well as the strictness of evidence rules in other court systems, information is only likely to be admissible if it is collected by someone with training in both the rules of evidence and proper methods of computer data collection. A **computer forensics expert** is a professional who is trained to collect and evaluate computer evidence in ways that are likely to be admissible in court. Computer forensics experts, for instance, have special equipment for copying the contents of hard drives in ways that are technically prevented from making any changes to the original disk drive. Mistakes in computer data collection typically will invalidate evidence, and the courts will not allow the evidence to be presented to the jury at all.

A computer forensics expert is a professional who is trained to collect and evaluate computer evidence in ways that are likely to be admissible in court

Admissibility of Evidence
   Unreliable evidence may be kept from juries
   Belief that juries cannot evaluate unreliable evidence properly
   Example: hearsay evidence

Federal Rules of Civil Procedure
   Guide U.S. courts
   Now have strong rules for evaluating the admissibility of electronic evidence

Computer Forensics Experts
   Professional trained to collect and evaluate computer evidence in ways that are likely to be admissible in court
   Meet with them before there is a need because the initial moments of an intrusion require correct action

Expert Witnesses
   Normally, witnesses can only testify regarding facts, not interpretations
   Expert witnesses may interpret facts to make them comprehensible to the jury in situations where juries are likely to have a difficult time evaluating the evidence themselves

FIGURE 9-8 Evidence and Computer Forensics (Study Figure)

In court testimony, normal witnesses may only testify about facts and may not try to interpret the facts for the jury. **Expert witnesses**, in contrast, may interpret facts to make the evidence comprehensible to the jury in situations where juries are likely to have a difficult time evaluating the evidence themselves. Certified forensics experts are expert witnesses.

Given the importance of admissibility, companies should use forensics experts when prosecution is anticipated. Given the importance of timelines, they should have prior discussion with their chosen forensics experts to understand what may be required. Also, their first step in any investigation should be contacting a forensics expert for advice. Normally, for instance, computer evidence is best preserved by unplugging the computer, but this is not always the case. Typically, computer forensics experts can collect data from an affected system and get it operational again for ongoing use.

TEST YOUR UNDERSTANDING

14. **a.** Why will courts not admit unreliable evidence?
    b. What is a computer forensics expert?
    c. What type of witness is allowed to interpret facts for juries?
    d. Why should companies work with forensics professionals before they have a need for them?

U.S. Federal Cybercrime Laws

Although the United States is a sovereign country, it is, in many ways, a confederation of individual states that have ceded some power to the national government. We have already seen that although federal laws cover some things, there often need to be state laws to supplement federal laws. However, we will focus on U.S. federal cybercrime laws because they are the most widely used.

Computer Hacking, Malware Attacks, Denial-of-Service Attacks, and Other Attacks (18 U.S.C. § 1030)

In the United States, the main federal law regarding hacking is United States Code Title 18, Part I (Crimes) Section 1030—**18 U.S.C. § 1030**. Although this section does not specifically use the terms *hacking*, *malware*, and *denial-of-service attacks*, these are its main focuses.[10]

HACKING   Section 1030 prohibits the intentional access of protected computers without authorization or exceeding authorization. **Protected computers** include "government computers, financial institution computers, and any computer which is used in interstate or foreign commerce or communications."[11] Note that this definition does not include all U.S. computers, although if an attack takes place against a computer in another state, this usually comes under the purview for the U.S. government.

DENIAL-OF-SERVICE AND MALWARE ATTACKS   Section 1030 also prohibits the "transmission of a program, information, code, or command that intentionally causes damage without authorization to a protected computer." This paragraph prohibits denial-of-service (DoS) attacks, most malware attacks, and various other types of damaging automated attacks.

(Continued)

---

[10] Section 1030 is the result of a series of laws, including the Computer Fraud and Abuse Act of 1986, the National Information Infrastructure Protection Act of 1996, and the Homeland Security Act of 2002.

[11] The Computer Crime and Intellectual Property Section, United States Department of Justice, *The National Information Infrastructure Protection Act of 1996: Legislative Analysis*, http://www.cybercrime.gov/1030analysis.html.

Legal Considerations (Continued)

The Situation

In some ways, including laws, the United States is more of a confederation of states than a single country

State laws are very important in many cases

18 U.S.C. § 1030

United States Code Title 18, Part I (Crimes) Section 1030

Actions prohibited

Hacking

Malware

Denial of service

Protected computers

Applicability is limited to protected computers

Include "government computers, financial institution computers, and any computer which is used in interstate or foreign commerce or communications."

Often require damage threshold for prosecution

The FBI may require even higher damages to prosecute

18 U.S.C. § 2511

Prohibits the interception of electronic messages, both en route and after the message is received and stored

Allows e-mail service providers to read the content of mail

A company can read employee mail if it owns the mail system

Other Federal Laws

Many traditional federal criminal laws may apply in individual cases

For example, fraud, extortion, and the theft of trade secrets

These laws often have far harsher consequences than cybercrime laws

FIGURE 9-9 Federal Cybercrime Laws (Study Figure)

DAMAGE THRESHOLDS In Section 1030, there usually are **damage thresholds** (minimum amounts of damage) that must occur before attackers are in violation of the law. The damage threshold often is only a few thousand dollars, and it is easy to do that much damage accidentally. However, the Federal Bureau of Investigation (FBI), which prosecutes most federal cybercrime, usually will not pursue prosecution unless the amount of damage is much higher.

Confidentiality in Message Transmission

We have just seen that 18 U.S.C. § 1030 deals with multiple types of cybercrime. However, other parts of the federal code are also important in prosecuting cybercrime. For example, **18 U.S.C. § 2511** prohibits the interception of electronic messages, both en route and after the message is received and stored.

The law does allow e-mail service providers to read e-mail. This means that a company owning its e-mail system may read employee e-mail without asking its employees' permission. However, if the company outsources e-mail, this freedom may not exist.

Other Federal Laws

Of course, the federal government has many other laws involving fraud, extortion, the theft of trade secrets, and many other matters. If computer intrusions involve these other laws, the penalties in these other laws—which usually are substantially higher—will apply.

TEST YOUR UNDERSTANDING

15. **a.** What section of which title of the United States Code prohibits hacking?
    b. What other attacks does it prohibit?
    c. Does it protect all computers?
    d. What are damage thresholds?
    e. What types of acts does 18 U.S.C. § 2511 prohibit?

INTRUSION DETECTION SYSTEMS

Attacks often proceed invisibly from the viewpoint of humans—merely changing magnetic patterns on disks or electronic patterns in memory. As we saw in Chapter 6, an **intrusion detection system (IDS)** is software and hardware that captures suspicious network and host activity data in event logs and provides automatic tools to generate alarms as well as query and reporting tools to help administrators analyze the data interactively during and after an incident.

> *An intrusion detection system (IDS) is software and hardware that captures suspicious network and host activity data in event logs and provides automatic tools to generate alarms and query and reporting tools to help administrators analyze the data interactively during and after an incident.*

An IDS is like a security camera in a building. A security camera may provide real-time intrusion detection if someone is monitoring the camera, and it provides tapes that can be examined after an incident, but security cameras in buildings do not replace door locks or safes. Similarly, an IDS is only an element in the security architecture. It does not stop intrusions; it only detects them. To use other terminology, it is a detective control, not a preventative control.

Event logging for suspicious events

Sometimes, send alarms

A detective control, not a preventative or restorative control

Usually, too many false positives (false alarms)

    Can be reduced by tuning the IDS not to give meaningless alerts

    Example, a UNIX attack in an all-Windows environment

    Example, a Windows Server 2000 attack if a server farm only uses newer versions of Windows server

---

FIGURE 9-10   Intrusion Detection Systems (IDSs) (Study Figure)

As Chapter 6 noted, the major problem with IDSs is **false positives**, that is, false alarms. Like the boy who cried "Wolf" too often, IDSs tend to be ignored if they generate many false positives, just as most people ignore car alarms.

TEST YOUR UNDERSTANDING

16. **a.** What is an IDS?
    b. Is an IDS a preventative, detective, or restorative control?
    c. What are false positives?
    d. Why are false positives problems for IDSs?

Functions of an IDS

Figure 9-11 shows that an IDS has four major functions: logging, automated analysis by the IDS, administrator actions, and management.

LOGGING (DATA COLLECTION)   The logging function captures discrete activities, such as the arrival of a packet or an attempt to log in. Each activity is time stamped and stored in a sequential file sorted by time. This file holds the raw data that IDSs administrators must analyze to respond correctly.

AUTOMATED ANALYSIS BY THE IDS   IDSs do a good deal of automated analysis throughout the day. Administrators tend to be unaware of this analysis unless the IDS issues a warning based on what it finds during automated analysis.

Attack Signatures   Several general methods are available for the IDS to find patterns in the large amount of data in its log files. The simplest IDS analysis is the use of attack signatures. These identify known attack patterns. This works much of the time but fails to detect attacks that do not have signatures in the signature database.

Anomaly Detection   The most sophisticated techniques involve anomaly detection, in which the IDS looks for deviations from historical traffic patterns. Anomaly

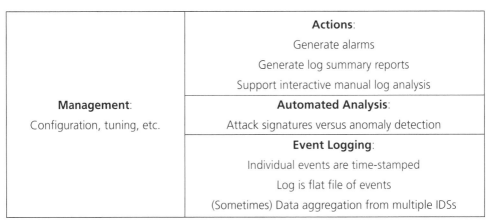

Management: Configuration, tuning, etc.	**Actions**:
	Generate alarms
	Generate log summary reports
	Support interactive manual log analysis
	Automated Analysis:
	Attack signatures versus anomaly detection
	Event Logging:
	Individual events are time-stamped
	Log is flat file of events
	(Sometimes) Data aggregation from multiple IDSs

FIGURE 9-11   Functions of a Simple IDS

detection can detect new threats that do not yet have attack signatures, but it is less precise than attack signatures.

ACTIONS Finally, there are the actions taken by the IDS and by the people using it.

    Alarms Merely collecting and analyzing data accomplishes nothing. IDSs must use results from analysis to interact with humans. Most obviously, they generate **alarms** if analysis indicates a dangerous condition.

    The IDS should only generate alarms for high-threat conditions. If an IDS were to send alarms for *all* threats, security administrators would be flooded with alerts. (Think of hair-trigger car alarms.) Some firms find that even high-threat alarms are too numerous (and too frequently incorrect) and throw away their IDSs.

    Alarms should not be generalized indicators that something appears to be wrong.

- Alarms should be as specific as possible, giving the user a description of what the problem is.
- There should be a way to test the alarm for accuracy, and
- The alarm should give advice about what the security administrator should do.

    Log Summary Reports IDSs only send alarms for high-risk threats. They merely log other threats. However, security administrators need to understand these lesser threats as well. IDSs usually produce **log summary reports** that list various types of suspicious activity. They also indicate threat priority by type of threat or by statistical analysis indicating high frequency. IDS administrators need to study these reports at least daily.

    Support for Interactive Manual Log Analysis In addition, IDSs help humans make sense of data collected by providing **interactive manual log analysis** tools to look through the log files. This allows security administrators to "drill down" into log files to better understand an ongoing or completed attack and to filter out irrelevant entries. For instance, a security analyst might look at all attacks against e-mail servers in the last three hours.

MANAGEMENT The final function is management. IDSs are not like toasters. You cannot just plug them in and expect them to provide security by themselves. As we will see later, a firm must do many things to manage an IDS. Poor management will create excessive work and may render the IDS useless.

TEST YOUR UNDERSTANDING

17. **a.** What are the four functions of IDSs?
   b. What are the two types of analysis that IDSs usually do?
   c. What types of action did this section mention?
   d. What information should alarms contain?
   e. What is the purpose of log summary reports?
   f. Describe interactive log file analysis.

Distributed IDSs

In a simple IDS, all four functions exist in a single device. Although stand-alone IDSs exist, they are of limited use. To understand a security incident, it normally is necessary to see the broader picture of which packets are flowing through the network and what is happening at multiple hosts. It is normal for a single host to reboot. If several hosts reboot in a few minutes, however, this should be a serious wake-up call. Figure 9-12 shows a distributed IDS that can collect data from many devices at a central manager console (client PC or Unix workstation).

AGENTS Each monitoring device has a software **agent** that collects event data and stores them in log files on the monitoring devices. Sometimes, agents also do some analysis and alarm reporting.

MANAGER AND INTEGRATED LOG FILE The **manager** program is responsible for integrating the information from the multiple agents that run on multiple monitoring devices. To do so, the manager must collect log files from various devices and integrate them into a single **integrated log file** (or at most a few log files). The manager must analyze the log file data, generate alarms, and allow humans to do interactive data queries.

BATCH VERSUS REAL-TIME DATA TRANSFER The agent can transfer log files to the manager in two ways. The least expensive is **batch transfer**, in which the agent waits until it has several minutes or several hours of data and then sends a block of log file data to the manager. Batch-mode transfers place the least load on the network because sending large blocks of data instead of sending each transactions is efficient. It also minimizes the number of disruptions of the manager. (Every interruption on a host requires considerable CPU activity.)

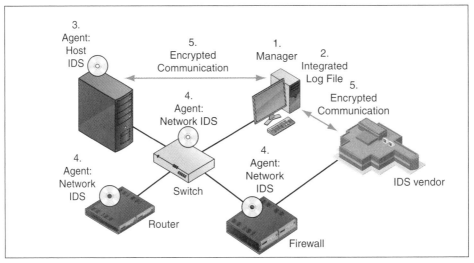

FIGURE 9-12 Distributed IDS

In contrast, in **real-time transfers**, each event's data goes to the manager immediately. This is attractive because one of the first things that many hackers do after taking over a device is to delete or at least disable event logging. If the attacker succeeds in doing that, and if the last batch-mode transfer was done some time before the attacker hacked the system, then data for all of their activities will be lost. With real-time transfers, only the activities after the deletion or disabling of event logging will be lost.[12]

SECURE MANAGER-AGENT COMMUNICATION   Communication between the agents and the manager should be secure, with authentication, integrity checking, confidentiality, and anti-replay protection. If an attacker can hack a computer and spoof an agent or manager, the result will be chaos.

VENDOR COMMUNICATION   The vendor also has a role in this process. Vendors periodically create new filtering rules. Companies must downloaded them and install them on all IDSs, usually via the manager. Communication between the vendor and the manager also needs to be secure, with authentication, integrity checking, confidentiality, and anti-replay protection.

TEST YOUR UNDERSTANDING

18. **a.** What is the advantage of a distributed IDS?
    b. Name the elements in a distributed IDS.
    c. Distinguish between the manager and agents.
    d. Distinguish between batch and real-time transfers for event data.
    e. What is the advantage of each type?
    f. What two types of communication must be secure?

Network IDSs (NIDSs)

So far, we have spoken vaguely of "agents." Now we will look at the two specific types of agents that companies use. As Figure 9-12 shows, there are two types of agents—network IDSs and host IDSs.

We will begin with **network IDSs (NIDSs)**, which capture packets as they travel through a network.

STAND-ALONE NIDSS   As Figure 9-12 shows, **stand-alone NIDSs** are boxes located at various points in the network. They read and analyze all network frames that pass by them. They essentially are corporate-owned sniffers.

SWITCH AND ROUTER NIDSS   In contrast, **switch NIDSs** and **router NIDSs** are switches and routers that have IDS software. Typically, these capture data on all ports.

STRENGTHS OF NIDSS   The strength of NIDSs is that they can see all packets passing through some locations in the network. Often, these packets are highly diagnostic of attacks.

---

[12] The most widely used network event data transfer standard is SYSLOG, which is available on almost all Unix system and which is available for Windows systems as well. SYSLOG has rules for which packets to logged and whether each rule's log entries should be held locally or sent to a remote SYSLOG server.

Network IDSs (NIDSs)
 Stand-alone device or built into a switch or router
 NIDSs see and can filter all packets passing through them
 Switch or router NIDSs can collect data on all ports
 A NIDS collects data for only its portion of the network
  Blind spots in network where no NIDS data are collected
 Cannot filter encrypted packets

Host IDSs (HIDSs)
 Attractions
  Provide highly detailed information for the specific host
 Weaknesses of Host IDSs
  Limited Viewpoint; Only one host
  Host IDSs can be attacked and disabled
 Operating System Monitors
  Collects data on operating system events
  Multiple failed logins
  Creating new accounts
  Adding new executables (programs—may be attack programs)
  Modifying executables (installing Trojan horses does this)
  Adding registry keys (changes how system works)
  Changing or deleting system logs and audit files
  Changing system audit policies
  User accessing critical system files
  User accessing unusual files
  Changing the OS monitor itself

FIGURE 9-13 Network IDSs (NIDSs) and Host IDSs (HIDSs) (Study Figure)

WEAKNESSES OF NIDSS However, NIDSs have a number of weaknesses that cause problems unless supplemented by non-network IDSs.

First, although switch and router NIDSs offer the possibility of internal data collection, no firm can afford to operate agents on all internal switches and routers. Consequently, all firms have blind spots where NIDSs cannot see packets. If only border NIDSs are used, in fact, then the entire internal network is one large blind spot.

Second, like firewalls, NIDSs cannot scan encrypted data. Although NIDSs can scan unencrypted parts of an encrypted packet (typically, an added IP header), this provides limited information. As encryption increases in popularity, the effectiveness of NIDSs will degrade proportionally.

TEST YOUR UNDERSTANDING

19. **a.** At what information do NIDSs look?
 b. Distinguish between stand-alone NIDSs and switch-based or router-based NIDSs.
 c. What are the strengths of NIDs?
 d. What are the two weaknesses of NIDSs?

Host IDSs

A firm has many host computers. The most critical hosts are the firm's servers. **Host IDSs** (HIDSs) work on data collected on the host computer.

ATTRACTION OF HIDSs The main attraction of HIDSs is that they provide highly specific information about what happened on a particular host. This is important for problem diagnosis.

WEAKNESSES OF HOST IDSs

Limited Viewpoint Host IDSs have two major weaknesses. First, a host IDS has a limited view of what is happening on the network. The same myopic focus that allows them to be specific also means they cannot see the broader picture. Repeated login failures on one host are a cause for concern. Repeated login failures on multiple hosts within a short time period are a much greater cause for concern.

Host IDSs Can Be Compromised In addition, host IDSs are subject to attack. As noted earlier, an attacker can delete or change log files, effectively making the attacker invisible to the HIDS.[13]

HOST IDSs: OPERATING SYSTEM MONITORS Most host IDSs are **operating system monitors**, which focus on operating system events. Here are some data typically collected by operating system monitor IDSs.

- Multiple failed logins.
- Creating new accounts.
- Adding new executables (programs—may be attack programs).
- Modifying executables (installing Trojan horses does this).
- Adding registry keys (changes how system works).
- Changing or deleting system logs and audit files.
- Changing system audit policies.
- User accessing critical system files.
- User accessing unusual files.
- Changing the OS monitor itself.

TEST YOUR UNDERSTANDING

20. **a.** What is the major attraction of a HIDS?
    b. What are the two weaknesses of host IDSs?
    c. List some things at which host operating system monitors look.

---

[13] Another way to analyze what has happened on the host is to use a file integrity checker. Chapter 3 explained that message digests can help users know if a message has been changed. File integrity checkers create message digests of all system files that are likely to be changed rarely or never. They can check this database periodically against newly generated message digests to determine whether there have been changes. Unfortunately, quite a few system files *do* change occasionally for legitimate reasons, so the number of false alarms is high until such files are ignored. Tripwire is the most widely used file integrity checker.

Log Files

TIME-STAMPED EVENTS   All log files have the same core format. Each is a flat file of log entries. Each **log entry** has a *time stamp* and an *event type*. Beyond that, log files may have other information to help diagnose the event. For instance, NIDS log files might contain basic packet field values. In turn, HIDS entries regarding suspicious file operations will name the file, the action performed on the file, and the user or program taking the action.

INDIVIDUAL LOGS   The trouble with log files from individual NIDSs or host IDSs is that each log file represents only a local view of activities at any moment. The slow scanning of many hosts on the network, for instance, is not likely to attract the attention of any single host or network-monitoring agent.

INTEGRATED LOGS   To provide a better view of events, companies usually import log file data from multiple host IDSs and NIDSs. In addition to storing all the log files on one computer, distributed IDSs attempt to aggregate all log entries from multiple sources into a single **integrated log file** that contains data from many places around the network for any given moment. Figure 9-15 shows one of these integrated lot files. The process of creating integrated log files is called **aggregation**.

Difficult to Create   If a company has NIDSs and HIDSs from multiple vendors, each IDS is likely to use a different format for log file entries. If this is the case, it will be extremely difficult and perhaps impossible to create an integrated log. However, few firms are likely to standardize on one vendor simply to be able to create integrated logs. In addition, some vendors deal only with host logging, stand-alone network logging, or switch or router logging.

Time Synchronization   If the times on the various IDSs are off by even a few thousandths of a second, it will be extremely difficult to see what is happening at a

---

Log Files
- Flat files of time-stamped events
- Individual logs for single NIDs or HIDs
- Integrated logs
  - Aggregation of event logs from multiple IDS agents (Figure 9-12)
  - Difficult to create because of format incompatibilities
  - Time synchronization of IDS event logs is crucial (Network Time Protocol)

Event Correlation (Figure 9-15)
- Suspicious patterns in a series of events across multiple devices
- Difficult because the relevant events exist in much larger event streams that are logged
- Usually requires many analysis of the integrated log file data

FIGURE 9-14 Analyzing Log Files (Study Figure)

Sample Log File (many irrelevant log entries not shown)

1.   8:45:05:47. Packet from 1.15.3.6 to 60.3.4.5 (NIDS log entry)

2.   8:45:07:49. Host 60.3.4.5. Failed login attempt for account Lee (Host 60.3.4.5 log entry)

3.   8:45:07:50. Packet from 60.3.4.5 to 1.15.3.6 (NIDS)

4.   8:45:50:15. Packet from 1.15.3.6 to 60.3.4.5 (NIDS)

5.   8:45:50:18. Host 60.3.4.5. Failed login attempt for account Lee (HIDS)

6.   8:45:50:19. Packet from 60.3.4.5 to 1.15.3.6 (NIDS)

7.   8:49:07:44. Packet from 1.15.3.6 to 60.3.4.5 (NIDS)

8.   8:49:07:47. Host 60.3.4.5. Successful login attempt for account Lee (HIDS)

9.   8:49:07:48. Packet from 60.3.4.5 to 1.15.3.6 (NIDS)

10. 8:56:12:30. Packet from 60.3.4.5 to 123.28.5.210. TFTP request (NIDS)

11. 8:56:28:07. Series of packets from 123.28.5.210 and 60.3.4.5. TFTP response (NIDS)

12. No more host log entries

(The log would not say this; it would merely stop sending events)

13. 9:03.17:33. Series of packets between 60.3.4.5 and 1.17.8.40. SMTP (NIDS)

14. 9:05.55:89. Series of packets between 60.3.4.5 and 1.17.8.40. SMTP (NIDS)

15. 9:11.22:22. Series of packets between 60.3.4.5 and 1.17.8.40. SMTP (NIDS)

16. 9:15.17:47. Series of packets between 60.3.4.5 and 1.17.8.40. SMTP (NIDS)

17. 9:20:12:05. Packet from 60.3.4.5 to 60.0.1.1. TCP SYN=1, Destination Port 80 (NIDS)

18. 9:20:12:07: Packet from 60.0.1.1 to 60.3.4.5. TCP RST=1, Source Port 80 (NIDS)

19. 9:20:12:08. Packet from 60.3.4.5 to 60.0.1.2. TCP SYN=1, Destination Port 80 (NIDS)

20. 9:20:12:11 Packet from 60.3.4.5 to 60.0.1.3. TCP SYN=1, Destination Port 80 (NIDS)

21. 9:20:12:12. Packet from 60.0.1.3 to 60.3.4.5. TCP SYN=1; ACK=1, Source Port 80 (NIDS)

FIGURE 9-15   Event Correlation for an Integrated Log File

particular moment in time—especially if the attack is automated and occurs quickly. The **Network Time Protocol (NTP)** allows this type of synchronization. All devices must be synchronized to a single internal NTP server.

EVENT CORRELATION   Often, single events are suspicious. If an application program tries to change a system executable, this is highly suggestive of an attack. In other cases, events are not suspicious individually because attackers tend to do many of the same things that ordinary users do. In such cases, only sequences of several events are likely to be suggestive of attacks. The analysis of multi-event patterns is called **event correlation**.

For instance, one manager noted with some interest that a server was having a large number of server message block authorization failures, indicating unsuccessful attempts to access files on another server.[14] When three other servers began to have large number of failed SMB authorizations, the investigation was kicked into high gear. The problem turned out to be the spread of a virus, Sircam, which spread partially by infecting network shares on other computers. This allowed the company to begin acting while the virus was just beginning to spread.

Figure 9-15 shows an integrated log file that contains information from network logs and a host operating system log. Only events pertaining to the attack are shown. In the thought questions, you will be asked to describe patterns of activities that are suspicious and whether they are suggestive of an attack or definitively prove an attack.

To get you started, note that the person logging in has two failed logins before succeeding. This could indicate password guessing. However, ordinary users sometimes mistype or forget their passwords, so the two failed logins are not collectively definitive. Note that there is enough time between login attempts to indicate a human actor. If the attempts were only hundreds of a second apart, that would suggest an automated attack and would be definitive proof that an attack is occurring.

MANUAL ANALYSIS   Finding useful patterns in integrated log files like the one shown in Figure 9-15 is not for the faint of heart. In addition, we have greatly simplified the task by removing irrelevant entries from the log file. The analyst must first sort through the log file looking for the relevant entries. This requires a high level of experience and analytical abilities.

TEST YOUR UNDERSTANDING

21. **a.** Why are integrated log files good?
    b. Why are they difficult to create?
    c. Explain the time synchronization issue for integrated log files.
    d. How do companies achieve time synchronization?
    e. What is event correlation?
    f. Distinguish between aggregation and event correlation.
    g. Why is analyzing log file data difficult?
    h. In Figure 9-15, how long is the delay between the first attempted login and the second?
    i. Does this indicate that the attack is a human attack or an automated attack?

Managing IDSs

Companies cannot just plug in IDSs and expect great results. Perhaps more than any other security technologies today, IDSs require constant attention. Companies without considerable security expertise and commitment to continuing outlays of time and money should not purchase IDSs.

TUNING FOR PRECISION   An important management concern is **precision**, meaning that the IDS should report all attack events and report as few false alarms as possible.

False Positives   As noted earlier in this chapter and in Chapter 6, IDSs tend to generate many false alarms, known technically as **false positives**. In many cases, false positives will outnumber true alarms ten-to-one or even more. In fact, the large

---

[14] NetForensics, "Case Study: Major New York Hospital System," undated. Accessed July 17, 2002. http://www.netforensics.com/healthcarecase.html.

Tuning for Precision
  Too many false positives
    False alarms
    Can overwhelm administrators, dull vigilance
  False negatives allow attacks to proceed unseen
  Tuning for false positives turns off unnecessary rules, reduces alarm levels of unlikely rules
    For instance, alarms for attacks against Solaris operating systems can be deleted if a firm has no Sun Microsystems servers
    Tuning requires a great deal of expensive labor
    Even after tuning, most alerts will be false positives

Updates
  Program, attack signatures must be updated frequently

Processing Performance
  If processing speed cannot keep up with network traffic, some packets will not be examined
  This can make some IDSs useless during attacks that increase the traffic load

Storage
  There will be limited disk storage for log files
  When log files reach storage limits, they must be archived
  Event correlation is difficult across multiple backup tapes
  Adding more disk capacity reduces the problem but never eliminates it

FIGURE 9-16 Managing IDSs (Study Figure)

---

number of false positives generated by IDSs is the major problem with IDSs today, causing many firms to stop using them after a trial period.

False Negatives IDSs also have many **false negatives**—failures to report true attack activities. False negatives are far more dangerous than false positives because they allow real attacks to continue undetected. However, because false negatives are not intrusive and often are undetected, their importance often is unappreciated.

Tuning A firm can dramatically reduce the number of false positives if it "tunes" its IDS. **Tuning** is turning off unnecessary rules and reducing the severity level in the alarms generated by other rules.

First, the firm should drop rules that make no sense in a particular environment. For instance, if an organization uses all Unix servers, why should its IDS test for and create an alarm for an attack designed to compromise the IIS webserver program (which runs only on Windows servers)? Even with tuning, false positives will tend to dominate alerts. Counterpane, a managed security company, found that even after tuning, only 14 percent were actual attacks.[15]

---

[15] Even with tuning, false positives will tend to dominate alerts. Counterpane, a managed security company, found that even after tuning, only 14 percent were actual attacks. Counterpane Internet Security, "Counterpane Internet Security's Customers Show Dramatic Improvement in Internet Security," April 11, 2002. http://www.counterpane.com/pr-500.html.

UPDATES   Companies must update their IDS attack signatures frequently. Often, vendors update their signatures weekly or even more often. Of course if a company tunes its IDS rules, it also must tune the rules in each update.

PROCESSING PERFORMANCE   Performance problems can make an IDS useless. First, it takes a large number of CPU cycles to process each event. As network traffic grows, and as the number of attack signatures increases, the IDS may lack the computational performance needed to process packets at high network loads.

If this happens, the IDS will skip some packets and so may miss attacks. Inadequate performance is especially bad during the many types of attacks, such as virus, worm, and DoS attacks, which increase network traffic dramatically. An IDS that functions well only when the system is not under attack is worthless.

STORAGE   Log files quickly become very large, so IDSs limit log file sizes. When disk storage nears capacity, the IDS transfers the log file to backup and starts a new log file. This limits the time spanned by each log file. An event that spans log files is difficult to analyze. Adding disk storage for log files can extend the time spanned by each log file, but the problem will remain.

TEST YOUR UNDERSTANDING

22. **a.** What is precision in an IDS?
    b. What are false positives, and why are they bad?
    c. What are false negatives, and why are they bad?
    d. How can tuning reduce the number of false positives?
    e. What does an IDS do if it cannot process all of the packets it receives?
    f. What may happen if a system runs out of storage space?
    g. Why is limiting the size of log files necessary but unfortunate?

Honeypots

One type of IDS is the honeypot. A honeypot is a fake server or entire network segment with multiple clients and servers. Legitimate users should never try to reach resources on the honeypot, so any attempted access to the honeypot is likely to be an attack. If an alarm is sent with every non-transient access attempt, the security administrator has a good chance of catching attackers. In practice, honeypots are used by primarily researchers studying attacker behavior by recording everything a visitor does or tries to do. Some corporate security administrators also find them useful.

TEST YOUR UNDERSTANDING

23. **a.** What is a honeypot?
    b. How can honeypots help companies detect attackers?

BUSINESS CONTINUITY PLANNING

Natural disasters such as floods and hurricanes, major building fires, and massive security incidents such as cyberterror or cyberwar could place the company's basic operation in jeopardy and could even threaten the survival of the firm. Every company should have a strong **business continuity plan** that specifies how a company will maintain or restore core business operations after disasters.

A business continuity plan specifies how a company plans to maintain or restore core business operations when disasters occur.

Business Continuity Planning

A business continuity plan specifies how a company plans to restore or maintain core business operations when disasters occur

Disaster response is restoring IT services

Principles of Business Continuity Management

Protect people first

Evacuation plans and drills

Never allow staff members back into unsafe environments

Must have a systematic way to account for all employees and notify loved ones

Counseling afterwards

People have reduced capacity in decision making during a crisis

Planning and rehearsal are critical

Avoid rigidity

Unexpected situations will arise

Communication will break down and information will be unreliable

Decision makers must have the flexibility to act

Communication

Try to compensate for inevitable breakdowns

Have a backup communication system

Communicate constantly to keep everybody "in the loop"

Business Process Analysis

Identification of business processes and their interrelationships

Prioritization of business processes

Downtime tolerance (in the extreme, mean time to belly-up)

Importance to the firm

Required by higher-importance processes

Resource needs (must be shifted during crises)

Cannot restore all business processes immediately

Testing the Plan

Difficult because of the scope of disasters

Difficult because of the number of people involved

FIGURE 9-17 Business Continuity Planning (Study Figure)

Updating the Plan
Must be updated frequently

Business conditions change and businesses reorganize constantly

People who must execute the plan also change jobs constantly

Telephone numbers and other contact information must be updated far more frequently than the plan as a whole

Should have a small permanent staff

FIGURE 9-17 (Continued)

A business continuity planning team with broad representation from departments across the firm creates the plan. The plan specifies what business actions will be taken, not simply what technological actions need to be taken.

In contrast to business continuity efforts, IT disaster recovery, as Figure 9-18 shows, is restoring IT functions after a disaster. IT disaster recovery may be part of a firm's broader business continuity effort after a disaster, or it may exist on its own—say, when there is a fire in a data center.

IT disaster recovery is restoring IT functions after a disaster.

TEST YOUR UNDERSTANDING

24. **a.** What do business continuity plans specify?
    b. Distinguish between business continuity plans and IT disaster recovery plans.

Principles of Business Continuity Management

Before diving into the specifics of business continuity planning, we should look at three basic principles that should underlie all thinking about business continuity.

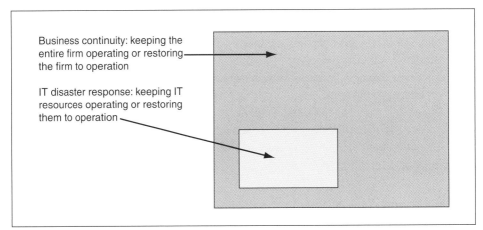

Business continuity: keeping the entire firm operating or restoring the firm to operation

IT disaster response: keeping IT resources operating or restoring them to operation

FIGURE 9-18 Business Continuity versus Disaster Response

PEOPLE FIRST   The first job of planning and event management is to provide for the safety of people.

- There should be evacuation plans and evacuation drills.
- The company should never allow staff members into an unsafe environment with building structural weaknesses or toxic chemicals.
- The company should have a systematic way to account for all staff immediately so that actions can be taken if people are missing. In addition, the company needs to make information about employee status available to loved ones.
- Afterwards, there will be a need for counseling.

REDUCED CAPACITY IN DECISION MAKING   Another basic principle is that people are not at their best cognitively during crises.[16] People under stress, emotional situations, and time pressures tend not to think things through well. Consequently, it is important to do as much planning ahead of time and to have people rehearse what they will do, making as many actions as possible as automatic as possible.

AVOIDING RIGIDITY   At the same time, rigid pre-planning should not lead to a loss of flexibility in response. Unexpected situations will arise frequently in a crisis, communication will be spotty, and information will be unreliable. If there is too rigid a structure, decision makers will not be able to react to these uncertainties. People on the front line with the most knowledge need to be able to make decisions. This should not mean that careful planning is unnecessary. As noted earlier in this chapter, adaptation within a strong plan usually is far better than total improvisation.

COMMUNICATION, COMMUNICATION, COMMUNICATION   In crises, communication inevitably breaks down because technology cannot survive building damage or prolonged periods without electrical power. Decision makers need to cope with communication breakdowns by having emergency back up communication systems. This includes such low-tech solutions as phone trees, in which each employee calls a fixed number of other employees to pass on important messages.

TEST YOUR UNDERSTANDING

25. **a.** What four protections can firms provide for people during an emergency?
   b. Why is accounting for all personnel important? (The answer is not in the text.)
   c. Why does human cognition in crises call for extensive pre-planning and rehearsal?
   d. Why is it necessary not to make plans and processes for crisis recovery too rigid?
   e. Why do communication systems tend to break down during crises?

---

[16] C. F. Harman, *International Crises; Insights from Behavioral Research*, New York: Free Press, 1972. Robert Billings, Thomas Milburn, and Mary Schallman. "A Model of Crisis Perceptions: A Theoretical and Empirical Analysis," *Administrative Science Quarterly*, Vol. 25, June 1980, pp. 300–316.

Business Process Analysis

IDENTIFICATION OF BUSINESS PROCESSES AND THEIR INTERRELATIONSHIPS The first step in creating a business continuity plan is to identify a firm's major processes and to rate the importance of each. A firm is a web of business processes, such as accounting, sales, production, and marketing. These processes are interdependent. Each must be identified. More significantly, the key interactions between business processes must be specified and understood.

PRIORITIZATION OF BUSINESS PROCESSES The next step is to prioritize business processes, so that the firm can restore the most important business processes first. A key factor is how sensitive a function is to downtime. The company must get order entry systems running quickly or sales will be lost. Billing can be down a little longer before it begins affecting the business. To complicate matters, some low-value business processes must be started first because one or more higher value business processes require them.

SPECIFY RESOURCE NEEDS In addition to prioritizing each process, planning should specify which resources each process needs. Due to disruptions during and after the disaster, the company may have to shift some of its remaining resources from lower priority processes to higher priority processes.

SPECIFY ACTIONS AND SEQUENCES The Wal-Mart case study near the beginning of this chapter notes that the plan specified some very precise actions, including getting cleanup supplies and security personnel to individual stores.

TEST YOUR UNDERSTANDING

26. **a.** List the four steps in business process analysis?
    b. Explain why each is important.

Testing and Updating the Plan

Once a business continuity plan is developed, using input from a wide variety of departments and external business partners, the company must test the plan. As noted earlier in this chapter, both walkthroughs (table-top exercises) and live tests are useful. Testing is more difficult for business continuity disasters than for major security incidents because disasters have much broader impact and involve so many people.

The company must update the plan frequently because business conditions change constantly and because businesses reorganize constantly. During a crisis is a bad time to wonder who must take over responsibilities assigned to a department that no longer exists. It is an even worse time to discover that your plan does not cover new business activities. Telephone numbers and other contact specifics change even more rapidly than other factors and should have monthly updates.

All of this updating requires a small permanent staff for business continuity. The staff will also act as the operational manager during a disaster.

TEST YOUR UNDERSTANDING

27. a. Why are business continuity plans more difficult to test than incident response plans?
   b. Why is frequent plan updating important?
   c. Why must companies update contact information even more frequently?
   d. For what two reasons is a business continuity staff necessary?

IT DISASTER RECOVERY

Business continuity planning lays out a general strategy for getting the company working again. In turn, **IT disaster recovery** looks specifically at the technical aspects of how a company can get IT back into operation.[17] IT disaster recovery may exist on its own, as in a data center fire, or may be part of a much larger business continuity effort in the case of disasters.

> *Disaster recovery looks specifically at the technical aspects of how a company can get IT back into operation using backup facilities.*

IT disaster recovery planning is critical to rapid and successful business continuity recovery. In the attack on the World Trade Center, two law firms near the center received heavy damage when the two towers collapsed.[18] One had a good IT disaster recovery program and was back to normal business operations in two days. The other did not and lost all of its computerized data. A year later, the second firm was still in the process of going through printed papers in warehouses to reconstruct its records. To partially replicate its data, it had to go to clients and even competitors.

Although many people view IT disaster recovery as "a concern for the techies," top management needs to have a good understanding of IT disaster recovery realities. In one insurance company, for instance, executives thought that they could be back to full operation in 48 hours.[19] However, the firm's IT disaster recovery executive knew that even the plan called for six days of recovery, and the plan had never even been run through to determine if it was feasible.

Also, as noted earlier in this chapter, every IT decision during response is a business decision. Decisions that seem purely technical may have major implications for the business that IT professionals may not accept and should certainly not have the final call on.

TEST YOUR UNDERSTANDING

28. a. What is IT disaster recovery?
   b. Why is it a business concern?

---

[17] Elizabeth Lennon's "Contingency Planning Guide for Information Technology Systems" is a comprehensive guide to disaster recovery planning. It is published by the Information Technology Laboratory of the National Institute of Standards and Technology, http://csrc.nist.gov/publications/nistpubs/index.html.

[18] Tiffany Kary, "From Ground Zero Up: How 9/11 Changed Disaster Planning," ZDnet.com, September 10, 2002. http://techupdate.zdnet.com/techupdate/stories/main/0,14179,2879843,00.html.

[19] Sandra Gittlen, "Today's Focus: Data Prioritization: Not as Easy as You Think," *Network World Newsletter: Sandra Gittlen on IT Education and Training*, May 22, 2002. E-mail newsletter.

IT Disaster Recovery

IT disaster recovery looks specifically at the technical aspects of how a company can get its IT back into operation using backup facilities

A subset of business continuity or for disasters the only affect IT

All decisions are business decisions and should not be made by mere IT or IT security staffs

Types of Backup Facilities

Hot sites

    Ready to run (power, HVAC, computers): Just add data

    Considerations: Rapid readiness at high cost

    Must be careful to have the software at the hot site up-to-date in terms of configuration

Cold sites

    Building facilities, power, HVAC, communication to outside world only

    No computer equipment

    Less expensive but usually requires too long to get operating

Site sharing

    Site sharing among a firm's sites (problem of equipment compatibility and data synchronization)

    Continuous data protection needed to allow rapid recovery

Office Computers

Hold much of a corporation's data and analysis capability

Will need new computers if old computers are destroyed or unavailable

    Will need new software

    Well-synchronized data backup is critical

People will need a place to work

Restoration of Data and Programs

Restoration from backup tapes: Need backup tapes at the remote recovery site

May be impossible during a disaster

Testing the IT Disaster Recovery Plan

Difficult and expensive

Necessary

FIGURE 9-19 IT Disaster Recovery (Study Figure)

Types of Backup Facilities

When a major computer facility becomes inoperable, the work has to be shifted to a **backup facility**, usually one at another location. Several types of backup facilities exist. Each type has strengths and weaknesses.

HOT SITES An attractive backup facility is a **hot site** that is ready to go in an emergency. A hot site is a physical facility with power, **HVAC** (heating, ventilation, and air conditioning), hardware, installed software, and up-to-date data. As soon as people can move in, the hot site can take over the full operation of the damaged site. With a skeleton crew, basic operation can begin even earlier.

Hot sites are attractive when processes have little downtime tolerance. They can be back in operation rapidly, and there rarely are the major delays that can occur when software is difficult to install on the computers used in other types of backup facilities. However, hot sites also are extremely expensive, and ensuring that the software at the backup site is configured in the same way as the original software is difficult.

COLD SITES   In turn, **cold sites** offer physical facilities, electrical power, and HVAC, but they are empty rooms with connections to the outside world. To use a cold site, the company has to procure, bring in, and set up hardware; install software; and mount data. By the time all of this happens, the company could be bankrupt. Cold sites are less inexpensive than hot sites, but companies must assess realistically how useful they would be in practice.

SITE SHARING WITH CONTINUOUS DATA PROTECTION (CDP)   Although hot sites are attractive, they are expensive to keep open and require time to become operational. Companies that have multiple data centers can shift the most critical work of a damaged center to another center in the firm. This is never automatic, however. The company needs a way to install programs and data files on machines in other sites.

If site sharing uses synchronized software at both sites with continuous data protection (CDP), which we saw in Chapter 7, recovery can be instantaneous. However, a site will rarely be able to take on the complete duties of both sites, so the response plan must prioritize applications.

As an example of site sharing within a firm, UAL Loyalty Services has two data centers that do site sharing in the Chicago area.[20] To keep data at the two sites synchronized in real time, the company uses a gigabit-per-second metropolitan area network. In addition to providing disaster recovery, continuous data protection provides the ultimate in general backup.

LOCATION OF THE SITES   One problem with site sharing is how far apart to locate the sites. If they are in the same city, both may be shut down by the same disaster. If they are too far apart, moving personnel between sites may be impossible. If a firm has many sites, it can address both problems. For instance, when Hewlett-Packard consolidated its 85 data centers into just 6,[21] it placed 2 in each of three cities—Atlanta, Houston, and Austin. The cities are sufficiently far apart that a disaster that hits more than one of these cities is unlikely. This means that most disasters will only cost HP a third of its server capacity. The pairs in each city would be within 15 miles of each

[20] James Cope, "Put Your IT Eggs in Different Baskets," *Computerworld*, July 15, 2002. http://www.computerworld.com/securitytopics/security/story/0,10801,72638,00.html.

[21] Candace Lombardi, "HP Plans Data Center Consolidation," CNET News.com, May 17, 2006. http://news.cnet.com/2110-1011_3-6073187.html.

other—near enough to shift staff but far enough apart to allow one site in each pair to survive anything but a regional disaster.

TEST YOUR UNDERSTANDING

29. **a.** What are the main alternatives for backup sites?
    b. What is the strength of each?
    c. What problem or problems does each raise?
    d. Why is CDP necessary?

Office PCs

Although severs are critical, office PCs probably hold most of a firm's business information and analysis capabilities. A fire is as likely to destroy an office area or several office areas as it is to destroy a server room.

DATA BACKUP   In a disaster, there often is no way to move many desktop PCs out of harm's way. One firm only uses notebook computers, which are easily moved, but this will be ineffective in a building fire in the middle of the night. The only real solution is to have centralized backup for PC files and to enforce up-to-date file synchronization.

NEW COMPUTERS   If most PCs are lost, a company will need new computers and will need them very quickly. Prior arrangements with the firm's equipment vendors can smooth this process.

A new computer is not enough. It must have application software, so it is important for firms to keep their installation media or, if they have standard configurations, to have disk images of these standard configurations accessible after a disaster.

WORK ENVIRONMENT   Another issue is finding a place for people to work. A common option is to secure rooms in a hotel that has good Internet access. Work at home is another option, but this eliminates the human interactions that are especially critical in the fluid and uncertain environment after a disaster. People may also do better emotionally in an environment with their familiar coworkers.

TEST YOUR UNDERSTANDING

30. What three things should a firm do about disaster recovery planning for office PCs?

Restoration of Data and Programs

Earlier in this chapter, we looked at the archival backup of program and data files. The companies must **restore** these files at the backup computer site.

Restoration from backup tapes is one way to move files to the backup site. If this is the goal, then the backup site must have the proper equipment to do the restoration. In addition, companies must deliver backup tapes to the backup site rapidly. This can be difficult to do during natural disasters or if the backup site is far from the storage site for backup tapes.

Of course, if the company uses continuous data protection, which we saw earlier in the chapter, then no recovery is necessary. The backup system is immediately ready to go to take over.

TEST YOUR UNDERSTANDING

31. **a.** What must be done to restore data at a backup site via tapes?
    b. How does this change if a firm uses continuous data protection?

Testing the IT Disaster Recovery Plan

Just as business continuity plans need testing, companies also need to test IT disaster recovery plans in as realistic a way as possible. In addition, companies must test rehearse their IT disaster recovery procedures to improve response speed and accuracy.

CONCLUSION

Synopsis

This book has been organized around the plan–protect–respond cycle. Most chapters dealt with the response phase. This final chapter completes the cycle by discussing response to both traditional security incidents and disasters.

The chapter began with a case of exemplary response to a disaster. This was Wal-Mart's handling of the Hurricane Katrina disaster in 2005. Wal-Mart has a dedicated disaster response department that pulls in experts from many fields when a disaster is about to occur. Wal-Mart's disaster expertise did not come easily. It developed its response method over a long period of time that included a number of disasters.

After the Wal-Mart case, we discussed some basic incident and disaster response terminology and concepts. We focused on a four-level severity scale for incidents—false alarms, minor incidents that can be handled by the on-duty IT staff, major incidents that require the convening of the firm's CSIRT, and disasters that affect IT alone or threaten business continuity for the entire firm. For all incidents and disasters, speed and accuracy are critical. These require extensive planning and rehearsals.

We then looked at response for major security incidents. We discussed a number of stages, including detection, analysis, escalation, containment, recovery, apology, punishment, and postmortem evaluation. We also discussed the organization of the CSIRT. For punishment, we discussed the difficulty of criminal prosecution, compared to the (relative) simplicity of disciplining employees.

This was followed by a box on legal considerations, which began with the difference between criminal and civil law. It then discussed jurisdictions in the United States at the federal and state levels and international cybercrime law. It also discussed rules of evidence and computer forensics. The box ended with a discussion of federal laws dealing with hacking, denial-of-service attacks, malware attacks, and the interception of electronic messages in transit and in storage.

The next section dealt with IDSs. We looked at the four functions of IDSs. We also looked at distributed IDSs using HIDSs and NIDSs. We looked at aggregated log files and the difficulty of event correlation. We discussed the problems of tuning and the difficulties of doing event correlation across multiple saved log files.

The chapter ended with a discussion of business continuity planning and IT disaster response. For IT disaster response, it is important to restore server functionality at other sites, preferably by site sharing with CDP. Business continuity response in disasters that threaten the operation of the business is a far more complex task. A great deal of planning is needed for success.

Thought Questions

1. You are advising a small company. a) Would you recommend using a firewall? Explain. b) Would you recommend using antivirus filtering? Explain. c) Would you recommend an intrusion detection system? Explain.

2. When IDSs generate alerts, it can send them to a console in the security center, to a mobile phone, or via e-mail. Discuss the pros and cons of each.

3. Examine the integrated log file shown in Figure 9-15. a) Identify the stages in this apparent attack. b) For each stage, describe what the attacker seems to be doing. c) Decide whether the actions in this stage work at human speed or at a higher speed, indicating an automated attack. d) Decide whether the

evidence in each stage is suggestive of an attack or conclusive evidence. e) Overall, do you have conclusive evidence of an attack? f) Do you have conclusive evidence of who committed the attack?

4. A firm is trying to decide whether to place its backup center in the same city or in a distant city. List the pros and cons of each choice.

5. To get out of taking exams, students occasionally phone in bomb threats just before the exam. Create a plan to deal with such attacks. This should take one single-spaced page. It should be written by you (a policy advisor) for your dean to approve and post in your college.

Troubleshooting Question

1. After you restore files following an incident, users complain that some of their data files are missing. What might have happened?

Perspective Questions

1. What was the most surprising thing you learned in this chapter?

2. What was the most difficult material in this chapter for you?

Module A

Networking Concepts

INTRODUCTION

> *Note: This module can be covered front-to-back for a fuller review of networking concepts. However, many teachers will only cover the parts of it they feel their students need to review.*

Sometimes, an attacker can simply walk up to a computer. In most cases, however, attackers must reach their victims via networks. Some attacks even aim *at* networks, trying to bring down local area networks (LANs), wide area networks (WANs), and even the global Internet. This module provides an overview of networking concepts to help readers of this textbook when they come across networking concepts in other chapters. Obviously, this chapter can only cover a limited number of networking concepts. Specifically, it focuses on aspects of networking that are most relevant to security.

> *In some cases, the security implications of a networking concept are noted. If so, they are set off in a paragraph like this.*

Before beginning, we should note three important terms that pervade the module:

- First, this module often uses the term **octet**. There is nothing mysterious about octets. An octet, pure and simple, is a byte—a collection of eight bits. Networking grew out of electrical engineering, where octet is the preferred term.
- The second term is **host**. Any device attached to the global Internet is called a host. This includes large servers host, of course, but it also includes client PCs, PDAs, Internet-capable mobile phones, and even Internet-accessible appliances such as coffee pots.
- Third, we will distinguish between the terms **internet** and **Internet**. We will capitalize the term when referring to the global Internet. Spelled in lower case, *internet* refers to either the internet layer in the TCP/IP architecture or a collection of networks that is *not* the global Internet.

TEST YOUR UNDERSTANDING

1. **a.** What is an octet?
   b. What is a host?
   c. Is a home PC connected to the Internet a host?
   d. Distinguish between the terms *internet* and *Internet*.

A SAMPLING OF NETWORKS

This section looks briefly at a series of increasingly complex networks, giving the reader an overview of what networks are like in the real world.

A Simple Home Network

Figure A-1 shows a simple home PC network. The home has two personal computers. The network allows the two PCs to share files and the family's single laser printer. The network also connects the two computers to the Internet.

THE ACCESS ROUTER   The heart of this network is its **access router**. This small device, which is about the size of a hardback book, has several functions:

- First, it is a switch. When one PC in the home sends messages (called frames) to the other PC, the switch transfers the frames between them.
- Second, the access router has a wireless access point that serves wireless computers. The upstairs computer is a wireless computer.
- Third, the access router is a true router. A router connects a network to another network; in this case, it connects the home network to the global Internet.
- Fourth, the access router has a Dynamic Host Configuration Protocol (DHCP) server. To use the Internet, each host needs an Internet Protocol (IP) address. The access router's DHCP server gives each home PC an IP address.

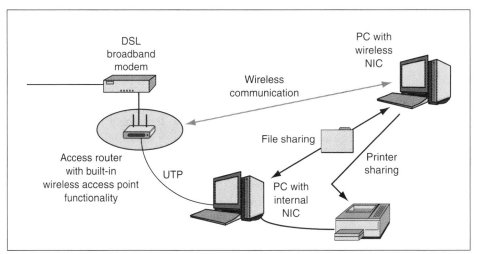

FIGURE A-1   A Simple Home Network

- Fifth, the access router provides network address translation (NAT), which hides internal IP addresses from potential attackers. Some access routers also have a static packet inspection (SPI) firewall for added security.

Wireless access points are dangerous because the radio signals they emit spread widely. If the user does not configure strong security on the access point and on all wireless stations, anyone will be able to read the traffic and do other mischief.

NAT provides a surprisingly large amount of protection automatically. Even people with one PC may find it attractive to use an access router to gain this protection.

It is important to configure computers for security. Although NAT by itself is strong, and although a growing number of access routers also provide stateful packet inspection firewalls, some attacks will inevitably get through to computers. The PCs in the home must have strong PC firewalls, antivirus programs, and antispyware programs. Such programs also must be updated whenever security patches are released by operating system vendors or application program vendors.

PERSONAL COMPUTERS   Each of the two PCs Figure A-1 needs circuitry to communicate over the network. Traditionally, this circuitry came in the form of a separate printed circuit board, so the circuitry was called the computer's network interface card (NIC). In most computers today, the networking circuitry is built into the computer; there is no separate printed circuit board. However, the circuitry is still called the computer's NIC.

UTP WIRING   The downstairs PC connects to the access router via copper wiring. Specifically, it uses **4-pair unshielded twisted pair (UTP)** wiring. As Figure A-2

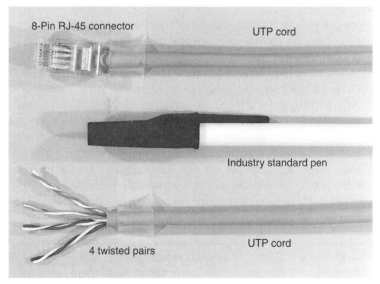

FIGURE A-2   Unshielded Twisted Pair Wiring (UTP) Cord

shows, a UTP cord contains eight copper wires organized as four pairs. The two wires of each pair are twisted around each other several times an inch to reduce interference.

Some early versions of twisted-pair wiring had metal foil or mesh shielding around each individual pair and also around the four pairs as a whole. This shielded twisted pair (STP) wiring was almost completely immune to external interference. However, the *unshielded* twisted pair wiring shown in Figure A-2 now dominates the market. This is because heavy external interference is rare in corporations and because UTP is far cheaper than STP. To handle 10 Gbps Ethernet, however, new "Category 7" wiring will return to STP technology.

INTERNET ACCESS LINE   The home network needs an **Internet access line** in order to connect to the Internet. In Figure A-1, this access line is a DSL high-speed access line, and the home connects to this access line via a small device called a DSL modem. (The DSL modem connects to the access router via a UTP cord; it connects to the wall jack via an ordinary telephone cord.) Other Internet access technologies include slow telephone modems, fast cable modems, and even wireless Internet access systems. Most of these technologies are called broadband access lines, and the modems are called **broadband modems**. In general, broadband simply means "very fast," although it also has a technical meaning in radio transmission.

TEST YOUR UNDERSTANDING

   2. **a.** What are the functions of an access router? Explain each function in one sentence.
       b. Describe the technology of 4-pair UTP wiring.
       c. What is an Internet access line?
       d. What is a broadband modem?
       e. Why is wireless transmission dangerous?

A Building LAN

The home network shown in Figure A-1 is a **local area network (LAN)**. A LAN is a network that operates on a customer's **premises**—the property owned by the LAN user. (For historical reasons, "premises" is always written in the plural.) In the case of the home network, the premises consist of the user's home. Figure A-3 shows a larger LAN. Here, the premises consist of a corporate office building.

On each floor, computers attach to a workgroup switch via UTP cords or a wireless access point. **Workgroup switches** are switches that connect computers to the network. Each workgroup switch (there is one on each floor) connects directly to a core switch in the basement equipment room. (A **core switch** connects switches to other switches.) When a computer on one floor sends a frame to a computer on another floor, the frame goes to the workgroup switch on the sender's floor, down to the core switch in the basement, up to the workgroup switch on the receiver's floor, and then to the destination computer.

UTP is easy to wiretap, allowing attackers to read all packets flowing through the cord. To prevent wiretapping, telecommunications closets should be kept locked at all times, and UTP cords should be run through thick metal wiring conduits wherever possible.

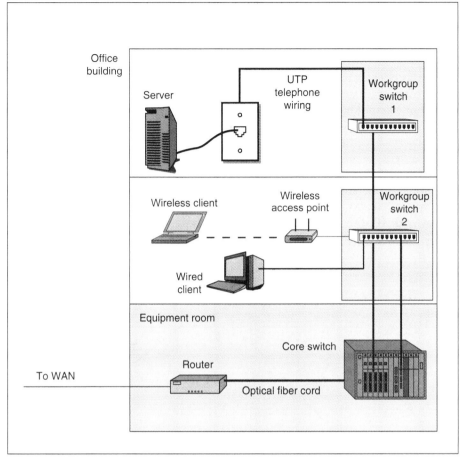

FIGURE A-3   Building LAN

UTP also generates weak radio signals when traffic flows through it. It is possible to read these signals from some distance away. However, this is a rare threat because expensive equipment is needed to read wire radiation.

Typically, attackers do not even need to tap wires in order to break into networks physically. In most building LANs, anyone entering the building can plug a notebook into any wall jack with a UTP cord. To thwart such an attack, most switches today have 802.1X capability that requires any device connecting to a wall jack to authenticate itself before being allowed to transmit beyond the switch. However, this authentication is ineffective without a sophisticated access and identity management control system.

TEST YOUR UNDERSTANDING

3. **a.** What is a local area network?
   b. What is the customer premises?
   c. Distinguish between workgroup switches and core switches.

    d. Why is UTP dangerous?
    e. Why is 802.1X needed?

A Firm's Wide Area Networks (WANs)

While LANs operate within a company's premises, commercial **wide area networks (WANs)** connect different sites—typically the multiple sites of a single corporation. Corporations do not have the regulatory rights of way needed to run wires through public areas, which they would need to do in order to connect their different sites. For WAN service, companies must use commercial companies called **carriers** that do have these rights of way.

    Figure A-4 shows that most firms use WANs from multiple carriers. In the figure, some of the company's sites are connected by **point-to-point leased lines** leased from a telephone company. The company also subscribes to **public switched data network (PSDN)** services that switch frames between several sites. These

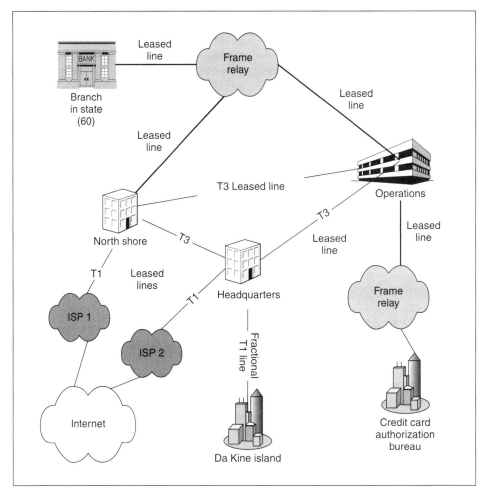

FIGURE A-4 Wide Area Networks (WANs)

switched network services use the Frame Relay technology. The company uses two separate Frame Relay networks—one to connect its own sites to each other and one to connect it to another firm.

Security professionals generally believe that carrier technology offers good security. Unlike the Internet, which allows anyone to connect to it, only commercial firms may connect to carrier WANs. This makes attacker access very difficult. However, attacker access is not impossible. For example, if an attacker hacks a computer owned by the carrier, this may permit access to individual WANs run by the carrier. Even hacking the computer of a subscriber can give the attacker access to the subscriber's portion of the carrier WAN.

In addition, the carrier alone knows how it routes traffic through its network. This should stymie attackers even if they somehow get access to the network because they will not know how to get around in the network. However, such "security through obscurity" is considered a very bad thing by security professionals because it is possible for attackers who hack carrier computers to get access to routing information.

Overall, however, effective carrier security usually is quite strong. Attackers usually have much simpler attack vectors.

TEST YOUR UNDERSTANDING

4. **a.** Distinguish between LANs and WANs.
   b. Why do companies use carriers for WAN transmission?
   c. What two WAN technologies are illustrated in the figure?
   d. Why is carrier WAN traffic generally considered safe?

The Internet

By the end of the 1970s, there were many LANs and WANs in the world. Many of the WANs were nonprofit networks that connected universities and research institutions. Unfortunately, computers on one network could not talk to computers on other networks. To address this problem, the Defense Advanced Research Projects Agency (DARPA) created the **Internet** and the TCP/IP standards that govern it. By definition, an internet is a "super network" that connects thousands individual networks together ("inter" means "between"). Initially, only noncommercial networks could connect to the Internet. Later, commercial networks were allowed to join the Internet, transforming the Internet into what we know today.

Figure A-5 shows that devices called **routers** connect individual networks together. Initially, these devices were called gateways. The term *gateway* was used in some early standards, but most vendors have now adopted the name router. One major exception is Microsoft, which still tends to call routers "gateways."

Any computer on any network on the Internet can send messages to any computer on any other network on the Internet. Messages that travel within a single network—a LAN or a WAN—are called **frames**. Messages that travel all the way from one computer to another across the Internet are called **packets**.

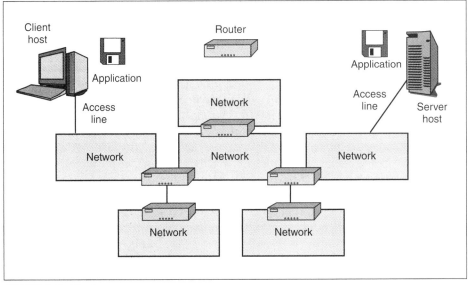

FIGURE A-5 The Internet

If you are confused about the fact that there are two types of messages—frames and packets—consider Figure A-6. Note that the packet travels all the way from the source host to the destination host. Along the way, the packet is carried inside a different frame in each network.

The global Internet uses transmission standards that are known as the TCP/IP standards. Many firms use those standards to build separate internal TCP/IP internets

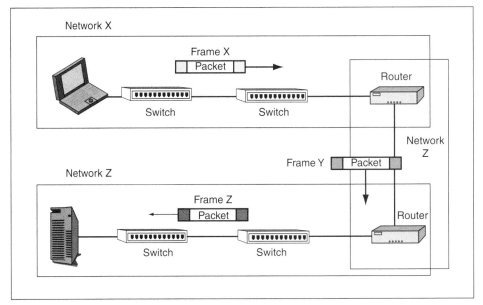

FIGURE A-6 Frames and Packets

for their own communication. These are called *intra*nets to distinguish them from the *Inter*net. As noted earlier, we will use the term *internet* with a lower-case "i" to designate any internet that is not the global Internet.

> Initially, security on intranets was fairly light because it was assumed that external attackers would have a difficult time getting into corporate intranets. However, if a hacker takes over an internal computer connected to the intranet, light security becomes a serious problem. Consequently, most firms have been progressively hardening their intranet security.

Figure A-7 shows that individual homes and corporations connect to the Internet via carriers called **Internet Service Providers (ISPs)**. The Internet has many ISPs, but they all connect at centers that are usually called Network Access Points (NAPs). These connections permit any computer on any ISP to reach any computer on any other ISP.

Some people are surprised to learn that nearly all ISPs are commercial organizations run for profit. Another point that sometimes surprises people is that there is no central point of control over the Internet's operation, although there is centralized control over the naming of Internet host computers and networks (for instance, *cnn.com*).

> When the Internet was designed in the late 1970s, there was a conscious decision not to add security because doing so would be burdensome. As a consequence of its lack of security technology and open access to almost anyone, the Internet today is a security nightmare. Companies that transmit sensitive information over the Internet need to consider cryptographic protections.

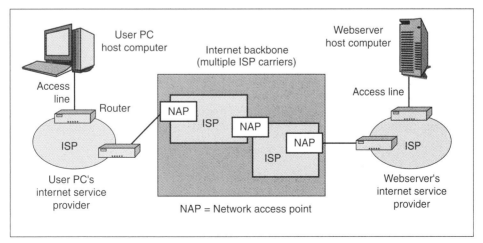

FIGURE A-7 Internet Service Providers (ISPs)

TEST YOUR UNDERSTANDING

5. **a.** Which organization created the Internet?
   b. What is the function of a router?
   c. Distinguish between frames and packets.
   d. If two hosts are separated by five networks, how many packets will there be along the way when a host transmits a packet to another host?
   e. If two hosts are separated by five networks, how many frames will there be along the way when a host transmits a packet to another host?
   f. Why was intranet security initially light?

Applications

Although both networks and internets are important, users only care about applications. Personal applications include the World Wide Web, e-mail, and music downloading, to name just three. Corporations use some of these applications, but they also use many business-specific applications, such as accounting, payroll, billing, and inventory management. Business applications are often transaction-processing applications, which are characterized by high volumes of simple repetitive transactions. The traffic volume generated by transaction-processing and other business-oriented applications usually far outweighs the traffic volume of personal applications in the firm.

> *All programs have bugs, some of which are security vulnerabilities. Businesses use many applications, and keeping track of application vulnerabilities and constantly patching many applications is an enormous task that is all too easy to put off or to complete only partially. Also, each application must be configured with options that have high security, and security must be managed on each application (for instance, antivirus and spam blocking in e-mail).*

TEST YOUR UNDERSTANDING

6. **a.** What type of applications usually generates the most traffic in an organization?
   b. Why is managing application security time-consuming?

NETWORK PROTOCOLS AND VULNERABILITIES

The products of different network vendors must be able to interoperate (work together). This is only possible if there are strong communication standards to govern the way hardware and software processes interact. With such standards, two programs on different hosts will be able to interoperate effectively regardless of what companies wrote and sold them.

Inherent Security

Standards raise four security issues. One is whether the standard itself is inherently secure because of the way it operates. For instance, the TCP standard discussed later in this module is difficult to attack because an attacker cannot send a false TCP message unless he or she can guess the sequence number of the next message. This is normally very difficult to do. However, if the attacker sends an RST message, which terminates a connection, this protection is greatly reduced. In fact, it is fairly easy to send RST messages that close legitimate open connections. Security that results from the inherent operation of a standard is called incidental security.

Security Explicitly Designed into the Standard

A second issue is security explicitly designed into the standard. Most standards were initially created without any security. If security was added in later versions, it was often done in an awkward way. For instance, IP, which is the main protocol for delivering packets over the Internet, originally had no security. The IPsec standards were created to address this weakness, but IPsec is burdensome and not widely used.

Security in Older Versions of the Standard

Third, even when security is added to a standard, it usually is added only to later versions of the standard. If a company uses an older version of the standard, it is limited in terms of the security it can implement.

Defective Implementation

A fourth issue is the security of defective standards implementations in vendor products. These defective implementations may create vulnerabilities that attackers can exploit even if the standard itself is highly secure.

TEST YOUR UNDERSTANDING

7. List the four security problems with protocols. Write one sentence describing each.

CORE LAYERS IN LAYERED STANDARDS ARCHITECTURES

Standards are complex. A common way to deal with complex problems is to break them down into smaller parts. Figure A-8 shows that standards are divided into three **core layers**. Collectively, these layers have the functionality needed to allow any application program on one host on one network of an internet to interoperate with another other program on another other host on any other network of the internet.

The highest core layer governs the interactions of *applications*. For instance, World Wide Web access is governed by the Hypertext Transfer Protocol (HTTP).

Super Layer	Description
Application	Communication between application programs on different hosts attached to different networks on an internet.
Internetworking	Transmission of packets across an internet. Packets contain application layer messages.
Network	Transmission of frames across a network. Frames contain packets.

FIGURE A-8 Three Core Standards Layers

In World Wide Web access, the two application programs—the browser on the client PC and the webserver program on the webserver—have to send messages governed by the HTTP standard.

The middle core layer is the *internet core layer*. Standards at this layer govern how packets are delivered across an internet, including the global Internet. One of the main standards at the internet core layer is the Internet Protocol (IP).

The lowest core layer is the *single-network core layer*. Standards at this layer govern the transmission of frames across the switches and transmission lines in a single network (a LAN or WAN).

TEST YOUR UNDERSTANDING

8. **a.** What are the three core standards layers?
   b. Distinguish between the single-network core layer and the internet core layer.
   c. At what core layer do you find LAN standards?
   d. At what core layer do you find WAN standards?
   e. At what core layer do you find standards for the global Internet?

STANDARDS ARCHITECTURES

Standards are created by standards agencies. The first action of a standards agency is to produce a broad layering plan called a **standards architecture**. Next, standards agencies create standards for the individual layers. Figure A-9 shows two popular layered standards architectures and relates these standards architectures to the three core layers we just saw.

TEST YOUR UNDERSTANDING

9. What is a standards architecture?

The TCP/IP Standards Architecture

The **Internet Engineering Task Force (IETF)** is the standards agency for the Internet. Its standards architecture is called **TCP/IP**—a name taken from two of its most important standards, TCP and IP. Figure A-9 shows that TCP/IP has four layers.

Super Layer	TCP/IP	OSI	Hybrid TCP/IP-OSI
Application	Application	Application	Application
		Presentation	
		Session	
Internet	Transport	Transport	Transport
	Internet	Network	Internet
Single network	Subnet access	Data link	Data link
		Physical	Physical

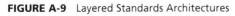

FIGURE A-9 Layered Standards Architectures

The bottom layer—the subnet access layer—corresponds to the single-network core layer. The top layer is the application layer, which corresponds to the application core layer. The two middle layers—the **internet** and **transport** layers—correspond to the internet core layer. TCP/IP is primarily used to govern internetworking. Dividing the internet core layer into two TCP/IP layers permits greater division of labor in standards development. The fifth and highest layer is the application layer.

IETF documents are publicly available at no charge. Most of these documents are **requests for comments (RFCs)**. Some RFCs are Internet Official Protocol Standards, but not all are. Periodically, an RFC specifies a current list of **Internet Official Protocol Standards**. To find an RFC, search for it in any search engine. For instance, to find the initial RFC for the Internet Protocol, search for "RFC 791" in any search engine.

TEST YOUR UNDERSTANDING

10. **a.** Which organization creates Internet standards?
    b. What is the name of its standards architecture?
    c. What is an RFC?
    d. How can you tell which RFCs are Internet Official Protocol Standard?

The OSI Standards Architecture

The other standards architecture shown in the figure is **OSI**, which is rarely spelled out by its full name, the Reference Model of Open Systems Interconnection. OSI is governed by two standards agencies. One is **ISO**, the International Organization for Standardization. The other is **ITU-T**, the International Telecommunications Union–Telecommunications Standards Sector. (No, the official names and the official acronyms do not match.)

Figure A-9 shows that OSI divides the three core layers into a total of *seven* layers. OSI single-network standards use the bottom two OSI layers—the physical and data link layers, which we will discuss in more detail later. OSI's market dominance is so strong at the physical and data link layers that the IETF rarely develops standards at these layers. The "subnet access" indication in the TCP/IP framework basically means, "Use OSI standards here." The OSI network and transport layers correspond to the internet and transport layers of TCP/IP. OSI divides the application core layer into three layers—session, presentation, and application.

TEST YOUR UNDERSTANDING

11. **a.** Which two standards agencies govern OSI? (Just give their acronyms.)
    b. Distinguish between OSI and ISO.
    c. How many layers does the OSI architecture have?
    d. Which of these layers are similar to the layers in TCP/IP?
    e. Compare the TCP/IP application layer with comparable OSI layers.

The Hybrid TCP/IP–OSI Architecture

Which of these two standards architectures is dominant? As Figure A-9 shows, the answer is, "Neither." What nearly all firms use today is the **hybrid TCP/ IP–OSI standards architecture**, which Figure A-9 also illustrates. This hybrid architecture uses

OSI standards at the physical and data link layers and TCP/IP standards at the internet and transport layers. Corporations also use standards from some other standards architectures at the internet and transport layers, but TCP/IP standards dominate.

At the application core layer, the situation is complex. Both OSI and TCP/IP standards are used, often in combination. In fact, OSI application standards often reference TCP/IP application standards and vice versa. Although OSI and TCP/IP are often viewed as rivals, this is not the case at all. Several other standards agencies also create application core layer standards, complicating the picture even further.

TEST YOUR UNDERSTANDING

12. **a.** What architecture do most firms actually use?
    b. In the hybrid TCP/IP-OSI architecture, which layers come from OSI?
    c. Which come from TCP/IP?
    d. From what standards architecture do application layer standards come?

SINGLE-NETWORK STANDARDS

As noted above, OSI standards are dominant in the two single-network layers—the physical and data link layers. These are the two layers that define LAN and WAN standards. Figure A-10 shows how the physical and data link layers are related.

TEST YOUR UNDERSTANDING

13. What two layers define LAN and WAN standards?

The Data Link Layer

The path that a frame takes through a single network is called a **data link**. The source computer sends the frame to the first switch, which forwards the frame to the next switch along the data link, which forwards the frame further. The last switch along

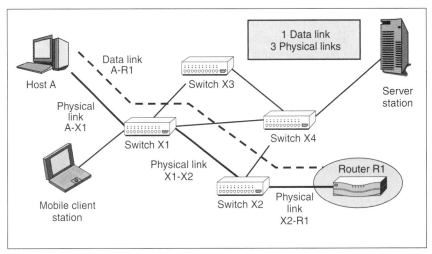

FIGURE A-10 Physical and Data Link Layers

the data link passes the frame to the destination computer (or router, if the packet in the frame is destined for a computer on another network).

TEST YOUR UNDERSTANDING

14. What is a data link?

The Physical Layer

UTP   **Physical layer** standards govern the physical connections between consecutive devices along the data link. Earlier, we saw one popular transmission medium, unshielded twisted pair wire. UTP dominates in links between computers and workgroup switches (see Figure A-3). UTP signals typically involve voltage changes. For instance, a high voltage may indicate a 1, while a low voltage may indicate a 0. (Actual voltage patterns are much more complex.)

OPTICAL FIBER   A popular transmission medium for longer distances is optical fiber, which sends light signals through thin glass tubes. Optical fiber signals actually are very simple. In each clock cycle, the light is turned on for a 1 or off for a 0.

UTP cords act like radio antennas when they carry signals. Some of the signal always radiates out, allowing people to intercept UTP signals by placing devices near (but not touching) the cord. In contrast, optical fiber requires physically tapping into the fiber cords.

WIRELESS TRANSMISSION   Wireless transmission uses radio waves. This permits mobile devices to be served in ways never before possible. Wireless transmission is used for both LAN and WAN transmission.

Radio waves spread widely, even when dish antennas are used. Consequently, it is very easy for eavesdroppers to listen in on radio transmissions and do other mischief. Radio signals must be strongly encrypted to prevent eavesdropping, and the parties must be strongly authenticated to prevent impostors from sending false radio messages.

Radio signaling is very complex. Most radio signaling uses spread-spectrum transmission, in which the information is sent over a wide range of frequencies. In wireless local area networks, spread spectrum transmission is used to improve propagation reliability. Radio transmission suffers from many propagation problems, many of which only occur at certain frequencies. If the signal is spread across a wide spectrum of frequencies, it will remain intelligible even if there are strong problems at some frequencies.

> *The military uses spread-spectrum transmission for security. Military spread-spectrum transmission works in such a way that makes intercepting transmissions very difficult. Civilian spread-spectrum transmission, in contrast, is designed to make connecting simple. Civilian spread-spectrum transmission on its own offers no security.*

SWITCH SUPERVISORY FRAMES Switches spend almost all of their time forwarding frames. However, switches must spend some of their time exchanging **switch supervisory frames** with one another, in order to keep the network running efficiently. For example, in Ethernet, which dominates LAN standards, if there are loops among the switches, the network will malfunction. If a switch detects a loop, it sends supervisory frames to other switches. The switches in the network then communicate until they determine how to close selected ports on certain switches to break the loop. This process is governed by the Spanning Tree Protocol or by the newer Rapid Spanning Tree Protocol.

> *Attackers can attack the switches in a network by impersonating a switch and sending to the network's real switches a flood of false supervisory messages indicating the presence of a loop. The switches may spend so much of their time reorganizing the network that they become unable to serve legitimate traffic. They also can use several other supervisory protocols to make switches unavailable for processing normal frames. The 802.1AE LAN security standard is designed to limit switch-to-switch communication to authenticated switches, thus preventing attacks based on impersonating switches.*

TEST YOUR UNDERSTANDING

15. **a.** Distinguish between physical links and data links.
    b. What advantage of optical fiber over UTP was listed in the text?
    c. Why is spread spectrum transmission used in wireless LANs?
    d. Why are switch supervisory frames needed?
    e. Why does optical fiber have better inherent security than UTP?
    f. What dangers does radio create?
    g. Does spread-spectrum transmission in commercial wireless LANs provide security?
    h. Why is the 802.1AE standard necessary?

INTERNETWORKING STANDARDS

As noted earlier, the IETF divided the internetworking core layer into two layers—the internet and transport layers. Figure A-11 shows how these two layers are related.

The internet layer governs how routers forward packets until these packets finally reach the destination host. The main standard at the internet layer is the Internet Protocol (IP).

The designers of TCP/IP realized that they could not predict what services the single networks connecting routers would provide. Consequently, IP was made a

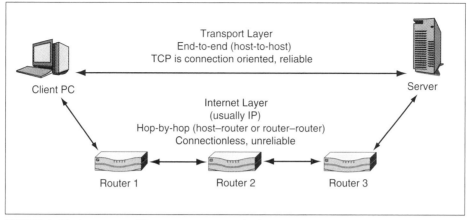

FIGURE A-11 Internet and Transport Layer Standards

simple best-effort protocol, in order to assume minimal functionality in the single networks along the way. There are no guarantees that packets will arrive at all, or, if they do arrive, that they will arrive in order.

To make up for the limitations of IP, a transport layer was added. The main standard designed for this layer—the Transmission Control Protocol (TCP)—was created as a high-capability protocol that would fix any transmission errors, ensure that packets arrived in order, slow transmission when the network became overloaded, and do several other things. For applications that do not need these capabilities, a simpler standard was created—the User Datagram Protocol (UDP).

TEST YOUR UNDERSTANDING

16. **a.** Why was IP made to be a very simple standard?
    b. Why was complexity needed in the TCP standard?

THE INTERNET PROTOCOL (IP)

The **Internet Protocol (IP)** has two main functions. First, it governs how packets are organized. Second, it determines how routers move packets to the destination host.

The IP Version 4 Packet

The dominant version of the Internet Protocol today is **Version 4 (IPv4)**. This version has been in use since its creation in 1981 and will continue to be used for many years to come.

A packet is a long stream of 1s and 0s. This stream would be far too long to show on a sheet of paper, so the IP header normally is shown by drawing several rows, with 32 bits in each row. The first row shows bits 0 through 31. (Binary counting usually begins at 0.) The next row shows bits 32 through 63.

The header is divided into smaller units called **fields**. Fields are defined by their bit position in the packet. For example, the first four bits (bits 0 through 3) constitute the version number field. To represent IPv4, this field's value is 0100, which is 4 in binary arithmetic.

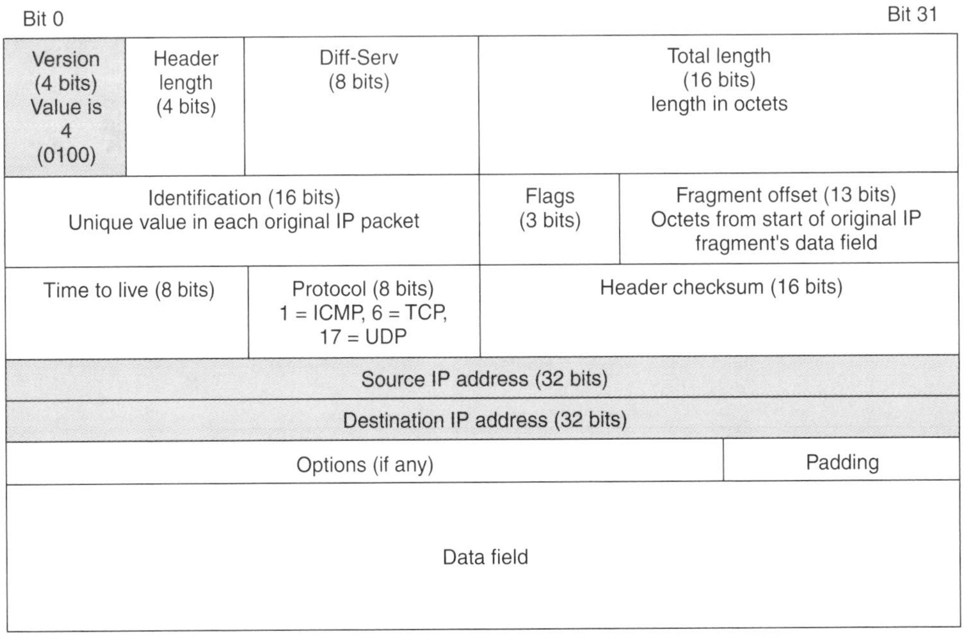

Bit 0   Bit 31

Version (4 bits) Value is 4 (0100)	Header length (4 bits)	Diff-Serv (8 bits)	Total length (16 bits) length in octets	
Identification (16 bits) Unique value in each original IP packet			Flags (3 bits)	Fragment offset (13 bits) Octets from start of original IP fragment's data field
Time to live (8 bits)	Protocol (8 bits) 1 = ICMP, 6 = TCP, 17 = UDP		Header checksum (16 bits)	
Source IP address (32 bits)				
Destination IP address (32 bits)				
Options (if any)				Padding
Data field				

FIGURE A-12   The Internet Protocol (IP) Packet

The First Row

In the newer version of the Internet Protocol, IP Version 6 (IPv6), the value is 0110. The next field is the header length field. This indicates the length of the header in 32-bit units. As Figure A-12 shows, a header without options has five 32-bit rows; in this case, the header length field would have the value 0101 (5 in binary).

> *The use of options in IP is uncommon. In fact, options tend to indicate attacks. A value larger than five in the header length field indicates that the packet header has options; therefore, it indicates that the packet is suspicious.*

Next comes the one-octet diff-serv (differential services) field, which was created to allow different levels of services (priority, etc.) to be given to different packets. However, this field typically is not used.

Finally, the total length field gives the length of the entire IP packet in octets. Given the 16-bit length of this field, the maximum number of octets in the IP packet is 65,536 (2^{16}). Most IP packets, however, are far smaller. The length of the data field is the total length minus the length of the header in octets.

The Second Row

If an IP packet is too long for a single network along the way, the router sending the packet into that network will **fragment** the packet, dividing its contents into a number of smaller packets. To permit reassembly on the destination host, all packets created from the original packet are given the same identification field value in the original packet. The data octets in the original packets are numbered, and the number of the first data octet in each packet is given a fragment offset value (13 bits long). There are three one-bit flag fields. One of these—the more fragments flag—is set to 1 in all but the last packet, in which it is 0. The information in these three fields allows the destination host to place the packets in order and to know when there are no more packets to arrive.

IP fragmentation is rare and can be used by attacker. It is therefore suspicious when it occurs. In fact, most operating systems automatically set the don't fragment *flag, which tells routers along the way to discard a packet rather than fragment it if it is too large for the next network along the way.*

The Third Row

The third row begins with an ominous-sounding **time to live (TTL)** field, which has a value between 0 and 255. The sending host sets the initial value (64 or 128 in most operating systems). Each router along the way decreases the value by 1. If a router decreases the value to 0, it discards the packet. This process was created to prevent misaddressed packets from circulating endlessly around the Internet.

To identify hosts, attackers will ping many IP addresses (as discussed later). A reply tells the attacker that a host exists with that IP address. In addition, by guessing the initial TTL value (usually 64 or 128) and looking at the TTL value in the arriving packet, the attacker can guess how many router hops separate the attacker's host from the victim host. Sending pings to many different IP addresses can help the attacker map the routers in the target network. Firms can change their host operating systems' default TTL values to confuse attackers.

Next, the data field of the IP packet may contain a TCP segment (message), a UDP datagram (message), or something else, such as the Internet Control Message Protocol (ICMP) messages we will see later. A value of 1 in the **protocol field** indicates that the data field contains an ICMP message. In turn, 6 indicates a TCP segment, and 17 indicates that the data field contains a UDP header.

The **header checksum** field allows the receiver to check for errors. The sender performs a calculation based on the values of other fields; the resulting number is then the value of the header checksum field. The internet process on the destination host redoes the calculation. If the two numbers are different, then there must have been an error along the way. If this is the case, the router or destination host simply discards the packet.

Options

Options are possible in IPv4, but they are rarely used. In fact, when they are used, they are suspicious from a security point of view.

TEST YOUR UNDERSTANDING

17. a. If the IP header length field's value is 6 and the total length field's value is 50, how long is the data field? Show your work.
   b. What is the general function of the second row in the IPv4 header?
   c. Why is a TTL field needed?
   d. If a router receives a packet with a TTL value of 1, what will it do?
   e. What does the protocol field in the IP header tell the destination host?
   f. How is the header checksum field used?
   g. Are IPv4 options used frequently?
   h. Why is fragmentation a threat indication?
   i. How can attackers use the TTL field to map a network?

The Source and Destination IP Addresses

When you send a letter, the envelope should have an address and a return address. The analogous addresses in IP headers are the source and destination **IP addresses**. Note that IP addresses are 32 bits long. To accommodate human reading, these 32 bits are divided into four 8-bit "segments," and each segment's bits are converted into a decimal number between 0 and 255. The four segment numbers are then separated by dots. An example is 128.171.17.13. Note that dotted decimal notation is only a memory and writing crutch for inferior biological entities (people). Computers and routers work with 32-bit IP addresses directly.

Many forms of firewall filtering are based on IP addresses. To thwart such protections and to hide their identities, many attackers spoof their packet's source IP address, that is, replace the real IP address with a false IP address.

Masks

The Internet contains tens of thousands of **networks**. One of these networks is the University of Hawaii Network. Another is the Microsoft network. Each ISP also is a network on the Internet.

Most organizations that have Internet networks subdivide these networks into **subnets**. For example, at the University of Hawaii, each college has its own subnet. One of these subnets is the Shidler College of Business subnet. A subnet may have many hosts.

Reflecting this hierarchical nature of the Internet's organization (the Internet, networks, and subnets), Internet addresses are hierarchical. They have a network part that specifies a host's network on the Internet, a subnet part that specifies the host's subnet on that network, and a host part that specifies a particular host on that subnet. For instance, in the address 128.171.17.13, 128.171 is the network part for all hosts at the University of Hawaii. All IP addresses at the University of Hawaii begin with 128.171. Shidler is subnet 17, so all hosts in the Shidler College of Business begin with 128.171.17. Voyager is a host in the College. Its full IP address is 128.171.17.13.

At the University of Hawaii, the network part is 16 bits long, the subnet part is 8 bits long, and the host part is 8 bits long. However, network, subnet, and host parts vary in size. For a router to send an incoming packet back out, it needs to know either the packet's network part or its combined network and subnet parts. Because part lengths vary, it must know an address's mask, which gives the required information. For instance, the network mask for the University of Hawaii is 255.255.0.0. (A collection of eight bits that is all 1s has the value 255.) Therefore, the network mask is sixteen 1s followed by sixteen 0s. For the Shidler College of Business, the subnet mask is 255.255.255.0. This means that the combined network and subnet parts are 24 bits long. Note in the IP header that there is no room for a mask. Routers exchange masks separately.

IP Version 6

Although IP Version 4 is widely used, its 32-bit IP address size causes problems. This relatively "small" size limits the number of possible IP addresses. In addition, when IP addresses were distributed, most addresses were assigned to the United States because the Internet was invented there. In fact, some individual U.S. universities received more IP addresses than all of China.

To address the limitations of the 32-bit IP address size, a new version of the Internet Protocol was created. This was **IP Version 6 (IPv6)**. Figure A-13 shows the IPv6 packet organization.

One obvious change is that IPv6 addresses are much larger—128 bits. Each IPv6 address, then, must be written as four 32-bit rows. This large address size provides enough IP addresses to allow almost every device to be a host on the Internet— including toasters and coffee pots.

The version number field is four bits long, and its value is 6 (0110). There are also a traffic class field similar to the diff-serv field in Version 4 and a flow label field that together are 20 bits long. These two fields allow the packet to be assigned to a category based on the packet's category (priority level, security level, etc.). All packets in a certain category would be assigned the same flow label and would be treated the same way by routers. However, this capability is not widely used.

On the next row, there is a 16-bit payload length field. "Payload" is another name for data field. Next comes the next header field, which we will see next. The

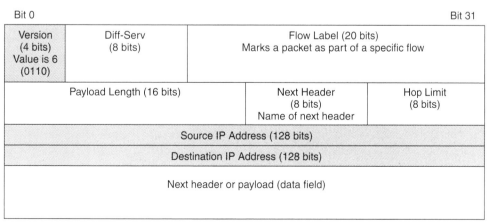

FIGURE A-13 IP Version 6 Packet

second row ends with the hop limit field, which serves the same function as the time to live (TTL) field in IPv4.

   A major innovation in IPv6 is the next header field. IPv6 allows multiple headers. For instance, IPsec security is implemented with a security header. While options are unusual in IPv4, IPv6 uses additional headers extensively. The next header field tells what the next header is. Each subsequent header has a next header field that either identifies the next header or indicates that there is no next header.

TEST YOUR UNDERSTANDING

18. **a.** How long are traditional IP addresses?
    b. What are the three parts of an IP address?
    c. Why are masks needed?
    d. What is the main advantage of IPv6?

IPsec

IP, which was created in the early 1980s, initially had no security at all. In the 1990s, the Internet Engineering Task Force developed a general way to secure IP transmission. This was IP security, which normally is just called IPsec (eye-pea-SEK). IPsec is a general security solution because everything within the data field of the protected packet is secure. This includes the transport message and the application message contained in the transport message. The IP packet, entirely or in part, is also secured, depending on the IPsec operating mode. Originally developed for IPv6, IPsec was extended to IPv4 as well, becoming a completely general security solution. IPsec provides transparent protection to all transport and application layer protocols, meaning that these higher-layer protocols are protected without their even knowing that IPsec is working.

> *IPsec operates in two modes. In transport mode, there is protection all the way from the source host to the destination host. In tunnel mode, there is only protection between sites and none within sites. Transport mode gives stronger protection but is much more expensive to implement. In addition, firewalls cannot easily filter transport mode traffic, which is unreadable unless the firewall has the decryption key for the communication.*

TEST YOUR UNDERSTANDING

19. **a.** In what sense is IPsec a general protection strategy for all internet, transport, and application protocols?
    b. Does IPsec work with IPv4, IPv6, or both?
    c. Compare IPsec transport mode and tunnel mode.

THE TRANSMISSION CONTROL PROTOCOL (TCP)

As noted earlier, the **Transmission Control Protocol (TCP)** is one of the two possible TCP/IP protocols at the transport layer. Figure A-14 shows a TCP message, which is called a **TCP segment**.

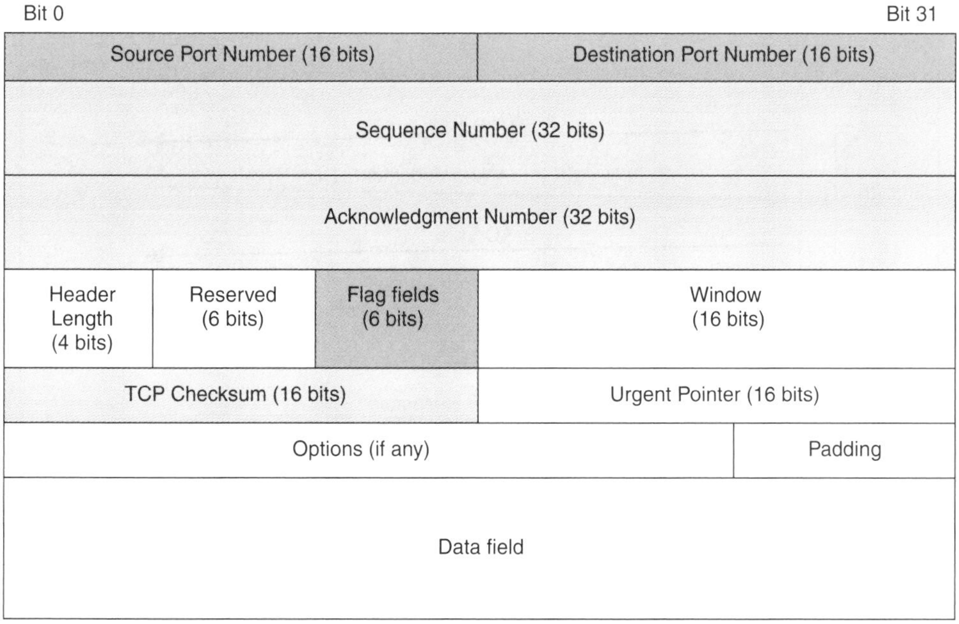

Bit 0   Bit 31

Source Port Number (16 bits)		Destination Port Number (16 bits)	
Sequence Number (32 bits)			
Acknowledgment Number (32 bits)			
Header Length (4 bits)	Reserved (6 bits)	Flag fields (6 bits)	Window (16 bits)
TCP Checksum (16 bits)		Urgent Pointer (16 bits)	
Options (if any)			Padding
Data field			

Flag fields are 1-bit fields. They include SYN, ACK, FIN, RST, PSH, and URG

FIGURE A-14   Transmission Control Protocol (TCP) Segment

TEST YOUR UNDERSTANDING

20. a. How many TCP/IP transport layer protocols are there?
   b. What is a TCP message called?

TCP: A Connection-Oriented and Reliable Protocol

CONNECTIONLESS AND CONNECTION-ORIENTED PROTOCOLS   Protocols are either connectionless or connection oriented.

- **Connection-oriented** protocols are like telephone conversations. When you call someone, there is at least tacit agreement at the beginning of a conversation that you are both willing to speak. For example, such expressions as "Hold, please" and "Can I call you back?" indicate an unwillingness to talk at the moment. Similarly, there is at least tacit agreement that you are done talking at the end of the conversation. (Simply hanging up is considered rude.)
- **Connectionless protocols**, in turn, are like e-mail. You do not need to get someone's permission to send them an e-mail. You just send it.

TCP is a connection-oriented protocol. Figure A-15 shows a sample TCP connection. In TCP, three messages are sent to open a connection. The originator of the connection transmits a TCP SYN segment to indicate that it wishes to open a TCP session. The other transport process sends back a TCP SYN/ACK segment that acknowledges the connection-opening message and indicates that it is willing to open the connection. The originating side then sends an ACK segment to indicate reception of the SYN/ACK segment.

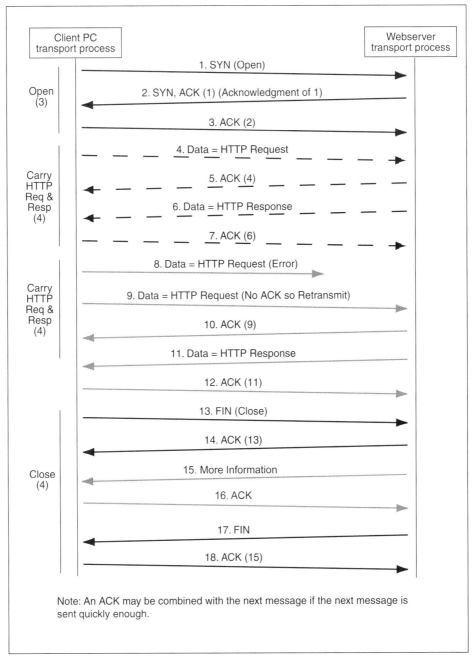

FIGURE A-15 Messages in a TCP Session

Attackers can use TCP connection openings to execute denial-of-service attacks, which make a server unable to respond to legitimate traffic. The attacker sends a SYN segment to open a connection to the victim server. The victim server responds with a SYN/ACK message. The victim server also sets aside resources for the connection. The attacker never responds with an ACK, so this is called a half-open

SYN attack. If the attacker floods a server host with SYN segments, the victim server will reserve so many resources that it will be overloaded and unable to serve legitimate connection-opening attempts. The server may even crash. This is called a TCP half-open attack.

In TCP, ending a conversation normally takes four messages. One side sends a FIN segment, which the second party acknowledges. Then, the second party sends a FIN segment, which the first side acknowledges. The first side will not send any new information after it sends the original FIN segment. It will continue to send acknowledgements for segments sent by the other party.

There is another way to end a session. At any time, either party can send an RST (reset) segment. An RST message ends the conversation abruptly. There is not even an acknowledgement. It is like hanging up in the middle of a telephone conversation. RST messages can also be used to reject connection-opening attempts.

Attackers often preface an attack by attempting to identify the IP addresses of running hosts—much like thieves "casing" a neighborhood. One way to do this is to send TCP SYN segments to hosts. A host that rejects a SYN segment often sends back an RST message. As noted earlier, TCP segments are carried in the data fields of IP packets. The source IP address in the packet delivering the TCP RST segment will be that of the internal host. Whenever the attacker receives an RST segment, it can verify the existence of a working host at that packet's IP address. Firewalls often stop RST segments from leaving a site to prevent them from reaching attackers.

RELIABILITY   In addition to being connectionless or connection oriented, protocols are either reliable or unreliable. A **reliable** protocol detects and corrects errors. An **unreliable protocol** does not. Some unreliable protocols do not even check for errors. Others check for errors but simply discard a message if they find that it contains an error.

TCP is a reliable protocol. It actually corrects errors. This process takes place over three steps.

- When a transport process sends a segment, it first calculates a value based on the values in various fields in the segment. It places this value in the TCP checksum header field. It then sends the segment.
- Second, the receiving transport process performs the same calculation. If the two resultant values are different, an error must have occurred. In cases of error, the receiving process simply drops the segment. If the values match, however, the segment must be correct. The receiving process sends an acknowledgment segment back to the original sending transport process.
- Third, if the transport process that sent the original segment gets an acknowledgment, it does nothing. However, if it does not receive an acknowledgment within a certain period of time, it retransmits the segment.

TEST YOUR UNDERSTANDING

21. **a.** Describe a TCP session opening.
    b. Describe a normal TCP closing.
    c. Describe an abrupt TCP closing.
    d. Describe how reliability is implemented in TCP.
    e. Describe a TCP half-open DoS attack.
    f. What information does a RST segment give an attacker?

Flag Fields

The term **flag field** is a general name for a one-bit field that is logical (true or false). To say that a flag field is **set** means that its value is 1. To say that a flag field is not set means that its value is 0.

The TCP header contains a number of flag fields. One of these is the SYN field. To request a connection opening, the sender sets the SYN bit. The other party sends a SYN/ACK segment, in which both the SYN and ACK bits are set. Other flags are FIN, RST, URG, and PSH.

TEST YOUR UNDERSTANDING

22. **a.** What is a flag field?
    b. What does it mean to say that a flag field is set?

Sequence Number Field

The **sequence number** field value allows the receiver to put arriving TCP segments in order even if the packets carrying them arrive out of order (as can happen when a segment is retransmitted). Sequence numbers are also used in acknowledgments, albeit indirectly. In TCP transmission, every octet that is sent is counted. This octet counting is used to select each segment's sequence number as shown in Figure A-16.

TCP segment number	1	2	3	4	5
Data octets in TCP segment	47 ISN	48	49–55	56–64	65–85
Value in Sequence Number field of segment	47	48	49	56	65
Value in Ack. No. field of acknowledging segment	48	NA	56	65	86

Note: ISN = initial sequence number (randomly generated).

FIGURE A-16 TCP Sequence and Acknowledgment Numbers

- For the first segment, a random initial sequence number (ISN) is placed in the sequence number field. This is 47 in the figure.
- If a segment contains data, the number of the first octet contained in the data field is used as the segment's sequence number. For instance, segment 3 contains octets 49 through 55. Therefore, its sequence number is 49.
- For a purely supervisory message that carries no data, such as an ACK, SYN, SYN/ACK, FIN, or RST segment, the sequence number is increased by one over the previous message. The second section, which is a SYN/ACK segment, therefore receives the sequence number 48.

One dangerous attack is TCP session hijacking, in which an attacker takes over the role of one side. This allows the hijacker to read messages and send false messages to the other side. To accomplish session hijacking, the attacker must be able to predict sequence numbers. If a segment arrives with an inappropriate sequence number, the receiver will reject it. TCP session hijacking is likely to be successful only if the initial sequence number is predictable. Few operating systems today pick initial sequence numbers in a predictable way, but predicable sequence numbers were common in earlier operating systems, a few of which are still in use.

TEST YOUR UNDERSTANDING

23. a. A TCP segment carries octets 23,802 through 23,875. What is its sequence number?
   b. The next segment is a FIN segment that carries no data. What is its sequence number?
   c. What does an attacker have to predict to be able to do TCP session hijacking?

Acknowledgment Number Field

When a receiver sends an acknowledgment, it of course sets the ACK bit. It also puts a value in the **acknowledgement number** field to indicate *which* segment is being acknowledged. This is needed because the sender sends many segments and because acknowledgements may be delayed.

You might think that the acknowledgement number would be the sequence number of the segment being acknowledged. Instead, it is the number of the *last* octet in the data field *plus one*. When Segment 3 in Figure A-16 is acknowledged, for example, its last octet is 55, so the acknowledgment number is 56. In other words, the acknowledgment number gives the octet number of the *first octet in the next segment* to be sent.

TEST YOUR UNDERSTANDING

24. A TCP segment carries octets 23,802 through 23,875. What will be the acknowledgement number in the TCP segment that acknowledges this segment?

Window Field

Flow control limits the rate at which a side sends TCP segments. The TCP **window** field allows one side to limit how many more octets the other side may send before getting another acknowledgement. The process is somewhat complex. In the case of acknowledgements, the sender sets the ACK bit and fills in the acknowledgement *and* window size fields.

The window field helps control congestion. Initially, the window field is given a small value. Often, the sender will have to send one segment and will not be able to send another segment until the first one is acknowledged. This prevents the sender from flooding the network with traffic. If there are no errors, the window field value is increased gradually, so that each side can send several messages before having the first segment acknowledged. If segments are lost due to congestion, however, each side immediately drops back to a small window size.

Options

Like the IPv4 header, the TCP header can have options. However, while IP options are rare and suspicious, TCP uses options extensively. One common option, often sent with the initial SYN or SYN/ACK segment, is the maximum segment size (MSS) option. This gives the other side a limit on the maximum size of TCP segment data fields (not on segment sizes as a whole). The presence of TCP options, then, is not suspicious in itself.

TEST YOUR UNDERSTANDING

25. a. What is the purpose of the TCP window field?
  b. How does the window field automatically control congestion?
  c. Does TCP use options frequently?

Port Numbers

We have now looked at most fields in the TCP header. However, we have skipped the first two fields—the source and destination port number fields—in order to save them for last.

PORT NUMBERS ON SERVERS **Port number** fields mean different things for clients and servers. For a server, a port number represents a specific application running on that server, as Figure A-17 shows. Most servers are multitasking computers, which

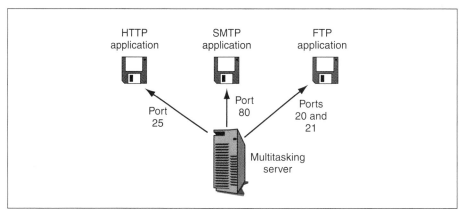

FIGURE A-17 Multitasking Server Host and Port Numbers

means that they can run multiple applications at the same time. Each application is specified by a different port number.

For instance, on a server, a webserver application program may run on TCP Port 80. Incoming TCP segments that have 80 as their destination port number are passed to the webserver application. Actually, TCP Port 80 is the **well-known port number** for webserver programs, meaning that it is the usual port number for the application. Although webservers can be given other TCP port numbers, this makes it impossible for users to establish connections unless they know or can guess the nonstandard TCP port number.

The TCP port range from 0 to 1023 is reserved for the well-known port numbers of major applications, such as HTTP and e-mail. For instance, Simple Mail Transfer Protocol mail server programs usually are run on TCP Port 25, while FTP requires two well-known port numbers—TCP Port 21 for supervisory control and TCP Port 20 for the actual transfer of files.

PORT NUMBERS ON CLIENTS Client hosts use TCP port numbers differently. Whenever a client connects to an application program on a server, it generates a random **ephemeral port number** that it only uses for that connection. On Windows machines, the ephemeral TCP port numbers range is 1024 to 4999.

> *The Microsoft port number range for ephemeral port numbers differs from the official IETF range for ephemeral port numbers, which is 49152 to 65535. The use of nonstandard ephemeral port numbers by Windows and some other operating systems causes problems for firewall filtering.*

SOCKETS Figure A-18 shows that the goal of internetworking is to deliver application messages from one application on one host to another application on another host. On each machine, there is a TCP port number that specifies the application

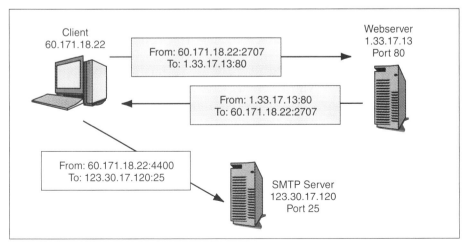

FIGURE A-18 Sockets

(or connection) and an IP address to specify a computer. A **socket** is a combination of an IP address and a TCP port number. It is written as the IP address, a colon, and the TCP port number. A typical socket, then, would be 128.171.17.13:80.

Firewalls often do filtering based on sockets. This is particularly true in static packet inspection (SPI) firewalls.

Attackers often do socket spoofing—both IP address spoofing and port spoofing. For instance, in TCP session hijacking, if the attacker wishes to take over the identity of a client, it must know both the client's IP address and ephemeral port number. Of course, these fields are transmitted in the clear (without encryption) in TCP, so an attacker with a sniffer that captures and reads traffic flowing between the client and server can easily obtain this information.

TEST YOUR UNDERSTANDING

26. **a.** A packet has the source socket 1.2.3.4:47 and the destination socket 10.18.45.123:4400. Is the source host a client or a server? Explain.
    b. Is the destination host a client or a server? Explain.
    c. A server sends a packet with the source socket 60.32.1.79:25. What kind of server is it? Explain.
    d. What is socket spoofing?

TCP Security

Like IP, TCP was created without security. However, while IPsec has made IP secure, the IETF has not created a comprehensive way to secure TCP specifically. One reason for this is IPsec's ability to secure all transport layer traffic transparently, without modification to transport layer protocols. The IETF has made IPsec the centerpiece of its security protections as a single security standard to handle upper-layer security. According to this logic, communicating partners that want TCP security should implement IPsec.

However, few TCP sessions are protected by IPsec. Consequently, some pairs of users employ an option in TCP to add an electronic signature to each TCP segment. This signature proves the identity of the sender. This option, described in RFC 2385, requires the two parties to share a secret value. This option is awkward because it provides no automatic way to share and change keys, and it does not provide encryption or other protections. The option is used primarily in the Border Gateway Protocol (BGP), which we will see briefly later. BGP messages are delivered in the data fields of TCP segments. BGP always uses one-to-one TCP connections, the communicating parties usually know each other quite well, and the two parties usually have long-term relationships, which makes key exchange less burdensome and risky. Outside of BGP, however, the RFC 2385 TCP electronic signature option does not appear to be used significantly. Even in BGP, it is widely seen as very weak security and often is not used at all.

TEST YOUR UNDERSTANDING

27. **a.** Does TCP have comprehensive security comparable with IPsec for IP?
    b. Why is a lack of an automatic key exchange a problem for TCP electronic signatures?

THE USER DATAGRAM PROTOCOL

As noted earlier, TCP is a protocol that makes up for the limitations of IP. TCP adds error correction, the sequencing of IP packets, flow control, and other functionality that we have not discussed.

Not all applications need the reliable service offered by TCP. For instance, voice over IP messages have to be delivered in real time. There is no time to wait for the retransmission of lost or damaged packets carrying voice. In turn, the Simple Network Management Protocol (SNMP), which is used for network management communications, sends so many messages back and forth that the added traffic of connection-opening packets, acknowledgements, and other TCP supervisory segments could overload the network. Consequently, voice over IP, SNMP, and many other applications do not use TCP at the transport layer.

Instead, they use the **User Datagram Protocol (UDP)**. This protocol is connectionless and unreliable. Each UDP message (called a UDP datagram) is sent on its own. There are no openings, closings, or acknowledgements.

As a consequence of the simplicity of UDP's operation, the UDP datagram's organization is also very simple, as Figure A-19 illustrates. There are no sequence numbers, acknowledgment numbers, flag fields, or most of the other fields found in TCP.

There are source and destination port numbers, a UDP header length to allow variable-length UDP datagrams, and a UDP checksum. If the receiver detects an error using the checksum, it simply discards the message. There is no retransmission.

The fact that both TCP and UDP use port numbers means that whenever you refer to port numbers for well-known applications, you also need to refer to whether the port numbers are TCP or UDP port numbers. This is why the well-known port number for webservers is *TCP* port 80.

Like TCP, UDP has no inherent security. Companies that wish to secure their UDP communication must use IPsec.

TCP's sequence numbers make TCP session hijacking very difficult. The receiver will discard messages with the wrong sequence numbers even if the source and destination sockets are correct. UDP lacks this protection, making UDP a somewhat more dangerous protocol than TCP.

Bit 0   Bit 31

Source Port Number (16 bits)	Destination Port Number (16 bits)
UDP Length (16 bits)	UDP Checksum (16 bits)
Data field	

FIGURE A-19 User Datagram Protocol (UDP)

TEST YOUR UNDERSTANDING

28. a. What is the attraction of UDP?
b. What kind of applications specify the use of UDP at the transport layer?
c. Why is UDP more dangerous than TCP?

TCP/IP SUPERVISORY STANDARDS

So far, we have looked at standards that deliver a stream of packets across an internet and that perhaps check for errors and provide other assurances. However, the TCP/IP architecture also includes a number of supervisory protocols that keep the Internet functioning.

Internet Control Message Protocol (ICMP)

The first supervisory protocol on the Internet was the **Internet Control Message Protocol (ICMP)**. As Figure A-20 shows, ICMP messages are delivered in the data fields of IP packets.

The best-known ICMP message types are the ICMP **echo** and **echo reply** messages. Suppose that a host sends an ICMP echo message to an IP address. If a host is active at that address, it may send back an ICMP echo reply message. This process is often called **pinging** because the most popular program for sending ICMP echo messages is called Ping. The echo message is a very important tool for network management. If the network manager suspects a problem, he or she will ping a wide range of host addresses to see which of them are reachable. The pattern of responses can reveal where problems exist within a network.

Attackers also love to ping a wide range of host IP addresses. Replies can give them a list of hosts that are reachable for attacks. Another popular network management and attack tool is traceroute (or tracert on Windows PCs). Traceroute is similar to ping, but

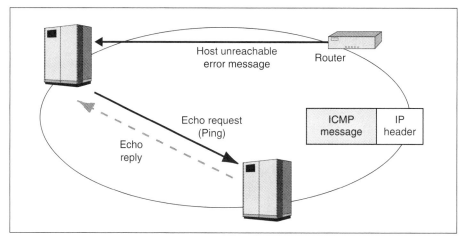

FIGURE A-20   Internet Control Message Protocol (ICMP)

traceroute also lists the routers that lie between the sending host and the host that is the target of the traceroute command. This helps an attacker to map the network. Border firewalls often drop echo reply messages leaving the firm to the outside.

Many ICMP messages are error messages. For instance, if a router cannot deliver the packet, it may send back an ICMP error message to the source host. This error message will provide as much information as possible about the type of error that occurred.

If an attacker cannot ping destination hosts because a firewall stops echo replies, the attacker often sends IP packets that are malformed and so will be rejected. The ICMP error message is delivered in an IP packet, and the source IP address in this packet will reveal the IP address of the sending router. By analyzing error messages, the attacker can learn how routers are organized in a network. This information can be very useful to attackers. Border firewalls often drop all outgoing error messages. In fact, they usually drop all outgoing ICMP messages except for echo messages.

TEST YOUR UNDERSTANDING

29. a. What is the TCP/IP internet layer supervisory protocol?
  b. Describe ping.
  c. Describe ICMP error messages.
  d. What information does ping give an attacker?
  e. What information does tracert give an attacker?
  f. What information does an ICMP error message give an attacker?

The Domain Name System (DNS)

To send a packet to another host, a source host must place the destination host's IP address in the destination address field of the packets. Often, however, the user merely types the host name of the destination host, for instance, cnn.com.

Unfortunately, host names are only nicknames. If the user types a host name, the computer must learn the corresponding IP address. As Figure A-21 shows, a resolver program on the host wishing to send a packet to a target host sends a **Domain Name System (DNS)** request message to the DNS server. This message contains the host name of the target host. The DNS response message sends back the target host's IP address. To give an analogy, if you know someone's name, you must look up their telephone number in a telephone directory. In DNS, the human name corresponds to the host name, the telephone number corresponds to the IP address, and the DNS server corresponds to the telephone directory.

DNS is critical to the Internet's operation. Unfortunately, DNS is vulnerable to several attacks. For example, in DNS cache poisoning, an attacker replaces the IP address of a host name with another IP address. After cache poisoning, a legitimate user who contacts a DNS server to look up the host name will be given the false IP address, sending the user to the attacker's chosen site. Denial-of-service attacks are also too easy to accomplish. RFC 3833 lists a number of DNS security issues.

> *Several attempts to strengthen DNS security have been developed, under the general banner of DNSSEC. However, both the original DNSSEC specifications (especially RFC 2535) and the newer DNSSEC bis specifications (RFCs 4033–4035) have proven to be insufficient. Developing a security standard that is sufficiently backwardly compatible for Internet-scale implementation has proven to be extremely difficult.*

If the original DNS server does not know the host name, it contacts another DNS server. The DNS system contains many DNS servers organized in a hierarchy. At the top of the hierarchy are 13 DNS root servers. Below these are DNS servers for top-level domains, such as .com, .edu, .IE, .UK, .NL, and .CA. Each top-level domain administrator maintains several top-level DNS servers for its domain. Second-level domain names are given to organizations (for instance, Hawaii.edu and Microsoft.com). Each organization with a second-level domain is required to maintain one or more DNS servers that know the host names of computers within its domain.

> *If attackers could bring down the 13 root servers, they could paralyze the Internet. Widespread paralysis would not occur immediately, but in a few days, the Internet would begin experiencing serious outages.*

TEST YOUR UNDERSTANDING

30. **a.** Why would a host contact a DNS server?
    b. If a local DNS server does not know the IP address for a host name, what will it do?
    c. What kind of organization must maintain one or more DNS servers?
    d. What is DNS cache poisoning?
    e. Describe the status of DNSSEC.
    f. Why are root servers attacked?

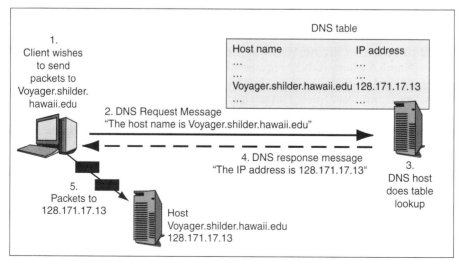

FIGURE A-21 Domain Name System (DNS) Server

Dynamic Host Configuration Protocol (DHCP)

Server hosts are given permanent **static IP addresses**. Client PCs, however, are given temporary **dynamic IP addresses** whenever they use the Internet. The **Dynamic Host Configuration Protocol (DHCP)** standard that we saw earlier in the module makes this possible. A DHCP server has a database of available IP addresses. When a client requests an IP address, the DHCP server picks one from the database and sends it to the client. The next time the client uses the Internet, the DHCP server may give it a different IP address.

> *The fact that clients may receive different IP addresses each time they get on the Internet causes problems for peer-to-peer (P2P) applications. A presence server or some other mechanism must be used to find the other party's IP address. A lack of accepted standards for presence (including presence security) is a serious issue now that P2P applications are widespread. In fact, most security considerations in P2P presence servers have involved presence servers trying to* avoid *discovery by legitimate authorities.*

TEST YOUR UNDERSTANDING

31. a. What kind of IP addresses do servers get?
   b. Why are DHCP servers used?
   c. Will a PC get the same dynamic IP address each time it uses the Internet?
   d. Both DHCP servers and DNS servers give IP addresses. How do these IP addresses differ?

Dynamic Routing Protocols

How do routers on the Internet learn what to do with packets addressed to various IP addresses? The answer is that frequently talk to one another, exchanging information about the organization of the Internet. These exchanges must occur frequently because the structure of the Internet changes frequently as routers are added or dropped. Protocols for exchanging organization information are called **dynamic routing protocols**.

There are many dynamic routing protocols, including the Routing Information Protocol (RIP), Open Shortest Path First (OSPF), the Border Gateway Protocol (BGP), and Cisco Systems' proprietary EIGRP. As Figure A-22 shows, each is used under different circumstances.

- RIP and OSPF are *interior* TCP/IP dynamic routing protocols, meaning that they are used within an anonymous system. (Roughly speaking, an anonymous system is a large organization or ISP.) RIP is too limited for large organizations. OSPF is highly functional, efficient in large organizations, and (when used properly) highly secure.
- EIGRP is also an interior dynamic routing protocol, but it is a *multiprotocol* interior dynamic routing protocol. This means that it is not limited to IP routing. It can also handle NetWare IPX routing, IBM SNA routing, AppleTalk packet routing, and the packets of other standards architectures.

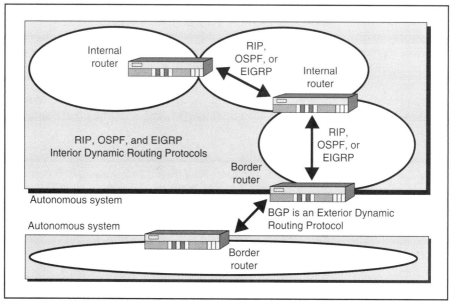

FIGURE A-22 Dynamic Routing Protocols

- BGP is an exterior TCP/IP dynamic routing protocol, meaning that it is used between different autonomous systems. While a firm is free to use whatever interior dynamic routing protocol it wishes, autonomous systems must negotiate what exterior dynamic routing protocol to use. (In most cases, the larger system's negotiation stance is, "Use this or else.") BGP is the only widely used exterior dynamic routing protocol.

If an attacker can impersonate a router, he or she can send false dynamic routing protocol messages to other routers. These false messages could cause the routers to misdeliver their packets. The attacker could even cause packets to pass through the attacker's computer, in order to read their contents.

The protocols listed above have widely different security features, and different versions of each protocol have different levels of security functionality.

BGP is especially important because it runs the Internet. If attackers can spoof BGP communications, they can do massive damage. They can even do a surprising amount of damage by accident. In 2008, a Pakistan ISP, prompted by Pakistan's efforts to control indecent content, decided to black-hole YouTube. It grabbed all YouTube traffic in Pakistan and directed it to nonexistent IP addresses. Unfortunately, its BGP announcement that it was the best way to reach YouTube spread outside of Pakistan and shut YouTube down worldwide for a few hours.

TEST YOUR UNDERSTANDING

32. **a.** Why are dynamic routing protocols needed?
    b. What is the main TCP/IP interior dynamic routing protocol for large networks?
    c. What is the main TCP/IP exterior dynamic routing protocol?

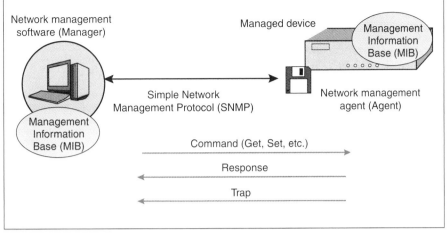

FIGURE A-23   Simple Network Management Protocol (SNMP)

    d. Why is Cisco's EIGRP attractive?
    e. Is a company free to select its interior dynamic routing protocol, exterior dynamic routing protocol, or both?
    f. How could an attacker use dynamic routing protocols to attack a network?

Simple Network Management Protocol (SNMP)

Networks often have many elements, including routers, switches, and host computers. Managing dozens, hundreds, or thousands of devices can be nearly impossible. To make management easier, the IETF developed the **Simple Network Management Protocol (SNMP)**. As Figure A-23 shows, the manager program can send SNMP GET messages to tell managed devices to send back certain information. The manager can even send SET messages that can change the configurations of remote devices. This allows the manager to fix many problems remotely.

> *Many firms disable remote configuration because of the damage that attackers could do with it. For instance, SET can be used to get routers to misroute some or all packets or route all packets through an attacker's sniffer.*

TEST YOUR UNDERSTANDING

33. a. What is the purpose of SNMP?
    b. Distinguish between the SNMP GET and SET commands.
    c. Why do many organizations disable the SET command?

APPLICATION STANDARDS

Most applications have their own application layer standards. In fact, given the large number of applications in the world, there is a multitude of application layer standards. This means a multitude of potential security issues at the application level.

Application Exploits

By taking over applications, hackers gain the permissions of the exploited program

A multitude of application standards

Consequently, a multitude of security issues at the application level

Many Applications Need Two Types of Standards

One for the transmission of messages, one for the content of application documents

For the World Wide Web, these are HTTP and HTML, respectively

For transmission, e-mail uses SMTP, POP, and IMAP

For message content, e-mail uses RFC 2822 (all-text), HTML, and MIME

FTP and Telnet

Have no security

Passwords are transmitted in the clear so can be captured by sniffers

Secure Shell (SSH) can replace both securely

Many Other Application Standards Have Security Issues

Voice over IP

Service-oriented architecture (SOA); web services

Peer-to-peer applications

FIGURE A-24 Application Standards (Study Figure)

As corporations get better at defending against attacks at lower layers, attackers have switched their focus to applications. If an attacker can take over an application running with high privileges, he or she usually obtains these privileges. Many applications run at the highest privileges, and attackers that compromise them "own the box."

HTTP AND HTML Many applications have two types of standards. One is a transport standard to transfer application layer messages between applications on different machines. For the World Wide Web, this is the **Hypertext Transfer Protocol (HTTP)**. The other is a standard for document structure. The main document structure standard for the WWW is the **Hypertext Markup Language (HTML)**.

Netscape, which created the first widely used browser, also created a security standard to protect HTTP communication. This was Secure Sockets Layer (SSL). Later, the Internet Engineering Task Force took over SSL and changed the name of the standard to Transport Layer Security (TLS).

E-MAIL For E-mail, in turn, popular transfer standards are the **Simple Mail Transfer Protocol (SMTP)** for sending e-mail and **POP** and **IMAP** for downloading e-mail to a client from a mailbox on a server. Popular document body standards include RFC 2822 (for all-text messages), HTML, and MIME.

An obvious security issue in e-mail is content filtering. Viruses, spam, phishing messages, and other undesirable content should be filtered out before they reach users and can do damage.

Another security issue in e-mail is the securing of messages flowing from the sending client to the sender's mail server, from the sender's mail server to the receiver's mail server, and from the receiving mail server to the receiving client. Fortunately, there are security standards to protect these message flows. The leading standards are SSL/TLS and S/MIME. Unfortunately, the IETF has been unable to agree upon a single security standard. This lack of standards clarity has hurt the adoption of e-mail security.

When web mail, which uses HTTP and HTML for e-mail communication, is used, SSL/TLS can work between the sender and the sender's mail server and between the receiver's mail server and the receiver. Transmission between the e-mail servers is another issue. Of course, senders can send encrypted message bodies directly to receivers. However, this prevents filtering at firewalls.

TELNET, FTP, AND SSH   The two earliest applications on the Internet were the **File Transfer Protocol (FTP)** and **Telnet**. FTP provides bulk file transfers between hosts. Telnet allows a user to launch a command shell (user interface) on another computer. Neither of these standards has any security. Of particular concern is that both send passwords in the clear (without encryption) during login. The newer **Secure Shell (SSH)** standard can be used in place of both FTP and Telnet while providing high security.

OTHER APPLICATION STANDARDS   There are many other applications and therefore application standards. These include voice over IP (VoIP), peer-to-peer applications, and service oriented architecture (Web service) applications, among many others. Most new applications have challenging security issues. Application security has become perhaps the most complex aspect of network security.

TEST YOUR UNDERSTANDING

34. **a.** Why are there usually two protocols for each application?
   b. In e-mail, distinguish between SNMP and POP.
   c. Why are Telnet and FTP dangerous?
   d. What secure protocol can be used instead of Telnet and FTP?
   e. What is the security standards situation in e-mail?

CONCLUSION

When the Internet was created in the early 1980s, its standards almost completely ignored security. In the first idyllic years of the Internet, this benign neglect made sense. Attacks, while not absent, were merely a nuisance. During the 1990s, when the Internet grew explosively, attackers gravitated to the Internet rapidly. Since then, there has been an arms race between attackers and corporate defenders.

Most attacks take place over networks, including both the Internet and internal networks. The objective of this module has been to cover important networking concepts that security specialists need to understand to work effectively. Within the module text, the security implications of various networking concepts were noted briefly.

GLOSSARY

27000. See **ISO/IEC 27000**.

802.11i. Very strong core security protocol protecting communication between an access point and a wireless client.

802.1X. Standard for requiring authentication before a device may attach to a switch or access point. Use in access points requires an extension, 802.11i.

802.1X mode. In WPA and 802.11i, mode of operation in which a central authentication server is used and the access point is the authenticator.

Abuse. Activities that violate a company's IT use policies or ethics policies.

Acceptable use policy. Policy that summarizes key points of special importance to users.

Access card. A plastic card that usually is the size of a credit or debit card. Used for authentication.

Access control. The policy-driven control of access to systems, data, and dialogues.

Access control list. List of rules for allowing or not allowing access.

Access control. The policy-driven control of access to systems, data, and dialogues.

Access control models. In military security, rules for handling multilevel security.

Accountability. Holding a particular person responsible for a resource or action.

Accreditation. In FISMA, the acceptance by an accreditation official of a certification that a particular system meets FISMA requirements.

ACL. See **access control list**.

Administrator. The super account in Microsoft Windows.

Admissible. In evidence, suitable to be presented in court.

Advanced Encryption Standard. Preferred symmetric key encryption standard today. Key lengths of 128 bits, 192 bits, or 256 bits. Places a relatively light processing burden on devices that use it.

AES. See **Advanced Encryption Standard**.

Alarm. An alert sent by an automated system when there is an indication of problems.

Anomaly detection. Attack detection based on unusual patterns in network traffic.

Application proxy firewall. Firewall that examines the content of application messages and provides other protections.

Archiving. Storing backed-up data for extended periods.

Attack signature. Characteristic of an attack. Used by firewall to detect attacks.

Auditing. 1) Collecting information about the activities of each individual in log files for immediate and later analysis. 2) A process involving sampling in order to develop opinions on the health of controls, not to find punishable instances of noncompliance.

AUP. See **acceptable use policy**.

Authentication. Assessing the identity of each individual claiming to have permission to use a resource.

Authenticator. Device to which a computer attaches to get network access. Usually a switch or an access point.

Authorizations. Specific permissions that a particular authenticated user should have, given his or her authenticated identity.

Autorun. On USB memory sticks, the ability of programs to run as soon as the stick is inserted, without user intervention.

Bandwidth limitation. Limits the amount of network capacity that a type of suspicious traffic may use.

Bank account theft. Taking money from a victim's bank account.

Baseline. A detailed description of what should be done but not how to do it.

Batch transfer. Transferring information occasionally, in large amounts.

Best practices. Descriptions of what the best firms in the industry are doing about security.

Biometric authentication. Authentication based on bodily measurements and motions.

Black hole. (Verb) To drop all packets from a particular IP address.

Black market websites. Places where attackers sell information and goods.

Blended threats. Malware that propagates both as viruses and worms.

Block encryption. Dividing a plaintext message into blocks and encrypting each block in series.

Border firewall. Firewall at the border between a site and the outside world.

Bots. Attack programs stored on many computers. Can be told to attack victims and can be updated to add functionality or fix bugs.

Breach. Successful attack.

Brute-force guessing. Trying all possible passwords or keys to find the right one.

Brute-force key cracking. Trying all possible keys until the cryptanalyst finds the right key.

Business continuity. The continued operation of the firm or the restoration of operation.

CA. See **certificate authority**.

Carding. See **credit card number theft**.

Career criminals. Attackers who attack for purely criminal motives.

Case law. Court interpretations of laws.

CDP. See **continuous data protection**.

Central authentication server. Maintains a central authentication database and checks credentials for many authenticators.

Central firewall management system. System that pushes filtering rules out to individual firewalls based on firewall policies.

Certificate authority. An organization that provides digital certificates.

Certificate revocation list. A list of serial numbers of a certificate authority's revoked digital certificates.

Certification. In FISMA, stating that a particular system meets FISMA requirements. Conducted by the agency owning the system or by an outside agency. System still must be accredited.

Chain of attack computers. A series of computers taken over by an attacker. Victim cannot trace an attack all the way back to the attacker's computer.

Chain of custody. The documented history of all transfers of the evidence between people and of all actions taken to protect the evidence while in each person's possession.

Challenge message. In authentication, a string sent by the verifier to the supplicant.

Chief security officer (CSO). Common title for the director of IT security.

CIA. Confidentiality, integrity, and availability.

Cipher. A specific mathematical process used in encryption and decryption.

Cipher suite. In SSL/TLS, a candidate set of methods and options to be used in a dialogue.

Ciphertext. What plaintext is enciphered into in encryption for confidentiality.

Civil law. Deals with interpretations of rights and duties that companies or individuals have relative to each other.

Classic risk analysis calculation. Method presented in Chapter 2 for doing risk analysis calculations.

Click fraud. A criminal website owner creates a program to click on the link repeatedly. Each of these bogus clicks takes money from the advertiser without generating potential customers.

CobiT. Governance framework used for high-level governance in IT.

Codes. Confidentiality methods in which code symbols represent complete words or phrases. Codes are not ciphers.

Cold sites. Physical backup facilities with electrical power, and HVAC, but that are empty rooms with connections to the outside world. To use a cold site, the company has to procure, bring in, and set up hardware; install software; and mount data.

Common word passwords. Passwords made from dictionary words or names. Easily cracked by dictionary attacks.

Complex passwords. Passwords that use a combination of letters, digits, and other keyboard characters.

Compliance laws and regulations. Laws and regulations that create requirements to which corporate security must respond.

Comprehensive security. Closing all routes of attack to their systems to attackers.

Compromise. Successful attack.

Computer forensics expert. Person certified to be able to give expert witness testimony, which includes the interpretation of facts and not simply the presentation of facts.

Computer security incident response team. Team used to handle major incidents. Has members from various parts of the firm.

Confidentiality. Protections that prevent people who intercept messages from reading them.

Connections. Persistent conversations between different programs on different computers.

Containment. In incident response, stopping the damage.

Continuous data protection. Continuous data backup to another site so that the other site can take over processing within minutes.

Contract workers. People who work for a firm for brief periods of time and are not employees.

Control. Tool to thwart an attack.

Cookie. Small text string stored on your computer by a website for later retrieval.

Corporate security policy. A brief statement that emphasizes a firm's commitment to strong security.

Corrective countermeasures. Tools to get the business process back on track after a compromise.

COSO. Governance framework used for high-level governance in the corporation.

Countermeasure. Tool to thwart an attack.

Credentials. Proofs of identity sent from the supplicant to the verifier.

Credit card number theft. Stealing credit card numbers. You actually looked this up?

Criminal law. Deals with the violation of criminal statutes (laws).

CRL. See **certificate revocation list**.

Cryptanalyst. Someone who cracks encryption.

Cryptography. The use of mathematical operations to protect messages traveling between parties or stored on a computer.

Cryptographic system. A packaged set of cryptographic countermeasures for protecting dialogues.

Cryptographic system standard. A standard for a particular type of cryptographic system.

Cryptographic VPN. See **virtual private network**.

CSIRT. See **computer security incident response team**.

CSO. See **chief security officer**.

Cybercrime. The execution of crimes on or against a computer or a network.

Cyberterror. Attacks by terrorists.

Cyberwar. Computer-based attacks made by national governments.

Data destruction. Destroying data by destroying a medium or writing over it with drive-wiping software.

Data Encryption Standard. Symmetric key encryption cipher with 56-bit keys.

Data extrusion management. Tools to prevent the unauthorized sending of sensitive data outside the corporation.

Data mining spyware. Spyware that searches through your disk drives for sensitive information.

Deception. In biometrics, when someone attempts to deceive a biometric access device.

Decryption. The process of converting ciphertext to plaintext.

Deep packet inspection. Inspecting all layer content in a packet.

Defendant. Party charged in a criminal or civil trial.

Defense in depth. Requiring an attacker to break through multiple countermeasures to succeed.

Demilitarized zone. Subnet that contains all of the servers and application proxy firewalls that must be accessible to the outside world.

Denial-of-service (DoS) attack. Attack attempts to make a server or network unavailable to serve legitimate users by flooding it with attack packets.

DES. See **Data Encryption Standard**.

Detective countermeasures. Tools that identify when a threat is attacking and especially when it is succeeding.

Dictionary attack. Cracking passwords by comparing them to dictionary terms.

Diffie–Hellman key agreement. A keying method that does not use encryption. The two sides exchange keying information, but an eavesdropper reading the exchanged keying information cannot compute the key.

Digital certificate. A file that gives a party's name and public key securely.

Digital rights management. Restricts what people can do with data.

Digital signature. Electronic signature that authenticates a single message with public key encryption and that gives message integrity as a by-product. Produced by signing the message digest with the sender's private key.

Direct-propagation worm. Worm that can jump to a computer that contains a specific vulnerability.

Directory server. Server that stores information about people and resources in a company, including security information for checking access credentials.

Disconnection. Disconnecting a compromised computer from the Internet or turning it off.

Discretionary access control. In military security, departments have discretion to alter access control rules set by higher authorities.

Disk image. A copy of an entire disk. Can be copied onto another machine.

Distribution. A version of LINUX including a kernel and other programs.

DMZ. See **demilitarized zone**.

DoS Attack. See **denial of service** attack.

Driving forces. Things that require a firm to change its security planning, protections, and response.

DRM. See **digital rights management**.

Due diligence. Examining the security system of a potential business partner before entering into data exchanges with that person.

Dumpster™ diving. An attacker goes through a firm's trash bins looking for documents, backup tapes, floppy disks, and other information-carrying media.

EAP. See **Extensible Authentication Protocol**.

EAP-TLS. Extended EAP standard using TLS that requires both the client and the authenticator to have digital certificates.

Eavesdropper. Someone who intercepts a message and reads it.

ECC. See **elliptic curve cryptography**.

Egress filtering. Firewall filtering for packets leaving a network.

Electronic signature. A string of bits added to a message sent during the ongoing communication stage to authenticate the sender and provide a message integrity check.

Elliptic curve cryptography. A widely used public key encryption cipher.

Encapsulating security payload. In IPsec, a header and trailer that mark the limitations of protection for content in a packet.

Encryption for confidentiality. Encryption that prevents interceptors from reading information.

Enterprise mode. Name given by the Wi-Fi Alliance to 802.1X mode in WPA and 802.11i.

Escalation. Passing responsibility for an incident to a more capable higher-level group.

ESP. See **encapsulating security payload**.

European Union (E.U.) Data Protection Directive. A broad set of rules ensuring privacy rights in Europe.

Event correlation. Sorting data from many intrusion detection systems in time so that events that occur at the same time can be seen as occurring together.

Evil twin access points. A PC that has software to allow it to masquerade as an access point. Executes a man-in-the-middle attack against the wireless client and a legitimate access point.

Exception handling. A procedure for handling exceptions in a particular circumstance. Actions are limited and documented.

Exhaustive search. Trying *all possible keys* until he or she finds the correct one.

Expert witness. Person certified to be able to give expert witness testimony, which includes the interpretation of facts and not simply the presentation of facts.

Exploit. Term related to break-ins. Refers to software used to break in or the act of breaking in.

Extended EAP standard. Extension to the Extensible Authentication Protocol that provides security to interactions between a wireless device and a wireless access point before authentication begins.

Extensible Authentication Protocol. Protocol to govern the specifics of authentication interactions.

Extortion. Attack in which the perpetrator tries to obtain money or other goods by threatening to take actions that would be against the victim's interest.

Face recognition. Biometric recognition based on a person's facial features.

Fail safely. If a protection fails, it does so in a way that does not compromise security, even if this means causing inconvenience.

Failure to enroll. When a person cannot enroll in a biometric system.

False acceptance rate. The percentage of people who should not be matched who are.

False negative. Not recognizing a true incident.

False open attack. Denial-of-service attack in which the attacker sends SYN segments but never responds to SYN/ACK replies.

False positive. Calling an innocent even a security problem. False alarm.

False rejection rate. The percentage of people who should be matched that are not.

FAR. See **false acceptance rate**.

Federal Rules of Evidence. Restrictions on evidence presentation in U.S. federal trials.

Federal Trade Commission. U.S. federal agency that prosecutes companies that fail to protect the privacy of customer information.

Federated Identity Management. System in which two companies can pass identity assertions to each other without allowing the other to access internal data.

File/directory data backup. Backing up the data in certain files and directories.

Financial theft. The misappropriation of assets or the theft of money.

Fingerprint recognition. Biometric recognition based on fingerprint patterns.

Firewall appliances. Pre-packaged firewalls.

Firewall policies. Policies to be executed on firewalls.

FISMA. Federal Information Security Management Act. Imposes security processes on government agencies and contractors.

Fixes. Work-arounds, patches, or other ways to deal with a vulnerability.

Forensics evidence. Evidence that is acceptable for court proceedings.

Fraud. Attacks that deceive the victim into doing something against the victim's financial self-interest.

Fraud and abuse triangle. Method of behavioral awareness that suggests that to commit bad actions, people need opportunity, motive, and the ability to rationalize their actions.

FRR. See **false rejection rate**.

FTC. See **Federal Trade Commission**.

Full backup. Backing up all specified files and folders.

GLBA. See **Gramm–Leach–Bliley Act**.

Governance frameworks. Specify how to do planning, implementation, and oversight.

GPO. See **group policy object**.

Gramm–Leach–Bliley Act. Act that requires strong data protection in financial institutions.

Group. In permissions, all members of the group receive permissions assigned to the group.

Group policy objects. In Windows, security policies that can be pushed out to individual hosts.

Guideline. Discretionary implementation guidance.

Hacker scripts. Programs written by hackers to help them hack computers.

Hacking. Intentionally accessing a computer resource without authorization or in excess of authorization.

Hacking root. Taking over the super user account.

Hand geometry recognition. Biometric recognition based on the shape of the hand.

Handshaking stages. In cryptographic systems, a set of three stages that takes place before ongoing communication: negotiating security methods and options, initial authentication, and keying.

Hash. In hashing, the result of hashing. The hash is a bit stream of short fixed length.

Hashing. A mathematical operation that, when applied to a long bit string, produces a bit stream of short fixed length.

Health Information Portability and Accountability Act. Act that requires strong data protection in health institutions.

HIDS. Host intrusion detection system.

HIPAA. See **Health Information Portability and Accountability Act**.

HMAC. See **key-hashed message authentication code**.

Hoaxes. E-mail messages that give false information.

Honeypot. A virtual network or host into which attackers are lured so that their behavior can be understood.

Host firewall. Software firewall on a client or server.

Host hardening. A group of actions to make a client or server more difficult to attack.

Host intrusion detection system. Intrusion detection system that reads all traffic going into and out of a host and that measures actions taken on the host, such as file accesses.

Host-to-host VPN. Virtual private network that links two hosts.

Hot site. Physical backup facility with power, HVAC (heating, ventilation, and air conditioning), hardware, installed software, and up-to-date data.

HVAC. Heating, ventilation, and air conditioning.

Hybrid dictionary attacks. Dictionary attacks that try such simple modifications of common words.

Identification. Done when the verifier determines the identity of the supplicant.

Identity management. The centralized policy-based management of all information required for access to corporate systems by people, machines, programs, or other resources.

Identity theft. Attacks in which the thief impersonates the victim sufficiently well to engage in large financial transactions.

IDS. See **intrusion detection system**.

IETF. See **Internet Engineering Task Force**.

IKE. See **Internet Key Exchange**.

Implementation guidance. Guidance limits the discretion of implementers, in order to simplify implementation decisions and to avoid bad choices in interpreting policies.

Incident. Successful attack.

Incremental backup. Backing up all files and folders that were changed since the last full backup.

Independence. The ability of the security function to report on a security infraction without reprisal.

Information assurance. Assuring that damage will not occur. An oxymoron.

Ingress filtering. Firewall filtering for packets entering a network.

Inheritance. In permissions, automatically receiving the permissions of the parent directory.

Initial authentication. Authentication before ongoing communication.

Integrated log file. A centralized log file created from other log files.

Integrity. Means that attackers cannot change or destroy information.

Intellectual property (IP). Information owned by the company and protected by law.

Internal rate of return. A return on investment calculation method.

Internet Engineering Task Force. Agency that creates the TCP/IP standards used on the Internet and in most corporate networks.

Internet Key Exchange. A general protocol for protecting the establishment of security associations in cryptographic systems.

Interorganizational systems. When two companies link some of their IT assets.

Intrusion detection system. System that reads network traffic to find suspicious packets.

Intrusion prevention system. Firewall that uses intrusion detection system filtering methods to identify and stop high-confidence attacks.

IP address scanning. Sending probes to a range of IP addresses to identify victims.

IPS. See **intrusion prevention system**.

IPsec. A family of cryptographic system standards created by the IETF for security at the internet layer. Provides transparent protection to everything in the data field of a packet.

IPsec gateway. A site gateway that terminates IPsec tunnel mode operation.

IPsec policy servers. Servers that push a list of suitable policies to individual IPsec gateway servers or hosts.

Iris recognition. Biometric recognition based on the colored part of the eye.

IRR. See **net present value**.

Irreversible. Something that cannot be undone. Hashing is irreversible.

ISO/IEC 27000. Governance framework specifically for IT security. Really, a family of standards.

IT disaster recovery. Recovery from a disaster that affects IT.

Jurisdictions. Areas of responsibility within which government bodies can make and enforce laws but beyond which they cannot.

Kerberos. Authentication system that has three parties—a Kerberos key server, a supplicant host, and a verifier host.

Kerckhoffs' Law. In order to have confidentiality, communication partners only need to keep the key secret, not the cipher.

Key. A random bit stream that is used with a cipher in encryption and decryption.

Key escrow. Storing an encryption key so that it can be retrieved if it is lost.

Key features. Data extracted from a biometric scan. Stored as the user template in enrollment scans. For authentication scans, compared with the template.

Key length. The length of a key in bits. Longer keys take longer to cryptanalyze.

Key-Hashed Message Authentication Code. Electronic signature that authenticates a single message with hashing and that gives message integrity as a by-product.

Keying. Sending keys or secrets securely.

Keystroke capture program. Steals keystrokes as the user types them in and sends the keystrokes to the attacker.

Keystroke loggers. Spyware that captures all of your keystrokes.

Latent print. A fingerprint that is not visible to the eye.

LDAP. See **Lightweight Directory Access Protocol**.

Legacy security technologies. Security technologies that a company implemented in the past but that now are at least somewhat ineffective.

Lifecycle identity management. Managing identities from their creations to their deletions.

Lightweight Directory Access Protocol. Protocol for communicating with a directory server.

Live tests. Rehearsals in the team that actually takes incident-recovery actions instead of merely describing what they would do.

Log file. File containing information about events, such as the dropping of packets by a firewall.

Magnetic stripe cards. Authentication cards that contain data on a magnetic stripe.

Major incident. Incident beyond the abilities of the on-duty staff to handle. Requires the activation of the firm's computer security incident response team (CSIRT).

Malicious payloads. Malware payloads that are designed to do damage.

Malware. Generic name for evil software.

Managed security service provider. A company that provides a wide range of outsourced security functions.

Mandatory access control. In military security, departments have no ability to alter access control rules set by higher authorities.

Match index. Comparison between a user's template and key data from an access scan.

Material control deficiency. A material deficiency, or combination of significant deficiencies, that results in more than a remote likelihood that a material misstatement in the annual or interim financial statements will not be prevented or detected.

MD5. Nonsecure hashing algorithm.

Mens rea. Literally, "guilty mind," Intent. Often must be proven in criminal trials.

Mesh backup. Peer-to-peer service in which PCs automatically provide backup to other PCs.

Message digest. In digital signatures, the message digest is the hash of the entire plaintext message. Signing the message digest with the sender's private key gives the digital signature.

Message integrity. The ability to reject an altered message.

Message-by-message authentication. Provides authentication for each message after the handshaking stages are completed.

Metadirectory server. An server that manages information in multiple directory servers.

Minor incidents. Incidents that can be handled by the on-duty staff.

Mobile code. Code on a webpage that executes when the webpage is downloaded.

Money mules. People who transfer money for criminals.

Monitor. Collect data electronically on actions.

Motion detection. In closed-circuit surveillance camera system, only recording when there is motion or even a particular type of motion.

MPLS. See **MultiProtocol Label Switching**.

MS-CHAP. Initial authentication method used for logging into the server. Relies on the fact that the user and the server should be the only entities to know the user's password.

MSSP. See **Managed security service provider**.

Multifactor authentication. Requiring a supplicant to supply two or more sets of authentication credentials. May provide defense in depth.

Multilevel security. In military security, the classification of resources in such terms as public, confidential, secret, top secret, and top secret compartmentalized. Users must have the same or higher level of clearance.

MultiProtocol Label Switching. A protocol for increasing the efficiency of routed networks by determining the transmission path of all packets between two points before a conversation begins between those two points. Routes are hidden from subscribers, providing security by obscurity.

Mutual authentication. Authentication in which each party authenticates itself to the other party.

NAC. See **network access control**.

NAT. See **network address translation**.

Network access control. Checking the status of client PC's security before allowing it into a network; often also checking its security after access is allowed.

Network address translation. Process of hiding internal IP addresses and port numbers to thwart sniffers.

Network intrusion detection system. Intrusion detection system that reads all traffic passing through a network location.

Network Time Protocol. Protocol that allows multiple hosts to synchronize their clocks from a network time protocol server.

NIDS. Network intrusion detection system.

Nonce. A field in a message that contains a random number; the reply includes the same nonce. Useful in thwarting replay attacks.

Nonrepudiation. A sender cannot repudiate a message. Digital signatures have nonrepudiation; HMACs do not.

NTP. See **Network Time Protocol**.

OCSP. See **Online Certificate Status Protocol**.

One-time password. A password used only once.

Ongoing communication. Stage in a cryptographic system after initial handshaking exchanges have been completed.

Online Certificate Status Protocol. A protocol for querying a certificate authority about the revocation status of a particular digital certificate.

Outer authentication. In Extended EAP standards, provides confidentiality within which normal EAP authentication methods can operate.

Outsource. To pay another company to handle some security function.

Oversight is a term for a group of tools for policy enforcement.

Owner. The person who is accountable for a resource.

Owning a computer. Having total control over a computer.

Oxymoron. See **information assurance**.

Packet stream analysis. Analyzing streams of packets to look for suspicious content.

Passphrase. A long string of keyboard characters that is converted into a key in 802.11i and WPA pre-shared key mode.

Password. A keyboard string used to authenticate access to a user account.

Password reset. Giving a user who has forgotten his or her password a new password.

Password-cracking program. Program that tries all possible passwords until it cracks one or more passwords.

Password-stealing spyware. Spyware that attempts to steal passwords as you type them.

Patch. Piece of software that can be installed to close a vulnerability.

Patch management servers. Push patches out to hosts that need them.

Payloads. In malware, pieces of code that do damage.

Payment Card Industry–Data Security Standard (PCI-DSS). Controls that must be followed by companies that deal with credit cards.

PCI-DSS. See **Payment Card Industry–Data Security Standard**.

PEAP. See **Protected EAP**.

Permissions. Actions that a particular authenticated user can take, given his or her authenticated identity.

Personal identification number. A brief series of numbers (four to six) entered manually as a second form of authentication.

Personal mode. Name given by the Wi-Fi Alliance to pre-shared key mode.

Phishing attacks. Attacks that create authentic-looking websites or e-mail messages.

Piggybacking. Following someone through a secure door without entering a pass code. Also called tailgating.

PIN. See **personal identification number**.

PKI. See **public key infrastructure**.

Plaintext. The original message in encryption for confidentiality.

Plaintiff. Party who brings a civil lawsuit.

Plan–protect–respond cycle. Top-level security management process that consists of three stages: planning, protecting (defending), and responding (to breaches).

Policy. Statement of *what* should be done, not *how* it should be done.

Port scanning. Probes sent to identified host in order to determine which applications the host is running.

Post-mortem evaluation. Evaluating the lessons learned during incident or disaster response.

PPR. See **plan–protect–respond**.

Preserving evidence. Maintaining evidence in a way that does not compromise its useability in court.

Pre-shared key mode. Mode of operation in WPA and 802.11i in which all clients share the same initial key. Only useful if a firm has a single access point.

Pretexting. Claiming to be a certain person in order to get private information about that person.

Preventative countermeasures. Tools to keep attacks from succeeding.

Prime authentication problem. Checking a person's human credentials before giving access credentials.

Principle of least permissions. Principle that each person should only get the permissions that he or she absolutely needs to do his or her job.

Private key. In public key encryption, a key that only the owner knows. Knowledge of this key can be used in authentication.

Procedure. Specification of the detailed actions that must be taken by specific employees.

Process. 1) A planned series of actions. 2) Specification of the general actions that must be taken by specific employees.

Prosecutor. Official who brings charges in a criminal trial.

Protected computers. In U.S. federal law, include "government computers, financial institution computers, and any computer which is used in interstate or foreign commerce or communications."

Protected EAP. An extended EAP standard that uses TLS for outer authentication between the authenticator and the client but that does not require the client to do authentication with TLS.

Protection. Tool to thwart an attack.

Provisioning. Providing access credentials.

Proximity access token. Token that provides access simply by being near a computer or door.

Proxy. In an application proxy firewall, a program that filters a particular application.

PSK mode. See **pre-shared key mode**.

Public intelligence gathering. Obtaining information about a company by looking through a company's website and other public information.

Public key. In public key encryption, a key that is not secret. Knowledge of this key allows anyone to send the key owner a message encrypted for confidentiality.

Public key encryption. Encryption cipher that requires each party to have a private key and a public key. Plaintext encrypted with Party A's private key can be decrypted with Party A's public key. Plaintext encrypted with Party A's public key can be decrypted with Party A's private key.

Public key infrastructure. Technology and organization needed for digital certificates and public key processes.

Quantum key cracking. The use of quantum physics to do a massive number of key-cracking attempts almost instantly. Can crack very long keys almost instantly.

Quantum key distribution. The use of quantum physics to transmit a very long key between two partners securely.

RADIUS. A common type of authentication server protocol. Provides cryptographic security between the RADIUS server and the authenticator.

RAT. See **remote access Trojan**.

RBAC. See **role-based access control**.

RC4. Symmetric key encryption cipher with variable-length keys.

Real-time transfer. Transferring information as soon as it is created.

Reasonable risk. An appropriate level of use.

Recommended practices. Prescriptive statements about what companies should do.

Rehearsal. Executing a recovery plan when no incident has occurred to improve accuracy and speed.

Remote access Trojan. Trojan horse that gives the attacker remote control of a computer.

Remote access VPN. VPN that gives access to a remote user.

Replay attack. Attack in which an adversary intercepts an encrypted message and transmits it again later.

Request/authorization control. Requiring one person to make a request and a separate person to authorize it.

Response. Recovery according to plan.

Response message. In authentication, a string sent by the supplicating to the verifier.

Restoration. Restoring backed up data to its original host.

Retention policies. Policies for how long to store various types of backed-up information.

Return on investment. A family of methods for determining the value of an investment that produces value and requires costs over a period of time.

Reusable password. A password used many times. Most passwords are reusable passwords.

Revoke. For a certificate authority to rescind a digital certificate. A revoked digital certificate should not be used, even if it is in its valid period.

Risk acceptance. Implementing no countermeasures and absorbing any damages that occur.

Risk analysis. Comparing probable losses against the cost of security protections.

Risk avoidance. Not taking an action that is risky.

Risk reduction. Adopting active countermeasures, such as installing firewalls and hardening hosts.

Risk transference. Having someone else absorb the risk. The most common example of risk transference is insurance.

Rogue access point. Unauthorized access point, usually having no security.

ROI. See **return on investment**.

Role-based access control. Giving access to people based on their organizational roles.

Root. The super user account in UNIX.

Rootkits. Trojan horses that take over the root account and use its privileges to hide themselves.

Routed VPN. WAN service that hides routing information and limits access. This gives security but not cryptographic security.

RSA. The most widely used public key encryption cipher.

Sabotage. The destruction of hardware, software, or data.

Safeguard. Tool to thwart an attack.

SAML. See **Security Assertion Markup Language**.

Sanction. Punishment for breaking security policies or standards.

Sarbanes–Oxley Act. Law that creates strong accuracy requirements in financial reporting.

SB 1386. California law that requires the notification of any California resident whose personal information is stolen in a security breach.

Screening border router. Border router with firewall capabilities for stopping simple, high-volume attacks.

Script kiddie. A derogatory term that skilled hackers give to relatively unskilled hackers who use these pre-made attack scripts.

Section 1030. United States Code Title 18, Part I (Crimes) Section 1030—18 U.S.C § 1030. Criminalizes hacking, malware, denial-of-service attacks, and several other kinds of attacks.

Section 2511. In U.S. federal law, prohibits the interception of electronic communication en route and in storage. However, if companies operate their own e-mail systems, they are allowed to read e-mail.

Secure Hashing Algorithm. Family of hashing algorithms. The SHA-1 hashing algorithm is not secure.

Security association. In IPsec, is an agreement about what security methods and options two hosts or two IPsec gateways will use.

Security Assertion Markup Language. In federated identity management, a protocol for sending assertions between firms.

Security baselines. Written set of actions to achieve a security goal.

Security goal. Security condition the security staff wishes to achieve.

Security metrics. Measurable indicators of security success.

Segregation of duties. Requiring separate actions by two or more people to complete an act.

Sequence number. In replay attacks, an encrypted number in a message that allows the receiver to tell that a message is a duplicate.

Service pack. In Windows, a collection of updates and patches.

Session key. A symmetric key that is only used for a single communication session. The use of session keys limits the amount of information transmitted with the same key. (Only a session's worth of traffic.)

SHA. See **Secure Hashing Algorithm**.

Shadowing. Backing up the file you are working on automatically.

Shared passwords. An account password shared by two or more people. Thwarts the ability to know who took an action.

Shoulder surfing. Stealing a password by watching somebody type it.

Signing. In public key encryption for authentication, the act of encrypting something with the sender's private key.

Single point of vulnerability. An element of the architecture at which an attacker can do a great deal of damage by compromising a single system.

Single sign-on. A user authenticates himself or herself to the identity management system once. Thereafter, whenever the user asks for access to a specific server, there is no need for additional logins.

Site sharing. Having two or more corporate computer facilities back up each other so that if one fails, the other or others can take over immediately.

Site-to-site VPN. VPN that links two sites.

Smart card. Authentication card that contains a microprocessor.

Sniffer. Device inserted into a network; reads traffic passing through it to find useful data.

Social engineering. Attacks that trick the victim to take actions that are counter to security policies.

Spam. Unsolicited commercial e-mail.

SPI. See **stateful packet filtering**.

Spoofing. Impersonating another person, an IP address, or other entity.

Spread spectrum transmission. Spreads a signal over a wide range of frequencies. Done to reduce transmission impairments, not to provide security as it does in military uses.

Spyware. Trojan horse that gathers information about you and makes it available to an attacker.

SSID. Service Set ID. Designates a particular access point. Turning off SSID broadcasting does nothing to stop a drive-by hacker.

SSL. Secure Sockets Layer. See **SSL/TLS**.

SSL/TLS. Cryptographic system standard for communication between a browser and a host or a browser and SSL/TLS gateway.

SSL/TLS gateway. Gateway that gives remote access to a computer with a browser.

SSO. See **single sign-on**.

Standard. Mandatory implementation guidance.

Standard configuration. Specification for how client PCs should be configured, including important options, application programs, and, sometimes, the entire user interface.

State. Period, phase, or stage in a connection.

Stateful packet inspection. Firewall filtering based on the state of the connection (connection opening, ongoing communication, etc.).

Static packet filtering. Firewall filtering mechanism that looks at packets one at a time in isolation and that only looks at some fields in the internet and transport headers.

Strong symmetric keys. Key long enough (100 bits or longer) to make exhaustive key cracking prohibitively time consuming.

Substitution cipher. Cipher in which one character is substituted for another but the order of characters is not changed.

Super user account. Account with permissions to do anything on a host.

Supplicant. The party trying to prove its identity to the other.

Surreptitious recognition. Recognition done without the subject's knowledge.

Symmetric key encryption. Encryption with a cipher that uses a single key is used for encryption and decryption in both directions.

Systems administrator. Professional who manages one or more servers.

Systems life cycle. A system's entire life from creation through termination. Not simply the systems development life cycle.

Table-top exercise. Rehearsal in which managers and other key personnel get together and discuss, step by step, what each will do during an incident. Also called a walk-through.

Tailgating. Following someone through a secure door without entering a pass code. Also called piggybacking.

TCI. See **total cost of incident**.

Technical security architecture. All of the company's technical countermeasures and how these countermeasures are organized into a complete system of protection.

Template. In biometrics, biometric data for a particular user. Stored for later comparisons.

Threat environment. The types of attackers and attacks that companies face.

Ticket. In Kerberos, a bit string that gives certain access permissions.

Time stamp. Field that gives the time of a message's transmission. Useful in thwarting replay attacks.

TLS. Transport Layer Security. See **SSL/TLS**.

Token. Something that represents something else. An authentication token represents the person wishing to be authenticated. Offers a one-time password or plugs into a USB port.

Total cost of incident. Value that gives estimates the complete cost of a compromise, including the cost of repairs, lawsuits, and many other factors.

Trade secret espionage. Illegally obtaining trade secrets.

Trade secrets. Pieces of sensitive information that a firm acts to keep secret.

Traffic analysis. Measures traffic patterns for indications of sensitive material being sent outside the firm.

Transitive. If System A trusts System B and System B trusts System C, then System A will trust System C.

Transparent operation. Operation that occurs automatically, without any change in parties or devices and without the knowledge of these parties or devices.

Transport mode. In IPsec, a mode of operation that provides host-to-host security.

Transposition ciphers. Cipher in which the letters are moved around within a message, based on their initial positions in the message. However, the letters are not changed.

Transshippers. People who receive fraudulently ordered products and ship them to the ultimate attacker.

Triple DES. Symmetric key encryption standard that encrypts plaintext three times using the data encryption standard—using either two or three keys.

Trojan horse. Malware that hides itself by deleting a system file and taking on the system file's name.

Trust. When one system trusts another.

Trustee. Person to whom an accountable owner delegates the enforcement of security; accountability itself is not delegated.

Tuning. In intrusion detection systems, turning off rules that do not apply and increasing the severity threshold at which alarms will be generated.

Tunnel mode. In IPsec, a mode of operation that only provides security between IPsec gateways at two sites.

Two-factor authentication. Requiring a supplicant to supply two sets of authentication credentials. May provide defense in depth.

Unified threat management firewall. Combines traditional firewall filtering with antivirus protection and other protections.

UTM firewall. See **Unified threat management firewall**.

Valid period. Time period outside of which a digital certificate should not be accepted.

Vein recognition. Biometric recognition based on veins in the hand. Does not require physical contact.

Verification. Done when a supplicant claims to be a particular person, and the challenge is to measure the supplicant's biometric access data against the template of the person he or she claims to be.

Verifier. The party to whom the supplicant is trying to prove its identity.

Virtual private network. Cryptographic system that provides secure communication over an untrusted network (the Internet, a wireless LAN, and so forth.). This is a cryptographic VPN. There are also routed VPNs.

Viruses. Programs that attach themselves to legitimate programs on the victim's machine.

Voice recognition. Biometric recognition based on vocal patterns.

VPN. Cryptographic system that provides secure communication over an untrusted network (the Internet, a wireless LAN, and so forth). This is a cryptographic VPN. There are also routed VPNs.

VPN gateway. Host at a site boundary that terminates host-to-host and remote access VPNs.

Vulnerability testing. Attacking a system yourself to find security weaknesses.

Walk-through. Rehearsal in which managers and other key personnel get together and discuss, step by step, what each will do during an incident. Also called a table-top exercise.

Watch List. A group of people who should be given or denied access to a resource.

Watermark. Invisible information added to a document to allow it to be traced or filtered.

Weakest link failure. Exists if the failure of a single component of a countermeasure will render the countermeasure ineffective.

Windows Action Center. In Windows 7, a central place for checking and changing a computer's security status.

Windows Security Center. In Windows XP and Vista, a central place for checking and changing a computer's security status.

Wired Equivalent Privacy. Weak and fully cracked core security protocol designed to protect communication between an access point and a wireless client. Yes, wired, not wireless.

Wireless Protected Access. Moderately strong core security protocol protecting communication between an access point and a wireless client. Has been partially cracked.

Wizard hackers. Hackers who have very high skills.

Work-around. A manual fix for a vulnerability.

Worms. Full programs that do not attach themselves to other programs.

WPA. See **Wireless Protected Access**.

WPA2. Name given by the Wi-Fi Alliance to 802.11i.

Zero-day attack. Attack that occurs before the vulnerability it uses has been discovered or has had a patch developed.

INDEX